THE AMERICAN PRESIDENCY

The American Presidency

AN INSTITUTIONAL APPROACH
TO EXECUTIVE POLITICS

WILLIAM G. HOWELL

PRINCETON UNIVERSITY PRESS
PRINCETON & OXFORD

Published by Princeton University Press
41 William Street, Princeton, New Jersey 08540
99 Banbury Road, Oxford OX2 6JX

press.princeton.edu

All Rights Reserved

ISBN 978-0-691-22558-6
ISBN (pbk.) 978-0-691-22557-9
ISBN (e-book) 978-0-691-22559-3

Library of Congress Control Number: 2022946323

British Library Cataloging-in-Publication Data is available

Editorial: Bridget Flannery-McCoy
Production Editorial: Karen Carter
Jacket/Cover Design: Wanda España
Production: Erin Suydam
Publicity: Charlotte Coyne and Kate Hensley

Jacket/Cover Credit: The Presidential Seal, the White House, Washington DC.
dbtravel / Alamy Stock Photo

This book has been composed in Arno Pro

Printed on acid-free paper. ∞

Printed in the United States of America

10 9 8 7 6 5 4 3 2 1

BRIEF CONTENTS

CONTENTS

ACKNOWLEDGMENTS

AUTHORS DON'T WRITE BOOKS ALONE. And they certainly don't improve drafts of books alone. For that, they depend upon critical readers. I've benefited from more than my fair share. Doug Kriner, Stephane Wolton, and Andy Rudalevige all offered helpful comments on early drafts of this book. Andrew Reeves, Brandon Rottinghaus, and Saul Jackman gave this textbook trial classroom runs while it was still in manuscript form—thanks to them and their students for extraordinarily helpful feedback. Perhaps more than anyone, students in my own undergraduate classes on the American presidency at the University of Chicago (and before that, Harvard University and the University of Wisconsin) have shaped my thinking about this textbook, and about the institutional presidency more generally. I also thank the many anonymous reviewers who, at various stages, helped improve this book via targeted strikes on individual sentences and demands that entire chapters be rewritten. With her usual acumen, Kathryn Ciffolillo proofread the entire manuscript. Alexis Walker was a fantastic development editor—sharp, demanding, and (not least!) organized. Meanwhile at Pearson, Jeff Marshall, Melissa Mashburn, Ashley Dodge, Carly Czech, and Reid Hester all helped usher this manuscript into print.

For this textbook's original publication, I leaned heavily on a small army of graduate students for assistance in pulling together the original draft of this textbook, which Pearson first published in 2017. David Brent kicked things off, helping research and draft chapters 1 and 7, Jon Rogowski then did the same for chapter 4, and Tom Wood took the lead on chapter 5. Hannah Cook, Alfredo Gonzalez, Faith Laken, and Ethan Porter helped out with these and other chapters. Sarah Miller-Davenport, meanwhile, was a real partner in this production. The products of her labor—both in research and drafting—are most pronounced in chapters 2, 7, and 13. But in truth, her deft touch improved nearly every chapter in this volume. Lastly, I'm not sure this textbook would have made it to print had it not been for the herculean efforts of Susan Mallaney.

I also thank the many reviewers who, at various stages, helped improve the original version of this book through suggested revisions, both small and large. These scholars include: Bryan McQuide, Grand View University; Chunmei Yoe, Southeastern Oklahoma State University; Stella Rouse, University of Maryland; Dr. Malinda Wade, Southwest Tennessee Community College; Mark Druash, Tallahassee Community College; Joshua Meddaugh, University of Pittsburgh, Bradford; Rodd Freitag, University of Wisconsin, Eau Claire; Michaela Fazecas, University of Central Florida; Sabrina Hammel, Northeast Lakeview College; Carlos Diaz-Rosillo, Harvard University; Michael Lynch, University of Georgia; John Pitney, Claremont McKenna College; Amy Dreussi, University of Akron; Raymond Rushboldt, SUNY, Fredonia; Cecilia Manrique, University of Wisconsin, La Crosse; and Mikhail Rybalko, Maryland University.

In 2020, with the commercial textbook industry in flux, and wanting to make far more changes than my original publisher was able to accommodate, I recovered the rights to the textbook and took them to Princeton University Press. I am so glad I did. Bridget Flannery-McCoy gave me the support and space needed to completely overhaul the textbook. Nearly every section of every chapter has been altered in some significant way; the result is a more forceful, grounded, and comprehensive examination of our nation's most important political office. As my development editor, Danna Lockwood was immensely helpful, attentive to the structure and flow of the volume while marking up individual sentences and paragraphs. Jenn Backer was at once meticulous and indefatigable in copyediting this textbook. Kevin Baron, Sean Byrne, Shawn Patterson, Greg Shaw, Rick Waterman, and other anonymous reviewers offered superb suggestions for revisions, which I have done my best to incorporate. Gabe Foy-Sutherland, Zachary Garai, Katia Kukucka, and Ben Konstan provided excellent research assistance. Allison Von Borstel updated nearly every table and figure in the volume. Simon Lane made crucial interventions into the early chapters. And Mike Wiley's ideas—and in significant places, his prose—can be seen throughout this volume. He helped reimagine what this textbook could be; and he proved absolutely indispensable in realizing the vision.

Lastly, this book is dedicated to my children, Charles Howell and Frances Howell. Marcy and I stand amazed at all the light and spirit they bring to our family.

PREFACE

FOR MORE THAN TWENTY YEARS, I have taught courses on the American presidency in lecture halls and classrooms, in person and online, at a large public university and two private ones. No matter the setting, however, the twin objectives have remained the same. I aim to make sense of the single most important political office in the world's single most powerful country. At the same time, I use the presidency as a point of departure for broader thinking about our politics, as an opportunity to grapple with questions about political power, representation, democratic governance, and the policymaking process. This textbook represents the culmination of these undertakings.

Three convictions guide this textbook. The first is that many of the most pressing empirical debates about the presidency, and political science more generally, remain unresolved. Though political scientists have learned a great deal over the last century about our politics, foundational debates persist. As a consequence, this textbook presents the most current scholarship on the American presidency in ways that are simultaneously accessible and attuned to the limits of current understandings. The purpose of this textbook is not to transform students into political scientists with scholarly agendas on the American presidency. Rather, the purpose is to emphatically enjoin student participation in the ongoing enterprise of professional political scientists (as well as historians and social scientists) to make sense of our nation's politics through the lens of the executive branch.

The second conviction is that the U.S. presidency cannot be understood in isolation. If we want to make sense of the president's opportunities to influence public policy, to meaningfully engage the public, and to reshape our polity, we must remain attuned to the political context in which he (someday she or they)* operates: a political system in which

---

*A word on gendered pronouns. I've done my best to avoid them, but my success, such as it is, has only been partial and uneven. In part, this is because of the limited options built into the English language. The larger problem, though, is that we have had forty-five consecutive men occupy the American presidency—a fact that needn't limit our imagination for what is possible, but a fact that we must confront head-on and try to understand. For a long time, I've tried to have it both ways. And the best construction I've managed to formulate appears here: namely, when referring to the president in the third person singular, speak of "he (someday she or they)." This is fine and well, I suppose, but it also feels a bit like a dodge. Perhaps a president in the near future will be a woman or someone who is non-binary. Truth be told, I hope she or they will be. But as I write now, we continue to live with a historical legacy—and a scholarly one as well—that is steeped in gendered notions of leadership.

other individuals with authority of their own can—and do—intermittently delegate new powers to the president and constrain the president's ability to exercise old ones. The old adage that the presidency is what the president makes of it is grossly misleading. What the presidency is depends a great deal more on the strategies and actions of legislators, bureaucrats, judges, and the broader public than it does on the person who inhabits the White House at any given moment.

And this leads to the third governing theme of this textbook. The most striking features of executive politics, and the features that bear most crucially on the exercise of presidential power, are *institutional*. Descriptively, the office of the presidency is deeply embedded in a massive administrative apparatus, one that continues to grow, expand, and adapt to new challenges. Situated within this apparatus, presidents, all presidents, confront clear incentives to behave in well-defined ways, to draw upon a common body of resources, and to square off against other politicians (legislators, judges, bureaucrats) with institutionally defined resources and incentives of their own. To make sense of what presidents do, we must clarify the institutional context in which they work. For where they stand on any particular issue, in absolutely crucial ways, depends upon where they sit.

Concerns for the institutional presidency—both as political fact and as approach to understanding executive politics—permeate this textbook. Entire chapters are devoted to the original construction of the presidency and its historical evolution over time. When discussing individual presidents, less emphasis is placed on personal biography than on the institutional dynamics presidents attempt to navigate. The textbook beckons students to overlook the din of executive branch personalities, leadership styles, and social flourishes that capture so much media attention and focus instead on the decisions that presidents actually make. Explanations about executive politics, as a consequence, focus heavily on the resources, incentives, constraints, and opportunities that animate institutional analyses throughout the social sciences.

This is a full-service textbook. It covers all of the key topics of executive politics. It invites students to think about the Constitution as a document of institutional design; of historical changes in the office of the presidency as the product of institutional reformers; of elections as contests with clearly defined rules and procedures that affect not only who is ultimately selected as president but how this person will behave once in office; of members of Congress, judges, justices, and bureaucrats as strategic actors whose actions bear directly upon presidential fortunes; and of public policy, both its construction and implementation, as the product of successive generations of politicians, each operating in a particular political context and responding to the attendant political constraints and incentives. Though the approach may be distinct, the range of topics covered in this textbook is entirely conventional.

This also is a textbook with a point of view. It looks skeptically upon arguments rooted in psychology and evidence based in anecdotes. But the text does not cling to its perspective dogmatically, nor does it encourage its readers to do so. Though institutionally grounded, this textbook does not take a reductionist view of our politics. A great many matters of importance—both to presidents themselves and to the office of the presidency—

originate in domains that are not the typical subject of institutional analysis: personal ambitions, cultural norms, chance events. Again and again, therefore, the text invites students to probe just how far institutional arguments can take us, and to spot instances in which other factors that are more personal, more historically contingent predominate.

Two features, which appear in every chapter, are specifically designed to prompt students to evaluate both the insights and limitations of institutional arguments about the presidency. The first, "Thinking Institutionally," illustrates ways in which institutional considerations not only warrant recognition but also can inform how we think about the exercise of political power. In so doing, this feature explicitly asks students to consider the relevance of decidedly *non*-institutional factors in shaping executive politics. "Thinking Institutionally," therefore, encourages students to evaluate critically how personal convictions of individual presidents sometimes inform the design of the American presidency and the extent to which individual presidents' ideological commitments complement or perhaps even trump institutional considerations.

The institutional presidency is decidedly not a fixed quantity, born of the fanciful imaginations of our nation's Framers and carefully preserved by successive generations of politicians. In response both to the political undertakings of presidents themselves and to institutional reformers working outside of government, the institutional presidency remains perpetually a work in progress. The second feature, "Historical Transformations," illustrates ways in which unique moments in the political life of this country have altered some facet of the institutional presidency, and often in ways that did not at all conform with the wishes of those individuals originally involved. History, and sometimes happenstance, regularly intrudes in our politics. And so they do in this textbook's survey of the institutional presidency.

On offer, then, is a volume that draws on contemporary scholarship, recognizes the president's place in our system of separated and federated powers, and develops an institutional argument about executive politics. It is designed as much to inform and enlighten as it is to stimulate curiosity and debate. So doing, it is meant to support every aspect of undergraduate classes on the American presidency. I hope that it fosters interest and insight, and I welcome any feedback that you are willing to share.

THE AMERICAN PRESIDENCY

Thinking Institutionally about an American Presidency

WHY DO PRESIDENTS behave as they do? When do they succeed? When do they fail? What mark do they leave on our politics?

For answers to these questions, journalists, biographers, politicians, and a good number of scholars look to presidents themselves, in all their complexity. In their personalities, leadership styles, personal backgrounds, and idiosyncrasies, it is presumed, are the keys to unlocking their behavior. It is the individual, many political observers insist, who matters most; and so it is the individual president we must study if we are to understand our national politics.

The American Presidency takes an altogether different tack. Rather than scrutinizing the *president*, this textbook analyzes the *presidency*. It illuminates the institutional context in which presidents work, the institutional foundations of executive power, and the institutional incentives that shape and inform presidential decisions and action. Rules and norms, procedures and protocols, incentives and perspectives, and grants and limitations of authority sit at its heart.

To make headway on this project, we will need to define what we mean by "institution" and "institutional approach." Hold tight: we will do this shortly. First, though, we would do well to recognize an alternative understanding of executive politics. While this textbook assumes—and even argues on behalf of—an institutional approach to the American presidency, the vast preponderance of discussions in the mainstream media fixate on presidents themselves. Therefore, before we turn our attention in earnest to the institutional presidency, let us take stock of the personal president.

0.1 The Personal President

Public servant does not begin to capture what the president means to us. Not even close. Presidents are part rock star, part parent, and part national icon. No one looms larger in the national consciousness. No one is better recognized, more powerful, or more controversial.

Presidents give voice to and embody the nation's most cherished values. Presidents are repositories for our highest aspirations, symbols of what America is and what it might become. Presidents not only decide what the government should do but define who we are as a people. We turn to them for consolation and strength. We look to them to affirm our national identity. And we evaluate presidential candidates not only on their policy positions, values, and ideological commitments but also, say some, on the basis of the personal relationships we imagine having with them.

Little wonder, then, that the family histories, character traits, and moral convictions of presidents captivate our attention and imagination. By turns, we read deep meanings into Joe Biden's history of personal tragedy, Donald Trump's habits of mind and language, Barack Obama's multicultural heritage, George W. Bush's Texas swagger, Bill Clinton's smooth talk, and George H. W. Bush's World War II service. Indeed, depending on one's ideological and partisan bent, merely watching presidents on television can evoke a deep emotional attachment or boiling indignation.

The concept of the **personal presidency**, which draws our attention to the individual presidents who hold office with all their nuances and complexity, owes its enduring strength to two groups of opinion makers: pundits and academics. In this section we will canvass the views of these two groups and then critique their approach to studying the personal president.

0.1.1 The Personal President: Pundits

Pundits—journalists, talking heads, consultants, and public intellectuals—have long supposed that *what* the presidency is, at any given moment, crucially depends upon *who* the president is—upon the president's leadership style, worldview, sense of self, energy, political acumen, likeability, temperament, demeanor, cognitive skills, and all the rest that make them fully-fledged human beings. If we want to understand what goes on in the White House, pundits tell us, we would do well to scrutinize the person who resides there.

This personal approach to understanding the American presidency dominates print, digital, and televised media, where pundits relate the president's latest political decision, misstep, or scandal to some mix of personality and biography. Again and again, we have been told that the key to decoding presidents' actions lies in their backgrounds, their convictions and biases, and their strengths and weaknesses. To better understand what this personal approach calls our attention to, and what it chooses to omit, let's examine three recent presidents through its lens.

JOE BIDEN

Joe Biden took office following an election that, even by recent historical standards, was light on policy substance. Among those who supported him, many did so not because of what he promised to accomplish in the White House but because of who he was. The son of a Delaware car salesman, Biden had garnered a reputation as one of the most down-to-earth, straight-talking members of Congress. A lover of ice cream cones and a dear, grand-fatherly companion to former president Obama, Biden's nicknames included "Middle-Class Joe" and "Amtrak Joe," the latter referring to his low-budget train rides home from Washington, D.C. In public, Biden's lighthearted persona concealed his tragic past, including the untimely deaths of his first wife and children. According to his supporters, Biden's personal story, combined with his "maverick" sensibilities, made him a graceful and productive addition to the presidency.

Biden's detractors also had plenty to say about his character. To some, his folksy demeanor belied his deep and sinister ambition; Biden had, after all, either planned or launched a presidential campaign in 1980, 1984, 1988, 2004, 2008, 2016, and 2020. Where some saw a man eager to bond with colleagues and voters, others saw inappropriate physical contact with younger women—an allegation Biden would eventually have to address publicly. Most persistent was the rumor that Biden—seventy-seven years old at the time of his election, and a known stutterer—was lying to reporters about his mental and physical health. For all these reasons and more, detractors presumed that Biden's personal characteristics would doom his tenure in the White House.[1]

DONALD TRUMP

If ever a president attracted scrutiny, it was Donald Trump. Indeed, "scrutiny" is the least of it. Every night, it seemed, news anchors and their guests pored over the president's latest tweet or dictate in search of clues into what made this exceptional president tick. And so doing, they evaluated Trump in distinctly personal terms. The descriptors ran the gamut from shrewd and successful "conservative businessman" to "tax-cheating, investor-swindling, worker-shafting, dictator-loving, pathologically lying, attorneys general–bribing, philandering, mobbed up, narcissistic serial con artist."[2] On one essential point, however, there appears to have been some consensus: understanding a Trump presidency required understanding Trump himself—his wants and desires, his personality and style, his hang-ups and foibles. For this president, with so little political experience and so few ties to his putative party, the keys to understanding action and eventual achievement lay in the heart and mind of the man himself.

To better understand the mind and intention of this dealmaker-turned-president, political observers plumbed Donald Trump's childhood upbringing. According to many, the key to understanding Trump was his relationship with his real-estate-mogul father, Fred Trump, who taught him to save every penny and to negotiate fiercely.[3] Trump's father raised his son in the real estate industry and, through mentoring and financial support, laid the foundation for his success. For all the lessons imparted, however, the father-son relationship lacked warmth and compassion. As one family friend noted, the two often "talked right past each other."[4] This toxic blend of parental judgment and indifference, observers argued, sent Donald Trump into adulthood with a cutthroat drive to succeed and total impatience with failure.

Behind all of Trump's antics, said some, lay a deep and nagging insecurity about what others thought of him. For many, Trump's unyielding self-regard and utter preoccupation with personal slights, no matter how petty, betrayed a man ill at ease with himself. His was a world informed by television ratings, crowd sizes, poll results, and electoral returns, which kept at bay the childhood demons that lived within him. When the facts did not cooperate, Trump either disregarded them or made up altogether new ones. And, when others did not join in, Trump—our nation's "toddler in chief"[5]—took to throwing tantrums. Trump's outspoken contempt for the "fake media," political experts, and the DC establishment, at its heart, revealed a sad and lonely man-child desperately longing for approval.

None of this is to say that there was a consensus view about Trump. To the contrary, Americans disagreed vehemently with one another about his motivations and character. Critics saw in Trump little but impulsiveness, immaturity, and self-regard. Supporters saw irreverence, independence, and determination. For most, though, a straight line could be drawn between the personal qualities of the man and the presidency he administered. The relationships he fostered with foreign nations, the political negotiations he charted domestically, and the policy agenda he articulated all flowed—quite naturally—from his own traits, experiences, styles, and obsessions. The origin of Trump's presidency was Trump himself.

BARACK OBAMA

The higher the stakes of a topic or debate, the more personal the coverage of presidential actions seems to become. In the summer of 2011, with the country facing a default on its national debt, President Obama's maneuvers to end partisan bickering and avoid default were largely evaluated in personal terms. Conservative commentators opined by turns that the president was being too "chill," too "passive," or possibly too "passive-aggressive" in his handling of the crisis.[6] And in the opinion pages of the *Wall Street Journal*, former Reagan speechwriter Peggy Noonan explained Obama's inability to reach an agreement with Republican leaders in these terms: "He really dislikes [them], and he can't fake it." Noonan then contrasted Obama to a previous Democratic president with whom Republicans had been willing to negotiate: "Bill Clinton understood why conservatives think what they think because he was raised in the South. He had a saving ambivalence."[7]

Some of the most vitriolic criticisms of Obama's character and temperament, however, came from pundits on the ideological Left. On his *Conscience of a Liberal* blog, commentator and Nobel laureate Paul Krugman spelled out what he found to be Obama's biggest limitation in framing the issue: "At this point, we just have to accept it as a fact of life: Obama doesn't, and maybe can't, do outrage—no matter how much the situation calls for it."[8]

These personal criticisms came to a head after the president signed a debt relief bill, hastily put together by Congress at the eleventh hour, which was seen by most as favoring Republicans. For example, a scathing op-ed in the *New York Times* titled "What Happened to Obama?" argued that he "has pursued the [political path] with which he is most comfortable given the constraints of his character," indicating a "deep-seated aversion to conflict." The problem was not merely political but existential—the president simply did not "know who he is or what he believes in."[9]

The *Times* criticisms are particularly interesting, given that the character traits under attack—his unflappable demeanor among them—were the same qualities that had, in the eyes of many, made Obama such a compelling presidential candidate. In its 2008 endorsement, the *Times* editorial board praised Obama's "cool, steady hand."[10] Before it even began, then, the Obama presidency was thought to be synonymous with the personal characteristics of the man himself; these expressed characteristics, rather than being shaped and informed by larger political, cultural, and racial dynamics, originated from within Obama himself.

PRESIDENTS PAST

Biden, Trump, and Obama were hardly the first presidents to be judged by the punditry in strictly personal terms. Both admirers and detractors also referred to George W. Bush as a man whose decisions were based on conviction rather than strategic calculation. A 2004 magazine profile described Bush's first term in office as an "extraordinary blend of forcefulness and inscrutability, opacity and action."[11] And a commentator who knew Bush well summed up the widespread assessment of him as president and person: "Those who love him say 'leader, decisive, passionate.' His detractors say 'angry, petulant.' But everybody agrees that there's something in his gut, something that's really driving him."[12]

Such has been the thinking of past presidents, as well. Though amplified by changes in the media, the nation's preoccupation with the president's psychology and personality has deep historical roots. Americans have always remembered our most famous presidents by identifying them with distinct personality traits: Old Hickory (Andrew Jackson), Honest Abe (Abraham Lincoln), the Schoolmaster (Woodrow Wilson), the Big Lub (William Howard Taft), Cautious Cal (Calvin Coolidge), Give 'Em Hell Harry (Harry Truman), Camelot (John F. Kennedy), Tricky Dick (Richard Nixon), and The Great Communicator (Ronald Reagan).

Since its inception, in fact, a veritable cult of personality has dominated discussions of the presidential office. During the Constitutional Convention of 1787, George Washington was widely seen as the obvious choice for president because of his superior personal qualities, especially his humility and aversion to power. Indeed, one convention delegate went so far as to argue that it was these very personal characteristics that had created the office of the presidency: "Many of the members [of the convention] cast their eyes toward General Washington as President and shaped their Ideas of the Powers to be given to a President, by their Opinions of his Virtue."[13] (See chapter 1 for an assessment of this argument.)

From Washington onward, presidents have been judged not by the success of their policies but by the content of their character. Legendary journalist H. L. Mencken once described Franklin D. Roosevelt as having "an ingratiating grin upon his face like that of a snake-oil vendor at a village carnival."[14] And Norman Mailer consistently attributed Lyndon Johnson's failure in Vietnam to character, calling Johnson an "ugly, tragic man," motivated by "vanity" and plagued by an "alienation" from himself that underscored the "depths of [his] insanity." Not that these traits were necessarily all bad. "Better to have a President who is a large and evil man," Mailer assured us, "than one who is small and ignoble."[15]

0.1.2 The Personal President: Academics

Among academics, too, the personal approach to understanding the presidency has held considerable sway. For much of the twentieth century, in fact, this approach dominated scholarly research on the American presidency. Taking their cues from personality theory and cognitive psychology, many authors of books on the American presidency devoted a chapter to each president, typically in chronological order. Prominent presidency scholars developed "types" and "schemata" of presidents on the basis of their emotional predispositions, key moments in their biographies, and leadership styles.[16] Though their conclusions varied, all of these scholars paid close attention to each president and the personal quirks and idiosyncrasies that made the president human.

Presidential Power and the Modern Presidents, the single most influential tract written on the American presidency during the last half century, posits presidents' "professional reputation" and "public prestige" as the essential determinants of their success or failure. To be sure, its author, Richard Neustadt, recognized that institutions, political actors, and public expectations shape presidential politics. He did not explore the character and design of political institutions at any length, however. Rather, he relegated political institutions to the background, holding that it is the person, ultimately, who must rise above these institutions. As Neustadt put it, the president must be an individual of "extraordinary temperament," one with "a sense of purpose, a feel for power, and a source of confidence."[17]

Consider, too, James Barber's typology of American presidents. In Barber's view, presidents' "personalities [are] engaged—not peripherally, but centrally—in fights" over policy; and as a consequence, presidents' "actions cannot be understood apart from the passions each poured into his task[s]."[18] Barber sought to categorize the types of presidential character that exist, in order to explicate "what in the personal past foreshadows the Presidential future."[19] Barber illuminated the details of presidents' personal histories, examining the future implications of, for example, ten-year-old Richard Nixon's letter to his mother and Jimmy Carter's reactions upon hearing Dylan Thomas read aloud.

In our survey of scholarship on the personal presidency, we must not overlook Fred Greenstein. In the last quarter century, no one has written at greater length or with more aplomb about the personal president than Greenstein. Documenting the tenures of every president, Greenstein directs our attention to each person's communicative proficiency, organizational capacity, political skill, policy vision, cognitive style, and emotional intelligence, for in such attributes, he insists, lie the explanations of their accomplishments.[20]

In Greenstein's work, as in so much that is written on American presidents, each president receives his own chapter—for each president must be evaluated and understood on his own terms.

0.1.3 The Personal President: A Brief Critique

Among pundits, the personal president continues to predominate. Among academics, though, its influence is on the decline. Over the last two decades, presidency scholars have focused instead on the formal tools at the president's disposal, the president's place in history, the growth of the "presidential branch" of government, and the efforts of presidents to oversee the bureaucracy. This shift in scholarly attention is eminently justified. For all the attention it receives, the personal president too often fails to deliver a reliable framework for making sense of what presidents do during their time in office and what meaning it has for our politics.

Let's elaborate:

- *The personal approach does not adequately account for the basic fact that the office of the presidency is embedded in a highly institutionalized setting.* This context has grown dramatically over at least the last century, whether measured by the sheer number of federal bureaucrats, advisors, and civil service employees working in the executive branch or by the size and number of its administrative agencies and departments. The structures within the federal bureaucracy crucially define the information presidents have about domestic and foreign policy and thus partially determine their ability to devise new policy solutions. These structures also present extraordinary management challenges with which each president must grapple, as explored in greater detail in chapter 10.

- *The personal approach gives insufficient attention to the judicial and legislative checks that all presidents face when they assume office.* When trying to advance a policy agenda, presidents regularly bargain with members of Congress, and when trying to protect past policy achievements, presidents must find ways to block congressional opponents. Similarly, the fate of a president's policy agenda lies in part within the judiciary, which has ample opportunities to either strike down or legitimate presidential actions and policies. The limits of presidential action are not defined by failures of imagination. Rather, they derive from other political actors deploying their own political authority in the service of altogether different political objectives.

- *The personal approach downplays the extraordinary ways in which public opinion both constrains and informs what any president is able to accomplish while in office.* If we want to understand the positions a president takes on race relations, bank bailouts, or the conflict in Ukraine, it will not do merely to look into the president's eyes and divine his or her deepest beliefs. Nor will it do to attribute the broader class of presidential actions—the ways in which they communicate with the public, the content of public speeches they make, and the like—to each president's idea about what it means to be president. Public opinion crucially defines the specific policy proposals that come out of the White House and the routines and rituals that fill the president's daily schedule.

- *The personal approach fails to grasp the ways in which presidential behavior arises from the institutional structures that presidents confront.* The choices offered to presidents depend on, and are constrained by, other political actors. The terms by which presidents evaluate these choices, in turn, are defined as much by institutional pressures as by what they might independently think. And their ultimate choices reflect, in addition to their personal policy preferences, strategic calculations about what is possible. The incentives, resources, and powers that do so much to shape presidential behavior are not born of the individuals who inhabit the White House. Rather, they are built into the institutions that constitute and surround their temporary place of residence. If we want to understand executive politics—indeed, if we want to understand politics at all—we would do well to put these institutions at the forefront of our attention.

0.2 The Institutional Presidency

Today, the most prominent scholarship on the American presidency embraces this institutional approach. Some of this scholarship is historical in nature. Some employs game theory to examine the strategic behaviors of presidents. Still other scholarship relies upon large data sets to uncover basic patterns in the presidency. Despite differences in methodology, however, nearly all of this scholarship puts the institutions that compose and surround the presidency at the center of its analysis.

In keeping with this approach, *The American Presidency* puts you, the reader, in the position not of the psychologist, journalist, or biographer but of the institutionalist. An **institutionalist** takes as a starting point the facts that the presidency is embedded within institutions and that presidential power is mediated by those institutions. As we shall soon see, however, the institutionalist does not merely recognize the existence of institutions. The institutionalist also thinks in distinctly institutional terms.

0.2.1 What Is an Institution?

What exactly is an institution? Most of us would agree that libraries (as well as churches, universities, and banks) are "institutions," and, for most of us, the buildings in which they are housed speak to their institutional nature. Take away the walls, roof, front desk, and even the books, however, and the notion of a library as an institution still has meaning. Its institutional quality is a step removed from its physical embodiment—at once more durable and abstract than what we can see and touch. Properly considered, an **institution** consists of a well-ordered set of practices, rules, and relationships that play a well-defined role in governing the actions and choices of individuals working within them.*

How exactly institutions "govern" individuals' actions and choices can vary from case to case. Rules and even laws may stipulate the range of acceptable choices put before some individuals in an institutional environment. But so, too, might norms, values, and historical precedent.

Just how "well ordered" must a collection of practices and relationships be to qualify as an institution? The dividing line between the *institutional* and *non-institutional* is not always neat. For example, emerging democracies are regularly governed by "weak institutions," that is, political bodies that may exert a tremendous amount of power but do not either constitute a "well-ordered set of practices" or perform a "well-defined role."

Just how strongly do institutions govern individual behaviors? Here, too, it depends. Institutional actors are not defined exclusively by the institutions in which they operate, and institutions themselves evolve over time, the subjects of both purposeful reform and sheer happenstance.

The durability, shape, and strength of institutions assuredly vary over time and place. Institutions are at once malleable and persistent, and the dividing line that separates an institution from its environment often more closely resembles a poorly attended hedge than a fortified brick wall.

But for all their variability, institutions powerfully and persistently shape the behaviors of those who work within them, including presidents and their staff. Indeed, as we shall see, institutions make presidents as much as presidents make institutions.

0.2.2 What Is the Institutional Presidency?

If the presidency is understood as an institution, we, as analysts, must steadfastly reject Woodrow Wilson's famous declaration that "the president is at liberty, both in law and in conscience, to be as big a man as he can. His capacity will set the limit."[21] How big a president can be depends on all sorts of factors, but the ones that matter most have little to do with the person in office. The possibilities afforded to each president are baked into the office of the presidency and the larger political context in which it is situated, not into the officeholder alone.

When thinking about the **institutional presidency**, we must offer an account not only of the initial creation of the presidency but also of its subsequent evolution. Panning outward, we must recognize other key institutions—Congress, the judiciary, and the federal bureaucracy—with which the institutional presidency must work. Further, we must rec-

---

* This definition closely adheres to that of Avner Grief and David Latin, who note that "we define institutions as a system of human-made, nonphysical elements—norms, beliefs, organizations, and rules—exogenous to each individual whose behavior it influences that generates behavioral regularities." Avner Grief and David Latin, "A Theory of Endogenous Institutional Change," *American Political Science Review* 98, no. 4 (2004): 633–52, 635.

ognize other institutions, such as the media, state election boards, lobbying organizations, and interest groups, all of which influence elections, public opinion, and political culture. All these institutions shape the resources, incentives, and opportunities that define the institutional presidency. We will not always manage to distinguish the exact boundaries that separate the presidency from all the other institutions with which it interacts, nor will we always be able to parse the distinct influence that presidents wield in this expansive institutional environment. An institutional approach to studying the presidency, however, provides a focal point for a deeper institutional examination of American politics as a whole.

0.2.3 What Is an Institutional Approach to Studying the Presidency?

What does an institutionalist do? What does it mean to take an institutional approach to studying the presidency? The work of institutional analysis proceeds at three levels.

THE FIRST LEVEL OF INSTITUTIONAL ANALYSIS

This level is purely descriptive: the institutionalist inventories the agencies, departments, and commissions that surround and, in various ways, serve the president. A good portion of this task, therefore, simply involves cataloguing the various components of the executive branch. But there is more. Acknowledging that institutions are not static entities, the institutionalist recognizes the ways in which administrative structures arise, adapt, and sometimes cease to exist. The executive branch has undergone incredible transformations over the past two centuries. The institutionalist must offer some kind of explanation for these changes, tracing the presidency from its constitutional origins through the Progressive Era, FDR's New Deal, Truman's Fair Deal, and on to contemporary calls for its reform.

THE SECOND LEVEL OF INSTITUTIONAL ANALYSIS

Institutionalists are not content to merely describe the institutions, past and present, that make up the executive branch. They also are committed to identifying how these institutions shape presidential behavior. To do so, the institutionalist pays less attention to the idiosyncratic characteristics and personal histories of individual presidents and more to the office's underlying incentives and overriding institutional contexts, as well as to the resources the office makes available to all presidents. The institutionalist follows political scientist Terry Moe's counsel to "stop thinking of the presidents as people, and to start thinking about them generically: as faceless, nameless, institutional actors whose behavior is an institutional product."[22]

The effect of this approach, in the main, is to downplay the unique qualities of individual presidents and to emphasize instead continuities across presidential administrations. Where variation in presidential behavior is observed, the institutionalist looks for changes in the institutional environment in which presidents work.

This is not to say that all presidents are alike or that the consequences of presidential elections are trivial. Democratic and Republican presidents can be expected to have radically different policy agendas; and for that reason alone, elections matter greatly. The psychological origins of their choice of agendas, however, lie beyond the institutionalist's purview. The institutionalist does not try to decipher why some presidents would prefer to see deeper federal investment in oil exploration versus alternative energy technologies. Rather, the institutionalist either takes these policy preferences as given and tries to make sense of presidents' efforts to act upon them or clarifies how these policy choices reflect strategic considerations about how best to navigate a system of government in which power is perennially divided and contested.

Nor is this to argue that all aspects of presidential behavior have institutional origins. A president's manner of speaking or reading habits, for example, may have little to do with political institutions (though, in fact, they just might). For the most part, however, such aspects of presidential behavior neither bear upon the doings of government nor invite coherent and verifiable explanation.

For the institutionalist, then, the focus of study is presidential decisions rather than the president. The institutionalist does not investigate what lies hidden within the deepest recesses of a president's head or heart. The institutionalist studies actions, broadly defined, that bear upon a president's performance in office. Institutionalists train their attention on the observable features of a president's tenure in office and ignore the childhood insecurities, foibles, varieties of faith, and personal ambitions that make up the chief executive's internal life.

THE THIRD LEVEL OF INSTITUTIONAL ANALYSIS

Institutional thinking also occurs at a third and deeper level—and it is here that things get really interesting. The institutionalist takes seriously the notion that institutions do not merely constrain behavior but also inform it. Consequently, the institutionalist scrutinizes political factors that encourage judges to avoid antagonizing the president, the ways in which congresspersons' concerns about reelection allow the president to exert more power over foreign policy than over domestic policy, and the conditions under which presidents pursue a legislative versus a unilateral policy strategy. In each of these scenarios, the institutionalist recognizes the ways in which a president's observed behaviors reflect not only the president's preferences but also the preferences, powers, and anticipated actions of other political actors with influence and autonomy of their own.

0.3 Outline of the Book

For the most part, the topical coverage of *The American Presidency* is like any other textbook on the presidency. It examines all of the main subjects that routinely show up in undergraduate courses on the American presidency: constitutional foundations, the processes of nominating and electing a president, the various inter- and intrabranch political struggles that constitute executive politics, and presidential efforts to influence the contents of foreign and domestic policy.

What sets this title apart from others is its distinctly institutional view of the American presidency. While this perspective has some implications for *what* topics are examined, the bigger effect is on *how* they are examined. Hence, we examine the presidential veto not simply as a tool of presidential power but as an institution unto itself—one with its own rules, norms, and ability to shape policy outcomes. When discussing presidential vetoes, *The American Presidency* does not merely define vetoes, identify where they are mentioned in Article I, describe how their usage has changed over time, and then discuss a handful of high-profile examples of interbranch showdowns. It analyzes the logic of veto bargaining and blame-game politics, the ways in which veto threats can elicit concessions from Congress, and the conditions under which bare majorities within Congress will send a bill over to the White House fully expecting the president to veto (and thereby kill) it.

This title also goes to greater lengths than most to lay out a variety of theories of presidential power, each of which has well-defined institutional foundations. By drawing upon these theories and investigating the critical debates among political scientists and presidency scholars, this volume goes beyond the broad institutional concepts that it champions in order to assess specific predictions about the particular conditions under which *all* presidents will exert more or less influence.

The American Presidency also devotes greater attention to some of the topics that make a regular, albeit brief, appearance in standard undergraduate courses. Chapter 16, for instance, focuses exclusively on the wartime presidency. It does so for reasons that relate directly to the overarching theme of the book: major wars have had a profound influence on the design of the modern presidency by inviting presidential involvement in new policy domains, expanding the size of the administrative state, and fundamentally altering aspects of the president's relationship with Congress and the judiciary. Moreover, the relationship between war and the American presidency has been the subject of renewed scholarly interest over the past decade. It is about time, then, for this topic to receive its due in a book on the American presidency.

To be sure, there are some features of American politics generally, and executive politics in particular, about which the institutional approach has very little to say. For that reason, the lessons from psychology, leadership styles, presidential character, and the like receive significantly less coverage here than in other books on the American presidency. When these topics do appear, they are critically evaluated rather than merely described in order to illustrate the ways in which political observers too often misattribute the sources of presidential successes and failures.

Two boxed features appear in every chapter and are explicitly designed to encourage institutional thinking that is at once incisive and reflective:

- Thinking Institutionally boxes address a variety of foundational questions: Do facts about the personalities of current or future presidents shape the institutional design of the presidency? Do presidents inherit the political universe, or are they able to remake it? What are the stakes of presidential elections? To what extent does a policy proposal represent the sincere preferences of a sitting president? Are there any domains of presidential politics (e.g., diplomacy) that are fundamentally personal in nature? Each Thinking Institutionally box either illustrates or challenges key aspects of this title's institutional argument and encourages critical reflection on the larger thematic issues at play.

- Historical Transformations boxes identify historical events that have played an important role in the original design and, more frequently, subsequent evolution of the institutional presidency. Institutions are neither handed down from on high nor set in stone. They are created and adapted by men and women responding to the challenges, demands, and interests of their day. Thus, the Historical Transformations feature pays special attention to the circumstances surrounding institutional change. These case studies cover such topics as the influence of Shays' Rebellion on the thinking of the Framers of the U.S. Constitution, the immediate and lasting impacts of the riots outside the 1968 Democratic convention in Chicago, and the profound changes wrought by foreign wars.

It should now be clear that this is a title with a definite point of view. It is not, however, intended to be dogmatic. Quite the contrary. It is meant to foster critical engagement with arguments about executive politics, clarify what the institutional approach adequately explains, and own up to what it does not. The institutional approach to studying the presidency can only take us so far in explaining why some candidates win presidential elections, why some presidents make mistakes early in their administrations while others hit their stride right away, why some Supreme Court nominees are chosen rather than others, and why some presidents appeal to the public through some media outlets and not others. Nor does the institutional approach resolve, once and for all, deep and long-standing debates about presidential powers. Indeed, as we shall see right away in chapter 1, while the Framers of our Constitution were committed institutionalists, they disagreed vehemently about just how the presidency ought to be designed and what powers ought to be conferred upon it. In the chapters that follow, other blind spots will be noted and investigated.

Conclusion

Whereas most discussions surrounding the president and presidential politics focus on the personalities that either occupy or seek entrance to the White House, *The American Presidency* assumes a distinctly institutional approach: it focuses on the office of the presidency rather than the identities of presidents.

An institutional approach proceeds at multiple levels. First, it shines a bright light on the institutions that constitute the executive branch, as well as the other institutions—Congress, the judiciary, the bureaucracy, the media, and interest groups—that intermittently constrain and support presidents. At a deeper level, though, it illuminates the ways in which institutions shape presidents' behavior and the very goals they pursue, for where presents sit in American government crucially defines what they see and how they act. In short, this title holds that the foundations of presidential power are institutional, not personal, in nature.

Key Terms

personal presidency　　**institution**
institutionalist　　**institutional presidency**

Questions for Discussion

1. What kinds of things does an institutional approach to studying the presidency ask us to ignore? At what cost do we do so?
2. Does an institutional approach to studying the presidency require us to take a deterministic view of American politics and political development? If so, why? If not, why not?
3. Are there ways in which the personal and institutional approaches to studying the presidency can be reconciled with each other?
4. Many voters profess a preference for "outsider" candidates for the presidency, ones who promise to shake things up and disrupt politics as usual. To what extent can the institutional presidency be expected to temper the influence—and ambition—of these candidates upon assuming office?

Suggested Readings

Aberbach, Joel D., and Mark A. Peterson, eds. *Institutions of American Democracy: The Executive Branch*. New York: Oxford University Press, 2005.

Edwards, George C., and William G. Howell, eds. *The Oxford Handbook of the American Presidency*. New York: Oxford University Press, 2011.

Edwards, George C., John H. Kessel, and Berk A. Rockman, eds. *Researching the Presidency: Vital Questions, New Approaches*. Pittsburgh: University of Pittsburgh Press, 1993.

Shapiro, Robert, Martha Joynt Kumar, and Lawrence Jacobs, eds. *Presidential Power*. New York: Columbia University Press, 2000.

Notes

1. Marc Fisher, "The Two Sides of Joe Biden," *Washington Post*, January 13, 2021, https://www.washingtonpost.com/politics/the-two-sides-of-joe-biden/2021/01/12/ec0ea9d8-4f8c-11eb-bda4-615aaefd0555_story.html.

2. Dan P. McAdams, "The Mind of Donald Trump," *Atlantic Monthly*, June 2016, 12–13; Matthew Dessem, "Here's Everything Samantha Bee Has Called Donald Trump on *Full Frontal*," *Slate*, November 5, 2016, http://www.slate.com/blogs/browbeat/2016/11/05/here_s_everything_samantha_bee_has_called_donald_trump.htm.

3. Mary Trump, *Too Much and Never Enough: How My Family Created the World's Most Dangerous Man* (New York: Simon & Schuster, 2020).

4. Michelle Dean, "Making the Man: To Understand Trump, Look at His Relationship with His Dad," *Guardian*, March 26, 2016, https://www.theguardian.com/us-news/2016/mar/26/donald-trump-fred-trump-father-relationship-business-real-estate-art-of-deal.

5. Daniel Drezner, *Toddler in Chief: What Donald Trump Teaches Us about the Modern Presidency* (Chicago: University of Chicago Press, 2020).

6. Peggy Noonan, "Declarations: Obama and the Debt Crisis," *Wall Street Journal*, June 4, 2011, Eastern edition, A.15; Jonathan S. Tobin, "Obama Still Politicizing the Debt Crisis," *Commentary*, July 29, 2011, https://www.commentarymagazine.com/jonathan-tobin/obama-politicizing-debt-crisis/; Ross Douthat, "The Diminished President," *New York Times*, July 31, 2011, Late edition, A.21.

7. Noonan, "Declarations: Obama and the Debt Crisis."

8. Paul Krugman, "Meh, Bleh, and Eek," *New York Times*, July 26, 2011, http://krugman.blogs.nytimes.com/2011/07/26/meh-bleh-and-eek/.

9. Drew Westen, "What Happened to Obama?" *New York Times*, August 6, 2011, SR.1.

10. "Barack Obama for President," *New York Times*, October 23, 2008, A.30.

11. Ron Suskind, "Faith, Certainty and the Presidency of George W. Bush," *New York Times Magazine*, October 17, 2004, http://www.nytimes.com/2004/10/17/magazine/17BUSH.html.

12. "43rd President Is 'Gut Player' Who Eschews Personal Change," NBC News, August 28, 2004, https://www.nbcnews.com/id/wbna5762240.

13. Pierce Butler, as quoted in Jack N. Rakove, *Original Meanings: Politics and Ideas in the Making of the Constitution* (New York: Random House Digital, 1997), 244.

14. Marion Elizabeth Rodgers, *Mencken: The American Iconoclast* (New York: Oxford University Press, 2005), 430.

15. Norman Mailer and Michael Leonard, *Conversations with Norman Mailer* (Jackson: University Press of Mississippi, 1988), 113, 146.

16. In addition to the studies summarized below, see, for example, Alexander George and Juliette George, *Presidential Personality and Performance* (Milton Park: Routledge, 2019); Erwin Hargrove, *Presidential Leadership: Personality and Political Style* (New York: Macmillan, 1966).

17. Richard E. Neustadt, *Presidential Power and the Modern Presidents: The Politics of Leadership from Roosevelt to Reagan* (New York: Free Press, 1991), 203.

18. James David Barber, *Politics by Humans: Research on American Leadership* (Durham: Duke University Press, 1988), 46.

19. Barber, *Politics by Humans*, 11.

20. Fred Greenstein, *The Presidential Difference: Leadership Style from FDR to George W. Bush* (Princeton: Princeton University Press, 2000), 5.

21. Woodrow Wilson, *Constitutional Government in the United States* (New Orleans, LA: Quid Pro Books, 1908), 40.

22. Terry Moe, "Presidents, Institutions, and Theory," in *Researching the Presidency: Vital Questions, New Approaches*, ed. George C. Edwards, John H. Kessel, and Bert A. Rockman (Pittsburgh: University of Pittsburgh Press, 1993), 379.

PART I

Foundations

1

Constitutional Origins

WHEN THE U.S. CONSTITUTION was officially ratified on June 21, 1788, a new, post-Revolutionary republic, and with it an American presidency, was born. How this American presidency would look and what powers American presidents would have, however, were not preordained. The Framers did not import *the* presidency—an ideal type, fully formed and completely actualized—into the American system from elsewhere. Rather, they created *a* presidency, one type among many possible.

In conceiving this new office, the Framers looked to distance themselves from the English model of monarchical rule and instead learn from the fledgling attempts at democratic governance at home. They drew heavily on Enlightenment works of legal and political philosophy, and were profoundly influenced by their experiences with colonial governorships and Revolutionary-period state constitutions.* Their most immediate experience with national governance, however, can be found in the Articles of Confederation. And so it is with these Articles that we begin our examination of the institutional presidency.

1.1 The Articles of Confederation

Composed by the Continental Congress at the height of the American Revolution, the "Articles of Confederation and Perpetual Union" established the first national constitution by which the affairs of the new confederation of independent states would be conducted. In its achievements, and even more in its shortcomings, the **Articles of Confederation** set an important precedent for an executive branch of the federal government whose eventual form would be inscribed in the U.S. Constitution ten years later. (For a review of key events in the founding of a new American republic, see the timeline in figure 1.1.)

---

* As Clinton Rossiter notes: "The materials with which [the Framers] worked were the colonial governorships and thus, more remotely, the British monarchy; the various solutions to the problem of executive power in the first state constitutions; the administrative departments that had developed under the Articles of Confederation; and the writings of such exponents of balanced government as Locke and Montesquieu." Clinton Rossiter, *The American Presidency* (New York: New American Library, 1960), 54.

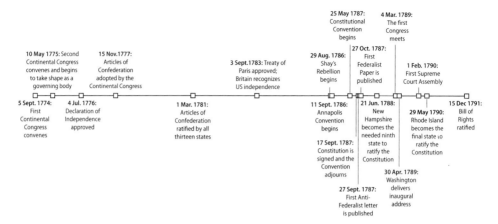

25 May 1787: Constitutional Convention begins

4 Mar. 1789: The first Congress meets

10 May 1775: Second Continental Congress convenes and begins to take shape as a governing body

15 Nov.1777: Articles of Confederation adopted by the Continental Congress

3 Sept.1783: Treaty of Paris approved; Britain recognizes US independence

29 Aug. 1786: Shay's Rebellion begins

27 Oct. 1787: First Federalist Paper is published

1 Feb. 1790: First Supreme Court Assembly

5 Sept. 1774: First Continental Congress convenes

4 Jul. 1776: Declaration of Independence approved

1 Mar. 1781: Articles of Confederation ratified by all thirteen states

11 Sept. 1786: Annapolis Convention begins

21 Jun. 1788: New Hampshire becomes the needed ninth state to ratify the Constitution

29 May 1790: Rhode Island becomes the final state to ratify the Constitution

15 Dec 1791: Bill of Rights ratified

17 Sept. 1787: Constitution is signed and the Convention adjourns

30 Apr. 1789: Washington delivers inaugural address

27 Sept. 1787: First Anti-Federalist letter is published

FIGURE 1.1. Historical timeline of the founding of the American Republic. Major events and milestones in the creation of the American Republic, from the founding of the Continental Congress to the ratification of the Bill of Rights.

1.1.1 Weaknesses of the Articles of Confederation

The Articles of Confederation, drafted in 1777 (but not fully ratified until 1781), established a national government that proved unable to address the substantive challenges of post-Revolutionary America: massive debt, domestic insurrection, popular dislocations, foreign threats, and a good deal more besides.

Despite a titular gesture toward "Perpetual Union," the Articles did little more than create a "firm league of friendship" among the states. Having banded together for the sole purpose of liberating themselves from the British crown, individual states had little appetite for relinquishing power to a new, centralized government after the war had been won. Instead, states tended to jealously guard their autonomy, and the Articles of Confederation generously permitted them to do so. "Each State retains its sovereignty, freedom and independence, and every power, jurisdiction, and right, which is not by this confederation expressly delegated to the United States, in Congress assembled" (Article II). The central government under the Articles lacked power to regulate commerce, establish a judiciary, collect taxes from individuals, or compel states to contribute to a national treasury in order to pay Revolutionary debts.

Under the Articles of Confederation, the federal government lacked an institutional structure through which it might execute its powers. Only a single governmental body—a national Congress modeled after the Continental Congress—was provided for. Each of thirteen state delegations had a single vote in the Confederation Congress. But as the only federal institution authorized by the Articles, the Confederation Congress had to fulfill all federal government functions on its own. First and foremost, it served as a legislature, with the power to write new laws. Though nominally empowered as a "deliberating, executive assembly" to declare war and conduct foreign relations, the Confederation Congress was subject to strict constraints, especially the requirement of a supermajority (nine of the thirteen possible votes) to pass any legislation. In its eight years of existence, the Confederation Congress only managed to pass a total of twenty-five ordinances, most of which pertained to maritime trade and piracy, the establishment of post offices, relations with Native Americans, and the internal organization of Congress itself. The remainder of the items the Confederation Congress passed were merely "recommendations" for its member states.[1]

Congress also had to attend to all judicial responsibilities, since the federal government was supposed to adjudicate disputes among states.[2] To do so, Congress set up provincial courts in the states where juries would try cases. Appeals were initially brought back to Congress for voting, but eventually the Confederation Congress established (through ordinance) an official appeals court consisting of three judges.[3] Disputes between states largely focused on maritime issues such as which state had rights to the seas and how prizes captured from enemy vessels should be allocated. In wartime, Congress was given substantial authority to adjudicate disputes, but as time went on, states became increasingly reluctant to abide by Congress's rulings.

Under the Articles, Congress did have a president. Indeed, eight different men would each serve one-year terms under the Confederation. The president, however, did not exercise the kind of executive power that is associated with the presidency today. Instead, the role was largely ceremonial. Like the Speaker of the House today, the president of the Confederation Congress refrained from participating in debate and voted only as a tie-breaker. Unlike current House Speakers, however, presidents under the Articles had no power to assign delegates to committees, no control over the political agenda, and no leverage to influence members to vote one way or another. Even the term "president" was deliberately chosen to signify someone assigned to preside over Congress, not someone with broad jurisdictional powers.

Members of the Confederation Congress soon recognized the need for some formalized system by which executive decisions could be made and its delegated powers carried out. Congress initially delegated executive authority to committees, such as the Committee on Foreign Affairs. Congress appointed select delegates to these committees, similar to the way contemporary congressional committees are formed. As the Revolutionary War dragged on, however, committee delegates were less and less able to cope with the burdens of government. As a result, in 1781 the Confederation Congress authorized the creation of four executive departments—War, Marine, Foreign Affairs, and Finance—with a single individual appointed to run each. In theory, these departments functioned the way contemporary executive cabinets do today: each department head gathered information and devised possible courses of action before advising Congress. Under the Articles of Confederation, however, these departments remained subsidiary divisions of Congress.

In a sense, the Articles merely codified the arrangement under which the states had already been working since their initial agreement to unite (at the First Continental Congress in 1774). Once the Revolution was over, however, it became increasingly clear that the Articles, and the federal government it supported, were no longer serviceable. Under the Articles of Confederation, the fledgling United States suffered three near-calamitous failures: two in foreign affairs, one in domestic matters.

The first failure: To finance the Revolutionary War, the Continental Congress had borrowed millions of dollars from foreign creditors. Since the central government had no power to compel taxation, the states, all of which were dealing with monetary and credit issues of their own, refused to supply the national government with funds to pay the nation's debts. As a consequence, foreign creditors began refusing U.S. trade. American ambassadors in Europe, such as Thomas Jefferson in France and John Adams in Britain, failed to convince their European counterparts to sign even modest trade agreements because European nations remained deeply skeptical that the United States had the domestic authority to follow through on its promises.

The second failure: Congress's second foreign affairs failure occurred upon the high seas. In the eighteenth century, the Mediterranean Sea was a hotbed of pirate activity often supported, either tacitly or explicitly, by the coastal states of North Africa. As subjects of the British crown, American ships had once been protected from pirates by Britain's powerful navy, as well as by hefty British bribes. Without this protection, U.S. ships sailing into the Mediterranean through the Strait of Gibraltar in the 1780s were repeatedly captured and plundered by pirates.

In July 1785, Algerian pirates captured two American schooners and impressed twenty-one crew members into servitude under Muhammad V, the ruler of Algiers. Thomas Jefferson and other American leaders expressed outrage, but the United States could not raise a fleet to bring back the hostages. Facing no threat of military reprisal, Muhammad demanded a ransom of $1 million (one-fifth the federal budget at the time)[4] in exchange for the hostages' safe return. Congress sent a commissioner, John Lamb, to negotiate with Muhammad, who eventually agreed to lower the ransom to $60,000. But infighting and disagreement ultimately prevented Congress from appropriating even this reduced amount, and the captured Americans remained in Algeria for another decade.[5]

Enslaved merchant crews proved to be a fitting symbol for the fractures and failures of the post-Revolution Confederation. United in common purpose, thirteen American colonies had only two years earlier defeated the most powerful empire in the world. Yet now, with the Revolutionary War over, the not-so-united United States could not adequately attend to threats posed by looting bands of pirates.

The third failure: Diplomatic and military setbacks abroad were troubling enough, but the Confederation government's ultimate undoing stemmed from conflicts within its own borders. Once the Revolutionary War officially ended with the Treaty of Paris in 1783, interstate conflicts erupted over claims to highly sought-after unincorporated western territories. In several cases, tensions between settlers on the western frontier escalated to the point of violence. Those same settlers also lived under constant threat of raids by Native Americans, against whom federal troops provided virtually no protection. The federal government's inability to protect its citizens became most apparent in the conflict known as Shays' Rebellion (detailed in this chapter's Historical Transformations feature).

By the second half of the 1780s, the damage to the federal government's reputation proved unacceptable. Congress had been shown to be completely ineffective at addressing foreign and domestic threats to the nation's security. Sectarian disputes had routinely been left unresolved in assembly. In the face of persistent threats from outside its borders, the national government was falling apart from within.

Historical Transformations: Shays' Rebellion

In Massachusetts, during the fall and early winter of 1786, nearly 3,000 men organized themselves into impromptu militias and began harassing officials in the state government. Most were farmers suffering from high tariffs on their stock and produce. Many, including their leader Daniel Shays, were former soldiers who had not been paid by the federal government for their service in the Revolutionary War. Their grievances were clear, as was the violence they perpetrated. The open question centered on the government's ability to respond effectively to an uprising.

Massachusetts governor and commander in chief James Bowdoin failed to assemble a state militia of sufficient size to quell this armed insurrection. The Confederation Congress, meanwhile, proved to be too impoverished and too slow to solve the crisis. Although other states worried that the violence of Shays' Rebellion might spread across their borders, their representatives in Congress could not agree on who should pay the military costs to raise a national force. Astonishingly, then, it was left to a group of wealthy, independent Boston merchants to raise and finance a volunteer army to disperse the rebels.

Shays' Rebellion is widely regarded as a pivotal transformation in the years between the end of the American Revolution in 1781 and the start of the Constitutional Convention in 1787. As historian Gordon Wood recognized, the intensity and scope of the uprising, "dramatically clarifying what was taking place in nearly all the states," persuaded pundits and political leaders across the nation that their confidence in their post-Revolutionary state constitutions as "model[s] of political perfection" had been misplaced. Up until the moment when Daniel Shays and his followers forced their way onto the national stage, so much complimentary attention had been paid to the efficacy of state constitutions that a majority of leaders at the time had been able to safely ignore the constitutional weaknesses of the Articles of Confederation.

After the rebellion, as Wood succinctly remarked, "state governments, however well structured, no longer seemed capable of creating virtuous laws and citizens." Moreover, the revolt in Massachusetts made it clear that however strong state institutions were, they would continue to be ineffective so long as they lacked a strong national institutional structure to undergird them. "In vain must be all our exertions to brace up our own [state]

Continued on next page

FIGURE 1.2. Daniel Shays, a captain in the Continental Army during the Revolutionary War, was the symbolic leader of agrarian protests against tax and debt collections in 1786 and 1787. The protests erupted in multiple states, but most were concentrated in western Massachusetts, where a series of poor harvests and a bad economy threatened the livelihood of farmers. *Source:* North Wind Picture Archives/ Alamy.

Government without we have a better federal System than at present,"[6] wrote Stephen Higginson, a lieutenant general in a Boston regiment that helped put down the rebellion. Higginson's sentiment reflected that of many Americans who now felt a pressing need for a strong *national* executive office—one that could support and maintain the peace. And for that, a new Constitution was required.

1.1.2 The Call to Amend the Articles of Confederation

The failures of the federal government had less to do with the incompetence or inexperience of its leaders and more to do with the structure of government. Historians point to the "weak, purely legislative" functions of Congress under the Articles of Confederation, which repeatedly failed to render even the few executive decisions it was empowered to make.[7]

The inadequacies of Congress, especially in executive matters, were not lost on political observers of the time. As early as 1781, prominent nationalists such as Alexander Hamilton had called for the reform of "the present futile and senseless confederation."[8] William Livingston, the governor of New Jersey, admitted that the authors of the Articles had been so frightened of monarchical power that they had failed to account for the government's need to maintain a reliable executive authority. Wrote Livingston, "we improvidently raised a battery against an attack that could never be made upon us, & accordingly constituted the Executive branch too weak & inefficacious to operate with proper energy & vigour."[9] Having witnessed the inefficiencies of Congress firsthand, executive department officers such as Robert Morris and John Jay were similarly disenchanted with the Articles. "Mismanagement" would always plague the Confederation Congress, Morris wrote, "because no man living can attend the daily deliberations of Congress and do executive parts of business at the same time."[10] Jay went one step further, explicitly outlining why "the Construction of our Federal Government is fundamentally wrong. To vest legislative, judicial, and executive Powers in one and the same Body of Men . . . can never be wise. In my Opinion those three great Departments of Sovereignty should be forever separated, as to serve as Checks on each other."[11]

Initial attempts to amend the Articles of Confederation and institute an independent executive proved futile. In the summer of 1785, the Massachusetts state legislature petitioned Congress to organize a convention for the sole purpose of revising the Articles of Confederation. According to the Massachusetts legislature, the Articles simply were "not adequate to the great purpose they were originally designed to effect."[12] Yet the state's own delegates in Congress refused the petition on the grounds that the current confederation embodied the republican ideal of state freedom that, if disrupted, would lead to tyranny.[13] Even moderate proposals for amending the Articles failed to gain traction within Congress.[14]

In the wake of such failures, the Virginia state assembly, led by James Madison, sent word to the other twelve states that a national conference would be held at Annapolis, Maryland, in September 1786. Ostensibly about trade, the assembly in actuality was meant to rally support for a wholesale revision of the Articles of Confederation. In response to Virginia, only four other states—New York, Pennsylvania, New Jersey, and Delaware—bothered to send delegations. Still, the Annapolis Convention proved to be a turning point. In Annapolis, Madison joined with Hamilton and other important political figures in issuing a call to action. As he put it, the states shall "meet at Philadelphia on the second Monday in May [of 1787], to take into consideration the situation of the United States, to devise such further provisions as shall appear to them necessary, to render the constitution of the Federal Government adequate to the exigencies of the Union."[15] The key players were coming together.

Madison's call resonated within both the general public and the upper echelons of political leadership, all of whom began to see that local fates were intimately tied to national ones. The confederation as then constituted could not achieve its aim, as stated in Article III, of providing for the states' "common defense, the security of their liberties, and their mutual and general welfare." In the wake of Shays' Rebellion, none other than George Washington, who had retired from public life after the Revolution, began pressing his colleagues for reform.[16] In the face of mounting pressure, Congress once again took up the Madison-Hamilton proposal for a convention in Philadelphia. This time, the proposal to initiate a convention to restructure the federal government was approved.

The speed with which public sentiment shifted toward the establishment of an independent executive body is nothing short of astonishing. Only a decade prior, any concentration of executive power was considered a mere prelude to tyranny. But the nation's experience during the first few years after the Revolution confirmed the importance of a strong executive.[17] Whereas the debate surrounding the Articles of Confederation had been about how to limit centralized executive authority at all costs, the question for the delegates in Philadelphia was the opposite: How could a vigorous executive institution exist within a republican framework of government?

1.2 An American Presidency, Defined

In May 1787, delegations from twelve of the thirteen states convened in Philadelphia, Pennsylvania, with only Rhode Island declining to participate. The convention's fifty-five delegates were nearly all members of the social and economic elite, including large landowners, small farmers, lawyers, merchants, doctors, and scientists. Even an ordained minister was present. Many were heroes of the Revolution: twenty-nine had fought in the Continental Army; eight had signed the Declaration of Independence. New Jersey's Jonathan Dayton (age 26) was the youngest member of the convention; the physically ailing Benjamin Franklin (age 81) was by far the oldest. Along with an array of backgrounds and regional affinities, the delegates came to Philadelphia with very different opinions about how to design a new national government.

Yet on one matter, at least, all the delegates agreed: it was time to fix what Madison called "the existing embarrassments and mortal diseases of the Confederacy."[18] In the opinions of most, this would involve a great deal more than just shoring up the formal powers of existing governmental institutions. It required creating altogether new ones, which very much included a strong executive office. As historian Jack Rakove points out, "the nearest thing to a first principle" among the delegates to the Constitutional Convention "was the desire to enable the executive to resist legislative 'encroachments.'"[19] Even those Framers wary of concentrated power such as Edmund Randolph recognized the "great requisites for the Executive department" were "vigor, despatch & responsibility."[20]

Agreeing on the need for change is one thing; settling on the nature of change is quite another. Due to the difficulties of eighteenth-century travel, the delegations all arrived in the city at different times, making a **quorum**—the number of members of an assembly needed in order for a binding vote to occur—at times difficult to achieve. Those present would revisit, again and again, proposals for the creation of an independent executive branch of government. Indeed, few topics divided them more. In the words of Alexander Hamilton, "There is hardly any part of the system which could have been attended with greater difficulty in the arrangement of it than this."[21]

Conflicting concerns animated the debates at the Constitutional Convention. On the one hand, Anti-Federalists, who opposed the ratification of the Constitution, held firmly to a deep distrust of concentrated power, an abiding belief in the importance of individual liberty, and a recognition of the merits of limited government. For many of those in attendance, concentrations of executive authority were too reminiscent of monarchy, which they associated with avarice, vice, and corruption. They predicted that a presidency would usher in "ambition with idleness—baseness with pride—the thirst for riches without labor—aversion to truth—flattery—treason—perfidy—violation of engagements—contempt of civil duties—hope from the magistrate's weakness: but above all the perpetual ridicule of virtue."*

On the other hand, some Framers, citing as evidence the scourge of recent domestic insurrections, maintained that individual liberty was at risk in the absence of a strong federal government capable of both writing *and* implementing laws. Alexander Hamilton took exactly such a position, warning in *Federalist* 70 that "[a] feeble executive implies a feeble execution of the government. A feeble execution is but another phrase for a bad execution; and a government ill executed, whatever it may be in theory, must be, in practice, a bad government." If the new nation was to effectively respond to emergent crises, it would need a newly empowered presidency.

For Framers like Hamilton (figure 1.3), the predominant concern lay in the possibility of legislative, not executive, overreach. While there was a consensus that the presidency must inject much-needed energy into the federal government, nearly all of the delegates in Philadelphia, as well as all three authors of the *Federalist Papers* (Hamilton, James Madison, and John Jay), assumed that Congress would remain the primary branch of government. Madison referred to the "general supremacy" of legislatures in *Federalist* 43 and to their "impetuous vortex" of power in *Federalist* 48; Governor Edmund Randolph of Virginia insisted that the powers exercised in legislatures to "swallow up the other branches" be taken as a "maxim."[22]

An American presidency was born of these two competing imperatives: deep distrust of concentrated power and recognition of the need for effective, energetic governance. The imprint of these dueling claims can be seen in the revision plans that several states brought to the convention. The essential provisions of three plans appear in table 1.1 for cross-comparison. In the end, none of the plans was adopted wholesale, nor were any defeated outright. Instead, elements of each were adopted piecemeal in the construction of an American presidency. At the convention itself, each imperative animated four dimensions of the debate on the presidency:

---

* The concerns of Anti-Federalists about a strong, unitary president were spelled out in the *Letters of Cato*, written, some think, by New York governor George Clinton, who opposed the ratification of the Constitution. The Federalists' case for a strong president, meanwhile, is laid out in *The Federalist Papers*, most forcefully those written by Alexander Hamilton in papers 67–77.

FIGURE 1.3. Alexander Hamilton. Among the nation's founders, Hamilton offered the most robust defense of a strong national government and, with it, a strong presidency. *Source:* John Trumbull/Library of Congress Prints and Photographs Division [LC-DIG-det- 4a26166].

1. the relative independence of the executive, legislative, and judicial branches of government;
2. the division of powers across the various branches of government;
3. the number of presidents who would govern; and
4. the mode of presidential selection and succession.

1.2.1 Executive Independence

The ambivalence of convention delegates toward executive power emanated from broader meditations on the nature of humankind. Would individuals occupying an office of great power work to advance the nation's interests rather than pursue their own private gains? Would appeals to a higher nature produce a steady stock of the "right" people—benevolent presidents, akin to Plato's philosopher kings, who would reliably recognize and correct for their own biases and ignorance and work doggedly on behalf of the nation as a whole? If so, power could be fearlessly vested in a single executive office.

The Framers rejected this line of argumentation. For them, the baser qualities of human nature, such as greed and ambition, could not be discarded. Moreover, it would be impossible to design a system of government that ensured that the "right" individuals would be elected to office. In the end, as the historian Richard Hofstadter notes, "a properly designed state, the Fathers believed, would check interest with interest, class with class, faction with faction, and one branch of government with another in a harmonious system of mutual

TABLE 1.1. The Executive Branch: Three Different Proposals

	Virginia Plan	New Jersey Plan	British Plan
Presenter	Edmund Randolph (drafted by James Madison)	William Paterson	Alexander Hamilton
Date Presented	May 29, 1787	June 15, 1787	June 18, 1787
Executive Selection	appointed by national legislature	appointed by national legislature	elected by electors chosen by people from each election district
Executive Succession	limited to one term of unspecified duration	limited to one term of unspecified duration	lifetime appointment, pending "good behavior"
Executive Structure	single individual	committee of unspecified number of individuals	single individual
Executive Responsibilities	• "execute the National laws" • veto power, shared with judicial branch	• "general authority to execute the federal acts" • appoint federal officers and federal judges • direct military operations	• "the execution of all laws passed" • veto power • direct military operations • make treaties, shared with the Senate • appoint federal department heads • nominate other federal officials, with Senate confirmation • grant pardons

frustration."[23] A contestation of competing interests, commitments, and worldviews, it was thought, would elevate the public good.

In this regard, the influences of Enlightenment thinkers John Locke (1632–1704) and Baron de Montesquieu (1689–1755) are palpable. In order to protect individual liberties, the Framers recognized, a system of **checks and balances** was needed, with each branch of government maintaining the requisite powers to guard against encroachments on its own prerogatives, which stood the best chance of ensuring a balance of power within government and the protection individual liberties beyond. To realize these objectives, the executive branch could be neither a subsidiary nor an extension of the legislature. Rather, it must have autonomy—that is, independence—with the resources to act in its own interests and, where necessary, to challenge and sometimes even negate those of the other branches of government.

In *Federalist* 51, Madison outlined three principles governing the creation of an independent executive:

1. Each branch of government, as much as possible, should retain control over the appointment of officials within it.
2. Compensation for members within each branch should depend, as little as possible, upon the discretion of other branches of government.
3. Each branch of government should be given the means, and personal motives, to guard against encroachments.

This third point is so important that it is worth quoting Madison at length:

> In framing a government which is to be administered by men over men, the great difficulty lies in this: you must first enable the government to control the governed; and in the next place oblige it to control itself. A dependence on the people is, of no doubt, the primary control on the government; but experience has taught mankind the necessity of auxiliary precautions.[24]

The independence of each branch of government, coupled with distinct and genuine powers, would lay the groundwork for a presidency that acted as a viable check on judicial and legislative authority, just as the judicial and legislative branches checked the presidency.

Henceforth, executive independence would be formally secured through elections—the president would now be elected by the people (if indirectly), not by Congress. Moreover, the president would be entrusted with the executive powers of the national government, and the **veto power** would rest solely with the chief executive rather than with a council selected by Congress. In addition, and not trivially for the times, Congress could not change a standing president's salary, nor could any individual serve simultaneously as president and as a member of the House or Senate. With the Constitution's ratification in 1788, the American presidency became, if not a coequal branch of government, then at least an independent one.

1.2.2 Executive Responsibilities, Divided and Shared

Though presidents would retain exclusive control over a few **enumerated powers**—those explicitly stated in the Constitution—some of these powers would be shared, and each branch would be afforded opportunities to affect the goings-on within the others.

As figure 1.4 shows, the new Constitution granted to presidents certain exclusive powers which they alone would hold. Only presidents under this new system of government could grant pardons, veto bills from Congress, and command the military. That these powers were exclusive, however, does not mean that they were complete. In fact, many such powers were only partial in form. While presidents could prevent legislation by issuing vetoes, for example, such vetoes could be overridden with a two-thirds majority in Congress.

The Constitution assigned other powers for both the presidency and Congress to share. Though presidents had the power to appoint individuals to the federal bureaucracy and judiciary, many of these appointments would be subject to the advice and consent of the Senate. And though the president would be commander in chief, the power to wage war would ultimately be shared with Congress, who had the sole authority to declare war and appropriate funds for military ventures. Figure 1.4 depicts a similar relationship between Congress and the judiciary, both of whom possess some mix of exclusive and shared powers. As explored at greater length in later chapters, presidential interactions with Congress and the judiciary would fundamentally shape the opportunities available to—and the decisions made by—the executive in the ongoing give-and-take of governing. Powers, under this system, would be both separated and shared.

The setup of this system was no accident. The Framers recognized the need for a division of legislative, executive, and judicial responsibilities, but they also appreciated the many ways in which these responsibilities blended into one another. Though assigned different stations and powers, each branch of government would affect the workings of government. A president en-

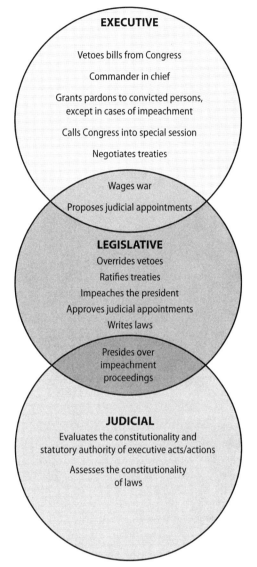

FIGURE 1.4. Constitutionally enumerated powers. Listed here are the most explicit constitutionally enumerated powers granted to the three branches of government.

joyed substantial independence but could not reasonably expect to be left alone. In fact, when administering some responsibilities, presidents depended upon the active approval—expressed in various ways—of members of Congress. And when going it alone, presidents had to proceed with considerable caution lest Congress or the courts amend, defund, or simply overturn their actions.

Not all formal powers granted to the president, though, are divided and shared. One, in particular, sits squarely with the president alone. Article II, Section 2 of the Constitution entrusts the president with "the power to grant reprieves and pardons for offenses against the United States, except in cases of impeachment." Under this provision, the president can grant full and conditional pardons, amnesties, and commutations of prison sentences to both individuals and large groups of individuals who have committed federal offenses.[25] For some of the Framers, the **pardon power** was meant to correct failures of the American legal system or temper justice with mercy in cases that deserve clemency.[26] Just as English kings had retained the power to overturn any sentence, these Framers thought that presidents should have the authority to grant clemency as they saw fit. For others, though, practical considerations about governance were of paramount concern. By giving the president the power to pardon, it was thought, the president might quell insurrections by assuring insurgents that they could avoid punishment should they surrender, as occurred at the close of the Civil War. In a similar vein, the promise of a pardon might be used to secure needed testimony from an individual who would otherwise face federal prosecution.[27]

In many ways, the power to pardon is nearly absolute. Unlike the veto, the pardon power is subject to neither *ex ante* nor *ex post* legislative review.[28] Similarly, the judiciary plays no formal role in evaluating the merits of any presidential power. For all intents and purposes, the only procedural check on the president's pardon power is impeachment, a topic that we discuss at further length below.

The boundaries of the pardon power, moreover, are remarkably expansive.[29] Presidents are free to pardon nearly anyone they choose—including, some have argued, their colleagues, family members, and themselves. Presidents can pardon people for federal crimes for which they have already been convicted, as well as crimes for which they have been merely charged. And with the sole exception of cases concerning impeachment, presidents can issue pardons for any federal offense whatsoever.

The president's pardon power is notable for both its expansiveness and its exceptionality. No other power granted to the president is nearly as vast or complete. And no other power sits so squarely within the executive branch alone. Presidents can issue pardons with considerable abandon. In nearly every other domain of governance, however, presidents must compromise, negotiate, bargain, or hedge—lest other branches of government, with powers of their own, disregard them, stand in their way, or undo their handiwork after the fact.

IMPEACHMENT

The Framers afforded the power of impeachment to the legislative branch as the ultimate guard against executive tyranny (defined by Madison in *Federalist* 47 as the "accumulation of all powers, legislative, executive, and judiciary, in the same hands, whether of one, a few, or many, and whether hereditary, self-appointed, or elective").[30] In light of the dangers of concentrated authority, and despite competing proposals to make only subordinate officers impeachable,[31] the Framers of the Constitution imported impeachment from English law and redesigned it as an institutional fail-safe, a process of ousting a tyrannical president in times when the country is unable to wait for the upcoming election to vote out the sitting president.[32] To be clear, the Framers believed that elections ought to be the primary mode of political accountability. They also recognized, though, that the costs of waiting until the next election could sometimes be prohibitive.

The Framers divided the process of forcing a president from office into two steps: impeachment and removal. Impeachment begins in the House of Representatives when a member or group of members of the House declare a charge of impeachment against the president.[33] The House Judiciary Committee then investigates the charges leveled against the president to determine if sufficient grounds for impeachment exist[34]—namely, if the person in question engaged in "treason, bribery, or other high crimes and misdemeanors." Following an investigation into the matter, the Judiciary Committee then submits a report about the specific misconduct to the full chamber. The House then votes on the Judiciary Committee's report to determine if the president's conduct warrants a trial.

If a simple majority of the representatives present votes to impeach the sitting president on one, several, or all of the articles presented, the case proceeds to the Senate.* The Senate first summons the official in question and sets a trial date. Under the Constitution, the Chief Justice presides over the impeachment trial if the official in question is the president.[35] Senate proceedings mirror those of a judicial hearing. Evidence is presented, arguments are made on both sides, and the Senate determines what information is relevant to each charge leveled against the officer. Following the trial, the Senate meets in a closed session to deliberate. The trial process culminates when the Senate votes on each article of impeachment separately. If two-thirds of the senators present vote to convict the president on one or more of the articles presented, the president is removed from office.[36]

What constitutes impeachable offenses? At one point in the constitutional drafting process, the stipulated grounds for impeachment consisted only of two clearly defined crimes, treason and bribery,[37] before the Framers ultimately landed on the much broader "treason, bribery, or other high crimes and misdemeanors." The inclusion of the catchall phrase "high crimes and misdemeanors" lends further credence to the idea that the Framers saw impeachment as a broad fail-safe against executive tyranny, and not as punishment for specific crimes.

In addition to safeguarding against corruption and treason, impeachment is meant to prevent presidents from committing other "high crimes"—which, depending on the interpreter, may refer to either serious criminal offenses or the crimes of high-ranking officials.[38] Meanwhile, the term "misdemeanors" extends the bounds of impeachable offenses to include conduct while in office that renders a president decidedly unfit to serve. To the Framers, misdemeanors represented a breach of public trust and not (as in our modern legal system) a minor crime. Given the vagueness of the phrase and without clear consti-

---

* As Alexander Hamilton explains in *Federalist* 65, the Framers assigned the power of removal to the Senate because "the Convention thought the Senate the most fit depositary of this important trust. Where else than in the Senate could have been found a tribunal sufficiently dignified, or sufficiently independent? What other body would be likely to feel confident enough in its own situation, to preserve unawed and uninfluenced the necessary impartiality between an individual accused, and the representatives of the people, his accusers?" Alexander Hamilton, "Federalist No. 65," *The Federalist Papers.*

tutional definitions or historical precedent for guidance, attempts to demystify "high crimes and misdemeanors" have thus far been unsuccessful. (For a history of the use of impeachment, see chapter 8.)

This, though, we know with some certainty: impeachment was not designed to combat private conduct that the public views as poor judgment, nor to oust presidents over ill-advised decisions or unpopular policy positions. Rather, impeachment was designed to remedy dangerous offenses and abuses of the office of the presidency. Despite the ambiguity of the phrase, the Framers settled on "high crimes and misdemeanors" because they felt that it best captured the range of criminal and non-criminal impeachable offenses. Impeachable offenses, thus, might best be understood as abuses of official power or misconduct committed while in office that imperiled the safety and security of the nation.

Notice that the Framers gave the impeachment power to Congress alone. Though they certainly recognized the possibility that "tyrannies of the majority" might arise on Capitol Hill, the Framers did not see fit to empower the president to remove legislators from office. The reason for this asymmetric assignment of power is simple: the Framers saw the presidency, structured as a unitary actor, as particularly susceptible to the power-hungry ambitions of men; and given as much, they could not be entrusted with this extraordinary authority. The Framers generally agreed that Congress, as a collective decision-making body, would be the more responsible steward of this power and that this power should be used to constrain and punish presidents, unelected administrators, and unelected judges.

1.2.3 A Singular Executive

Even after the principles of executive independence and checks and balances had been established, a great deal of disagreement about the internal design of the presidency persisted. Some, such as delegate James Wilson of Pennsylvania, who would later become one of the nation's first Supreme Court justices, advocated for a presidency that would consist of a single individual who would oversee a federal bureaucracy—a **unitary executive**. Others, such as Edmund Randolph of Virginia, pushed for a multimember executive committee—a **plural executive**. Unsurprisingly, the arguments over design once again pitted the standard concerns about unbridled and concentrated authority against the desire for effective, coherent executive governance.

By vesting executive power in a single person, some feared, the Framers would potentially create what Randolph called "the foetus of monarchy."[39] A president who was "a favorite with his army,"[40] who displayed extraordinary charisma, or who curried the favor of a particularly powerful segment of the American populace might manage to seize control of the country and turn himself into a king. To be sure, that outcome was not preordained. But as long as the executive branch was governed by one person, Randolph and others worried, ambitious men might gather unto themselves the essential powers of the federal government. As subsequent chapters will make clear, Randolph was not altogether wrong to worry.

Randolph and his supporters eventually lost out to advocates for a unitary executive. In the lead-up to the Constitutional Convention, most delegates recognized that an executive committee would be less effective and less responsible than a single individual.* During the course of the convention, the Framers disparagingly referenced weak state constitutions, such as that of Randolph's Virginia, that had multiple executives. Even those Framers who doubted the superiority of a unitary executive recognized that it provided the best chance to contain the expansion of legislative authority, which many delegates presumed to be the greatest threat to the delicate balance of powers across the various branches of government. A multiheaded presidency, Madison wrote before the convention, was "too numerous and expensive; [its] organization [too] vague and perplexed" to keep a legislature in check.[41] What a representative republic required was a "single magistrate" who, in the words of James Wilson, would "giv[e] most energy, dispatch and responsibility to the office."[42]

More than anyone else, Hamilton articulated the benefits of a strong, unitary presidency. Indeed, for Hamilton, the very fate of the federal government depended upon it. As he argued in *Federalist* 70, "Energy in the executive is a leading character in the definition of good government." Hamilton went on to emphasize the need for executive alacrity and acuity, especially in times of war, thereby equating good governance with both speed and efficiency—exactly what the legislature under the Articles of Confederation could not provide. Though Hamilton's arguments did not win over every delegate, he nonetheless managed to shape the contours of the presidency, in scholar Clinton Rossiter's words, as "an office of remarkable vigor and independence."[43]

Thinking Institutionally: Did the Personal Inform the Institutional?
The Case of George Washington

When the delegates to the Constitutional Convention convened in Philadelphia in May 1787, they unanimously elected George Washington as president to oversee their deliberations. It was a smart, if obvious, selection. As commander in chief of the Continental Army during the Revolutionary War, Washington had a national reputation as the ideal American leader: a gentleman of dignity, modesty, and valor. His presence at the convention gave the proceedings legitimacy, and his support of the drafted Constitution made it more palatable to state legislatures. The "living embodiment [of] classical Republican virtue," whose "face was clearly visible to everyone" in the convention hall,[44] Washington assuaged concerns that the proposed presidency would lapse into a kingship. Indeed, observers at the time were certain that, without Washington's support, the Constitution never would have been ratified. James Monroe,

Continued on next page

---

* Or as historian Charles Thach put it, "executive efficiency and responsibility vary inversely in proportion to the size of the executive body." Charles Thach, *The Creation of the Presidency, 1775–1789: A Study in Constitutional History* (1923; Baltimore: Johns Hopkins University Press, 1969), 74.

writing to Thomas Jefferson, confided, "Be assured, [Washington's] influence carried this government."[45]

Yet while Washington's importance to the ratification process is clear, his impact on the actual drafting of the Constitution remains ambiguous. As president of the convention, his role was to gavel sessions to order but otherwise remain "above the fray."[46] Washington therefore abstained from the often-heated convention debates and spoke on record only twice: once to thank the delegates for the honor of serving as president of the proceedings and again, during the last session, to give his input on a fairly minor matter of representation.

In spite of his relative silence, some historians have argued that Washington's immense popularity and unimpeachable character reassured the Framers about the risks of vesting executive powers in one individual. The basis for such claims comes almost entirely from a single letter written by South Carolina delegate Pierce Butler. Butler protested that the powers of the executive branch ended up being "greater than I was disposed to make them," adding that he doubted that "they would have been so great had not many of the members cast their eyes toward General Washington as President; and shaped their Ideas of the Powers to be given to a President, by their Opinions of his Virtue."[47]

Did personal considerations inform deliberations about matters of institutional design? Just weeks before the convention, Madison wrote to Washington about the executive office, confessing that he had "scarcely ventured to form [his] own opinion either of the manner in which it ought to be constituted or of the authorities with which it ought to be cloathed."[48] When James Wilson first made a motion "that the Executive consist of a single person," the delegates delayed discussion of the matter, "seeming unprepared for any decision on it."[49] Did the Framers really have no conception of how to institutionalize executive power until the most obvious example of executive authority, the restrained and singular General Washington, stepped into the void? Should it be assumed that the Framers would never have settled upon a strong, unitary presidency had the trusted Washington not been sitting in their midst?

Many of the most influential delegates to the convention harbored clear conceptions of how the institution of the presidency ought to be constructed. Before the convention, John Jay, who would later become the first Chief Justice of the U.S. Supreme Court, wrote of a three-branch federal system in which "the executive branch should stop short of a monarchy, but only slightly."[50] Alexander Hamilton and John Dickenson likewise expressed their admiration for Britain's system of limited monarchy.[51] Finally, during the convention debates, the vast majority of delegates, well aware that the need to draft a new constitution arose from the weak, or nonexistent, executive established under the Articles of Confederation, expressed worries about the executive being too feeble rather than too strong.

From the outset, the delegates recognized that their charge was to build the nation's government anew. They therefore took the long view of the American

FIGURE 1.5. While presiding over the Constitutional Convention, Washington said very little. Still, some historians suggest, his mere presence lent the proceedings legitimacy; these historians further argue that Washington's reputation substantially influenced the institutional design of the office. The bases for such a conclusion, though, warrant scrutiny. *Source:* History/Newscom.

presidency and executive power. They were committed institutionalists, set upon building a legal document for posterity. Deliberations were steeped in legal and historical analyses, not in the comforting thought that Washington would be the first president. At the heart of the model of government that they would create lay a belief in the importance of institutional checks and balances on executive power, not on the idea that a virtuous individual would banish the influence of vice. This core tenet of the new government was eloquently summarized by none other than Washington himself: "Men are very apt to run into extremes . . . it is a maxim founded on the universal experience of mankind, that no [man] is to be trusted farther than [he] is bound by [his] interest; and no prudent statesman or politician ventures to depart from it."[52]

If Washington did embody, in character and temperament, their notion of the presidential ideal—an executive who "would rise above party turmoil to embody a disinterested notion of the public good"—the Framers also recognized that the heroic General Washington was exceptional in this regard.[53] Even John Adams, who was one of Washington's few contemporary critics, marveled that "he seeks information from all quarters and judges more independently than any man I ever knew."[54] The Framers fully recognized that they could not count on people such as Washington always to win the presidency and that, if the goal were to create a political system that could exist in perpetuity, they would have to think institutionally, not individually.[55]

1.2.4 Executive Selection and Succession

The Framers pondered the ways in which a president might be selected. They considered allowing state governors or state legislatures to elect the president, but they remained concerned that the practice would encourage presidents, beholden to state electors, to elevate local interests above the national interest. At the convention, therefore, the chief debate about selection and succession centered on whether to let Congress choose the president or to allow the people to decide. The former, of course, would be a violation of the basic principle, already adopted, of a system of independent checks and balances. If Congress were to select the president, what would prevent its members from choosing a lackey? For as James Wilson noted, congressional election would leave the executive "too dependent to stand [as] the mediator between the intrigues & sinister views of the representatives of the Representatives and the general liberties & interests of the people."[56] On the other hand, allowing the people to choose their own leader evoked numerous other concerns. In a country the size of the early United States, without the ease of transportation and communication we now enjoy, would individual citizens even be aware of qualified candidates for national office?

Although Washington had gained national recognition as commander in chief during the Revolutionary War, it was unlikely—the Framers anticipated—that there would be many opportunities for a potential president to acquire personal distinction. Additionally, existing imbalances between the northern and southern states, and between smaller and larger states, meant that presidents, who presumably were to represent the entire country, might be elected by popular majorities concentrated in particular geographic regions.* Smaller southern states simply would not agree to an electoral system that they perceived as rigged against them.

Beyond logistical and political concerns, the Framers had little faith in the abilities of average citizens to recognize the qualities needed to fill the office of chief executive or to resist emotional appeals. Edmund Randolph attributed the country's problems at the time to "the turbulence and follies of democracy." Hamilton similarly argued that the masses "seldom judge or determine right." Gouverneur Morris of New York, not to be outshone, exclaimed, "The mob begin to think and reason. Poor reptiles!"[57] The office of the executive that the Framers envisioned would grant autonomy and substantive power to the officeholder. But would that officeholder, they worried, be subject to the whims of an unruly citizenry? To ensure not, the Framers ruled out direct democracy and set to work on designing an altogether new way of electing a president.

---

*This was not an entirely unfounded fear. Of the first six presidents, four were from the most populous state (Virginia) and two were from the third most populous (Massachusetts).

THE ELECTORAL COLLEGE

The use of an **Electoral College**—a deliberative body entrusted by voters to make decisions about presidential candidates on their behalf—was created to solve two problems. First, a body of electors would provide a needed corrective for the mistakes that poorly informed voters were bound to make. This rationale is recognized in *Federalist* 68, in which Alexander Hamilton sought to persuade the American public of the merits of the college:

> It was equally desirable, that the immediate [presidential] election should be made by men most capable of analyzing the qualities adapted to the station, and acting under circumstances favourable to deliberation, and to a judicious combination of all the reasons and inducements which were proper to govern their choice. A small number of persons, selected by their fellow-citizens from the general mass, will be most likely to possess the information and discernment requisite to such complicated investigations.

Elections based on candidate-centric appeals to the public, Hamilton worried, would reward office seekers who possessed "talents for low intrigue, and the little arts of popularity." A somber Electoral College of eminent citizens, it was thought, would not be so easily distracted by such trivialities.

The second rationale for the Electoral College was that it could mitigate the anxieties of smaller states that feared a loss of influence and autonomy in this newly created Republic. The Electoral College assigned electors to each state, but it did not do so strictly on the basis of the state's population. Because every state was guaranteed at least three electors (given their two senators and at least one member of the House), the populations of especially small states were disproportionately represented in the selection of presidents. Moreover, should college electors fail to come to a majority consensus behind a single presidential candidate, the Constitution required that the House of Representatives resolve the matter, with each state delegation having a single vote. Here again, smaller states were the distinct beneficiary of this arrangement, which many expected to regularly decide the outcome of presidential elections.

Concerns about race and slavery also loomed large in these deliberations.[58] At the time of the convention, the populations of northern and southern states were roughly equal, with one vexing and abominable caveat: much of the South's population was enslaved. This was true of nearly half of South Carolina's population, none of whom were allowed to vote. Not only did the North have more eligible white voters, but it also extended voting rights to its Black citizens—lending it a potentially massive advantage in presidential elections. This advantage did not go unnoticed by southern delegates. Madison, a Virginian, complained that "the right of suffrage was much more diffusive in the Northern than the Southern states; and the latter can have no influence on the election on the score of the Negroes."[59]

When designing the Electoral College, southern states could not accept a system that advantaged their northern counterparts, with whom they vehemently disagreed on the issue of slavery. Nor would they willingly grant slaves the right to vote. The compromise? Attach a state's electors to the size of its representation in Congress. While drafting Article

I, the Framers had already agreed on the **three-fifths clause**, in which congressional representation was calculated "by adding to the whole Number of free Persons . . . three fifths of all other Persons." Applying this clause to the Electoral College, southern states added three-fifths of all slaves to their populations—greatly empowering themselves and equalizing the number of electors across north and south.

So what are the properties of the Electoral College under the terms of the Constitution? Each state is granted a number of electors equal to the number of representatives and senators that they are entitled to elect to the U.S. Congress. The Constitution does not require that the appointment of electors be determined by popular election. Instead, it simply mandates that "Each State shall appoint, in such Manners as the Legislature thereof may direct, a Number of Electors."[60] States also retained broad discretion in deciding how the votes of electors are aggregated.*

STATE ELECTIONS FOR A NATIONAL OFFICE

The Constitution further permits considerable variation in the administration of the **franchise** (the right to vote) in different states, with different rules on voter eligibility, ballot access for candidates, polling machinery, and availability of early voting.† With such heterogeneity in the electoral composition and voting laws, it is perhaps useful to regard a presidential election as fifty-one simultaneous state-level elections, rather than a single national contest.‡

The first iterations of presidential elections in the fledgling States are an excellent example of this heterogeneity. In some states the popular vote determined presidential electors, while in others the state legislature appointed electors. Methods of selection also fluctuated from one election to the next as state legislatures flipped their states back to legislative selection in order to ensure their party's supremacy.[61] By 1824 the nation had largely settled

---

*During times of electoral and legal impasse, as in Florida during the 2000 presidential election, state governments have exercised the right to preempt an electoral result and appoint electors via an act of state government.

† This stipulation persists to this day, when perhaps the clearest differences are apparent in the question of felon enfranchisement: in Vermont, for instance, prisoners may vote and even run for office while incarcerated, while in Florida, a former prisoner is required to petition the governor in person to reacquire voting privileges. Such differences are discussed at further length in chapter 6.

‡ The rules governing the election of presidents have changed a great deal over time. In 1804, following the advent of political parties and an 1800 election fiasco in which Aaron Burr and Thomas Jefferson tied at seventy-three electoral votes each, Congress passed the Twelfth Amendment, requiring that separate ballots be cast for president and vice president. The practice of allowing the House to select the president when no clear majority presented itself in the Electoral College was promptly suspended after the scandal of John Quincy Adams's election in 1824 over Andrew Jackson. Termed the "corrupt bargain," the election of 1824 was widely suspected to have been decided on a quid pro quo, in which Speaker of the House Henry Clay convinced the House to vote in Adams's favor in exchange for an appointment as secretary of state. And, following Franklin Delano Roosevelt's four terms in office in the 1930s and 1940s, presidents were permitted to run for office, and win, only twice. (In chapters 5 and 6, we discuss these and other developments at greater length.)

on the popular vote (18 of 24 states); by 1832 only South Carolina had not implemented a state popular vote, a position they would retain until after the Civil War.

One could not necessarily vote simply because a given state used the popular vote, though. Enfranchisement, too, varied widely by state, somehow even more so than selection methods. The general standard in 1789 was that only white, male, taxpaying, land-owning citizens over the age of twenty-one could vote in *every* state that permitted it. However, what taxes needed to be paid, or what quantity of land constituted "landowning," was unregulated and left up to individual states. Additional stipulations such as literacy tests also varied on a state-by-state basis. Some states occasionally delved beyond this, too, including allowing women or Black citizens to vote. However, these exceptions were frequently overturned with legislative administration changes. Such was the case with New Jersey, which prior to 1807 allowed "all inhabitants of this colony, of full age, who are worth fifty pounds . . . and have resided within the county . . . for twelve months" to vote.[62] Thereafter, new restrictions were adopted and the New Jersey franchise shrunk dramatically.

OATH OF OFFICE

Article II, Section 1 of the Constitution concludes with the presidential oath of office—the only section of the entire document to appear in quotation marks. Before executing the duties of the office of the presidency, presidents-elect must put their hand on a sacred text of their choosing, raise their right hand, and say: "I do solemnly swear (or affirm) that I will faithfully execute the Office of President of the United States, and will to the best of my Ability, preserve, protect and defend the Constitution of the United States."[63] Having done so, a president-elect becomes a president in fact.

The roots of the president's oath of office trace back to England, where government officials took religious oaths both to the Crown and to the Church.[64] The Framers removed the religious component—though George Washington added "so help me God" to the end, and every president has followed suit[65]—and fashioned an oath of office that required presidents to commit themselves instead to the Constitution. As Alexander Hamilton argued in *Federalist* 27, the oath of office was meant not only to signify the transfer of power from one administration to the next but to bind the president to the Constitution through "the sanctity of an oath."[66]

Among constitutional law scholars, there is an ongoing debate about whether the oath of office confers or constrains presidential power. Those in the former camp argue that by assigning responsibilities to the office of the presidency, the oath unavoidably expands its powers. For these scholars, the oath constitutes a mandate to preserve the Union,[67] establishes an implicit duty to defend the presidency against legislative encroachment,[68] and directs the president to refuse to execute laws that are unconstitutional.[69] Moreover, the requirement that presidents "preserve" the Constitution implicitly recognizes their power to exercise legal review over the other branches and thereby prevent behaviors that threaten the constitutional order.[70]

Other scholars, by contrast, argue that the oath acts as a clear restraint on presidential power. As a binding vow, the oath of office subordinates presidents to the Constitution, limiting their powers to those outlined within the founding document. If a president violates the oath by acting in such a way that threatens the Constitution or the survival of the Union, Congress may deem the president unfit to uphold the duties of the executive office.*

SUCCESSION

It was not until the final days of the Constitutional Convention that the Framers broached the question: What happens if the president dies while in office? Becomes disabled? Resigns? Who will replace him?

Talk of presidential succession arose only within the context of the vice presidency, as the Framers debated what roles the secondary office should have. As with most constitutional questions, the Framers were informed by the leading political philosophy of their time. Charles Montesquieu—whom Madison had called "the oracle who is always consulted and cited"—had written extensively on the shortcomings of Russian succession rules, which allowed the czar to appoint his own successor. Hoping to lend stability in a time of political turmoil—yet wanting to avoid giving presidents too much power over their own untimely succession—the Framers largely deferred to Congress on the matter.

Though Article II, Section 1 places the vice president first in line for succession, it also states that "Congress may by Law provide for . . . what Officer shall then act as President" should the vice president be unable to serve. In 1792, the second Congress passed the Presidential Succession Act, which placed the president pro tempore of the Senate and the Speaker of the House, in that order, next in line of succession after the vice president. Two more Presidential Succession Acts were passed—in 1886 and 1947—before the final succession line was established: after the vice president, the Speaker of the House, followed by the Senate's president pro tempore. If necessary, the secretary of state is fourth in line, followed by the heads of other executive branch departments (in the order of the department's creation).

To date, these rules have been invoked for nine presidents—eight of whom were assassinated or died during their terms. But death is not the only potential reason for succession. According to Article II, succession can be triggered "in Case of the Removal of the President from Office, or of his Death, Resignation, or Inability to discharge the Powers and Duties" of the office. The Twenty-Fifth Amendment, ratified in 1967, helped clarify the term "inability." At any time, the amendment said, the president can submit to Congress a written declaration that he is unable to perform his duties, at which point the vice president becomes the acting president. If the president is unable to write such a declaration—say, if he

---

* Though the oath was mentioned in the impeachment proceedings for Andrew Johnson, Richard Nixon, Bill Clinton, and Donald Trump, the House of Representatives has never formally charged a president with violating the oath of office.

has fallen into a coma or in some other way become incapacitated—a majority of the cabinet members can vote to transfer his authority to the vice president.

1.3 Textual Meanings

For a good long while, scholars, jurists, and politicians have argued about the most appropriate way to interpret the Constitution.[71] At the risk of gross simplification, the debate has pitted two camps against one another. On one side are **originalists**, who fixate on the Constitution's plain text.[72] Originalists warn against the pathologies of extrapolating beyond the text's original meaning and insist that the constitutional order can only be preserved when judges and justices focus narrowly on the Framers' intent when they drafted Article II. On the other side, meanwhile, are advocates of a **Living Constitution** that imparts meanings that flexibly change over time.[73] Proponents of this view make much of the fact that the Framers could not, by their own recognition, foresee all future conflicts and that interpretations of their writing would, of necessity, evolve.[74]

Examples can be found of presidents in both of these interpretivist camps. In the modern era, though, they tend to break along partisan lines. Republicans routinely count themselves among the originalists, whereas Democrats put their faith in a Living Constitution. All presidents, however, read into the Constitution certain **inherent powers**—which, though neither stated nor straightforwardly implied by the Constitution's text, grant them broad discretion over both foreign and domestic policy.[75] They do so, of course, in different ways, with Republicans arguing that the Framers fully intended to vest the president with sweeping authority over numerous policy domains, and with Democrats underscoring the importance of constitutional adaptation over time. But as we discuss at length in chapter 4, presidents from both parties push outward on the boundaries of their power, and the Constitution provides a wealth of arguments and justifications for doing so.

How is this possible? How can presidents who interpret the Constitution through such different methods nonetheless draw common conclusions about its meaning? The answer comes in two parts, each of which highlights a different feature of Article II. First, its language is notoriously vague, particularly on vital matters of presidential power. Rather than demarking clear and unmistakable limits, the Framers settled on language that could reasonably support a broad array of interpretations. And second, the meanings of Article II depend not only on its contents but also on its omissions. In places of constitutional silence, presidents have found ways to interpret consent, and they thereby marshal justifications for vesting additional authority in an office about which the Framers had relatively little to say.

1.3.1 Ambiguity

In certain respects, Article II of the Constitution is tremendously precise. It specifies exactly how the president and vice president are to be elected. It identifies who can run for the presidential office and who will succeed to the presidency should a sitting president die or leave office. It lays out the specifics of the treaty ratification process. It discusses the terms by which presidents' salaries can be adjusted.

On other issues, however, Article II of the Constitution is altogether vague. It is no exaggeration, in fact, to say that ambiguity is the defining characteristic of the president's enumerated powers—or, at least, of those powers that matter most, such as the vesting clause, the take-care clause, and a variety of foreign policy powers. The Constitution does not so much confer well-delineated powers upon the president as it recognizes the president's rightful claim to an array of broad titles and responsibilities. Depending on how one chooses to read these titles and responsibilities, one can draw radically different conclusions about the constitutional bases for either a strong or weak presidency.

The **vesting clause** of Article II merely asserts that "the executive Power shall be vested in a President of the United States." (Similar vesting clauses in Articles I and III grant legislative powers to Congress and judicial powers to the Supreme Court, respectively.) Exactly which powers are vested in the president, however, is not specified. Equally ambiguous is the Constitution's further instruction, in language that is commonly called the **take-care clause**, for presidents to "take Care that the laws [of the United States] be faithfully executed."

All the Constitution says definitively about the vesting and take-care clauses is that the president is one person, entrusted with carrying out the laws Congress has passed. Yet the clauses are not limited to just these basic enumerations. How do these clauses function in practice? A great deal rides on how we answer this question, along with a host of ancillary ones. For instance, how quickly must a president implement a new law? If a president believes that a law is unconstitutional, is he or she still bound to execute it? What if Congress enacts a law that a president vehemently disagrees with? How much discretion does a president have to interpret laws that are fairly described as vague? As outside observers, how are we, the public, to know when a president has exceeded the legal requirements of any law that the chief executive is duty-bound to execute?

The cloud of ambiguity thickens further when we consider that presidents are responsible for implementing, not merely one law at a time, but the entire body of statutory law at all times. Given conflicting laws—one, say, that creates incentives for domestic energy producers to increase oil reserves and another that raises clean air and water standards—what is the president to do? Implement the law that was enacted more recently? The one that is more precise? Or the one that, in the president's judgment, better serves the nation's interests?

The vagueness of Article II is not confined to these two clauses. Ambiguity also permeates the language defining the president's foreign policy powers. In cases of sudden attacks against the United States on U.S. soil, everyone agrees that presidents have a fair measure of discretion to exercise military force as they see fit. Strictly speaking, though, Article II does not explicitly grant emergency powers to presidents. Although presidential authority to independently exercise military force was first identified in Madison's notes on the Constitutional Convention and later codified by the courts, just how far this authority can take a president remains an open question.

When is a president "repelling sudden attacks," and when is he or she using force unconstitutionally? If U.S. vessels are attacked on the high seas, may a president command an immediate military response? If so, how much force can be exercised? Does it matter whether the vessels are government property or the property of a private U.S. corporation? Can U.S. vessels pursue a fleeing enemy? Can they seize an aggressor ship or its crew and cargo? Can they pursue adjacent ships that pose potential (but not immediately actual) risks? Does it matter whether these ships hail from the same nation as the original aggressor?

These are not merely hypothetical questions. In 1801, an American naval schooner in the Mediterranean received fire from a ship hailing from Tripoli and promptly responded in kind. The American schooner managed to disable the Tripolitan ship, but, aware that they were fighting without congressional authorization, the U.S. commander opted not to go beyond the line of defense and subsequently liberated the pirate ship. The deficits of this arrangement were apparent to all. In an address to Congress later that year, Jefferson suggested that "by authorizing measures of offense also, [the legislature would] place our force on an equal footing with that of its adversaries."[76] Jefferson worried that, in an ongoing struggle with Barbary pirates, the strict limits placed on the president's war powers by Congress put the lives of U.S. soldiers and the material interests of the nation at risk.

Or consider another example in the arena of foreign policy. In 1793, when war broke out between Britain and France, President Washington unilaterally issued a proclamation "declaring that the United States was neutral in the conflict and warning Americans that they would face legal sanction if they assisted one of the belligerents."[77] The basis for this neutrality proclamation was neither a law passed by Congress nor an explicitly enumerated power. Rather, Washington cited the broad authority enclosed in the vesting clause. Did Washington have the authority to act as he did? Or was this another example of executive overreach?

These questions lack obvious answers. Moreover—and this is the crucial point—Article II of the Constitution does little to clarify them. Though it is possible to derive some general principles from the Constitution, presidents must invariably look beyond the founding document for guidance to answer them.

In part, the ambiguity of Article II was born from political compromise. The Framers, unable to agree on specifics, allowed both advocates of a strong federal government and champions of states' rights to return to their constituents and claim victory. The Constitution's ambiguity also reflects the uncertainties and ambivalence that the Framers themselves could not resolve when trying to balance a perceived need for a powerful and independent executive against fears of either tyranny or mob rule.* Furthermore, ambiguity is a necessary part of any constitution. For a constitution to last—that is, for future generations to continue to respect its basic principles when confronting challenges that its au-

---

* What it means to be "intentionally ambiguous," of course, is itself ambiguous. For a longer discussion on possible understandings, see William G. Howell, *Thinking about the Presidency: The Primacy of Power* (Princeton: Princeton University Press, 2013), 62–65.

thors could not possibly have anticipated—its language must permit a measure of flexibility and adaptability.

This latter point, however, can take us only so far. While rigidity is to be avoided in any constitution, the relative clarity of Article I (which lays out Congress's formal structure and powers) and of Article III (which defines the structure and powers of the judiciary) stands in sharp relief against the vagueness of Article II. This vagueness was not a foregone conclusion, and, as we shall see, it had significant consequences for the future development of the office of the presidency, as well as for subsequent presidents' conceptions of their responsibilities and powers.

1.3.2 *Silence*

On some issues involving presidential power, the Constitution is vague. On others, it is altogether silent. The Constitution does not give the president explicit emergency powers. Nor does it say anything about the president's authority to unilaterally set public policy. What are we to make of such omissions? Does silence indicate prohibition? Or might it tacitly imply permission? Depending on one's answer, radically different conclusions follow about the appropriate boundaries of Article II powers.

Viewed one way, the Framers explicitly recognized only those enumerated powers that they agreed were indispensable.[78] In this way, the contents of Article II set a floor on the president's authority, not a ceiling. It would be a mistake, as such, to infer opposition from silence. For a variety of reasons, the Framers did not explicitly recognize sources of presidential power that future generations would rightly view as legitimate. Cognizant of their inability to foresee all future contingencies, the Framers recognized that they, by necessity, were writing an incomplete governing contract. Moreover, important benefits flow from leaving less-than-indispensable issues in a state of irresolution. Through silence, after all, future politicians would have the permission they needed to expand or restrict executive powers. Understood this way, the Constitution must be silent in order to endure; and in this silence, presidents can justifiably claim that which the Framers themselves chose not to enumerate.

Take, for example, the president's vast arsenal of unilateral powers, which are the subject of chapter 9. The term "executive order" is never mentioned in the Constitution, yet this particular tool, and many other equivalents, is an indispensable means of presidential policymaking. Though the Framers designed Congress to act as the nation's lawmaking body, executive orders, born of constitutional silence, allow presidents to redirect the doings of government without prior congressional consent. The Framers could have explicitly prohibited these powers. They also could have prescribed them. Having done neither, they opened up a space where authority and power might be productively conceived. In this sense, at least, silence proved generative.

Other scholars take a very different view, insisting that we do not read into constitutional silence. The Bill of Rights, after all, concludes with the Anti-Federalist statement that "the powers not delegated to the United States by the Constitution . . . are reserved to the states."[79] Given this clause, constitutional silence would appear to establish clear limits—that is, a ceiling—on the national government's authority generally, and the president's specifically. Any authority that is not expressly granted to the federal government should redound to the states, not to the president.[80] Rather than allowing future generations to interpret silence as tacit permission for the presidency to expand its reach into new realms, the Framers equated silence with prohibition.

As a matter of legal interpretation, none of this is settled. Jurists and scholars have not come to any consensus about the significance of constitutional silence. Routinely, though, presidents have viewed silence—much like ambiguity—as an invitation to claim more power for themselves. For presidents, after all, the stakes of constitutional interpretation have less to do with fidelity to the Framers' intent, a principled method of interpretation, or some notion of truth and more to do with their material capacity to follow through on campaign promises, advance a policy agenda, and ultimately build a legacy worthy of emulation. While constitutional law scholars disagree about the appropriate mode of interpreting Article II and its contents, presidents speak with one voice: where the Constitution plainly confers power, presidents gladly accept it; and where the Constitution is either silent or ambiguous, presidents conjure justifications that accommodate their most sweeping ambitions.

1.3.3 Context and Meaning

Constitutional law scholars continue to disagree about fundamental aspects of the American presidency. The nature of the Constitution—in both its ambiguities and omissions—can intensify these debates, but it is not their only source. Still unresolved are questions of how to read the *entire* Constitution: Are some provisions more important than others? Should everything be read within the wider context of the document? If so, what happens when two clauses contradict each other? How one answers these questions has important implications for one's evaluation of executive power. Divergent methods of reading the Constitution—some based on just a single clause or two, others that emphasize the larger context—can drastically alter one's understanding of the institutional presidency.

Article II's provision that the "executive Power shall be vested" in the president presents the biggest source of disagreement over the size and scope of presidential authority. As we have already seen, this clause is shrouded in a great deal of ambiguity, into which advocates of either a strong or weak president can read support for their cause. How one interprets the vesting clause, however, turns on more than just one's preferred meaning of the word "executive." For some constitutional scholars, it also depends upon what is said elsewhere in the text.

One view is that the executive clause vests all power that is executive in nature in the president, limited only by the executive powers elsewhere in the text (mostly in Article I, Section 8) and in the explicit limitations enclosed in Article II. In an essay supporting Washington's aforementioned neutrality proclamation, Hamilton wrote, "The general doctrine then of our constitution is, that the Executive Power of the Nation is vested in the

President; subject only to the *exceptions* and qualifications which are expressed in the instrument."[81] This *substantive* view of the vesting clause is supported by the context of the legislative and judicial vesting clauses. The legislature is limited to the legislative powers "herein granted," while the judiciary is limited to cases only within its jurisdiction. The Framers included no such limitation for the executive, suggesting that they intended a broad mandate of executive power.

A second, *nonsubstantive* view of the clause is that it merely identifies the person unto whom the enumerated executive powers are entrusted. Proponents of the nonsubstantive position claim that a substantive reading of the vesting clause renders much of Article I redundant. Why, asks Justice Oliver Wendell Holmes, would the Framers bother to stipulate that

> the President shall be commander-in-chief; may require opinions in writing of the principal officers in each of the executive departments; shall have power to grant reprieves and pardons; shall give information to Congress concerning the state of the union; shall receive ambassadors; shall take care that the laws be faithfully executed—if all of these things and more had already been vested in him by the general words?[82]

These are not merely academic disputes. To see the stakes involved, consider the **Unitary Executive Theory (UET)**. This modern theory states, in brief, that the president possesses singular control over the entire executive branch of government. It envisions the executive branch as an extension of the president's will and that any efforts to impede this will constitute unconstitutional encroachments. To justify such conclusions, UET relies on a narrow reading of the Article II's vesting clause. From this one clause, some legal scholars have defended the president's power to declare war, surveil the population, ignore congressional laws, and more. But others, who are inclined to interpret the vesting clause's meaning within the context of the larger Constitution, support a more moderate version of the theory or bristle at the mere notion of a unitary executive. The manner by which one reads the Constitution, it turns out, profoundly affects one's understanding of the presidency.

Those who would read the vesting clause largely in isolation are significantly more inclined to tolerate vast claims of presidential power. In the words of Supreme Court Justice Antonin Scalia, who landed squarely in this camp, the vesting clause "does not mean some of the executive power, but all of the executive power."[83] In his dissent of *Morrison v. Olson* (1988), Scalia suggested a two-tiered process by which to determine a law's constitutionality: first, one must evaluate whether a law entails action that is purely executive; and second, one must assess whether it "deprive[s] the President of the United States of exclusive control over the exercise of that power." If a law vested executive power in any person other than the president, said Scalia, the Court must render it "void."

Robert Delahunty and John Yoo, who previously served in the Department of Justice and is a prominent defender of a robust UET, elaborated on Scalia's two tiers. They specified that any "ambiguities" in the allocation of executive power between Congress and the president "must be resolved in favor of the executive branch."[84] They defended this position on the grounds that Article I is restrictive in the powers it grants Congress, while Article II's vesting clause offers no such restrictions. This logic contains several implications, all of which are favorable for the president's power. Chiefly, executive branch agencies cannot be independent from the president, nor can they have congressional oversight. In other words, using no more than a single clause in Article II, Delahunty and Yoo support the president's ability to behave in all sorts of ways that are unaccountable to Congress.

Reading the exact same Constitution, other scholars arrive at wholly different conclusions. For example, Justice Samuel Alito favors a more moderate version of UET, explaining that the theory "doesn't have to do with the scope of executive power. . . . It has to do with who within the executive branch controls the exercise of executive power."[85] This distinction may seem slim, but legal scholar Saikrishna Prakash's more expansive reading of the Constitution helps draw it out. He wrote that the vesting clause must grant full, unenumerated executive powers to the president alone.[86] If not, Prakash reasoned, the rest of Article II would be redundant, as it goes on to describe a singular executive.

Part of what separates this moderate version of UET from its radical counterpart, therefore, is its readers' attention to the larger Constitution. In Prakash's view, executive power is neither unlimited nor uninfringeable by Congress. He acknowledges Article I provisions that grant power to Congress and says that they "necessarily trump" a broad reading of Article II's vesting clause. To declare war, nominate judges, and make key appointments, the president must seek congressional approval as explicitly stated by the Constitution. By undertaking a more comprehensive outlook in constitutional interpretation, Prakash reads the vesting clause in the context of Article I, resulting in a far less expansive role for the presidency.

Opponents of UET argue that the *full* context of the Constitution provides an even more restrained interpretation of the vesting clause. Columbia Law professor Peter Strauss examined other constitutional provisions that can inform one's judgment of UET. First among these provisions is the opinions clause, allowing the president to "require the Opinion, in writing, of the principal Officer in each of the executive Departments."[87] To Strauss, this clause implies a degree of separation between the president and the implementation of law in the executive branch.[88] In other words, the Framers never expected the president to be the sole director of public policy but rather an *overseer* who appointed and sought advice from other officials. The second provision Strauss examined was the take-care clause, which stipulates that the president must "take care that the laws be faithfully executed." Strauss then highlights the necessary and proper clause, which gives Congress the power to structure the executive branch, and which allows for the creation of independent agencies shielded from presidential interference (except, of course, for the requesting of written opinions). Together, these provisions convinced Strauss and others that "the text of the Constitution settles no more than that the President is to be the overseer of executive government."[89]

Alternatively, some opponents of UET cite the "Framers' intent"—a method of constitutional interpretation in which the reader imagines what the Framers would think about a current issue. Of course, the Framers did not think (or speak) in unison. In many ways, they were deeply divided, and one should exercise caution when describing what the Framers "intended." Nonetheless, documents outside the Constitution can help shed light on certain clauses. Madison, for example, wrote that "nothing is more natural or common than first to use a general phrase, and then to explain and qualify it by a recitation of particulars"—a major blow for UET supporters who focus exclusively on the vesting clause.[90] Conservative legal scholar Ilya Somin used the "Framers' intent" to further scrutinize UET. In his view, the theory allows for too much power in the hands of a single person, precisely the situation the Founding Fathers sought fervently to avoid.[91]

In an important 20th Century Supreme Court case, the courts sided with Somin, Strauss, and other UET opponents. In *Morrison v. Olson*, the Court reviewed the constitutionality of independent agencies within the executive. Following the Watergate scandal, Congress passed the Ethics in Government Act of 1978 allowing for independent counsels to investigate high-ranking government officials.[92] By not answering to the president, however, these counsels struck a blow against the UET. A decade later, when a member of President Reagan's Department of Justice refused to produce documents subpoenaed by an independent counsel, the case went to the Supreme Court.[93] In a 7–1 ruling, the Court upheld the constitutionality of independent counsels. Moreover, the justices ruled that UET "depends upon an extrapolation from general constitutional language which we think is more than the text will bear."[94] Congress is entitled to appoint and fire independent executive officials "so long as they do not unduly trammel on executive authority."[95]

The ruling was an affront not only to UET and its proponents but to the method of constitutional reading and interpretation that kept it alive. Though *Morrison v. Olson* may not have fully resolved the questions posed earlier—are some provisions more important than others?—it did caution against overly broad interpretations of narrow passages. It reaffirmed the value of the *entire* Constitution and cautioned against extrapolating too broadly from any single clause or provision.

Conclusion

The Constitution, Edward Corwin famously recognized, is "an invitation to struggle."[96] The Constitution does not resolve the tensions between individual liberty and state authority, between centralized and decentralized authority, or between effective governance and protected rights. Rather, the Constitution formalizes these tensions and thereby creates a framework within which subsequent generations can grapple with them. As Arthur Schlesinger reminds us, "The Constitution [is] an extraordinary document. But a document is only a document, and what the Constitution 'really' [means]—i.e., [means] in practice—only practice could disclose."[97]

The president's powers are not rooted strictly and solely in the text of the Constitution. Interpretations of these powers are the product of political struggle. They reflect the interests, powers, and incentives of the different branches of government. The practice of presidential politics, as we shall soon see, has been crafted and recrafted over the course of the nation's history, even if it was first born in the imaginations of our nation's Framers some two centuries ago.

Key Terms

Articles of Confederation
quorum
checks and balances
veto power
enumerated powers
pardon power
unitary executive
plural executive
Electoral College

three-fifths clause
franchise
originalism
Living Constitution
inherent powers
vesting clause
take-care clause
Unitary Executive Theory

Questions for Discussion

1. Is discerning the Framers' intent an achievable and worthwhile goal when settling legal disputes?
2. Does the Constitution's take-care clause empower presidents, or is it merely a job description?
3. Presented by Alexander Hamilton, the British Plan featured a lifetime appointment of presidents, pending "good behavior." Why might the Framers have decided against this proposal? Why might Hamilton have preferred it?
4. Is the ambiguity of Article II a weakness, a strength, or both?
5. If the Framers were, in fact, "institutionalists," does that mean that they paid no attention to the characters and convictions of those individuals who would likely assume power in the newly formed government? Is it possible to reconcile the personal with the institutional?
6. Does the Constitution establish a template for resolving competing claims between the need for effective leadership and abiding concerns about tyranny? Or does the Constitution amount to the equivalent of a conversation starter, an invitation for each generation of politicians to formulate answers of its own?

Suggested Readings

Berkin, Carol. *A Brilliant Solution: Inventing the American Constitution*. New York: Mariner Books, 2003.

Hamilton, Alexander, James Madison, and John Jay. *The Federalist Papers*. Ed. Clinton Rossiter. Intro. Charles R. Kessler. New York: Penguin Putnam, 1961; Signet, 2003.

Lowe, Ben. *Political Thought and the Origins of the American Presidency*. Tallahassee: University Press of Florida, 2021.

Maier, Pauline. *Ratification: The People Debate the Constitution, 1787–1788*. New York: Simon & Schuster, 2011.

McConnell, Michael. *The President Who Would Not Be King: Executive Power under the Constitution*. Princeton: Princeton University Press, 2020.

McDonald, Forrest. *The American Presidency: An Intellectual History*. Lawrence: University Press of Kansas, 1994.

Nelson, Eric. *Royalist Revolution: Monarchy and the American Founding*. Cambridge, MA: Harvard University Press, 2014.

Rakove, Jack N. *Original Meanings: Politics and Ideas in the Making of the Constitution*. New York: Alfred A. Knopf, 1996.

Thach, Charles. *The Creation of the American Presidency, 1775–1789: A Study in Constitutional History*. 1923. Indianapolis: Liberty Fund, 2009.

Notes

1. Richard P. McCormick, "Ambiguous Authority: The Ordinances of the Confederation Congress, 1781–1789," *American Journal of Legal History* 41, no. 4 (1997): 411–39.

2. Jack Rakove, *Revolutionaries: A New History of the Invention of America* (Boston: Houghton Mifflin Harcourt, 2011), 253.

3. McCormick, "Ambiguous Authority."

4. "CPI Inflation Calculator," Officialdata.org, https://www.officialdata.org/us/inflation/1785.

5. The most comprehensive book on America's struggles with Barbary pirates is Gregory Fremont-Barnes's *The Wars of the Barbary Pirates: To the Shores of Tripoli: The Rise of the US Navy and Marines* (New York: Osprey Publishing, 2006).

6. Stephen Higginson to Nathan Dane, June 16, 1787, "Letters of Stephen Higginson, 1783–1804," in *Annual Report of the American Historical Association, 1896*, vol. 1 (Washington, DC: Government Printing Office, 1897), 759–60, quoted in Gordon S. Wood, *The Creation of the American Republic, 1776–1787* (Chapel Hill: University of North Carolina Press, 1969), 466.

7. Sidney Milkis and Michael Nelson, *The American Presidency: Origins and Development, 1776–2011*, 6th ed. (Washington, DC: Congressional Quarterly Press, 2011), 6. For a dissenting view, see Merrill Jensen, *The Articles of Confederation* (Madison: University of Wisconsin Press, 1940).

8. "Historical Notice" preceding Alexander Hamilton, James Madison, John Jay, and John Church Hamilton, *The Federalist: A Commentary on the Constitution of the United States* (Philadelphia: J. B. Lippincott, 1864), xxvii.

9. William Livingston to Baron van der Capellen, November 18, 1783, in *The Papers of William Livingston*, vol. 5, ed. Carl E. Prince (Trenton: New Jersey Historical Commission, 1979–1988), 56–57, quoted in Jack N. Rakove, *Original Meanings: Politics and Ideas in the Making of the Constitution* (New York: Random House, 2010), 250.

10. Robert Morris to John Jay, February 4, 1777, in *Letters of Delegates to Congress, 1774–1789*, vol. 6, ed. Paul H. Smith et al. (Washington, DC: Library of Congress, 1976–2000), 216, quoted in Rakove, *Original Meanings*, 254.

11. John Jay to Thomas Jefferson, August 18, 1786, in *The Papers of Jefferson*, vol. 10, ed. Julian P. Boyd (Princeton: Princeton University Press, 1954), 272, quoted in Rakove, *Original Meanings*, 255.

12. *Boston Independent Chronicle*, February 6, 1783, quoted in Wood, *Creation of the American Republic*, 361.

13. Elbridge Gerry, Samuel Holton, and Rufus King to Governor James Bowdoin, September 3, 1785, in *Letters of Members of the Continental Congress*, ed. Edmund Cody Burnett (Washington, DC: Carnegie Institution, 1921), described in Forrest McDonald, *The American Presidency: An Intellectual History* (Lawrence: University Press of Kansas, 1994), 146.

14. Edmund Cody Burnett, *The Continental Congress* (Westport, CT: Greenwood Press, 1975), 663–65.

15. James Madison, quoted in Milkis and Nelson, *The American Presidency*, 8.

16. Wood, *Creation of the American Republic*.

17. Charles Thach, *The Creation of the American Presidency, 1775–1789: A Study in Constitutional History* (1923; Indianapolis: Liberty Fund, 2009), 49.

18. James Madison, April 1, 1787, in *The Writings of James Madison: 1769–1783*, vol. 1, ed. Gaillard Hunt (New York: G. P. Putnam's Sons, 1900), 335, quoted in Wood, *Creation of the American Republic*, 471.

19. Rakove, *Original Meanings*, 259.

20. As quoted in Michael McConnell, *The President Who Would Not Be King: Executive Power under the Constitution* (Princeton: Princeton University Press, 2020), 56.

21. Alexander Hamilton, "Federalist No. 67," in *The Federalist Papers*, ed. Clinton Rossiter, intro. Charles R. Kessler (New York: Penguin Putnam, 1961; Signet, 2003).

22. Max Farrand, ed., *The Records of the Federal Constitution of 1787*, 1937 rev. ed., vol. 1 (New Haven: Yale University Press, 1966), 26–27, proceedings of May 29, notes of James McHenry.

23. Richard Hofstadter, *The American Political Tradition: And the Men Who Made It* (New York: Alfred Knopf, 1948; Vintage Books, 1989), 11.

24. James Madison, "Federalist No. 51," *The Federalist Papers*.

25. Leonard B. Boudin, "The Presidential Pardons of James R. Hoffa and Richard M. Nixon: Have the Limitations on the Pardon Power Been Exceeded?" *University of Colorado Law Review* 48 (1976): 1–40.

26. Paul Rosenzweig, "A Federalist Conception of the Pardon Power," Heritage Foundation, December 4, 2012, https://www.heritage.org/the-constitution/report/federalist-conception-the-pardon-power.

27. Alexander Hamilton, "Federalist No. 74," *The Federalist Papers*.

28. *Ex parte Garland*, 71 U.S. (4 Wall.) 333, 380 (1866).

29. Boudin, "The Presidential Pardons of James R. Hoffa and Richard M. Nixon."

30. James Madison, "Federalist No. 47," *The Federalist Papers*.

31. McConnell, *The President Who Would Not Be King*, 51–60.

32. Raoul Berger, *Impeachment: The Constitutional Problems* (Cambridge, MA: Harvard University Press, 1974), 299–300.

33. U.S. Const., art. I, § 2.

34. T. J. Halstead, "An Overview of the Impeachment Process," CRS Report 98–806 A (Washington, DC: Congressional Research Service, 2005), https://www.everycrsreport.com/reports/98-806.html.

35. U.S. Const., art. I, § 3.

36. Halstead, "An Overview of the Impeachment Process."

37. McConnell, *The President Who Would Not Be King*, 58.

38. Daniel P. Franklin et al., *The Politics of Presidential Impeachment* (Albany: State University of New York Press, 2020).

39. For minutes of the Convention of 1787 including Randolph's quote, see "The Founders' Constitution: Volume 3, Article 2, Section 1, Clause 1, Document 4," in *The Records of the Federal Convention of 1787*, 4 vols., ed. Max Farrand (New Haven: Yale University Press, 1937).

40. "An Old Whig V," *Philadelphia Independent Gazetteer*, November 1, 1787, quoted in Rakove, *Original Meanings*, 273.

41. James Madison, "From James Madison to Caleb Wallace, 23 August 1785," The National Archives: Founders Online (University of Virginia Press), http://founders.archives.gov/documents/Madison/01-08-02-0184.

42. "Madison Debates: June 1," Avalon Project of Yale University, https://avalon.law.yale.edu/18th_century/debates_601.asp.

43. Clinton Rossiter, *The American Presidency* (New York: New American Library, 1960), 59.

44. Wood, *Creation of the American Republic*, 206.

45. James Monroe to Thomas Jefferson, July 12, 1788, in *The Papers of Jefferson*, vol. 13, ed. Julian P. Boyd (Princeton: Princeton University Press, 1956), 35, quoted in Wood, *Creation of the American Republic*, 209.

46. Joseph J. Ellis, *His Excellency: George Washington* (New York: Random House, 2005), 177.

47. Pierce Butler to Weedon Butler, May 5, 1788, in *The Records of the Federal Convention of 1787*, vol. 3, rev. ed., ed. Max Farrand (New Haven: Yale University Press, 1937), 302, quoted in Rakove, *Original Meanings*, 244.

48. James Madison to George Washington, April 16, 1787, in *Papers of James Madison*, vol. 9, ed. Gaillard Hunt (Chicago: University of Chicago Press, 1975), 385, quoted in Rakove, *Original Meanings*, 255.

49. *Records 1787*, 1:64–66, 66–69, quoted in Rakove, *Original Meanings*, 257.

50. Ellis, *His Excellency*, 176.

51. Rakove, *Original Meanings*, 256.

52. George Washington to Henry Laurens, November 14, 1778, in *The Writings of George Washington from the Original Manuscript Sources, 1745–1799*, vol. 13, ed. John C. Fitzpatrick (Washington, DC: Government Printing Office, 1931–1939), 254–57, quoted in Joseph J. Ellis, *Founding Brothers: The Revolutionary Generation* (New York: Random House, 2003), 132–33.

53. Rakove, *Original Meanings*, 247–48.

54. "Letter from John Adams to Sylvanus Bourne," August 30, 1789, The National Archives: Founders Online (University of Virginia Press), http://founders.archives.gov/documents/Adams/99-02-02-0737.

55. For a longer discussion of this case, see William G. Howell, *Thinking about the Presidency: The Primacy of Power* (Princeton: Princeton University Press, 2013), 58–62.

56. McConnell, *The President Who Would Not Be King*, 54–56.

57. Hofstadter, *American Political Tradition*, 6–7; Gouverneur Morris to John Penn, May 20, 1774, in *American Archives*, 4th ser., vol. 1, ed. M. St. Clair Clarke and Peter Force (Washington, DC: M. St. Clair Clarke and Peter Force, 1837–46), 342–43, in *The Founders' Constitution*, web ed., vol. 1, ed. Philip B. Kurland and Ralph Lerner (1986; Chicago: University of Chicago Press, 2000).

58. Paul Finkelman, "The Proslavery Origins of the Electoral College," *Cardozo Law Review* 23, no. 4 (2002): 1145–58.

59. Finkelman, "The Proslavery Origins of the Electoral College," 1155.

60. U.S. Const., art. II, § 1.

61. John L. Moore, ed., *Congressional Quarterly's Guide to U.S. Elections*, 2nd ed. (Washington, DC: Congressional Quarterly Press, 1985).

62. "Did You Know: Women and African Americans Could Vote in NJ before the 15th and 19th Amendments?" National Park Service, https://www.nps.gov/articles/voting-rights-in-nj-before-the-15th-and-19th.htm.

63. U.S. Const., art. II, § 1, cl. 8.

64. Vic Snyder, "You've Taken an Oath to Support the Constitution, Now What?: The Constitutional Requirement for a Congressional Oath of Office," *University of Arkansas at Little Rock Law Review* 23, no. 4 (2001): 909.

65. Donald R. Kennon, "Taking the Oath of Office," White House History Historical Association, Fall 2004, https://www.whitehousehistory.org/taking-the-oath-of-office.

66. Alexander Hamilton, "Federalist No. 27," *The Federalist Papers*.

67. Jerrold L. Steigman, "Reversing Reform: The Handschu Settlement in Post–September 11 New York City," *Journal of Law and Policy* 11, no. 2 (2003): 745–99.

68. Roy E. Brownell II, "The Constitutional Status of the President's Impoundment of National Security Funds," *Seton Hall Constitutional Journal* 12 (2001): 1.

69. Steven G. Calabresi and Saikrishna B. Prakash, "The President's Power to Execute the Laws," *Yale Law Journal* 104, no. 3 (1994): 541.

70. Michael Stokes Paulsen, "The Most Dangerous Branch: Executive Power to Say What the Law Is," *Georgetown Law Journal* 83 (1994): 217.

71. For a useful summary, see Brandon J. Murrill, "Modes of Constitutional Interpretation," CRS Report R45129 (Washington, DC: Congressional Research Service, 2018), 1–25, https://fas.org/sgp/crs/misc/R45129.pdf, www.crs.gov.

72. Antonin Scalia and Bryan A. Garner, *Reading Law: The Interpretation of Legal Texts* (St. Paul, MN: Thomson/West, 2012), 85.

73. Austin W. Bramwell, "Against Originalism: Getting over the US Constitution," *Critical Review* 16, no. 4 (2004): 431–53.

74. Peter Berkowitz, "Reading into the Constitution," *Policy Review* 173 (2012): 81.

75. Louis Fisher, "Invoking Inherent Powers: A Primer," *Presidential Studies Quarterly* 37, no. 1 (2007): 1–22.

76. Thomas Jefferson, "First Annual Message," December 8, 1801, available online at the American Presidency Project: https://www.presidency.ucsb.edu/documents/first-annual-message.

77. McConnell, *The President Who Would Not Be King*, 236.

78. Martin Loughlin, "The Silences of Constitutions," *History Review* 237 (2018): 266.

79. U.S. Const., amend. X.

80. Laurence H. Tribe, "Toward a Syntax of the Unsaid: Construing the Sounds of Congressional and Constitutional Silence," *Indiana Law Journal* 57 (1981): 515.

81. Alexander Hamilton, "Pacificus No. 1" (spelling corrected).

82. *Myers v. United States*, 272 U.S. 52, 228–29 (1926) (Holmes, J. dissenting).

83. *Morrison v. Olson*, 487 U.S. 654 (1988).

84. Robert J. Delahunty and John C. Yoo, "The President's Constitutional Authority to Conduct Military Operations against Terrorist Organizations and the Nations That Harbor or Support Them," *Harvard Journal of Law and Public Policy* 25 (2001): 487.

85. John Harrison, "The Unitary Executive and the Scope of Executive Power," *Yale LJF* 126 (2016): 374.

86. Saikrishna Prakash, "The Essential Meaning of Executive Power," *University of Illinois Law Review* (2003): 701.

87. U.S. Const., art. II, § 2, cl. 1.

88. Peter L. Strauss, "Presidential Rulemaking," *Chicago-Kent Law Review* 72 (1996): 965.

89. Strauss, "Presidential Rulemaking," 985.

90. Prakash, "The Essential Meaning of Executive Power," 701.

91. "Testimony of Peter M. Shane," Hearing of the Senate Judiciary Committee, U.S. Congress (2018).

92. Nick Bravin, "Is *Morrison v. Olson* Still Good Law? The Court's New Appointments Clause Jurisprudence," *Columbia Law Review* 98, no. 4 (1998): 1103–44.

93. *Morrison v. Olson*, 487 U.S. 654 (1988).

94. Karl M. Manheim and Allan Ides, "The Unitary Executive," *Los Angeles Lawyer* (September 2006).

95. Steven G. Calabresi and Kevin H. Rhodes, "The Structural Constitution: Unitary Executive, Plural Judiciary," *Harvard Law Review* 105, no. 6 (1992): 1153–1216.

96. Edward Corwin, *The President: Office and Powers, 1787–1957*, 4th ed. (New York: New York University Press, 1957), 171–75; Arthur M. Schlesinger Jr., *The Imperial Presidency* (1973; Boston: Houghton Mifflin, 2004), 13.

97. Schlesinger, *The Imperial Presidency*, 13.

2

The Ascendance of an
Institutional Presidency

ARTICLE II OF THE CONSTITUTION provides the architectural foundation of the institutional presidency, but our nation's Framers left it to successive reformers and politicians to define, develop, and shape our national politics, in which the presidency, over time, would play an increasingly important role.

Starting from the very beginning with George Washington, every president has left some mark on the institutional presidency and the terms under which his successors would wield power. Not until the first half of the twentieth century, however, did the presidency that we now know come into view. Four factors, at once interrelated and independent, have profoundly changed the institution of the presidency since the dawning of the 1900s:

1. the push for government activism by advocates of Progressive Era reforms;
2. the efforts to rationalize bureaucracy by the pioneers of scientific management;
3. the advent of total war; and
4. the expansion of social movements.

After briefly discussing nineteenth-century presidents, in this chapter we explore the ways in which each of these factors, singly and jointly, ushered in a more expansive and powerful executive office that sits squarely in the middle of our national politics.

2.1 Nineteenth-Century Presidents

In nearly every facet of American life—social, economic, and geographic—the nineteenth century transformed the United States and tested the durability of its Constitution.[1] In 1799, the United States was comprised of sixteen states, most of which sat along the Atlantic coast. By 1899, the number of states had grown to forty-five, not counting the territories of Puerto Rico, Alaska, Hawaii, and Cuba. Over the century, the U.S. population increased fifteenfold. Technological advances in agriculture and transportation brought an explosion of interstate commerce. Wind and animal power were replaced by steam and oil. Congress, dedicated to the cause of economic expansion, granted public lands and cash assistance to railroad companies—investments that would only hasten the pace of urbanization and industrialization.

Through most of these developments, however, the presidency continued to sit at the peripheries of our national politics.[2] Presidents in the nineteenth century played a relatively minor role in a federal government dominated by its legislative branch.[3] Congress, not the president, set the federal policy agenda. In those rare instances when presidents advocated for specific bills, Congress was unlikely to oblige them because presidents were seen as dutiful administrators bound to faithfully execute laws conceived, drafted, and enacted on Capitol Hill.[4]

In addition to wielding little political influence, nineteenth-century presidents also maintained a relatively low public profile. Rarely did presidents appeal directly to the American public, preferring, instead, to communicate in writing to Congress.[5] And according to one analysis of newspaper articles from 1820 to 1876, presidents received more press coverage than Congress only during elections.[6] Between elections—when the hard work of governance was done—the media shifted its focus back on Congress, the apparent source of power in Washington. President Woodrow Wilson later referred to this period as one of "congressional government." Taking aim at the notion that power had been balanced between the three branches, Wilson wrote that "in ordinary times, it is not from the executive that the most dangerous encroachments are to be apprehended. The legislature is the aggressive spirit."[7]

None of this is to say, of course, that all nineteenth-century presidents were weak in any absolute sense. Some, in fact, accomplished extraordinary things. Thomas Jefferson purchased the Louisiana Territory from France[8]—a decision that doubled the size of the country yet, in Jefferson's own words, was likely outside his constitutional authority.[9] As the first president to be neither nominated nor elected by Congress but rather by popularly chosen electors, Andrew Jackson vetoed a bill to recharter the national bank, whose existence had long been a source of tension between the parties.[10] Meanwhile, President James Polk instigated and then executed the Mexican-American War and exerted newfound influence over the national budget.[11]

While each of these administrations made a profound mark on the nation, none can be said to mark the beginning of a robust institutional presidency that stands at the center of American political life. Further, these presidents did little to expand the reach of the executive branch: nearly 90 percent of the growth in federal employment between 1816 and 1861 could be attributed to the Post Office.[12] And for the vast preponderance of the nineteenth century, Congress retained its control over the apparatus of government. Members of the president's cabinet spent much of their time on Capitol Hill, negotiating with the standing committees who oversaw their day-to-day assignments.[13] At the end of the nineteenth century, the presidency operated at the margins of national politics—much as it did at the beginning.

But what about Abraham Lincoln? Not only did Lincoln exercise more authority than any president in the nineteenth century, he accomplished more than nearly any president since. At the time of his inauguration in 1861, seven states—South Carolina, Mississippi, Florida, Alabama, Georgia, Louisiana, and Texas—had formally seceded from the Union. After the Battle of Fort Sumter, the first conflict of the Civil War, Lincoln's overriding aim became the preservation of the Union and its Constitution, a task he executed largely without permission or guidance from Congress. Two months into his presidency, while Congress was not in session, Lincoln ordered massive expansions of the army and navy, despite Congress's constitutional power "To raise and support Armies."[14] Likewise, despite the Constitution's provision that "No Money shall be drawn from the Treasury, but in Consequence of Appropriations made by Law," Lincoln unilaterally ordered his treasury secretary to advance two million dollars to war-related activities.[15]

As the war continued, Lincoln claimed still more authority. On New Year's Day, 1863, he signed the Emancipation Proclamation, abolishing slavery in all Confederate states that had not yet been defeated. In September of the same year, he issued another proclamation suspending the writ of habeas corpus—which allows citizens to contest their unlawful imprisonment—throughout the United States. Members of Congress were aghast at a presidency many saw as a budding dictatorship. "No one at a distance," wrote one Republican representative, "could form any conception of the hostility of the Republican members to Lincoln at the time of final adjournment . . . [Ohio Republican] Senator Wade said the country was going to hell, and that the scenes witnessed in the French Revolution were nothing in comparison with what we should see here."[16]

How, then, could Lincoln not be said to have transformed the institutional presidency? The answer is reasonably clear: Lincoln himself disavowed any such intention. Before assuming office, Lincoln retained an abiding skepticism of a strong presidency. A member of the Whig Party, he was propelled into politics by what he saw as a usurpation of power by the Jackson administration. In Congress, Lincoln staunchly opposed Polk's unilateral handling of the military.[17] Once in office, he never repudiated these views. Reflecting back on his wartime actions, Lincoln confessed: "I felt that measures otherwise unconstitutional might become lawful by becoming indispensable to the preservation of the Constitution through the preservation of the nation."[18] But Lincoln's wartime actions were never meant to establish precedent for his peacetime successors. It is no accident that presidents after Lincoln—Johnson, Grant, Hayes, and Garfield—were, in the words of one scholar, "nothing more than products of their time." In the decades following the Civil War, the public still looked to Congress, not the president, to formulate federal policy.[19] While Lincoln might have permanently remade the course of history, he did not (and did not seek to) remake the presidency.

The institutional presidency we see today—central not just to federal policymaking but also to the everyday lives of American citizens—came later. It does not owe its existence to the views of a particular president, nor to the steady accumulation of power by presidents like Lincoln. Rather, the circumstances of the twentieth century—chief among them urbanization, industrialization, rising immigration, and the emergence of monopolies—produced in the public a new set of demands for their government. Starting in the Progressive Era, the presidency found its moorings and extended its reach.

2.2 The Progressive Era and Institutional Change

By the eve of the twentieth century, the United States had become a very different country from the one in existence at its founding. The republic of self-reliant farmers championed by nearly every president from Jefferson, in 1801, to Lincoln, in 1861, had long been under siege from the relentless onrush of modern industrial capitalism. By 1900, newly formed corporations—Union Pacific Railroad, Standard Oil, and U.S. Steel, to name but a few—amassed unprecedented capital by limiting competition and streamlining manufacturing.

The nation's physical and cultural landscape had been transformed in the process. Prairies had surrendered to surging metropolises where immigrant workers labored in factories to produce commodities for a rising middle class. Railroads and telegraph lines, reaching even the most isolated pockets of rural America, had knit the sprawling nation together through an ever-expanding web of media, markets, and transportation. A newly aggressive foreign policy accompanied this economic growth. Throughout the latter half of the nineteenth century, the United States had extended its reach across the world stage. As new national labor laws and waves of European immigrants fueled domestic capacity for production, the United States dramatically increased its manufacturing exports. Business leaders pushed for increased access to raw materials in Latin America and for entry into new markets in Asia. Having definitively inserted itself into the race for empire, together with all the leading Western powers of the day, the United States entered an age of imperialism and acquired control over numerous overseas territories in the Caribbean and the Pacific, including Puerto Rico, the Philippines, and Hawaii.

Against this background of social and economic upheaval, Americans entertained new notions of state. For many Americans, the old rules of governance and of limited government seemed ill-suited to the challenges of the day. The countless disruptions wrought by the new industrialism gave rise to a diverse assembly of activists who promoted an array of reforms, ranging from temperance and labor rights to attempts at social engineering. These reform activities came to define a roughly forty-year period now known as the **Progressive Era,** which was marked by an expansion of presidential powers, a growth of civil service protections, and more interventionist government policy.

Faith in the capacity of government to take on the problems of American life was a core sentiment of progressive reformers.* The Pure Food and Drug Act of 1906, for example, was enacted after journalists in New York and Chicago exposed the appallingly fraudulent and unhealthy practices of American food and drug manufacturers; and its passage demonstrated the broad appeal of progressive ideas as a means of improving the lives of citizens. Most progressives were convinced that individuals in an increasingly interdependent society had only limited autonomy and that stronger state institutions were needed to

---

* Today, the word "progressive" has come to mean "liberal." No such association is intended here. "Progressive reformers" merely refers to the academics, businesspeople, journalists, and activists who pushed for policy changes during the Progressive Era.

promote the common good. A number of progressive reforms, therefore, sought to end municipal corruption, give women the right to vote, and increase government transparency. Still others attempted to restrict immigration and enshrine the role of unelected experts in policymaking. And as both proponent and subject of reform, the presidency occupied a prominent place in the imaginations of progressives.

2.2.1 Theodore Roosevelt's Stewardship

With William McKinley's assassination in 1901, Vice President Theodore Roosevelt assumed the presidency and brought with him a new philosophy of governance. Though observers at the time noted the vigor and dynamism with which he carried out the duties of the office, it was not until *The Autobiography of Theodore Roosevelt* was published in 1913 that Roosevelt's own governing philosophy was revealed in full. Casting himself in the mold of Presidents Lincoln and Jackson, Roosevelt wrote in the autobiography that the president, and indeed every executive officer, was "a steward of the people bound actively and affirmatively to do all he could for the people."[20]

This **stewardship theory**, as it came to be called, defined Roosevelt's presidency. Past presidents had derived their power from Article II of the Constitution. For Roosevelt, however, the Constitution did not tell him what he could do; it only told him what he could *not* do in service of the people. Where the Constitution was silent, then, the president was free to do as he chose. Precisely because Article II was both short and ambiguous, this reformulation of the office's relationship to the Constitution dramatically expanded the possibilities for presidential leadership.

Implicit in Roosevelt's vision of the presidency was a challenge to the notion that the president, under the terms of the Constitution, should normally yield to congressional authority on domestic issues. Increasingly, Roosevelt and many other progressives had come to see Congress as an obstacle to reform. Its members, they judged, were too short-sighted and too indebted to local interests to govern effectively or to represent the nation as a whole. It was thus the job of the president, the only politician elected by the nation as a whole, to do "the work of the people, breaking through the constitutional form."[21]

Roosevelt, a Republican himself, often found himself at odds with the conservative Republican leadership in Congress, which attempted to thwart much of his progressive domestic policy agenda. So, in 1905, when conservatives in the Senate prevented a floor vote on Roosevelt's proposal to strengthen the ability of the Interstate Commerce Commission (ICC) to regulate railroad shipping rates, the president embarked on an extensive public relations campaign to drum up support for rate regulation among voters in the Midwest and Southwest. By the time the ICC bill came up for a vote in 1906, public favor for the bill—and for the president—was so widespread that only three senators voted against it.[22]

While Roosevelt rallied the public to his cause in ways that broke from nineteenth-century precedents (for more on this, see chapter 12), he also believed in strengthening presidential authority through formal—that is, institutional—means. Roosevelt and his

FIGURE 2.1. The Panama Canal. In both domestic and foreign affairs, Theodore Roosevelt breathed vigor and ambition into the presidency. Nowhere were his efforts on greater display than in the building of the Panama Canal. *Source:* Library of Congress Prints and Photographs Division [LC-DIGppmsca- 26113].

allies waged no organized progressive campaign to amend the Constitution, but they worked tirelessly to change both how the office operated and the larger governmental landscape. Roosevelt broke new ground, for example, by taking advantage of executive orders (unilateral policy directives that bypass Congress) to push through domestic reforms. In 1908, for instance, he issued an executive order—a "midnight forests" order—that set aside sixteen million acres of western land for conservation the night before an anti-conservation bill passed in Congress.[23]

Roosevelt and his allies also sought to establish lasting federal bureaucracies that would relieve the executive branch of local patronage. Under Roosevelt, no fewer than 60 percent of civil servants became subject to the merit system, with hirings and promotions based on performance on competitive exams rather than on political affiliation.[24] By the time he left office, federal employment rolls had swelled by 33 percent (from 275,000 positions in 1901 to 365,000 in 1909), but cronyism was far less common.

Roosevelt's foreign policy was even more muscular than his domestic agenda. Roosevelt firmly believed that it was the president's job not only to effect change at home but to enhance the nation's international standing abroad. He shaped an aggressive foreign policy centered around three principles: "broadly defined US interests, US Power, and Anglo-American leadership."[25] In order to uphold these values, Roosevelt vastly expanded the U.S. Navy and engaged internationally to a degree not seen by prior presidents.

Among the most enduring of his foreign policy ventures was helping to stir up a secessionist movement in Panama that culminated in its formal separation from Colombia in 1903, which in turn ensured American preeminence over what would later become the Panama Canal Zone (figure 2.1). This level of international engagement established a precedent that (after a brief stint with isolationism in the 1920s) would go on to shape and define U.S. foreign policy for the latter half of the twentieth century.

Roosevelt's actions in the foreign policy arena, beyond shaping America's role in global geopolitics, managed to clarify the president's role in foreign policy. Rather than delegating, "[he] charted the broad course of American diplomacy and attended personally to the significant details of its execution."[26] The modern presidency has followed this trajectory: the United States has placed itself in the center of global geopolitics, just as presidents have placed themselves at the center of American foreign policy. As one popular historian succinctly summarizes, "As America's role as world leader increased, so has the power of the president."[27]

This increase in presidential power was very much in keeping with Roosevelt's designs. Whereas Lincoln took pains to underscore the exceptional circumstances that temporarily justified his wartime actions, Roosevelt's expansionist foreign policy—and with it, his vigorous pursuit of domestic policy and the stewardship theory that he promoted—established a template for executive governance ever more.

Historical Transformations: The Stewardship Theory Weathers Its First Rejoinder

Presidents are often judged against the challenges they inherit. Some presidents come to power during war. Others, during economic or public-health crises. These presidents are forever remembered as having overcome (or not) the challenges that stood before them. When William Howard Taft entered office in 1909, he inherited a challenge that may very well have been insurmountable: carrying on the legacy of Theodore Roosevelt.

As Roosevelt's secretary of war, William Taft was handpicked by the outgoing president to build on their administration's achievements: standing up to large monopolies, conserving the environment, and asserting America's interests abroad. Few scholars, however, would claim that Taft accomplished these goals. His unwillingness to take on Congress or the party leadership, his reverence for the rule of law and the judicial system, and his deep aversion to controversy resulted in multiple defeats. Whereas Roosevelt had revolutionized the president's relationship with the public, taking his agenda directly to the people, Taft adopted a modest communications strategy akin to that of nineteenth-century presidents. Even during the 1908 election, he planned to run a "front-porch" style campaign in which he avoided travel and let his most famous surrogates—most notably, President Roosevelt—speak on his behalf.[28] More importantly, Taft's understanding of the presidency itself—its relationship to the Constitution, the powers it conferred—controverted Roosevelt's, and left Taft little room to advance his predecessor's policy agenda.

In his post-presidency book, *Our Chief Magistrate and His Powers*, Taft articulated a **literalist theory** of the presidency. "The true view of the Executive function," Taft wrote, "is that the President can exercise no power which cannot be fairly and reasonably traced to some specific grant of power or justly implied and included within such express grant."[29] In other words, the Constitution (and through occasional delegations,

Congress) delineates those powers that the president is meant to exercise. Absent such a delineation, Taft argued, "there is no undefined residuum of power" for presidents to claim.[30]

Nearly point by point, Taft's literalist view of the presidency repudiated Roosevelt's stewardship theory. Indeed, Taft viewed Roosevelt's theory as not merely wrongheaded but dangerous. "My judgement is that the view of . . . Mr. Roosevelt, ascribing an undefined residuum of power to the President is an unsafe doctrine and that it might lead under emergencies to results of an arbitrary character. . . . The wide field of action that this would give to the Executive one can hardly limit."[31]

It is no coincidence that Taft's presidency has largely slipped from historical memory. His reticence to exercise power—boldly, and in the service of national objectives, as Roosevelt would have it—yielded an administration devoid of major accomplishments. In one of the earliest disappointments of his presidency, Taft tried to work with Congress to lower tariffs, which many in his party saw as a boon for large monopolies. In place of the sweeping reductions he promised in his 1908 campaign, however, the bill was quickly taken over by Republican moderates, who made it more palatable to businesses and even raised tariffs on several goods. Despite his threat to veto an insufficient bill, Taft soon backed down and even praised it as "the best tariff bill the Republican party ever passed."[32]

Failures like these obliterated Taft's reputation among progressive Republicans. Roosevelt, who had all but handed Taft the keys to the White House, became sufficiently frustrated to leave the Republican Party and run in 1912 under the "Bull Moose" banner, ultimately splitting the Republican vote and handing the election to Democrat Woodrow Wilson. With just eight electoral votes, Taft suffered one of the worst electoral performances of any incumbent president in history.

The 1912 election was not just the defeat of a single president. Far more than that—it was the downfall of Taft's view of presidential power. Despite his consistent legislative failures, voters in 1912 could very well have welcomed the return to normalcy embodied by Taft. That is, after the startling assertiveness of Roosevelt's presidency, voters might have wanted to revert to the nineteenth-century way of doing things: Congress as the main governing body, the president a quiet spectator. This did not happen. As we will see, Wilson's victory in 1912—and then Franklin Delano Roosevelt's two decades hence—affirmed the public's appetite for strong, ambitious presidents. Taft's literalist perspective ultimately rendered an unavailing critique, and the stewardship theory, in time, set the terms by which all presidents were evaluated.

2.2.2 Woodrow Wilson: Progressivism Continued

Running under the banner of the newly formed Progressive Party, Roosevelt lost the presidential election of 1912 to Democrat Woodrow Wilson. Despite his loss, the 1912 race nonetheless represented an endorsement of Roosevelt's vision of the presidency and of his progressive politics. As president, Wilson behaved much like Roosevelt. He took to new heights the Rooseveltian quest to expand and professionalize federal institutions as well as the Rooseveltian strategy of direct public appeals. Wilson made frequent public appearances and earned a reputation as a captivating speaker. As the first president to hold press conferences, Wilson also set a new precedent for White House public relations.*

On December 2, 1913, in a controversial move, Wilson gave the State of the Union Address within the chambers of Congress, restoring a practice not seen since 1801, at the very end of John Adams's presidency. As a former professor of political science, Wilson saw the State of the Union speech as an opportunity squandered by nineteenth-century presidents. Wilson thought that the speech, if delivered in person and in Congress, would focus the public's attention on issues that Congress might otherwise be inclined to sidestep.

During his time as president, Wilson tackled a wide range of progressive reforms. With the Underwood Tariff Act of 1913, he lowered tariffs for the first time since the American Civil War.† Through the passage of the Federal Trade Act in 1914, he helped create the Federal Trade Commission, whose mandate was to curb unfair and illegal business practices by issuing "cease and desist" orders. Wilson then spelled out these "unfair and illegal" practices in the 1914 Clayton Anti-Trust Act. Wilson pursued banking reform, most notably through the 1913 creation of the Federal Reserve System, which established an independent central bank that was charged with overseeing monetary policy. He also worked with Congress to give worker's compensation to federal employees, to secure a maximum eight-hour workday for railroad employees, and to outlaw child labor with the Keating-Owen Act (though this act was ruled unconstitutional in 1918). By the end of Wilson's first term, a significant amount of progressive legislation had been passed, affecting broad swaths of the domestic economy, farming, labor, veterans' affairs, the environment, and conservation.

The transformation of the presidency during the Progressive Era was based more on a shift in precedent than an alteration of the formal characteristics and powers of the office. Roosevelt and Wilson succeeded in changing popular ideas about the presidency—and expectations for how the president should wield the powers already constitutionally granted—without the benefit of any changes to the Constitution. The model of a more vigorous, public presidency that they both promoted set the standard for all presidents to come. After the Progressive Era, presidents were expected to steer the national policy agenda using whatever means they could muster, whether through Congress, through public opinion, or through federal agencies. Meanwhile, as the federal government expanded in concert with the broadening of presidential power, the figure of the president became the face of American nationhood. The president's command over the machinery of government thus amplified his influence in politics. Presidents who managed to enact lasting

---

*An important area in which Wilson differed from Roosevelt concerned their visions of the president's appropriate relationship to his political party. Rather than challenging party leadership, Wilson believed the president should assume the role as head of his party, currying its allegiance and exerting discipline when necessary to maintain cohesion.

† The process by which presidents' legislative agendas come to fruition is discussed in detail in chapter 8.

institutional change ensured that their voices would continue to be heard once they left office. Those who came later would need to find their own ways to be heard above the din.

2.3 Scientific Management and Institutional Change

If the early decades of the twentieth century had largely been defined by the progressive agendas of Theodore Roosevelt and Woodrow Wilson, the 1920s ushered in a period of conservative retrenchment overseen by three Republican presidents—Warren G. Harding, Calvin Coolidge, and Herbert Hoover—who were committed to laissez-faire economics and limited government and averse to continuing the expansion of the federal government initiated by Roosevelt and Wilson. In the 1930s, things would be different: in 1933, Franklin Delano Roosevelt ascended to the presidency and promptly set in motion a new round of structural reforms. Among these reforms was a significant reorganization of the executive branch using the ideas of scientific management.

2.3.1 A Brief, and Ultimately Discredited, Conservative Resurgence

At the end of Wilson's presidency, the United States recoiled from the uncertainty and upheaval associated with Progressive legislation and, significantly, with World War I. Republican presidential candidate Warren Harding promised a "return to normalcy," one marked by a smaller, less interventionist federal government and a presidency that returned to its rightful place in the constitutional order. Harding and his two Republican successors, Calvin Coolidge and Herbert Hoover, delivered on such promises. The ultimate repudiation of their tenures in office, though, paved the way for the institutionalization of a distinctly modern presidency.

Politically, the policy preferences of the three presidents who held office in the 1920s looked quite different from their Progressive predecessors. Harding and Coolidge, in particular, sought to scale back the government's intrusions into the domestic economy through tax cuts and deregulation. Hoover, who held office during the Great Depression, harbored considered views about how markets ought to function, but he strongly preferred that the state limit itself to encouraging businesses to adopt new practices rather than mandating them. It was not until very late in his presidency—too late, it turns out, to stem the tide of sentiment against him—that Hoover supported legislation that provided direct government investment in the economy.

These three presidents also took a much more modest view of their office than did either Roosevelt or Wilson. Presidents, these Republicans thought, were not meant to meddle in the affairs of Congress. As Hoover would write in his memoirs, "I had felt deeply that no President should undermine the independence of the legislative and judicial branches by seeking to discredit them."[33] As a result, neither he nor his fellow Republican presidents of that decade barnstormed the country on behalf of a chosen cause. Unlike Harding, Coolidge and Hoover each developed direct relations with the media and larger public. None, however, saw fit to challenge the autonomy of Congress, the courts, or the party organizations.

Still, the 1920s were not entirely lacking in institutional achievements. Notably, and as discussed at greater length in chapter 8, Congress enacted the Budget and Accounting Act of 1921, which ceded important new responsibilities to the president in the drafting of an annual budget. And in *Myers v. United States*,[34] the Supreme Court recognized the president's sweeping authority to remove executive appointees from office. As these examples indicate, however, during this period of conservative retrenchment, the work of building an institutional presidency fell primarily to Congress and the Supreme Court.

After dying in office, Harding's legacy was scarred by revelations of personal and political scandals, which are discussed at greater length in chapter 10. The free-spirited (i.e., unregulated) economic expansion of the Coolidge administration would promptly run aground with the stock market crash of 1929. And Hoover's principled refusal to use the arm of the state to tackle the Great Depression met with widespread public rebuke. To replace this moribund policy was one of "bold, persistent experimentation"[35] and a philosophy of action that would transform the office of the presidency.

2.3.2 *Franklin Delano Roosevelt: Engineering a New American State*

The steps Theodore Roosevelt and Wilson had taken to increase the role of the president in shaping domestic affairs were broadened under Franklin Delano Roosevelt—so much so, in fact, that many historians credit FDR for ushering in the **modern presidency**, a more powerful and institutionalized presidency.* (For a critique of this notion, see this chapter's Thinking Institutionally feature.) FDR drew on the spirit of the Progressive Era to tackle an unprecedented threat to the social and economic order, but he surpassed the achievements of his Progressive predecessors in engineering the institutions of state. Where earlier Progressive presidents had faced a society in flux, FDR confronted one in deep crisis. The Great Depression, precipitated by the market crash of 1929, had thrown a quarter of the U.S. workforce out of work, devastated farm incomes, and blighted banking and industry nationwide. To meet these challenges, many thought, the machinery of government needed fixing.

During his first hundred days in office, FDR sent Congress a record number of proposals for federal action aimed at providing immediate, targeted economic relief, restoring public confidence in the banking system, and easing unemployment. He also made liberal use of executive orders. Immediately after taking office, he declared a bank holiday, outlawed the hoarding of gold, and called Congress into a special session. Viewing the Depression as a national catastrophe that could be overcome only through strong presidential leadership, FDR appealed to Congress to grant him "broad executive power to wage a war against the emergency, as great as the power that would be given to [him] if we were in fact invaded by a foreign foe."[36]

---

* Other historians credit Theodore Roosevelt or Woodrow Wilson as originators of the modern presidency.

FIGURE 2.2. The New Deal. In reorganizing and expanding the executive branch, FDR also sought to expand his influence in government more generally. This tendency attracted considerable criticism, as in this cartoon, which depicts the New Deal as a Trojan horse for tyranny. Copyright Fotosearch/Getty Images. Reproduced with permission.

Like the administrations of Theodore Roosevelt and Wilson, but far more aggressively, the FDR administration undertook numerous reforms and invented new government agencies under the rubric of the **New Deal**, a massive legislative agenda that cemented the notion of the federal government as a tool for mediating the social and economic life of the nation. FDR spearheaded public works programs, relief for the unemployed, a national pension system known as Social Security, new protections for workers, and more. Some political observers were taken aback by the powers the new president claimed through his New Deal. (For one such example, see figure 2.2.) But for most, his actions and ambitions constituted a welcome departure from his predecessor's benign neglect.

At the same time, FDR elevated the profile of the presidency through a dramatic reorganization of the executive branch. He recognized early on that organizational inefficiency was one of the biggest obstacles to the effective implementation of New Deal policies and programs: with so many new programs springing into existence, often with overlapping mandates, the New Deal apparatus proved dynamic but unwieldy. As best he could, FDR sought to discipline and direct the swelling federal juggernaut. Lacking many official mechanisms for executive oversight, FDR made do throughout his first term by poaching staff from various departments and agencies and by cultivating a sense of competition among New Deal administrators.[37]

THE BROWNLOW COMMITTEE

One of the major projects of FDR's second term was to corral the federal government's many new agencies and bring them under a formal system of presidential supervision. Shortly after his reelection in 1936, FDR appointed a committee of public administration experts, headed by Louis Brownlow, to offer recommendations on providing the president with "controls commensurate with his responsibilities."[38] In their findings, the **Brownlow Committee** emphasized the need for a stronger managerial president.[39] The committee assumed that greater efficiency went hand in hand with greater presidential authority. It hunted for ways to apply the techniques of **scientific management** to the executive branch—that is, ways to organize the federal government the way one would organize a large factory. By using modern tools of management, the committee believed that the federal government could be made more efficient and effective.

In a final report submitted to Congress as a bill in 1937, the Brownlow Committee plainly declared that "the president needs help" and offered a multipoint program designed to provide it. One of the report's most significant recommendations was the creation of a new institution, the **Executive Office of the President (EOP)**. Brownlow further recommended that the Bureau of the Budget be reassigned from the Treasury Department to the EOP, where the president would have more control over its appointments. Showing its allegiance to scientific management principles, the Brownlow report further stipulated that EOP aides "should be possessed of high competence, great physical vigor, and a passion for anonymity." Other Brownlow Committee recommendations included the elimination of the Civil Service Commission, support for additional aides who would report directly to the president, and the consolidation of numerous federal agencies, which would then be put under the direct control of the president. The report also tackled the thorny question of congressional oversight of executive agencies, arguing that the executive branch should have sole authority over expenditures, once the legislative branch had appropriated funds for a particular program.

Initially, the Brownlow report ignited a backlash in Congress. Opponents branded it the "dictator bill," and the controversy surrounding FDR's efforts to enlarge the Supreme Court and pack it with judges sympathetic to his agenda (a topic discussed at greater length in chapter 11) further undercut the bill's reception. As a result, the House and the Senate failed to reach an agreement on an amended Brownlow bill during the 1937 legislative session.

By 1939, however, congressional distrust of the president seemed to have abated, and the two chambers passed the **Executive Reorganization Act** of 1939, a watered-down version of Brownlow's original recommendations. The checks on presidential prerogatives included a congressional veto on overhaul plans, rejection of EOP absorption of the comptroller general's office, exclusion of twenty-one agencies from executive consolidation, and a two-year limit on implementation. Nonetheless, Congress did agree to some of FDR's demands for more influence over federal operations. Most significantly, Congress approved the Brownlow Committee's terms for the establishment of the EOP, including the transfer of the Bureau of the Budget, and authorized the president to enlarge the White House staff so that, by 1941, fifty-three persons were employed in the president's office—up from only two during Thomas Jefferson's presidency.[40] The newly constituted EOP would wield significant power in managing domestic economic policy leading up to World War II. It would come to play an even larger role in the decades that followed.

Thinking Institutionally: The "Modern Presidency" as an Analytic Category

Scholars have long attempted to sort the American presidency into distinct categories for observation. Various strains of literature refer to an "imperial" presidency, an "imperiled" presidency, a "plebiscitary" presidency, and even an "impossible" presidency.[41] (Let us not forget, of course, the institutional presidency.) These conceptions are valuable insofar as they draw our attention away from the eccentricities of individual presidents and, instead, invite us to consider broad periods in presidential leadership, situating individual officeholders within a reasonably well-defined political or historical context.

While some of these categories have been abandoned, one has been remarkably long-lived: the "modern" presidency. Gaining traction in the early 1980s, promoters of the modern presidency divide presidents into two camps: "traditional" presidents, who held office during the eighteenth, nineteenth, and early twentieth centuries; and "modern" presidents, who held office from 1933 onward.

The distinction is rooted in some very real observations about changes in the office of the presidency. According to Fred Greenstein, who helped popularize the concept, the modern presidency differs from its traditional counterpart in four key respects:[42]

1. Modern presidents are expected to set the legislative agenda and actively exercise the veto.
2. Modern presidents have more opportunities to create policy unilaterally.
3. Modern presidents can rely on a dramatically larger personal staff and a vast bureaucracy.
4. Modern presidents are the most visible symbols of government. Deserved or not, they receive credit or blame for the state of the nation.

Continued on next page

Notably, Greenstein does not claim that modern presidents are invariably more powerful or more successful than their predecessors. The expansion of the formal tools coincided with nigh impossible expectations that the president will be the nation's champion of the public good.

These expectations—mostly about what presidents *should* do, rather than what they *can* do—are the hallmark of the modern presidency.

Like all categories, the notion of a distinctly modern presidency is the subject of scholarly disagreement. In *The Myth of the Modern Presidency*, David Nichols argues that the fundamental elements of the presidency can all be traced back to the Constitution, which did not change during the FDR presidency. Suggesting new legislation, controlling the bureaucracy, acting unilaterally—these tasks were carried out by nineteenth- and twentieth-century presidents alike. And while it is undoubtedly the case that the powers and responsibilities of recent presidents have grown, Nichols attributes this growth solely to the expansion of government. "Relative to the tasks that government performs," writes Nichols, "modern presidents do no more—and no less—than Presidents have done in the past."[43]

Other scholars push back against any category that situates a hard, dividing line in presidential history. In their view, the notion of a modern presidency unfairly treats all post-FDR presidents as a coherent group—overemphasizing their similarities, underemphasizing their very real differences, and ignoring parallels between them and their nineteenth-century predecessors.[44] Moreover, the need to label presidents in this way can lead to constant and unwarranted updating, including claims by some that we have surpassed the modern presidency and entered the "postmodern" presidency.[45] Claims such as these, usually written to describe whichever president is currently in office, are hurriedly revised or thrown out just as soon as a new president assumes office.

How, then, should we think about the modern presidency category? Of course, we should look critically upon any effort to categorize. What falls under one category should differ substantially from what falls under another. But on this score, the traditional/modern dichotomy has real merit. As we have seen in this chapter, the presidency *was* transformed in the twentieth century, especially in the four areas Greenstein identified. The transformation did not happen all at once; and important parallels between presidents across this divide can still be drawn. But as we explore further in future chapters, presidents' relationships with Congress, the bureaucracy, the public, and their own unilateral powers look markedly different in the modern era than they did before. Moreover, this transformation did not merely track the growth of the presidency alongside the overall growth of the federal government, as Nichols argues. Rather, over time, and especially while FDR was in office, presidents greatly increased their power vis-à-vis Congress and the courts.

For these reasons, the modern presidency can indeed be a useful concept for thinking about the presidency, and the following chapters will mention it from time to time. You will notice, however, that it is not the organizing concept of this book. Our focus remains the institutional presidency. Unlike the modern presidency, the institutional presidency does not delineate a clear temporal divide. Rather, the institutional presidency is constantly shifting—dramatically, at times, as during the Progressive Era—according to the powers vested in and the expectations directed toward the office itself, and also according to changes in the structural design and composition of institutions that surround the presidency. To determine the effectiveness of any one president, we must look, for example, to the partisan makeup of Congress and the Supreme Court, the structure of the bureaucracy, the media landscape, and more. The onset of the modern presidency undeniably accompanied significant changes in the president's relationships with these other institutions. And for this reason alone, it is not just a scholarly conceit. Rather, the notion of a modern presidency speaks to—perhaps somewhat clumsily, and obviously incompletely—very real developments in the American presidency.

2.4 War and Institutional Change

Does "war make states"?[46] It is an idea attributed to the great social scientist Charles Tilly, and its validity has long been debated. Lending support to Tilly's claims, World Wars I and II were watershed events in the history of the United States, not least because of their lasting impact on the scope and powers of the administrative state. In both wars, U.S. presidents had to respond to the challenge of waging massive military campaigns abroad by expanding the productive capacities of industry at home. To achieve the necessary degree of mobilization, new regulatory and administrative agencies were plainly needed, over and above those recently put in place to deal with the pressing circumstances of the Progressive Era and the Great Depression. If World War I can be regarded as the nation's introduction to **total war**, a military conflagration that affects and mobilizes nearly every sector of society, then World War II can be seen as an acceleration and expansion in kind—with dramatic consequences for the institutional design of government.

2.4.1 World War I

Although the United States managed to stay out of World War I (1914–18) for the first three years of fighting, its involvement in the conflict beginning in April 1917 would prove transformative for the nation. After a series of developments that strained America's policy of nonintervention—including several German submarine attacks on U.S. merchant ships and Germany's secret attempt at an anti-American alliance with Mexico—Wilson announced an end to American neutrality in 1917.

From the beginning, it was clear that Wilson envisioned a war mobilization effort that would dwarf any that had come before. In an address on April 2, 1917, the president sought a congressional declaration of war, calling for nothing less than "the organization and mobilization of all the material resources of the country" in order to "make the world safe for democracy."[47] Congress responded with a formal declaration of war against Germany

FIGURE 2.3. Civic volunteerism. In World War I, nearly all Americans were called upon to serve and sacrifice. Even children's breakfast cereals were implicated in the president's war effort. *Source:* Library of Congress Prints and Photographs Division [LC-USZC4–10218].

on April 4 and, in May, passed the Selective Service Act of 1917, which authorized the president to enforce a new military draft and to send approximately five million American soldiers to the European front.

At the same time, the home front underwent changes both sudden and extreme. Wilson's assertion of presidential authority to wage total war worked in parallel with moves to centralize political power within a strong federal state. While Wilson courted Congress's support for wartime measures, deliberately avoiding some of the more blatant power grabs that he associated with Lincoln's Civil War presidency, he nonetheless saw himself as the undisputed overseer of wartime operations in Europe and at home. As Wilson saw it, "the responsibility of conducting the war and safeguarding the nation" ultimately fell upon the president.[48]

Making liberal use of executive orders and taking advantage of a reasonably compliant Congress, Wilson created dozens of new federal agencies that pushed the executive branch into realms previously considered private. The War Industries Board (WIB), for instance, worked with numerous industries to ensure the continual production of raw materials deemed essential for war mobilization. The National War Labor Board (NWLB) oversaw relations between labor and management in just about every enterprise, at once urging companies to accede to labor's demands for higher wages and better hours and persuading unions to limit strikes and agitation against open-shop rules (wherein eligibility for employment is not contingent on union membership). A host of other agencies—Fuel Administration, Railroad Administration, and Food Administration among them—maintained strict oversight of a staggering array of business practices affecting wages, prices, production levels, allowable profits, and product standardization.

The war, Wilson claimed, demanded deference to the state. But the president walked a fine line between mandating and merely encouraging it. True to his Progressive ideals, Wilson believed in state regulation of business, but he was uncomfortable exerting too many economic controls. Although newly established war agencies were vested with significant authority, Wilson often worked to foster state cooperation with, rather than appropriation from, private enterprise. Meanwhile, Wilson sought to nurture a spirit of civic voluntarism by asking Americans to contribute to the war effort of their own volition (figure 2.3).

At the same time, his administration maintained a culture of vigilance in which dissent was not merely discouraged but was viewed as treasonous. The Committee on Public Information, appointed by Wilson and organized to disseminate propaganda, used sensationalistic imagery to convince Americans of the brutality of the German enemy and to compel women and other non-combatants to sacrifice for the war effort. Posters claimed that the nation could "beat back the Hun" if people bought enough "liberty bonds," if they lived the maxim that "food is ammunition" that is not to be wasted, and if they allowed "Uncle Sam" every reasonable license to ferret out draft evaders. Wilson also advocated for and signed into law the Espionage Act of 1917, allowing his administration to clamp down on domestic speech that the government deemed contrary to the war effort.

Most of Wilson's wartime agencies were terminated after the war's end. Their influence, however, would persist a good deal longer. For example, the Justice Department's Bureau of Investigation enforced crackdowns on political dissent during the war, but its activities—in targeting immigrant labor agitators, for one thing—would continue long afterward, with the agency eventually becoming the nation's leading domestic intelligence agency, the Federal Bureau of Investigation (FBI). The principle of progressive taxation, in which the rich pay a higher portion of their income to the government than the middle and lower classes, also became a central component of the political landscape. Wilson's discourse of obligation-based citizenship also persuaded many Americans that the federal government was the appropriate guarantor of social and economic order.

2.4.2 World War II

Although Wilson ignited popular support for America's entry into World War I, Americans were decidedly reluctant to enter into any other military engagements once that war was over. Throughout the 1930s, as Nazi Germany gathered allies, FDR faced deep congressional opposition to any policy that might address the threat. Over the course of the decade, Congress confirmed its isolationist leanings by passing a series of neutrality acts, so when a second world war erupted in Europe in 1939, the United States did not join the fight.

As the war in Europe intensified, FDR bucked congressional isolationists and made limited moves to support America's allies, especially Great Britain. In 1940, without seeking congressional approval, FDR initiated the Destroyers for Bases Agreement to transfer American warships to the Royal Navy in exchange for free long-term leases on British military bases.* A year later, FDR pushed the much broader Lend-Lease Act through Congress, which provided significant American military support to the Allied cause.

---

*Roosevelt had the endorsement of the Supreme Court in his efforts to override congressional isolationism. A few years earlier, in *United States v. Curtiss-Wright Export Corp.*, 299 U.S. 304 (1936), the Supreme Court had articulated what is now the standard interpretation of the Court's reasoning in this case (even if it is at some distance from its actual reasoning): a vision of expansive presidential authority in matters of international relations. In its 1936 decision on the case—which involved the constitutionality of a law authorizing the president to prevent the export of American weapons to countries engaged in armed conflict—the Court stated that the president served as the nation's "sole organ" in foreign affairs. A year later, in *United States v.*

When the Lend-Lease bill went to the floor in March 1941, congressional votes were cast largely along party lines, with the Democratic majority in both houses carrying the bill to passage. After the bombing of Pearl Harbor in December 1941, however, even the most hardened isolationists in Congress united behind the president. At FDR's behest, a massive war mobilization effort quickly got underway, in which virtually every policy instrument at the president's disposal was linked to the war effort.

During World War II, the president seized a wide range of emergency powers that allowed him to:

- set prices and wages;
- regulate labor-management relations;
- require workers in "nondeferrable" employment to be transferred either into the armed forces or into jobs deemed essential to the war effort;
- impose martial law on the territory of Hawaii;
- force over 100,000 people of Japanese descent into internment camps throughout the western United States;
- compel workers to join unions in any place of employment already covered by a union contract;
- requisition private property;
- mandate the length of the work week;
- demand, under threat of criminal punishment, that specific businesses meet orders placed by the government;
- suspend or amend regulations governing radio communications;
- ration food, tires, gasoline, and other scarce commodities;
- oversee the quality and quantity of goods produced by different industries; and
- assume primary control, where necessary, over the production of plants deemed central to the war effort.

Reflecting a capitulation to FDR's executive authority that seemed unfathomable before the attack on Pearl Harbor, the other two branches of government largely fell in line.

Like Wilson, FDR lined up an assembly of wartime administrative agencies—including the National War Labor Board, War Production Board, Office of Price Administration, National Housing Agency, Board of Economic Warfare, War Manpower Commission, Office of Defense Transportation, Office of Economic Stabilization (later the Office of War Mobilization), and Office of Censorship—to carry out his domestic policy. Also like Wilson, FDR launched most of them through executive orders or other unilateral directives, rather than through the more cumbersome legislative process.

But FDR went several steps beyond Wilson. To appreciate just how massive FDR's wartime expansion of the executive branch was, consider figure 2.4, which graphs the historical number of civilians employed by the federal government. Notably, the figure only

---

Belmont, 301 U.S. 324 (1937), the Court ruled that the president had the right to negotiate binding agreements with other nations and ignore the treaty process, which mandated congressional approval.

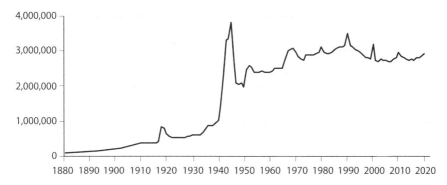

FIGURE 2.4. Total number of civilian employees in federal government. The size of the federal government increased dramatically over the course of the twentieth century, and nearly all of this growth occurred within the executive branch. While Congress added staffers and the judiciary grew modestly, the executive branch employment numbers increased by millions. Note the dramatic increase during World War II. *Source:* U.S. Bureau of the Census, Historical Statistics of the United States, U.S. Office of Personnel Management, and the Federal Reserve Bank of St. Louis.

shows *non-military* employees; FDR's impact on the administrative state went far beyond the number of soldiers he recruited. At the onset of the twentieth century, fewer than a quarter of a million employees worked in the federal government, and nearly all held positions in the executive branch. At the end of the war, that number peaked at nearly four million employees—and never retreated to its prewar levels.

While the most recent trend line in figure 2.4 seems to show signs of an overall decrease in federal employment—from a peak of roughly 3.5 million employees in the late 1980s—this decline hides substantial increases in federal spending conducted via private contractors who are not normally counted as government employees. The federal government, both in its staffing and activities, is now orders of magnitude larger than it was at the start of the twentieth century.

The administrative apparatus that FDR constructed enabled him to extend the reach of the federal government into just about every facet of American life. For example, the revived National War Labor Board (NWLB) under FDR was definitively more muscular than its World War I antecedent. Created in January 1942 by executive order, the new NWLB could mandate binding arbitration—in stark contrast to the World War I agency, which relied on persuasion and moral coercion to manage labor relations.

Significantly, the attack on Pearl Harbor came at a time when FDR's pro-labor agenda, the linchpin of his New Deal coalition, was flagging. During 1940 and 1941, FDR's efforts to supply America's European allies with arms and other material, requiring increased production from American workers, had exacerbated tensions between labor and management. Unions were escalating their demands for closed shops (wherein all employees of a given workplace would be required to join the union), and strikes and walkouts were on the rise. Business interests, in the meantime, had gained traction in Congress, which was threatening to pass various anti-labor measures. A compromise bill that FDR had sent to Congress failed, while a conservative proposal for preventing strikes passed in the House a few days before Pearl Harbor. The December 7 bombing quickly silenced this business-labor quarreling. Within days, virtually every important labor leader pledged not to strike for the duration of the war, and pending anti-labor legislation in Congress was jettisoned.

As they had been after World War I, many federal agencies created during World War II were dissolved once the fighting ended. The wartime state, however, did not simply evaporate, nor did the United States retreat into isolationism. Instead, as tensions between the United States and the Soviet Union mounted in the years after the war, Americans embraced their nation's expanded role on the world stage and underwrote a national security state that was ready for any new confrontation that might arise.* Meanwhile, veterans' benefits—the so-called GI Bill—helped reshape American society, as loans and payments for college, loans for homeownership, and other forms of government aid provided millions of former soldiers with access to the middle class.

World War II had enduring consequences for the American state.[49] Future presidents would confront a public that continued to look to its government to solve all manner of problems and challenges that previously had been thought to be the exclusive province of private or civic action. It is no accident, then, that many of the regulatory agencies erected during the war did not promptly disband at its conclusion. Instead, they carried on much as they had, just as others melded into the new, more expansive administrative landscape of the postwar era. The institutional presidency—both the structure itself and the public expectations that undergird it—was permanently altered.

2.5 The Long Civil Rights Movement and Institutional Change

Institutional change is not the exclusive province of external pressures or elite politics. Sometimes, it comes from domestic, grassroots movements that—with time and effort—garner resources and attention from the federal government. Movements such as women's suffrage, immigrant rights, industrial workers' rights, and farmworkers' rights promulgated important institutional changes. In this section we focus on one of the most consequential: the long civil rights movement.

The roots of civil rights achievements preceded the dramatic and familiar events of the 1950s and 1960s. Indeed, the organizational capacities of civil rights movements were built decades prior. The National Association for the Advancement of Colored People (NAACP), for instance, was founded in 1909, more than a half century before the passage

---

* The United States also significantly underwrote the rebuilding of postwar Europe, allocating approximately $13 billion (1948 dollars) under a program known as the Marshall Plan, or the European Recovery Program (ERP). This led to the modern system of non-military foreign aid, now a significant part of the American foreign policy apparatus.

of landmark civil rights legislation. Early NAACP members sought to raise awareness of racial violence and injustice and, according to their original charter, "to promote equality of rights and eradicate caste or race prejudice among citizens of the United States; to advance the interest of colored citizens; to secure for them impartial suffrage; and to increase their opportunities for securing justice in the courts, education for their children, employment according to their ability, and complete equality before the law." Within a decade, the organization sponsored national events, opened over 300 branches around the country, and enlisted more than 90,000 members.[50]

The NAACP worked alongside other grassroots civil rights organizations in search of broad, societal change. The presidency rather quickly came within their sights. At a time when congressional action on civil rights seemed all but impossible, the presidency offered at least the chance that racial violence and inequity might be recognized. And as the Progressive Movement and World War I transformed the office of the presidency into a steward of the people, the NAACP recognized its potential benefit for the cause.

Change did not come easily—or quickly. Initial victories came predominantly in the form of symbolic gestures, and they were routinely followed by setbacks. In 1912, a beleaguered Woodrow Wilson saw fit to briefly pander to the Black electorate, securing more Black American votes than any previous Democratic candidate.[51] Once in office, however, Wilson intermittently defended segregationist policies. Not to be dissuaded, social activists organized protests that made for front-page news. Years later, these continued efforts paid minor dividends when President Herbert Hoover increased the number of Black appointees to federal positions; though here again, the gains proved short-lived and illusory. During his administration, after all, Hoover restructured the Republican Party to strip Black partisans of any power or influence. As Russell Riley notes, "the political and demographic developments of the 1920s materially altered the incentive structures governing presidential behavior toward African Americans."[52] In this way, partial gains gave way to decided setbacks. Throughout, though, the presidency remained a primary target of social movement activity.

It wasn't until Franklin Delano Roosevelt's administration that the entreaties of social movement activists finally spurred sustained presidential action—and with it, a transformed American presidency. Change, though, did not happen the moment Roosevelt assumed office. When the affable former governor of New York was elected in 1932, civil rights was hardly his priority. Rather, concerns about economic recovery and the building of a national welfare state dominated his agenda, as they would his first two terms in office. The passage of his New Deal reforms—on which the recovery of the nation depended—was of paramount concern. And these reforms would not have passed without the support of southern Democrats in Congress, who steadfastly opposed anything that threatened their elaborate system of racial segregation in the South.

Roosevelt's fragile alliance with southern Democrats yielded legislation that, though helpful for the economy, precluded the advancement of minority rights. In the South, Black Americans were legally denied Social Security benefits, the protection of labor laws,

FIGURE 2.5. The long civil rights movement. A. Philip Randolph's threatened march on Washington proved instrumental in securing new civil rights policy—and with it, institutions charged with implementing it. *Source:* Library of Congress.

federal home loans, and more.[53] Meanwhile, Roosevelt refused to endorse civil rights legislation that, today, seems entirely uncontroversial. In 1934, amid widespread violence against Black citizens, Roosevelt refused to even endorse an anti-lynching law, saying only that "I frankly haven't got sufficient clarity in my own mind" about the bill.[54]

Still, civil rights leaders continued to pressure the president. Presiding over a much more powerful movement than had existed only decades prior, allies of A. Philip Randolph—an activist and organizer for a predominately Black labor union—ratcheted up their demands for presidential action. And with the outbreak of World War II, Randolph and his associates found the leverage they needed to realize political change.

In October 1940, Roosevelt signed an order requiring that Black Americans be drafted into the army at similar rates as whites—but still be deployed in segregated regiments.[55] Leaders like Randolph were infuriated by the rank hypocrisy of the administration's stance on racial integration, and they demanded that the president sign an executive order abolishing discrimination in the federal workforce. The National Urban League, an organization focused on economic and political justice, amplified the egregious double standard employed by the administration and underscored the need for presidential action.[56]

Beginning in January 1941, with the president refusing to sign an executive order, Randolph published editorials in several newspapers calling for a March on Washington, scheduled for July 1 of that year. Backed by the National Urban League, more than a hundred thousand Black supporters were set to take part, answering Randolph's call for a "thunderous march" that would "shake up white America."[57] Roosevelt pleaded for patience and invited Randolph to the White House in late June, but Randolph did not back down. His March on Washington would mark the first time a protest had focused so singularly on the White House, and Roosevelt wanted desperately to avoid it.

Ultimately, Roosevelt recognized that he could ignore civil rights no longer. On June 24, placing the demands of Randolph and other activists over southern Democrats in Congress, the president signed *Executive Order 8802: Prohibition of Discrimination in the Defense Industry*. With the order came the establishment of the Fair Employment Practices Committee (FEPC), tasked with enforcing new nondiscrimination rules in all federal agencies involved in the war effort. Responsible solely to the president—and financed by a "special projects fund" in Roosevelt's new Executive Office of the President—the FEPC represented the first racially progressive policy action undertaken by the federal government since the little-noticed Morrill Act of 1890, and before that the enactment of the Thirteenth, Fourteenth, and Fifteenth Amendments.

Despite legitimate complaints about the capacity of the small, eight-member staff of the FEPC, the passage of Order 8802 had significant and enduring implications for the institutional presidency. In important respects, the FEPC served as a model for Lyndon Johnson's Equal Employment Opportunity Commission (EEOC). Both commissions worked alongside the courts to enforce anti-discrimination laws, but Johnson's EEOC improved upon the FEPC by regulating employment outside the federal government. A direct line also can be traced from the FEPC to FDR's appointment of Black policymakers and experts in the executive branch,* Truman's desegregation of the military, Eisenhower's defense of school integration and support for the Civil Rights Act of 1957, and eventually the passage of the Civil Rights Act of 1964. Each presidential action, spurred by the work of social movements, legitimized future action and set the stage for the sweeping institutional changes of the 1960s.

More immediately, the FEPC laid the groundwork for additional presidential actions in the years ahead. Importantly, expectations mounted for presidents to actively support civil and racial rights. No longer did presidents have the freedom to decide *whether* they would address civil rights; the open question, instead, centered on *how* they would incorporate civil rights into their platform. Through its very existence, Roosevelt's executive order admitted an assumption of presidential responsibility. If presidents can transform the policy landscape through unilateral action, they also must assume some obligation for the things they choose to preserve. If a problem or challenge can be named, social activists recognized, presidents can be blamed.

By reformulating citizens' understanding of their relationship to the state, the obligations of government, and the duties of those who hold power, the long civil rights movement set the terms under which presidents would engage the public—the plans they would be expected to lay, the policies they would be expected to formulate. Having impressed Roosevelt into action, future leaders of and organizers within the civil rights move-

---

* Known collectively as the "Black Cabinet," membership included Eugene Jones, a leader of the National Urban League.

ment could rightfully demand that future presidents explain what they would do to address the problem of race in America—and these presidents would have to answer.

More than any other time in American history, the civil rights movement of the mid-1960s left an indelible mark on the federal government. In five short years, President Lyndon Johnson signed into law a spate of landmark laws expressly designed to dismantle white supremacy and open up new opportunities for marginalized populations. By banning discrimination on the basis of race and sex, enforcing school integration, ensuring equal access to public housing, and a good deal more besides, the Civil Rights Act (1964), Voting Rights Act (1965), and Fair Housing Act (1968) remain among the most significant laws ever passed by the United States Congress.

In the wake of these laws' enactment, new infrastructure was needed to implement them. Within the Justice Department, the Civil Rights Division grew from roughly a dozen staff members at the time of its creation in 1957 to over five hundred members a decade later, litigating against racial discrimination in nearly all areas of public and private life.[58] A host of new agencies added to the regulatory apparatus under the president's control. In 1964, the newly created EEOC worked alongside the judiciary to investigate and enforce claims of workplace discrimination. One year later, the Department of Housing and Urban Development (HUD) was established as a cabinet-level agency, charged with overseeing federal efforts at combating housing segregation nationwide. These agencies still exist today, representing a lasting change to the institutional landscape in which presidents operates.

Scholars widely recognize that few of these policy and institutional advancements would have occurred without the political pressure applied by civil rights groups such as the NAACP, the Congress of Racial Equality, the Southern Christian Leadership Conference, and the Student Nonviolent Coordinating Committee.[59] Lunch-counter sit-ins, university teach-ins, boycotts, freedom rides, and marches around states and the nation's capital forced a national reckoning on race, just as civil rights leaders pressured elected officials—very much including the president himself—to adopt specific policies intended to dismantle the historical vestiges of slavery and the contemporary scourge of Jim Crow. Because of the organization, public outreach, and lobbying of social movements in America, race became the purview of the institutional presidency.

Conclusion

The institutional presidency has always been a work in progress. Over the first half of the twentieth century, however, the office was utterly transformed. Recognizing the manifest failures of government to meet modern challenges, Progressive reformers reimagined—and then reconstituted—the American state, paying particular attention to the presidency. Urbanization and inequality, followed shortly thereafter by the tumult of war and racial upheaval, inspired new theories about what government ought to do and how it ought to operate. These theories posited an institutional presidency—organized and emboldened—as the fulcrum of a more responsive government.

In important respects, the evolution of the institutional presidency continues. Public expectations of presidents show no signs of abating, the adjoining branches of government vest new authority and responsibilities in the presidency, and successive presidents leave enduring marks on the branch of government they oversee. In the following chapter, therefore, we examine the presidency as it exists today—its structure, its long-standing institutions, and, most noticeably, its sheer magnitude.

Key Terms

Progressive Era	**Brownlow Committee**
stewardship theory	**scientific management**
literalist theory	**Executive Office of the President**
modern presidency	**Executive Reorganization Act**
New Deal	**total war**

Questions for Discussion

1. In what ways did progressive calls for a more activist government support arguments of scientific management? In what ways did these two movements conflict with each other?
2. How do social movements, which typically function outside of government, remake the purposes and design of the administrative state?
3. If wars predictably increase the size of government, why might the return to peacetime not confer an equivalent decline?
4. Why might the Spanish-American War (1898) not have expanded presidential power in the same way as the first and second world wars?
5. Why might the Brownlow Committee have recommended that members of the EOP possess a "passion for anonymity"?
6. In what ways did Taft's literalist theory lend itself to a weak presidency?
7. Why might so many scholars attribute the "modern presidency" to FDR? Why not Theodore Roosevelt? Or, for that matter, Lincoln?
8. Is stewardship theory still a useful concept for examining the presidency? To what extent do today's presidents preach—or simply conform to—its central tenets?

Suggested Readings

Arnold, Peri E. *Making the Managerial Presidency: Comprehensive Reorganization Planning, 1905–1996.* Rev. ed. Lawrence: University Press of Kansas, 1998.

Dickinson, Matthew J. *Bitter Harvest: FDR, Presidential Power and the Growth of the Presidential Branch.* New York: Cambridge University Press, 1996.

Francis, Megan Ming. *Civil Rights and the Making of the Modern American State.* New York: Cambridge University Press, 2014.

Milkis, Sidney, and Daniel Tichenor. *Rivalry and Reform: Presidents, Social Movements, and the Transformation of American Politics*. Chicago: University of Chicago Press, 2019.

Skowronek, Stephen. *Building a New American State: The Expansion of National Administrative Capacities, 1877–1920*. New York: Cambridge University Press, 1982.

Notes

1. Paul Finkelman, ed., *Encyclopedia of the United States in the Nineteenth Century* (New York: Scribner, 2001).

2. Theodore J. Lowi, *The Personal President: Power Invested, Promise Unfulfilled* (Ithaca: Cornell University Press, 1985).

3. On this point, dissenting views certainly exist. See, for example, David K. Nichols, *The Myth of the Modern Presidency* (University Park: Pennsylvania State University Press, 1994); Michael J. Korzi, "The Seat of Popular Leadership: Parties, Elections, and the Nineteenth-Century Presidency," *Presidential Studies Quarterly* 29, no. 2 (1999): 351–69; Daniel Galvin and Colleen Shogan, "Presidential Politicization and Centralization across the Modern-Traditional Divide," *Polity* 36, no. 3 (2004): 477–504; William D. Adler, "The Historical Presidency: 'Generalissimo of the Nation': War Making and the Presidency in the Early Republic," *Presidential Studies Quarterly* 43, no. 2 (2013): 412–26; and Jon C. Rogowski, "Presidential Influence in an Era of Congressional Dominance," *American Political Science Review* 110, no. 2 (2016): 325–41.

4. Jeffrey E. Cohen, "The Impact of the Modern Presidency on Presidential Success in the U.S. Congress," *Legislative Studies Quarterly* 7, no. 4 (1982): 515–32.

5. Jeffrey Tulis, *The Rhetorical Presidency* (Princeton: Princeton University Press, 1987). For alternative views of nineteenth-century presidential rhetoric, see Melvin C. Laracey, *Presidents and the People: The Partisan Story of Going Public* (College Station: Texas A&M University Press, 2002); Richard J. Ellis and Alexis Walker, "Policy Speech in the Nineteenth Century Rhetorical Presidency: The Case of Zachary Taylor's 1849 Tour," *Presidential Studies Quarterly* 37, no. 2 (2007): 248–69.

6. Samuel Kernell and Gary C. Jacobson, "Congress and the Presidency as News in the Nineteenth Century," *Journal of Politics* 49, no. 4 (1987): 1016–35.

7. Woodrow Wilson, *Congressional Government: A Study in American Politics* (Cambridge, MA: Riverside Press, 1885), 35–36.

8. It is somewhat ironic, of course, that Jefferson's presidency proved so consequential. The Virginian, after all, had spent much of his career trying to undermine the authority of the executive branch. Congress, he believed, was "the fundamental organ, the mainspring of government," and the institution best equipped to represent the coalition of farmers and frontiersmen his party represented. Wilfred Ellsworth Binkley, *President and Congress* (New York: Vintage Books, 1962), 61.

9. Jefferson to John Breckinridge, August 12, 1803, in *The Portable Thomas Jefferson*, ed. Merrill D. Peterson (New York: Viking Press, 1975), 494–97.

10. Binkley, *President and Congress*, 83.

11. Robert Merry, *A Country of Vast Designs: James K. Polk, the Mexican War and the Conquest of the American Continent* (New York: Simon & Schuster, 2009).

12. Michael Nelson, "A Short, Ironic History of American National Bureaucracy," *Journal of Politics* 44, no. 3 (1982): 768.

13. Nelson, "A Short, Ironic History of American National Bureaucracy," 747–78.

14. U.S. Const., art. I, § 8.

15. U.S. Const., art. I, § 9. For an examination of the constitutionality of these and other actions, see Daniel Farber, *Lincoln's Constitution* (Chicago: University of Chicago Press, 2011).

16. Quoted in Binkley, *President and Congress*, 146.

17. Binkley, *President and Congress*, 134.

18. Binkley, *President and Congress*, 155.

19. Vincent De Santis, "American Polities in the Gilded Age," *Review of Politics* 25, no. 4 (1963): 551–61, 554.

20. Theodore Roosevelt, *Theodore Roosevelt: An Autobiography* (New York: Scribner, 1927), 357.

21. Henry Jones Ford, *The Rise and Growth of American Politics—A Sketch of Constitutional Development* (New York: Macmillan, 1898), 292–93.

22. Sidney Milkis and Michael Nelson, *The American Presidency: Origins & Development, 1776–2011*, rev. ed. (Washington, DC: Congressional Quarterly Press, 2012), 221–24.

23. Theodore Roosevelt, *The Works of Theodore Roosevelt*, vol. 15 (New York: Scribner's, 1926), 256–57, in Milkis and Nelson, *The American Presidency*, 232.

24. Eric Rutkow, *American Canopy: Trees, Forests, and the Making of a Nation* (New York: Scribner's, 2012), 164.

25. William N. Tilchin, "For the Present and the Future: The Well-Conceived, Successful, and Farsighted Statecraft of President Theodore Roosevelt," *Diplomacy & Statecraft* 19, no. 4 (2008): 658–70.

26. Tilchin, "For the Present and the Future."

27. Stephen E. Ambrose, "The Presidency and Foreign Policy," *Foreign Affairs* 70, no. 5 (1991): 137.

28. Michael J. Korzi, "William Howard Taft, the 1908 Election, and the Future of the American Presidency," *Congress & the Presidency* 43, no. 2 (2016): 227–54.

29. William Howard Taft, *Our Chief Magistrate and His Powers* (New York: Columbia University Press, 1925), 139–40.

30. Taft, *Our Chief Magistrate and His Powers*, 140.

31. Taft, *Our Chief Magistrate and His Powers*, 144.

32. Quoted in Patricia Bauer, "Payne-Aldrich Tariff Act," *Encyclopaedia Britannica*, https://www.britannica.com/topic/Payne-Aldrich-Tariff-Act.

33. Herbert Hoover, *The Memoirs of Herbert Hoover: The Great Depression, 1929–1941*, vol. 3 (New York: Macmillan, 1952), 104.

34. 272 U.S. 53 (1926).

35. Franklin D. Roosevelt, *The Public Papers and Addresses of Franklin D. Roosevelt*, vol. 2 (New York: Random House, 1938), 646.

36. As quoted in Milkis and Nelson, *The American Presidency*, 291.

37. John P. Burke, *The Institutional Presidency* (Baltimore: Johns Hopkins University Press, 1992), 6–8.

38. Minutes of the meeting of the President's Committee on Administrative Management, May 9 and 10, 1936, Roosevelt Library, quoted in Peri E. Arnold, *Making the Managerial Presidency: Comprehensive Reorganization Planning, 1905–1996*, rev. ed. (Lawrence: University Press of Kansas, 1998), 97.

39. Burke, *The Institutional Presidency*, 10.

40. Burke, *The Institutional Presidency*, 13.

41. Craig A. Rimmerman, "The 'Post-Modern' Presidency: A New Presidential Epoch?" *Western Political Quarterly* 44, no. 1 (1991): 221–38.

42. Fred I. Greenstein, "Change and Continuity in the Modern Presidency," in *The New American Political System*, ed. Anthony King (Washington, DC: American Enterprise Institute for Public Policy Research, 1979), 45–86.

43. Nichols, *The Myth of the Modern Presidency*, 7.

44. Stephen Skowronek, "Notes on the Presidency in the Political Order," *Studies in American Political Development* 1 (1986): 286–302.

45. Michael Nelson, "Is There a Postmodern Presidency?" *Congress & the Presidency* 16, no. 2 (1989): 155–62.

46. Charles Tilly, "War Making and State Making as Organized Crime," in *Bringing the State Back In*, ed. Peter Evans, Dietrich Rueschemeyer, and Theda Skocpol (Cambridge: Cambridge University Press, 1985), 170.

47. The full text of Wilson's speech is available at http://historymatters.gmu.edu/d/4943.

48. Woodrow Wilson, quoted in Arthur Leonard, ed., *War Addresses of Woodrow Wilson* (Boston: Ginn and Company, 1918), 38.

49. Robert Higgs, *Crisis and Leviathan* (New York: Oxford University Press, 1987).

50. "Our History," NAACP, https://naacp.org/about/our-history.

51. Kendrick A. Clements, *The Presidency of Woodrow Wilson* (Lawrence: University Press of Kansas, 1992), 31.

52. Russell L. Riley, *The Presidency and the Politics of Racial Inequality: Nation-Keeping from 1831 to 1965* (New York: Columbia University Press, 1999), 129.

53. Sidney Milkis and Daniel Tichenor, *Rivalry and Reform: Presidents, Social Movements, and the Transformation of American Politics* (Chicago: University of Chicago Press, 2019), 117.

54. Milkis and Tichenor, *Rivalry and Reform*, 119.

55. Hugh Davis Graham, *The Civil Rights Era* (New York: Oxford University Press, 1990), 10.

56. Guichard Parris and Lester Brooks, *Blacks in the City: A History of the National Urban League* (Boston: Little, Brown, 1971).

57. A. Philip Randolph, "Call to Negro America to March on Washington for Jobs and Equal Participation in National Defense," *Black Worker* 14 (May 1941).

58. Brian K. Landsberg, *Enforcing Civil Rights: Race Discrimination and the Department of Justice* (Lawrence: University Press of Kansas, 2001), 2.

59. See, for example, Taylor Branch's seminal trilogy on the civil rights movement: *Parting the Waters: America in the King Years, 1954–63* (New York: Simon & Schuster, 1989); *Pillar of Fire: America in the King Years, 1963–65* (New York: Simon & Schuster, 1999); *At Canaan's Edge: America in the King Years, 1965–68* (New York: Simon & Schuster, 2006).

3

The Modern Institutional Presidency

THE EXPLOSIVE GROWTH of the executive branch constituted the most significant development in U.S. state-building in the twentieth century—and possibly ever. Whereas Congress and the courts increased modestly in size, the executive branch constructed hundreds of new administrative units, employed millions of new civil servants and contractors, and oversaw trillions more in federal outlays. Sitting alone atop this massive branch is a president awash in institutions—some of his own making, many not, but all with resources, rules, norms, and procedures that structure and define both limits and possibilities of presidential governance. As future chapters will make clear, these institutions confer both benefits and burdens for the president. In this chapter, however, we undertake a simpler task: to inventory the institutional setting in which presidents govern and to take stock of just how active and expansive the institutional presidency has become.

3.1 The Basic Architecture

The contemporary institutional presidency consists of a good deal more than the president and his advisors—which was basically all that existed for much of the eighteenth and nineteenth centuries. Today, hundreds of agencies that employ millions of people define its scope, purposes, and character. By the middle of the twentieth century, its essential architecture was in place, consisting of three components:

1. the EOP, the president's command-and-control center;
2. a growing number of executive departments, each charged with overseeing essential policy domains; and
3. many more independent agencies and government corporations.

Figure 3.1 shows the basic organizational structure of the modern executive branch. In addition to its sheer size, the first thing to notice is its hierarchical design.[1] Whereas Congress is a collective decision-making body that consists of 535 voting members spread across two chambers, the presidency is situated at the peak of a reasonably well-defined

FIGURE 3.1. The organizational structure of the executive branch. The president sits alone atop a sprawling executive branch. Through appointments and oversight, the president shapes the activities of executive departments, the heads of which serve on the cabinet. The president's influence over independent agencies and government corporations is more tenuous. The years in which administrative units were originally created appear in parentheses. Additionally, there were over fifty independent agencies and government corporations, not all of which are listed here. *Source:* U.S. General Services Administration.

executive hierarchy.* As the figure shows, there are not hundreds of lines connecting the president to the various government agencies; instead, a single line runs through the Executive Office of the President (EOP), which the president relies on to streamline communication with the rest of the executive branch. Below the president and the EOP are cabinet-level departments, government corporations, and independent agencies, three distinct subgroups that will be explained in the following sections.

The influence the president wields over this structure is assuredly imperfect. But no one within the executive branch—indeed, no one within the American government—can claim to hold a more exalted position than the president.

---

* The executive branch, to be sure, is not the presidency. Indeed, a great deal separates presidents from the larger executive branch of government, and the president's influence over the administrative units of the executive branch is imperfect, a condition that we will consider at some length in chapter 10. Still, an essential fact persists: a lone president presides at the very top of an executive hierarchy.

3.1.1 The Executive Office of the President

When new presidents take office, they inherit institutions whose express purpose is to support, protect, and advance their policy objectives. Foremost among them is the EOP, the staff of which reports directly to the president. First conceived by the Brownlow Committee, the EOP is designed to serve the president's core interests, which explains why some scholars refer to the EOP as the "presidential branch" of government.[2]

The EOP houses a batch of administrative units with responsibilities and powers unto themselves. Based on their influence over public policy, the most significant units include:

- the **White House Office (WHO)**, which organizes the president's schedule, manages press relations, and develops political strategy;
- the **Council of Economic Advisors (CEA)**, which, as its name implies, advises the president on economic matters;
- the **Office of Management and Budget (OMB)**, which oversees regulatory matters and helps the president write an annual budget proposal; and
- the **National Security Council (NSC)**, which reports directly to the president on perceived foreign threats and offers policy recommendations on how best to meet them.

In addition, the EOP houses the Office of the U.S. Trade Representative, the Office of Policy Development, and the Office of Science and Technology Policy, among other units.

Over the course of the twentieth century, growth within the EOP proceeded at a steady but not constant pace. Between 1964 and 1969, the EOP experienced a massive jump in employees, due largely to the hiring of new staff to oversee aspects of Lyndon Johnson's Great Society programs. During this period, upwards of six thousand employees worked in the EOP. When Richard Nixon assumed office in 1969 he sought to streamline the EOP, which at the time was staffed by personnel who did not share his domestic policy objectives. In the decade that followed, all eleven EOP units created in the 1960s—including the Economic Opportunity Council, the National Council on the Arts, and the Office of Economic Opportunity—were either abolished, redesigned, or reassigned.

Within the EOP, administrative units attend to a wide variety of policy domains, both foreign and domestic. Domestically, these units cover issues ranging from environmental and energy regulation to AIDS policy, and from gender equality issues to drug use prevention. On the foreign policy front, units cover issues involving trade, security policy, economic development, and global communications. And if that were not enough, the scope of issue domains carries us, with the National Space Council, out into the beyond. It is primarily through these units that presidents craft their policy agendas.

To further illuminate the size and complexity of the EOP, figure 3.2 highlights the subunits within just one of its offices, the White House Office (WHO). The WHO is home to the president's closest advisors and confidants—including the Office of Chief of Staff and Office of the First Lady—but it also contains a range of other political and policy units. Some of

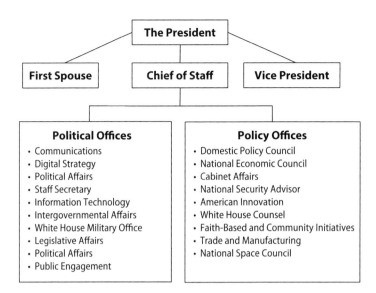

FIGURE 3.2. The political and policy subunits of the White House Office. This is just one unit within the Executive Office of the President, in which the president's point-person is the chief of staff. Support service staff are not included in this figure. *Source:* U.S. General Services Administration.

these units, such as the Office of Cabinet Affairs, help the president coordinate with other parts of the government, while others such as the National Economic Council directly assist the president's policymaking functions. All of these units report to the chief of staff, who in turn reports to the president. The depth and diversity of the WHO are typical of other EOP units, whose many subunits could similarly be broken down and examined.

Every president since FDR has contributed new institutions to the EOP, which tally twenty-five at present. Some of the offerings, such as the Council on Personnel Administration and the President's Board of Consultants on Foreign Intelligence Activities, proved short-lived, operating for just a few years. Others, such as the National Economic Council and the Intelligence Oversight Board, functioned for decades. And two, the White House Office and the OMB (previously the Bureau of the Budget), have persisted since 1939.

What we find, then, is an executive branch and EOP whose institutional units are increasing in number, responsibilities, and size. Administrative units, to be sure, continually evolve and mature. Periodically, they also split, merge, or terminate. But the thicket of institutions that presidents must navigate grows ever denser.

3.1.2 The Cabinet

The oldest and largest organizational units in the executive branch are cabinet-level departments, which write and implement policies in broad areas of government responsibility. The head of a cabinet-level department is usually referred to as its "secretary," whom the president appoints subject to the Senate's approval. These secretaries, along with the vice president and select other officials, make up the president's **cabinet**. Presidents maintain direct control over their cabinet secretaries and, as with all executive-branch officials they appoint, cabinet heads can be dismissed at any time without Senate approval.*

At the nation's founding, in 1789, Washington oversaw only three cabinet-level departments: Treasury, War (now Defense), and State. During the nineteenth century, Interior (1849), Justice (1870), and Agriculture (1862) were added. In the latter half of the twentieth century, however, the number of cabinet-level departments really took off, with the addition of the Department of Health, Education, and Welfare, later Health and Human Services (1953), Housing and Urban Development (1965), Transportation (1967), Energy (1977), Education (1979), Veterans Affairs (1989), and, finally, Homeland Security (2002). Today, a total of fifteen cabinet-level departments exist.

Department responsibilities vary widely. And so do their budgets. In fiscal year 2022, the Department of Health and Human Services tops the list of spending, as it manages an annual budget of $1.64 trillion.[3] This funding covers Medicaid and Medicare as well as allotments to operate agencies such as the Food and Drug Administration, the National Institutes of Health, and the Centers for Disease Control and Prevention. Next up is Defense, whose budget is just over $713 billion.[4] Education, Energy, and Housing and Urban Development, by contrast, are the three smallest departments in budgetary terms: combined, they spend roughly $188 billion each year.[5]

Thinking Institutionally: The Fight over Homeland Security

It matters greatly how a federal institution is structured. Whether it is a cabinet-level department, an agency, or an organization within the EOP, the relative autonomy built into an institution and the kind of oversight to which it is subject—presidential or congressional—affect how well it is funded, how it operates, and how partisan it is. At the same time, the wider political environment (including the balance of partisan power in Washington), the level of public commitment to an institution's mission and scope, and the nature of the events precipitating its creation can influence the institution's specific contours.

The stakes of institutional design were brought into sharp relief during the 2001–2 debates over whether or not to establish a new cabinet-level department: the Department of Homeland Security. A series of attacks executed by the terrorist group Al-Qaeda in New York City and Washington, D.C., on September 11, 2001, prompted a national reevaluation of domestic security policy. Americans were shocked that foreign militants

Continued on next page

---

* This ability was solidified in 1926 with *Myers v. United States*, a Supreme Court case that approved President Woodrow Wilson's decision to remove Postmaster Frank Myers without senatorial approval (for a sense of timeline, note that Wilson's presidency ended in 1921, and he had been dead since 1924).

were able to launch such a devastating assault on U.S. soil: How could Al-Qaeda's plan have escaped the scrutiny of American intelligence experts?

Though it would later come out that both the Federal Bureau of Investigation (FBI) and Central Intelligence Agency (CIA) had warned George W. Bush's administration that Al-Qaeda was organizing a strike in the United States, much of the blame for September 11 fell on the intelligence community, not the White House. A report on September 26, 2001, from the House Permanent Select Committee on Intelligence asserted that there was "a fundamental need for both a cultural revolution within the Intelligence Community as well as significant structural changes." Claiming that the intelligence agencies were relying on paradigms dating back to the Cold War, the report insisted that intelligence gathering must be considered as important as military defense and recommended a more cohesive intelligence network. "This is not a time to preserve the status quo," it warned.[6]

Most policymakers in Washington recognized the need for a new federal body that would coordinate intelligence and devise responses to domestic security threats, but almost as soon as plans began circulating, a heated battle erupted over its design. On September 21, Senate Intelligence Committee chairman Bob Graham proposed the creation of a new office that would be housed within the EOP but ultimately be accountable to Congress. The White House objected to what it saw as congressional overreach, and a few weeks later, on October 8, President Bush issued an executive order creating a new EOP institution: the Office of Homeland Security (OHS). He appointed Pennsylvania governor Tom Ridge, a long-time political ally, to direct the new office. By stipulating that Ridge would be considered a special assistant to the president, Ridge and any future OHS directors would not require Senate confirmation and the office's activities would not be subject to congressional oversight.

Many in Congress thought that Bush's plan for the OHS was too vague and too limited. Within days, a bipartisan group of senators led by Arlen Specter, who had switched party affiliation more than once, and Joseph Lieberman, a prominent Democrat-turned-Independent, proposed yet another iteration: a cabinet-level department whose director would be subject to Senate confirmation and whose work would be overseen by Congress. Bush opposed the Senate bill and continued to push for the office he envisioned, requesting $38 million in congressional appropriations for OHS in early 2002.

To the surprise of many in Congress, in June of that year, the White House released a new proposal for a cabinet-level institution that would supersede the recently formed OHS: the Department of Homeland Security (DHS). The DHS would have four divisions, one each to oversee border security, emergency protection, weapons of mass destruction, and intelligence. It would consolidate nearly two dozen federal agencies, programs, and research institutes under one umbrella, leaving both the CIA and FBI to continue as separate entities.

Many lawmakers in Washington favored Bush's DHS plan, not least because it provided much of the congressional oversight lacking in his original OHS proposal.

But because DHS would absorb several organizations housed within other cabinet departments—including the Secret Service and the Customs Service, both formerly within the Treasury—debate over the proposal fell within the jurisdiction of no fewer than eighty-eight congressional committees and subcommittees.

In the months that followed, members of Congress raised a number of objections to Bush's outline for the DHS, many of them centering on the issue of congressional oversight. The White House wanted autonomy to transfer funds between DHS accounts, to reorganize DHS operations, and to hire and fire DHS employees. While Republicans were generally supportive of the DHS as Bush had formulated it, Democrats opposed its proposed personnel policy, arguing that DHS staff should have the same level of job protection as other federal employees.

Democrats lost political leverage in the 2002 midterm elections, when Republicans took control of the Senate and expanded their advantage in the House. Less than a month later, Democrats in Congress helped pass the bill to create the DHS, and the Senate quickly approved Tom Ridge as the first secretary of Homeland Security. Two decades later, the Department of Homeland Security is one of the largest and most powerful cabinet departments in the executive branch, with over 240,000 employees and an expansive mandate to exercise authority over matters ranging from immigration to natural disaster relief.[7]

The pathway to the Department of Homeland Security's creation must be viewed in light of a batch of domestic political circumstances. At each step, though, the president and members of Congress argued about the optimal design of the new department and the opportunities each would have to control it.

3.1.3 Independent Agencies and Government Corporations

The executive branch consists of still more administrative units beyond cabinet-level departments and offices housed in the EOP. Operating outside of both are **independent agencies** and **government corporations**, which appear in the bottom administrative tier in figure 3.1.

Unlike cabinet secretaries, whom the president can freely nominate and fire, heads of independent agencies and government corporations must have well-defined qualifications and hold office for fixed periods. These restrictions on hiring and firing tend to protect them from the efforts of presidents and members of Congress to meddle in their affairs.

INDEPENDENT AGENCIES

Independent agencies perform all sorts of functions. They manage the museums of the Smithsonian Institution and, through the Peace Corps, they send college graduates to volunteer in countries all over the globe. The National Aeronautics and Space Administration (NASA) oversees space exploration, the Social Security Administration issues millions of checks each year, and the U.S. Postal Service delivers the mail. Recently, still more independent agencies have been created, including the U.S. Election Assistance Commission and the Office of the National Counterintelligence Executive.

Other independent agencies perform regulatory functions. The first federal-level independent regulatory agency, the Interstate Commerce Commission, was created in 1887 to oversee the network of American railways at a time when industrial behemoths dominated the domestic economic landscape. The Administrative Procedures Act (APA) of 1946 established the administrative framework for independent regulatory agencies, some of the most important of which include the Consumer Product Safety Commission (1972), the Securities and Exchange Commission (1934), the Federal Trade Commission (1914), and the Federal Communications Commission (1934). Of more recent vintage is the Consumer Financial Protection Bureau, which is the subject of this chapter's Historical Transformations feature.

GOVERNMENT CORPORATIONS

Still further removed from presidential and congressional control are government corporations (GCs).[8] These organizations, which are relatively recent additions to the executive branch, most closely resemble private companies. Unlike private companies, however, government corporations receive steady streams of government funding and are subject to modest government oversight. Typically, government corporations provide public services not adequately addressed by the private marketplace. Prominent examples of government corporations include the National Railroad Passenger Corporation (Amtrak), the Federal Deposit Insurance Corporation (FDIC), and Fannie Mae and Freddie Mac.[9] Although these organizations are run like companies, their boards of directors are appointed by the president and confirmed by the Senate.

Though it has fluctuated over time, presidential control over these GCs has generally remained weak. GCs must be individually chartered through an act of Congress alone. Moreover, upon creation, they are not necessarily subject to executive branch oversight but rather are overseen by a proximate committee or agency.[10] For example, while the Federal Financing Bank exists within the Department of the Treasury, the Export-Import Bank is independent and thereby shielded from executive interference. What level of influence a given GC's host commands varies according to its charter, though Congress's Government Accountability Office (GAO) retains universal auditing rights via the Government Corporation Control Act of 1945.

The president's only oversight role involves receiving an annual budget proposal and submitting it to Congress upon review and revision.[11] Because funding is streamlined in this way, presidents have even less discretion than they would over, say, departmental agencies. This setup exists because GCs provide essential services (railway, banking, etc.) that need to be funded regardless of a president's priorities. As a result, GC budgets are explicitly protected from political tampering. Hence, presidents cannot simply allocate money in accordance with their agenda as they would for agencies or other bodies under their direct control.

Historical Transformations: The Consumer Financial Protection Bureau

Sometimes a president must spend years advocating for the creation of a new federal institution—and make numerous compromises along the way. Such was the case with the Consumer Financial Protection Bureau (CFPB), a federal independent agency established in 2010 to regulate the lending and debt collection practices of banks, credit card companies, mortgage lenders, and numerous other financial services companies.

The CFPB was conceived out of crisis, yet its formation followed a slow and convoluted path. The agency was proposed as a response to the collapse of the American housing market, which, in 2008, caused stock markets to plunge worldwide and millions of Americans to lose their homes. Many economists blamed the crisis on lax lending practices and deceptive mortgage terms that lured home buyers with small down payments and historically low initial interest rates. Housing prices soared as increasing numbers of Americans, under the misconception that real estate values would only continue to climb, purchased homes. In the meantime, financial firms started buying up mortgages, bundling them together, and selling the financial products to investors on the open market. When mortgage lenders raised interest rates, however, homeowners began defaulting on their mortgages and investors incurred huge losses, causing a downward spiral in global financial markets.

To help prevent such a crisis from occurring again, reformers called for an overhaul of the financial regulatory system and for new transparency in credit services. The CFPB was conceived as one arm of a new regulatory regime. The idea for the bureau originated with Elizabeth Warren, now a U.S. senator, who was, at the time, a professor at Harvard Law School. She was also chairwoman of a congressional oversight panel created to monitor the federal government's Troubled Assets Relief Program (TARP), a federal initiative to invest in banks, automobile manufacturers, and other companies deemed vital to a stable economy.

In an atmosphere of growing distrust of both the federal government and the financial industry, Warren proposed an agency that would apply the same regulatory standards to lending and credit as had been in place for material commodities for decades. "It is impossible to buy a toaster that has a one-in-five chance of bursting into flames and burning down your house. But it is possible to refinance an existing home with a mortgage that has the same one-in-five chance of putting the family out on the street— and the mortgage won't even carry a disclosure of that fact to the homeowner," wrote Warren. "Why are consumers safe when they purchase tangible consumer products with cash, but when they sign up for routine financial products like mortgages and credit cards they are left at the mercy of their creditors?"[12]

President Obama announced his support for a consumer financial protection agency modeled on Warren's brainchild on June 17, 2009. The new consumer financial protection body would "rebuild trust in our markets" as an independent watchdog headed by a director appointed by the president and assisted by an advisory board. Among other

Continued on next page

powers, the agency would restrict or ban mandatory arbitration clauses that compel borrowers to waive their right to sue, enforce increased transparency in loan contracts, and implement existing laws aimed at ensuring equal access to credit. The agency would also have jurisdiction over mortgage companies not owned by banks that "fall into a regulatory 'no man's land.'"[13]

Not surprisingly, the powerful banking lobby—that is, its political arm of influence—balked at the idea. Over the next several months, financial reform legislation, spearheaded by congressional Democrats, progressed in the House but stalled in the Senate. Senator Chris Dodd (D-CT), the Democratic sponsor of the Senate bill, sought Republican votes by floating the possibility of placing the consumer protection agency under the Federal Reserve, which would diminish some of its ability to act as an independent watchdog. But Senate Republicans put forth their own proposal to create a "Council for Consumer Financial Protection." This version of the proposed agency would have no director and would instead consist of a group of six members, including the chairman of the Federal Reserve, the comptroller of the currency, the chairman of the Federal Deposit Insurance Corporation (FDIC), and three "independent consumer protection experts," thereby inviting onto the council the bank regulators that the original board was intended to hold accountable.[14]

Congress finally passed financial reform legislation, known as the Dodd-Frank Wall Street Reform and Consumer Protection Act, on July 21, 2010, more than a year after Obama officially endorsed it. The Consumer Financial Protection Bureau (CFPB), established as part of the new legislation, retained many of the attributes of Obama's original proposal—except that it would now be an independent agency within the Federal Reserve rather than an autonomous federal agency.

The Senate vote for Dodd-Frank fell along partisan lines, with only three moderate Republicans voting in favor. After the bill's passage, however, Republicans continued to try to block the CFPB, first by making it clear that Elizabeth Warren, Obama's first choice to head the new agency, would never obtain Senate confirmation. In July 2011, Obama nominated Ohio attorney general—and five-time *Jeopardy!* champion—Richard Cordray as CFPB director. Although his nomination received a majority of votes in the Senate, Republicans, knowing that the CFPB could not operate without a director, derailed Cordray's appointment through use of the filibuster, a parliamentary maneuver that is discussed at greater length in chapter 8. On January 4, 2012, President Obama installed Cordray as CFPB director through a recess appointment, a maneuver that allows the president to circumvent congressional proceedings, and a topic that receives further coverage in chapter 11. Obama renominated Cordray when Congress reconvened in January 2013, but it took until July 16 for the Senate to confirm him to a five-year term, finally closing the door on the three-year journey to create a new agency within the federal government.

After years of leading the agency, Cordray stepped down as CFPB director on November 24, 2017, but not before promoting CFPB deputy director Leandra English to acting director. That same day, President Trump installed a vocal critic of the CFPB, Office of Management and Budget (OMB) director Mick Mulvaney, as acting director, setting up a showdown for control of the incipient agency. Both English and Mulvaney claimed to be the legitimate head of the CFPB, forming the crux of a legal battle realized in the case *English v. Trump*. English claimed that the language of Dodd-Frank explicitly makes the deputy director the acting director upon the "absence or unavailability" of the director, while Trump argued, per the Federal Vacancies Reform Act (FVRA), that the president has the authority to designate an acting CFPB director. Days later, a U.S. district judge allowed Mulvaney to assume the role of acting director while the case awaited a ruling in the courts. Meanwhile, Mulvaney requested an allowance of $0 from the Federal Reserve for the agency, called for staff to execute their mission—consumer protection—with "humility," and implied that legal limitations were the sole factor restraining him from shuttering the bureau entirely.[15] On June 16, 2018, Trump formally nominated Kathleen Kraninger to replace Mulvaney as director of the CFPB, and English dropped her lawsuit and resigned.[16]

The CFPB's brief history exhibits all of the politics of bureaucratic structure. To create the new regulatory agency, Obama had to offer numerous concessions in order to placate opponents of the agency and secure its eventual passage. Even then, though, the agency wasn't in the clear. For just as soon as another president rose to power—one who took a much dimmer view of the agency's merits—an open fight ensued over who would control it. It was a fight, moreover, with material consequences for the institutional presidency and the administrative state. As discussed at greater length in chapter 10, Trump—like many presidents before him—used his appointment powers not merely to alter the rules and policies that emanated from federal agencies but also to restructure, and in some cases dismantle, the agencies themselves.

3.2 Partners to the President

Not everyone who works in the executive branch is a subordinate to the president. Unlike most other government officials, the vice president and first spouse stand alongside the president: the vice president as running mate, the first spouse as life partner.

Their offices have few (if any) formal obligations, and during their time in the White House, the public expects them to accomplish far less than the president. But despite their relatively undemanding roles, contemporary vice presidents and first spouses assume a host of responsibilities. They spearhead initiatives of their own design and, where possible, they assist in advancing the president's most high-profile agenda items. As we open our aperture from the individual president and take stock of the larger institutional presidency, therefore, we should also scrutinize the rising political significance of the president's two most noteworthy partners.

3.2.1 *The Office of the Vice President*

On a structural level, the vice president is the officer of the federal government next in rank to the president: should the president die in office, the vice president is meant to assume the president's place. Because they run for office on a shared ticket, moreover, the president and vice president are typically viewed as the key members of a team governing the executive branch.*

A team they may be, but they certainly do not constitute a team of equals. To the contrary, the vice presidency has historically been a much-maligned institution. Only recently, in fact, have vice presidents found ways of making their own independent marks on the nation's governance.

THE EARLY VICE PRESIDENCY

The Constitution devotes little space to the institution of the vice presidency. Formally, the office is meant to serve just three key functions:

1. to preside over the Senate, casting a vote only in the event of a tie;
2. to help tally the electoral ballots cast for president and vice president; and
3. to succeed a president who is removed, dies, resigns, or is unable to perform the duties of the office.

The vice presidency amounted to little more than an afterthought at the Constitutional Convention. The Framers, after all, did not hold an especially high view of the office. As delegate Roger Sherman succinctly put it, "If the vice-President were not to be President of the Senate, he would be without employment."[17]

For much of the office's early history, the vice presidency seemed like little more than a repository for failed political ambitions. John Adams, the first to occupy the office, put it this way: "My country has in its wisdom contrived for me the most insignificant office that ever the invention of man contrived or his imagination conceived."[18] He also famously suggested "Your Superfluous Highness" as a suitable form of address for office occupants.[19]

The nation's early vice presidents were selected primarily on the basis of the electoral help they would provide; having performed this function on Election Day, their service,

---

*The Constitution—curiously, and perhaps revealingly—does not include any provision regarding vice-presidential succession. Over the course of the nation's history, the office has been vacant for nearly thirty-eight years. By the mid-twentieth century, however, as vice presidents like Nixon (under Eisenhower) picked up more and more responsibility, a consensus arose that the vice presidency should never be vacant. Eisenhower had bouts of disability and illness (something that had plagued earlier presidents while in office, as well), and Truman had to assume the highest office just a few months after joining the Roosevelt administration, when FDR died of a stroke on April 12, 1945. But it was the assassination of John F. Kennedy, the youngest elected president in history, that propelled Congress, in 1967, to amend the Constitution and stipulate formal rules of vice-presidential succession. Under the terms of the Twenty-Fifth Amendment, the president can appoint a vice president to fill a vacant office, subject to approval by both chambers of Congress.

for the most part, was deemed complete. Throughout the nineteenth century, vice presidents kept offices on Capitol Hill, not at the White House, and rarely attended meetings with other executive branch staff.

When Theodore Roosevelt assumed the vice presidency in 1901, he worried that it would be nothing more than "a stepping stone to . . . oblivion."[20] Woodrow Wilson held a similar notion. He once said of the vice presidency, "The chief embarrassment in discussing this office is, that in explaining how little there is to be said about it, one has evidently said all there is to say."[21] Wilson's vice president, Thomas Marshall, evidently concurred. The vice president, he said, is a man "conscious of all that goes on but has no part in it."[22] Marshall later wrote in his memoirs that, seeing as he did not want to work anymore, he "wouldn't mind being Vice President again."[23] Truman's second-term vice president,* Alben Barkley, told a similar joke about the vice presidency, which went something like this: "A woman had two sons. One of them went away to sea and the other one became Vice President and neither of them was ever heard from again."[†]

THE RISE OF THE MODERN VICE PRESIDENCY

For all their bellyaching, early vice presidents did participate in some aspects of executive governance. Marshall, for one, attended and presided over some cabinet meetings while Wilson was abroad. And the vice presidents who followed varied in the responsibilities they took on, occasionally rising above the largely ceremonial trappings of the office to accomplish something in their own rights. Progress, though, was slow: while FDR was busy enlarging and transforming the presidency, his first vice president, John Nance Garner (1933–41), saw his own office in less transformational terms, famously stating that the vice presidency was "not worth a bucket of warm spit" and was "almost wholly unimportant."[24]

Despite being another vice-presidential malcontent, Garner, in a slight improvement over vice presidents of the past, was strategically deployed by the president to negotiate with Congress over aspects of his New Deal. In fact, FDR explicitly sought to expand the role of vice president into an "additional set of eyes and ears," consulting with Garner on things of genuine importance.[25] After Garner, who would later break with the administration over, among other things, FDR's pursuit of an unprecedented third term, FDR made use of his second vice president, Henry Wallace (1941–45), as a foreign emissary and policy advisor during World War II.

In the decades that followed, the vice presidency underwent important institutional changes. Vice presidents became members of the National Security Council as early as

---

* Truman did not have a first-term vice president, having himself succeeded from the position upon FDR's death.

† In the mid-twentieth century, scholar Clinton Rossiter referred to the vice presidency as a "hollow shell of an office, an impotent and uncomfortable heir apparency sought by practically no one we should like to see as President." He then summed matters up this way: "The vice-presidency as it exists today is simply not worth having." Clinton L. Rossiter, "The Reform of the Vice-Presidency," *Political Science Quarterly* 63, no. 3 (1948): 383.

1949 and of the Homeland Security Council in 2002. In 1961, vice presidents were given space in the Executive Office Building at the White House. They also benefited from more formal organization of staff and office. In 1970, for the first time, a federal budget for the vice president's office was secured. During the 1960s and 1970s, the vice-presidential staff rose from fewer than twenty members to seventy permanent positions and an annual budget of $2 million.[26]

The Carter administration marked another turning point in the growth of the vice presidency. To empower the position, Carter instituted a tradition of weekly lunches with Walter Mondale, his vice president. Mondale was the first vice president to maintain an office in the West Wing, thereby completing, as he put it, the "executivization" of the office.[27] Mondale is also credited with forging a new precedent for vice-presidential contributions to the executive branch, leaving a legacy of increased expectations and encouraging prospective presidents to select running mates of a presidential caliber.[28]

Even as vice-presidential responsibilities grew, irritations persisted. When Nelson Rockefeller assumed the office in 1974 (under Ford), he commented that he had known every vice president since Henry Wallace and asserted that "they were all frustrated, every one of them,"[29] at still being limited to fulfilling largely diplomatic and ceremonial roles, taking foreign trips and goodwill tours, raising funds for the party, and making appearances at funerals. Late into the 1970s, observers proposed to abolish the vice presidency because it served "no vital function."[30]

VICE-PRESIDENTIAL AMBITION FULFILLED

For all intents and purposes, the vice presidency did not come into its own until long after the institutional presidency had been established. Any questions of the office's significance and advisory capacity were finally put to rest with the vice presidency of Dick Cheney. Under Cheney's leadership, the office was set on an increasingly ambitious trajectory, one that has persisted ever since. Like the president, the vice president now has a national security advisor, a press secretary, a chief of staff, and additional aides and advisors.

As a former member and minority whip of the House, White House chief of staff for Gerald Ford, and secretary of defense for George H. W. Bush, Cheney had forged a diverse and impressive résumé before joining George W. Bush's team. Consequently, Cheney was not satisfied with a position that served "no vital function"; he sought to transform the office well beyond what his predecessors had imagined. Throughout his tenure, Cheney earned himself such titles as "deputy president" and "co-president." Some went so far as to claim that Cheney's role in the White House surpassed that of the president himself.

These claims were not entirely unfounded. A passionate advocate of the administration's foreign policy, particularly in the aftermath of the September 11 attacks, Cheney routinely spoke on behalf of the White House to the press. And beyond advocating for White House policy, Cheney became a crucial part of crafting it as well. Where previous vice presidents had distanced themselves from the legislative branch—besides casting tie-breaking votes when necessary—Cheney routinely attended meetings of the Senate Republican Conference and coordinated the party's legislative efforts.[31]

Cheney also established and maintained his own policy and legal counsel, whose deliberations and initiatives were largely kept secret from the president.* According to one account, Cheney's use of an independent counsel allowed him to advance policies without the president's explicit approval.[32] This independence was especially helpful during the "War on Terror," in which Cheney's team was instrumental in opening a detention center in Guantánamo Bay and depriving prisoners of war of Geneva Convention protections.[33] Often, the vice president expanded his own authority by bolstering the president's unilateral powers. Arguing, for example, that the president had unilateral authority over the treatment of suspected terrorists, Cheney's legal team indirectly empowered the vice president. By operating independently and dictating policies without direct presidential oversight, the Office of the Vice President exercised many powers intended for the Oval Office.

Through actions like these, Cheney defined a new vice presidency, one whose authority was no longer limited to its proximity to the president. Subsequent occupants of the office benefited from Cheney's handiwork. For example, Vice President Joe Biden served essential legislative functions during the Obama presidency. With more than thirty years of experience in the Senate, Biden was instrumental in passing the Budget Control Act in 2011, helping to avert a government shutdown. He took the lead in the (ultimately failed) effort to enact sweeping gun control legislation after the shooting at Sandy Hook Elementary School, in which twenty children were murdered in 2012. Internationally, Biden was tasked with delivering on one of President Obama's signature campaign promises: exiting the war in Iraq. "Joe, you do Iraq," the president reportedly said during a national security meeting in 2009, delegating a massive responsibility typical of today's vice presidents.[34]

In 2017, Vice President Mike Pence entered the office with more governing experience than his president. Having served in the House of Representatives and as governor of Indiana, Pence was named chairman of the White House Coronavirus Task Force in February 2020—placing him in charge of the single most important issue for President Trump's failed reelection bid. And though Pence can hardly be blamed for Trump's loss, he joins a much longer line of vice presidents working to legitimize and expand their office.

When joining his presidential ticket, Kamala Harris negotiated the same deal with Joe Biden that Biden had negotiated with Obama: namely, that the vice president would be "the last person" in the room for every important decision.[35] Once in office, Harris rather promptly assumed important responsibilities. She pushed for the administration's Covidequity task force and broader education efforts to reach vaccine-hesitant minority populations. She advocated for the inclusion of community development financial institutions in the president's American Rescue Plan.[36] And with few constitutional restrictions, the door sits ajar for Harris—as well as future vice presidents—to exert more and more influence over the president's policy agenda.

---

* Generally speaking, the White House Counsel is intended to serve both the president and vice president.

3.2.2 *The Office of the First Spouse*

Before the second half of the twentieth century, the first spouse occupied only a marginal role in national politics. With no formally enumerated powers or responsibilities, she took part in the preservation and beautification of the White House and presided over a variety of social functions. Like the vice presidency, however, the Office of the First Spouse has become increasingly important both in political and in policy realms. Spouses—thus far, exclusively wives—now do a great deal more than play host and dutiful partner.* Their office budgets, staff, and influence exceed those of some of the president's official advisors.[37] As President Harry Truman long ago opined, "I hope someday someone will take time to evaluate the true role of wife of a president, and to assess the many burdens she has to bear and the contributions she makes."[38]

EARLY FIRST SPOUSES

For much of American history, there was no Office of the First Spouse. Mentioned nowhere in the Constitution, the first spouse had no institutional function, staff, or formal responsibilities. Indeed, even the term "First Lady" did not become popular until the Hayes administration (1877–81).[39] Early spouses such as Louisa Adams (wife of John Adams) described their roles as "Smilin' for the Presidency," with almost no influence in government.[40]

Receiving no guidance from the Constitution, public expectations of the first spouse were largely defined by the earliest women to occupy the office. And save, perhaps, Mary Todd Lincoln, first spouses were held in high regard. Most found a place for themselves in the White House, as Martha Washington, for instance, played the roles of "public figure, social hostess, and presidential confidante."[41] Privately, however, Washington expressed dissatisfaction with the duties she had given herself (and thus her successors), once confessing that she felt more "a state prisoner than anything else."[42]

The march toward political influence took time. Early signs of progress—including when Edith Roosevelt, Theodore Roosevelt's wife, acquired her own staff—did not substantially change public expectations for the first spouse. Even with a staff of her own, Roosevelt made a point of staying out of the public eye. She avoided the press, once remarking that "a lady's name should appear in print only three times, at her birth, marriage, and death."[43] To some observers, Roosevelt's quiet restraint made her "the perfection of invisible government."[44]

---

* Some early presidents who were widowers or bachelors, or who had spouses die in office, had other women assume the role of first lady. James Buchanan's niece and Andrew Jackson's daughter-in-law, for instance, acted as "first lady" for these respectively unwed and widowed presidents. See Robert P. Watson, "The First Lady Reconsidered: Presidential Partner and Political Institution," *Presidential Studies Quarterly* 27, no. 4 (1997): 808.

FIGURE 3.3. First spouse. Eleanor Roosevelt, wife of FDR, played a vital role not only in managing the president's communication efforts but in advancing policy initiatives of her own. *Source:* Library of Congress.

SETTING A PRECEDENT

Over time, first spouses added to their list of political responsibilities. Another Edith, Edith Wilson, established important precedents for the first spouse after her husband suffered a severe stroke in 1919. During his illness, she assumed the tasks of chief of staff, filtering information and access to the president while he recovered. She also worked tirelessly for an urban housing bill for which her death, some thirty-seven years after her husband's, served as impetus for passage. Over a decade after Wilson's tenure in office, the highly educated and accomplished Lou Hoover became the first presidential spouse to deliver addresses over the radio, supporting President Herbert Hoover's policies, volunteerism, and the Girl Scouts.[45]

The legacy of one of our nation's most famous first spouses, Eleanor Roosevelt, benefits from the sheer amount of time she held the office (figure 3.3). Residing in the White House for over twelve years, she held regular press conferences (nearly 350 in all) in which she demanded that news outlets allow female reporters to cover policy content instead of just "style" issues. She also held the first formally appointed position for a first spouse, albeit an unsalaried one, serving for a time as an assistant head of the Office of Civilian Defense.

With a physically disabled husband, Eleanor Roosevelt traveled both domestically and abroad for the administration. She gave frequent speeches and lectures, inspected New Deal program sites, and visited overseas military bases. When FDR died in office in April 1945, she continued to advocate a host of civil and human rights reforms.

Policy matters, however, have not preoccupied all modern first spouses. Though she holds the record for largest staff of any first lady, Jacqueline Kennedy focused mainly on

White House beautification and preservation. She created a committee to restore the White House, raised private contributions to fund the renovation, and advocated the establishment of a permanent White House curator. Her successor, Claudia Alta Taylor "Lady Bird" Johnson, took on similar projects, albeit outside the White House, and frequently represented the administration in ceremonies and social gatherings.

EMPOWERING THE FIRST SPOUSE

The tenures of Jacqueline Kennedy and Lady Bird Johnson did not mark a permanent shift in the office of the first spouse. Just as Walter Mondale asserted a more vigorous vice presidency during the Carter administration, so too did Rosalynn Carter infuse her office with newfound energy and responsibility. She employed twenty staff members, allowing her to play the part of "advisor, emissary, social director, activist, and campaigner."[46] She was the first in her position to be present at a cabinet meeting. Her advocacy work for women took place within the administration and beyond, as she kept tabs on female appointments and reviewed executive reports pertaining to women's issues before they were sent to Congress.[47] In 1977, she traveled to seven Latin American countries as an official representative of the United States. According to her husband, she had "substantive talks" with Latin American heads of state on such varied issues as human rights, nuclear proliferation, the arms race, drug trafficking, and trade.[48]

Aiding Rosalynn Carter was the first official institutionalization of the Office of the First Spouse: the White House Personnel Authorization Act of 1978 (WHPAA). The bill, meant to streamline the size and staffing of the executive branch, formalized the role of the first spouse and gave the office a substantial staff.[49] The newly founded Office of the First Spouse would be situated in the East Wing of the White House and, under the direction of the first spouse's chief of staff, provide first spouses the tools to perform their increasing duties. In this way, institutional change proceeded, rather than preceded, the individual initiative of pioneers like Edith Wilson and Eleanor Roosevelt.

Hillary Rodham Clinton was the beneficiary, and in many ways the culmination, of these changes to the Office of the First Spouse.[50] Rather than stray away from the limelight as Edith Roosevelt had done, Hillary Clinton publicly took on health care reform, heading the task force on the president's most important legislative initiative. Her policy remit was so large, in fact, that Hillary Clinton was granted a paid informal advisor position in the White House. Her husband, Bill Clinton, would joke that voters were getting "two for the price of one" due to her broad policy influence.[51]

In part, Clinton's accomplishments as first spouse stemmed from her willingness to modify and expand her office. She became the first to locate her office directly in the West Wing of the White House, acquired more funding than the office had ever seen, and fully integrated her staff within the policy apparatus of the president.[52] According to her chief of staff, the workers in her office (allocated by the WHPAA) participated in all the relevant policy meetings held by the president's staff. As a result, she was able to fully engage in the policymaking process and advance her health care agenda. Thanks to Clinton's aggressive expansion of the Office of the First Spouse and involvement in policymaking, a federal court for the first time declared the first spouse a federal employee.

First spouses may not always occupy the forefront of executive branch politics, but the modern Office of the First Spouse accomplishes far more than selecting china and Christmas decor. Since Clinton's tenure in office, all first spouses have devoted time and resources to a "noncontroversial charitable cause" that affects the daily lives of Americans.[53] Throughout her husband's presidency, Laura Bush focused her efforts on child literacy in the United States, including by testifying before Congress for improved teacher training and salaries. As the first African American first spouse, Michelle Obama spoke publicly about issues involving race, sex, and class. She launched campaigns on healthy eating, national service, arts education, veteran wellness, and education for young women. Perhaps most notable among these was her 2010 "Let's Move" initiative, encouraging parents to support healthy lifestyles. Melania Trump, like other modern first spouses, met with the wives of foreign leaders, such as Israeli prime minister Benjamin Netanyahu and Japanese prime minister Shinzo Abe, in various diplomatic meetings. Domestically, she took an active role through her "Be Best" campaign—an effort to combat cyber bullying. Jill Biden promoted the federal government's vaccination campaign, advanced a variety of education initiatives, and traveled the country and world at a pace that "was on par with the president's."[54] In doing so, these four women fulfilled the duties of an Office of the First Spouse unrecognizable to its earliest inhabitants. As one historian put it, the first spouse "has gone from being primarily a hostess to being an important spokesperson for [the president's] political agenda."[55]

3.3 For Any Policy, a Crowded Field of Institutions

All presidents who wish to advance policy change must contend with a full suite of institutions—departments, agencies, government corporations, and so forth—that intermittently support and undermine their efforts. The presidency, in this sense, derives its institutional character from the richly institutional context in which it is embedded. Its opportunities for influence are routinized, and its relationships with other executive branch employees are rationalized. Presidential incentives both derive from and depend upon this larger institutional environment in important ways. To see this, let's consider the institutional governance of just one policy area: climate change.

As in all policy domains, the president sits at the top of the executive hierarchy devoted to climate change. The time he is able to spend on this issue, however, is obviously limited. Working for the president within the EOP is an array of officials and working groups whose mission it is to address climate change head-on.

In the Obama administration, an Assistant to the President for Energy and Climate Change—known colloquially as the energy "czar"—ran the White House Office for Energy and Climate Change Policy. The Council on Environmental Quality coordinated with agencies and other White House offices on the development and implementation of environmental policy. The Climate Change Adaptation Task Force, which Obama convened in one of his first executive moves, issued regular reports on how the federal government can strengthen policies to adapt to climate change. This task force was co-chaired by the Council on Environmental Quality, the Office of Science and Technology, and the National Oceanic and Atmospheric Administration, and it includes representatives from more than twenty other federal agencies. Additionally, the Domestic Policy Council occasionally weighs in on various aspects of climate change policy.

A complicated bureaucratic tangle, to say the least.

Increasingly, too, the U.S. Environmental Protection Agency (EPA) monitors the causes and effects of climate change. In 2010, for instance, the EPA instituted new fuel efficiency standards for cars and trucks. Then, in June 2014, the EPA proposed the Clean Power Plan, the first-ever carbon pollution standards for existing power plants, with the intention of reducing carbon pollution by 30 percent by 2030. Created in 1970 and now employing nearly 15,000 people,[56] the EPA functions as an independent agency, but its head administrator, whose appointment requires Senate confirmation, usually joins departmental secretaries as a member of the president's cabinet.

Among cabinet-level departments, Energy assumes important responsibilities over the development of new technologies and alternative energy sources meant to address various forms of environmental degradation, including climate change. Working just below the secretary of energy are a batch of assistant secretaries who oversee issues, more and less directly, of climate change policy, including environmental management, nuclear energy, fossil fuels, energy efficiency, and renewable energy. Working below each of these assistant secretaries are many more deputy assistant secretaries and their staffs, assistant deputy assistant secretaries, and tens of thousands of full-time scientists and administrators.

The Department of the Interior (DOI) also weighs in on climate change policy. Responsible for overseeing billions of acres of public lands, the DOI monitors the effects of climate change on wildlife relocation patterns, glacial melting, the outbreak of fires, and the spread of invasive species. Within the DOI, the Climate Change Response Council supports and disseminates scientific findings that relate to climate change. Eight regional Climate Science Centers study the local effects of climate change and coordinate efforts to address them. Moreover, the DOI is developing a network of "landscape conservation cooperatives" to develop and disseminate strategies for dealing with the various effects of climate change.

And of course, as the Office of the Vice President has emerged as a valuable ally to the president, its influence on climate policy has grown. During the Clinton presidency, Vice President Al Gore was a particularly strong advocate for environmental reform. Gore personally advocated for the United States' adoption of the Kyoto Protocol, which would have committed the country to reducing its greenhouse gas emissions. Gore also spearheaded the GLOBE Program, which educates children worldwide about environmental stewardship. And while vice presidents have only ever bolstered their president's stance on climate change—rather than pursue policies of their own—their cooperation nonetheless requires extensive coordination and planning from the Oval Office.

In this one policy domain, then, we find a dense thicket of institutional structures, through which any president interested in influencing climate change policy must carve a path. The institutional presidency, it should be abundantly clear, is no monolith, and the president is far from the only actor within it. Rather, the institutional presidency is a sprawling assembly of administrative units with overlapping divisions of labor and contested sources of authority. To effect change, the president must corral and, to the extent possible, command the many departments, agencies, and government corporations that populate a policy domain.

Conclusion

From a handful of policy advisors throughout the nineteenth century to a robust hierarchy of offices and agencies dedicated solely to the White House, the presidency today operates in a highly institutionalized setting. As political scientists Lyn Ragsdale and John Theis have observed, "The presidency has entered a period in which the institution makes presidents as much if not more than presidents make the institution."[57] No matter how personal a president's appeal may be, no matter how closely a president's campaign promises reflect the cultural zeitgeist of the time, and no matter how sincere a president may have been when making those promises, once elected, a president is immersed in institutions. As we shall see in chapter 4, these institutions constitute a crucial part of presidents' political power.

Key Terms

White House Office   cabinet
Council of Economic Advisors   independent agencies
Office of Management and Budget   government corporations
National Security Council

Questions for Discussion

1. In what ways does the proliferation of executive institutions reinforce the emergence of a distinctly institutional presidency? Are there ways in which such proliferation might undermine it?
2. What does the fight over the Department of Homeland Security reveal about the instincts and capabilities of presidents and legislators to design and oversee the executive branch?
3. Why is it important that presidents be given less control over government corporations than other kinds of agencies?
4. What incentives do vice presidents and first spouses have to expand their offices?
5. If the cabinet has existed since 1789, what is the point of the Executive Office of the President?
6. Why might some EOP offices persist across multiple administrations, while others are relatively short-lived?

Suggested Readings

Borrelli, MaryAnne. *The Politics of the President's Wife*. College Station: Texas A&M University Press, 2011.

Burke, John P. *The Institutional Presidency*. Baltimore: Johns Hopkins University Press, 1992.

Hart, John. *The Presidential Branch*. 2nd ed. New York: Chatham House Publishers, 1995.

Hult, Karen, and Charles Walcott. *Empowering the White House: Governance under Nixon, Ford, and Carter*. Lawrence: University Press of Kansas, 2004.

Walcott, Charles, and Karen Hult. *Governing the White House: From Hoover through LBJ*. Lawrence: University Press of Kansas, 1995.

Notes

1. For a more complete listing, see *U.S. Government Manual, 2006–2007*, National Archives and Records Administration, Office of the Federal Register (Washington, DC: Government Printing Office, 2006), 361–554, https://www.govinfo.gov/app/details/GOVMAN-2006-06-01.

2. John Hart, *The Presidential Branch*, 2nd ed. (New York: Chatham House, 1995).

3. "2022 Department of Health and Human Services Budget-in-Brief," United States Department of Health and Human Services, https://www.hhs.gov/sites/default/files/fy-2022-budget-in-brief.pdf.

4. "National Defense Budget Estimates for FY 2022," Office of the Under Secretary of Defense (Comptroller), August 2021, https://comptroller.defense.gov/Portals/45/Documents/defbudget/FY2022/FY22_Green_Book.pdf.

5. "FY 2021 Congressional Action," U.S. Department of Education, https://www2.ed.gov/about/overview/budget/news.html; "Department of Energy FY 2022 Congressional Budget Request: Budget in Brief," Office of Chief Financial Officer, U.S. Department of Energy, June 2021, https://www2.ed.gov/about/overview/budget/news.html; "2022 Congressional Justifications," U.S. Department of Housing and Urban Development, https://www.hud.gov/sites/dfiles/CFO/documents/Consolidated_2022CJ.pdf.

6. "Report to Accompany the Intelligence Authorization Act for Fiscal Year 2002," H.R. Rep. No. 107–328, Permanent Select Committee on Intelligence (2001).

7. "About DHS," Department of Homeland Security, May 4, 2012, https://www.dhs.gov/about-dhs.

8. *U.S. Government Manual, 2006–2007*, 361–554.

9. All in all, the 2006–7 edition of the *U.S. Government Manual* lists 110 independent agencies and government corporations. However, the actual number may be larger than 110; actual counts vary significantly. See *Government Corporations: Profiles of Existing Government Corporations*, GAO/GGD-96–14 (Washington, DC: Government Accountability Office, 1995), http://www.gao.gov/archive/1996/gg96014.pdf.

10. "Federal Government Corporations: An Overview," CRS Report RL30365 (Washington, DC: Congressional Research Service, 2011), https://www.everycrsreport.com/reports/RL30365.html.

11. "Federal Government Corporations: An Overview."

12. Elizabeth Warren, "Unsafe at Any Rate," *Democracy* (Summer 2007), https://democracyjournal.org/magazine/5/unsafe-at-any-rate/.

13. "Financial Regulatory Reform: A New Foundation: Building Financial Supervision and Regulation," Department of the Treasury, 2009, https://www.treasury.gov/initiatives/Documents/FinalReport_web.pdf.

14. Sewell Chan, "Republicans Offer Alternative Financial Overhaul," *New York Times*, April 27, 2010, http://thecaucus.blogs.nytimes.com/2010/04/27/republicans-offer-alternative-financial-overhaul/.

15. Alan Rappeport, "Mick Mulvaney Calls for 'Humility' from Consumer Financial Protection Bureau," *New York Times*, January 23, 2018, sec. U.S., https://www.nytimes.com/2018/01/23/us/politics/mick-mulvaney-consumer-financial-protection-bureau.html.

16. Emily Flitter, "Consumer Bureau Official Who Sued Trump to Step Down and Drop Her Suit," *New York Times*, July 6, 2018, B.2.

17. As quoted in Harold C. Relyea, "The Law: The Executive Office of the Vice President: Constitutional and Legal Considerations," *Presidential Studies Quarterly* 40, no. 2 (2010): 328.

18. John Adams in C. F. Adams, ed., *The Works of John Adams*, vol. 1 (Boston: Little, Brown, 1850), 289.

19. Marie D. Natoli, "Perspectives on the Vice Presidency," *Presidential Studies Quarterly* 12, no. 4 (1982): 598–602.

20. "Vice President of the United States (President of the Senate)," United States Senate, http://www.senate .gov/artandhistory/history/common/briefing/Vice_President.htm.

21. Woodrow Wilson, *Congressional Government* (New York: Meridian Books, 1956), 162.

22. Joseph F. Menez, "Needed: A New Concept of the Vice-Presidency," *Social Science* 30, no. 3 (1955): 143.

23. Tony Horwitz, "The Vice Presidents That History Forgot," *Smithsonian Magazine* (July 2012), https:// www.smithsonianmag.com/history/the-vice-presidents-that-history-forgot-137851151/.

24. Patrick Cox, "John Nance Garner on the Vice Presidency: In Search of the Proverbial Bucket," Center for American History, University of Texas at Austin, http://www.cah.utexas.edu/documents/news /garner.pdf.

25. Mark O. Hatfield with the Senate Historical Office, "Vice Presidents of the United States: Henry Agard Wallace (1941–1945)," in *Vice Presidents of the United States, 1789–1993* (Washington, DC: Government Printing Office, 1997), 399–406.

26. Paul C. Light, "The Institutional Vice Presidency," *Presidential Studies Quarterly* 13, no. 2 (1983): 198–211.

27. Relyea, "The Law," 331.

28. Joel K. Goldstein, "The Rising Power of the Modern Vice Presidency," *Presidential Studies Quarterly* 38, no. 3 (2008): 374–89.

29. Nelson Rockefeller, quoted by the *New York Daily News*, August 3, 1975, as cited in Natoli, "Perspectives on the Vice Presidency," 599.

30. Marie D. Natoli, "Abolish the Vice Presidency?" *Presidential Studies Quarterly* 9, no. 2 (1979): 202–6. Natoli argues its vital function is in institutionalized succession. Similarly, Adkison sees its function in apprenticeship. Danny M. Adkison, "The Vice Presidency as Apprenticeship," *Presidential Studies Quarterly* 13, no. 2 (1983): 212–18.

31. Nina Totenberg, "Cheney: A VP with Unprecedented Power," National Public Radio, January 15, 2009, https://www.npr.org/templates/story/story.php?storyId=99422633. Previous vice presidents had attempted to coordinate with the legislative branch and been reproached. As former vice president Walter Mondale put it, this coordination provides "a tip-off to the executive branch about what the Senate's going to do" and thereby subverts our system of checks and balances.

32. Barton Gellman and Jo Becker, "'A Different Understanding with the President,'" *Washington Post*, June 24, 2007, A.1.

33. Joel K. Goldstein, "The Contemporary Presidency: Cheney, Vice-presidential Power, and the War on Terror," *Presidential Studies Quarterly* 40, no. 1 (2010): 102–39.

34. Evan Osnos, "The Biden Agenda," *New Yorker*, July 28, 2014, https://www.newyorker.com/magazine /2014/07/28/biden-agenda.

35. Tim Hains, "Biden: I Told Harris She'd Be the Last Person in the Room, 'That Means She Gets Every Assignment,'" *RealClear Politics*, March 24, 2021, https://www.realclearpolitics.com/video/2021/03/24 /biden_i_told_kamala_harris_shed_be_the_last_person_in_the_room_that_means_she_gets_every _assignment.html.

36. Edward-Isaac Dovere, "What Kamala Harris Has Learned about Being Vice President," *The Atlantic*, May 17, 2021, https://www.theatlantic.com/politics/archive/2021/05/kamala-harris-vice-president -impossible/618890/.

37. Robert P. Watson, "The First Lady Reconsidered: Presidential Partner and Political Institution," *Presidential Studies Quarterly* 27, no. 4 (1997): 805–18.

38. As quoted in Karen O'Connor, Bernadette Nye, and Laura Van Assendelft, "Wives in the White House: The Political Influence of First Ladies," *Presidential Studies Quarterly* 26, no. 3 (1996): 835. Daniel C. Diller and Stephen L. Robertson, *The Presidents, First Ladies, and Vice Presidents: White House Biographies, 1789–2005* (Washington, DC: Congressional Quarterly Press, 2005).

39. Diller and Robertson, *The Presidents, First Ladies, and Vice Presidents*.

40. Janet M. Martin, *The Presidency and Women: Promise, Performance, & Illusion* (College Station: Texas A&M University Press, 2003).

41. Anthony J. Eksterowicz and Robert P. Watson, "Treatment of First Ladies in American Government and Presidency Textbooks: Overlooked, Yet Influential, Voices," *PS: Political Science and Politics* 33, no. 3 (2000): 589–95.

42. Christine Sadler, "America's First Ladies," in *Records of the Columbia Historical Society*, vol. 66/68 (Washington, DC: Historical Society of Washington, DC), 99.

43. Robert P. Watson, "'Source Material': Toward the Study of the First Lady: The State of Scholarship," *Presidential Studies Quarterly* 33, no. 2 (2003): 425.

44. Allida M. Black, "The Modern First Lady and Public Policy: From Edith Wilson through Hillary Rodham Clinton," *OAH Magazine of History* 15, no. 3 (2001): 15.

45. Lewis L. Gould, "Modern First Ladies and the Presidency," *Presidential Studies Quarterly* 20, no. 4 (Fall 1990): 677–83.

46. Faye Lind Jensen, "An Awesome Responsibility: Rosalynn Carter as First Lady," *Presidential Studies Quarterly* 20, no. 4 (1990): 769.

47. Martin, *The Presidency and Women*.

48. Kathy B. Smith, "The First Lady Represents America: Rosalynn Carter in South America," *Presidential Studies Quarterly* 27, no. 3 (1997): 540–48.

49. MaryAnne Borrelli, Kathryn Dunn Tenpas, and Lauren A. Wright, "Smoothing the Peaceful Transition of Democratic Power," Report 2017–07, The White House Transition Project, 2017, http://whitehousetransitionproject.org/wp-content/uploads/2016/03/2017_07_WHAT_HAPPENS_NEXT.pdf.

50. Black, "The Modern First Lady," 18.

51. Valerie A. Sulfaro, "Affective Evaluations of First Ladies: A Comparison of Hillary Clinton and Laura Bush," *Presidential Studies Quarterly* 37, no. 3 (2007): 486–514.

52. Anthony J. Eksterowicz and Kristen Paynter, "The Evolution of the Role and Office of the First Lady: The Movement toward Integration with the White House Office," *Social Science Journal* 37, no. 4 (2000): 547–62.

53. Sulfaro, "Affective Evaluations of First Ladies."

54. Darlene Superville, "Jill Biden's Travels Show Range of Missions and Emotions," Associated Press, July 3, 2021, https://apnews.com/article/joe-biden-jill-biden-coronavirus-pandemic-sports-baseball-92fc409d69e0103596bf0a47c42dd260.

55. "Laura Welch Bush," The White House, http://www.whitehouse.gov/1600/first-ladies/laurabush.

56. "EPA's Budget and Spending," U.S. Environmental Protection Agency, https://www.epa.gov/planandbudget/budget.

57. Lyn Ragsdale and John Theis, "The Institutionalization of the American Presidency, 1924–92," *American Journal of Political Science* 41, no. 4 (1997): 1316.

4

Power and the Institutional Presidency

THE PRESIDENCY IS AN IMPOSSIBLE JOB. On one hand, modern presidents are saddled with huge responsibilities and oppressively large public expectations. On the other, they possess few explicit constitutional powers. Such is the essence of the **presidential dilemma**: expected to do everything, presidents are formally empowered to do far less.[1]

As we discussed in chapter 1, the Constitution is intentionally guarded in its conception of presidential authority. And while Progressive reformers such as Theodore Roosevelt managed to expand this authority in meaningful ways, their twentieth-century innovations also multiplied the number of policy domains for which today's presidents are held responsible.

How, then, are presidents supposed to meet the extraordinary expectations put before them? Relying upon vague constitutional mandates obviously will not suffice. Rather, presidents must seek, conserve, and legitimize power wherever they can find it. And so they do. While individual presidents hold a wide array of concerns—passing policies, winning elections, and all the rest—what unites presidents is the desire for greater power. If we are to understand both the behaviors of presidents as institutional actors and the design of the institutional presidency itself—our twin goals in this title—we need to make sense of presidential preoccupations with power.[2]

4.1 What Is Political "Power"?

Scholars of American politics differ in their understanding of **political power**. Some, such as Robert Dahl, assume a largely procedural notion of power—that is, the capacity of one political actor to convince another to do something he or she otherwise would not do. In this title, however, we take a slightly different tack. When gauging the exercise of presidential power, we focus explicitly on outcomes, be they laws written, policies implemented, or actions taken. Power, thus conceived, is the capacity to shape government policies through political action, whether threatened or taken.

Presidential power may be exercised in the service of any number of objectives—sometimes altering existing government practices, sometimes thwarting the efforts of other political actors. This power is often harnessed to change the status quo: to reshape and redirect government and to legitimize new uses of public authority. Power matters just as much, however, when it is deployed to *protect* the status quo. Rather than change policy, presidents may use their power to keep their political opponents from doing so.

Power may manifest itself in different ways. Presidents may induce other political actors, by either persuasion or coercion, to do things (and thereby realize new outcomes) that they would otherwise not be inclined to do. Alternatively, they may convince political actors to do nothing at all (and thereby preserve existing outcomes), even when they are predisposed to action.

Presidential power, however, need not involve efforts to manipulate the actions of other political actors. Instead, presidential power may involve direct, unilateral action, as when they fire incompetent or obstructionist bureaucrats or dismantle administrative agencies with which they disagree. At other times, unilateral directives may give way to persuasive appeals, as when a president unilaterally intervenes in a policy domain and launches a new programmatic initiative, and then leans on legislators to authorize the spending needed for the program's continued operation.

All of these potential sources and characterizations of presidential power have a common reference point: outcomes. By wielding power, presidents ensure that the behavior of the federal government, and by extension the livelihoods of Americans, is materially different than it would be if only Congress and the courts were in charge. As we monitor presidents' efforts to claim and assert power, we must train our attention on the outcomes they produce—the content, interpretation, and implementation of government policy.*

4.2 Great Expectations

Let's begin with a simple question: Why do presidents want more power than they have? Our answer is twofold: first, because people have extraordinary expectations of presidents; and, second, because presidents do not have nearly enough power to meet these expectations.

We evaluate our presidents according to what we expect them to accomplish, and these expectations are vast. We want our presidents to stimulate our national economy while protecting local ones, and we chide them when either shows signs of weakness. We call on presidents to bolster innovation and simultaneously to stamp out corruption. We demand that presidents, as the main stewards of the nation's welfare, resuscitate our housing and automobile industries but, at the same time, reduce the national debt. We count on presidents, as commanders in chief, to wage wars abroad while remaining attentive to foreign policy challenges beyond the battlefields. We look to presidents, as national figureheads,

---

* Given the sheer number of actors involved in the policymaking process, it is often nearly impossible to describe the contributions of any individual, including the president. Moreover, when assessing presidential power, it is easy to be distracted by the secondary considerations that too often preoccupy pundits and social scientists: lamentations, for instance, about the near inevitability of policy compromises, the fickleness of public opinion, and the inscrutability of government processes. Moving forward, though, we must not lose sight of some basic conceptual matters: power is as power does; and outcomes, rather than the visible actions that accompany them, establish the basis for gauging its relevance.

to be among the first on scene at natural or man-made disasters, to offer solace to the grieving, and to assign meaning to lives lost and ruined.

From the very beginning, the nation's presidents faced a host of daunting challenges. In his brief First Annual Message to Congress—now known as the **State of the Union Address**—President Washington talked about security, foreign affairs, immigration, innovation, infrastructure, education, and the standardization of weights, measures, and currency. With the exception of the last item, all the issues that Washington prioritized remain on the current president's agenda.

In the modern era, however, the issues the president is expected to address have proliferated. As we saw in chapters 2 and 3, twentieth-century presidents constructed a more institutionalized presidency to meet the challenges of monopolization, war, economic calamity, and racial inequality. So doing, they not only improved the capacity of their successors to tackle issues like these but also reinforced expectations that they would necessarily do so. With each addition to the institution of the presidency, the presidential mandate, along with public perception of the scope of presidential leadership, grew larger.

Subsequent presidents have had little choice but to accept these developments and govern accordingly. Public expectations of the presidency, after all, are remarkably resilient. Even if they were so inclined, presidents can do very little to temper them. To the contrary, presidents spend nearly the entirety of their time in office trying to keep pace with the awesome array of expectations that the public holds of them. And where presidents affect their composition, it is nearly always through expansion and propagation.

Consequently, presidents today must offer policy solutions on trade, health care, the environment, research and development, government transparency, government efficiency, energy, and taxation. They must clean our air and water, protect our borders, build our infrastructure, promote the well-being of our elderly, improve the literacy rates of our children, guard against droughts and floods, and prevent the spread of nuclear weapons.

So great are the public's expectations of the president, in fact, that most Americans mistakenly conflate the presidency with the entirety of our national government. They invest presidents with their highest aspirations for the country as a whole, for their communities and families, and sometimes for their own private lives. They harangue presidents to say more, to do more, to be more. Although they occasionally pay homage to limited government and constitutionalism, Americans much more readily beseech their presidents to take charge and lead. As political scientist Lyn Ragsdale puts it, "The image of a president is thus of a person who is omnicompetent (able to do all things) and omnipresent (working everywhere)."[3]

The extraordinary demands for aid and service placed on presidents originate from no fewer than five sources: leaders in the executive branch, Congress, a president's political party members and supporters, citizens, and representatives from abroad.[4] To succeed, presidents must find ways to placate all of these interested parties, no matter how unreasonable their individual demands or how inconsistent their collective claims.

According to political historian Clinton Rossiter, presidents "wear many hats," a familiar but inapt metaphor in that presidents cannot return any of their responsibilities to the rack. By constitutional mandate, Rossiter observed, presidents serve as chief of state, chief

FIGURE 4.1. Presidential responsibility and blame. Presidents are expected to attend to every conceivable public problem, want, or need. *Source:* https://www.latimes .com/politics/la-xpm-2012-sep-21-la-na-tt-presidential-power-20120920-story .html.

executive, commander in chief, chief diplomat, and chief legislator, but their responsibilities do not end there. Presidents also serve as chief of their party, voice of the people, protector of the peace, manager of prosperity, and world leader. The burden of these ten functions, Rossiter insisted, is nothing short of "staggering," even "monstrous."[5]

In short, there is hardly any domain of public life where presidents can comfortably defer to the judgment of others—that is, where they can insist that taking action on a particular matter is above their pay grade. More than half a century ago, Harry Truman kept a placard on his desk inscribed with the words "The BUCK STOPS here!" It was not a show of vanity: it was a gross understatement. As figure 4.1 editorializes, every trouble and inconvenience, in one way or another, would seem to fall within the president's purview.

4.3 Power and Executive Action

The individuals who become president may not readily profess an appetite for power. They may affirm only the most modest of ambitions—to serve the public good, say, or to give back to the country. But given where they sit in government, and given the extraordinary expectations put before them, even the most reluctant presidents realize that they need more power than they have. As Richard Nixon's advisor John Connally once told him: "If the legislature wants to give you a new power—you take it. Put it in the corner like an old shotgun. You never know when you might need it."[6]

THE BIG STICK IN THE CARIBBEAN SEA

FIGURE 4.2. President as commander in chief. In his presidency, Theodore Roosevelt sought to project strength and vigor. "Speak softly," he liked to say, "and carry a big stick." This image of a larger-than-life commander asserting the nation's interests on the global stage helped establish the mold for modern presidents. *Source:* Everett Collection/Alamy.

The president's interest in power, then, is largely instrumental in nature. Presidents amass power not for its own sake but for what it allows them to do—whether straightaway or, as Connally counsels, sometime around the bend. If they are to withstand political scrutiny, presidents must act, and they must do so visibly, forthrightly, and expediently. Deliberation and analysis are not substitutes for action.

To reap the praise of today's public and tomorrow's historians (the two audiences that matter most to presidents), executive action must have three qualities. First, *presidential action must be open for all to see.* The public distrusts presidents who recoil from public view: it demands a commander in chief (figure 4.2), not a manager in chief. Presidents who are perceived to manage rather than command, particularly in the face of emergent crises (think Herbert Hoover or Jimmy Carter), cannot expect to keep company with the greats. (For a perspective on Herbert Hoover's presidential legacy, refer to the Historical Transformations feature in this chapter.)

Second, *presidential action must be decisive and, whenever possible, swift.* The less light that shines between an observed challenge and the president's response, the better. Equivocation, particularly in the face of crisis, will never do. While presidents need not rise to every challenge in an instant, they must convey to the public from the get-go that they have plans ready to set into motion and the resources to accomplish what is required. Even when justified, delay invites criticism, and nothing more reliably induces snickering from the opposing camp than appearing to be caught off guard.

Third, *presidential action must be forthright and unapologetic.* In the face of setbacks, presidents must gather their resolve and press onward. Excuses that follow failure, no matter how valid, almost never resonate. Presidents must never be defensive, and they must never concede that the people's fate is left to chance alone. Even amid military catastrophe and economic ruin, presidents must insist that the nation's brightest days lie ahead, that the industry and imagination of the American people will never dim, and that the shining city upon a hill, as Ronald Reagan put it, awaits us still.

In their finest moments, presidents stand tall and issue calls to arms (as George W. Bush did, through a megaphone no less, atop the rubble of the collapsed twin towers of the World Trade Center), defy international convention in the service of some larger good (as Barack Obama did when ordering a surgical strike to take out Osama bin Laden without assent from the Pakistani government),[7] and demonstrate how the federal government can act, must act, in the face of utter calamity (as FDR did twice, first in the aftermath of the Great Depression and then in response to the imperialistic designs of European and Asian regimes). Presidents in these kinds of moments appear—how else to put this?—distinctly presidential.

Alternatively, when presidents appear indifferent or are slow to answer the call of duty, they face the wrath of a dissatisfied public. Near the end of his term, Donald Trump found himself the unwilling Doctor in Chief during the Covid-19 pandemic. Though the virus's spread to the United States was largely inevitable, Trump refused to tackle it with the full weight of the presidency. Asked about the short supply of coronavirus testing kits, Trump replied, "I don't take responsibility at all."[8] He instead delegated authority almost entirely to state governors, telling them that "you are going to call your own shots" on when and how to reopen.[9] With the federal government sitting idly, the public received conflicting and at times misleading information on how to remain safe. Ultimately, though it is impossible to say with certainty, it was public dissatisfaction with Trump's pandemic response that doomed his reelection campaign.

The American public demands action, then, and the president seeks the power to act. Alas, presidential action does not invariably lead to improvements in public welfare. To the contrary, presidents sometimes face extraordinary incentives to act when non-action, or at least delayed action, might better serve the national interest. It is important not to conflate the political imperatives of meeting the presidential imperative with the production of good policy or the protection of American interests.

Just and effective resolutions to some crises may require deliberation, caution, and care. As a result, presidential preoccupations with power can, in some circumstances, distort and degrade national interests. In the rush to act, presidents may promote policies that are ineffective or even downright harmful, or that exacerbate deep and growing imbalances in our system of separated powers. In justifying seizures of power with dubious arguments about history or the Constitution, presidents may simultaneously erode the public trust and the constitutional foundations on which this trust is built.

Perhaps the most relevant domestic example of this effect in the early twenty-first century was President Obama's response to the Great Recession.[10] In the throes of the worst economic crisis in almost a century, there were widespread expectations that the Obama administration needed to "solve" the recession and get America back on track.[11] Under this immense, legacy-defining pressure, and with economic conditions getting worse by the day, Obama rushed through his 2009 American Recovery and Reinvestment Act (ARRA). This bill attacked the recession on both the supply and demand sides, subsidizing consumers in an attempt to jump-start aggregate demand and bailing out large corporations in an effort to build back supply chains.[12]

Many economists, however, dispute the efficacy of these programs and argue that a rash response intended to satiate public demands for action may have hindered America's economic recovery. A substantial body of economic research suggests that immediate, short-term fiscal stimuli see only temporary, short-term effects: they don't change the overall trajectory of a recovery and can actually slow it down by saddling the country with debt.[13]

Did the president's actions prolong the recession?[14] It is at least possible. Different schools of economic thought argue different sides of the debate. For our purposes, though, a simpler matter is at stake: the sky-high expectations that presidents face during times of crisis require action; and sometimes this action generates outcomes that may be counterproductive. What the public wants and needs are not synonymous. What is politically expedient for presidents, as such, yields outcomes that do not always improve the public's welfare.

Historical Transformations: Hoover and Presidential Failure

Americans expect their presidents to "act presidential"—to seize the mantle of leadership without hesitation and to command public discourse with relaxed confidence, squared shoulders, and aspirational rhetoric. Sometimes, though, presidents disappoint public expectations of what it means to lead. And when they do, the consequences for their legacies can be devastating.

The repudiation of Herbert Hoover's presidency (1929–33) is a case in point. After gliding into the presidency on a wave of national optimism—and with an inspiring life story of his own—Hoover would leave office four years later with the Great Depression in full swing and his reputation in tatters. By then, small camps of homeless people dotted the American landscape. "Hoovervilles," as these were called, were a living testimony to his disgraced name. Everything, it seemed, was the president's fault. Popular comedian Will Rogers joked that if a man bit into an apple and found a worm, he would find reason to blame Hoover.[15]

It was ironic that Hoover, of all people, would be discredited for failing to take action. After all, his rise to prominence was due in part to his image as the archetypal self-made man who went from being the orphaned son of a blacksmith to a millionaire mining tycoon before his fortieth birthday. He first garnered notice when he organized a

Continued on next page

FIGURE 4.3. From a Great Depression that left millions utterly destitute arose shantytowns that came to be known as "Hoovervilles." Shown here is one located in Central Park in New York City. Copyright 1933 Bettmann/Getty Images. Reproduced with permission.

massive private humanitarian relief effort during World War I. He then served in a series of federal posts. Although he retained no press agents or publicity officers, Hoover's profile was the sort that most politicians only dream about. In 1928, when his name was raised for the Republican nomination, which he eventually won unopposed, the *New York Times* described him as the "most unpolitical man in public life." He was, readers were told, above partisanship and personal pettiness, dedicated only to the pursuit of competence. Indeed, this dedication made him the "busiest man in Washington."[16]

Despite being a Republican who owed his fortune to private enterprise, Hoover was not a free-market ideologue. His efforts to rationalize wartime food policy were firmly in line with the Progressive ethos of centralized state authority, regulation, and scientific management. In keeping with his own narrative of personal betterment, he was a staunch advocate of the power of capitalism to effect social change. He believed, however, that the relationship between the government and private enterprise should be based, as much as possible, on volunteerism and that regulations should be used sparingly, it at all. With hard work and smart planning, Hoover thought, success would follow.

His nomination for president came after nearly a decade of runaway growth on Wall Street aided by the pro-business policies of the Republican Party. In accepting the Republican nomination in 1928, Hoover famously, if ironically, declared, "We in America today are nearer to the final triumph over poverty than ever before in the history of any land. The poorhouse is vanishing from among us." Soon, he believed, all Americans would reap the benefits of Republican administration of the economy, which would deliver "a chicken in every pot and two cars in every garage."[17]

Such wildly optimistic predictions would come back to haunt Hoover. Less than a year into his presidency the stock market crashed, and he was forced to reconcile his faith in capitalism with the exigencies of a global financial catastrophe.[18] His initial voluntaristic approach to the Depression proved wholly inadequate to the enormity of the crisis. Personal entreaties to business leaders to keep workers working could not roll back the tide of unemployment. His later capitulations to government intervention in the economy—in the form of government-secured loans and federal investment in public works, most notably the Hoover Dam—likewise failed to alleviate the nation's economic misery. The Emergency Relief and Construction Act, one of Hoover's last-ditch efforts to rescue the economy before he lost the presidency to FDR in 1932, hardly made a dent. According to many critics at the time and since, Hoover's attempts at managing the economy were simply too little, too late.

The things he had left "undone," opined a writer for the Catholic magazine *Commonweal*, defined Hoover's failures.[19] He seemed resigned to his own powerlessness. He publicly compared the job of president with that of a repairman facing a dike, endlessly trying to stop leaks as new ones sprung.[20] At times he blamed Congress for not coming to his aid, but he never blamed his own action—or lack thereof—for the nation's miseries. The popular press took to calling him President Reject—a leader who, in the midst of crisis, was eager to oppose solutions without ever proposing alternatives.[21] Unable to tame the growing crisis, Hoover would retreat into denialism, telling journalist Raymond Clapper, "Nobody is actually starving. . . . The Hobo's, for example, are better fed than they have ever been."[22]

Yearning for Hoover to support just one governmental program—any program—to combat the crisis, his allies in the media could do nothing to forestall his growing unpopularity. His ideological restraint proved fatal.[23] He was outspoken in his hostility toward government aid to the poor and unemployed, insisting alternately that such assistance would foster dependency and that it was unnecessary. By the time Roosevelt defeated him in a landslide victory in 1932, Hoover was viewed by many Americans as not only heartless but an utter failure. "Democracy is a harsh employer," he later recalled.[24]

After the White House, Hoover remained active in public life, chairing committees during the Eisenhower and Truman administrations that overhauled the organization of the executive branch. Yet Hoover's post-presidency accomplishments never made up for his lost reputation. His failed presidency serves as a persistent reminder to his successors of the imperatives of executive action in the modern era.

4.4 Evaluating the President's Powers

What formal constitutional power do presidents have at their disposal to meet such extraordinary demands? The answer, especially in the modern era, has been "not enough." As Rossiter tellingly put it, the president's "authority over the administration is in no way equal to his responsibility for its performance."[25]

4.4.1 Constitutionally Enumerated Powers

As discussed in chapter 1, the forty-six presidents who have served since the Constitutional Convention have enjoyed an abundance of constitutional authority, at least when compared to the ten presidents who labored under the Articles of Confederation. Under the presidential powers enumerated in the Constitution, presidents can issue pardons and vetoes, exercise all of the attendant powers of a commander in chief, and even, in extraordinary circumstances, convene and adjourn Congress. Additionally, presidents can, "with the Advice and Consent of the Senate," make treaties with foreign nations and appoint federal judges and government officials.

To say that the president's constitutionally enumerated powers exceed those of Confederation presidents is not to claim that they were (or are) sufficient for the challenges at hand. Several powers now amount to very little at all. For example, although presidential pardons are not subject to either congressional or judicial review, presidents historically have used them sparingly, and rarely in ways that have significant policy consequences. Similarly, while the provision to convene and adjourn Congress may have bestowed meaningful leverage on presidents when the national legislature met for just half of each year, as it did during the eighteenth and nineteenth centuries, in contemporary times Congress is in session for significant portions of every month except August, so the power to convene its members hardly exalts the president's stature.

The remaining powers explicitly conferred on presidents under the Constitution either react to or are shared with another branch of government. Although presidents are free to veto legislation, they cannot formally introduce new bills in Congress or directly engage in any of the daily negotiations that occur in both chambers. To intervene in the legislative process, presidents must rely upon congressional surrogates who, most commonly, come from the ranks of their own party. Presidents, as such, act at the tail end of the legislative process, capable of vetoing bills they do not like but can only indirectly promote their preferred policy agendas. In negotiating treaties and in appointing judges and bureaucrats, of course, presidents can move their agendas forward. In both instances, though, their actions are subject to formal Senate approval and as such may be blocked. If the Senate refuses to approve treaties or appointments, presidents must either concede defeat or, as we shall see in chapter 9, find ways to work around Congress.

Not that the president's veto, treaty, and appointment powers are inconsequential. On the contrary, as subsequent chapters will make clear, these powers matter a great deal. A substantial body of scholarship convincingly documents, both empirically and theoretically, how presidents can wield these three powers in order to materially affect the composition of legislation, the terms of foreign agreements, and the makeup of government.[26]

Still, presidents equipped with just the powers enumerated in the Constitution are much like soldiers sent to war with a paintball gun. They may get by for a while, but as soon as their enemies gather and mount an offensive, presidents are bound to lose.

Dissatisfied with their constitutional lot, several presidents have taken steps to expand their authority, particularly during the early twentieth century. As we saw in chapters 2 and 3, President Theodore Roosevelt promoted a deliberately broad view of his constitutional powers—a view he passed down to his successors, who reengineered the executive branch to meet the challenges of their time. These efforts resulted in a massive institutional apparatus unimaginable to most nineteenth-century presidents, and one that dramatically elevated presidents' standing vis-à-vis Congress.

That these efforts were consequential, however, does not mean that they permanently filled the gap between public expectations and enumerated powers. They certainly did not. Rather, presidents like FDR provided a framework upon which subsequent administrations would continue to build. Just as new agencies would be added to the already established Executive Office of the President, so too would presidents rely on past precedent to lay claim to new sources of authority. In the following section, we lay out exactly how presidents make these claims. That they do so at all, though, demonstrates the perpetual deficits of their constitutionally enumerated powers, as well as the unfinished project of the modern institutional presidency.

4.4.2 Additional Sources of Power

If the presidential powers explicitly enumerated in Article II of the Constitution do not give presidents sufficient power to meet modern expectations, where can they find it? The short answer: in statutes enacted by Congresses, both past and present; in actions taken by their predecessors; and in vague articulations of the public good. In all these places and more, presidents claim the political (and sometimes legal) justifications they need to advance policy change.

Examples abound of presidents unearthing existing delegations of authority or manufacturing altogether new ones. Let's consider a few. The first comes from Bill Clinton's time in office. At the end of his first term in office—and facing a reelection campaign against Republican senator Bob Dole—President Clinton found himself at a standstill with Congress. At issue were, of all things, 1.8 million acres of federal land in southern Utah. Clinton desperately wanted to convert the land (the Grand Staircase-Escalante) into a national monument; polls had shown broad support for the proposal among environmental voters, who were key to Clinton's reelection. Controversially, however, the proposal would prevent access to nearly seven billion tons of underground coal reserves. For this reason (and perhaps not wanting to give Clinton a victory), the Republican-held Congress opposed the president's proposal, with Utah senator Orrin G. Hatch saying that "there would be real hell to pay" if the monument were created.[27]

Rather than accept defeat, Clinton looked for other ways to get what he wanted. By itself, constitutional authority would not be enough. Article II says little that relates even tangentially to a president's ability to create national monuments. What Article II does say, however, is that the president "shall take Care that the Laws be faithfully executed."[28] With this phrase in mind, Clinton scanned existing laws that, if faithfully executed, would allow him to create the monument. Clinton discovered what he needed in the 1906 Antiquities Act—a modest, five-hundred-word law signed by Theodore Roosevelt that allows presidents to "declare by public proclamation historic landmarks . . . situated upon the lands owned or controlled by the Government of the United States."[29] Used by Roosevelt to designate the Grand Canyon National Park, the Antiquities Act was carefully written to maximize presidential discretion over public lands. Interestingly, the act does not say whether future presidents are authorized to reverse monument declarations. Thus, not only was the law a source of political power for Clinton; it was a source of permanent power, as all 1.8 million acres of the Grand Staircase-Escalante National Monument remain federally protected today.

President Obama, too, found himself hamstrung by Congress in his first term in office. In 2012, the fight for education reform had reached a tipping point. Congress had failed for five years to rewrite President Bush's No Child Left Behind (NCLB) law, which critics argued set unfair standards for teachers and placed too much emphasis on standardized testing.[30] (One requirement was that 100 percent of children be proficient in reading and math by 2014, which was out of reach for nearly all high-performing teachers.) However unpopular the law had become, though, the divided Congress seemed unwilling to let President Obama make his mark on education policy.

As with Clinton and the Antiquities Act, Obama looked for previously enacted laws that could empower his education agenda. Ironically, he did not have to look farther than NCLB itself. As part of the law, the president could issue waivers to states, relieving them of their obligation to meet federal standards. Creatively, Obama decided to issue these waivers conditionally, in return for states' adopting his own standards. His secretary of education created eighteen commitments that states had to make in order to receive the waivers, such as creating college-readiness standards like the "Common Core" and emphasizing charter schools.[31] Announcing his new waiver policy, President Obama said, "I've urged Congress for a while now, let's get a bipartisan effort to fix this. Congress hasn't been able to do it. So I will."[32] Initially, only ten states accepted these waivers. Just two years later, forty-three states had received them—representing a massive shift in federal education policy, even in the absence of congressional involvement.

As we will discuss at greater length in chapter 9, President Trump was no less inventive than his predecessors when it came to the search for power. Throughout his 2016 campaign, Trump promised immigration reform and, specifically, a "big beautiful wall" along the U.S.-Mexico border.[33] But after Democrats seized control of the House in 2018, it seemed unlikely that Congress would be willing to pay for it. Despite his best efforts—including forcing the longest government shutdown in American history—Trump failed to convince

Congress of the wall's merits.[34] House Democrats passed a spending bill that included $1.375 billion for border security, far short of the $25 billion Trump demanded for his wall.

Trump's ace in the hole? A decades-old law known as the National Emergencies Act. Throughout history, presidents had exercised their most sweeping powers during national emergencies, such as when President Franklin Roosevelt halted all financial transactions during the Great Depression. Seeing the potential danger of leaving the president's emergency powers unchecked, the 1976 National Emergencies Act was designed to rein in this unilateral authority. Before presidents could activate their emergency powers, the act required that they publish their emergency declarations in the *Federal Register* and state specifically what powers they intended to use. There was one loophole, however: the law said nothing about what constitutes a national emergency.[35]

Trump used this loophole to his advantage. Issuing Proclamation 9844, "Declaring a National Emergency Concerning the Southern Border of the United States," Trump claimed that U.S.-Mexico immigration constituted a "humanitarian crisis."[36] He used the proclamation to divert billions of dollars in emergency funding from the Department of Defense toward construction of the border wall. Thus, Trump used the National Emergencies Act—designed to limit presidential power—to accomplish something Congress would not have done otherwise. Hundreds of miles of border wall were constructed during Trump's tenure, and to date he remains the only president to use emergency funds for a project that Congress had explicitly rejected.[37]

These examples are hardly exceptional. In ways that are at once creative and alarming, presidents push outward on the boundaries of their power in order to realize their policy objectives. They create new federal offices, agencies, and departments whose directors report directly to them and bend their institutional authority to achieve specific goals—such as using torture or wiretaps without warrants—in policy areas that might not otherwise fall within their formal purview. They might issue an executive order to raise the minimum wage requirements for federal contractors, for instance, which would have sweeping consequences for employment practices well beyond the federal bureaucracy. Or they might circumvent Congress's power to declare war by authorizing covert military operations.

Presidents who resisted the imperatives of power—James Buchanan, William Taft, and Herbert Hoover—were repudiated by their contemporaries and largely forgotten by subsequent generations. Meanwhile, presidential candidates who forswore the use of certain instruments of presidential power during campaigns quickly learned to appreciate their merits once in office. Compare, for instance, candidate Obama's principled arguments for the sparing use of unilateral powers with President Obama's subsequent employment of them. Obama's approach to executive and national secrecy issues, which is discussed in this chapter's Thinking Institutionally feature, underwent a similar evolution.

Though steadfast in their pursuit of power, presidents rarely grab it in lavishly orchestrated public displays. We do not find them announcing radical new directives before hordes of reporters in Rose Garden signing ceremonies. Rather, they often insert themselves quietly into new policy arenas, reorganizing the bureaucracy, issuing new rules, devising new forms of unilateral directive, guarding information, and resisting, as much as they can, calls for greater transparency. Moreover, when they do come forward to announce a change in policy that neither Congress nor the courts have formally endorsed, presidents speak as though their authority is perfectly well established—a fait accompli— and as though no new powers are being claimed at all.

When appealing openly to Congress, presidents may advocate only modest policy changes; when exercising unilateral powers, they may alter the existing policy landscape only incrementally; when fabricating new powers for themselves, they may appear especially conciliatory to the expressed wishes and concerns of Congress and the courts. Most of the time, presidents do not flaunt their power. But this, too, is a strategic consideration, for power of this kind, quietly nurtured and obliquely referenced, leaves imprints on our policy and politics often not appreciated until long after a president has left office.

Although the single-minded pursuit of power—both its attainment and maintenance— may not inspire all presidential actions, the necessity of bargaining for influence is a staple of the modern institutional presidency. This is not to say that presidents care only about power—rather, it says that concerns about power logically accompany their motivations, whether enacting policy, extending or undoing the work of their predecessors, responding to a perceived public mandate, or securing their place in history. Americans place incredible burdens on the president to accomplish great things. To accomplish anything, presidents need power. That fact alone explains why they seek it.

Thinking Institutionally: Obama and the Power of Secrecy

Don't be fooled. Presidents seek power even when they go out of their way to present themselves as champions of executive transparency and cross-branch cooperation. Secrecy is its own form of power: it allows presidents to pursue actions or long-term policy goals at their discretion, without having to justify their means either to Congress or to the public. When a policy or action is all but invisible, criticisms are hard to muster.

Few presidents are immune to the allure of secrecy. Over the course of George W. Bush's presidency, reports trickled out regarding the widespread incarceration and torture of suspected Islamist militants, usually in overseas detention centers such as at Guantánamo Bay or in so-called "black sites" maintained by the CIA in nations known for human rights abuses, where American law supposedly did not apply. The details of these counterterrorism tactics remained hidden, however, while the Bush administration claimed the need for secrecy in the face of a powerful enemy.

Candidate Obama rejected this line of thinking. A former constitutional law lecturer at the University of Chicago, he called for "reestablishing our credibility as a nation committed to the rule of law, and rejecting a false choice between fighting terrorism and respecting habeas corpus."[38] He promised to shut down the Guantánamo Bay prison. Once in office, Obama initially made an even broader case for openness. In his inaugural address in early 2009, he proclaimed that "those of us who manage the public's dollars" will "do our business in the light of day, because only then can we restore the vital trust between a people and their government."[39]

Two years later, Guantánamo was still in operation, and a bill was introduced by Senators Carl Levin and John McCain to explicitly authorize the U.S. government to hold terrorism suspects without trial, whether they had been captured "in the course of hostilities" or not. One might have assumed that President Obama would oppose such legislation, which came under attack from a significant number of senators in both parties, among them Dianne Feinstein and Rand Paul, who argued that detention without trial was unconstitutional.

Indeed, before he met with members of the Senate Armed Services Committee to hash out a revised draft of the McCain-Levin bill, Obama threatened to veto it. The modified bill, however, did not incorporate any new civil liberties protections. Rather, it was even *less* supportive of the rights of detainees than the bill originally proposed. Obama called for the removal of a provision that would have exempted American citizens from military detention, and he also pushed to limit restrictions on the president's authority to act as the ultimate arbiter of detainee rights. As journalist Glenn Greenwald wrote at the time, "The White House's North Star on this bill—as they repeatedly made clear—was Presidential discretion: they were going to veto the bill if it contained any limits on the President's detention powers."[40] Whatever Obama's preferred policy on detention, his actions were part and parcel of his larger pursuit of presidential power.

Obama's record on other forms of government transparency also departed from his campaign rhetoric. Like the Bush administration, the Obama administration claimed the right to engage in covert, extrajudicial assassinations of suspected terrorists, including American citizens. It came down harshly on government whistleblowers and on leakers of classified information, released fewer records under the Freedom of Information Act than did Bush, and censored hundreds of pages of email correspondence about its Open Government Directive.

In short, despite many campaign promises to the contrary, after becoming president Obama unabashedly embraced secrecy, the institutional facts of presidential life having won out over the theoretical concerns of concentrated power.

4.5 Constraints and Backlash

Presidents expand their power when they unilaterally bypass the legislative process; when they build and rebuild the administrative apparatus that surrounds them; when they emphasize loyalty in appointing individuals to positions in the federal bureaucracy; when they engage directly with the public; when they lobby Congress for broader authority; and when they invoke the Unitary Executive Theory—the legal argument that presidents legitimately retain unrivaled control over the executive branch—to justify their actions.* None of this maneuvering, however, implies that presidents exercise all the power they would like. Ample scholarship emphasizes the historical contingencies and institutional constraints that limit a president's ability to exercise unilateral powers, centralize authority, politicize the appointments process, issue public appeals, or refashion the political universe.

Presidents begin their terms with high-minded goals, policy to-do lists, and outlines for programs they have imagined implementing for years. These goals, lists, and outlines, however, are routinely stymied by political forces at home and abroad. Presidents' policy initiatives collapse on the long and laborious road to legislative acceptance; their appeals to the public fall on deaf ears; their efforts to project power abroad fail to convince foreign states to ally themselves with the United States or foreign foes to stand down.

Some impediments to presidential action come from within governments; others arise from outside. As Lincoln once remarked, "I claim not to have controlled events, but confess plainly that events have controlled me."[41] For Lincoln, it was civil war that consumed his presidency. More recently, presidents have needed to manage persistent unrest in the Middle East, sudden economic free falls, school shootings, urban protests, and global pandemics. These events may redirect or derail executive planning, interfering with a president's ability to get other things done. Presidents have plenty of political reasons to appear in command. In point of fact, however, they spend a good portion of their time in office treading turbulent waters. As Gary Andres, Patrick Griffin, and James Thurber write, "Instead of trying to predict what the next president can accomplish in the first hundred days, we should ask if he will be able to get anything done at all. Given the built-in checks on both the president and Congress, a president who succeeds with even small agenda items in Congress deserves more plaudits and accolades than are currently afforded by the press, pundits, and scholars."[42]

Fresh off reelection in 2004, George W. Bush famously quipped that he intended to spend liberally the **political capital**—a vague and contested notion that public vestments of trust and approval bestow rights to political accommodation—that comes with victory.† Bush promptly marshalled his available resources to restructure Social Security through privatization, but he failed so completely that Congress never voted on a single element of his second-term legislative master plan.

Obama suffered a similarly trying fate at the hands of congressional Republicans. During the final six years of his presidency, a period in which the Republicans controlled at least one chamber of Congress, a bare majority of House Republicans managed to delay, derail, or block the president's efforts to enact gun control legislation, immigration reform, a jobs bill, and all manner of appointments. While campaigning and fundraising on behalf of Democratic congressional candidates for the 2014 midterm elections, Obama mused, "Realistically, I'd get a whole lot more done if [Democrat] Nancy Pelosi [were] Speaker of the House."[43]

---

* The unitary theory of the executive is discussed at greater length in chapters 1 and 9.

† See also the notion of a "mandate," which is discussed at greater length in chapter 6.

Even when their party controls Congress, however, presidents still struggle to advance portions of their policy agendas. Reflecting back on his presidency, Jimmy Carter sheepishly admitted, "Maybe I was overly confident when I was inaugurated about what I could do." Carter found himself at odds not only with congressional Republicans but also with various segments of his own Democratic Party. "I couldn't get a single Democrat to sponsor my legislation that I wanted for reorganizing the government," he recalled.[44] When that challenge passed, Carter promptly confronted another legislative failure and then another—on environmental policy, energy policy, health policy, and on and on.*

Like Carter, Donald Trump also ran headlong into institutional constraints and divisions that persist even during periods of unified government. After assuming office with a Republican majority in both the House and Senate, Trump set to work on fulfilling his campaign promise to repeal and replace Obama's signature domestic policy achievement, the Affordable Care Act.[45] Rushed from the start, however, the effort first hit speed bumps and then drove straight into a ditch. The Trump administration spent only sixty-three days working on their first legislative proposal, the American Health Care Act (AHCA), and devoted less than three weeks to debating the actual text.[46] Some members of the Republican House Freedom Caucus, including Kentucky senator Rand Paul, criticized the bill for its subsidies, labeling it "Obamacare Lite." Other Republicans chafed at the prospect of cutting Medicaid benefits for their poorer constituents. Lacking the votes to pass the bill in the House, the first attempt at "repeal and replace" was quickly tabled. President Trump blamed the failure on a lack of bipartisan support from House Democrats, but a broader truth remains: even with a unified government, substantial reform is often beyond the president's reach.

Sometimes, presidents meet a fate even worse than political obstruction. Rather than temporarily block presidential ambitions, political opponents take measures to permanently weaken the presidency. This is particularly likely when presidents reach for too much power, when their actions and rhetoric violate basic norms of decency and forbearance, when their claims appear not just excessive but dangerous. Should they press their case too far, too aggressively, presidents risk backlash.

Before Trump, few if any modern presidents had engaged in more blatant abuses of their power than Richard Nixon. It was his presidency that caused the historian Arthur Schlesinger to rethink his views about executive power and raise alarm bells about the emergence of an **Imperial Presidency**—that is, a presidency that runs roughshod over legal and legitimate checks on executive authority.[47] From his clandestine war in Cambodia to his use of impoundment powers for decidedly political purposes to his "dirty tricks" perpetrated against his political enemies, Nixon exercised power with utter abandon.[48] Ultimately, his presidency collapsed amid the Watergate scandal, the details of which are

---

* Though Republicans were more averse to the Democratic president's policies, House Democrats still only voted with Carter roughly 70 percent of the time. By comparison, House Democrats voted with Obama, during his first term in office, roughly 85 percent of the time. See Lyn Ragsdale, *Vital Statistics on the Presidency*, 3rd ed. (Washington, DC: Congressional Quarterly Press, 2008), table 9–8.

covered in chapter 8. What is worth noting here, though, is that Nixon's actions did not just lead to his political undoing. They also triggered a backlash against presidential powers as members of Congress sought a more permanent solution to Nixon's illegalities and offenses. Over the course of several years, Congress passed the War Powers Resolution of 1973, which sought to limit a president's ability to wage war; the Budget and Impoundment Control Act of 1974, which curtailed the president's ability to block congressional spending; and the Ethics in Government Act of 1978, which strengthened the government's ability to investigate and punish violations of the public trust. These laws were not meant to merely frustrate a single president. Though their legacies would prove spotty, and possibly even counterproductive,[49] these laws were intended to permanently alter the balance of power between the first and second branches of government.

4.6 An Enduring Interest in Power

Presidents do not hold all the power they would like. When deploying that which is within reach, presidents are routinely frustrated by Congress and courts. And when brashly claiming too much power, these adjoining branches of government are periodically stirred to action, setting new rules, protocols, and strictures that only exacerbate the leadership dilemma that stands at the very heart of the American presidency.

Still, these constraints and setbacks do not quash a president's interest in power. Just the opposite, in fact. It is precisely because presidents face so many obstacles in securing desired outcomes that they work so hard to expand the powers available to them. The weak assembly of enumerated powers in the Constitution spurs the search for more influence; political limits, too, fuel the president's ongoing quest for still more power.

As we saw in chapter 1, the Framers of the Constitution chose to institute a system whereby each branch of government was capable of curtailing the authority of the other two. Both Congress and the judiciary have the right—some might say the obligation—to rein in the president, given their constitutionally defined powers to make law and to rule on the constitutionality of those laws. Through legislation and court rulings, Congress and the courts can attempt to curb not just the policy actions of individual presidents but the presidency's very claims to power.

Examples abound. In addition to the aforementioned congressional resurgence of the 1970s, in 1998 the Supreme Court stripped the president of a newly acquired (and congressionally delegated) line-item veto (the power to veto parts of a law without vetoing the law in its entirety) in *Clinton v. City of New York*. And in 1954, Congress nearly passed the Bricker Amendment, which would have dramatically curtailed a president's ability to forge agreements with other nations independently. In chapters 8 and 11, we discuss these and other examples at length.

Judicial and legislative efforts to curb presidents, however, have had mixed success. Though majorities, and even supermajorities, occasionally clip the wings of presidents mid-flight, the sense of outrage that fuels congressional action eventually dissipates, and often rather abruptly.

Since 1974, for example, members of Congress have done precious little to uphold the strict requirements of the War Powers Resolution. In the half century since Congress failed, by a single vote, to pass the Bricker Amendment, presidents have relied on executive agreements—agreements with foreign countries that, unlike treaties, do not require the Senate's formal ratification—with rising frequency. And though they can no longer use a line-item veto to remove elements of laws with which they disagree, presidents nonetheless have developed other means of communicating their intentions not to implement particular parts of particular laws—through **signing statements**, for example, which are formal pronouncements issued by a president upon signing a bill into law.

Although Congress and the courts have the wherewithal to stall, even halt, a president's power grabs, just as often legislators and judges relinquish their own powers, either by refusing to exercise their discretionary authority or by explicitly transferring authority to a president. Over the years, Congress has authored legislation that delegates to the president extraordinary powers over the domestic economy, the exercise of military force, the budget, state emergencies, foreign trade, and more. Sometimes such delegations of power are narrowly defined and laden with various reporting requirements. Just as frequently, though, Congress confers broad authority on presidents to define and resolve policy challenges almost entirely as they see fit.

Once powers are granted to—or won by—a president through legislation or judicial review, they are rarely retracted. Sitting on the books at any time are sweeping delegations of authority, many of which have been in place for decades. Consider the literally hundreds of emergency powers expressly granted to the president by acts of Congress over the course of the twentieth century. These powers have enabled presidents to set wage and price controls, intervene unilaterally in labor-management disputes, establish limits on housing rents, impound funds formally appropriated by Congress, and much more.[50] Though quick to delegate emergency powers, Congress has proved unreliable in formally withdrawing them after an emergency has ended. As a consequence, delegations of power enacted during crises long since passed remain on the books for presidents to employ at will. Not until the National Emergencies Act (1976) did Congress get around to imposing much discipline on the body of law delegating emergency powers to the president. (For a longer discussion of this topic, see chapter 9.)

It is inconceivable that presidents would delegate to others their own constitutional authority to execute the law, although members of Congress have often freely handed over extraordinary lawmaking powers to presidents. It is equally inconceivable that presidents would stand quietly by as either the judicial or legislative branch infringed on their authority, although both branches have often done so when presidents have infringed on theirs. Successive presidents with radically different policy agendas have acted entrepreneurially to expand their influence over foreign and domestic affairs and have fiercely guarded their authority against perceived judicial and legislative encroachments. For presidents, the search for and defense of power are matters of first-order importance.

Conclusion

The acquisition, consolidation, and institutionalization of power are the modus operandi of presidents. Though individual presidents, in their rhetoric, may preach prudence and humility, their actions usually accord with the universal incentives for presidents to seek and nurture power. Meanwhile, limits on presidential power can be unpredictable and contingent on any number of factors external to the presidency—the partisan makeup of Congress, for example, or the political leanings of members of the Supreme Court. As we discuss the relationship of the president to these other branches in chapters 8, 9, and 11, therefore, readers can expect the political power dynamics described here to resurface.

Key Terms

presidential dilemma   **political capital**

political power   **Imperial Presidency**

State of the Union Address   **signing statements**

Questions for Discussion

1. What are the advantages of defining political power in terms of outcomes? Can you think of any alternative ways to define the term?
2. Do presidents care about power for power's sake? Or do presidents value power for what, instrumentally, it delivers for them?
3. In what ways, if at all, do concerns about power relate to other objectives that presidents may have, such as advancing good public policy or strengthening their respective political parties?
4. In what ways do power considerations help explain continuities across presidential administrations? In what ways do they help explain differences?
5. Should presidents worry that, by wielding power in service of a new issue domain, they only reinforce and expand the public's expectations for their involvement?
6. Are there limits to a president's appetite for power? If so, what is their source?

Suggested Readings

Crenson, Matthew, and Benjamin Ginsberg. *Presidential Power: Unchecked and Unbalanced.* New York: W. W. Norton, 2007.

Howell, William G. *Thinking about the Presidency: The Primacy of Power.* Princeton: Princeton University Press, 2013.

Landy, Marc, and Sidney Milkis. *Presidential Greatness.* Lawrence: University Press of Kansas, 2013.

Rudalevige, Andrew. *The New Imperial Presidency: Renewing Presidential Power after Watergate.* Ann Arbor: University of Michigan Press, 2006.

Schlesinger, Arthur M., Jr. *The Imperial Presidency.* 1973. Boston: Houghton Mifflin, 2004.

Notes

1. Michael A. Genovese, *The Presidential Dilemma: Leadership in the American System* (New York: Harper-Collins College Publishers, 1995).

2. This chapter draws from William G. Howell, *Thinking about the Presidency: The Primacy of Power* (Princeton: Princeton University Press, 2013).

3. Lyn Ragsdale, "Studying the Presidency: Why Presidents Need Political Scientists," in *The Presidency and the Political System*, 9th ed., ed. Michael Nelson (Washington, DC: Congressional Quarterly Press, 2010), 36–37. See also Fred Greenstein, "What the President Means to Americans," in *Choosing the President*, ed. James Barber (New York: American Assembly, 1974), 130–31; Gene Healy, *The Cult of the Presidency: America's Dangerous Devotion to Executive Power* (Washington, DC: Cato Institute, 2008).

4. Richard E. Neustadt, *Presidential Power and the Modern Presidents: The Politics of Leadership from Roosevelt to Reagan* (New York: Free Press, 1991).

5. Clinton Rossiter, *The American Presidency* (New York: New American Library, 1960).

6. As quoted in Rick Perlstein, *Nixonland: The Rise of a President and the Fracturing of America* (New York: Scribner, 2009), 600.

7. For a recent critical assessment of this history, see Seymour M. Hersh, "The Killing of Osama bin Laden," *London Review of Books* 37, no. 10 (2015): 3–12, http://www.lrb.co.uk/v37/n10/seymour-m-hersh/the-killing-of-osama-bin-laden.

8. Caitlin Oprysko, "'I Don't Take Responsibility at All': Trump Deflects Blame for Coronavirus Testing Fumble," *POLITICO*, March 13, 2020, https://www.politico.com/news/2020/03/13/trump-coronavirus-testing-128971.

9. Kevin Liptak, Kristen Holmes, and Ryan Nobles, "Trump Completes Reversal, Telling Govs 'You Are Going to Call Your Own Shots' and Distributes New Guidelines," CNN, April 16, 2020, https://www.cnn.com/2020/04/16/politics/donald-trump-reopening-guidelines-coronavirus/index.html.

10. For a compendium of examples in foreign affairs, see Brent Staples, *Restraint in International Politics* (New York: Cambridge University Press, 2019).

11. William Galston, "President Barack Obama's First Two Years: Policy Accomplishments, Political Difficulties," *Brookings Institution*, November 4, 2010, https://www.brookings.edu/research/president-barack-obamas-first-two-years-policy-accomplishments-political-difficulties/.

12. James Feyrer and Bruce Sacerdote, "Did the Stimulus Stimulate? Real Time Estimates of the Effects of the American Recovery and Reinvestment Act," National Bureau of Economic Research Working Paper 16759 (2011).

13. John B. Taylor, "The Role of Policy in the Great Recession and the Weak Recovery," *American Economic Review* 104, no. 5 (2014): 61–66.

14. Feyrer and Sacerdote, "Did the Stimulus Stimulate?"

15. Glen Jeansonne, "The Real Herbert Hoover," *Historically Speaking* 12, no. 4 (2011): 26–29.

16. L. C. Speers, "The Sort of Man Herbert Hoover Is," *New York Times*, January 29, 1928, 3.

17. "A Chicken in Every Pot" political ad and rebuttal article, *New York Times*, October 30, 1928, from the National Archives Catalog, https://research.archives.gov/id/187095.

18. Louis Liebovich, *Bylines in Despair: Herbert Hoover and the Press* (Westport, CT: Praeger Press, 1994), 109.

19. Liebovich, *Bylines in Despair*, 109.

20. "From Hero to Scapegoat," Herbert Hoover Presidential Library and Museum, https://files.eric.ed.gov/fulltext/ED388564.pdf.

21. Richard Norton Smith and Timothy Walch, "The Ordeal of Herbert Hoover," *Prologue Magazine* 36, no. 2 (2004), http://www.archives.gov/publications/prologue/2004/summer/hoover-2.html.

22. Clapper's forty-minute interview with Hoover was on February 27, 1931. Olive E. Clapper, *Washington Tapestry* (New York: Whittlesey House, 1946), 3–4.

23. Liebovich, *Bylines in Despair*, 142.

24. William E. Leuchtenberg, *Herbert Hoover* (New York: Henry Holt and Company, 2009).

25. Rossiter, *American Presidency*, 246.

26. See, for example, Charles Cameron, *Veto Bargaining: Presidents and the Politics of Negative Power* (New York: Cambridge University Press, 2001); Glen Krutz and Jeffrey Peake, *Treaty Politics and the Rise of Executive Agreements: International Commitments in a System of Shared Powers* (Ann Arbor: University of Michigan Press, 2010); and David E. Lewis, *The Politics of Presidential Appointments: Political Control and Bureaucratic Performance* (Princeton: Princeton University Press, 2008).

27. Timothy Egan, "Clinton Enters Utah Battle over Fate of Wilderness Area," *New York Times*, September 17, 1996, A.12.

28. U.S. Const., art. II, § 3.

29. Quoted in Mark Kelso, "The Contemporary Presidency: A Lasting Legacy? Presidents, National Monuments, and the Antiquities Act," *Presidential Studies Quarterly* 47, no. 4 (2017): 804.

30. Motoko Rich, "Holding States and Schools Accountable," *New York Times*, February 9, 2013, A.25.

31. Patrick McGuinn, "From No Child Left Behind to the Every Student Succeeds Act: Federalism and the Education Legacy of the Obama Administration," *Publius: The Journal of Federalism* 46, no. 3 (2016): 392–415.

32. McGuinn, "From No Child Left Behind to the Every Student Succeeds Act," 399.

33. Rebecca Morin, "A Quick History of Trump's Evolving Justifications for a Border Wall," *POLITICO*, January 8, 2019, https://www.politico.com/story/2019/01/08/trumps-evolving-reasons-border-wall -1088046.

34. Mihir Zaveri, Guilbert Gates, and Karen Zraick, "The Government Shutdown Was the Longest Ever: Here's the History," *New York Times*, January 9, 2019, https://www.nytimes.com/interactive/2019/01/09/us /politics/longest-government-shutdown.html.

35. Glenn E. Fuller, "The National Emergency Dilemma: Balancing the Executive's Crisis Powers with the Need for Accountability," *Southern California Law Review* 52, no. 5 (1979): 1453–1512.

36. President Donald Trump, Proclamation, "Declaring a National Emergency Concerning the Southern Border of the United States, Proclamation 9844 of February 15, 2019," *Federal Register* 84, no. 34 (February 20, 2019): 4949–50.

37. Charlie Savage, "Presidents Have Declared Dozens of Emergencies, but None Like Trump's," *New York Times*, February 16, 2019.

38. As quoted in Anthony Gregory, *The Power of Habeas Corpus in America: From the King's Prerogative to the War on Terror* (New York: Cambridge University Press, 2013), 248.

39. Barack Obama, "Inaugural Address," January 20, 2009, https://obamawhitehouse.archives.gov/the -press-office/2013/01/21/inaugural-address-president-barack-obama.

40. Glenn Greenwald, "Obama to Sign Indefinite Detention Bill into Law," *Salon*, December 15, 2011, https://www.salon.com/2011/12/15/obama_to_sign_indefinite_detention_bill_into_law/.

41. Alan Greenblatt, "Why Obama (and Any President) Fails to Meet Expectations," National Public Radio, March 12, 2013, http://www.npr.org/blogs/itsallpolitics/2013/03/12/174104878/why-obama-and-any -president-fails-to-meet-expectations.

42. Gary Andres, Patrick Griffin, and James Thurber, "The Contemporary Presidency: Managing White House–Congressional Relations: Observations from Inside the Process," *Presidential Studies Quarterly* 30, no. 3 (2000): 563.

43. "Obama: 'I'd Get a Whole Lot More Done If Nancy Pelosi Is Speaker,'" CBS News, April 4, 2013, http:// washington.cbslocal.com/2013/04/04/obama-id-get-a-whole-lot-more-done-if-nancy-pelosi-is-speaker/.

44. George Edwards, "Exclusive Interview with President Jimmy Carter," *Presidential Studies Quarterly* 38, no. 1 (2007): 2.

45. Carl Hulse, "'Repeal and Replace': Words Still Hanging Over G.O.P.'s Health Care Strategy," *New York Times*, January 15, 2017, A.11.

46. Jonathan Cohn, "The Death of Trumpcare Is the Ultimate Proof of Obamacare's Historic Accomplishment," *Huffington Post*, March 26, 2017, http://www.huffingtonpost.com/entry/health-care-republicans-repeal-obamacare_us_58d81295e4b03787d3598bf6.

47. Arthur M. Schlesinger Jr., *The Imperial Presidency* (1973; Boston: Houghton Mifflin, 2004).

48. John A. Farrell, *Richard Nixon: The Life* (New York: Doubleday, 2017).

49. Louis Fisher, *Congressional Abdication on War and Spending* (College Station: Texas A&M University Press, 2000).

50. Harold C. Relyea, "National Emergency Powers," CRS Report 98–505 (Washington, DC: Congressional Research Service, 2007), http://www.fas.org/sgp/crs/natsec/98-505.pdf.

PART II
Selection

5

The Nomination of
Presidential Candidates

WILLIAM "BOSS" TWEED, a notorious, machine politician* from the 1860s and 1870s, once said about elections: "I don't care who does the electing, so long as I get to do the nominating." For a good long time, Tweed did the nominating in New York City. And so did other party officials all across the nation. But no longer. From "King Caucus" to the proliferation of primaries, from campaign finance laws to voting procedures, a changing assembly of rules and institutions has redefined how parties field candidates for the presidency.

Who, then, picks today's presidential candidates? As it turns out, the answer is a good deal more complicated than "the people." In this chapter, we examine the nomination process, which begins at the time presidential candidates launch their campaigns and ends with the national conventions where parties formally select their nominees. And in the next chapter, we consider general elections, which carry all the way to Election Day itself. In both, we see how changes in institutional rules and practices reshape the dynamics of candidate selection—affecting not only who votes and who runs but, ultimately, who finds a home in the White House.

5.1 Presidential Nominations: Institutions of the Past

The Constitution does not explain how presidential candidates are to be nominated. As it happens, this oversight did not much matter in 1789 or in 1792 when, in the first two presidential elections, George Washington ran unopposed. But by 1796, after Washington had declined to seek a third term, political parties (which the Framers had also failed to recognize or incorporate in the Constitution) began fashioning their own nominating procedures. With the emergence of parties, the first stage in the institutionalization of presidential nominations commenced. Three phases proceeded from there.

---

* A machine politician is an individual who belongs to a political organization, a "machine," that exercises significant control over a political party in a certain area. William Tweed was the leader of Tammany Hall, the political machine of the Democratic Party in New York City.

5.1.1 King Caucus: 1796–1824

In 1796, leaders of the Federalist Party met informally to nominate John Adams to succeed George Washington. The Democratic-Republicans, by contrast, convened their members in Congress to nominate Thomas Jefferson. Four years later, in 1800, both parties used **congressional caucuses**—formal groups of co-partisans within Congress that make joint decisions about legislative affairs and electioneering—to select presidential nominees. Because Congress was in session, with party adherents already assembled in Washington, D.C., congressional caucusing provided an expedient way of selecting party nominees.

This period, roughly between 1796 and 1824, was called the era of **King Caucus** as candidates for the presidency were nominated by party elites who were all members of Congress. States with the largest populations had significant influence in choosing nominees in the era of King Caucus because the size of any state's congressional delegation was based on population. Moreover, all delegations at the time tended to favor potential nominees from their home states over those born elsewhere. Small wonder, then, that in every election from 1796 to 1820, Democratic-Republican caucuses put candidates on the presidential ticket from the large slaveholding state of Virginia.

For all its merits, the congressional caucus as a nominating institution generated two related objections: first, because congressional caucuses excluded ordinary citizens from the selection of party nominees, they were said to be undemocratic; and second, because only party elites in Congress participated, congressional caucuses were said to be unrepresentative of the party's rank-and-file membership.

Such concerns about King Caucus came to a head in 1824, when four candidates—John Quincy Adams (MA), Henry Clay (KY), William Crawford (GA), and Andrew Jackson (TN)—sought the Democratic-Republican nomination. That year, when the credibility of the party caucus as a nominating institution was fading, only a quarter of congressional Democratic-Republicans caucused. Crawford won the caucus nomination even though he had recently suffered a debilitating stroke. The three other candidates, each with robust local bases of support, challenged Crawford's nomination. All four Democratic-Republicans competed in the general election, where Crawford finished third, bested by both Jackson (who received the most electoral votes) and Adams.

None of the candidates received a majority of electoral votes, and so, per the Constitution, the House of Representatives assumed responsibility for deciding the election. After repeated rounds of voting in which no candidate emerged the winner, John Quincy Adams ultimately prevailed in what came to be known as the "corrupt bargain," wherein Adams agreed to give the position of secretary of state to Henry Clay (who was Speaker of the House) in return for the votes of Clay's supporters.[1] The public outcry over Adams's ascendency, fomented by Jackson and others, was intense. That Adams, who had lost both the popular and electoral votes in the general election, had been made president eroded the credibility of King Caucus and signaled its doom (table 5.1).

In 1828, no nominating caucuses were held. Instead, in a procedure that decentralized and democratized the nominating institution, state legislatures named presidential candi-

TABLE 5.1. The Election of 1824

Candidate	Political Party	Popular Vote (%)	Electoral Vote	House Vote (state delegations)
John Quincy Adams	Democratic-Republican	30.5	84	13
Andrew Jackson	Democratic-Republican	43.1	99	7
William H. Crawford	Democratic-Republican	13.1	41	4
Henry Clay	Democratic-Republican	13.2	37	—

Note: Though all of the candidates for the presidency in 1824 were Democratic-Republicans, the individual who won the party's caucus (Crawford) placed third, receiving just 13 percent of the popular vote. When the House of Representatives convened to choose a winner from the top three candidates, second-place Adams came out on top.

Source: Historical Election Results, Electoral College, National Archives and Records Administration.

dates. In a rematch between Adams (now the nominee of the newly formed National-Republican Party) and Jackson (the nominee of the newly formed Democratic Party), Jackson prevailed.

5.1.2 National Party Conventions, Local Control: 1832–1912

The idea of staging a national **nominating convention** in which each party formally selects its nominee had been discussed as early as 1822. Ten years later, in 1832, the recently formed Democratic Party inaugurated a new phase in presidential nominations by hosting the first-ever national party convention in U.S. history.

Curiously, though, the 1832 convention nominated not a presidential candidate but a vice-presidential one. It was a foregone conclusion that Andrew Jackson would again be the Democratic nominee for president. John C. Calhoun (SC), who had been elected four years earlier as Jackson's vice president, resigned in early 1832, opening a spot on the ticket for someone new. The Democrats opted to hold a convention to nominate a replacement for Calhoun, and in May 1832 the first Democratic National Convention took place in Baltimore. Martin Van Buren, an established Jackson insider, easily secured the nomination.* Ever since, major parties have formally nominated candidates at national party conventions, where each state sends **delegates** to cast votes for both president and vice president.[2]

In the nineteenth and early twentieth centuries, state legislators, not the general public, selected delegates to send to national party conventions. By appointing local party loyalists to national party conventions, state legislators curried the favor of local **party bosses**, elite members of political machines, on whose support they depended for their own reelections. This arrangement strengthened the role of bosses in national politics and gave them a great deal of say over who would occupy the White House.

---

* In addition to serving as vice president during Jackson's second term in office, Van Buren would go on to win the presidency for himself in 1836.

Throughout most of the nineteenth century, political parties were loose assemblies of factions built around geographic and economic interests. As a result, parties occasionally named nominees with nearly no national exposure. In 1844, for instance, the Democrats were deeply divided over the annexation of Texas. When delegates assembled for the party's national convention, no fewer than seven candidates were in the running. As the convention approached, former president Martin Van Buren (1837–41) from New York was the clear front-runner. His objection to annexing Texas, however, evoked substantial opposition among convention delegates from regions where annexation was favored. After seven ballots without a majority, a new name was added: James Knox Polk, a senator from Tennessee. Rather astonishingly, Polk quickly emerged as the compromise candidate and secured the required number of votes on the ninth ballot. Though his name was familiar to party leaders, he was unknown among the general public—so much so, in fact, that the opposition Whig Party, which was the precursor to the Republican Party that emerged after the Civil War, adopted "Who is James K. Polk?" as its campaign slogan that year.

Polk was not the only obscure nominee to emerge from a major party's national convention in the nineteenth century. In 1852, the Democratic national party convention opened with four viable candidates supported by distinct constituencies:

- Lewis Cass, the unsuccessful Democratic Party nominee for president in 1848, was backed by northerners for his support of the Compromise of 1850, which temporarily settled disputes about the balance of new pro-slavery and pro-freedom states to be admitted into the Union from territory acquired in the Mexican-American War.
- Stephen Douglas, from Illinois, enjoyed support among railroad interests and so-called expansionists, who advocated for a larger U.S. territory.
- James Buchanan was popular in his home state of Pennsylvania and perhaps the candidate most friendly to the South.
- William Marcy was backed by his home state of New York, which controlled more electoral votes than any other state at the time.

After repeated ballots, and a clear demonstration that the differences among these vested interests and their candidates would not be overcome, an alternative candidate, Franklin Pierce from New Hampshire, eventually secured the party's nomination and won the general election.

He was not alone. At the time of their nominations, Abraham Lincoln in 1860, Horatio Seymour in 1868, Rutherford B. Hayes in 1876, and James A. Garfield in 1880 also were all dark horses—virtual unknowns who unexpectedly won or made strong showings at their party conventions. Each emerged as a consensus candidate when delegates could not settle on any better-known candidate.

5.1.3 Trial-and-Error Primaries: 1912–1968

At the dawn of the twentieth century, political activists began to call for changes to existing nomination practices. Progressives—a diverse assembly of reformers who opposed political graft and wanted to invest more authority in the people—hoped to replace the national party conventions with a system in which voters select a party's nominee through state-administered elections—that is, a **direct primary** system, also known more simply as a primary system.

Primary elections, progressives argued, would check the control of party organizations, party bosses, and political elites and thereby facilitate a purer expression of the public will and increase the quality of candidates. Wisconsin passed the first direct-primary law in 1903 and, by 1917, forty-four of the remaining forty-seven states followed suit.

For a variety of reasons, the institution of direct primaries did not immediately alter presidential politics. For starters, reform proved short-lived. After World War I, the high costs of administering primary elections, combined with low levels of voter turnout, led many states to abandon them. Furthermore, even when primaries were in operation, candidates did not actively campaign for primary votes. Doing so was considered a sign of weakness, particularly among candidates with high name recognition. Most importantly, however, convention delegates at the time were not bound by primary election outcomes. As a result, the formal selection of a party's presidential nominee often had little to do with primary politics.

The 1912 presidential campaign provides a case in point. By late 1911, many progressive Republicans were disillusioned with incumbent Republican president William Taft. Convinced that Taft would not vigorously advance social and economic reforms, Senator Robert LaFollette and former president Theodore Roosevelt actively sought to take the Republican nomination from him. Though Roosevelt announced that he would not compete in any primaries, he nonetheless signaled his willingness to accept the nomination if it were awarded to him, thereby giving his supporters the go-ahead to campaign on his behalf.

Of the states holding primaries, Roosevelt triumphed in all but two, even winning Taft's home state of Ohio. Taft's supporters, however, maintained control over Republican Party insiders, who replaced Roosevelt delegates with Taft delegates at the national party convention and named Taft the Republican nominee. Not to be outdone, Roosevelt founded a new party—the Bull Moose Party—and ran as its nominee in the general election, splitting the Republican popular vote and handing the election to Democrat Woodrow Wilson.

Similar events characterized the Democratic nomination in 1952, when Senator Estes Kefauver challenged incumbent president Harry Truman. Kefauver defeated Truman in the New Hampshire primary, after which Truman bowed out of the race. Still, Democratic elites, including Truman, did not trust Kefauver, convinced that his views were too populist and that a Kefauver victory would substantially weaken the Democratic Party's chances in the general election. None of the obvious alternatives—including Georgia senator Richard Russell, Ambassador Averell Harriman, and Vice President Alben Barkley—were palatable to Democratic Party officials. Kefauver went on to win twelve of the fifteen state primaries then held and was the favorite heading into the national party convention, at which point the party reached out to Adlai Stevenson, a moderate governor from Illinois. Though he expressed reservations, Stevenson stopped short of withdrawing his name from consideration. At the convention, state and national party bosses rallied behind Stevenson, who became the nominee on just the third ballot.

5.2 Presidential Nominations: The Modern Institution

Primaries sometimes provided party elites with valuable information about the broader appeal of presidential candidates and offered the candidates new opportunities to engage the public directly. As long as state and national party leaders maintained control over how delegates voted at national party conventions, however, the relevance of primaries would remain largely symbolic. Since primaries had failed to increase the public's influence over the selection of major party nominees for president, further reforms to the institution were proposed in the 1960s.

In response to the chaos and violence surrounding its 1968 national convention, the Democratic Party formed the **McGovern-Fraser Commission** to develop a new set of rules that would govern the future nominations of presidents by both parties. Based on the commission's recommendations, the Democratic Party implemented a series of reforms aimed at increasing the transparency of the primary process, raising the participation of underrepresented groups, and decreasing the representation of state organizations on state delegations.[3] Through these reforms, the commission hoped to augment the influence of ordinary citizens and generate party nominees who better reflected the views of rank-and-file party members.[4] (For more on the 1968 Democratic National Convention in Chicago, which led to the McGovern-Fraser political reforms, see the Historical Transformations feature in this chapter.)

Historical Transformations: 1968, Chicago under Siege

The protests that broke out on the streets of Chicago during the 1968 Democratic National Convention reflected the disenchantment that many Americans felt with the country's direction and its institutions, including those that determined how presidents were nominated.[5] The political reforms that were enacted after the protests, on the recommendation of the McGovern-Fraser Commission, were intended to transform the electoral politics of the American presidency in meaningful and lasting ways.

In the year that preceded the 1968 convention, protests against an escalating war in Vietnam erupted across the country. In late 1967, antiwar groups attempted to recruit antiwar Democrats to enter the race for the party's presidential nomination. A fair number signed on to challenge Lyndon Johnson, despite the fact that no incumbent president in the twentieth century had been denied the nomination if he sought it. The fact that Johnson—on whom the gross errors of the war were blamed—was expected to be the party's nominee again in 1968 compelled Senator Eugene McCarthy from Minnesota, a vocal opponent of the war, to enter the race. Others soon followed, particularly after the Tet Offensive, which resulted in a spike in U.S. casualties, a new draft call, and the resignation of Secretary of Defense Robert McNamara.

Initially McCarthy did not poll well, largely because of low name recognition. Although McCarthy invested significant resources in New Hampshire, Johnson defeated him in the March 12 primary. The small margin of Johnson's victory, however, was a perceived

FIGURE 5.1. The street violence between police and protesters that coincided with the Democratic National Convention in Chicago in 1968 convinced many people of the need for institutional reforms to the processes by which parties chose their presidential nominees. Copyright 1968 Bettman/Getty Images. Reproduced with permission.

blot on the incumbent president. Shortly thereafter, Senator Robert Kennedy, another antiwar candidate, entered the race. When Johnson announced his decision not to seek reelection—a surprise to all—Hubert Humphrey, Johnson's loyal vice president, launched his own campaign for the office.

The candidates' decisions about how to campaign reflected, in large measure, their respective bases of support. McCarthy's core constituents were young activists and intellectuals; Kennedy's most ardent supporters were Catholics and African Americans. All of these groups could be mobilized to vote in primaries but would be dramatically underrepresented at the convention.

Humphrey, on the other hand, had support from party elites and labor unionists who would have seats at the convention. As the establishment candidate, Humphrey therefore decided to sit out the primaries altogether; his fate would be settled by the party bosses at the national convention. When Kennedy was assassinated in June 1968, Humphrey had only McCarthy to beat.

The Democratic National Convention was set to begin in Chicago during the last week of August. For much of the previous year, activists had held protests and demonstrations across the city, motivated both by antiwar sentiment and by civil rights and housing issues.

With the Democratic convention in full swing, tensions between the demonstrators and police mounted—and then turned violent. Clashes between protesters and police

Continued on next page

that began in Grant Park spilled over into the streets of Chicago, and TV crews were on hand to broadcast the crackdown nationally. While activists battled police outside, chaos reigned on the convention floor. Humphrey arrived confident of the support of the party, but antiwar delegates—unconvinced that a Humphrey administration would change course on the war—moved to put forward Senator George McGovern's name for consideration. McGovern supporters promptly aligned with McCarthy's in a bid to derail the almost-certain Humphrey nomination, but the insurgency failed. Humphrey easily won the delegate count and became the party's nominee.

For both Humphrey and the Democratic Party, the campaign quickly went south. Media coverage of the rioting outside cemented the image of the Democratic Party in many people's minds as the party of disorder. Within the party, opponents of the war railed against Humphrey and the party establishment. As a result, four years after Johnson's landslide victory in 1964, Humphrey lost the general election to Richard Nixon, whose law-and-order politics seemed to many the needed antidote to national disintegration.[6]

To many, the process by which the Democratic Party had selected its presidential nominee appeared tainted. Humphrey, it seemed, was nominated solely because he was able to leverage support from a less than fully accountable party machine. The people, however, inconveniently refused to remain quiet, and the result was a public relations nightmare. Party leaders appeared deaf to the voices of the rank and file.

Motivated by the need to refurbish the party's image and to address the deeper challenges of acknowledging diversity within the party, the Democrats convened the McGovern-Fraser Commission, from which, in a summer of historical transformation, our modern primary system was born.

5.2.1 The Pool of Primary Candidates

The question of who runs for president very much depends upon who selects the party's nominees. During the days of King Caucus, only individuals with close ties to national legislators—and especially those from large, populous states—could hope to secure their party's nomination. Similarly, beginning in 1828, nominating conventions filtered out candidates who lacked relationships with state legislators and local party bosses. Even as the nation began experimenting with direct primaries, successful candidates still spent much of their time persuading party insiders—rather than the voters themselves—that they could unite party factions and win the general election.

By changing how parties select their nominees, McGovern-Fraser permanently altered the kinds of people who run for president. As we will discuss later, relationships with party insiders still weigh heavily on the nomination process; after McGovern-Fraser, however, these relationships alone no longer made or broke a candidacy. The reforms meant that

FIGURE 5.2. Candidates seeking the 2020 Democratic nomination. A particularly crowded field of Democratic candidates sought their party's nomination for the 2020 presidential election. So many, in fact, that candidates had to share the debate stage separately on consecutive nights. *Source:* Doug Mills/The New York Times/ Redux.

outsider candidates—those without strong name recognition or financial backing—could readily compete for the nomination. Similarly, the reforms opened the door for a more diverse pool of candidates including racial minorities and women who, though still underrepresented in presidential politics, traditionally lacked the kinds of insider relationships that were necessary to compete.

Unsurprisingly, as barriers to entry eased, the number of candidates for president increased. In 2008, more than sixteen candidates competed in the Iowa caucuses, with at least four viable candidates from each party, including Hillary Clinton, John Edwards, Barack Obama, and Bill Richardson on the Democratic side, and Rudy Giuliani, John McCain, Mitt Romney, and Fred Thompson on the Republican side. In 2012, seven major Republican candidates ran in Iowa. By July 2015, five Democrats and seventeen Republicans were slated to run in Iowa[7]—so many, in fact, that President Obama quipped, "I've lost count of the number of Republicans running. They have enough for an actual Hunger Games."[8] Even more extreme, at the start of the 2020 primary cycle there were enough Democrats vying for the nomination—twenty-one by the time of the first debate—to merit splitting the candidates into two separate debate groups (figure 5.2).[9]

Of course, plenty of factors still dissuade individuals from seeking their party's nomination for president. All candidates, for example, must assess whether they have any reasonable chance of winning.* In this regard, one strategic consideration looms large: incumbency. In the modern era, members of the same party rarely challenge incumbent presidents for their party's nomination. When challenges do occur, they usually signal deep divisions within the party. The incumbent Democrat Jimmy Carter faced a challenge from within his own party in 1980, and Republicans tried to wrest the nomination from George H. W. Bush in 1992: Carter and Bush both eventually secured their party's nomination but lost the general election.

More candidates tend to seek a nomination, and the quality of the pool of eligible candidates tends to be much stronger, when an incumbent is not in the field. In **open elections**, as in 1988, 2000, 2008, and 2016, all years in which no incumbent ran for reelection, the pathway to the nomination tends to be much more competitive.

The state of the economy and public approval of the party that occupies the White House also weigh heavily in decisions to seek a nomination. When the economy is strong and an incumbent president's party is popular, a weaker assembly of opposition candidates comes forward. When the economy is flagging, however, and the public holds an incumbent president's party in low regard, the opposing party can be expected to field a stronger group of contenders.[10]

Of course, none of the considerations affecting the decision to run is set in stone. In some cases, an incumbent president's perceived strength, not his weakness, plays into the hands of an especially entrepreneurial challenger. The popularity of George H. W. Bush in late 1991, fresh off a victory in the Persian Gulf War, deterred many well-known Democrats, including New York governor Mario Cuomo, from seeking the nomination. When Cuomo vacillated, an opportunity for Bill Clinton, governor of Arkansas at the time, opened up. He entered the race and won the Democratic nomination, even though he lacked national name recognition. By summer 1992, the country was in a mild recession, helping Clinton win an easy victory in the general election. Had other Democrats anticipated the downturn in the nation's economy, the 1992 election might well have given us a President Cuomo rather than a President Clinton.

5.2.2 Open Primaries, Closed Primaries, and Caucuses

Because they were adopted at the state level, and because state law governs the behavior of Republicans and Democrats alike, virtually all of the McGovern-Fraser reforms ended up applying to both parties. The specific reforms, however, vary slightly by state. In some

---

* Of course, not all candidates see winning as the principal reason for running. In nearly every election, at least one Democratic or Republican candidate formally seeks the nomination, not with a serious view to winning it but because the race provides a platform from which to air deeply held policy views. This increases the candidate's national exposure and influences the political agenda for the coming Congress and presidency. Recent examples of such candidates include Representative Ron Paul (R-TX) in both 2008 and 2012, Representative Dennis Kucinich (D-OH) in 2004 and 2008, and Al Sharpton (D) in 2004.

states, primaries are open; in others, they are closed. In an **open primary**, any voter can participate in either party's primary election regardless of party affiliation; in a **closed primary**, voting is open only to registered party members. In states with primaries, voters go to polling stations to cast votes. Other states, however, hold **caucuses**, in which party members deliberate openly about the merits of different candidates. Depending on the state, voting in caucuses may proceed either openly or by secret ballot.

In 2012 and 2016, thirty-seven states held primaries to select nominees for president, while the remaining thirteen states held caucuses.* In 2020 the number of states with primary elections rose to forty-seven, with only three caucusing holdouts.[11] Puerto Rico holds primaries while the other U.S. territories—Guam, American Samoa, the Northern Mariana Islands, and the Virgin Islands—hold caucuses.

5.2.3 The Primary Electorate

By most reasonable standards, the primaries and caucuses of the modern era have democratized the nominating process. In the last twenty years, voter participation in presidential primaries has increased modestly. Whereas only 20 percent of registered voters turned out during the 2000 primary season, roughly 30 percent did so in 2008.[12] In 2016, roughly two in three registered voters participated in the New Hampshire primary, a new record for the Granite State. The state's numbers inched upward by about three percentage points in 2020, when a highly competitive field of candidates sought the Democratic nomination.[13]

In addition, presidential primaries and caucuses tend to bring **retail politics**—a style of political campaigning in which candidates interact directly, and usually informally, with voters at public events—to the fore. Especially in early season contests, candidates go door-to-door to introduce themselves to local residents and gather in local diners, barns, and town halls to discuss the issues of the day.[14]

It is not immediately clear, however, that the interests of average citizens receive any greater consideration in modern-era primaries than they did when party elites ruled the nominations.[15] Despite potential improvements in recent years, primaries and caucuses tend to elicit the participation of only a small subset of the voters who turn out for the general election. As figure 5.3 shows, turnout rates for primary elections are a fraction of those in general elections.†

Turnout is especially poor in states that hold caucuses, which require citizens to vote at a specific time of day and stay at the caucus center until everyone has been counted—a process that can take hours. (Contrast this to primaries which, ideally, allow citizens to vote quickly and at a time that is most convenient for them.) In 2020, four states switched from caucuses to primaries and saw swift and significant increases in turnout.[16]

---

*Because incumbent president Barack Obama opted to seek reelection in 2012, no serious challenger arose in the Democratic Party, and four states actually canceled their primaries.

†Because it only shows turnout levels in primary elections when both parties held primaries, however, figure 5.3 likely understates the true differences in turnout between primary and general elections.

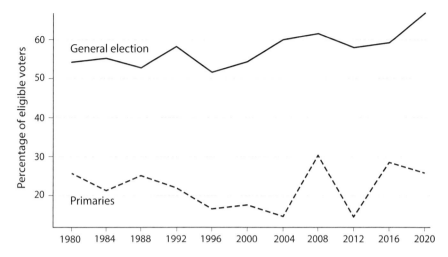

FIGURE 5.3. Primary versus general election turnout, 1980–2020. Turnout figures are calculated as a percentage of eligible voters in all primaries and caucuses. Because of state-specific restrictions on voting during the nomination phase, the total eligible population of voters in caucuses and primaries is smaller than that in the general election. As a result, the figures reported here may understate just how low turnout rates tend to be. *Sources:* Primary data 1980–2016: Pew Research Center, https://www.pewresearch.org/fact-tank/2016/06/10/turnout-was-high-in-the-2016 -primary-season-but-just-short-of-2008- record/. General data 1980–2016: The American Presidency Project, https://www.presidency.ucsb.edu/statistics/data/voter-turnout-in-presidential -elections. General data 2020: Dr. Michael P. McDonald, University of Florida, http://www .electproject.org/home/voter-turnout/voter-turnout-data.

For a long time, people worried that low turnout rates had an adverse effect on the quality of general election candidates. That is, they assumed that primary voters—small in number, unusually energetic about politics—hold more extreme views than the rest of their party, resulting in primaries that select only the most polarizing candidates. Troubling as this may seem, however, low turnout rates need not come at the expense of citizens who forgo their local primaries or caucuses. According to a recent paper coauthored by John Sides, Chris Tausanovitch, Lynn Vavreck, and Christopher Warshaw, primary voters are not meaningfully different (in terms of demographics or ideology) from members of their party who only vote in the general election.[17] Though primary voters are indeed more excited about elections, Sides and coauthors find, they tend to hold similar views about public policy as do their co- partisans who tend to vote only in the general election. Thus, even though primaries have relatively low turnout rates, they may still be reasonably adept at representing the views of the broader electorate.

5.2.4 The Nominating Season

State primaries and caucuses are held in the first two quarters of presidential election years. Because the earliest of these nominating contests usually occurs in January or early February, nearly a year before the general election, and because the early contests are important

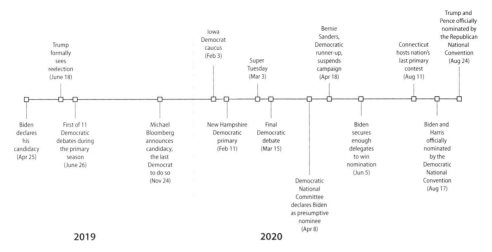

FIGURE 5.4. Campaign timeline for the 2020 presidential nomination. To become the nominee, a candidate must secure votes from a majority of the delegates who assemble in late summer at their party's national convention.

barometers of support, candidates begin their campaigns in the preceding year when the presidential election is far removed from most voters' minds.

Figure 5.4—a timeline of the 2020 season, from candidates' entries to the formal nomination—shows just how long the road to election has become. Though Joseph Biden entered the race in late April 2019, he would have to wait another two months until meeting his fellow candidates on the debate stage, the first significant event of the primary calendar. What figure 5.4 does not show, however, are the two candidates—John Delaney and Andrew Yang—who launched their campaigns as early as August 2017 in hopes that the additional *two years* of electioneering would give them an advantage over their opponents.

Were it not for McGovern-Fraser, this timeline would appear both shorter and less eventful. In the 1968 election, for example, only fourteen states and the District of Columbia held primaries. The nominating season began on March 12, 1968, and ended three months later on June 11. Richard Nixon, who won the Republican nomination and ultimately the presidency, did not launch his campaign until February 1968, a full nine months later than Joe Biden entered the 2020 election.

5.2.5 *Allocation of Delegates*

To win the nomination, candidates must secure a majority of their party's delegates. But beware: even if candidates perform well among regular voters, they may still drastically underperform when it comes time to count delegates. There are a couple reasons for this.

First, not all delegates are created equal. Under the rules of many states, so-called "pledged" delegates are legally obligated to cast their ballots for the candidate to which they are assigned based on primary or caucus results. By contrast, "unpledged" delegates, also known as **superdelegates**, are not bound to vote for any particular candidate. A superdelegate is usually a member of the U.S. House of Representatives or the U.S. Senate, a state or territorial governor, a member of the party's national committee, or another state or national party leader. Superdelegates may announce their support for a candidate at any time, though such announcements are nonbinding and their votes are not formally recorded until the convention. As a matter of strict accounting, pledged delegates today significantly outnumber superdelegates. But when a race is close, superdelegates can tip the scales for one candidate or another.

In the spring of 2008, some political observers wondered whether superdelegates might award the Democratic nomination to Hillary Clinton. As Obama assembled a narrow yet persistent lead in the pledged delegate count, the Clinton camp continued to insist that its candidate offered the party superior odds of winning the general election in the fall. Superdelegates, theoretically, could have provided Clinton with enough votes to put her over the top at the convention had they opted to jettison their party's front-runner.[18]

Differing rules across states and parties can also affect candidates' delegate counts. Whereas some states award delegates on a winner-take-all basis, others award theirs proportionally, or as a hybrid of these two approaches. In a winner-take-all state, the candidate who wins the most votes receives *all* of the state's pledged delegates—even if they won by only a few percentage points. In practice, performing *just well enough* in a winner-take-all can give a candidate an insurmountable lead in delegates, one reason the Democratic Party does not allow winner-take-all allocation in its primary process.

By awarding delegates proportionally, a state's delegates are divided among the candidates relative to how well they perform. Only the poorest-performing candidates receive no delegates at all. In the 2020 New Hampshire primary, for instance, candidates had to win at least 10 percent of the total primary vote in order to receive any delegates. The top candidates, Bernie Sanders and Pete Buttigieg, both garnered nine delegates, having won 25.7 and 24.4 percent of the vote, respectively. They were trailed by Amy Klobuchar, who won six delegates. However, Elizabeth Warren and Joe Biden, the eventual nominee, failed to cross the threshold, with each receiving 9.2 percent and 8.4 percent, respectively.[19] As such, they secured no delegates.

Differences in allocation rules help explain why, in some years, the Republican nomination is settled much earlier than the Democratic nomination. The winner-take-all rule for allocating delegates leads to a rather quick narrowing of the field: Republican candidates who lose early primaries have a much more difficult time sustaining financial and popular support. The proportional rule for allocating delegates, by contrast, allows candidates who finish in second and third place to continue their campaigns for longer periods of time. As long as they continue to secure meaningful numbers of delegates from states along the way, their campaigns retain viability.[20]

5.2.6 Party Conventions

As shown in figure 5.4, the primary season concludes with the Democratic and Republican national conventions. It is here that the parties formally nominate their candidates for president. In the nineteenth century and well into the twentieth, party conventions were protracted, heated affairs because the parties, especially the Democrats, often had geo-graphically dispersed but entrenched factions to appease. Settling on a ticket regularly stretched over days of balloting, with party bosses gathering privately in backrooms to negotiate outcomes.

Modern-day conventions, however, bear little resemblance to the raucous gatherings that predated the McGovern-Fraser reforms. Held in mid- to late summer, conventions today mark the end of the primary season and the beginning of the general election cam-paign. By this point the country already knows who the nominees are, and convention rules and party platforms are set. Designed to rally the faithful, today's party conventions shine a bright (and hopefully flattering) light on the party's presidential nominee. Vivid displays of pageantry and patriotism showcase party messages, but voting on the presiden-tial nominee is strictly a formality.*

Hardly the "smoke-filled rooms" they once were, today's conventions are coronations—spaces for parties to celebrate their nominees and curry the support of the broader elector-ate. If there is any scheming involved in these conventions, it usually serves to appease, rather than confound, the party's constituents. This is evident in how the party selects its convention sites. After McGovern-Fraser, the two parties had all the more reason to host its conventions in cities that reflected the broader interests of their voters. In 2000, for in-stance, the Democrats held their convention in Los Angeles in order to shore up their sup-port in California; in that same year, Republicans held theirs in Philadelphia, likely because Pennsylvania was an important swing state. In 2016—the last fully in-person conventions, given the pandemic in 2020—the two parties once again located their conventions in swing states, with Democrats headed to Philadelphia and Republicans to Cleveland.

Meanwhile, as a direct result of McGovern-Fraser, convention delegates have tended to more closely resemble the demographic makeup of the parties' rank and file. The per-centage of female delegates to the Democratic Party's nominating conventions tripled between 1968 and 1972, although women were still (and continue to be) under-represented relative to the larger electorate. The 1972 election also saw increases in the numbers of African Americans and younger voters in attendance and a decrease in the number of more affluent delegates.[21]

While neither party's delegates for the 2016 conventions were especially representative of the country's voting population as a whole, convention delegates did tend to mirror their party's demographics. For instance, African Americans comprised 25 percent of the dele-gates to the Democratic convention and 1 percent of the delegates to the Republican con-vention.[22] Today's conventions—attended by individuals who not long ago were denied the right to vote—serve as a visible reminder of how the primary process has changed.

---

* Received wisdom holds that conventions grant their candidates an approval "bump" generated by the abundance of positive imagery conveyed mostly unfiltered by the media. A study of all conventions between 1960 and 2000 found that convention bumps do, indeed, exist; however, the effect is limited since the separate effects of each party's convention largely offset each other. See James Stimson, *Tides of Consent* (Cambridge: Cambridge University Press, 2004), 128.

5.3 Institutional Biases in Candidate Selection

The modern system of presidential primaries—largely created by the McGovern-Fraser reforms of the late 1960s—looks quite different from the institutional arrangements that preceded it. By all accounts, the reforms successfully democratized the nomination process, shifting power from a small group of political and economic elites to, for the most part, any citizen who wishes to engage and cast a ballot.

The above description is accurate but also incomplete. The pool of candidates and voters is indeed much larger and more diverse than it used to be. But even though more people have a say in the nomination, some voters still matter more than others. Due to a number of institutional factors—some relating to the basic layout of the primary calendar, others to the strength of political parties—the most popular candidate does not always win. Instead, the winner is often the one who can gain support from the groups who matter most: party insiders, wealthy campaign contributors, and, not least of all, the voters in Iowa and New Hampshire.

5.3.1 The Early State Advantage

Together, Iowa, with its six electoral votes, and New Hampshire, with its four, constitute less than 4 percent of the total number of electoral votes needed (270) to win the presidency in the general election. Voters in these states also differ rather dramatically from the national citizenry. In 2020, for instance, 56 percent of the people who participated in the Iowa caucus were female, 53 percent had received a college degree, and 91 percent were white—figures, all, that vastly exceed national averages. And things did not become any more representative in the New Hampshire primaries that followed, where 57 percent were female, 67 percent college educated, and 89 percent white.[23]

Why, then, do Iowa and New Hampshire attract so much media attention every four years? And why do candidates pour so many resources into these two states? Wouldn't candidates be better served by focusing their attention on larger, more representative states?

The answer, it turns out, is no. The outsized importance of Iowa and New Hampshire is not merely imagined. It is quite real. By tradition, the Iowa caucuses and the New Hampshire primary are the nation's first scheduled nominating contests. And in a system of staggered primaries and caucuses, wherein donors, voters, journalists, and the candidates themselves continually update expectations on the basis of past performance, candidates have real incentives to focus their energies and resources on these early contests. The significance of these two states, it turns out, has less to do with the electoral votes they bestow and more to do with the public expectations that they inform.

To see this, consider the experience of one promising candidate who opted to forgo these early contests. After announcing his candidacy for the 2008 presidential nomination in February 2007, former New York City mayor Rudolph Giuliani quickly achieved front-runner status and retained his lead in the polls for almost all of that year. In mid-2007,

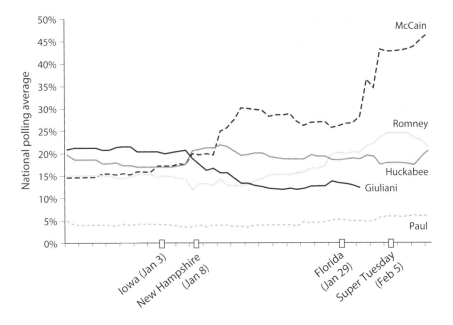

FIGURE 5.5. Early state advantage in the 2008 race for the Republican nomination. Giuliani was the clear front-runner leading up to the 2008 presidential primaries. When he opted out of the first three contests, however, Giuliani's standing quickly eroded. After winning the New Hampshire primary, McCain never looked back. (Early primary contests in Wyoming, Michigan, Nevada, and South Carolina not labeled.) *Source:* RealClearPolitics, "2008 Republican Presidential Nomination," https://www.realclearpolitics.com/epolls/2008/president/us/2008 _republican_presidential_nomi nation-2741.html.

however, he made the fateful decision to buck tradition. His campaign chose to focus its attention on larger states, such as Florida and California, and to ignore the early contests in Iowa and New Hampshire.

By the second week in January, Americans learned that Giuliani had won only 3 percent in the Iowa caucus and 9 percent in the New Hampshire primary. The effects of Giuliani's early losses carried into later states, particularly Florida, where his campaign had spent the bulk of its time and money. After capturing less than 15 percent of the vote in the Sunshine State, Giuliani realized that he had no path to victory. Rather suddenly, the most famous mayor in the country, and the early presidential front-runner, promptly exited the race (figure 5.5).

Giuliani's experience highlights the importance of **momentum** in presidential nominating contests.[24] Though early wins certainly do not guarantee a nomination, they help to burnish a candidate's image as the all-important front-runner and consequently stir up enthusiasm, generate increased media attention, and energize activists and volunteers. Early wins also help candidates raise money: donors have every incentive to back the eventual nominee, not the also-rans, and to do so as early as possible. Early wins in Iowa and New Hampshire therefore provide financial windfalls that enhance a candidate's ability to compete in subsequent races.

As a consequence, wins tend to beget wins.[25] As political scientist Larry Bartels puts it, momentum is "like a football game, in which you say to the first team that makes a first down with ten yards, 'Hereafter your team has a special rule. Your first downs are five yards. And if you make three of those you get a two-yard first down. And we're going to let your first touchdown count 21 points. Now the rest of you bastards play catch-up under the regular rules.'"[26]

Early victories have helped fuel many an upstart campaign. In 1968 Eugene McCarthy's strong performance in New Hampshire helped convince President Lyndon Johnson, the incumbent, not to seek reelection; in 1976 Jimmy Carter's early wins in Iowa and New Hampshire catapulted him to the top of the Democratic field; and in 2008 Barack Obama's victory in Iowa landed him the support of many Americans who approved of his message but had been skeptical about his ability to attract white voters.

The converse is also true. Candidates who perform poorly in early caucuses and primaries tend to drift further and further behind. Anticipating a long downward spiral, many simply quit the race. Following poor performances in the Iowa caucuses and New Hampshire primaries in 2016, for example, Republican contenders Carly Fiorina, Mike Huckabee, Chris Christie, Rand Paul, and Rick Santorum all dropped out of the race, as did Democrat Martin O'Malley. Likewise in 2020, once-promising campaigns of numerous Democratic contenders, including Andrew Yang and Senator Elizabeth Warren, promptly disbanded after poor performances in these early states. Since Iowa began hosting caucuses in 1972, the state's winner has gone on to win the party's nomination approximately half the time—another strong indication that early losses do not bode well for presidential hopefuls.[27]

What drives momentum, you will notice, has less to do with the candidates themselves and more to do with the structure of the primary season. Momentum does not derive from a psychological boost in confidence that early winners experience, which enables them to perform better in subsequent debates and campaign stops. Rather, the logic of momentum—and all that it implies about candidate performance and strategy—is built into a system of staggered primaries and caucuses, wherein key stakeholders continually update their expectations on the basis of past performance. If every state held its primary on the same day, the logic of momentum would understandably unravel. There would be no "early" winners, and victories in states like Iowa and New Hampshire would deliver only a handful of electoral votes. Instead, in our system where the first and last primaries take place several months apart, donors redirect their giving to early winners, with the hopes of currying their favor.

Journalists also devote more coverage to these early winners. Consequently, voters in later contests are more likely to hear from and about these early winners, giving them a clear edge. And quite apart from the campaign advantages that early wins confer, voters have independent reasons for rallying behind the early victors in the primary season. Quite rationally, these voters may infer that victors in Iowa and New Hampshire are of higher quality, and hence stand a better chance in the general election. In this way, winning becomes something of a self-fulfilling prophecy.

FRONT-LOADING PRIMARIES

The logic of momentum depends upon the institutional structure of the nominating process. But momentum, by turns, also generates feedback effects that have the potential to reshape the very process that supports it. The disproportionate significance of states that hold early primaries and caucuses, after all, encourages other states to move up the dates of their contests. Observing all the attention given to Iowa and New Hampshire, other states want to get into the action. So they appeal to party leaders to allow them to move their own contests up, which has the effect of front-loading the primary season.

In 2000, only three states held primaries or caucuses before February 10. In 2004, more than a dozen did.[28] When additional states expressed interest in moving up the dates of their 2008 contests, the Democratic National Committee (DNC) overruled most, allowing only Iowa, New Hampshire, Nevada, and South Carolina to stage their votes before February 5. Two states, Florida and Michigan, nonetheless scheduled their primaries for late January and were punished by the DNC with a temporary loss of their convention delegates. Undeterred, the president of the Florida Senate explained, "I'd much rather have a say in the nomination process as opposed to the coronation process."[29]

Rather than move their own contests up, other states have attempted to meet the challenges of momentum by joining forces. In 1988, for instance, Democratic leaders in the South hoped to increase the influence of the region in the nominating process by arranging for primaries and caucuses in Texas, Florida, Tennessee, Oklahoma, Mississippi, Kentucky, Alabama, and Georgia to be held on the same day, Tuesday, March 8. By their calculation, the vote tallies on **Super Tuesday**, the Tuesday in February or March of a presidential election year during which the largest number of states hold their primaries and caucuses, would force the party to coalesce around a centrist candidate who would appeal to conservative southern voters without alienating liberal voters in the North.

These developments have created a primary process that is simultaneously drawn out and bunched up. While the bulk of states schedule their contests in February and March, the remainder host theirs either concurrently or just days apart. Consequently, the primary season intermixes lulls with periods of frantic activity—an advantage for candidates who use the downtime to fundraise but a pitfall for candidates who need the "bounce" that only strong finishes can provide.

KICKSTARTING CAMPAIGNS

Candidates have struggled to adapt to the front-loading and bunching of primaries and caucuses.[30] Many candidates now spend months, and sometimes years, recruiting support in states with early primary season calendar dates. In figure 5.6, we see this phenomenon play out in two primary contests: 1980 and 2020. In 1980, shown in gray, candidates were relatively slow to enter the race. The winning candidate, Ronald Reagan, announced his campaign on November 13, 1979—roughly a year before Election Day. By contrast, candidates for the 2020 primary, shown in black, entered much earlier on average;

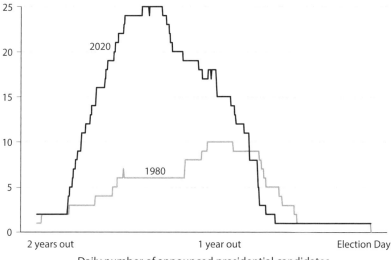

FIGURE 5.6. Daily number of announced presidential candidates, 1980 and 2020 primaries. The figure aggregates the number of candidates running by day leading up to the presidential election in 1980 and 2020. Notice how many more candidates ran in 2020 and how early candidates threw their hat in the race. *Sources:* Data for 2020 come from "Timeline of Announcements in the Presidential Election, 2020," Ballotpedia, https://ballotpedia.org/Timeline_of_announcements_in_the _presidential_election,_2020; data for 1980 were aggregated from campaign announcements and withdrawal articles for each declared candidate.

the crowded field reached its peak in November 2019, though a total of 21 candidates had already entered the field before May.

Increasingly, it seems that it is never too soon to launch a presidential campaign. With exclusive access to caucus goers, and plenty of time to build name recognition and local connections, early candidates vie for support in the Iowa caucuses. Note, however, that these are merely *relative* advantages. If nearly everyone enters early—as was the case in 2020—no one candidate enjoys the spoils. But conversely, if a candidate decides to enter months or even weeks later than everyone else, they risk being left behind.

EXCEPTIONS TO THE EARLY STATE ADVANTAGE

Many candidates rise and fall in presidential primaries according to the dictates of momentum. It would be a mistake, though, to conclude that early wins in every primary necessarily and irrevocably pave the way to an eventual nomination.

Consider the Democratic primaries leading up to the 2020 presidential election. Both Bernie Sanders and Pete Buttigieg seemed to have momentum on their sides, each garnering about a quarter of the vote in the first two contests of the primary season. Joe Biden,

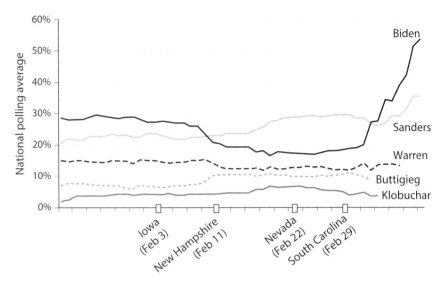

FIGURE 5.7. Lack of early state advantage in the 2020 race for the Democratic nomination. Despite crushing losses in the early contests of Iowa and New Hampshire, Joe Biden's later wins—particularly in South Carolina—propelled him to the nomination. *Source:* "2020 Democratic Presidential Nomination," *RealClearPolitics,* https://www.realclearpolitics.com/epolls/2020/president/us/2020_democratic _presidential_nomination-6730.html.

who entered the race with a clear front-runner status in national polling, earned just 15 percent of the vote in Iowa and 8 percent in New Hampshire. If momentum was at work, it appeared to be working entirely against him. This was reflected in the polls; just a week after his fourth-place finish in Iowa, Biden lost his front-runner status to Sanders. After his fifth-place finish in New Hampshire, and a twenty-five point loss in Nevada, the gap between him and Sanders only grew wider (figure 5.7).

Unlike the experience of Rudy Giuliani, however, these early losses did not consign Biden to the loser's circle. Biden kept his sights on South Carolina—the fourth state in the nominating contest—where he claimed an astonishing 50 percent of the vote, a nearly thirty-point victory over Sanders.[31] In a matter of days, Biden regained his lead in the polls while several of his top contenders—including Buttigieg, whose standing in the polls hardly moved after his victories in Iowa and New Hampshire—dropped out of the race. Reminding the populace that "We are very much alive," Biden went on to win the majority of the subsequent primaries and eventually the party nomination.[32]

5.3.2 The Influence of Parties

From the early state advantage, we gather that electoral rules can inadvertently favor some campaigns over others. Candidates can adapt to these rules, entering the race sooner and campaigning harder in early states. But what happens when the bias is intentional? Can candidates adapt when political institutions deliberately throw their support behind one of their competitors?

They can, and they must. Or so argues a group of prominent political scientists in their book *The Party Decides*, which delves into what has been called "the invisible primary." Taking place long before voters in Iowa and New Hampshire cast their ballots, the invisible primary is the process by which party insiders build a consensus around who they believe ought to be their nominee—or more precisely, whom they will try to propel through the voting contests and on to the convention.

POLITICAL PARTIES AS COALITIONS

If political parties, rather than voters, pick presidential candidates, we should take a moment to understand what parties really are. Parties are closely associated with their leadership organizations—that is, the Republican National Committee (RNC) and the Democratic National Committee (DNC). These governing committees are composed almost entirely of elected officials (governors, members of Congress, etc.), CEOs, and professional fundraisers.[33] In addition to raising money and drafting their respective party platforms, these committees are responsible for organizing their national conventions.

As we saw in section 5.2, the importance of national conventions has diminished with time. Once the place for party insiders to gather and nominate presidents, conventions have become little more than televised, four-day formalities.[34] No longer private strongholds of high-ranking deliberation and dealmaking, modern conventions are very public spaces for delegates to declare, officially, what the voters have already decided.

Given these developments, it would seem that party insiders have very little say over presidential primaries. However, as the authors of *The Party Decides* point out, parties are far more expansive than what we have described so far. In addition to party committees, they include "a coalition of interest groups, social group leaders, activists, and other 'policy demanders'" that shapes government policy.[35] Among Republicans, examples include the National Rifle Association, the American Action Network, and the National Right to Life Committee. Among Democrats: the American Federation of Teachers, the Sunrise Movement, EMILY's List, and Planned Parenthood. According to the authors, these groups—unions, religious organizations, activist movements, and more—form an integral part of political parties.

The inclusion of social groups and activists in the larger party apparatus is not a new concept in American politics. As early as the 1790s, two activist groups (then called "Democratic Clubs") organized around the concept of popular sovereignty, a pillar of the Republican agenda. Soon thereafter dozens of clubs formed, each with its own political agenda. These groups became powerful voices in party politics, not only contributing to elections but influencing their results. Today, these social groups have tremendous sway over the media and donor class.

With this more expansive definition of political parties, it is easier to see the influence they can have on presidential primaries. Crucially, though, social groups and party leadership are successful insofar as their efforts are coordinated. An increasing number of interest groups, each with its own policy priorities, can lead to unproductive infighting. To avoid this, political parties must choose a single candidate to support throughout the election. The process by which this happens is called the invisible primary.

THE INVISIBLE PRIMARY

Also referred to as the "exhibition season," the invisible primary begins before voters set foot in a voting booth. The authors of *The Party Decides* equate this primary to "a long-running national conversation" that takes place "in newspapers, on Sunday morning television talk shows . . . and most recently in the blogosphere."[36] (The "blogosphere" might be better thought of as Twitter, but the point remains.) There are no strict dates for this primary, but its winners are deemed front-runner candidates for the (visible) primary season that follows.

Candidates must assemble, fund, and promote their campaigns to receive much attention by the media. For them, the purpose of the invisible primary is to earn support from their party. This support can be financial, but it can also take the form of endorsements, name recognition, access to fundraising networks, and volunteer labor. These things are crucial for any candidate who hopes to survive fifty states' worth of primaries and caucuses.

Winning the invisible primary, however, comes with some downsides. The victor must balance allegiance to specific, interest group–approved issues with a popularly supported agenda. And if the victor makes it to the White House, the party coalitions that endorsed and contributed to the campaign will expect a return on their investment and "demand policy responses to accompany their support."[37]

How, then, does the party finally choose a winner of the invisible primary? There is no concrete decision-making process. No ballots are completed, nor is there an official list of organizations involved. Sometimes the results of the invisible primary seem obvious from the beginning. Before the 2016 Democratic primary, few party insiders doubted that Hillary Clinton would be their nominee. Making room for Clinton, Democrats like Joe Biden refused to run.[38] Other times, the results are not so obvious. Though some voices are more influential than others, the authors of *The Party Decides* note that "anyone can join [the invisible primary] simply by paying attention, attending party gatherings, and chiming in."[39] Put simply, the invisible primary is a time of competitive, cacophonous communication that ultimately produces a winner. Unless, of course, it does not.

AN EXCEPTION TO THE INVISIBLE PRIMARY

Donald Trump's ability to win the Republican Party nomination for president, and then to emerge triumphant in the general election to follow, defied conventional understandings of electoral dynamics, very much including those involving the invisible primary. Staking out ground as a populist insurgent in a field crowded with Republican Party stalwarts,

Trump managed to captivate the imaginations of a significant portion of the primary electorate without garnering much support at all from party elites, newspaper editors, or wealthy donors. As it turned out, he didn't need to. Voters flocked to his rallies and the media fixated on his every statement, propelling the firebrand to the top of the ticket and then to the presidency—and leaving entire classes of political pundits and party officials utterly flummoxed in his wake.

How is it possible that Trump won the Republican nomination? Part of the answer surely involves the media. Trump did not need money to transfix the gaggle of reporters that followed him. Throughout this period, its appetite for more stories on the freewheeling, plain-speaking candidate seemed insatiable. In nearly every week between November 2015 and April 2016, the height of caucus and primary season, over 50 percent of cable news stories on the Republican race featured Trump. He also received more coverage than any other Republican candidate in print and online news stories.[40]

Besides the media, however, another factor worked in Trump's favor: the GOP's failure to unify behind one of his opponents. As was mentioned earlier, party leadership can successfully choose its nominee only insofar as its efforts are coordinated. And unlike invisible primaries of the past, the GOP in 2016 refused to take a clear stance in support of another candidate. Trump took advantage of this indecision—riding a wave from the media's sideshow attraction to the Republican convention, and eventually to the White House. Meanwhile, one of the authors of *The Party Decides* published an op-ed in which he pondered why the GOP "had barely taken any action" despite their apparent distaste for Trump and concluded that, whatever the reason, "this year's election has not followed our script."[41]

5.4 Campaign Spending

Fundraising constitutes a crucial component of any successful presidential campaign. Especially during the primary election, money helps candidates build national exposure and endear themselves to party elites. But candidates must be careful about the amount of money they accept and from whom; for much like the other elements of primary elections discussed in this chapter, campaign finance is governed by legal rules and ethical standards.

These rules track the steady rise in presidential campaign expenditures and have occupied a larger share of our political discourse in recent years, with some arguing that we must "get big money out of politics." However feasible this demand may (or may not) be, it comes from a place of genuine concern: Who picks the presidential nominees? The majority of voters, or a handful of wealthy campaign contributors?

In this section, we first question whether these concerns are overblown—that is, whether money actually determines who becomes a party's nominee. Seeing that it most certainly does, we then examine how a single Supreme Court decision, ***Citizens United v. Federal Election Commission***,[42] can transform the role of money in how we pick the president.

5.4.1 Money Matters

Randall Adkins and Andrew Dowdle coined the term "money primary" to describe the fundraising battle that takes place between presidential contenders before the primary season officially begins.[43] Because corporations are forbidden by law from contributing directly to presidential candidates, the bulk of these fundraising efforts focus on individual donors. Under the most recent amendments to the 1974 Federal Election Campaign Act (FECA),* individuals can contribute up to $2,900 per candidate in each election cycle.[44] But as Adkins and Dowdle point out—and as figure 5.8 demonstrates—these seemingly paltry sums add up quickly.

Adkins and Dowdle find that most fundraising occurs before the actual primary season, and the candidate who wins this early competition usually attains the nomination. From 2008 to 2016, almost all of the presidential primary victors raised the most money. John McCain, Mitt Romney, Barack Obama (twice over), and Hillary Clinton (in 2016) all outraised the rest of the field in their contests. In 2016, Donald Trump defied this trend, and at certain points in the 2020 campaign, Joe Biden was similarly outspent by his rivals. But these two are unlikely the start of a new trend; after all, nearly 80 percent of contested primaries end with a victory for the candidate who raised the most money.[45]

Does money *cause* political success, or does it merely accompany its incidence? As it turns out, the question is exceedingly difficult to answer. Though the two are definitely correlated, it could simply be that more popular candidates attract more donations. Thus, money might be the result of candidate quality, not the cause. Another possibility is that high-dollar donors, seeking premier access to officeholders, withhold their donations until a clear front-runner emerges. Again, in this scenario, candidate success would be responsible for successful fundraising, not the other way around.

To disentangle cause from effect, it is useful to begin by examining how and why campaigns spend money. The first and most obvious reason is to buy things. Campaigns spend large sums on offices, full-time staff, transportation, printing, focus groups, social media, advertising, and more. Money also allows candidates to build a "ground game," or person-to-person campaigning that engages volunteers, reaches out to individual voters, and establishes a presence in local communities.

Scholars have long struggled to prove the benefits of such investments. For example, in the 2020 Democratic primary, over one billion dollars was spent on advertising alone. One

---

* Under the original statute, the FECA required strict disclosure of the sources of campaign contributions, placed restrictions on candidates' ability to use their personal finances in an election campaign, and founded the Federal Election Commission to monitor campaigns' compliance with these laws. The most consequential facet of these laws was their regulation of political advertising—specifically, what types of advertisements could be financed with money raised under FECA's auspices. Among the most notable FECA restrictions, meanwhile, were limits on individual contributions: individuals could donate no more than $1,000 to a candidate per election (adding up to a total of $2,000 per campaign cycle—$1,000 for the primary season, which FECA considers a separate election, and $1,000 for the general election) and up to $20,000 to a political party per year, with yearly political contributions limited to a total of $25,000.

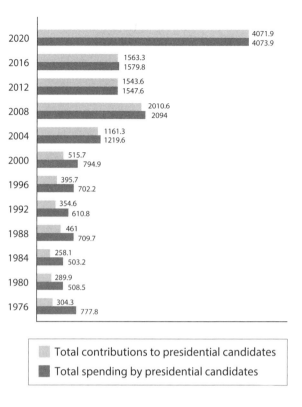

FIGURE 5.8. Fundraising for presidential elections, 1976–2020. Presidential elections have grown more and more extravagant in recent years, as candidates note the apparent relationship between fundraising and electoral success. Note: Spending and contributions in the figure are in 2020 dollars. *Source:* Center for Responsive Politics and the Federal Election Commission. Data from 1976 to 2016 available at https://www.statista.com/statistics/216793/fundraising-and -spending-in-us-presidential-elections/; data from 2020 can be found at https://www.fec.gov /updates/statistical-summary-21-month-campaign-activity-2019–2020-election-cycle/.

would assume that advertisements help persuade voters and boost candidates' name recognition, especially during primaries, when voters are still beginning to form opinions about the field.[46] But in one of the most optimistic studies about the effects of advertising, Yale University's Alan Gerber found that ads boost an incumbent's standing in the polls by only a few percentage points—until the following week, when the effects disappear entirely.[47]

A second reason campaigns fundraise, separate from what money can buy, is because of the signal it sends about the candidate's viability.[48] Before campaigns purchase their first TV spots or reveal their professionally designed logos, candidates with large war chests gain media attention. Meanwhile, those who struggle to fundraise are not considered serious. Voters typically have limited information with which to distinguish primary candidates, so fundraising can be a powerful tool to communicate legitimacy.

Candidates recognize the symbolic value of strong fundraising numbers and seek to broadcast them at every opportunity. In the 2016 and 2020 primaries, for example, Senator

Bernie Sanders set records for his ability to collect donations from working-class voters. Between October 2015 and January 2016, he pulled in no less than $50 million in small donations; over the 2020 election cycle small donations made up over 53 percent of his campaign finances, for a total of $114,813,781.[49] During every rally, Sanders made sure to emphasize these numbers, often asking the audience, "Anyone know what our average contribution is? That's right. Twenty-seven dollars."[50]

Voters are not the only ones who pick up on these signals. Party elites, too, pay close attention to candidates' fundraising totals. More than most, they want to ensure that the party's future leader can direct donors to down-ballot races. It is not surprising, therefore, that they have reserved certain privileges for candidates who can fundraise. In the 2020 Democratic primary, for example, candidates were denied entrance to the televised debates unless they met thresholds for the amount of money raised and the number of individual donors who contributed.*

Notably, this version of the "money primary" sounds a lot like the "invisible primary" we discussed in section 5.3.2. Most money is raised before the primary season formally begins, and it matters insofar as it curries favor among those who can influence election outcomes. An alternative story involves the logic and momentum and the early state advantage, which were discussed in section 5.3.1. By this account, early fundraising success translates into more money for advertising and staff, which in turn attracts more money, as success builds on itself until a winner is determined.

Whatever the precise relationship between money and success may be, the former undeniably contributes to the latter. Indeed, money matters. But how and why it matters depends entirely on the institutions that decide not just how much candidates can take in but how they can spend it. In the next section, we look at how a single change to campaign finance rules, handed down by the Supreme Court, can drastically affect the influence of money—and everyday voters—in politics.

5.4.2 Citizens United v. FEC (2010)

In 2008, Democratic contestants Hillary Clinton, John Edwards, and Barack Obama together spent more than $20 million on advertising in Iowa; Republican candidate Mitt Romney alone spent more than $7 million. In 2012, however, candidates' direct spending on advertising plummeted in Iowa. Collectively, the candidates for the Republican

---

* For the first debate, candidates either needed to reach 1 percent support in three valid polls or attain 65,000 unique donors, with at least 200 in twenty different states. By the seventh debate, candidates needed to pass both the polling requirement (5 percent support in four approved national polls or 7 percent support in two approved early state polls) and the fundraising requirement (225,000 unique donors with at least 1,000 in twenty different states). Zach Montellaro, "Here Are the Qualifications for the First 2020 Democratic Debates," POLITICO, May 9, 2019, https://www.politico.com/story/2019/05/09/2020-democratic -candidates-debate-qualifications-1305150; Madeleine Carlisle, "6 Democratic Candidates Will Face Off in the Last Debate before the Iowa Caucuses Tonight: Here's What to Know," Time, January 12, 2020, https://time .com/5760818/january-democratic-debate/.

nomination spent only slightly more than $10 million, and Romney—the big spender in 2008—spent less than $2 million. The cause of this decline had little to do either with the individual proclivities of the candidates or with a voter backlash against paid advertising. Rather, this change in spending patterns was the result of a landmark Supreme Court ruling.

Citizens United centered on a key provision of the 2002 **Bipartisan Campaign Reform Act**, known colloquially as McCain-Feingold. Among other regulations on the use of **soft money**—spending and contributions that are not directed to the campaign of a specific candidate—McCain-Feingold prohibited corporations from broadcasting communications that mention the name of a political candidate within thirty days of a primary election or within sixty days of a general election.

In 2008, Citizens United, a conservative nonprofit organization, produced a film that criticized Democratic candidate Hillary Clinton, but McCain-Feingold prohibited Citizens United from airing it. Citizens United challenged McCain-Feingold, and in a landmark 5–4 decision, the Supreme Court ruled in its favor. Justice Anthony Kennedy wrote the majority opinion, in which he argued that the First Amendment "prohibits Congress from fining or jailing citizens, or associations of citizens, for simply engaging in political speech." In handing down its decision, the Court ruled that there was no constitutional basis for distinguishing the rights of individuals from the rights of collections of individuals (such as corporations or unions or, for that matter, commercial filmmakers) when it comes to political expression.

As a result of the ruling, an altogether new type of fundraising institution came onto the political scene: the **super PAC**. Unlike the more traditional **political action committee (PAC)**, a super PAC is permitted to raise unlimited sums of money from individuals and from corporations, unions, and associations. Though super PACs must report their donors, they have greater flexibility in doing so than traditional PACs (which must report donors monthly). As long as a super PAC abstains from making any direct contributions to political candidates or from coordinating its activities with any candidate, it can spend any amount of money in either the primary season or the general election.

The early effects of *Citizens United* on presidential politics could be seen in 2012, particularly among Republicans. Harold Simmons, a banking mogul, and Sheldon Adelson, an owner of casinos, each donated $20 million to Crossroads GPS, a super PAC that spent around $160 million on behalf of Republican candidates in the 2012 race. David and Charles Koch, owners of the world's largest private chemical company and founders of another conservative super PAC, Americans for Prosperity, spent $40 million for Republicans and Republican causes in that race. These contributions alone nearly equaled the total of all donations given by individual contributors to John McCain, the eventual Republican nominee in 2008. (For more about the *Citizens United* decision and its effect on the 2012 Republican primary races, see this chapter's Thinking Institutionally feature.)

Institutional changes to campaign finance law, however, did not end with the ruling handed down in *Citizens United*. In 2014, *McCutcheon v. Federal Election Commission*

TABLE 5.2. Pre-Convention Individual Contributions to Presidential Candidates (in millions), 2012–2020

2012 Candidates		2016 Candidates		2020 Candidates	
Barack Obama	$341.31	Hillary Clinton	$250.69	Joe Biden	$390.21
Mitt Romney	$198.55	Bernie Sanders	$231.82	Donald Trump	$231.46
Ron Paul	$39.93	Ted Cruz	$92.04	Bernie Sanders	$202.55
Newt Gingrich	$24.00	Ben Carson	$63.46	Elizabeth Warren	$155.89
Rick Santorum	$22.46	Donald Trump	$50.10	Pete Buttigieg	$102.89
Herman Cain	$16.02	Marco Rubio	$45.36	Amy Klobuchar	$49.88
Michele Bachmann	$7.46	Jeb Bush	$33.59	Andrew Yang	$41.19
Timothy Pawlenty	$5.68	John Kasich	$19.14	Kamala Harris	$39.53
Jon Huntsman	$3.73	Carly Fiorina	$12.05	Cory Booker	$22.81
Buddy Roemer	$0.37	Rand Paul	$10.23	Beto O'Rourke	$18.45

Note: The candidate who raises the most individual contributions during the primary season regularly emerges as the party's nominee. In the last several presidential races, these amounts ran into the hundreds of millions of dollars. The clear exception to this pattern, however, was the 2016 primary election, when the winning Republican candidate raised considerably less in individual contributions than his main competitors.
Source: Federal Election Commission.

(FEC)[51] altered the aggregate limits on campaign donations. Although the $2,900 cap on individual contributions, per candidate, per election cycle, remained in place, *McCutcheon* altered the total amount an individual could give directly to candidates and to committees. Arguing that aggregate limits on campaign donations violate the First Amendment, the Court ruled, by a 5–4 margin, to end them.

Chief Justice Roberts, who authored the majority opinion in *McCutcheon*, reasoned that caps constrain "an individual's right to participate in the public debate through political expression and political association." As he saw it, if newspapers could endorse however many candidates they like, individuals ought to have the right to do the same.[52] Opponents of the ruling fear that the *McCutcheon* decision, coupled with *Citizens United*, opens the floodgates on campaign spending, privileging the voices of the wealthy at the expense of average citizens. Indeed, precisely these concerns became main talking points during Bernie Sanders's campaign for the 2016 Democratic nomination for president.

Citizens United, it bears noting, was hardly the first effort by the federal judiciary to relax limits on campaign spending. In 2007, in *Federal Election Commission v. Wisconsin Right to Life, Inc.*,[53] the Supreme Court established broad exemptions to the restrictions on "electioneering communications," which had been erected by the Bipartisan Campaign Reform Act (BCRA). In its ruling, the Court replaced the BCRA standard with one in which "an ad is the functional equivalent of express advocacy only if the ad is susceptible of no reasonable interpretation other than as an appeal to vote for or against a specific candidate."

In other words, the 2007 ruling meant that outside groups could now run "issue ads"—which mention a politician's stance on an issue without expressly advocating support or opposition—in the weeks leading up to an election. Until *Citizens United*, it was still illegal to run an election-time ad with the words, "Senator X opposes free speech. Vote against Senator X." Thanks to *FEC v. Wisconsin Right to Life*, however, groups could sponsor a nearly identical ad with the words, "Senator X opposes free speech. Call Senator X to tell him how you feel."

Thinking Institutionally: The Unintended Consequences of Campaign Finance

Simple changes to the rules of politics can have wide-ranging and unintended consequences; and changes to the rules governing campaign spending are no different. In its decision to remove limits on certain kinds of campaign donations in *Citizens United v. FEC*, the Supreme Court made much of the imperatives of free political speech, but the justices did not anticipate the effects of their ruling on presidential campaigns.

Some of these effects can be seen in the realm of campaign advertising. Although all political candidates publicly profess disdain for negative advertising, privately they recognize its utility. In the past, however, candidates always had to weigh the immediate benefits of negative advertising against the public relations challenges associated with repeatedly launching nasty attacks on the competition. No longer. Thanks to *Citizens United v. FEC*, candidates can let super PACs assume the messy business of negative assaults.

In the spring of 2012, when Republican candidates were in the midst of their fight for the presidential nomination, one study found that more than three-quarters of the ads produced by super PACs in support of the race's four major candidates were negative, compared with just over half directly aired by the campaigns for the same four candidates. A whopping 92 percent of the ads produced by the Romney-supporting super PAC Restore Our Future were negative.[54] During the general election campaign, Obama's chief political strategist, David Axelrod, pointed to the free-spending ways of super PACs as an explanation for how negative the race between the president and his challenger had turned.[55]

Super PACs may have altered the dynamics of presidential advertising campaigns in yet another way by affecting the timing of ad placements. Research shows that last-minute ads are generally more effective than ads broadcast earlier in a campaign.[56] Should a candidate stand to benefit from a late media blitz, super PACs may have the resources, when individual contributors do not, to fund advertising that may make the difference on Election Day.

The advent of super PACs may have yet farther-reaching effects on presidential campaigns. Since super PACs allow individuals and corporations to donate large sums—often in the millions of dollars—in support for a candidate, their proliferation reduces the incentive for candidates to solicit small individual contributions. In the 2012 election cycle, many super PACs, such as Winning Our Future (pro-Newt Gingrich), Restore Our Future (pro-Romney), and Endorse Liberty (pro-Ron Paul),

FIGURE 5.9. In *Citizens United v. FEC*, the Supreme Court opened up altogether new ways for corporations to finance political campaigns. In so doing, some charged, the Court undermined the most basic principles of democratic representation. Copyright 2012 Mike Flinn. Reproduced with permission.

were explicitly connected to individual candidates. Super PACs figured just as prominently in the 2016 election. Great America PAC (pro-Trump), Priorities USA Action (pro-Clinton), and Right to Rise USA (pro-Bush) all raised tens of millions of dollars in service of one favored candidate. And though no super PAC supported Bernie Sanders, the upstart challenger for the Democratic nomination went out of his way to excoriate their influence on American politics. As other candidates shifted their attention from soliciting individual contributions to courting powerful donors to super PACs, Sanders opined that the voices of wealthy individuals and corporations overwhelmed those of ordinary citizens—and our democracy was worse for it.

5.5 Selecting a Running Mate

Once the presidential nominees have been chosen, the first order of business, seen by many as the single most anticipated event of the post-primary campaign season, is the selection of a vice-presidential candidate. Speculation about the short list comes fast and furious, replacing, for a time, the interparty "horse-race" coverage that has come to dominate discussions about the race for the presidential nomination. These, though, are distinctive features of only contemporary presidential elections.

In the early years of the Republic, electors of the Electoral College cast votes for two candidates, with the candidate receiving the second-most electoral votes automatically becoming vice president. The problem with this arrangement, of course, was that electors could not readily coordinate on the selection of president and vice president.* The Twelfth Amendment, ratified in 1804, modifies the operation of the Electoral College so that electors cast separate votes for president and vice president.

In the years leading up to McGovern-Fraser, running mates were usually announced at the convention, shortly after the presidential nominee was chosen. Presidential nominees often selected running mates at the last minute, and chiefly for their ability to win support from party elites. At an uncertain convention, the VP selection was a valuable tool for candidates who wanted to secure their majorities. In the words of one presidency scholar, the vice presidency was "an invaluable piece of bait that could be used to attract last-minute support from favorite sons, second-tier candidates, interest-group representatives, and state party leaders."[57]

Today, presidential nominees have much more freedom (and time) in how they pick their running mates. Given that nominees are now known long before the convention, and last-minute convention dealings no longer change the election results, nominees can choose a vice president they feel is most prepared to help them govern—or even step into the role of president if necessary.[58] Such was the motivation behind Bush's selection of Dick Cheney in 2000. Cheney was the quintessential insider, having served as chief of staff under President Ford, as a member of Congress from Wyoming, and as secretary of defense under George H. W. Bush. Similarly, the selection of Joe Biden helped Obama assemble a team of well-placed Washington insiders who could effectively manage the many challenges that would face the winner of the 2008 election.

Governing experience, however, is not the only consideration when picking a running mate. Nominees also have an eye toward the general election, the weaknesses of their campaign, and—though it may not be as powerful a force as it once was—the preferences of party insiders.

5.5.1 Balancing the Ticket

The principal consideration when selecting a running mate is balancing the ticket. Sometimes regional balance is required—a northerner, for example, might choose a southerner. Sometimes nominees seek balance with respect to energy or youthfulness. Sometimes a

---

*And soon enough, this flaw presented tangible problems. In the election of 1800, Federalists John Adams and Charles Pinckney and Democratic-Republicans Thomas Jefferson and Aaron Burr were all candidates for executive office. When the Electoral College convened, each Democratic-Republican elector planned to cast one vote for Jefferson and one vote for Burr. To ensure a Jefferson victory, one elector was instructed not to cast one of his votes for Burr. That elector failed to obey, and the election resulted in a tie between Jefferson and Burr, each credited with seventy-three electoral votes. The House of Representatives stepped in and settled the presidency on Jefferson, with Burr named his vice president.

moderate might pick an ideological extremist; as this, too, may afford some measure of balance. Balance can take many forms, but ultimately, it means choosing a running mate who will complement—some might say *compensate for*—specific qualities of the presidential candidate. On an ideally balanced ticket, the running mate can appeal to audiences who have misgivings about the presidential candidate.

It isn't difficult to find historical examples of ticket balancing. In 1960 and 1988, the Democratic nominees for president—Massachusetts senator John F. Kennedy and Massachusetts governor Michael Dukakis, respectively—chose running mates from Texas, a strong attempt at geographical balance. In 1988 (George H. W. Bush), 2008 (John McCain), and 2012 (Mitt Romney), the Republican nominees were universally perceived to lack energy on the campaign trail. By selecting young and charismatic running mates (Dan Quayle in 1988, Sarah Palin in 2008, Paul Ryan in 2012), the three nominees added energy to the ticket and generated positive press coverage for their unconventional picks.[59]

Whatever form it might take, ticket balancing is far more than a matter of preference. It almost always serves to offset a candidate's weaknesses in some way or assist a candidate's transition into the White House. When Democratic nominee Barack Obama, often criticized for his lack of foreign policy experience, chose Joe Biden as his running mate in 2008, his campaign gained much needed gravitas, as he was much younger and less experienced than his Republican opponent. (Biden was widely regarded as one of the Senate's top foreign policy experts at the time.)

One of the most important forms of ticket balancing concerns ideology. Consider, for example, Republican nominee Donald Trump. In the decades prior to running for president, Trump had staked out public positions on gay marriage, abortion, and other issues that ran contrary to Republican orthodoxy. In the summer of 2016, therefore, he attempted to allay concerns within his party about his wayward ideological commitments by appointing Mike Pence, whose conservative credentials were unimpeachable. A former conservative radio and television talk show host, Pence won the governorship of Indiana in 2012 and set promptly to work cutting taxes, affirming traditional notions of marriage, and expanding the rights of gun owners. In Pence, many conservatives found the assurance they needed in order to support Trump for the presidency, leading religiously conservative Republicans, a demographic that had expressed reluctance in the face of Trump's candidacy, to rally behind the newly balanced ticket.[60]

5.5.2 Battleground Magnates

When Hillary Clinton set about picking a running mate, she listed her top considerations as follows: "Number one, is this a person who could be president literally tomorrow? Secondly, is this a person that I could work with day in and day out . . . to serve our country? And third, can this person help me win?"[61] With Senator Tim Kaine of Virginia, Clinton believed she could answer all three questions affirmatively.

Before joining Clinton, Kaine had won every election in which he had ever run. He had an affable, folksy demeanor. But more importantly, in his home state of Virginia, a key battleground in the upcoming election, he was widely adored. Kaine was not the first running mate chosen (at least in part) because of a belief that he could deliver his home state in the general election. Just four years earlier, it was thought that Romney's selection of Paul Ryan—a representative from Wisconsin—could hand the swing state to Republicans.

But Romney lost Wisconsin. And while Clinton did in fact win Virginia, she did so by the narrowest of margins—claiming just 49.7 percent of the popular vote statewide. What went wrong? As it turns out, most analyses find that a running mate's home-state advantage lies somewhere between minute and zero.[62] It is no coincidence, therefore, that many recent VP picks did not hail from a swing state. Joe Biden, Sarah Palin, Mike Pence, and Kamala Harris all came from reliably Democratic or Republican strongholds. Thus, while nominees may still sometimes pick running mates from battleground states, home-state advantage is likely only one of several factors leading to such a decision.

5.5.3 Descriptive Representation

In the run-up to the 2020 election, then-candidate Joe Biden publicly voiced his commitment to selecting a woman as his vice-presidential running mate. Speaking toward the tail end of the Democratic primary season, at the CNN-Univision debate in DC, Biden stated that "if I'm elected president, my Cabinet, my administration will look like the country, and I commit that I will, in fact . . . pick a woman to be vice president."[63] Several months later, the Democratic Party nomination safely in his pocket, Biden expanded on that statement: "I am not committed to naming any (of the potential candidates), but the people I've named, and among them there are four Black women."[64]

In the end, Biden chose California senator Kamala Harris, a Black, Asian American woman. Harris was not the first woman selected for such a role. In 1984, Walter Mondale selected Congresswoman Geraldine Ferraro to be his running mate; and twenty-four years later, in 2008, John McCain chose Sarah Palin, the governor of Alaska.[65] Unlike these past choices, however, Biden's was forecasted far in advance. Combined with the sociopolitical backdrop of this announcement, this represented a significant appeal to descriptive representation (that is, representation not just of ideological but of gender and ethnic characteristics) and ultimately a boon to the Biden campaign.

Both internal (party) and external (national) circumstances factored into Biden's announcement and decision. Nationally, with the prominent coverage of the killing of Black men by police and "Black Lives Matter" rallies occurring all across the nation, public outcries against structural racism and police violence occupied significant space on the political, media, and social landscapes.[66] Beyond the astuteness of making this choice alongside the present social justice backdrop, Biden himself had earned liberal scorn for certain policy choices and votes he had made while a senator. For example, in 1994 he supported crime legislation leading to harsher sentencing along racial lines, a significant weakness for the Biden platform in terms of winning over more progressive voters.[67]

In choosing Kamala Harris as his running mate, Biden both acknowledged and shored up some of his campaign's political liabilities. Even before selecting Harris, however, his vocal commitment to descriptive representation sent a signal to his party about the kind of administration he wanted to lead: one in which inclusivity and diversity mattered, and the concerns of his party's most liberal members would have a home.

Conclusion

While a president's term is four years, presidential campaigns have become a nearly permanent feature of the political landscape. As soon as newly elected presidents take office, talk turns to their replacements: Who will run? What chance do they have of winning? Answers to these questions, it turns out, depend on the set of electoral rules under which candidates compete.

When it comes to picking the president, not every vote counts equally. Though early primaries and caucuses tend to be in smaller states with fewer delegates at stake, voters in these states tend to matter a lot more than their counterparts in later states. Additionally, wealthy voters can contribute money and sponsor advertisements, which in turn elevate their preferred candidates in the eyes of the influential party establishment.

For candidates, the path to the party's nomination runs through all of these groups. It is not enough to be charismatic or well-liked by a large number of voters; winning candidates must often be charismatic, well-liked, *and* preferred by the individuals who have the most say over the primary process. Only then can they clinch their party's nomination.

Key Terms

congressional caucuses	caucuses
King Caucus	retail politics
nominating convention	superdelegates
delegates	momentum
party bosses	Super Tuesday
direct primary	*Citizens United v. Federal Election Commission*
McGovern-Fraser Commission	Bipartisan Campaign Reform Act
open election	soft money
open primary	super PAC
closed primary	political action committee (PAC)

Questions for Discussion

1. Historically, what political forces contributed most to the emergence of the modern presidential primary system?

2. In what ways has the emergence of direct primaries increased the likelihood that presidential candidates will represent the broad interests of the American people? In what ways have direct primaries diminished this likelihood?

3. Has the emergence of super PACs accentuated or reduced the significance of momentum in the primary process?

4. Did institutional rules that stifled the voices of certain segments of the Democratic Party contribute to the unrest at the 1968 nominating convention in Chicago, or, in your view, were larger disagreements about the Vietnam War primarily responsible?

5. The Supreme Court has reaffirmed the principle that money constitutes a form of speech, no matter who (or what) delivers it. If we accept this argument, does it necessarily follow that more money improves public deliberations about who should serve as president?

Suggested Readings

Bartels, Larry. *Presidential Primaries and the Dynamics of Public Choice.* Princeton: Princeton University Press, 1988.

Cohen, Marty, David Karol, Hans Noel, and John Zaller. *The Party Decides: Presidential Nominations Before and After Reform.* Chicago: University of Chicago Press, 2009.

Cowan, Geoffrey. *Let the People Rule: Theodore Roosevelt and the Birth of the Presidential Primary.* New York: W. W. Norton, 2016.

Edwards, George C. *Why the Electoral College Is Bad for America.* 3rd ed. New Haven: Yale University Press, 2019.

Kamarck, Elaine. *Primary Politics: Everything You Need to Know about How America Nominates Its Presidential Candidates.* 3rd ed. Washington, DC: Brookings Institution Press, 2018.

Norrander, Barbara. *The Imperfect Primary: Oddities, Biases, and Strengths of U.S. Presidential Nomination Politics.* 3rd ed. New York: Routledge, 2019.

Notes

1. For more on the controversial 1824 election, see Jeffrey A. Jenkins and Brian R. Sala, "The Spatial Theory of Voting and the Presidential Election of 1824," *American Journal of Political Science* 42, no. 4 (1998): 1157–79.

2. For a history of party conventions from 1831 to the present, see *National Party Conventions, 1831–2008* (Washington, DC: Congressional Quarterly Press, 2009).

3. For more on how the McGovern-Fraser reforms addressed the representative quality of party nominating conventions, see Austin Ranney, "Turnout and Representation in Presidential Primary Elections," *American Political Science Review* 66, no. 1 (1972): 21–37.

4. For an extended discussion of twentieth-century party reforms, see Austin Ranney, *Curing the Mischiefs of Faction: Party Reform in America* (Berkeley: University of California Press, 1975).

5. For fuller discussions of the events that contributed to the riots during the 1968 Democratic convention, see David Farber, *Chicago '68* (Chicago: University of Chicago Press, 1988); and Frank Kusch, *Battleground Chicago: The Police and the 1968 Democratic National Convention* (Chicago: University of Chicago Press, 2008).

6. For a full account of the 1968 presidential election, see Theodore H. White, *The Making of the President 1968* (New York: HarperCollins College Publishers, 2010).

7. The earliest to announce, Sen. Ted Cruz (R-TX), did so in March 2015.

8. Gardiner Harris, "Obama, in Wisconsin, Takes on Scott Walker," *New York Times*, July 3, 2015, A.12.

9. "2020 Democratic Party Debate Schedule," Election Central, https://www.uspresidentialelectionnews .com/2020-debate-schedule/2020-democratic-debate-schedule/.

10. For more on how the public regards an incumbent president and the conditions that lead potential challengers to enter the race, see Thomas M. Holbrook, "Campaigns, National Conditions, and U.S. Presidential Elections," *American Journal of Political Science* 38, no. 4 (1994): 973–98, and Arthur H. Miller and Martin P. Wattenberg, "Throwing the Rascals Out: Policy and Performance Evaluations of Presidential Candidates, 1952–1980," *American Political Science Review* 79, no. 2 (1985): 359–72. For more on the relationship between the economy and election outcomes, see Morris P. Fiorina, "Economic Retrospective Voting in American National Elections: A Micro-Analysis," *American Journal of Political Science* 22, no. 2 (1978): 426–43; and Gerald H. Kramer, "Short-Term Fluctuations in U.S. Voting Behavior, 1896–1964," *American Political Science Review* 65, no. 1 (1971): 131–43. For more on how electoral incentives relate to presidential policymaking, see Larry M. Bartels, *Unequal Democracy: The Political Economy of the New Gilded Age* (Princeton: Princeton University Press, 2008), 98–126; William D. Nordhaus, "The Political Business Cycle," *Review of Economic Studies* 42 (1975): 169–90; and Edward R. Tufte, *Political Control of the Economy* (Princeton: Princeton University Press, 1978).

11. Amanda Zoch, "Elections 2020: Shifting from Caucuses to Primaries," National Conference of State Legislatures, February 13, 2020, https://www.ncsl.org/blog/2020/02/13/elections-2020-shifting-from -caucuses-to-primaries.aspx.

12. http://www.ncsbe.gov/ncsbe/voter-turnout.

13. Nathaniel Rakich, "Historic Turnout in 2020? Not So Far," *FiveThirtyEight*, March 17, 2020, https:// fivethirtyeight.com/features/historic-turnout-in-2020-not-so-far/.

14. For an interesting look at retail politics in the 1996 New Hampshire Republican primary, see Lynn Vavreck, Constantine J. Spiliotes, and Linda L. Fowler, "The Effects of Retail Politics in the New Hampshire Primary," *American Journal of Political Science* 46, no. 3 (2002): 595–610.

15. For more on the representativeness of presidential primary voters, see David W. Brady, Hahrie Han, and Jeremy C. Pope, "Primary Elections and Candidate Ideology: Out of Step with the Primary Electorate?" *Legislative Studies Quarterly* 32, no. 1 (2007): 79–105; John G. Geer, "Assessing the Representativeness of Electorates in Presidential Primaries," *American Journal of Political Science* 32, no. 4 (1988): 929–45; and Barbara Norrander, "Ideological Representativeness of Presidential Primary Voters," *American Journal of Political Science* 33, no. 3 (1989): 570–87. For more on how the rules that govern voter participation in primaries affect candidate selection, a topic not covered here, see Elisabeth R. Gerber and Rebecca B. Morton, "Primary Election Systems and Representation," *Journal of Law, Economics, and Organization* 14, no. 2 (1998): 304–24.

16. German Lopez, "Voter Turnout Surged in Super Tuesday States That Ditched Caucuses," *Vox*, March 4, 2020, https://www.vox.com/policy-and-politics/2020/3/4/21164591/super-tuesday-election-results-voter -turnout-caucus.

17. John Sides, Chris Tausanovitch, Lynn Vavreck, and Christopher Warshaw, "On the Representativeness of Primary Electorates," *British Journal of Political Science* 50, no. 2 (2018): 677–85.

18. For more on the 2008 Democratic delegate count and relationship between primary elections and the convention votes of unpledged delegates, see Josh M. Ryan, "Is the Democratic Party's Superdelegate System Unfair to Voters?" *Electoral Studies* 30, no. 4 (2011): 756–70.

19. "Live Election Results: New Hampshire Primaries 2020," *POLITICO*, https://web.archive.org/web /20200626233513if_/https://www.politico.com/2020-election/results/new-hampshire/.

20. For more on the consequences of delegate selection rules, see Stephen Ansolabehere and Gary King, "Measuring the Consequences of Delegate Selection Rules in Presidential Nominations," *Journal of Politics* 52, no. 2 (1990): 609–21.

21. John W. Soule and Wilma E. McGrath, "A Comparative Study of Presidential Nominating Conventions: The Democrats 1968 and 1972," *American Journal of Political Science* 19, no. 3 (1975): 501–17.

22. Sarah Frostenson, "Half of the Democratic Delegates Were People of Color: For Republicans, It Was Only 6%," *Vox*, July 29, 2020, https://www.vox.com/2016/7/29/12295830/republican-democratic-delegates-diversity-nonwhite.

23. For more statistics on the composition of these electorates, see "Iowa Caucus: Who Different Groups Supported," *New York Times*, https://www.nytimes.com/interactive/2020/02/03/us/elections/results-iowa-caucus-polls.html; "New Hampshire Exit Polls," CNN, https://www.cnn.com/election/2020/entrance-and-exit-polls/new-hampshire/democratic.

24. Classic explanations of the role of momentum include John A. Aldrich, "A Dynamic Model of Presidential Nomination Campaigns," *American Political Science Review* 74, no. 3 (1980): 651–69; and Larry Bartels, *Presidential Primaries and the Dynamics of Public Choice* (Princeton: Princeton University Press, 1988).

25. For a technical treatment of how momentum affects the dynamics of sequential elections, see Steven Callander, "Bandwagons and Momentum in Sequential Voting," *Review of Economic Studies* 74, no. 3 (2007): 653–84. For a less technical exposition, see Rebecca B. Morton and Kenneth C. Williams, *Learning by Voting: Sequential Choices in Presidential Primaries and Other Elections* (Ann Arbor: University of Michigan Press, 2001).

26. Bartels, *Presidential Primaries*, 4.

27. Katie Akin, "Historically, Do Iowa Caucus Winners Go on to Earn Their Party's Nomination, Become President?" *Des Moines Register*, January 5, 2020, https://www.desmoinesregister.com/story/news/elections/presidential/caucus/2020/01/05/do-iowa-caucus-winners-win-presidency-party-nomination-general-election/4410195002/.

28. David W. Chen, "New Jersey Moves to Hold Early Primary," *New York Times*, June 24, 2005, B.1.

29. Mike Haridopolos in Brendan Farrington, "Florida Primary Election 2012: State Broke Rules Again to Hold Early Contest," *Huffington Post*, January 31, 2012, http://www.huffingtonpost.com/2012/01/31/florida-primary-election-rules_n_1243879.html.

30. For a book-length treatment of this topic, see William G. Mayer and Andrew E. Busch, *The Front-Loading Problem in Presidential Nominations* (Washington, DC: Brookings Institute, 2004).

31. Domenico Montenaro, "4 Takeaways from Biden's Big Win in South Carolina," National Public Radio, March 1, 2020, https://www.npr.org/2020/03/01/810813892/4-takeaways-from-joe-bidens-big-win-in-south-carolina.

32. Lauren Leatherby and Sarah Almukhtar, "Democratic Delegate Count and Primary Elections Result 2020," *New York Times*, September 14, 2020, https://www.nytimes.com/interactive/2020/us/elections/delegate-count-primary-results.html.

33. "About the Democratic Party," Democratic National Committee, https://democrats.org/who-we-are/about-the-democratic-party.

34. Howard Reiter, *Selecting the President: The Nomination Process in Transition* (Philadelphia: University of Pennsylvania Press, 1985).

35. Marty Cohen et al., *The Party Decides: Presidential Nominations Before and After Reform* (Chicago: University of Chicago Press, 2008).

36. Cohen et al., *The Party Decides*.

37. Bryon E. Shafer, *Bifurcated Politics: The Evolution and Reform of the National Party Convention* (Cambridge, MA: Harvard University Press, 1988).

38. Amy Chozick and Maggie Haberman, "Hillary Clinton Camp Is Making Moves to Check Joe Biden," *New York Times*, October 1, 2015, A.1.

39. Cohen et al., *The Party Decides*.

40. Nicholas Confessore and Karen Yourish, "$2 Billion Worth of Free Media for Donald Trump," *New York Times*, March 15, 2017, https://www.nytimes.com/2016/03/16/upshot/measuring-donald-trumps-mammoth-advantage-in-free-media.html?searchResultPosition=1; John Sides and Kalev Leetaru, "A Deep Dive into the News Media's Role in the Rise of Donald J. Trump," *Washington Post*, June 24, 2016, https://www.washingtonpost.com/news/monkey-cage/wp/2016/06/24/a-deep-dive-into-the-news-medias-role-in-the-rise-of-donald-j-trump/.

41. Hans Noel, "Why Can't the G.O.P. Stop Trump?" *New York Times*, March 1, 2016, https://www.nytimes.com/2016/03/01/opinion/campaign-stops/why-cant-the-gop-stop-trump.html.

42. 558 U.S. 310.

43. Randall E. Adkins and Andrew J. Dowdle, "The Money Primary: What Influences the Outcome of Pre-Primary Presidential Nomination Fundraising?" *Presidential Studies Quarterly* 32, no. 2 (2002): 256–75.

44. For a complete and current listing of contribution limits, see "The FEC and the Federal Campaign Finance Law," Federal Elections Commission, http://www.fec.gov/pages/brochures/fecfeca.shtml.

45. Adam Bonica, "Professional Networks, Early Fundraising, and Electoral Success," *Election Law Journal: Rules, Politics, and Policy* 16, no. 1 (2017): 153–71.

46. Michael Pfau et al., "Influence of Communication during the Distant Phase of the 1996 Republican Presidential Primary Campaign," *Journal of Communication* 47, no. 4 (1997): 6–26.

47. Alan S. Gerber et al., "How Large and Long-lasting Are the Persuasive Effects of Televised Campaign Ads? Results from a Randomized Field Experiment," *American Political Science Review* 105, no. 1 (2011): 135–50.

48. James J. Feigenbaum and Cameron A. Shelton, "The Vicious Cycle: Fundraising and Perceived Viability in US Presidential Primaries," *Quarterly Journal of Political Science* 8, no. 1 (2012): 1–40.

49. "Summary Data for Bernie Sanders, 2020 Cycle," OpenSecrets, Center for Responsive Politics, https://www.opensecrets.org/2020-presidential-race/bernie-sanders/candidate?id=N00000528.

50. Philip Bump, "Bernie Sanders Keeps Saying His Average Donation Is $27, but His Own Numbers Contradict That," *Washington Post*, April 29, 2019, https://www.washingtonpost.com/news/the-fix/wp/2016/04/18/bernie-sanders-keeps-saying-his-average-donation-is-27-but-it-really-isnt/.

51. 572 U.S. 185.

52. Adam Liptak, "Supreme Court Strikes Down Overall Political Donation Cap," *New York Times*, April 3, 2014, A.1.

53. 551 U.S. 449.

54. Felicia Sonmez, "Negative Ads: Is It the Campaigns, or the Super PACs?" *Washington Post*, March 22, 2012, http://www.washingtonpost.com/blogs/post-politics/post/negative-ads-is-it-the-campaigns-or-the-super-pacs-thursdays-trail-mix/2012/03/22/gIQAOf8VTS_blog.html.

55. Olivier Knox, "David Axelrod: Romney, Super PACs to Blame for Campaign's 'Negative' Tone," ABC News, July 25, 2012, http://abcnews.go.com/Politics/OTUS/david-axelrod-romney-super-pacs-blame-campaigns-negative/story?id=16853325.

56. Gerber et al., "How Large and Long-lasting Are the Persuasive Effects of Televised Campaign Ads?"

57. William G. Mayer, *In Pursuit of the White House 2000: How We Choose Our Presidential Nominees* (New York: Chatham House, 2000), 346.

58. Mark Hiller and Douglas Kriner, "Institutional Change and the Dynamics of Vice Presidential Selection," *Presidential Studies Quarterly* 38, no. 3 (2008): 401–21.

59. For more on the strategic considerations presidential candidates use when selecting running mates, see Lee Sigelman and Paul J. Wahlbeck, "The 'Veepstakes': Strategic Choice in Presidential Running Mate Selection," *American Political Science Review* 91, no. 4 (1997): 855–64; and Hiller and Kriner, "Institutional Change and the Dynamics of Vice Presidential Selection."

60. McKay Coppins, "God's Plan for Mike Pence," *Atlantic Monthly* 321, no. 1 (2018): 44–53.

61. Chris Cillizza, "Everything You've Heard about Picking a Vice President Is Wrong," CNN, August 10, 2020, https://www.cnn.com/2020/08/10/politics/joe-biden-vp-pick-kamala-harris/index.html.

62. See, for example, Robert L. Dudley and Ronald B. Rapoport, "Vice-Presidential Candidates and the Home State Advantage: Playing Second Banana at Home and on the Road," *American Journal of Political Science* 33, no. 2 (1989): 537. See also Christopher J. Devine and Kyle C. Kopko, "Presidential versus Vice Presidential Home State Advantage: A Comparative Analysis of Electoral Significance, Causes, and Processes, 1884–2008," *Presidential Studies Quarterly* 43, no. 4 (2013): 814–38.

63. Kate Sullivan, "Biden Says He Will Pick Woman to Be His Vice President," CNN, March 15, 2020, https://www.cnn.com/2020/03/15/politics/joe-biden-woman-vice-president/index.html.

64. Kate Sullivan and Sarah Mucha, "Joe Biden Says He Is Considering Four Black Women to Be His Running Mate," CNN, July 21, 2020, https://www.cnn.com/2020/07/21/politics/joe-biden-four-black-women-vice-president/index.html.

65. Lila Thulin, "The Woman Who Paved the Way," *Smithsonian Magazine*, August 10, 2020, https://www.smithsonianmag.com/history/geraldine-ferraro-unprecedented-1984-campaign-vice-president-180975491/.

66. Michael Scherer and Jenna Johnson, "Joe Biden Pressed Again to Name a Black Woman as His Running Mate," *Washington Post*, August 10, 2020, https://www.washingtonpost.com/politics/joe-biden-pressed-again-to-name-a-black-woman-as-his-running-mate/2020/08/10/d383d786-db2d-11ea-8051-d5f887d73381_story.html.

67. Scherer and Johnson, "Joe Biden Pressed Again to Name a Black Woman as His Running Mate."

6

General Elections

AFTER THE NATIONAL PARTY CONVENTIONS—after the bright lights have turned off, the balloons have dropped, and the delegates have gone back to their hotel rooms—party nominees must move quickly and assuredly into the general election. There is no time to waste, as the timeline in figure 6.1 demonstrates. Unlike primaries, where candidates wait nearly a year before the first ballots are cast, the general election spans just over two months, beginning with the conventions and ending on Election Day in early November. Also unlike the primaries, candidates cannot rely on momentum in a few early states to propel them to victory. In the general election, Election Day happens just once—and it's win or lose.

For all the suspense and fanfare that surrounds general elections, it may surprise some readers that political scientists can predict the popular vote for president—very much including that of 2016—with remarkable accuracy months, even years, in advance.[1] In the words of Stuart Stevens, a senior Republican strategist who managed Mitt Romney's presidential bid in 2012, "the secret to success in political consulting is to work for candidates who were going to win anyway."[2]

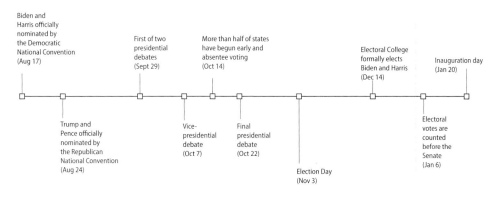

FIGURE 6.1. The 2020 general election. Party nominees have only a few short months to transform their campaigns—which had been tailored to the unique challenges of the primaries—into proper general election campaigns. If successful, their vote totals will be confirmed by the Electoral College, and they will be sworn in at the Capitol in January.

General elections are predictable because, in actuality, two factors play an outsized role in their outcomes: the composition of the electorate and the state of the economy. Though the specific policy positions articulated in any campaign may reflect the priorities of particular candidates, the ways in which candidates shape and revise these positions, the strategies they use to advance them, and their ultimate success and failure depend upon these fundamental forces of American politics.

6.1 Presidential Electorates

To become president, party nominees must appeal to a much larger and more ideologically diverse electorate than they encountered in the primary. But unlike the primary, candidates need not win over voters in every state. Institutional features of the Electoral College, in fact, result in campaigns heaping their limited resources on voters in just a handful of competitive states. And as the composition of the presidential electorate has changed over time—again, in response to changes in a host of voting rules—candidates have adjusted their platforms and appeals accordingly.

6.1.1 Tacking to the Ideological Middle

Having devoted the primaries to courting the party's faithful, presidential candidates must reach a broader national electorate in the general election. Because the typical voter in general elections is a great deal more conservative than the typical Democratic primary voter and a great deal more liberal than the typical Republican primary voter, candidates from both parties must move to the ideological middle just as soon as they secure their nominations.

The move to the general election can require nothing short of a transformation in candidate identity, and one that must be realized with a high degree of finesse. The required shifts—in tone, emphasis, and even policy—invariably incite criticism and, when not handled deftly, ridicule. Statements made during the primaries can haunt a candidate in the general election, where the challenge is not to establish liberal or conservative credentials but to appear in step with the mainstream. Mitt Romney in 2012 and Joe Biden in 2020, the last two challengers to incumbent presidents, were saddled with accusations of flip-flopping in the general election. In fact, however, given the rules that govern primaries and general elections, flip-flopping is better understood as an unavoidable consequence of the institutional presidency than as a character flaw of any given presidential candidate.

As one of the most centrist candidates among the Republicans running for the 2012 nomination, Romney had been under a great deal of pressure to establish authentically conservative credentials. Fighting it out with hardliners such as Michele Bachmann, who sought to brand the sitting president, Barack Obama, as a socialist, and Ron Paul, widely known for his staunch libertarian views on the economy and foreign affairs, Romney had swerved right during the primaries.

During the Republican primary debates, for example, Romney downplayed the obvious parallels between the health care reform that he had signed into law as governor of Massachusetts and Obamacare. In another appeal to the party base, Romney went on the offensive on the issue of immigration: he accused Texas governor Rick Perry of making Texas a "magnet" for undocumented immigrants by allowing them to receive in-state tuition at public universities,[3] and he suggested that the United States make immigration enforcement policies so severe that undocumented immigrants would "self-deport."[4]

In March 2012, however, following his success in the bruising primary, Romney's senior advisor Eric Fehrnstrom publicly described the campaign's intention to "hit a reset button for the fall campaign. Everything changes. It's almost like an Etch-A-Sketch. You can kind of shake it up and restart it all over again."[5] And that's precisely what Romney did.

In the run-up to the general election, Romney tempered and even rejected many of his earlier stances. He touted Massachusetts health care reform as "a model for the nation." He also overtly courted Latino voters, avoiding any further mention of "self-deportation" and telling them that "we share the same goal, the same vision, and the same belief in American greatness that draws so many people to our shores."[6]

When Romney announced during the first presidential debate on October 3, 2012, that he never had any intention of cutting taxes for the top 1 percent of American earners, his opponent, incumbent President Obama, seemed unnerved. Obama had likely been expecting Romney to defend a pledge made earlier to "cut taxes on everyone across the country by 20 percent, including the top 1 percent."[7] Instead, the former Massachusetts governor mocked the president's attempts to differentiate their tax policies, saying, "Look, I've got five boys. I'm used to people saying something that's not always true but just keep on repeating it and ultimately hoping I'll believe it. But that is not the case. I will not reduce the taxes paid by high-income Americans."[8] Obama campaign advisor David Axelrod later told CBS's *Face the Nation* that the president had been "taken aback at the brazenness with which Governor Romney walked away from so many of the positions on which he's run."

Romney's revisionism was not unusual for a candidate in the general election. Obama, too, adjusted his own ideological stance after the 2008 primaries. While he had emphasized his antiwar credentials before receiving the party nomination, by the summer he was touting a tough stance on Iran to Israeli lobbyists. In fact, when party conventions end and the general election begins, *all* presidential candidates reliably tack toward the ideological middle. Democrats who spent the primaries brandishing their liberal credentials reinvent themselves as moderates. Republicans who, just months earlier, insisted that they offered the only true conservative voice among their party's possible nominees suddenly temper their stridency.

This shift need not always accompany an overhaul of candidates' policy platforms. Often, it works just as well to signal, via campaign rhetoric, a candidate's commitment to moderation and bipartisanship. Using text analysis software on nearly eight hundred speeches delivered during the 2008 and 2012 presidential races, researchers found that candidates Obama, McCain, and Romney all substantially toned down their rhetoric after the primaries, by both deemphasizing divisive issues and reframing issues to make them

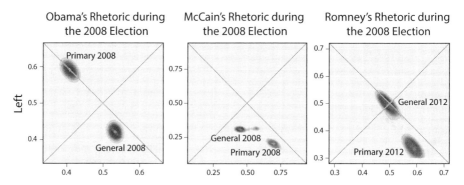

FIGURE 6.2. Changing presidential rhetoric. The lower right section of each figure represents a high proportion of conservative (right) rhetoric and a low proportion of liberal (left) rhetoric, while the upper left represents a high proportion of liberal rhetoric and a low proportion of conservative rhetoric. The intersection of the two lines represents rhetoric that I balanced between liberal and conservative. All candidates moved toward a more balanced rhetoric for the general election, with Obama (in 2008) and Romney (in 2012) making the largest adjustments. The + marks the median for each category. *Source:* Brice D. L. Acree et al., "Etch-a-Sketching: Evaluating the Post-Primary Rhetorical Moderation Hypothesis," *American Politics Research* 48, no. 1 (2018): 99–131.

more palatable to centrist voters (figure 6.2).[9] Moreover, the authors found that, to the extent that the candidates changed their issue positions, they did so largely by announcing new policies rather than revising old ones. For example, John McCain waited until after the Republican convention to propose a tax credit for owners of zero-emission vehicles, as did Romney for a proposed temporary visa program for migrant workers.

Some researchers, it bears noting, have uncovered findings that cast doubt on the need to retreat to the ideological middle. Examining the relationship between candidates' ideologies and electoral outcomes, these researchers have found that more extreme positions do little[10] or nothing[11] to help candidates succeed in the primaries. In the general election, however, extreme positions can be a death knell for aspiring officeholders. If true, these results suggest that candidates would do well to assume moderate positions in the primaries and hold them through the general election.

Why, then, do candidates feel the need to adopt more extreme positions in the primaries? Do they misunderstand the needs of their primary voters, or is something else at play? One explanation involves the "invisible primary" we discussed in chapter 5. According to this line of thinking, candidates adopt far-left or far-right positions to appease the informal networks of donors, activists, and power brokers that make up their political parties.[12] Even before the primary begins, support from these groups may be crucial to launching a campaign—even if they demand policy positions to which primary voters are indifferent and general election voters are hostile.

Advisedly taken or not, when candidates adopt extreme policy positions in the primaries, they subsequently need to tack to the ideological middle in the general election.

Even in the 2016 election—one of the most divisive and vitriolic in modern history—both Hillary Clinton and Donald Trump went out of their way to shun the more extreme positions they had assumed during the primaries. Whereas Trump launched his primary bid with a promise to keep out the "rapists" and "drug dealers" who were pouring through the border, his general election candidacy framed border security only as part of a broader campaign for the restoration of law and order and not the alienation of what would be a key voting bloc come Election Day. And whereas the problems of climate change, rising inequality, and big banks—all lightning rods for the political left—featured prominently in her primary campaign, Clinton did not give these issues nearly as much attention in the general. The reason for these shifts, again, has nothing to do with the candidates intrinsically. Rather, it relates directly to the institutional demands of the U.S. electoral system.

6.1.2 Swing States

Though presidential candidates seek an office that represents the entire country, their campaigns tend to focus on distinct subsets. Ideologically, as was just discussed, candidates target voters situated somewhere between the extremes of the liberal-conservative spectrum. And owing to the particular structure of the Electoral College, candidates narrow their focus not just ideologically but geographically as well.

Because nearly all states award delegate votes on a winner-take-all basis, presidential candidates focus almost exclusively on **swing states**—states where Republicans and Democrats have similar levels of support, making the outcome of a contest there uncertain. The three most populous states—California, Texas, and Florida—together represent more than 20 percent of the Electoral College. Because the outcome of their electoral votes is all but foreordained, however, voters in these states often host no candidate rallies and receive little if any campaign advertising. Of the seven states with the largest Electoral College delegations, only Florida, Ohio, and Pennsylvania, all swing states, were regularly visited by presidential candidates during the last three election cycles.

The implications for mass participation in politics are discouraging. While all fifty states have a lawful role in the election of the president, voters in only a handful of states are actively engaged by the campaigns and made to feel politically influential.* The Obama campaign spent $314.8 million on television advertising from April 11, 2012, to

---

* Recognizing these problems, many people have sought a wholesale reform of the Electoral College. (For a particularly trenchant critique, see George C. Edwards, *Why the Electoral College Is Bad for America*, 2nd ed. [New Haven: Yale University Press, 2011].) For instance, the National Popular Vote Compact is an initiative advocated by former state and federal legislators. (Those interested in this particular proposal should read Derek Muller, "The Compact Clause and the National Popular Vote Interstate Compact," *Election Law Journal* 6, no. 4 [2007]: 372–93; or see the group's website at www.nationalpopularvote.com.) As soon as the right combination of states signs on—their total Electoral College votes must add up to at least 270—the participating states have agreed to award their respective electors to whichever candidate has won the national popular

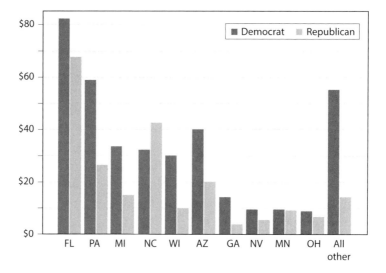

FIGURE 6.3. The disproportionate attention directed to competitive states in the 2020 election. Television advertising (presented in tens of millions of dollars) spent in ten competitive states in the 2020 presidential election vastly exceeded spending in the remaining forty. Domenico Montenaro, "Presidential Campaign TV Ad Spending Crosses $1 Billion Mark in Key States," National Public Radio, October 13, 2020, https://www.npr.org/2020/10/13/923427969 /presidential-campaign-tv-ad-spending-crosses-1-billion-mark-in-key-states; "Presidential General Election Ad Spending Tops $1.5 Billion," Wesleyan Media Project, October 29, 2020, https://mediaproject.wesleyan.edu/releases-102920/#table1.

Election Day, with 99.6 percent of that money targeting voters in swing states. During the same period, Romney spent $147.8 million (99.9 percent of his total television advertising budget) on ads in the same states.[13] In the 2020 election, the campaigns directed the majority of television ad spending to ten competitive states (figure 6.3).

A similar trend appears when examining candidates' campaign stops, the majority of which take place in swing states (figure 6.4). In the last two months of the 2020 campaign, Biden and Harris collectively held 92 rallies around the country. Sixty-six of these, or 72 percent, were held in the swing states of Arizona, Florida, Georgia, Michigan, North Carolina, Pennsylvania, and Wisconsin.[14] Of the 135 rallies held by Trump and Pence, 93, or 69 percent, were held in these same states. Over the same time period, not a single rally took place in New York, Illinois, Alabama, and many other non-competitive states.

One might expect voters to criticize candidates who spend all their time in a handful of states, ignoring the rest of the country. In reality, just the opposite happens: voters attack candidates when they don't spend *enough* time in the battleground states. After her loss in

vote. Nine states, constituting about a quarter of all 538 Electoral College votes, have passed laws binding them to this method of vote allocation.

FIGURE 6.4. The disproportionate attention directed to competitive states in the 2020 election. Candidates also directed the majority of their time to a handful of states. Bill Ruthhart and Jonathon Berlin, "Campaign Trail Tracker: Where Trump, Biden and Their Running Mates Have Traveled in Presidential Race's Final Weeks," *Chicago Tribune*, November 5, 2020, https://www.chicagotribune.com/politics/ct-viz-presidential-campaign-trail-tracker-20200917-edspdit2incbfnopchjaelp3uu-htmlstory.html.

the 2016 campaign, Hillary Clinton was roundly condemned for her lack of presence in Wisconsin. The first candidate since 1972 not to visit the state, Clinton went on to lose Wisconsin by less than one percentage point. Reflecting on the outcome, Clinton lamented that "with a margin like that, everyone can have a pet theory about why I lost. It's difficult to rule anything out."[15]

Never mind the fact that winning Wisconsin would not have given Clinton the necessary electoral votes to win the presidency. Never mind, too, that Clinton won the nationwide popular vote by nearly three million votes. This distinction matters little given the winner-take-all structure of the Electoral College, which has handed the presidency to the popular vote loser in four presidential elections: 1876, 1888, 2000, and 2016. Given a choice between winning the voters and winning the Electoral College, the answer is easy—and it directs candidates to the swing states again and again.

6.1.3 Appealing to a Changing National Electorate

Tacking to the ideological middle and campaigning hard in swing states are permanent features of presidential elections. As we will see, however, the electorate itself has undergone drastic transformations throughout American history. As the franchise has been extended to citizens of different socioeconomic statuses, races, and sexes, many campaigns have adapted to win over the new voting groups. Other campaigns, meanwhile, have found ways to undermine the franchise itself, altogether eliminating the need to appeal to a changing electorate.

HISTORICAL CHANGES TO THE AMERICAN ELECTORATE

During George Washington's first election in 1789, the right to vote was highly restricted.[16] Eligible voters were white, male, property-owning, taxpaying citizens over the age of 21.* As if this group were not exclusive enough, states set their own standards regarding the property value, taxes, and additional fees necessary to cast a ballot.[17] Many states assigned their presidential electors by legislative selection—altogether eliminating the need to hold a popular vote. As such, in 1789, only 18 percent of Americans over the age of 18 (the voting-age population, or VAP) met base voting requirements, and only 2 percent actually voted.[18]

As seen in figure 6.5, the country has come a long way since 1789. The number of voters would fluctuate for much of the next thirty years, as states switched back and forth between forms of popular vote and legislative selection for the Electoral College.[19] It was not until 1824 that the popular vote caught on, and with it came an expansion of voting rights. By 1856, over 34 percent of the VAP was eligible to vote—representing near-total white male suffrage, regardless of property ownership.

For Black Americans and former slaves, however, suffrage was not guaranteed until long after the Civil War. Though the Voting Rights Act of 1866 extended the vote to all male citizens over the age of 21, it was not until the ratification of the Fourteenth and Fifteenth Amendments in 1868 and 1870, respectively, that the right to vote could not be "denied or abridged . . . on account of race, color, or previous condition of servitude."

For women, suffrage came much later. Before the Nineteenth Amendment was ratified in 1920, only fifteen out of the forty-eight states extended voting rights to women. Additionally, six states permitted women to vote only in presidential elections.[20] Not only did the Nineteenth Amendment massively expand the size of the electorate; it represented the largest single step toward universal suffrage in the history of the United States. An unprecedented 82 percent of the VAP was eligible to vote in the 1920 election, up from 47 percent just four years earlier.

But what was true on paper was not a reality for many Americans. Literacy tests and poll taxes—common forms of voter suppression—were still widespread in the South.[21] Among its many accomplishments, the Civil Rights Act of 1964 outlawed unequal voter registration requirements. Later, the Twenty-Fourth Amendment (1964) banned the use of poll taxes in federal elections, and the Voting Rights Act (1965) banned literacy tests, state-level poll taxes, and any rule that denied voting rights "on account of race or color."[22] Finally, in 1971, the Twenty-Sixth Amendment officially lowered the voting age from 21 to 18. By 1972, nearly 99 percent of citizens over the age of 18 were eligible to vote—a yet-unbroken record in the history of American elections.

---

*Not to mention other regulations certain states had in place, such as education requirements or literacy tests.

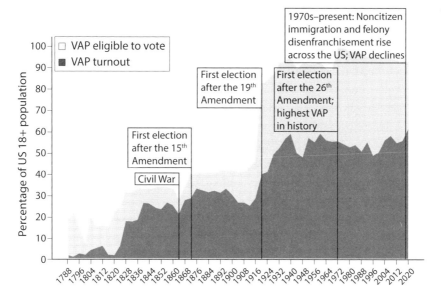

FIGURE 6.5. The national franchise, 1790–2020. Major advancements in the franchise—the Fifteenth, Nineteenth, and Twenty-Sixth Amendments, among others—have transformed both the number and demographics of people who can select the president. In 1789, only 18 percent of American adults (almost all of them white, male property owners) were eligible to vote, but only 2 percent actually did. Today, more than 90 percent of the voting-age population (VAP) can cast a ballot. Far fewer do. *Sources:* "The United States Census: Statistics of the Population of the United States," U.S. Census Bureau; Dave Leip, "Dave Leip's Atlas of U.S. Presidential Elections: United States Presidential Election Results," https://uselectionatlas.org; Curtis Gans, *Voter Turnout in the United States, 1788–2009* (Washington, DC: Congressional Quarterly Press, 2011); Michael P. McDonald, "National General Election VEP Turnout Rates, 1789–Present," United States Elections Project.

Despite these major efforts to expand the franchise, only 93 percent of the VAP was eligible to vote in the 2016 election—nearly six points *lower* than in 1972. What caused this backward slide? Part of the answer concerns the country's rising incarceration rate. In almost every state, incarcerated citizens are barred from voting, sometimes long after their sentences have been served. In three states—Iowa, Kentucky, and Virginia—felons are permanently disenfranchised. These voters totaled 6.2 million in 2020, or 2.3 percent of the VAP.[23] This number, which had increased every year from the late 1970s through 2016, declined after 2016 as states began implementing reforms to grant voting access to those with felony convictions.[24]

Noncitizens, too, are barred from voting. In 2019, 13.7 percent of the population was foreign-born (up from a low of 4.7 percent in 1970). Approximately half of that population were noncitizens, ineligible to vote yet included in the VAP.[25] Combined, the rising trends of incarceration and immigration have produced a less inclusive franchise in recent decades.

APPEALS TO NEW VOTERS: WOMEN

The gradual diversification of the electorate has had profound implications for candidates' general election strategies. Exclusive appeals to white, property-owning males have little value in modern campaigns; quite simply, these voters do not make up a large enough share of today's electorate to secure the presidency. Throughout history, candidates have had to appeal to newly enfranchised groups by incorporating new (or previously ignored) ideas into their speeches and policy platforms.

Perhaps nowhere is this more apparent than in the years before and after the Nineteenth Amendment was ratified, when women's suffrage nearly doubled the size of the electorate. Though they represented by far the largest group of newly enfranchised voters, initial appeals to women were tepid, and women's votes were seen merely as an extension of their husbands'.[26] With time, however, the presence of women in the electorate redefined the set of topics presidential candidates saw fit to discuss on the campaign trail.

Long before the Nineteenth Amendment was ratified, President Woodrow Wilson understood the impact women could have on future elections. Wilson publicly endorsed women's voting rights in 1918, prior to the midterm election, encouraging members of his Democratic Party to do the same. Nonetheless, when a suffrage bill failed in the Democrat-controlled Senate, it was interpreted as a failure of the party—and Wilson specifically—to commit to the suffragist cause.[27]

For Wilson's Republican challenger, Warren G. Harding, this failure posed a remarkable opportunity. Though Harding had never publicly allied himself with the suffragist movement before—in fact, he had skipped Senate debates on the subject—he began appealing to the women who felt disappointed by Wilson.[28] The Harding campaign took out family-oriented advertisements in women's publications such as *Needlecraft Magazine*, making grand declarations that the Republican ticket would oppose the League of Nations and keep their sons out of foreign wars.[29] (These ads, it was thought, would appeal to women's maternal instincts.) Two months after the Nineteenth Amendment was ratified, Harding won a landslide victory in the 1920 election—due in no small part to his support among politically active women.

And yet, while this story might seem like a victory for Harding and the Republican Party, turnout for women lagged behind that of their male counterparts in the 1920 election and for several years thereafter (as seen in the difference between eligible voters and voter turnout in figure 6.5). One explanation, detailed in the scholarship of J. Kevin Corder and Christina Wolbrecht, is that women had been taught from a young age to stay out of politics. Many believed it unbecoming for women to vote or even engage in political conversation—an obstacle that proved insurmountable for quite some time.[30]

Another explanation, again raised by Corder and Wolbrecht, is that mobilization efforts aimed at women were largely relegated to the local level. Political clubs for women, mostly sponsored by Republicans, fostered a sense of community activism and bolstered an already strong Republican lead going into the 1920 election. The League of Women Voters was also founded to inform women about politics and register them to vote.[31] These were important advancements, to be sure, but they also highlighted the lack of mobilization efforts undertaken at the national level. In the presidential race, campaign strategies and policy-based appeals to women were limited to family-oriented advertisements, whose effects were dubious at best.

Despite an early lack of individualized appeals, however, the addition of women to the electorate had a sizable effect on the set of political issues discussed by presidential campaigns.[32] As societal norms evolved and women gained more independence from their husbands, many enrolled in social welfare programs for themselves and their children. They also tended to express more egalitarian views than men. In response, successful politicians (even those who had been silent on the issue) made social welfare a key element of their campaign platforms. Women rallied behind the New Deal programs of the 1930s and Great Society reforms of the 1960s—solidifying their majority support for the Democratic Party.

Today, women consistently turn out to vote at higher rates than men.[33] And while family-oriented appeals to women persist (including appeals to the "yoga voter"[34] and "soccer mom"),[35] women remain a dominant force in presidential elections. In 2020, the Biden campaign website featured a stand-alone section titled "The Biden Agenda for Women" in which he pledged to expand access to health care, lower the cost of childcare, end domestic violence, and strengthen pay and benefits in careers disproportionately chosen by women.[36] In many ways, these promises—all of which received attention in Biden's in-person rallies—are reminiscent of the social welfare platforms in the 1930s and 1960s. But more broadly, they served as the Biden campaign's acknowledgment of the unique interests of female voters and the continuous efforts candidates must make to curry their favor.

APPEALS TO NEW VOTERS: BLACK AMERICANS

By the early 1960s, race and civil rights were familiar topics in national political debates. But relative to today, these debates did not map cleanly across partisan lines. As late as the mid-1950s, a majority of Black voters were Republicans.[37] (Dr. Martin Luther King Jr. lived much of his life a Republican, as did famed baseball player Jackie Robinson.) And in the 1960 election, Democrat John F. Kennedy won Texas, Mississippi, Alabama, and South Carolina—overwhelmingly white, southern states that would be almost impossible for a Democratic presidential candidate to win today. Why do things look so different now?

These changes have their roots in the Civil Rights Act of 1964 and the Voting Rights Act of 1965, which removed many of the barricades that had prevented Black voters from exercising their right to vote. By 1969, an estimated 61 percent of the Black voting-age population was registered to vote, up from 23 percent prior to the 1964 and 1965 acts.[38]

As Black voters became a more potent force in American politics, presidential candidates reevaluated their positions on race and civil rights. Throughout his 1964 campaign, for instance, President Lyndon B. Johnson was a staunch defender of the rights of Black Americans. He promised in his speeches to be a president for *all* Americans, emphasizing that until civil rights were achieved, "emancipation will be a proclamation but not a fact."[39] Johnson did not come to this position lightly, however. Even as he pushed Congress to pass the Civil Rights Act, Johnson worried that his opponent, Republican Barry Goldwater, would stoke racial tensions by exploiting white voters' opposition to the bill.[40] Moreover, when the bill finally passed, Johnson is credited as saying, "I think we just delivered the South to the Republican party for a long time to come."[41] The Democratic Party's embrace of civil rights, Johnson plainly worried, would push white voters into the Republican Party.

Even though Johnson won the 1964 election, his prediction about the South appears to have come true. Future Republican presidential candidates embraced the so-called "Southern Strategy," in which they doubled down on their appeals to southern white voters. Popularized by Nixon, the strategy originated with Goldwater, who argued in 1964 that his party "ought to forget the big cities" and "back up on school integration" to secure more white votes.[42] In the 1968 election, against a backdrop of nationwide race riots and the assassination of Martin Luther King Jr., Nixon distanced himself from racial progress and promised his supporters "law and order."[43] (Notably, this was the same Nixon who, a decade earlier, had endorsed the Civil Rights Act of 1957.)[44] In the end, Nixon's subtle appeals to white voters paid off; he swept the central swath of the United States, with the Democratic candidate, Hubert Humphrey, trailing far behind.[45]

In the wake of the Civil Rights and Voting Rights Acts, there emerged a new equilibrium in American politics. After Nixon was reelected in 1972, winning forty-nine out of fifty states, the GOP embraced the Southern Strategy. In the words of one of Nixon's strategists, "From now on, the Republicans are never going to get more than 10 to 20 percent of the Negro vote and they don't need any more than that."[46]

Today, the Republican Party continues to dominate among southern white voters. Democratic presidential candidates, meanwhile, receive roughly 90 percent of the Black vote in recent elections.[47] None of this, of course, was preordained. The strategic decisions of candidates Johnson and Nixon, adapting as best they knew how to the electorate they inherited, have had lasting effects on presidential elections.

VOTER SUPPRESSION

Strategic appeals like those outlined above—President Harding's family-oriented advertisements to women, or President Nixon's "law and order" message—do not tell the whole story of candidates' interactions with the electorate. Sometimes, when the forces of electoral change operate to their disadvantage, candidates and their parties try to alter the voting rules in their favor.

Voter suppression has played an unmistakable role in American elections. As we discussed earlier, southern states (then controlled by Democrats) used poll taxes and literacy tests to restrict Black enfranchisement after the Civil War. Though these restrictions were later deemed illegal, voter suppression tactics have adapted with the Supreme Court's blessing. Over the last decade, the Court has "systematically reduced the scope and reach of the [Voting Rights Act]" to the point where "the Voting Rights Act regime . . . is gone, and it's not coming back."[48] Also in the past decade, many states have passed laws that make it harder for eligible voters to cast a ballot. Voter identification laws, cuts to early voting, and voter roll purges have disproportionately disenfranchised racial minorities who tend to vote for Democrats.

Most states have passed some form of voter ID law, enabling election officials to request identification at the polling station.[49] The severity of these laws varies by state; in its most severe form, as in states like Georgia, a ballot will not be counted unless the voter presents a valid form of ID.[50] In 2016, North Carolina judges ruled that these laws "target African Americans with almost surgical precision."[51] In 2017, Georgia also enacted an "exact match" law mandating that the name on a voter's ID perfectly match the state's registration records. Evidence from the 2018 midterm elections revealed that about 80 percent of affected voters were Black.[52]

In addition to voter ID laws, minority communities are disproportionately affected by voter roll purging, long lines at polling places, and precinct closures.[53] And because of racial disparities in the criminal justice system, minority voters are also disproportionately affected by felon disenfranchisement laws.[54]

Of course, this is not an exhaustive list of voter suppression tactics, which change as the electorate does, or as new opportunities arise. (Recall, for instance, President Trump's efforts to sow distrust in mail-in voting at the height of a pandemic.)[55] Though we may not be able to predict when and how voter suppression arises, we at least know why it does. Put simply, changes in the electorate create both winners and losers out of our national parties. At different points in history, both parties have been negatively impacted by extensions of the franchise. When that happens, and parties fail to appeal to new voters, new forms of disenfranchisement are used to diminish the electoral support for their opposition.

6.2 The Economy and the Presidential Vote

In U.S. presidential elections, like elections for most political offices, incumbents enjoy formidable advantages. Since 1900, only five incumbents—William Howard Taft, Herbert Hoover, Jimmy Carter, George H. W. Bush, and Donald Trump—have lost a bid for reelection. Taft excepted, voters' concerns about the national economy played a crucial role in the outcome of those cases. Fairly or not, voters regard the president as the nation's chief economic steward, responsible for the creation of jobs, the maintenance of price stability, and the promotion of consumer confidence. In typical elections, therefore, the state of the economy is among the best predictors of an incumbent's reelection prospects.

The effects of objective economic conditions and subjective economic perceptions on voter choice rank among the most studied topics in mass political behavior.[56] The research has proceeded via two methodological routes, one considering the effect of economic circumstances on individual voters' attitudes, the other investigating the effect of economic conditions on incumbent candidates' vote shares. The two approaches have generated remarkably consistent results, which underscore the relevance of economic considerations for presidential elections.

The first method was originally used in *The American Voter*, a seminal study of voter choice in the 1952 and 1956 presidential elections. In this study, Angus Campbell and his coauthors found that perceptions of an incumbent's economic management powerfully conditioned voters' attitudes toward him, even after taking partisanship into account. Pessimism about an administration's likely economic stewardship considerably reduced the probability of an individual's voting for the incumbent.[57] In 2007, political scientists replicated the original studies of *The American Voter* with data from the 2004 election and found similarly large economic effects. For example, Independents who felt the national economy had improved over the preceding four years were about four times more likely to support the incumbent President Bush as those who felt the situation had worsened.[58]

Almost as fundamental is Morris Fiorina's 1981 book *Retrospective Voting in American National Elections*, which exercised the second approach to studying the effects of the economy on electoral votes. Fiorina found that a party's perceived superiority in economic stewardship had almost as large an influence on voter choice as a voter's partisanship. Over the ensuing years, other scholars corroborated Fiorina's findings about the importance of unemployment and inflation patterns to presidential elections.[59] And still more research emphasizes the relevance of economic growth rates as important indicators of an incumbent's electoral prospects.* In this respect, American voters behave consistently with voters in other wealthy democracies—in one survey of the published literature, Michael Lewis-Beck and Mary Stegmaier found that French, British, and Danish voters similarly rewarded and punished incumbent politicians according to the performance of their national economies.[60]

Thinking Institutionally: Predicting the Results of Presidential Elections

---

In each presidential election a cottage industry of political scientists hauls out prediction models and lays bets on a winner. Nearly all of these models rely on **structural factors**, or basic facts about the state of the world, to make their predictions. Common structural factors include economic indicators, the involvement of the United States in a costly foreign war, or the fiscal situation stateside. Some models include additional political indicators, such as the duration of the incumbent party's current time in the White

---

*For instance, Christopher Wlezien and Robert Erikson found that the relationship between income growth and presidential vote grows stronger over the four-year presidential term—the effect is apparent eighteen months before an election and is at its apex in the twelve months preceding a presidential race. Christopher Wlezien and Robert S. Erikson, "Temporal Horizons and Presidential Election Forecasts," *American Politics Research* 24, no. 2 (1996): 492–505. Ray Fair finds a substantively similar effect for real per capita GDP growth, where every two-percentage-point increase in the rate of growth during the three quarters preceding the election leads to about a one-percentage-point increase in the incumbent presidential party's vote share. Ray C. Fair, "Presidential and Congressional Vote-Share Equations," *American Journal of Political Science* 53, no. 1 (2009): 55–72. This model for predicting the outcome of presidential elections is discussed further in the Thinking Institutionally feature in this chapter.

TABLE 6.1. Predictive Models for the 2020 Presidential Election

Model	Author(s)	Method	Predicted Winner	Predicted Popular Vote for Trump	Error
State Presidential Approval/ Economy	Enns and Lagodny	State-level presidential approval and economic variables	Biden	46.5	1.3
State by State	Jerome, Jerome-Speziari, Mongrain, and Nadeau	State-level economic variables and state-level presidential approval	Biden	48.3	−1.5
Leading Economic Indicators	Erikson and Wlezien	Change in leading economic indicators	Biden	45.0	1.8
Political Economy	Lewis-Beck and Tien	Presidential popularity; economic growth; whether incumbent party candidate previously elected	Biden	43.3	3.5
Prospective	Lockerbie	Prospective economic evaluations, duration of incumbent party's time in White House	Trump	55.2	−8.4

Source: PS: Political Science and Politics 54, no. 1 (2021): 47–110.

House.* None of the models takes into account campaign strategy, candidates' biographies, advertising, or the effects of an October surprise, which we will discuss later.

Table 6.1 describes the methods of five statistical models used to predict the 2020 election, arranged in order of their accuracy. As you can see, there are not any especially clear patterns. Whereas the Lewis-Beck and Tien model nearly perfectly predicted the outcome of the 2016 election (in which its error was just 0.1 percentage points), it was substantially less accurate in predicting the 2020 election. Likewise, there isn't any clear evidence that models that include measures of either a candidate's or the incumbent president's popularity perform any better than those models that include only a bevy of economic indicators. Indeed, the Enns and

* This cycle has been particularly apparent since 1960: when a party has held the executive for only a single term, six out of seven of that party's candidates have been successful in the subsequent election. When a party has held the executive for two terms or more, however, it has won only one of six elections. The strength of this effect is potentially confounded by the Twenty-Second Amendment, which precludes any person from seeking a third election to the presidency.

Continued on next page

Lagodny model, which performed best within our sample, and the Lockerbie model, which performed the worst, both used some combination of political and economic indicators.

Most of these models, it bears noting, were able to predict a victory for Biden, even if they could not pinpoint the popular vote. The 2020 election is not unique in this regard; the Lewis-Beck and Tien model, for example, correctly picked the winner in sixteen of the last nineteen presidential elections. Its remarkable success highlights the overriding importance of structural factors in determining electoral outcomes. For all the hubbub over the failure of polls and pundits to foresee Trump's rise to power, basic facts about the state of the economy and the incumbent party do a remarkable job of predicting election results.

But as the table also demonstrates, structural factors can only take us so far. Unpredictable and nonquantifiable factors—including the quality of political ads, campaign scandals, and more—may help explain the right-hand column in the table. These errors in this column are small but real. And in a closely divided election, they may make all the difference.

6.2.1 Pocketbook versus Sociotropic Voting

As we have seen, political scientists have come up with a number of different models to define the relationship between the economy and a presidential candidate's electoral fortunes. They also have developed a variety of ways to analyze the relevance of different economic indicators for individuals' vote choices. In the main, though, political scientists have posited two potential influences of the general economy on voting behavior: pocketbook voting and sociotropic voting.

Pocketbook voting refers to voters' focus on their personal economic circumstances. If a pocketbook voter has lost her job or had her hours reduced, she will be more likely to vote against an incumbent president or, in the case of an open election in which an incumbent is not running, against the incumbent president's party. This model does not assume that voters believe a president is *personally* implicated in a specific economic episode; voters are instead presumed to reason that better economic stewardship at the national level might have forestalled setbacks in their personal circumstances.

The alternative to pocketbook voting is **sociotropic voting**. Rather than judging the strength of the economy from personal experience, sociotropic voters rely upon direct observations of the world around them and media reports about economic indicators to determine whether the domestic economy is flourishing or foundering—and to decide, accordingly, which presidential candidate or party to support. As Morris Fiorina writes, "The [sociotropic] voter need not spend his life watching *Meet the Press* and reading the *New York Times*. He can look at the evening news and [independently] observe . . . the increasing price of a basket of groceries between this month and last."[61]

Which model of economic behavior is best supported by evidence? While politicians target voters with pocketbook appeals, evidence that they actually sway votes is not espe-

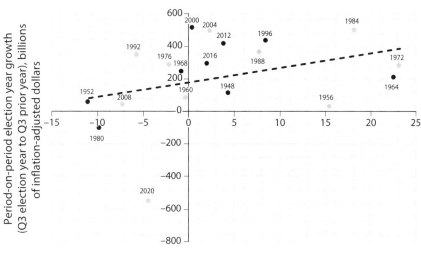

FIGURE 6.6. The economy and the vote. The y-axis measures the inflation-adjusted annual change in the nation's gross domestic product in billions of dollars between the third quarter of the election year and the third quarter of the prior year. The x-axis shows the incumbent party's margin of victory. The year of each data point is identified and shaded according the partisanship of the incumbent party (gray for Republican, black for Democrat). *Source:* Historical Tables, Bureau of Economic Analysis, Department of Commerce: https://apps.bea.gov/iTable/iTable.cfm?reqid=19&step=2#reqid=19&step=2&isuri=1&1921=survey.

cially strong. Empirically, researchers can rarely tie respondents' personal circumstances to their policy preferences, particularly after accounting for aggregate economic changes. It has been consistently shown, for instance, that individuals' personal finances do not affect their attitudes toward tax policy.

The evidence for sociotropic voting's impact on elections appears stronger. For example, in the wake of the quick and decisive success of Operation Desert Storm in 1991, the reelection of President George H. W. Bush was considered a foregone conclusion. But not long before the 1992 election, news about a $300 billion budget deficit and 10 percent inflation drove voters to elect the challenger, Bill Clinton. It seems, then, that while pocketbook considerations may weigh heavily on people's daily lives, they do not predominate when they go to the polls. As voters, people tend to evaluate presidential candidates on the basis of prevailing economic trends.

To see this more clearly, take a look at figure 6.6, which shows the relationship between election-year changes in the national gross domestic product and the vote share of the incumbent president (or, in cases when the incumbent did not run, then the vote share of his party).[62] Since 1932, a strong, positive relationship is observed, as noted by the linear regression line that reveals the relationship between these two quantities of interest. Though not all of the data points appear exactly on the line—the pandemic shutdown in 2020, you'll notice, yielded the biggest outlier—a clear pattern is nonetheless evident. When the economy expands during the course of an election year, the incumbent party, regardless of whether it was Democratic or Republican, secures a greater portion of the national vote share. And when the economy stalls or shrinks, the electoral fortunes of the party in power reliably diminish. The fate of presidential candidates, regardless of the personalities involved, routinely depends upon macro-level changes in the overall economy.[63]

6.2.2 Implications for Candidate Strategy

Savvy presidential candidates use the national economic situation to their advantage. When incumbents campaign during prosperous times, they routinely trumpet their prudent economic management. Challengers whose prospects are not aided by a focus on the economy, by contrast, often run what political scientist Lynn Vavreck calls an "insurgent campaign,"[64] which is explicitly designed to bring some other issue to the forefront of electoral discourse.*

When an insurgent campaign takes hold and an incumbent is slow to react, the damage can be difficult to overcome. Vavreck points to the 1976 and 2000 elections as two prime examples of successful insurgent campaigns. Despite sound economic performance in both periods, the challenger successfully exploited the incumbent's personal liabilities. In 1976, for example, Jimmy Carter successfully argued that his status as a Washington outsider would ensure a clean break from the Watergate scandal that had marred the reputation of the incumbent Republican Party. Similarly, the 2000 campaign of George W. Bush promised to end the divisive partisan squabbles that had marked the Clinton presidency.

In 2012, Mitt Romney exemplified what Vavreck calls a "clarifying candidate," that is, a challenger who shines a bright light on the economic shortcomings experienced by the country during an incumbent's tenure. A New England moderate whose Mormon faith jarred many of the southern evangelical voters within the Republican Party, Romney focused instead on his reputation as a managerial expert who had saved the 2002 Winter Olympics and served as governor of Massachusetts from 2003 to 2007. Consistent with Vavreck's predictions, Romney's campaign also relentlessly focused on the economy—claiming that the recovery from the 2008 financial crisis was too slow, that the president had not done enough to bring down unemployment, and that the deficit was dangerously high.

Obama stubbornly refused to concede Romney's premise that his administration had mismanaged the economy. Obama had assumed office in 2009 at the lowest point of a deep

---

* Almost always, Vavreck argues, insurgent campaigns select issues that share two features: first, they attract nearly unanimous support from voters, such as increased education funding, harsher penalties for criminals, or national energy independence; and second, they exacerbate some perceived weakness of an opposing candidate.

economic crisis, and even though the economy struggled to recover over the ensuing four years, Obama was able to defend his economic record. In an attempt to tar Romney with his ties to the financial industry, the president stressed the role of financiers in causing the economic crisis. Finally, Obama cast Romney as a conventional Republican whose policies closely matched those pursued by Bush before the crisis hit.

On Election Day, Obama's appeals resonated with the electorate. Among those who declared "unemployment" as the biggest economic problem for the nation, Obama won by 10 percentage points. Similarly, the president won by more than 30 points among voters who designated "the housing market" as the nation's biggest economic problem. Finally, by 15 percentage points, voters in exit polls blamed Bush over Obama for the economic crisis. In hindsight, Romney may have been better served by running as an insurgent candidate and emphasizing something other than economic stewardship, which by the campaign's end was broadly recognized as one of Obama's strengths.

6.3 The Small, but Consequential, Effects of Campaigns

Who are the voters? How is the economy doing? These questions form the bedrock of presidential elections. The answers to these questions help us understand both who is most likely to win and the strategies candidates adopt throughout the course of their campaigns. And as we saw in this chapter's Thinking Institutionally feature, using just these fundamental indicators, political scientists have come startlingly close to predicting the popular vote margins in recent elections.

Were we to turn on the television to learn about what is important in presidential elections, however, the electorate and the economy would garner comparatively little attention. Instead, we would likely see pundits—often employees of the campaigns themselves—discussing minute-by-minute changes in the polls, changes allegedly spurred by things such as gaffes in presidential debates, breaking-news scandals, and other campaign "game changers." In the 2012 election, no less than sixty-eight unique events were referred to as game changers.[65] A speech given by Ann Romney, Mitt Romney's wife, at the Republican National Convention registered as one. Romney's endorsement by the *Des Moines Register* was another. A resurfaced video of Obama delivering a speech in 1998 was, to far too many, yet another.

Looking back, it is unlikely that any of these events deserved their designated status of game changer. The resulting minute-by-minute swings in the polls, though exciting to watch, told us little about the trajectory of the 2012 campaign. And the reason is simple: the electorate and the economy do not drastically change from one minute to the next.

Campaign managers may spend days preparing their candidates for the debates or plotting media strategies in the face of an emerging scandal, but their efforts usually matter only at the margin. With effects small and fleeting, they can certainly make the difference in a tight race. Really, anything can. But even the most expensive item on a campaign budget, campaign advertising, cannot reliably rewrite the rules of presidential elections in one candidate's favor.

6.3.1 Campaign Advertising

Presidential campaigns spend money on many things; they hire staff, they rent offices, they invest resources to register likely supporters, and so on. Advertising, though, is generally regarded as the main ingredient of presidential campaigns. In the 2020 presidential election, the Trump campaign spent approximately 43 percent of its budget on advertising while the Biden campaign allotted more than half of its resources, approximately 55 percent, to advertising.[66]

For the average voter, advertising also is the dominant source of information about presidential candidates. If one were to ask a typical voter to provide an account of a recent presidential election, the answer would most likely reflect the tone and content of the campaigns' advertisements. This does not mean, however, that campaigns are correct to spend as much as they do on advertising, or even that ads are an effective way to win votes. As we will see, researchers have long been interested in the effects of campaign advertising, and their results do not obviously justify the exorbitant sums spent on it.

EVIDENCE ON THE GENERAL EFFICACY OF CAMPAIGN ADVERTISING

Political scientists who study the effects of political advertising on voter attitudes and candidate preferences confront significant challenges. To begin with, voters do not come to political ads as blank slates. Rather, the new information an ad provides must be balanced against the knowledge and attitudes voters possess *before* they watch it. Those with strong partisan preferences, in particular, tend to filter out or downplay information that contradicts their candidate's positions.

Campaigns and political supporters also do not spend advertising money randomly. As best they can, they target undecided and independent voters.[67] Because these voters tend to have a lower stock of political knowledge, however, the effects of advertising on this subpopulation may not apply to voters generally. As a result, studies of advertising that show big effects on undecided and independent voters cannot be reliably extrapolated to the larger population of voters in presidential elections.

To overcome these and other identification challenges, much of the best research relies on experimental methods, which allow the analyst to manipulate the exposure of ads to populations of interest. Important work in this area shows that most voters are quick to forget the new information that ads convey. Though the judgments or candidate preferences they derive from this information may persist.[68] Some political psychologists have dubbed this the "Online Model of Voting": voters process new information as they acquire it, updating their evaluations in either a positive or negative direction and subsequently discarding the information itself. When voters express their evaluation of a candidate, whether by voting or by providing an answer to a political survey, their evaluation will reflect a synthesis of all the political information they have acquired, despite the fact that they may remember little or none of its actual content.

Other research suggests that the average effects of advertising on vote choice are unlikely to be either large or lasting. One well-conducted field experiment published in 2011 randomly examined television advertising in the 2006 Texas gubernatorial election and found that the ads significantly influenced voter attitudes—at first. By the time a week had lapsed, however, ads had no significant relationship with voter opinions.[69] A subsequent experiment, examining election results in neighboring media markets, found a relationship between candidates' votes and the share of television ad space they had purchased. According to the authors, "the average citizen seeing about 22 more ads promoting one candidate rather than the other, increases the partisan difference in vote shares by about half a percentage point."[70] Effects like these—small but statistically significant—have been reasonably consistent regardless of when or where the ads are shown, their content, and the partisan leanings of the viewing audience.[71] Overall, campaign ads are mildly persuasive for some voters and ineffective for many others; across the electorate, campaign ads alone are unlikely to determine who serves as the next president.[72]

NEGATIVE CAMPAIGN ADVERTISING

The profusion of **negative advertisements** is, for many, the most odious development of modern elections. Voters from all parties roundly condemn them, and even candidates periodically lament their prevalence. Many observers object to negative advertisements on the grounds that they coarsen public discourse, focus on personal traits or other issues irrelevant to governance, and mislead and demotivate the electorate.*

These concerns were seemingly justified by the so-called "Willie Horton" ads, one of the most notorious negative ad campaigns in history (figure 6.7). In an effort to paint his opponent as weak on crime, Republican nominee George H. W. Bush leveled the racially charged attack against his Democratic opponent, Michael Dukakis. In the television version of the 1988 ad, an off-screen narrator tells the story of William Horton (renamed "Willie" by Bush's campaign manager), a Black man who committed rape and murder after being released from prison on a Dukakis-sponsored furlough program. "Weekend prison passes: Dukakis on crime," proclaims the narrator. Meanwhile, photos of a scowling Horton appear on-screen, his hair and beard overgrown after several weeks in solitary confinement. As Horton himself would confess years later, having seen the ad: "I would have been scared of me too."[73]

Backlash to the ad was fierce. Civil rights leaders including Jesse Jackson condemned it as racist, and the Bush campaign denied involvement. (This was long before the 2002

---

* In fact, it is not clear that all of these worries are justified. Analyses have found that negative ads tend to focus more on substance than other ads, and they offer voters more comparative claims that allow voters to easily distinguish candidates' policy positions. See John Geer, *In Defense of Negativity: Attack Ads in Presidential Campaigns* (Chicago: University of Chicago Press, 2006). Other analyses have suggested that negative ads can increase turnout. See Joshua D. Clinton and John S. Lapinski, "'Targeted' Advertising and Voter Turnout: An Experimental Study of the 2000 Presidential Election," *Journal of Politics* 66, no. 1 (2004): 69–96; Martin P. Wattenberg and Craig Leonard Brians, "Negative Campaign Advertising: Demobilizer or Mobilizer?" *American Political Science Review* 93, no. 4 (1999): 891–99; and Deborah Jordan Brooks, "The Resilient Voter: Moving toward Closure in the Debate over Negative Campaigning and Turnout," *Journal of Politics* 68, no. 3 (2006): 684–96.

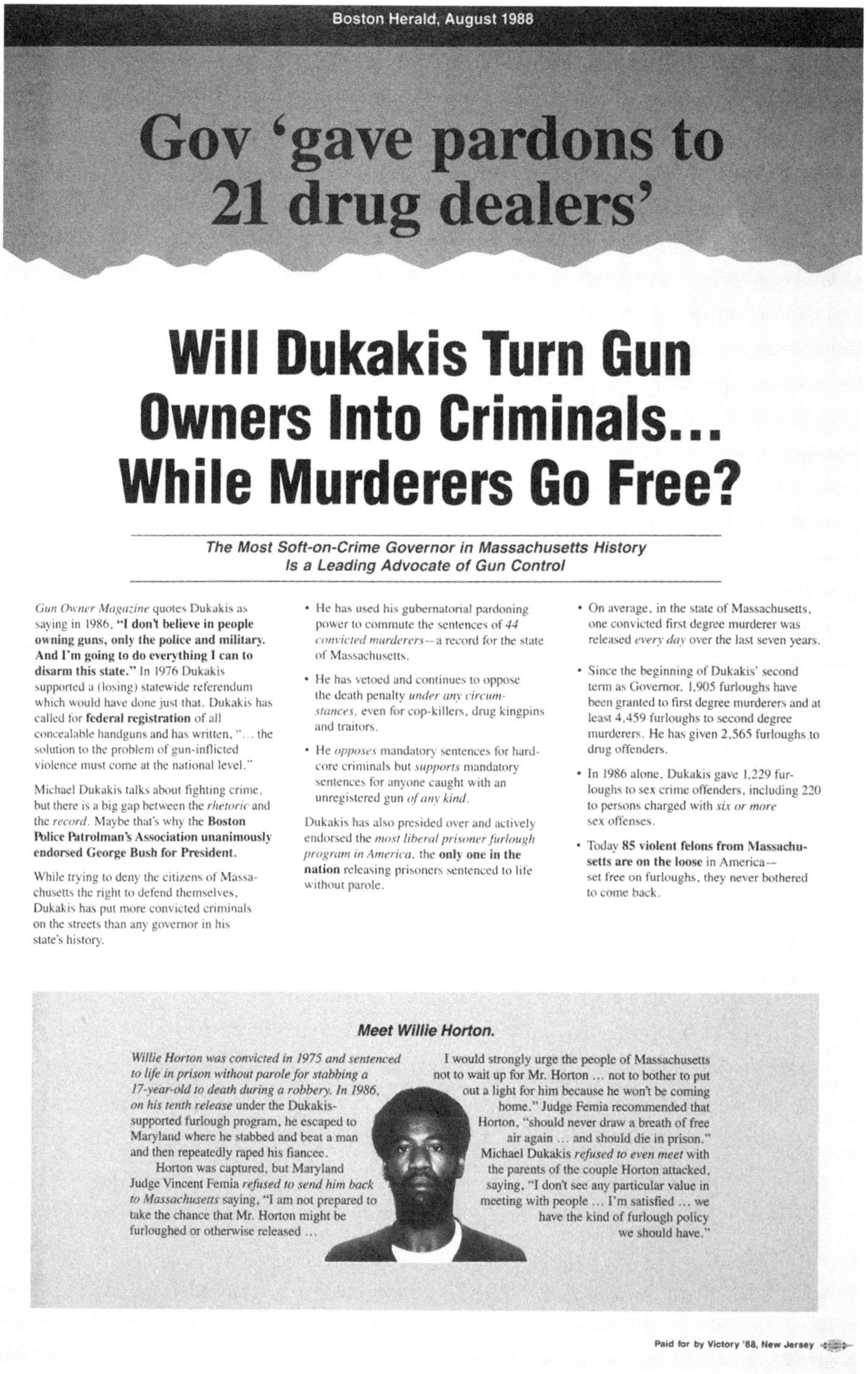

Gov 'gave pardons to 21 drug dealers'

Will Dukakis Turn Gun Owners Into Criminals... While Murderers Go Free?

The Most Soft-on-Crime Governor in Massachusetts History Is a Leading Advocate of Gun Control

Gun Owner Magazine quotes Dukakis as saying in 1986, **"I don't believe in people owning guns, only the police and military. And I'm going to do everything I can to disarm this state."** In 1976 Dukakis supported a (losing) statewide referendum which would have done just that. Dukakis has called for **federal registration** of all concealable handguns and has written, "... the solution to the problem of gun-inflicted violence must come at the national level."

Michael Dukakis talks about fighting crime, but there is a big gap between the *rhetoric* and the *record*. Maybe that's why the **Boston Police Patrolman's Association unanimously endorsed George Bush for President.**

While trying to deny the citizens of Massachusetts the right to defend themselves, Dukakis has put more convicted criminals on the streets than any governor in his state's history.

- He has used his gubernatorial pardoning power to commute the sentences of *44 convicted murderers*—a record for the state of Massachusetts.

- He has vetoed and continues to oppose the death penalty *under any circumstances,* even for cop-killers, drug kingpins and traitors.

- He *opposes* mandatory sentences for hard-core criminals but *supports* mandatory sentences for anyone caught with an unregistered gun of *any kind.*

Dukakis has also presided over and actively endorsed the *most liberal prisoner furlough program in America,* the **only one in the nation** releasing prisoners sentenced to life without parole.

- On average, in the state of Massachusetts, one convicted first degree murderer was released *every day* over the last seven years.

- Since the beginning of Dukakis' second term as Governor, 1,905 furloughs have been granted to first degree murderers and at least 4,459 furloughs to second degree murderers. He has given 2,565 furloughs to drug offenders.

- In 1986 alone, Dukakis gave 1,229 furloughs to sex crime offenders, including 220 to persons charged with *six or more* sex offenses.

- Today **85 violent felons from Massachusetts are on the loose** in America—set free on furloughs, they never bothered to come back.

Meet Willie Horton.

Willie Horton was convicted in 1975 and sentenced to life in prison without parole for stabbing a 17-year-old to death during a robbery. In 1986, on his tenth release under the Dukakis-supported furlough program, he escaped to Maryland where he stabbed and beat a man and then repeatedly raped his fiancee.

Horton was captured, but Maryland Judge Vincent Femia *refused to send him back to Massachusetts* saying, "I am not prepared to take the chance that Mr. Horton might be furloughed or otherwise released ...

I would strongly urge the people of Massachusetts not to wait up for Mr. Horton ... not to bother to put out a light for him because he won't be coming home." Judge Femia recommended that Horton, "should never draw a breath of free air again ... and should die in prison." Michael Dukakis *refused to even meet* with the parents of the couple Horton attacked, saying, "I don't see any particular value in meeting with people ... I'm satisfied ... we have the kind of furlough policy we should have."

FIGURE 6.7. William Horton and the 1988 presidential election. In an effort to paint his Democratic opponent as weak on crime, Republican nominee George H. W. Bush launched a racially charged attack ad in both print and television against Michael Dukakis in the 1988 presidential election. Bush went on to win the race. A number of scholars would later point to this negative ad, and the racial fear it conjured, as an important reason for Bush's victory. Copyright Frent Collection/Corbis-Getty Images. Reproduced with permission.

Bipartisan Campaign Reform Act, whose **Stand by Your Ad** provision required that advertisements feature a declaration by the candidate taking responsibility for it.)

Criticisms of the ad, however, hardly served as a deterrent for future presidential campaigns. Negative advertisements—including those that appeal to racial anxieties and animosities—have continued to be aired in the years since the 1988 election. In the 2012 race between Obama and Romney, 61 percent of television ads were negative. Interestingly, though, the tone and content of television ads in the 2020 election turned sharply positive. For all the controversy, vitriol, and disagreement that characterized that showdown between Trump and Biden, only 27 percent of television ads were negative.[74]

If Americans disdain political ads, why do they so frequently appear on our airwaves come election time? As it turns out, relative to the marginal effects of most campaign advertising, negative ads may be particularly well suited to persuade voters. Research from cognitive psychology points to a "negativity bias" in how humans process information, meaning that unpleasant news can more easily affect our mood than equivalent positive news.[75] Consequently, in addition to harming their impression of targeted candidates,[76] negative ads have been shown to boost voters' memory of political information.[77] Moreover, negative ads can be especially persuasive when they tap into feelings of fear and anxiety[78]—precisely the emotions evoked by the Horton ad.*

None of this, however, means that negative ads can derail the fundamental dynamics of presidential elections. Their effectiveness relies on a host of other factors. Incumbents, for example, have been shown to benefit less from negative ads than challengers.[79] The content of the ad is also important: substantive critiques are far more effective than personal attacks. And if an ad is perceived as irrelevant "mudslinging," voters' evaluations of *both* candidates can take a hit.[80] Though negative ads have their place in politics, they are hardly a fail-safe tool for candidates trailing in the polls.

6.3.2 Presidential Debates

The most visible events of a presidential election are debates, which are not easily controlled and thus often invite gaffes, heated argumentation, and overblown rhetoric. Accordingly, they are endlessly parsed by the news media, with reporters and pundits obsessing over who "won" the debate and what it will mean for the final election results.

Vice President Richard Nixon and Massachusetts senator John F. Kennedy met in Chicago for the first of three debates—and the first televised presidential debate in American history—on September 26, 1960. Nixon's staff reportedly regarded the debate as simply another campaign event and made no special effort to prepare their candidate

---

* The effectiveness of this specific ad is the subject of some controversy. According to some, appeals to racial fears are most effective when made implicitly, and the Horton ad, having made race explicit, lost its persuasiveness. Other authors have argued that explicit racial appeals are no more effective when made implicitly. See Tali Mendelberg, *The Race Card Campaign Strategy, Implicit Messages, and the Norm of Equality* (Princeton: Princeton University Press, 2001); and Gregory A. Huber and John S. Lapinski, "The 'Race Card' Revisited: Assessing Racial Priming in Policy Contests," *American Journal of Political Science* 50, no. 2 (2006): 421–40.

FIGURES 6.8 AND 6.9. Nixon and Kennedy in the 1960 televised debate. In the hot glare of television lights, Richard Nixon sweated profusely during a 1960 presidential debate with the dapper young Democratic nominee, John F. Kennedy. The visual distinction between the two, some say, left a powerful impression on the audience. *Sources:* Nixon: AP Images; Kennedy: Copyright 1960 Bettmann/Getty Images, reproduced with permission.

for television. Nixon, who had recently ended a twelve-day stint in the hospital for an infection and still had a low-grade fever, appeared unshaven, gaunt, and pallid (figure 6.8). He had apparently prepared for the debate entirely by reading policy briefs. Kennedy's staff, on the other hand, was said to have been highly sensitive to the opportunities and challenges posed by the televised event, carefully checking how their candidate's attire appeared on-screen and leading the senator through a series of mock debates beforehand (figure 6.9).

Watching the debate today, Kennedy does seem visibly healthier and younger than Nixon, whose face glistens with sweat. Kennedy also adopts a tone more consistent with that of modern political rhetoric, emphasizing lofty goals and traditional American values, whereas Nixon uses the staid traditional rhetoric of parliamentary debate.

The ensuing coverage of the debate made much of these differences, and a particular contention would pass into popular consciousness: among those who watched the debate on television, the advantage was overwhelmingly given to Kennedy; radio listeners, on the other hand, regarded Nixon as the victor. The implication was that Nixon, the more substantive candidate, was penalized for appearance and style, while Kennedy's on-screen charisma masked his inattention to policy details.

Like other popular claims about the effects of television, however, this claim about the Nixon-Kennedy debate has been made with almost no empirical support. The only poll cited to back it up is a survey by a commercial market research firm, which used a small and unrepresentative sample. No attempt was made to account for the demographic differences between radio and television audiences: the radio sample was overwhelmingly rural and Protestant, an audience that likely had a prior aversion to Kennedy, an urban Catholic.*

Regardless, this account of the debate's reception has shaped common wisdom about debates ever since: that they are potential turning points in a campaign; that they are principally a test of a candidate's capacity to appear presidential, rather than demonstrate policy mastery; and finally, that the public's evaluation of a debate will be powerfully conditioned by media coverage.

Press coverage of the presidential horse race regularly construes debates as the final opportunity for a languishing candidate to close the gap with the front-runner—or not. President Gerald Ford was said to have cemented his political fate in 1976 when he stated during a debate with Jimmy Carter that, all facts to the contrary, "there is no Soviet domination of eastern Europe, and there never will be under the Ford Administration."[81] President Reagan was thought to have won major points with viewers during the 1984 presidential debates when, after being asked if, at seventy-three, he was too old to be president, he quipped, "I will not make age an issue of this campaign. I am not going to exploit, for political purposes, my opponent's youth and inexperience."[82] Romney's performance in the first debate in 2012 was widely held to have upped the stakes of that race, effectively erasing the small but stable lead the president had established beforehand. In the second debate, however, Obama reportedly regained momentum by hitting back hard, hammering Romney for his politically inept comments about the "47 percent" who would vote for Obama "no matter what" in return for government entitlements and for his time at Bain Capital, "play[ing] by a different set of rules" designed for the ultra-rich.

---

* In an attempt to perform a more rigorous test of these claims, in a 2003 article Jamie Druckman randomly assigned subjects to watch and listen to the debate—those who watched the debate had a small pro-Kennedy preference, compared to radio listeners. But this too was an imperfect test. While Druckman carefully excluded subjects who had any prior knowledge of the debate, the 1960 encounter was easily the most famous of all presidential debates, and accordingly his findings might confound a television effect with respondents' vague impression that then-senator Kennedy was a consummate TV performer. Just as plausibly, these apparent Kennedy preferences might simply be mediating the stark difference in historical evaluation of the two presidents' respective legacies. See James Druckman, "The Power of Television Images: The First Kennedy-Nixon Debate Revisited," *Journal of Politics* 65, no. 2 (2003): 559–71.

Popular accounts of presidential elections are replete with such anecdotes. The actual significance of these moments, however, is doubtful. A study by Thomas Holbrook on debates attributes to them much less influence than do most political reporters. For one thing, according to the study, the debates conclude only weeks before Election Day, so they come too late in the election to change many people's minds.[83] In fact, due to early voting, some voters have already cast their ballot before the first debate has occurred. Moreover, debates are broadcast to viewers who are, for the most part, already fervently rooting for their preferred candidate and unlikely to be moved by even the most embarrassing misstep. Lastly, by the time of a debate, the other factors shown to have major consequences for electoral outcomes (namely, incumbency status and the economy) have already been baked into the election.

The 2016 presidential campaign offers additional support to Holbrook's claims. Nearly every pundit and pollster expected Clinton to win this race. And according to many political observers, the October debates put the final nails in the coffin of what many viewed as a poorly organized and undisciplined Trump campaign. The first debate, in particular, featured Trump rambling, easily distracted by Clinton's taunts, and lacking a clear message for undecided voters. After the debate, Republican Party official Bill Flores of Texas conceded that Trump "made some good points, but he wasn't as consistent as he could be."[84] Republican congressman Patrick Meehan of Pennsylvania said Trump "had an idea where he wanted to go" but didn't quite get there. "He started out strong but needed to be able to stay disciplined."[85] Or as Barack Obama put it, "I would say that the other guy [Donald Trump] doesn't have the preparation, the temperament or the core values of inclusion and making everybody have opportunities that would take our country forward."[86]

In each of their evaluations, they may have been right. It is not clear, though, that it mattered very much. Less than a month later, Trump won the Electoral College. And in the post-election commentary, hardly anyone suggested that his debate performances obstructed his pathway to the presidency.

6.3.3 Campaign Scandals

We've established that advertising and debates have marginal effects on voter choice. Let's turn now to scandals. Scandals, small and large, are something of a mainstay of presidential elections. Opposition researchers scour the pasts of their competitors. Enterprising journalists hound the candidates at every turn. And caught on a hot mic or momentarily letting their guard lapse, candidates may say something untoward, uncouth, or unwise. The revelation or gaffe can unleash a frenzy of media activity and personal attacks, putting a campaign on the defensive, if not derailing it entirely.

Consider, by way of example, Gary Hart's bid for the 1988 presidential election. At the time, the junior senator from Colorado was a front-runner to win the Democratic nomination, and Gallup had him beating the presumptive Republican nominee George H. W. Bush by 13 points in the general election.[87] In a *New York Times* interview,

Hart lamented the media's fascination with personal politics and inattention to substantive political issues. When asked about his womanizing past, Hart spoke off the cuff and told reporter E. J. Dionne Jr., "Follow me around. I don't care. I'm serious. If anybody wants to put a tail on me, go ahead. They'd be very bored."[88] Unfortunately for him, reporters from the *Miami Herald* did just that. After receiving an anonymous tip that Hart was having an affair with actress Donna Rice, the journalists staked out his Washington home and caught the two leaving the premises together.[89] Shortly thereafter, Hart suspended his campaign, ceding the Democratic nomination to the less well-known Massachusetts governor Michael Dukakis, and George H. W. Bush went on to win the election.

The next big scandal in a presidential election was not far off. Just four years later, in 1992, Arkansas governor Bill Clinton, who was seeking the Democratic nomination for president, was accused of sexual impropriety. Unlike Gary Hart's sex scandal, however, this one did not stick. The scandal centered around a woman named Gennifer Flowers, a cabaret dancer and former television reporter who told tabloids that she had been involved in an extramarital affair with Clinton for twelve years.[90] Clinton managed to weather this scandal, partly because of the way he and his wife, Hillary, responded to the allegations. In a joint interview on the popular television show *60 Minutes*, Hillary Clinton appealed to the American people: "I'm sitting here because I love him, and I respect him, and I honor what he's been through and what we've been through together. And you know, if that's not enough for people, then heck—don't vote for him."[91] But plenty of Americans did vote for him—enough, in fact, for him to win first the Democratic nomination and then the presidency itself. As historian Julian Zelizer recalled, "The truth is that many Americans didn't really care about the personal peccadilloes of politicians as long as their private actions didn't fundamentally clash with the political positions for which they stood."[92]

Scandals, it seems, have the power to derail some campaigns (in the case of Gary Hart) while other campaigns can make it out unscathed (in the case of Bill Clinton). How can we predict the results of scandals in advance? Does it come down to how well campaigns coordinate their response? Unlikely. First, it matters when the scandal erupts. Because voters tend to forget about scandals over time, candidates embroiled in last-minute scandals are more likely to face electoral consequences.[93] (For more on this, see the following section on "October surprises.") And second, it matters what kind of scandal it was; justly or not, scandals that impugn a candidate's character can have greater repercussions than those that concern a candidate's policy judgment.[94]

The effects of political scandals, however, cannot be divorced from the two fundamental factors of presidential elections: the electorate and the economy. When predicting whether a candidate will overcome a political scandal, it helps to first consider how the candidate is faring along these two dimensions. For a far-left or far-right challenger to a moderate incumbent, a scandal could mean the end of a campaign. For an incumbent running on a strong economic record, a major scandal might only be a minor setback. Research from the Watergate and Monica Lewinsky scandals bears this out: even amid these high-profile scandals, the standard economic indicators of inflation and employment were still the primary factors driving the two presidents' standing in the polls.[95]

Historical Transformations: Violating Norms of Financial Disclosure

Campaign scandals need not always involve a violation of American laws or values. Sometimes, they occur when candidates deviate from the well-established norms of presidential campaigns. In vital respects, public expectations about how presidents ought to behave, rather than formal strictures on how they must behave, help define the institutional presidency. And so it is with financial disclosures. There is nothing illegal about presidential candidates refusing to release their tax returns. Still, for the better part of forty years, presidential candidates had willingly done so. This practice, however, came to a screeching halt in 2016, when Donald Trump decided not to release his tax returns. And though all sorts of political activists and observers cried foul, none could compel him to do so either during the campaign or after he assumed office.

The standard practice of releasing tax returns traces back to, of all presidents, Richard Nixon. When he ran for the vice presidency under Dwight Eisenhower in 1952, Nixon was accused of mishandling campaign funds. In what is now known as the "Checkers Speech," Nixon assured his television audience that he had never abused a position of public service. He did admit to having been given a dog named Checkers, which, he conceded, could be construed as a political gift. Still, he cheekily insisted, he wasn't going to give her up.[96] To prove his trustworthiness, though, he released a financial summary statement and challenged the Democratic presidential and vice-presidential candidates to do the same, arguing that "if they don't, it will be an admission that they have something to hide."[97] The Democratic candidates, Adlai Stevenson and John Sparkman, released ten years of tax returns, and Eisenhower followed suit by releasing a summary statement of his own.

It wasn't until his second term as president that Nixon released his own tax returns.[98] The impetus for doing so, once again, was political self-preservation. In 1972, a Rhode Island newspaper, the *Providence Journal-Bulletin*, published a story revealing that Nixon and his wife had paid very small sums in taxes to the federal government.[99] Shortly thereafter, the *New York Times* published an article laying out the potential wrongdoing that Nixon was concealing, concluding that "only full financial disclosure could lay these questions to rest. The release of the president's income tax returns is the essential first step in this process."[100] It was in response to this charge that Nixon famously declared, "I am not a crook." He then went ahead and released his tax returns, which showed that he had paid only a 7 percent average tax for gross income between the years of 1969 and 1972.[101] To further limit the political damage wrought, Nixon agreed to pay back taxes totaling more than $400,000. It was the Watergate scandal, of course, that led to Nixon's undoing. But as tax historian Joseph Thorndike observes, Nixon's tax scandal "helped undermine faith in American political institutions, including not just the presidency but the federal tax system, too."[102]

Thereafter, presidential candidates routinely released their tax returns, and presidents and vice presidents had their taxes audited annually.[103] The only exception to this practice was Gerald Ford, who as a presidential candidate in 1976 released only summary tax data.[104] Unlike the summary data, tax returns reveal a complete picture of candidates' financial interests; more than simply stating their gross income and taxes paid, returns identify companies in which they have stakes, individuals to whom they owe money, amounts given to charity, and holdings kept in offshore locations.[105] Presidents were not legally obligated to provide this information. Instead, it was a norm that governed this feature of presidential elections. As Thorndike observes, the next forty years of presidential history has "turned Nixon's shame into something much more powerful: a norm of voluntary transparency observed by those presuming to seek the highest office in the land."[106]

But just as norms can be forged, so too can they be broken. On the campaign trail in 2016, Republican nominee Donald Trump admitted to paying "as little as possible" in taxes, and he resisted urgings to release his returns, including those from his fellow Republicans.[107] Initially, Trump claimed that he could not do so while he remained under audit, even though Nixon's tax returns were under audit when he established the norm of disclosure.[108] Even after the Internal Revenue Service publicly declared that an audit need not interfere with releasing tax returns, candidate Trump refused to budge.[109] And his election victory did not bring a change of heart. White House senior advisor Kellyanne Conway insisted that Trump would not release his tax returns, saying "we litigated this all through the election. People didn't care."[110] Even as calls for his tax returns intensified in the lead-up to Tax Day, culminating in protests in forty-eight states, with more than 25,000 attendees in DC alone, Trump resisted.[111]

To be sure, Trump's refusal to release his tax returns came at a political cost. Concerns about his financial dealings and potential conflicts of interest hounded his administration until the very end. But through his actions, Trump may have reshaped future expectations about financial disclosures. It is possible that the political furor surrounding Trump's decision not to share his tax returns may have imbued the norm with newfound meaning and import. On the other hand, though Trump's successor Joe Biden released his tax returns, the norm may be permanently weakened. Future candidates, seeing that the consequences for bucking tradition are not as severe as they imagined, may decide not to release their tax returns. Again, Thorndike: "The tradition is up for grabs right now. It's not clear that it will survive this."[112]

6.3.4 October Surprises

October surprises feature unexpected events or revelations late in a campaign cycle with the potential to affect the ultimate election outcome. The logic is simple enough: appearing in the waning days of a campaign, these events do not allow candidates to marshal an effective response; and for at least some voters, particularly those who remain undecided, this final piece of information may make the difference for their vote choice. Though we lack much systematic evidence of October surprises upending elections, a handful of prominent cases have breathed life into the myth—if not the reality—of their enduring relevance.

One of the earliest examples of an October surprise came in late October 1880, when a letter was published in which Republican presidential nominee James Garfield allegedly opined that employers have "the right to buy labor where they can get it cheapest."[113] This came during a time when many white workers were afraid of losing their jobs to cheaper Chinese immigrants. The letter blindsided Garfield in the final stretch of the election, but after investigation, its authenticity was questioned, as the man who Garfield allegedly wrote could not be found.[114] Though damaged, Garfield managed to eke out a victory just weeks later.

In some elections, candidates work furiously to quash an October surprise that might benefit the competition. This kind of preemptive behavior reached the pinnacle of dramatic heights in 1968, when Republican candidate Richard Nixon interfered with ongoing efforts to negotiate a last-minute peace deal to the Vietnam War. Nixon entered the fall with a commanding lead in the electoral projections, thanks to a Democratic voting base that was divided between Democratic nominee Hubert Humphrey and third-party candidate George Wallace. That September, however, the gap narrowed significantly as a series of missteps by Wallace drove Democrats back to Humphrey. Facing a narrowing margin for victory, Nixon's case for becoming president rested heavily on his ability to persuade voters that he would finally bring the Vietnam War to an end. At the time, though, then-president Lyndon Johnson was working toward a peace settlement, which Vietnam's president Nguyễn Văn Thiệu was reluctant to endorse.

Had President Johnson reached a settlement, one of Nixon's main campaign arguments would have been rendered moot. Worried about the electoral repercussions, Nixon directed Anna Chennault, the widow of a U.S. general from World War II, to act as a line of communication between Nixon and the Vietnamese government. Through Chennault, Nixon convinced Thieu to avoid signing any peace agreements until after the election, promising him a better deal. While conducting wartime surveillance of South Vietnam, the Johnson administration discovered what was later dubbed "the Chennault Affair." Concerns about domestic upheaval and the damage done to U.S. relations with South Vietnam prevented Johnson from releasing the details of the subterfuge.[115] An October surprise thus avoided, Nixon won the election handily.

Not all October surprises come in the form of scandals. John McCain had entered September 2008 polling slightly ahead of Barack Obama when a confluence of economic disasters brought his candidacy to a halt: in September, the investment company Lehman Brothers filed for bankruptcy; in the first week of October, the Dow Jones Industrial Average fell 18 percent; and on October 3, it was announced that the United States had lost 159,000 jobs.[116] The "Great Recession" actually began in December 2007, but the confluence of events in fall 2008 stunted McCain's chances of replacing his fellow Republican George W. Bush in the White House.[117]

The 2016 election delivered October surprises for both candidates. In early October, the *Washington Post* released a tape it had acquired from the television show *Access Holly-wood*, which recorded Donald Trump bragging about his ability to "grab [women] by the pussy" and "when you're a star they let you do it."[118] The fallout from his lewd remarks was swift: prominent Republicans including Kelly Ayotte, Paul Ryan, John McCain, Ted Cruz, Marco Rubio, and Jeb Bush denounced his behavior. Republican fundraiser Spencer Zwick indicated that "major GOP donors are pulling back support from Donald Trump and are now looking to fund an effort to back someone else as the Republican nominee."[119] The opposition party, though, was grappling with an October surprise of its own. At around the same time, the online group WikiLeaks released the transcripts of paid speeches Hillary Clinton had given to Wall Street firms and a slew of emails sent by her campaign manager, John Podesta.[120] Donald Trump responded to this leak by arguing that the emails showed definitive proof of "collusion" between the Clinton team and the Department of Justice.[121] Revealed portions of Clinton's speeches expressed support for hawkish foreign policy and indicated that she had "both a public and a private position" on policy issues.[122] Then, on October 28, FBI director James Comey informed Congress that emails found on the computer of the disgraced husband of Hillary Clinton's top aide required the investigation into the email scandal to be reopened.[123] A week later, Comey announced that the emails were immaterial and closed the investigation back down. In the interim, however, many citizens had cast early votes, all but sealing Clinton's electoral defeat.

Though commentators still blame Comey's announcement for Clinton's defeat, there is plenty of reason to look skeptically upon the accuracy of most October surprises. As Gabriele Gratton and his coauthors point out, politicians think strategically about when to leak bombshells about their opponents—often in ways that can be deceptive to the average voter.[124] If candidates know that the information they are leaking is false, or at the very least misleading, they tend to keep it secret until just before the election. That way, the media has very little time to discredit it. Conversely, if the information is accurate, candidates should want to release it as soon as possible, then sit back while the media scrutinizes their opponents. Examining a data set of past presidential elections, Gratton and his coauthors find that these dynamics are quite helpful in understanding last-minute scandals. The frequency of October surprises, they discovered, is driven by "fake" scandals that are discredited only after sufficient time has passed. In other words, when a candidate happens upon a "shocking discovery" about his opponent the week before the election, there is a good chance it is false.

What do these strategic considerations tell us about the effects of October surprises on election results? While unexpected economic downturns may be able to derail a campaign, scandalous October surprises likely have much smaller effects than we think. On paper, they may appear damning. But in practice, they often amount to very little. This would explain why, according to the little systemic evidence we have, October surprises do not seem to have much effect on the polls, at least not consistently—the exception being economic events.[125] On the one hand, last-minute disruptions would seem to be highly influential on elections; after all, they are fresh in the minds of voters as they go to the polls. But on the other, October surprises occur only after most voters have already formed and solidified their opinions, and they arise under clouds of suspicion about their veracity. These two realities work against each other, reducing the power of October surprises to reliably change election results.

6.4 Declaring a Winner

On Election Day, millions of Americans come out to select the next president—either by showing up at a polling place, mailing in their ballot, or casting their vote at a local drop box. For hours after the polls close, election workers from Maine to Alaska begin to tally the votes. Meanwhile, the major decision desks—at Fox News, CNN, and the Associated Press, among others—keep track of the electoral votes accumulated by each candidate. When one candidate obtains 270 electoral votes (a majority of the 538 votes possible),* a winner is declared.

Of course, this process does not always go according to plan. Some states report final results on the night of the election; others wait a good deal longer to do so. Sometimes, the closest contests can only be resolved via litigation. And even when the major decision desks have named a winner, the weeks between Election Day and Inauguration Day are replete with procedural and ceremonial events for declaring a winner—each providing a point of vulnerability for the electoral system, should norms be flaunted or rules ignored.

6.4.1 Counting Votes, Certifying Elections

When Americans cast their votes for president, they are actually selecting a slate of electors to vote on behalf of their state. Article II, Section 1 of the Constitution assigns state legislators the responsibility of appointing electors, although this function has since been delegated to political parties. Democratic and Republican state parties nominate competing slates of electors, only one of which is confirmed by the voters on Election Day. When a candidate wins a state, his or her party's electors are appointed as the state's official electors. The state finalizes this decision through a "Certificate of Ascertainment," which the governor mails to the Archivist of the United States.[126]

By mid-December, electors in each state meet in their respective capitols to formally cast their votes. Each elector must sign six "Certificates of the Vote," which are mailed to the president of the Senate (i.e., the vice president), the Archivist, their state's elections administrator, and the chief judge of the local district court. On January 3, the Archivist sends the Certificates of the Vote to both chambers of the new Congress in preparation for a joint session on January 6.

---

*Forty-eight states and the District of Columbia assign all their electors to the candidate who wins the popular vote in their state. Maine and Nebraska each assign two electors to the statewide winner, assigning the others to the winner of each congressional district.

Historically a ceremonial affair, the January 6 joint session certifies the president-elect's victory. The president of the Senate reads aloud the Electoral College votes of each state in alphabetical order. After a state's results have been read, a senator and representative may jointly (and in writing) object to its electoral vote tally. If an objection has been brought, alleging either that an elector's vote was not "regularly given" or that an elector's appointment was not "lawfully certified," the two chambers must separately deliberate and vote on the electors in question. For an objection to succeed, a majority of both chambers must vote in its favor. In exceptionally rare instances where a state introduces multiple slates of electors, the two chambers must decide which one to select; if no congressional action is taken, then the slate certified by the governor is counted.[127]

If, after all this, no candidate achieves the bare minimum of 270 electoral votes necessary for victory, the Twelfth Amendment provides for a contingent election beginning on January 6. The president then is elected by a majority of state delegations in the House of Representatives, and the vice president by a majority in the Senate.* Such a scenario has occurred only twice in the nation's history, in 1800 and 1824.† If the House cannot agree on a winner, its members hold successive votes until a compromise is reached; should this process drag on past Inauguration Day, the Senate's choice for vice president is sworn in as acting president.‡

Faithless electors—electors who vote for someone other than the winner of their state—can complicate matters in close elections. For example, George W. Bush won 271 electoral votes in 2000. Had just *two* of these electors broken ranks and voted for a third party candidate or abstained, a contingent election would have been initiated. Frequently, faithless electors cast their votes (or abstain) as a protest—of the Electoral College,[128] of the candidate to whom they were pledged,[129] of the District of Columbia's lack of congressional representation,[130] or for other reasons. Many states pass laws to prevent faithless electors by imposing fines, voiding their votes, or replacing them with new electors—laws that the Supreme Court recently upheld as constitutional in *Chiafalo v. Washington* (2020).[131] This ruling may very well limit the impact of faithless electors in the future, though many states still have not passed any protections against rogue electoral votes.

---

* In the House, which elects the president, each state delegation votes as a unit for one candidate, and no more than three candidates (the three with the highest number of Electoral College votes) can partake. For instance, suppose the 2020 election resulted in an Electoral College tie, 269 votes to 269. Twenty states had Democratic-majority delegations, twenty-seven had Republican-majority delegations, and three were exactly tied. If votes were cast on the party line, Donald Trump would win the contingent election in the House 27-20-3. In the Senate, only the top two candidates advance to the contingent election, and senators vote as individuals to elect the vice president.

† The sole exception would be the vice-presidential contingent election of 1837. For more, see "Contingent Election of the President and Vice President by Congress: Perspectives and Contemporary Analysis," CRS Report R40504 (Washington, DC: Congressional Research Service, 2020), https://sgp.fas.org/crs/misc/R40504.pdf.

‡ In the unlikely event that *both* the House and Senate deadlock and do not elect a president or vice president by Inauguration Day, the Speaker of the House assumes the role of acting president. There is no precedent for an election this close, though a narrowly won House and an evenly divided Senate could produce such a result.

6.4.2 Contested Elections

In most elections, the process of tallying and validating votes goes according to plan: votes are tallied, electors cast their ballots faithfully, a winner is declared without a contingent election, and the victor subsequently moves into the White House. Sometimes, though, things do not go so smoothly. In at least four presidential elections—1800, 1876, 2000, and 2020—uncertainty lingered long after Election Day.

THE 1800 ELECTION

The 1800 race between John Adams and Thomas Jefferson is generally regarded as the first peaceful transfer of power between political rivals in the United States.[132] Adams, the incumbent president, was a Federalist who had served as Washington's vice president. His disdain for Jefferson, a Republican, was well known; his allies publicly criticized Jefferson as "an Atheist in Religion and a Fanatic in politics."[133] Americans worried that, should Adams lose the election, he would refuse to resign, opening a rift in our national politics that, in time, could lead to a civil war.

In the end, Jefferson and the Republicans won the election, with one unlikely twist: Jefferson and his vice-presidential candidate, Aaron Burr, tied with exactly 73 electoral votes each.* For six days in early 1801, the House of Representatives failed to break the tie. The Republicans voted for Jefferson, and the Federalists lined up behind Burr, whom they saw as their only acceptable alternative. It was not until a group of Republican governors threatened violence that the Federalists capitulated, and Jefferson was elected the third president of the United States.

But tensions did not altogether subside. The question still remained whether Adams would concede defeat and step down from office. Adams answered the question unambiguously. Rather than contest the election, as some Federalists encouraged him to do, Adams accepted the Republican victory.[134] On the day of Jefferson's inauguration, he left the White House and took a carriage back home to Massachusetts.

THE 1876 ELECTION

The race between Republican governor Rutherford B. Hayes and Democratic governor Samuel Tilden seemed, at first, to have been won by Tilden.[135] Though he had secured a majority in the popular vote, Tilden's victory was upended by a Republican plot to overturn the results in a handful of close states. In Florida, Louisiana, and South Carolina, state officials produced two separate and conflicting slates of electors to vote on the candidates, and both tallies were sent to Congress to certify. In January of the following year, members

---

*Until the Twelfth Amendment was ratified in 1804, each elector was given two votes. The candidate who received the largest share of electoral votes became president, while the second-place candidate became vice president. It was possible, therefore, for members of opposing parties to co-occupy the White House or, as was the case in 1800, for presidents to tie with their vice-presidential candidates.

of Congress assembled a commission to choose which electors should be recognized—and thus, who should become president. The commission ultimately handed the election to Hayes.

Furious, Democrats in Congress threatened to delay the final authorization of Hayes's victory. Such a tactic would have sent the election to a vote in the House of Representatives, which then was controlled by Democrats. On March 2, however, just two days before the constitutionally defined inauguration date, Democrats brokered a deal that allowed Hayes to take office: in return for the presidency, Hayes and leading Republicans agreed to withdraw federal troops from the southern states, ending Reconstruction and the federal government's efforts—such as they were—to combat disenfranchisement, segregation, and violence against Black Americans.

THE 2000 ELECTION

The election of George W. Bush in 2000 remains one of the closest presidential elections in U.S. history. On election night, it was clear that Bush's opponent, Vice President Al Gore, had won the popular vote, but neither candidate had secured an Electoral College majority. In Florida, with its 25 electoral votes, the vote margin was so thin as to trigger a mandatory recount.

The results of the recount were completed on November 10, and they showed Bush with a miniscule lead of 327 votes (out of approximately 6 million cast).[136] Meanwhile, Gore's legal team demanded that an additional hand-recount be conducted in counties with disputed ballots. The Florida Supreme Court sided with Gore, giving three counties (Broward, Miami-Dade, and Palm Beach) until November 26 to submit their final tallies. When the deadline arrived, however, Florida secretary of state Katherine Harris, a Republican, officially certified Bush's victory before the full results from Miami-Dade and Palm Beach were counted.

Gore formally contested Harris's decision, and the Florida Supreme Court again ruled in his favor. On December 8, the court ordered recounts in counties with large "undervotes," or ballots that did not indicate a vote for president. Approximately 45,000 ballots met this description statewide.[137] Bush subsequently appealed this ruling to the U.S. Supreme Court, and on December 12, the Court sided with Bush. In a 5–4 ruling, the justices halted the recount, arguing that the initial ruling applied uneven standards across the electorate. (For more on this decision, see chapter 11's Thinking Institutionally feature.) Immediately thereafter, the vice president honored the decision and conceded the election to Bush, ending his campaign for president.

THE 2020 ELECTION

Despite Donald Trump's claims to the contrary, the 2020 election was not nearly as close as the 2000 election. Having lost to Joe Biden by seven million votes, Trump spent his final months in office alleging—both online and in the courts—that the results were "rigged" and that "Frankly, we did win this election. . . . This is a major fraud on our nation."[138] Throughout the transition, which is discussed at length in chapter 7,[139] significant portions of the American public worried that the president would ultimately refuse to leave office. Other portions encouraged the president to do so.

Though unsubstantiated, Trump's allegations involved all sorts of conspiracies that statewide voting systems had been manipulated and that undocumented immigrants voted in large numbers. In just a handful of battleground states, Trump and his lawyers filed more than sixty lawsuits—all of which were defeated or dismissed for lack of evidence.[140] Trump nearly won a single case over a pocket of votes in Pennsylvania, only to have the state's Supreme Court overturn the ruling weeks later.[141] Just two cases made it to the U.S. Supreme Court, and both times the justices ruled swiftly and definitively against the president.

Even after his own Justice Department concluded that there was no voter fraud "on a scale that could have effected a different outcome in this election," Trump continued pressuring state and local officials not to certify their vote tallies.[142] In Georgia, after a hand audit and machine recount confirmed Biden's victory in the state, Trump publicly criticized the governor and secretary of state as an "enemy of the people" who needed to "get tough" to overturn the "scam" election results. In a private phone call, Trump urged Georgia's secretary of state to "recalculate" the results and "find" enough votes for him to win.[143] The state officials, both Republican, did not comply.

Following his defeats in the courts and in state governments, Trump turned to his most reliable group of supporters: his voting base. On January 6, 2021, Trump encouraged thousands of protesters to march on the Capitol as Congress was counting and certifying the results of the Electoral College. Much like Trump's legal battles, the events that followed— the desecration, violence, and bloodshed—did not change the election's outcome. Late that evening, after Trump's supporters were removed from the grounds, members of Congress reentered their chambers and certified Biden's victory. (For more on the events of January 6 and the impeachment proceedings that followed, see chapter 8.)

It was only when all these efforts failed—in the court of law, in state election administrations, and, ultimately, in the court of public opinion—that Trump begrudgingly left the nation's capital on the morning of Biden's inauguration. He did so without ever acknowledging, much less congratulating, the incoming president. Trump's myriad failures leading up to the inauguration made it much more difficult, perhaps unsustainable, for him to press his case any longer while holding office. In the end, he was not forcefully removed from office—as some suspected he might be.[144] Rather, he left reluctantly but on his own volition.

6.4.3 Democratic Vulnerabilities

In contested elections such as these, it may be comforting to think that the "correct" result will inevitably prevail—that the strength of our institutions, or perhaps the divine wisdom of the founders, will ensure a peaceful handoff of presidential power in every instance. Our democracy offers no such assurances.

Notice that all four of these elections were settled through some measure of concession or compromise. In 1800, resolution came only after Adams willingly resigned. In 1876, a deal was brokered to hand Hayes the presidency (and the South the end of Reconstruction). In 2000, Bush became president not because Gore was forced to step aside but because Gore, believing that "partisan feeling must yield to patriotism," did so voluntarily.[145]

And so it was in 2020. Trump never formally admitted defeat, nor did he attend the inauguration of his successor, Joe Biden, as all modern presidents had done. In the end, Trump exited the White House on his own two feet, accompanied—not prodded—by an armed security detail. His departure was far from congenial, but it was voluntary. The 2020 election, like all elections before it, concluded with the consent of the losing candidate.

But what would happen if this consent were withheld? Truthfully, nobody knows. In the entire history of the presidency, there are no examples of candidates being forcibly removed from the White House after refusing to concede defeat and abdicate power. All we can say with certainty, however, is that there are no rules—no regulations, no laws, no designated institutions—guaranteeing that the duly elected candidate would be sworn in as president. Instead, the sanctity of American elections relies, to a frightening and under-appreciated extent, on a shared commitment to democratic norms.[146]

To appreciate the significance of this point, imagine that the 2020 election had come down to a single state. Imagine, too, that this state's popular vote had fallen within what officials call the "margin of litigation"—meaning that its outcome was close enough to warrant a fight in the courts.[147] In this scenario, Trump's refusal to concede would have been far more than symbolic: it could very well have swung the election in his favor.

As his lawyers pursued allegations of voter fraud in the courts, and his allies in the media broadcast these claims to the public, Trump could have turned his attention to the electors themselves. He could have encouraged electors to vote against their states' popular vote totals, or pressured conservative state legislatures to appoint a new slate of electors, as we saw in the Hayes-Tilden race. In an election with a clear victor, as 2020 was, such actions might not make a difference. But if the election had been closer—and faith in its results had been even lower—Trump might never have left the White House.

Scenarios like these are not pure fiction. Indeed, in 2000, the election was close enough that Al Gore could have deployed similar tactics. His refusal to do so was inspired by a norm dating back to the election of 1800: that one candidate will eventually, through concession or compromise, make way for the other. When Americans lose sight of this norm, or at least when a single candidate fails to internalize it, democracy itself stands at risk. In the words of Steven Levitsky and Daniel Ziblatt, "Without robust norms, constitutional checks and balances do not serve as the bulwarks of democracy we imagine them to be."[148]

None of this is to say, of course, that Trump's actions in 2020 could only do damage in a hypothetically close election. Indeed, his actions *were* damaging, and we may not know the full extent of this damage for years to come. Since 2020, the lies he told have festered in the public conscience and motivated a wave of anti-democratic behavior. Believers of the "Big Lie" about a stolen 2020 election subsequently ran for local offices around the country in positions that oversee elections.[149] Meanwhile, Republican legislatures in at least eight states passed bills to reduce the authority of governors and state secretaries to administer elections—disempowering, in other words, those who defied Trump in 2020.[150] In their place, these bills empowered state legislatures to hire and fire county election board members at will, an unprecedented level of control over state and local elections. These proposals only added to decades of Republican efforts to restrict voting rights, further politicizing the bipartisan norms that safeguard our elections.

When consistent rules and procedures are needed most—that is, when election results are uncertain—they ultimately prove insufficient, and we must rely upon candidates' own goodwill and magnanimity. Many Americans take for granted that losers will acknowledge their fate, step aside, and permit their opponent to assume power. Unavoidably, though, elections remain vulnerable to those who might not be so gracious in defeat. According to the historian Julian Zelizer, "We talk about it, some worry about it, and we imagine what it would be. But few people have actual answers to what happens if the machinery of democracy is used to prevent a legitimate resolution to the election."[151]

Conclusion

The forces that shape general election campaigns, as well as their ultimate success, ultimately fall outside candidates' immediate control. Within the parameters set by fundamental political and economic trends, minor consequences result from each campaign's tactical innovations. Unexpected political maneuvers and mishaps may have a small, temporary effect on voter preferences, and these effects may be amplified by the news media. But just as candidates cannot change the rules by which votes are tallied and a winner is declared, such developments rarely do much to alter the larger context in which a campaign operates. Indeed, the single most consequential decision available to a campaign may just be to peacefully and graciously concede defeat when the time comes.

Key Terms

swing states	negative advertisements
structural factors	Stand by Your Ad
pocketbook voting	October surprise
sociotropic voting	

Questions for Discussion

1. How do basic institutional differences between primary and general elections affect the behavior of candidates over the course of a presidential election?

2. In what ways does the Electoral College shape the campaign strategies of presidential candidates?

3. Suppose that the United States switches to a simple, first-past-the-post popular vote method for determining presidential election victors, and the Electoral College is retired. How might we expect presidential campaigns to change? How might presidents govern differently?

4. Pundits frequently remark on the "nationalization" and "polarization" of modern elections. Do these trends encourage candidates to move to the ideological center in hopes of attracting the median voter, or to maintain a more partisan campaign in order to turn out party loyalists en masse?

5. Assess the following claim: "The things that candidates control matter very little for their electoral prospects, while the things that are beyond their control matter a great deal."

6. In a democratic political system, how should we think about the fact that election outcomes systematically correlate with outcomes over which the president exercises very little control?

7. In the wake of *Citizens United v. FEC*, there was concern among citizens and political observers that the wealthy would be able to "buy" elections. Given the evidence described within this chapter, is this threat significant? Consider especially the impact of advertisements vis-à-vis structural or "fundamental" attributes of the general election race.

Suggested Readings

Edwards, George C. *Why the Electoral College Is Bad for America*. 2nd ed. New Haven: Yale University Press, 2011.

Erikson, Robert, and Christopher Wlezien. *The Timeline of Presidential Elections: How Campaigns Do (and Do Not) Matter*. Chicago: University of Chicago Press, 2012.

Hillygus, Sunshine, and Todd Shields. *The Persuadable Voter: Wedge Issues in Presidential Campaigns*. Princeton: Princeton University Press, 2008.

Jamieson, Kathleen Hall. *Packaging the Presidency: A History and Criticism of Presidential Campaign Advertising*. New York: Oxford University Press, 1996.

Sides, John, Chris Tausanovitch, and Lynn Vavreck. *The Bitter End: The 2020 Presidential Election and the Challenge to American Democracy*. Princeton: Princeton University Press, 2022.

Sides, John, and Lynn Vavreck. *Identity Crisis: The 2016 Presidential Campaign and the Battle for the Meaning of America*. Princeton: Princeton University Press, 2018.

Stromer-Galley, Jennifer. *Presidential Campaigning in the Internet Age*. New York: Oxford University Press, 2014.

Wolbrecht, Christina, and J. Kevin Corder. *A Century of Votes for Women: American Elections since Suffrage*. Cambridge: Cambridge University Press, 2020.

Notes

1. For a thorough discussion of this paradox, see Andrew Gelman and Gary King, "Why Are American Presidential Election Campaign Polls So Variable When Votes Are So Predictable?" *British Journal of Political Science* 23, no. 4 (1993): 409.

2. Stuart Stevens, *The Big Enchilada: Campaign Adventures with the Cockeyed Optimists from Texas Who Won the Biggest Prize in Politics* (New York: Simon & Schuster, 2001), 95.

3. Fox News/Google Republican Presidential Debate, September 22, 2011.

4. NBC News/Tampa Bay Times/National Journal Republican Presidential Debate, January 23, 2012.

5. Peter Grier, "Etch-A-Sketch: Can Mitt Romney Shake Off His Aide's Mr. Potato Head Gaffe?" *Christian Science Monitor*, March 21, 2012, https://www.csmonitor.com/USA/Politics/The-Vote/2012/0321/Etch-A-Sketch-Can-Mitt-Romney-shake-off-his-aide-s-Mr.-Potato-Head-gaffe.

6. Ashley Parker and Trip Gabriel, "Romney Exhibits a Change in Tone on Immigration," *New York Times*, June 21, 2012, A.1.

7. CNN Arizona Republican Presidential Debate, February 22, 2012.

8. Presidential Debate, October 3, 2012.

9. Brice D. L. Acree et al., "Etch-a-Sketching: Evaluating the Post-Primary Rhetorical Moderation Hypothesis," *American Politics Research* 48, no. 1 (2018): 99–131.

10. Andrew B. Hall and James M. Snyder, "Candidate Ideology and Electoral Success" (unpublished manuscript, September 29, 2015).

11. Shigeo Hirano et al., "Primary Elections and Partisan Polarization in the U.S. Congress," *Quarterly Journal of Political Science* 5, no. 2 (2010): 169–91.

12. Seth E. Masket, *No Middle Ground: How Informal Party Organizations Control Nominations and Polarize Legislatures* (Ann Arbor: University of Michigan Press, 2011).

13. "Mad Money: TV Ads in the 2012 Presidential Campaign," *Washington Post*, http://www.washingtonpost.com/wp-srv/special/politics/track-presidential-campaign-ads-2012/. The states considered swing states are Colorado, Florida, Iowa, Michigan, Nevada, New Hampshire, North Carolina, Ohio, Virginia, and Wisconsin.

14. Bill Ruthhart and Jonathon Berlin, "Campaign Trail Tracker: Where Trump, Biden and Their Running Mates Have Traveled in Presidential Race's Final Weeks," *Chicago Tribune*, November 5, 2020, https://www.chicagotribune.com/politics/ct-viz-presidential-campaign-trail-tracker-20200917-edspdit2incbfnopchjaelp3uu-htmlstory.html.

15. Hillary Rodham Clinton, *What Happened* (New York: Simon & Schuster, 2018), 304.

16. Timeline via: "U.S. Voting Rights Timeline," Northern California Citizenship Project, 2004, https://a.s.kqed.net/pdf/education/digitalmedia/us-voting-rights-timeline.pdf.

17. "Who Voted in Early America?" Constitutional Rights Foundation, September 1, 2020, https://www.crf-usa.org/bill-of-rights-in-action/bria-8-1-b-who-voted-in-early-america.

18. VEP and VAP data retrieved from "The United States Census: Statistics of the Population of the United States," U.S. Census Bureau; Dave Leip, "Dave Leip's Atlas of U.S. Presidential Elections: United States Presidential Election Results," 2020, https://uselectionatlas.org/2020.php; Curtis Gans, *Voter Turnout in the United States, 1788–2009* (Washington, DC: Congressional Quarterly Press, 2011); Michael P. McDonald, "National General Election VEP Turnout Rates, 1789–Present," United States Elections Project; and Michael P. McDonald and Samuel L. Popkin, "The Myth of the Vanishing Voter," *American Political Science Review* 95, no. 4 (2001): 963–74.

19. John L. Moore, ed., *Congressional Quarterly's Guide to U.S. Elections*, 2nd ed. (Washington, DC: Congressional Quarterly Press, 1985).

20. "Centuries of Citizenship: A Constitutional Timeline," National Constitution Center, https://constitutioncenter.org/timeline/html/cw08_12159.html.

21. For a recent and important study of historical patterns of voter suppression, see Luke Keele, William Cubbison, and Ismail White, "Suppressing Black Votes: A Historical Case Study of Voting Restrictions in Louisiana," *American Political Science Review* 115, no. 2 (2021): 694–700.

22. Voting Rights Act of 1965, Pub. L. 89–110, 79 Stat. 437.

23. Christopher Uggen et al., "Estimates of People Denied Voting Rights," October 15, 2020, https://www.sentencingproject.org/wp-content/uploads/2020/10/Locked-Out-2020.pdf.

24. Uggen et al., "Estimates of People Denied Voting Rights."

25. "CSPAN Presentation: The Foreign-Born Population of the United States," U.S. Census Bureau, December 2, 2011.

26. J. Kevin Corder and Christina Wolbrecht, "Did Women Vote Once They Had the Opportunity?" *Insights on Law and Society* 20, no. 1 (2019), https://www.americanbar.org/groups/public_education/publications/insights-on-law-and-society/volume-20/issue-1/did-women-vote-once-they-had-the-opportunity-/.

27. "U.S. Senate: A Vote for Women," U.S. Senate, https://www.senate.gov/artandhistory/history/minute/A_Vote_For_Women.htm.

28. Eugene P. Trani, "Warren G. Harding: Life in Brief," Miller Center, University of Virginia, October 4, 2016, https://millercenter.org/president/harding/life-in-brief.

29. "Presidential Campaign Advertisement, 1920," National Museum of American History, https://americanhistory.si.edu/collections/search/object/nmah_540782.

30. J. Kevin Corder and Christina Wolbrecht, *Counting Women's Ballots: Female Voters from Suffrage through the New Deal* (New York: Cambridge University Press, 2016), 13.

31. Corder and Wolbrecht, "Did Women Vote Once They Had the Opportunity?"

32. Corder and Wolbrecht, *Counting Women's Ballots*.

33. Ruth Igielnik, "Men and Women in the U.S. Continue to Differ in Voter Turnout Rate, Party Identification," Pew Research Center, September 2, 2020, https://www.pewresearch.org/fact-tank/2020/08/18/men-and-women-in-the-u-s-continue-to-differ-in-voter-turnout-rate-party-identification/.

34. Jessa Crispin, "The False Promise of the 'Yoga Voter,'" *New Republic*, April 25, 2019, https://newrepublic.com/article/153504/false-promise-yoga-voter.

35. Darren Samuelsohn, "Who Are the Soccer Moms of 2016?" *POLITICO Magazine*, July/August 2016, https://www.politico.com/magazine/story/2016/07/2016-election-battleground-swing-states-soccer-moms-nascar-dads-demographics-trump-clinton-214047/.

36. "The Biden Agenda for Women," Joe Biden for President: Official Campaign Website, September 22, 2020, https://joebiden.com/womens-agenda/.

37. Elwood Watson, "Guess What Came to American Politics? Contemporary Black Conservatism," *Journal of Black Studies* 29, no. 1 (1998): 73–92.

38. "Voting Rights for African Americans," Library of Congress, https://www.loc.gov/classroom-materials/elections/right-to-vote/voting-rights-for-african-americans/.

39. Vaughn Davis Bornet, *The Presidency of Lyndon Baines Johnson* (Lawrence: University Press of Kansas, 1984), 96–97.

40. Jeremy D. Mayer, "LBJ Fights the White Backlash," *Prologue Magazine: Quarterly of the National Archives and Records Administration* 33, no. 1 (2001), National Archives, https://www.archives.gov/publications/prologue/2001/spring/lbj-and-white-backlash-1.html.

41. Bill Moyers, *Moyers on America* (New York: New Press, 2004), 167.

42. Mayer, "LBJ Fights the White Backlash."

43. Ted Gest, *Crime & Politics: Big Government's Erratic Campaign for Law and Order* (New York: Oxford University Press, 2003), 14.

44. "RN, MLK, and the Civil Rights Act of 1957," Richard Nixon Foundation, January 15, 2017, https://www.nixonfoundation.org/2017/01/rn-mlk-and-the-civil-rights-act-of-1957/.

45. "Presidential Election of 1968," 270toWin, https://www.270towin.com/1968_Election.

46. James Boyd, "Nixon's Southern Strategy: It's All in the Charts," *New York Times*, May 17, 1970, https://www.nytimes.com/packages/html/books/phillips-southern.pdf.

47. Theodore R. Johnson, "How the Black Vote Became a Monolith," *New York Times Magazine*, September 20, 2020, MM28.

48. Guy-Uriel E. Charles and Luis E. Fuentes-Rohwer, "The Court's Voting-Rights Decision Was Worse than People Think," *The Atlantic*, July 8, 2021, https://www.theatlantic.com/ideas/archive/2021/07/brnovich-vra-scotus-decision-arizona-voting-right/619330/.

49. Jack Citrin, Donald Green, and Morris Levy, "The Effects of Voter ID Notification on Voter Turnout: Results from a Large-Scale Field Experiment," *Election Law Journal* 13, no. 2 (2014): 228–42.

50. "Voter Identification Requirements | Voter ID Laws," National Conference of State Legislatures, https://www.ncsl.org/research/elections-and-campaigns/voter-id.aspx.

51. Christopher Ingraham, "The 'Smoking Gun' Proving North Carolina Republicans Tried to Disenfranchise Black Voters," *Washington Post*, July 29, 2016, https://www.washingtonpost.com/news/wonk/wp/2016/07/29/the-smoking-gun-proving-north-carolina-republicans-tried-to-disenfranchise-black-voters/.

52. Theodore Johnson and Max Feldman, "The New Voter Suppression," Brennan Center, January 16, 2020, https://www.brennancenter.org/our-work/research-reports/new-voter-suppression.

53. Kevin Morris, "Voter Purge Rates Remain High, Analysis Finds," Brennan Center, August 21, 2019, https://www.brennancenter.org/our-work/analysis-opinion/voter-purge-rates-remain-high-analysis-finds.

54. Daniel Goldman, "The Modern-Day Literacy Test? Felon Disenfranchisement and Race Discrimination," *Stanford Law Review* 57, no. 2 (2004): 611–55.

55. Yochai Benkler et al., "Mail-In Voter Fraud: Anatomy of a Disinformation Campaign," Berkman Klein Center, Harvard University, October 2, 2020.

56. As of 2007, Michael Lewis-Beck and Mary Stegmaier found that over four hundred articles had been published on this question: "Economic Models of Voting," in *The Oxford Handbook of Political Behavior*, ed. Russell J. Dalton and Hans-Dieter Klingemann (Oxford: Oxford University Press, 2007), 518–37.

57. Angus Campbell et al., *The American Voter* (Chicago: University of Chicago Press, 1960), 398.

58. Michael S. Lewis-Beck et al., *The American Voter Revisited* (Ann Arbor, MI: University of Michigan Press, 2007), 376.

59. The most prominent examples are Robert S. Erikson, "Economic Conditions and the Presidential Vote," *American Political Science Review* 83, no. 2 (1989): 567–73; Gregory B. Markus, "The Impact of Personal and National Economic Conditions on the Presidential Vote: A Pooled Cross-Sectional Analysis," *American Journal of Political Science* 32, no. 1 (1988): 137–54; and Richard Nadeau and Michael S. Lewis-Beck, "National Economic Voting in U.S. Presidential Elections," *Journal of Politics* 63, no. 1 (2001): 159–81.

60. Michael Lewis-Beck and Mary Stegmaier, "Economic Determinants of Electoral Outcomes," *Annual Review of Political Science* 3, no. 1 (2000): 183–219. See also Robert S. Erikson, "Economic Conditions and the Congressional Vote: A Review of the Macrolevel Evidence," *American Journal of Political Science* 34, no. 2 (1990): 373–99; Lewis-Beck and Stegmaier, "Economic Models of Voting."

61. Morris Fiorina, *Retrospective Voting in American National Elections* (New Haven: Yale University Press, 1981), 10.

62. These data consist of annual changes in GDP, which include economic activity after Election Day. When examining GDP changes in the second and third quarters of an election year, which avoid this complication, the same pattern arises, albeit with one big outlier. Between 1932 and 2016, election-year changes in quarterly GDP correlated strongly and positively with the incumbent president's vote share. In 2020, however, the economy shut down and then reopened during this same period, generating altogether unprecedented levels of economic upheaval. There is no evidence that the massive upswing associated with the economy's reopening redounded to the electoral benefit of Trump—and certainly not in ways that accord with historical patterns.

63. For more on the systemic effects of economic changes on elections and the performance of government, see Robert Erikson, Michael Mackuen, and James Stimson, *The Macro Polity* (New York: Cambridge University Press, 2002).

64. Lynn Vavreck, *The Message Matters: The Economy and Presidential Campaigns* (Princeton: Princeton University Press, 2009).

65. John Sides and Lynn Vavreck, *The Gamble: Choice and Chance in the 2012 Presidential Election* (Princeton: Princeton University Press, 2014).

66. The data for these figures were produced using Sara Fischer, "Biden Is Highest-Spending Political Candidate on TV Ads," *Axios*, October 24, 2020, https://www.axios.com/biden-highest-political-ad-spender-ever-91b5c8a8-35f7-4650-b1c3-1a24e5fd0770.html; "Expenditures Breakdown, Donald Trump, 2020 Cycle," *OpenSecrets*, https://www.opensecrets.org/2020-presidential-race/donald-trump/expenditures?id=N00023864; and "Expenditures Breakdown, Joe Biden, 2020 Cycle," *OpenSecrets*, https://www.opensecrets.org/2020-presidential-race/joe-biden/expenditures?id=N00001669.

67. For more on targeting political independents, see Lynn Vavreck, "The Reasoning Voter Meets the Strategic Candidate: Signals and Specificity in Campaign Advertising, 1998," *American Politics Research* 29, no. 5 (2001): 507–29; Paul Freedman and Ken Goldstein, "Measuring Media Exposure and the Effects of Negative Campaign Ads," *American Journal of Political Science* 43, no. 4 (1999): 1189–208; and Martin P. Wattenberg and Craig Leonard Brians, "Negative Campaign Advertising: Demobilizer or Mobilizer?" *American Political Science Review* 93, no. 4 (1999): 891–99.

68. A leading example is Milton Lodge, Marco R. Steebergen, and Shawn Brau, "The Responsive Voter: Campaign Information and the Dynamics of Candidate Evaluation," *American Political Science Review* 89, no. 2 (1995): 309–26.

69. Alan S. Gerber et al., "How Large and Long-lasting Are the Persuasive Effects of Televised Campaign Ads? Results from a Randomized Field Experiment," *American Political Science Review* 105, no. 1 (2011): 135–50.

70. Jörg L. Spenkuch and David Toniatti, "Political Advertising and Election Results," *Quarterly Journal of Economics* 133, no. 4 (2018): 1981–2036, 1984.

71. Alexander Coppock, Seth J. Hill, and Lynn Vavreck, "The Small Effects of Political Advertising Are Small Regardless of Context, Message, Sender, or Receiver: Evidence from 59 Real-Time Randomized Experiments," *Science Advances* 6, no. 36 (2020), https://www.science.org/doi/10.1126/sciadv.abc4046.

72. For more on the effectiveness of campaign advertisements, see Matthew P. Motta and Erika Franklin Fowler, "The Content and Effect of Political Advertising in U.S. Campaigns," *Oxford Research Encyclopedia of Politics*, December 22, 2016, https://doi.org/10.1093/acrefore/9780190228637.013.217.

73. Beth Schwartzapfel and Bill Keller, "Willie Horton Revisited," *The Marshall Project*, May 13, 2015, https://www.themarshallproject.org/2015/05/13/willie-horton-revisited.

74. "End of Cycle Report," Wesleyan Media Project, https://mediaproject.wesleyan.edu/2020-summary -032321/. See also Motta and Fowler, "The Content and Effect of Political Advertising in U.S. Campaigns."

75. Martin Haselmayer, "Negative Campaigning and Its Consequences: A Review and a Look Ahead," *French Politics* 17, no. 3 (2019): 355–72.

76. Kim Leslie Fridkin and Patrick J. Kenney, "Do Negative Messages Work?" *American Politics Research* 32, no. 5 (2004): 570–605.

77. J. G. Geer and J. H. Geer, "Remembering Attack Ads: An Experimental Investigation of Radio," *Political Behavior* 25, no. 1 (2003): 69–95.

78. Ted Brader, "Striking a Responsive Chord: How Political Ads Motivate and Persuade Voters by Appealing to Emotions," *American Journal of Political Science* 49, no. 2 (2005): 388–405.

79. Richard R. Lau and Gerald M. Pomper, *Negative Campaigning an Analysis of U.S. Senate Elections* (Lanham, MD: Rowman & Littlefield, 2004).

80. Kim Leslie Fridkin and Patrick J. Kenney, "Do Negative Messages Work?" *American Politics Research* 32, no. 5 (2004): 570–605.

81. Gerald R. Ford, "Presidential Campaign Debate," October 6, 1976, Gerhard Peters and John T. Woolley, The American Presidency Project, http://www.presidency.ucsb.edu/ws/?pid=6414.

82. Ronald Reagan, "Debate between the President and Former Vice President Walter F. Mondale in Kansas City, Missouri," October 21, 1984, Peters and Woolley, The American Presidency Project, http://www .presidency.ucsb.edu/ws/?pid=39296.

83. Thomas M. Holbrook, "Political Learning from Presidential Debates," *Political Behavior* 21, no. 1 (1999): 67–89.

84. Rachael Bade, "Hill Republicans: At Least Trump Didn't Blow It," *POLITICO*, September 27, 2016, http://www.politico.com/story/2016/09/trump-first-debate-performance-paul-ryan-228784.

85. Bade, "Hill Republicans."

86. Sierra Marquina, "Barack Obama on the 2016 Presidential Debate: I'd Be 'Even More Gray' If I Let Donald Trump's Digs Get to Me," *Us Weekly*, September 27, 2016, http://www.usmagazine.com/celebrity-news /news/barack-obama-reacts-to-2016-presidential-debate-w442314.

87. Matt Bai, "How Gary Hart's Downfall Forever Changed American Politics," *New York Times Magazine*, September 18, 2014, MM37.

88. E. J. Dionne Jr., "Gary Hart, the Elusive Front-Runner," *New York Times*, May 3, 1987, 6028.

89. Tom Fielder, Jim McGee, and James Savage, "The Gary Hart Story: How It Happened," *Miami Herald*, May 10, 1987, https://undercover.hosting.nyu.edu/s/undercover-reporting/item/14428.

90. "The 1992 Campaign; Clinton Denounces New Report of Affair," *New York Times*, January 24, 1992, A.14.

91. Claire Lampen, "Who Is Gennifer Flowers? Bill Clinton's Affairs Are Still Problematic for Hillary Clinton," *Mic*, October 9, 2016, https://mic.com/articles/156292/who-is-gennifer-flowers-bill-clinton-s-affairs-are-still-problematic-for-hillary-clinton.

92. Julian Zelizer, "Bill Clinton's Nearly Forgotten Sex Scandal," CNN, April 6, 2016, http://www.cnn.com/2016/04/06/opinions/zelizer-presidential-election-campaign-scandals-bill-clinton/index.html.

93. Miguel M. Pereira and Nicholas W. Waterbury, "Do Voters Discount Political Scandals over Time?" *Political Research Quarterly* 72, no. 3 (2019): 584–95.

94. Scott J. Basinger, "Judging Incumbents' Character: The Impact of Scandal," *Journal of Political Marketing* 18, no. 3 (2018): 216–39.

95. D. J. Smyth and S. W. Taylor, "Presidential Popularity: What Matters Most, Macroeconomics or Scandals?" *Applied Economics Letters* 10, no. 9 (2003): 585–88.

96. Lee Huebner, "The Checkers Speech after 60 Years," *The Atlantic*, September 22, 2012, https://www.theatlantic.com/politics/archive/2012/09/the-checkers-speech-after-60-years/262172/.

97. Stephen Mihm, "Nixon's Failed Effort to Withhold His Tax Returns," *Bloomberg View*, August 2, 2016, https://www.bloomberg.com/view/articles/2016-08-02/nixon-s-failed-effort-to-withhold-his-tax-returns.

98. Lauren Carroll, "Most GOP Nominees since 1970s Have Released Their Tax Returns, Fox's Chris Wallace Says," Politifact, http://www.politifact.com/punditfact/statements/2016/may/18/chris-wallace/most-gop-nominees-1970s-have-released-their-tax-re/.

99. Joseph J. Thorndike, "JCT Investigation of Nixon's Tax Returns," The History and Role of the Joint Committee: The Joint Committee and Tax History, United States Capitol Historical Society, February 2016, http://uschs.org/wp-content/uploads/2016/02/USCHS-History-Role-Joint-Committee-Taxation-Thorndike.pdf.

100. "Still a Mystery," *New York Times*, November 17, 1973, http://www.nytimes.com/1973/11/17/archives/still-a-mystery.html.

101. "President Nixon's Troublesome Tax Returns (Copyright, 2005, Tax Analysts)," Tax Analysts, http://www.taxhistory.org/thp/readings.nsf/cf7c9c870b600b9585256df80075b9dd/f8723e3606cd79ec85256ff6006f82c3?OpenDocument.

102. Thorndike, "JCT Investigation of Nixon's Tax Returns."

103. Kevin G. Hall and Greg Gordon, "Thanks to Nixon, President Trump's Taxes Will Be Audited Automatically Every Year," *McClatchy*, November 29, 2016, http://www.mcclatchydc.com/news/politics-government/white-house/article117755838.html.

104. Morgan Quinn, "Trump Won't Release His Taxes—But These Presidents Did," GOBankingRates, October 24, 2016, https://www.gobankingrates.com/personal-finance/trump-release-taxes-presidents/.

105. Melissa Yeager and Richard Skinner, "Why Is the Tax Return a Big Deal and What Information Can You Learn from It?" Sunlight Foundation, July 27, 2016, https://sunlightfoundation.com/2016/07/27/why-is-the-tax-return-a-big-deal-and-what-information-can-you-learn-from-it/.

106. Joseph Thorndike, "Tax History: Voyeurism, Disclosure, and Why the Trump Apologists Are Wrong," Tax Analysts, July 18, 2016, http://www.taxanalysts.org/content/tax-history-voyeurism-disclosure-and-why-trump-apologists-are-wrong.

107. Valentina Zarya, "Trump Takes Heat on *Meet the Press* and *This Week* over Tax Plan," *Fortune*, October 4, 2015, http://fortune.com/2015/10/04/trump-tax-plan-3/.

108. Ryan Kelly, "Chart: Presidential Candidates' Tax Returns," *Roll Call*, October 21, 2016, http://www.rollcall.com/news/politics/number-tax-returns-each-candidate-released-since-nixon-trump-clinton.

109. Katy O'Donnell, "The Evolving Tale of Trump's Tax Returns," *POLITICO*, August 1, 2016, http://politi.co/2av54XI.

110. Jill Disis, "Presidential Tax Returns: It Started with Nixon. Will It End with Trump?" *CNN Business*, January 23, 2017, http://money.cnn.com/2017/01/23/news/economy/donald-trump-tax-returns/index.html.

111. Gregory Krieg, "From Tweets to the Streets: Nationwide Anti-Trump 'Tax Day' Marches Came Together on Social Media," CNN, April 14, 2017, http://www.cnn.com/2017/04/14/politics/trump-tax-day-march-protests/index.html; David van den Berg, "Trump Still Has No Plans to Release Returns Despite Protests," Tax Analysts, April 19, 2017, http://www.taxanalysts.org/content/trump-still-has-no-plans-release-returns-despite-protests.

112. As quoted in Disis, "Presidential Tax Returns."

113. Taylor Gee, "15 October Surprises That Wreaked Havoc on Politics," *POLITICO Magazine*, October 4, 2016, http://politi.co/2dI3cky.

114. "An 1880 'October Surprise,'" *Garfield Observer*, October 19, 2012, https://web.archive.org/web/20201027224543/https://garfieldnps.wordpress.com/2012/10/19/an-1880-october-surprise/.

115. John A. Farrell, *Richard Nixon: The Life* (New York: Doubleday, 2017).

116. "October Surprise: Does It Ever Swing a US Election?" BBC News, October 30, 2016, http://www.bbc.com/news/magazine-19887898.

117. Harry Enten, "How Much Do 'October Surprises' Move the Polls?" *FiveThirtyEight*, October 30, 2016, https://fivethirtyeight.com/features/how-much-do-october-surprises-move-the-polls/.

118. David A. Fahrenthold, "Trump Recorded Having Extremely Lewd Conversation about Women in 2005," *Washington Post*, October 8, 2016, https://www.washingtonpost.com/politics/trump-recorded-having-extremely-lewd-conversation-about-women-in-2005/2016/10/07/3b9ce776–8cb4–11e6-bf8a-3d26847eeed4_story.html.

119. "Tape of Trump's Crude Remarks about Women Rocks Campaign," Bloomberg, October 7, 2016, https://www.bloomberg.com/politics/articles/2016-10-07/tape-of-trump-speaking-crudely-about-a-woman-emerges.

120. "The Strange History of the October Surprise," *Smithsonian Magazine*, October 11, 2016, http://www.smithsonianmag.com/history/strange-history-october-surprise-180960741/.

121. Sabrina Siddiqui, "Clinton Campaign Dubs WikiLeaks 'Russian Propaganda' after Latest Hack," *Guardian*, October 11, 2016, https://www.theguardian.com/us-news/2016/oct/11/clinton-campaign-wikileaks-hack-russia-donald-trump.

122. "18 Revelations from Wikileaks' Hacked Clinton Emails," BBC News, October 27, 2016, http://www.bbc.com/news/world-us-canada-37639370.

123. John Cassidy, "James Comey's October Surprise," *New Yorker*, October 28, 2016, http://www.newyorker.com/news/john-cassidy/james-comeys-october-surprise.

124. Gabriele Gratton, Richard Holden, and Anton Kolotilin, "When to Drop a Bombshell," *Review of Economic Studies* 85, no. 4 (2017): 2139–72.

125. Enten, "How Much Do 'October Surprises' Move the Polls."

126. "Counting Electoral Votes: An Overview of Procedures at the Joint Session, Including Objections by Members of Congress," CRS Report RL32717 (Washington, DC: Congressional Research Service, 2016), https://crsreports.congress.gov/product/pdf/RL/RL32717/12; Miles Parks, "Biden's Victory Cemented as States Reach Key Electoral College Deadline," National Public Radio, December 8, 2020, https://www.npr.org/2020/12/08/942288226/bidens-victory-cemented-as-states-reach-deadline-for-certifying-vote-tallies.

127. See "Counting Electoral Votes."

128. One 1988 elector from West Virginia cast her ballot for Lloyd Bentsen and Michael Dukakis for president and vice president, respectively, rather than the reverse, to protest the Electoral College. See Sharen Shaw Johnson, "Capital Line: [Final Edition]," *USA Today*, January 5, 1989, A.4.

129. See "Contingent Election of the President and Vice President by Congress: Perspectives and Contemporary Analysis," CRS Report R40504 (Washington, DC: Congressional Research Service, 2020), https://sgp.fas.org/crs/misc/R40504.pdf.

130. In 2000, one elector from the District of Columbia abstained, protesting the District's lack of representation in Congress. See David Stout, "The 43rd President: The Electoral College; The Electors Vote and the Surprises Are Few," *New York Times*, December 19, 2000, A.31.

131. "Supreme Court Clarifies Rules for Electoral College: States May Restrict Faithless Electors," CRS Legal Sidebar LSB10515 (Washington, DC: Congressional Research Service, 2020), https://www.everycrsreport.com/files/2020-07-10_LSB10515_6b3c61fe0a75b99d7ae9cce4a901771ae3ce6a33.pdf.

132. Joanne B. Freeman, "The Election of 1800: A Study in the Logic of Political Change," *Yale Law Journal* 108, no. 8 (1999): 1959.

133. Alexander Hamilton to John Jay, May 7, 1880, https://founders.archives.gov/documents/Hamilton/01-24-02-0378.

134. John E. Ferling, *Adams vs. Jefferson: The Tumultuous Election of 1800* (New York: Oxford University Press, 2005).

135. Paul Leland Haworth, *The Hayes-Tilden Disputed Presidential Election of 1876* (Cleveland: Burrows Brothers, 1906).

136. "How We Got Here: A Timeline of the Florida Recount," CNN, December 13, 2000, https://www.cnn.com/2000/ALLPOLITICS/stories/12/13/got.here/index.html.

137. "Election 2000 Timeline," *Pittsburgh Post-Gazette*, December 17, 2000, 4.

138. James P. Pfiffner, "The Violent Transition of the Presidency, 2020–2021," *SSRN Electronic Journal*, 2021, https://doi.org/10.2139/ssrn.3770839.

139. For book-length treatments of the topic, see Michael Wolff, *Landslide: The Final Days of the Trump Presidency* (New York: Henry Holt, 2021); and Jonathan Karl, *Betrayal: The Final Act of the Trump Show* (New York: Dutton, 2021).

140. William Cummings, Joey Garrison, and Jim Sergent, "By the Numbers: President Donald Trump's Failed Efforts to Overturn the Election," *USA Today*, January 6, 2021, https://www.usatoday.com/in-depth/news/politics/elections/2021/01/06/trumps-failed-efforts-overturn-election-numbers/4130307001/.

141. Jacob Shamsian, "Trump and His Allies Filed More than 40 Lawsuits Challenging the 2020 Election Results; All of Them Failed," *Business Insider*, February 22, 2021, https://www.businessinsider.com/trump-campaign-lawsuits-election-results-2020–11.

142. Katie Benner and Michael S. Schmidt, "Barr Acknowledges Justice Dept. Has Found No Widespread Voter Fraud," *New York Times*, December 1, 2020, A.1.

143. Marshall Cohen, Jason Morris, and Christopher Hickey, "Timeline: What Georgia Prosecutors Are Looking at as They Investigate Trump's Efforts to Overturn the Election," CNN, August 5, 2021, https://www.cnn.com/interactive/2021/08/politics/trump-georgia-2020-election/.

144. Jan Wolfe, "Explainer: How and When Will Trump Leave Office?" Reuters, November 9, 2020, https://www.reuters.com/article/us-usa-election-eviction-explainer/explainer-how-and-when-will-trump-leave-office-idUSKBN27P19X.

145. Al Gore, Concession Speech, December 13, 2000, https://www.nytimes.com/2000/12/13/politics/text-of-goreacutes-concession-speech.html.

146. Lawrence Douglas, *Will He Go?: Trump and the Looming Election Meltdown in 2020* (New York: Twelve, Hachette Book Group, 2020).

147. Richard L. Hasen, *The Voting Wars: From Florida 2000 to the Next Election Meltdown* (New Haven: Yale University Press, 2012).

148. Steven Levitsky and Daniel Ziblatt, *How Democracies Die* (New York: Crown, 2018), 7.

149. Charles Homans, "In Bid for Control of Elections, Trump Loyalists Face Few Obstacles," *New York Times*, December 11, 2021, https://www.nytimes.com/2021/12/11/us/politics/trust-in-elections-trump-democracy.html.

150. Nick Corasaniti, "Republicans Aim to Seize More Power over How Elections Are Run," *New York Times*, March 24, 2021, https://www.nytimes.com/2021/03/24/us/politics/republicans-election-laws.html.

151. As quoted in Barton Gellman, "The Election That Could Break America," *The Atlantic*, April 7, 2021, https://www.theatlantic.com/magazine/archive/2020/11/what-if-trump-refuses-concede/616424/.

7

Transitions of Governance

FOR MOST PEOPLE, and even for those who dedicate their entire careers to politics, becoming president is an almost impossible objective. As we saw in the previous two chapters, an endless supply of obstacles confronts those who might try. Even if they raise enough money to launch a competitive campaign, garner enough support during their party's nominating process, perform well in the general election debates, and secure majorities in both the popular vote and the Electoral College, their victory may still be contested if they do not win by a sufficiently wide margin.

Should a candidate overcome all these hurdles, what follows is not a time for rest and recovery. Between their election in November and inauguration in January, presidents-elect must make many decisions, large and small, that will shape their presidencies. They must establish informational and decision-making channels, just as they must select their advisors, appoint cabinet members, hire a staff, and determine how they will translate campaign promises into tangible policy. Whereas winning the general election guarantees someone the presidency, the start of a *successful* presidency requires deliberate planning and coordination—work that presidents-elect complete during the **transition period**.

7.1 Planning the Transition

Early transitions, when presidents had much smaller cabinets and staffs, were not as complex as they are today. George Washington, for example, appointed only secretaries of state, war, and the treasury, as well as an attorney general. For his executive staff, Thomas Jefferson appointed only a messenger and a secretary. More than a half century later, Ulysses S. Grant had a staff of three, and after another half century Woodrow Wilson still had only seven full-time aides. It was not until 1857 that Congress even appropriated funds for White House staff, and it did so initially for a single presidential clerk. Until the mid-twentieth century, many staff members were personal aides rather than policy advisors: on several occasions, presidents hired relatives to perform clerical duties and paid them out of their own pockets.[1]

How times have changed. The executive branch carries out more functions than ever before, and contemporary presidents have to make upwards of 7,000 political appointments. Of these, more than 1,000 require Senate confirmation.[2] Though many appointees do not need to be chosen directly by the president or selected before Inauguration Day, such figures are reflective of the massive expansion of duties that presidents now confront when transitioning into office.

While responsibilities have increased, the allowed time to perform them has shrunk. The Twentieth Amendment, ratified in 1933, moved Inauguration Day from March 4 to January 20, cutting the window between election and inauguration in half and making post-election fishing trips (like those Herbert Hoover took) or Bermuda vacations (enjoyed by Woodrow Wilson) impossible. Today presidents-elect are simply swamped as they squeeze all kinds of preparations into just a couple of months.

The institutional presidency does not go on hiatus when a new person assumes the office. Before inauguration, presidents-elect must personally fill eighty to a hundred key positions that would be detrimental to leave vacant after January 20. Promptly at 12:01 p.m. on Inauguration Day, a newly elected president is expected to roll out an entirely new version of whitehouse.gov, the presidency's website; as a result, staffers charged with this digital transition have only a few weeks to identify the president's immediate policy priorities, draft language to communicate them, and scrub any mention of issues that the president would prefer to bury.[3] Through ongoing public performances and private negotiations, presidents must turn the policy agenda announced during the campaign into a realistic plan for governance. The moment they assume office, presidents need to be poised to hit the ground running.

7.1.1 Pre-Election Planning

Though the stakes of the transition period are impossibly high, presidents-elect do not have to figure out everything on their own. Well before Election Day, candidates start putting together transition teams, often comprised of staffers from prior administrations of the same party, operatives from the campaign, and long-time aides and confidants. As presidents face increased demands and responsibilities, the size and cost of transition teams have grown, and working groups of academics, consultants, and policy experts are formed to help.

Jimmy Carter was the first president-elect to put significant resources toward a transition before his election. As an outsider unfamiliar with the nuances of Washington and the complexities of the executive branch, he began planning in April of his election year, when it became clear he would be the Democrats' nominee.[4] A key aide from Carter's term as governor of Georgia led the transition team, which was largely kept separate from Carter's campaign operations.

George W. Bush also started planning his transition early, a full year and a half before his election in November 2000. Like Carter, he selected someone well known to him to lead the task: Dick Cheney, who served in his father's administration.[5] Even as Bush faced a lawsuit challenging his win of the Florida Electoral College votes, his transition team kept plugging away under the assumption that he would prevail. Their diligence paid off, helping Bush navigate the Washington scene despite his inexperience with national politics.

Likewise, Barack Obama began transition planning well before his election. His planning efforts might have begun as early as the spring of 2008; certainly, they were underway by mid-summer. We can't be certain because the director of Obama's transition operations, former Clinton chief of staff John Podesta, made sure his staff avoided the media.[6] Nevertheless, during the summer of 2008, there was minor controversy when the media caught wind of Obama's early transition planning. Some observers felt that he was "measuring the drapes too early"—planning for the exercise of power before power had actually been conferred.

Such accusations, however, are foolish. Condemning early planning as presumptuous is to mistake the importance and scope of the task at hand: presidents must be ready to undertake major policy initiatives and handle a range of foreign and domestic crises as soon as they enter the White House. Early planning helps ensure that all aspects of running the president's office, from staffing to budgeting, will go smoothly. As the Partnership for Public Service argues, "failing to plan for the transition can leave the country vulnerable" to a range of threats, from national security breaches to unstable financial markets.[7]

Given the stakes, the federal government now underwrites pre-election transition planning. Enacted in 2010, the Pre-Election Presidential Transition Act stipulates that recognized presidential candidates can access transition services and facilities before the general election takes place. The General Services Administration provides candidates with secure communications and offices of the sort that were previously provided only after the election.[8] The 2012 Republican nominee, Mitt Romney, was the first candidate to receive Transition Act assistance, which took the form of office space and supplies, including furniture, information services, computer equipment, and mobile phones, at a cost to taxpayers of $8.9 million.[9]

Additionally, the Presidential Transitions Improvement Act of 2015 dictates that a White House Transition Coordinating Council and Agency Transition Directors Council be established a full six months prior to the November election in order to facilitate increasingly complex presidential transitions.[10] This new law boasts a more streamlined transition process with a digital platform, new on-boarding systems, and greater participation by federal agencies.[11]

In 2016, Donald Trump made use of these funds, officially launching his transition team in early August of that year. According to many reports, however, neither Trump himself nor his surrogates did much by way of organizational preparation. Though the team employed more than a hundred staff, including a healthy supply of policy experts, the transition team did not work especially closely with the candidate or his campaign. As a result, when Trump won the general election later that fall and attention promptly turned to the transition, he appeared flat-footed and defensive. Trump promptly fired the head of his transition team, embattled New Jersey governor Chris Christie, and replaced him with his vice president-elect, Mike Pence. In the days that followed, his transition was marked by division and discord, as various factions within the Republican Party, the campaign team, and Trump's own family members vied for influence.

7.1.2 Personnel Decisions

Of the many transition tasks facing the president-elect, personnel decisions are among the most time-consuming. Potential appointees must be identified, thoroughly screened, and quickly trained to take over the duties of the outgoing staff. Presidents-elect delegate this staffing process to **professional vetters**, who are expected to perform thorough background checks on job candidates.

The vetting process, while imperfect, is meant to unearth potential issues that could cause the president embarrassment or the nominee to be rejected. Vetters examine a job candidate's public statements, voting record, investments, and tax returns. They ask about extramarital affairs, drug use, psychiatric treatment, organizational affiliations, and criminal history. They interrogate friends, family, neighbors, and coworkers. The sheer scope of the vetting process can be overwhelming: for every position there may be hundreds, or even thousands, of candidates considered.

Of the many appointments to be made, the president-elect personally fills only the highest, most consequential positions. The first of these decisions is made when, as a candidate, he or she must announce a running mate. This does not mean, of course, that vetters are not involved—quite the contrary. Former senator Evan Bayh (D-IN), a past vice-presidential contender, described the vice-presidential vetting process as "totally invasive. It's like having a colonoscopy, except they use the Hubble telescope on you."[12] As one vetter who worked for the campaign of John McCain bragged, "We had things in there that never came out. We had things that [McCain's running mate, Sarah] Palin[,] didn't even know about."[13] When Dick Cheney oversaw the vice-presidential vetting process for Bush's 2000 campaign—before accepting the job himself—he asked for over one thousand pages of material from each of the candidates.[14]

After the election, the president-elect moves on to cabinet appointments and senior White House staff. White House staff are usually drawn from the pool of campaign operatives, transition leaders and staff, and the president's personal networks. The transition team is also flooded by tens of thousands of résumés. Recent transition teams have received up to 1,500 applications per day.[15] For President Reagan's personnel chief, Pendleton James, sifting through job candidate portfolios was "like drinking water from a fire hydrant . . . your mouth is only that big and the rest just sputters and spills on the floor. There just isn't enough time."[16]

Presidents-elect are also personally bombarded by requests and recommendations from campaign staff, donors, interest groups, their parties, and Congress. "The House and Senate Republicans just start cramming people down your throat," James recalled. "Then the [White House] political office wants to find places for all the campaign workers. The collision is sometimes horrendous to behold."[17] Predictably, filling these positions takes time and planning, favoring those who start early.

Presidents-elect have to do more than choose individuals to fill the White House, however. They also need an organizational structure. Who will report to whom? How will decisions get made? "There is no White House organization," a Nixon aide observed. "It's what you make when you get there. There's no prescription. There are very few laws to restrict how you can organize. It's almost entirely left up to the president."[18] While a blank slate offers opportunities, it also presents enormous challenges. Presidents-elect must create this structure practically out of nothing while at the same time appeasing the many people who helped get them elected. As a result, modern presidents have tended to focus first on appointing chiefs of staff as well as a host of other senior advisors who serve as information gatekeepers.[19] Once these positions are filled, those at the top of the chain can start to fill lower-level positions, and the administration begins to take shape.

If incoming presidents do not take full advantage of the transition time to structure the executive office, they and their staffs may find themselves in a challenging position come Inauguration Day. For example, by the time President Clinton made key appointments, many in the Bush White House had already left, so the newcomers could not seek on-the-job training from those who had held the same posts in the previous administration. Because of its relatively late start, the Clinton administration also experienced difficulty with some of its Senate confirmations, which delayed appointments of staff needed to drive its policy agenda. To this day, the Clinton administration's failure to take decisive action during the transition serves as a cautionary tale to those seeking presidential office.

Thinking Institutionally: The Missteps of the 1992 Presidential Transition

Much has been made of Bill Clinton personally. Ambitious, gregarious, egocentric, and fitted with an outsized personality, he seemed born for the campaign trail—and, in fact, his 1992 bid for president was his twentieth electoral campaign.[20] As a candidate, Clinton promised to bring change to Washington, reform the nation's health care system, lift the ban against gays in the military, reduce the size of the White House, and cut taxes for the middle class, among other big plans.

Upon election, however, Clinton had his work cut out for him. While he amassed over twice as many electoral votes as George H. W. Bush, the incumbent, Clinton garnered only 5 percent more of the popular vote, or 43 percent overall.[21] He also attracted the lowest margin of congressional Democratic support in nearly three decades. Further, his presidency followed twelve years of Republican Party control of the White House. Much depended on the use he made of the transition period.

Despite the stakes involved, Clinton's transition is routinely cited as an example of what *not* to do when preparing to take office. Very little work was done regarding personnel during the pre-election transition period,[22] and the pace of appointments did not accelerate after the election.

Clinton named his chief of staff over a month after the election,* and he failed to select any cabinet nominees or other White House staff until six weeks after the election.[23] The president-elect reportedly believed staffing would come together on

---

* For comparison, around this same time during Obama's transition in 2008, his entire cabinet had been announced. Similarly, Obama's first chief of staff, Rahm Emanuel, accepted the president-elect's offer within days of his election.

Continued on next page

its own, and he later acknowledged in his autobiography that he spent hardly any time choosing his White House staff.[24] Six days before inauguration, Clinton finally announced more than fifty outstanding essential appointments that he still had not made.[25]

Even more importantly, early controversies surrounding nominees who required Senate confirmation interfered substantively with Clinton's ability to address his policy priorities. Zoë Baird and Kimba Wood, two different nominees for attorney general, were both rejected during Nannygate, the scandal about revelations that both had employed undocumented childcare workers. While transition staff sought a third candidate, a holdover from the Bush administration continued to head the Justice Department.[26] The controversy also stalled other nominees from moving forward, since their personal lives would now be investigated far more carefully. The result was that nearly six months into Clinton's administration, less than half of the positions requiring Senate confirmation were filled in the Department of Defense.[27]

Some of these difficulties arose because Clinton tapped important members of the transition staff to join his administration. Grueling confirmation hearings made it difficult for cabinet nominees to focus on other transition work, setting the administration up for a slow start after inauguration. More significantly, his transition director, Warren Christopher, was nominated to be secretary of state after the 1992 election and left the transition to prepare for his confirmation hearings. Another key transition team member, Richard Riley, who served as the transition's personnel director, was named secretary of education.

Clinton could have avoided these headaches had he chosen transition staff who would not be pulled out for other positions. Other presidents did exactly that. In 2020, for example, president-elect Biden selected Ted Kaufman, who had been his chief of staff in the Senate, to head his transition effort. Kaufman knew how Washington worked, was well versed in the art of transitioning, and—importantly—did not intend to join the incoming administration.

Instead of arming himself early on with a strong White House staff of Washington insiders, Clinton focused on his cabinet and policy priorities. When he did make his White House picks, he failed to follow the example of Reagan, who compensated for his outsider status by turning to experienced aides. Clinton's chief of staff, for instance, was Mack McLarty, a childhood friend with little relevant experience.

Were the many problems Clinton confronted during his transition the result of his individual personality and temperament, or were they inevitable, given the adversarial institutional environment he faced? Some of the problems surely reflect the difficult nature of transitions and the challenges of assuming power after 12 years of Republican control of the White House. At the same time, others probably derived from Clinton's own liabilities and miscalculations.

7.1.3 Prepping a Policy Agenda

A successful transition allows a new president to make productive use of the **honeymoon period**—the first weeks of a new administration during which presidents are expected to rapidly issue and enact new policies. To do so, presidents-elect must articulate a clear agenda before their inauguration, ensuring that on Day One nobody is scrambling to identify major goals or policy priorities. Time is of the essence. Over the course of a long campaign, candidates rack up tens, if not hundreds, of campaign promises, and the candidate who actually wins can expect to face all sorts of scrutiny by the press and public, who want to see results.

During their transition periods, presidents and their staff cannot expect to move forward on all their campaign promises. Instead, they must prioritize the dominant themes of the campaign—or even just a single issue—and quickly pursue these. Upon entering office in 1977, President Carter instructed his staff to make a list of every promise he had made during the election, and he planned to make progress on each one. The result was an aimless and incoherent policy agenda; Congress, unsure which of Carter's myriad proposals to consider first, was slow to give any consideration at all.[28]

To avoid mistakes like this, presidents-elect appoint transition teams to focus on specific policy areas.[29] These teams are usually comprised of people who will continue working in the new administration, advising the president on policy and seeking support from key legislators and their aides and advisors.[30] For these teams to be effective, they need to cultivate relationships on Capitol Hill. Through closed-door meetings, they aim to convince congressional leadership to work with the president-elect by outlining his or her policy agenda and seeking advice on how to enact it.[31]

More formal avenues for creating working relationships with Congress are built into the transition process itself. Presidents-elect set up official congressional liaison teams, such as the Office of Congressional Relations or the Office of Legislative Affairs, in an attempt to streamline their administration's interactions with Congress. The president-elect then strategically selects who among the staff will be responsible for serving on these teams, freeing up other staff to work on White House staff structure, the vetting process, and other personnel matters.[32]

Before taking office, the president-elect's staff also must monitor the activity of the outgoing administration. It is typical for incumbent presidents, in the waning days of their terms, to rush through a bevy of policies, usually in the form of unilateral directives such as executive orders or proclamations. Inevitably, some of these are meant to hamstring their successors.[33] For incoming presidents, then, the task is to learn about these last-minute policies and determine which must be undone and which they can live with. In 2001, for example, incoming president George W. Bush sought to advance his own unilateral directives on education, taxes, and faith-based initiatives. Early on, however, his attention was spent reviewing a series of climate-related orders written by his predecessor, Bill Clinton, in the previous months. It took time for his staff to review the merits of each order—time that should have been spent before the inauguration. Asked why Clinton's orders had come as a surprise to the administration, Bush's deputy chief of staff said, "But that assumes that at the same time you're running and trying to plan for a transition, that you're also carefully monitoring all the stuff they [the outgoing administration] are getting ready to plant. And frankly, no organization running for president has that kind of resources."[34]

When President Biden entered office in 2021, his administration had a clear idea which policies it would like to pursue, as well as the existing policies it would like to eliminate. On Day One, Biden signed a total of seventeen executive orders, proclamations, and memoranda (policy tools we will discuss at length in chapter 9).[35] Several were culminations of Biden's biggest campaign promises, including tackling Covid-19 through the appointment of a pandemic coordinator and new requirements for medical masks. Several others were drafted for the sole purpose of reversing actions taken by the Trump administration. The termination of construction of the border wall, rejoining the Paris Agreement on climate change, and ending the so-called "Muslim ban"—all of which fit within Biden's priorities of immigration and climate change—were aimed directly at his predecessor's top policy achievements.

In total, Biden signed thirty-three unilateral directives during his first week in office.[36] And while these directives addressed a range of issues, from racial equity to abortion and economic security, Biden's early legislative agenda focused on a single one: the Covid-19 stimulus. Months of preparation with policy advisors allowed Biden to unveil the $1.9 trillion proposal on January 14, a week before his inauguration. That way, rather than waste his honeymoon period quietly drafting his proposal, Biden got straight to work negotiating and advocating for his bill with Congress and the public. (For more on Biden's Covid-19 stimulus, see chapter 14.)

7.2 Managing Campaign and Party Operatives

During transitions, presidents-elect must shift from directing a mobile, high-energy, and close-knit campaign staff to overseeing an expansive executive office as well as the entire federal civil service. At the same time, they must repay debts to many of the supporters who helped get them elected. The obligations that accumulate over the course of the campaign often influence their staffing decisions.

7.2.1 Campaign Operatives

During their campaigns, major-party presidential contenders typically employ thousands of staff. By October 2012 of Obama's reelection campaign, for example, there were more than four thousand people on his campaign payroll.[37] These campaigns also enlist thousands of volunteers. Neither of these groups disappears after their candidate's election.

While not all campaign operatives expect a job in the new president's transition or administration, plenty do. Some have left jobs to work for the campaign and are looking to advance a career in politics or government. One of Reagan's advisors described the turnover of personnel from campaign to administration as "the most natural thing in the world," saying that campaign staff "work so long and so hard and become so much of the team that when the candidate wins, they automatically come in."[38]

Patronage appointments are one of the most important tools presidents-elect have at their disposal. In addition to wanting to reward supporters for their investment of time, political capital, and money, presidents-elect also recognize the benefits of their supporters' continued assistance once in office. Campaign operatives endorse the policy agenda outlined during the campaign, so presidents-elect can rely on them to be on their side when it is time to govern.

A post in the administration also encourages future campaign work from staffers, by both acknowledging their past service and focusing their continued attention. Many re-election campaigns see the return of staff from the first campaign, and this continuity can be essential to a president's success. It is also in the president's interest to preempt any betrayals. For many senior campaign staff, this isn't their first foray into party politics or government. Their networks are far-reaching, and they can easily go to the media with insider secrets should they feel shortchanged when it comes to appointments within the new administration. By rewarding their work, presidents keep them reeled in.

A study of over 1,000 of Obama's 2007–8 paid campaign staff found that more than 12 percent of them obtained jobs in the new administration.[39] Among senior campaign staff, the percentage is even higher. This study also found that campaign staff who contributed the most to Obama's electoral success were particularly likely to be given patronage appointments, and campaign staff working in battleground states were uniformly more likely to assume a job in the Obama administration than were staff working in non-battleground states. For staff working in non-battleground states, the prospects of securing a job in the president's administration correlated with the strength of local support shown for Obama on Election Day.

For many reasons, not least of which is the selective and strategic assignment of staff to campaign precincts around the country, these relationships cannot be interpreted causally. Better-quality staff may have been assigned to battleground states, and it may have been on the basis of their quality, and not their campaign assignment, that they were selected to continue on in the administration. Still, the correlations are striking, underscoring a rich and complex relationship between presidential staffing in campaigns and in governance.

Karl Rove is one example of campaign-strategist-turned-White-House-advisor, serving Texas governor and then U.S. president George W. Bush. Rove ingratiated himself with the Bush family, working first for George H. W. Bush and then playing an instrumental role in George W. Bush's successful run for the Texas governorship in 1994.[40] In the 2000 presidential race, Rove helped Bush raise a record-breaking campaign war chest and navigated the campaign to victory. Rove went on to serve as senior advisor to President Bush from 2000 to 2007 and deputy chief of staff from 2004 to 2007.[41] In his 2004 victory speech, freshly reelected President Bush referred to Rove as "the architect" of his campaign success.[42] Arguably, Rove was the architect of the Bush presidency as well, focusing intently on five policy components: education standards (achieved through the enactment of No Child Left Behind), a "faith-based initiative" funding religious organizations, the privatization of Social Security, the creation of a Medicare alternative, and a reformed immigration policy.[43] John DiIulio, a former presidential advisor, wrote in 2001, "Karl is enormously powerful, maybe the single most powerful person in the modern, post-Hoover era ever to occupy a political advisor post near the Oval Office."[44]

Perhaps. But Rove wouldn't be the last presidential advisor to wield enormous power in the White House. Steve Bannon served as CEO of Trump's 2016 presidential campaign and, like Rove, he leveraged this role into a position of influence in the White House, serving as the president's chief strategist. While Rove had a long political résumé, Bannon's was decidedly more eclectic. With an MBA from Harvard, a history as an investment banker at Goldman Sachs, a small fortune made from television investments, and a top role at the alt-right news website Breitbart, Bannon came to politics as an outsider, just like his candidate.[45] Bannon's role in the Trump campaign and subsequently the White House catapulted him, temporarily, into the mainstream of American politics.[46] Christopher Ruddy, Newsmax CEO and friend of President Trump, described Bannon as "the chief ideological officer" of the Trump administration.[47] And though Bannon's tenure in the White House ultimately did not last more than a year, his experience underscores how relationships developed before and during a campaign can yield important agenda-setting positions during an administration.

Much of the logic behind rewarding loyal campaign staffers also applies to influential party members, donors, and other people who helped the candidate win the election. Donors and other campaign contributors are therefore frequently appointees to ambassadorships and other diplomatic positions. Fully 36 percent of George W. Bush's ambassadorial appointments, for instance, were considered political appointments* rather than choices made on the basis of relevant knowledge or experience.[48] (The relationship between campaign giving and ambassadorial appointments is discussed at further length in chapter 10.)

7.2.2 When Campaigners Don't Help in Governance

Contemporary campaigns employ an increasingly professionalized cohort of political consultants, strategists, and pollsters. These merchandising specialists can have an extensive range of responsibilities, including introducing candidates to the masses, reframing candidates'

---

*While such figures might seem high, they are far lower than what was once the norm. As discussed at length in chapter 2, before civil service reform in the late nineteenth and early twentieth centuries, patronage was king, and campaign workers steadfastly expected employment rewards for their service. When civil service reform first went into effect in the late 1800s, it affected only 10 percent of the federal government's civilian employees. Today, more than 90 percent of a much larger federal workforce find themselves subject to the merit system these reforms put into place.

controversial past actions and policy positions to make them more electable, and even picking out neckties and shoes.[49] These professionals might be effective at running campaigns, but they are not likely to make impressive cabinet appointees.

The temperament of other campaign operatives, moreover, often does not suit the tasks of governing. Campaign staffers can be zealously partisan. While this may be necessary during the campaign, inside the White House it can create a partisan operation that troubles other, more moderate officials and alienates large swaths of the national electorate.[50]

7.2.3 Intraparty Rivals

In staffing the White House, the president-elect must consider how the various pieces will fit together into a coherent administration. Where can campaign and transition team leaders be placed? Will White House staff appointments clash with department head nominees? The president must also appease the larger party organization, including candidates who left the primaries feeling disgruntled. In this case, the president-elect can make appointments that help smooth over any lingering tensions within the party.

Abraham Lincoln is famous for the **team of rivals** he assembled after his election in 1860.[51] He filled three cabinet positions with his competitors for the Republican presidential nomination, appointing New York senator William Seward as secretary of state, Ohio governor Salmon P. Chase as secretary of the treasury, and Missouri statesman Edward Bates as the attorney general. And these were not the only rivals he employed in his administration. Lincoln spent his transition period filling his staff with people whose views ranged widely. Not everyone, for instance, shared his gradualist approach to ending slavery: several members of his administration were radical abolitionists. His staff disagreed not only with Lincoln but with each other, creating a ragtag coalition government that offered representation to a wide variety of Union perspectives as the nation dove headlong into war.

Lincoln was hardly the first president to fill his White House with political contrarians. By the time Lincoln was elected, in fact, White House rivalries had become commonplace. Having witnessed the debates and rivalries that marked the Constitutional Convention, George Washington welcomed several of its members into his administration. A continuous challenge of his administration was to smooth over the feud between Jefferson, his secretary of state, and Hamilton, his secretary of the treasury, and convince the two men to work together. In a letter to Jefferson, the president wrote: "How unfortunate, and how much is it to be regretted then, that whilst we are encompassed on all sides with avowed enemies and insidious friends, that internal dissentions should be harrowing and tearing our vitals."[52]

John Quincy Adams was the first president to reserve a cabinet position for one of his campaign opponents. (His secretary of state, Henry Clay, had won the fourth most electoral votes in the 1824 election.) And in the decade preceding Lincoln's election, three presidents—Millard Fillmore, Franklin Pierce, and James Buchanan—all reserved cabinet positions for men who had lost their party's nominating contest.

FIGURE 7.1. Barack Obama's transition. Keep your friends close, and your rivals even closer. Here, we see Obama flanked by Hillary Clinton (with whom he fought a bitter race for the Democratic nomination, and whom he would enlist as his secretary of state) and Robert Gates (a Republican, whom Obama would keep on as secretary of defense). *Source:* AP Images.

These trends continued into the twentieth century. After a near-loss in the 1960 election, Kennedy sought opportunities to disarm voters' fears about having a young, inexperienced, and Catholic president. He found one in Adlai Stevenson, who had campaigned against him in the primary. Voters knew Stevenson. Having won the Democratic nomination in both 1952 and 1956, Stevenson was popular among the party's liberal establishment. And though, according to one historian, both Kennedy and his brother Robert (Bobby) viewed Stevenson as "rather prissy and ineffective" and resented his unwillingness to endorse Kennedy in the primary, they offered him several positions in the administration, ultimately settling on Ambassador to the United Nations.[53]

Similar motivations guided Obama's decision to assemble a team of rivals in 2009 (figure 7.1). Indeed, by retaining the Republican Robert Gates as his secretary of defense, Obama went even further than past presidents in building an ideologically diverse administration. Obama also chose Joe Biden as his running mate in 2008 following Biden's own failed presidential bid. But Obama's most strategic—and, for many, surprising—choice was to appoint Hillary Clinton as secretary of state. Clinton, the well-established and well-known former first spouse and then senator from New York, had been Obama's main competitor during the primaries. Many felt that Obama, who only a few years before had been an obscure Illinois state senator, was too inexperienced to accept the Democratic nomination, which—rightfully Clinton's—had been captured by an upstart. By appointing Clinton, Obama helped patch the holes in his own party.

For all the benefits a team of rivals can confer, presidents also must be prepared for the costs it can convey. Too many competing viewpoints can slow deliberations and spread presidents' attention too thin. And when disagreements become overheated, it is the president's job to build consensus around a single option without damaging ties with those who would have chosen otherwise. As Secretary of State Henry Kissinger recounted after his years in the White House, "So much time, effort, and ingenuity were spent in trying to organize a consensus . . . there was too little left to consider the weaknesses of the plan."[54]

7.3 Soliciting Help from the Outgoing Administration

In any transition, the outgoing administration holds information that a newly elected president needs to assimilate. The outgoing staff are best suited to advise incoming staff on White House operations and organization, the best ways of working with the bureaucracy and Congress, and the most pressing foreign and domestic policy issues. They can provide intelligence briefings and training needed to ensure a smoother takeover. The outgoing administration can save the new administration some early fumbling—especially if the president's campaign and transition team are populated with a large number of people unfamiliar with the inner workings of the White House and Washington.

7.3.1 Responding to Events in Real Time

Some transfers of power take place during periods of relative stability. But for those that do not, the work is made much easier by cooperation between the incoming and outgoing administrations. With the actual instruments of power still beyond their reach, presidents-elect must be briefed on the very latest efforts to address unfolding crises. In this regard, the transition from George W. Bush to Barack Obama was just about as good as it gets.

When Obama was campaigning in 2008, the United States entered into the worst economic crisis the nation had seen since the Great Depression. With the collapse of global stock markets, massive home foreclosures, and skyrocketing unemployment dominated national discourse,[55] economists warned that the Great Recession could turn into a full-blown depression. Out of necessity, then, Obama began to address the economy well before inauguration. Shortly after the election, he announced that he would assign to his economic team the task of devising a two-year stimulus plan that would interrupt the downward spiral of panic that had seized stock markets and halted consumer spending. Throughout his transition, Obama coordinated efforts with congressional leadership to begin work on this plan.

Obama benefited from the cooperation of his predecessor. Facing an unfolding economic catastrophe that could not be neglected during the months-long transition, the Bush administration sought to prevent any interruption of federal services and programs. Early on, Bush instructed White House staff to direct this transition—at least as early as the summer of 2008, before the election had even taken place and before anyone could know whether a new party would assume control.[56] As a result, incoming appointees were briefed on their positions and agency priorities, marking a new level of cooperation between an outgoing and incoming administration.[57]

7.3.2 Information Transfers

With the growing complexity and scope of the institutional presidency, sharing information between administrations has become increasingly important. This is particularly true in the area of national intelligence. The limited public record and sensitive nature of most national security and foreign policy issues makes soliciting help from the outgoing administration essential.

Despite the obvious benefits of data sharing, it was not until the transition from Harry S. Truman to Dwight D. Eisenhower in 1952–53 that an outgoing administration systematically collected and presented a body of information to the incoming one.[58] Truman had been vice president for fewer than one hundred days when President Roosevelt died. Truman was shocked to learn how much information had been withheld from him as vice president: imagine his surprise, for example, when Henry Stimson, the secretary of war, briefed him on the Manhattan Project, the massive secret initiative to build the world's first atomic weapon. Remarking, "There were so many things I did not know when I became President," Truman decided that the presidential candidates in 1952 should have access to the nation's security intelligence. He therefore advised the CIA to brief Eisenhower and Adlai Stevenson as soon as they were selected as their party's candidates.[59] Truman explained his rationale, saying that the president

> now carries power beyond parallel in history. That is the principal reason why I am so anxious that it be a continuing proposition and that the successor to me and the successor to him can carry on as if no election had ever taken place. I am giving this president more information than any other president had when he went into office.[60]

In transitions since, some outgoing presidents have lived up to Truman's goal of making succession as seamless as possible. Just as the Bush administration worked closely with Obama on the economic crisis, it also devoted a great deal of attention to making sure that Obama would be fully briefed on issues involving national security. Days after Obama's election, Bush warned that terrorists "would like nothing more than to exploit this period of change."[61] President-Elect Obama subsequently received numerous security and terrorism briefings from Bush as well as from senior security and intelligence advisors.

The Bush White House even went so far as to prepare more than a dozen contingency plans to guide Obama through potential crises, should one occur in his first days in office. These plans outlined options for the president if, say, there were a nuclear explosion in North Korea or a terrorist attack on U.S. facilities abroad. The Bush administration also generated more than three dozen additional memos on other national security issues and briefed incoming senior officials while many of Obama's other appointments awaited Senate confirmation.[62]

Having benefited from Bush's assistance during his transition to office, Obama went out of his way to work closely with Trump during his. After meeting with Trump in the Oval Office just days after the election, Obama publicly announced that "my number one priority in the next two months is to try to facilitate a transition that ensures our President-Elect is successful." Recognizing the highly charged nature of the previous presidential election, he went on to say that "it is important for all of us, regardless of party and regardless of political preferences, to now come together, work together to deal with the many challenges we face." For his part, President-Elect Trump expressed gratitude for the gesture of goodwill. As he put it, "We discussed a lot of different situations, some wonderful and some difficulties. I very much look forward to dealing with the President in the future, including counsel. He explained some of the difficulties, some of the high-flying assets and some of the really great things that have been achieved."[63]

As discussed later in this chapter, however, this goodwill and cooperation dissipated rather quickly. The ascension of Trump to power proved just as tumultuous and divisive as his road to victory on Election Day.

When this transfer of knowledge fails to take place, presidents can find themselves in a real bind. Jimmy Carter, for instance, "discovered" a Soviet brigade in Cuba that had been stationed there since before the Cuban Missile Crisis in 1962. Upon learning about the troops, Carter assumed they had only been recently deployed, and he publicly chastised the Soviets for not respecting America's interests in the Western Hemisphere. The Soviets, meanwhile, could not believe that Carter was unaware of the brigade and assumed he was simply manufacturing a crisis.[64] Had he been alerted to this beforehand, Carter's administration might have avoided a tense diplomatic moment with the Soviets.

7.3.3 *When Cooperation Proves Difficult*

As the example from the Carter administration suggests, outgoing and incoming administrations do not always work together during key moments of transition.[65] The new administration can be disinclined to make use of the outgoing administration's vast knowledge reserve: instead of seeking help from the existing White House staff, presidents-elect may focus on how best to replace them.[66] Selected to run John F. Kennedy's personnel operation in 1961, Dan Fenn later recalled,

> We were a little bit hubristic—our impression was that there wasn't an awful lot that [the outgoing administration] could do for us that we couldn't do for ourselves. To us, at least, it was perfectly clear that presidents over two hundred years of American history had screwed everything up. The last thing we wanted to do was to pay the least bit of attention to the terrible Eisenhower administration.[67]

The outgoing administration, for its part, may harbor resentments after seeing their candidate lose a hard-fought election. After the contentious election of 2000—in which Al Gore won the popular vote by a small margin but lost a recount bid that turned over Florida's crucial twenty-five electoral votes to Bush—members of Bill Clinton's outgoing administration let their disdain be known with a series of sophomoric pranks. According to some reports, they stole doorknobs, vandalized bathrooms, and, most infamously, removed the letter W from dozens of computer keyboards.[68]

The greatest source of friction in these interparty transfers of power is the opposing goals of the incoming and outgoing presidents.[69] Members of the outgoing staff have justifiable reason to worry that their work is about to be undone by an incoming president with an entirely different agenda, leaving them with little incentive to help the new administration get started. This can result in an awkward contest of wills, in which the old administration makes "midnight appointments" or pushes through last-minute policies, while the president-elect gathers forces in the service of a perceived **electoral mandate**— that is, the implicit endorsement by voters of a candidate's policy objectives coupled with a presumption that other politicians therefore must table their objections and lend their support.[70]

RONALD REAGAN ENTERING AND LEAVING OFFICE

Throughout the 1980 campaign, Ronald Reagan railed against "big government" and attacked the incumbent, Jimmy Carter, as a spendthrift liberal intent on hobbling the free market through federal regulation and taxation. Not coincidentally, while campaigning, Reagan had difficulty interacting with the Carter White House. In fact, the Reagan team was reluctant, and sometimes even refused, to meet with members of Carter's administration, fueling a sense of distrust on both sides.[71]

At first, Reagan's campaign staff rejected intelligence briefings, saying Reagan wished to be free to criticize Carter's policies without running the risk of betraying sensitive information. It was only after war broke out between Iraq and Iran in September 1980 that Reagan finally consented to a CIA briefing on the situation.[72] Upon winning the election, of course, Reagan's transition team had to work with the very agencies it had criticized during the campaign, which brought its fair share of challenges.[73]

Even when a president-elect and incumbent come from the same party, smooth transitions are hardly guaranteed. Many assumed, for example, that George H. W. Bush's succession to the presidency after Reagan's two terms would be easy. For precisely this reason, his transition team was significantly smaller than the average. Whereas Reagan's transition staff hovered around 1,500 to 2,000 people, Bush's team was just over 150.[74] And why should Bush have thought to employ more manpower? He had just spent eight years as vice president and was expected to continue the work of the previous administration.

This very expectation, however, produced its own difficulties. Some critics viewed Bush as a "third-term president" who would simply pick up where Reagan left off.[75] Bush knew he would need to continue to curry favor with the Reagan base; therefore, he retained some of Reagan's people for his own administration. But he also wanted to distinguish himself from his predecessor and leave behind his own presidential legacy. Thus the people closest to him during the transition were his own staff, not Reagan's. He sought to fill the White House with new faces and in the process surprised and angered many veteran Reagan staff members whom he asked to leave.

LYNDON B. JOHNSON

Like George H. W. Bush, Lyndon Baines Johnson took over an administration in which he had been vice president. But if Bush suffered from being too close to the outgoing administration, Johnson faced the opposite problem in 1963. Not only did he have to strike the right balance between sensitivity and strong leadership during a time of national mourning over John F. Kennedy's assassination, he faced the added challenge of taking over an administration from which he had been largely excluded.

Kennedy, a patrician New Englander, had never liked the rough-hewn senator from Texas and only reluctantly added Johnson to the ticket in 1960 to appease Democratic Party leadership. Johnson, the "Master of the Senate," had been one of the most powerful people in Washington and a strong contender for the Democratic nomination himself, before he joined the Kennedy campaign. As vice president under Kennedy, however, Johnson saw his power and prestige slip. In fact, relations between the two men were so strained that Johnson worried he might be left off Kennedy's ticket in the 1964 elections.[76] Johnson went from being a favorite for the Democratic nomination in 1960 to settling for a subordinate post that, by 1963, was careening toward a dead end.[77]

Then Kennedy was assassinated in Dallas on November 22, 1963, and everything was thrown into flux. A pall was cast over the White House, Washington, D.C., and the entire nation. Johnson was sworn in on Air Force One just a few hours after the president was pronounced dead (figure 7.2).

While most presidents-elect have months to gather their resources and assemble a team of trusted advisors, Johnson's takeover was instantaneous and occurred at a moment when friends in the White House were hard to find. Johnson faced contemptuous advisors and White House aides who distrusted and disliked him. The most trying relationship of all, called "one of the great blood feuds in American political history," was with Bobby Kennedy, the U.S. attorney general as well as the late president's younger brother, and a man with presidential ambitions of his own.[78] How could Johnson simultaneously adjust to the presidency, deal with his adversaries, manage Congress, fulfill Kennedy's legacy, establish his own legacy, *and* run a successful campaign for the fast-approaching 1964 election?

Johnson, unlike typical presidents-elect, did not have campaign operatives to install in vacant White House staff positions or to appoint as senior officials. He did not have a transition period to hire additional personnel, ease into office, and communicate with the outgoing administration. As he recounted later, "I was catapulted without preparation into the most difficult job any mortal man could hold. My duties would not wait a week, or a day, or even an hour."[79] He was dependent on administration officials already in place—in fact, he desperately needed them to stay. These were advisors and department heads who held him in low regard, and under different circumstances Johnson would have relished showing them the door. But to dismiss them all would have been foolish— not only because they possessed insider information that he lacked but also because he needed to project an image of legitimacy and stability both to a country still in shock over

FIGURE 7.2. Lyndon Johnson's impromptu swearing-in ceremony. Just hours after John F. Kennedy's assassination on November 22, 1963, Lyndon Johnson took the oath of office on Air Force One with the widow of the slain former president by his side. *Source:* Library of Congress.

the loss of its elected leader and to his political allies and enemies, particularly those in the Kremlin.

Johnson, however, managed to quickly turn the situation to his advantage. His landmark legislative achievements, with the 1964 Civil Rights Act ranking at the top, were the result of his dogged efforts—combining charm and intimidation—to corral the necessary votes in Congress.[80] Johnson did not hesitate to draw upon Kennedy's reputation to galvanize popular support for the bills. Although Kennedy had been relatively inactive on the question of civil rights legislation, Johnson, in his first speech as president, told Congress, "No memorial oration or eulogy could more eloquently honor President Kennedy's memory than the earliest possible passage of the civil rights bill for which he fought so long."[81] Johnson famously lost the support of the southern Democrats by advocating for civil rights, but the legislation established his national reputation.

Johnson won election on his own later in the fall of 1964. In fact, he enjoyed one of the greatest popular wins in presidential election history over Barry Goldwater, a staunch conservative from Arizona. Johnson would not have been able to run such an effective campaign, however, had his administration remained in disarray following Kennedy's death. His election success was due in no small part to his deft management of the transition.

Historical Transformations: Our Nation's Most Contentious Transition

As we saw in chapter 6, Trump's refusal to concede in 2020 did not ultimately swing the election in his favor. This does not mean, however, that his behavior was inconsequential. As Trump sought to discredit Biden's victory, he encouraged his administration not to cooperate with Biden's transition team until the results were "official"[82]—an act that threatened not only Biden's planning efforts but the very norm of peaceful transitions.

It would seem a blessing, then, that at least one element of the transition does not depend on the goodwill of the outgoing president. According to the Presidential Transition Act of 1963, it is the head of the General Services Administration (GSA)—not the president—who ascertains the election's victor and initiates the transition process accordingly. Approval from the GSA is no symbolic gesture: it unlocks special privileges for the incoming president, including classified national security briefings, office space, and roughly $6.3 million to pay the salaries of transition staff.[83] GSA approval also allows the incoming president to formally schedule meetings with heads of executive branch agencies, such as the Food and Drug Administration and Centers for Disease Control.

In the past, GSA approval happened almost immediately. President Obama was elected on November 4, 2008, and declared the "apparent winner" by the GSA on November 5.[84] President Trump also received GSA approval in a single day.[85] President Biden, however, did not receive GSA approval until November 23—a full twenty days after Election Day (and thirteen days after the election was called by the decision desks of the major television networks).

Twenty days may not sound like a massive setback, but transition experts would say otherwise. "As it is, the transition period barely gives enough time to prepare the incoming leadership," wrote Denise Turner Roth, head of the GSA under Obama. "Every day lost sets the new administration further behind and can hamper its ability to effectively govern."[86]

Former White House chief of staff John Podesta called the delayed approval "dangerous."[87] As a counselor to Obama, Podesta saw firsthand the necessity of the transition process in preparing for a national emergency. During the 2008 financial crisis, Podesta met frequently with then–treasury secretary Henry Paulson, and members of the new administration spent "endless hours at the Treasury Department looking at the forecasts." In Podesta's view, this process was essential to the Obama administration's ability to craft a stimulus bill.

In her "letter of ascertainment" granting approval to Biden, GSA administrator Emily Murphy cited "legal challenges" as reason for the delay[88]—referencing, of course, the legal arguments Trump had been pursuing in the courts, all of which were later rejected.[89] Though there is no evidence that Trump himself coerced Murphy or other GSA officials, the delay was undoubtedly prolonged by his insistence that he had won.

Continued on next page

Even after Biden received GSA approval, Trump and his staff still did not cooperate with the incoming administration. Long into December, members of the Office of Management and Budget (OMB) refused to coordinate with the Biden transition team, claiming that "redirecting staff and resources to draft your team's budget proposals is not an OMB transition responsibility."[90] The Biden team disagreed. According to Yohannes Abraham, executive director of the Biden transition, "OMB's refusal to cooperate impairs our ability to identify opportunities to maximize the relief going out to Americans during the pandemic, and it leaves us in the dark as it relates to Covid expenditures and other gaps."[91]

Receiving little help from the outgoing administration, Biden's transition team found surprising success on its own. After receiving GSA approval, the transition team held more than five thousand meetings with federal agencies and congressional officials. Biden also announced 44 Senate-confirmed officials and 206 White House staff members before his inauguration day—more than Trump, Obama, and Bush combined. According to one expert, it was "the most productive transition from a personnel perspective in history."[92]

But while months of careful planning seemed to pay off for the Biden administration, the future of presidential transitions remains precarious. How will subsequent administrations conduct their transitions? One possibility is that they will succumb to partisan animosity—that distrust that hamstrings the efforts of their successors to gain information and insights from outgoing executive branch officials. As Trump's example demonstrated, this option may inflict little damage on the outgoing president, but it would add to the erosion of peaceful and cooperative transitions.

Alternatively, the Trump-Biden transition could have the opposite effect, reviving the norms of civility and cooperation during transitions. The task would fall to presidents who, like George W. Bush, prioritize uninterrupted White House leadership over partisanship. Seeing the dangers posed by the 2020 transition, especially during a national public health crisis, future presidents may proactively coordinate with their successors and instruct all members of the executive branch to do the same. Though both paths are plausible, it is far too early to know which one future administrations will choose.

Conclusion

As a brief respite between a punishing campaign and a demanding job, transitions would appear to be the most likely space for presidents to indulge their own tastes, wants, and habits, and to eschew the impositions of the institutional presidency.

They are not. In fact, in the last fifty years or so, transitions have become remarkably routinized. Though presidents-elect must draw upon their own skills and on personal networks, they count on a small army of advisors to guide them through the many decisions that await them: whom to keep and whom to let go from the campaign staff, whose support to solicit from the larger party, what elements of a policy agenda to prioritize, how to handle the outgoing administration, and on and on. With only three months to prepare, presidents must work doggedly during their transitions to systematize the organization they need in order to govern.

Transitions are worth examining both for what they portend for a president's time in office and for what they reveal about the institutional presidency. It is during transitions, after all, that presidents take the first, crucial steps toward governance, in choosing the individuals and establishing the protocols that will further their policy aspirations. And it is in transitions that we find some of the most essential institutional challenges of the modern presidency: how to reward past supporters while propelling an agenda; how to solicit the support and cooperation of political adversaries; and how to organize individuals in a political environment in which both power and demands for reward are bountiful. The institutional presidency thus does not go on hiatus during these transitions. Rather, it kicks into high gear.

Key Terms

transition period   **team of rivals**
professional vetters   **electoral mandate**
honeymoon period

Questions for Discussion

1. Imagine that you are an advisor to the next president-elect. What advice do you offer about the transition process? Specifically, name two steps that the president-elect—regardless of party, background, or personal leadership style—should take.

2. Continuing in your role as advisor to the president-elect, what are two missteps made by previous presidents that the incumbent president should avoid?

3. How is campaigning different from governing? How is it similar? What role do institutional dynamics play in the comparison?

4. When Clinton assumed office, Republicans had held the White House for twenty of the previous twenty-four years. Does this fact, which has nothing to do with Clinton's personal history or leadership style, shed light on any of the challenges he faced during his transition?

5. Suppose a presidential election is inconclusive, and the House of Representatives must elect the new president (per the Twelfth Amendment). For the vast majority of the transition period, there is no president-elect, and either candidate could win. How should each prepare for the presidency? How should governing institutions prepare for handling such a scenario?

Suggested Readings

Burke, John P. *Presidential Transitions: From Politics to Practice*. Boulder: Lynne Rienner, 2000.

Jones, Charles O. *Passages to the Presidency: From Campaigning to Governing*. Washington, DC: Brookings Institution, 1998.

Kumar, Martha Joynt. *Before the Oath: How George W. Bush and Barack Obama Managed a Transfer of Power*. Baltimore: Johns Hopkins University Press, 2015.

Kumar, Martha Joynt, and Terry Sullivan, eds. *The White House World: Transitions, Organization, and Office Operations*. College Station: Texas A&M University Press, 2003.

Pfiffner, James. *The Strategic Presidency: Hitting the Ground Running*. 2nd ed. Lawrence: University Press of Kansas, 1996.

Notes

1. John P. Burke, "The Institutional Presidency," in *The Presidency and the Political System*, 9th ed., ed. Michael Nelson (Washington, DC: Congressional Quarterly Press, 2010), 341–42.

2. Martha Joynt Kumar et al., "Meeting the Freight Train Head On: Planning for the Transition to Power," in *The White House World: Transitions, Organization, and Office Operations*, ed. Martha Joynt Kumar and Terry Sullivan (College Station: Texas A&M University Press, 2003), 8.

3. For discussions of the two most recent digital transfers, see Jim Puzzanghera, "A Speedy Presidential Transition on the Web," *Los Angeles Times*, January 21, 2009, http://articles.latimes.com/2009/jan/21/nation/na-inaug-website21; and Alyssa Bereznak, "The Digital Presidency of Donald Trump," *The Ringer*, February 8, 2017, https://www.theringer.com/2017/2/8/16036778/donald-trump-digital-presidency-barack-obama-e3072777675c.

4. John P. Burke, "The Contemporary Presidency: The Obama Presidential Transition: An Early Assessment," *Presidential Studies Quarterly* 39, no. 3 (2009): 575.

5. James P. Pfiffner, "Presidential Transitions," in *The Oxford Handbook of the American Presidency*, ed. George C. Edwards and William G. Howell (New York: Oxford University Press, 2009), 88.

6. Burke, "The Contemporary Presidency," 576.

7. Partnership for Public Service, "Ready to Govern: Improving the Presidential Transition" (Washington, DC: Center for Presidential Transition, 2010), ii.

8. Al Kamen, "Romney Working on the Transition," *Washington Post*, July 19, 2012, http://www.washingtonpost.com/blogs/in-the-loop/post/romney-and-obama-thinking-about-transition/2012/07/19/gJQAlrv4vW_blog.html.

9. Katy Steinmetz, "The Cost of Romney's Government-Assisted Transition: $8.9 Million," *Time*, December 19, 2012, http://swampland.time.com/2012/12/19/the-cost-of-romneys-government-assisted-transition-8-9-million/.

10. Carten Cordell, "Advocates Applaud New Presidential Transition Law," *Federal Times*, March 21, 2016, http://www.federaltimes.com/story/government/election/2016/03/21/obama-signs-new-presidential-transition-law/82071818/.

11. "FACT SHEET: Facilitating a Smooth Transition to the Next Administration," Barack Obama White House, November 10, 2016, https://obamawhitehouse.archives.gov/the-press-office/2016/11/10/fact-sheet-facilitating-smooth-transition-next-administration.

12. The Week Staff, "Inside the VP Vetting Process: A Guide to the Invasive Questions," *The Week*, July 20, 2012, http://theweek.com/article/index/230860/inside-the-vp-vetting-process-a-guide-to-the-invasive-questions.

13. Jason Zengerle, "Wanna Be Veep? Okay, but This Is Going to Hurt," *GQ*, August 2012, http://www.gq.com/news-politics/politics/201208/mitt-romney-vice-president-gq-july-2012?printable=true.

14. Zengerle, "Wanna Be Veep?"

15. Bradley H. Patterson and James P. Pfiffner, "The White House Office of Presidential Personnel," *Presidential Studies Quarterly* 31, no. 3 (2001): 429.

16. Patterson and Pfiffner, "The White House Office of Presidential Personnel," 429.

17. W. David Clinton and Daniel G. Lang, "What Makes a Successful Presidential Transition? The Case of Foreign Affairs," *Presidential Studies Quarterly* 23, no. 1 (1993): 49.

18. Quoted in Charles O. Jones, *Passages to the Presidency: From Campaigning to Governing* (Washington, DC: Brookings Institution, 1998), 84.

19. John P. Burke, *Presidential Transitions: From Politics to Practice* (Boulder, CO: Lynne Rienner, 2000), 7.

20. Jones, *Passages to the Presidency*, 47.

21. "Bill Clinton: Campaigns and Elections," American President: A Reference Resource, Miller Center, University of Virginia, http://millercenter.org/president/clinton/essays/biography/3; R. Gordon Hoxie, "Democracy in Transition," *Presidential Studies Quarterly* 23, no. 1 (1993): 27–36.

22. Glenn P. Hastedt and Anthony J. Eksterowicz, "Perils of Presidential Transition," *Seton Hall Journal of Diplomacy and International Relations* (Winter/Spring 2001): 67–85.

23. Partnership for Public Service, "Ready to Govern," 13.

24. "Transition 1992: Bill Clinton," IBM Center for the Business of Government, March 11, 2008, https://transition2008.wordpress.com/2008/03/11/transition-1992-bill-clinton/.

25. William J. Clinton, "Clinton White House Staff Appointments," January 14, 1993, http://www.c-spanvideo.org/program/37017–1.

26. John P. Burke, "Lessons from Past Presidential Transitions: Organization, Management and Decision Making," in *The White House World: Transitions, Organization, and Office Operations*, ed. Martha Joynt Kumar and Terry Sullivan (College Station: Texas A&M University Press, 2003), 34.

27. Partnership for Public Service, "Ready to Govern," iii.

28. James P. Pfiffner, "Presidential Transitions," in *Oxford Handbooks Online*, ed. George C. Edwards and William G. Howell, June 2009, https://doi.org/10.1093/oxfordhb/9780199238859.003.0005.

29. Burke, *Presidential Transitions*.

30. Corey Cook, "'The Contemporary Presidency': The Permanence of the 'Permanent Campaign': George W. Bush's Public Presidency," *Presidential Studies Quarterly* 32, no. 4 (2002): 757.

31. Kumar et al., "Meeting the Freight Train," 23.

32. Martha Joynt Kumar, "Recruiting and Organizing the White House Staff," *PS: Political Science and Politics* 35, no. 1 (2002): 38.

33. William G. Howell and Kenneth R. Mayer, "The Last One Hundred Days," *Presidential Studies Quarterly* 35, no. 3 (2005): 533–53, https://doi.org/10.1111/j.1741-5705.2005.00263.x.

34. Martha Joynt Kumar, "Getting Ready for Day One: Taking Advantage of the Opportunities and Minimizing the Hazards of a Presidential Transition," *Public Administration Review* 68, no. 4 (2008): 603–17, 608.

35. "Fact Sheet: President-Elect Biden's Day One Executive Actions Deliver Relief for Families across America amid Converging Crises," The White House, January 25, 2021, https://www.whitehouse.gov/briefing-room/statements-releases/2021/01/20/fact-sheet-president-elect-bidens-day-one-executive-actions-deliver-relief-for-families-across-america-amid-converging-crises/.

36. "Presidential Documents," *Federal Register*, https://www.federalregister.gov/presidential-documents.

37. "Key People—President Barack Obama," Obama for America, last modified June 14, 2013, http://www.p2012.org/candidates/obamaorg.html.

38. Martha Joynt Kumar, "The White House Is Like City Hall," in *The White House World*, ed. Kumar and Sullivan, 84.

39. Camille D. Burge and David E. Lewis, "Campaigning for a Job: Obama for America, Patronage, and Presidential Appointments," https://my.vanderbilt.edu/davidlewis/files/2011/12/burge-lewis-wisconsin.pdf, 13.

40. "Karl Rove—The Architect: Karl Rove's Life and Political Career," PBS, April 12, 2005, http://www.pbs.org/wgbh/pages/frontline/shows/architect/rove/cron.html.

41. Karl Rove, "Bio," http://www.rove.com/bio.

42. "Full Text: George Bush's Victory Speech," *Guardian*, November 4, 2004, https://www.theguardian.com/world/2004/nov/04/uselections2004.usa17.

43. Joshua Green, "Karl Rove in a Corner," *The Atlantic*, November 2004, https://www.theatlantic.com/magazine/archive/2004/11/karl-rove-in-a-corner/303537/; Joshua Green, "The Rove Presidency," *The Atlantic*, September 2007, https://www.theatlantic.com/magazine/archive/2007/09/the-rove-presidency/306132/.

44. As quoted in Julian Borger, "The Brains," *Guardian*, March 8, 2004, https://www.theguardian.com/world/2004/mar/09/uselections2004.usa1.

45. Ken Stern, "Exclusive: Stephen Bannon, Trump's New C.E.O., Hints at His Master Plan," *Vanity Fair*, August 17, 2016, http://www.vanityfair.com/news/2016/08/breitbart-stephen-bannon-donald-trump-master-plan; Joshua Green, "Trump Campaign CEO's Résumé Includes Goldman and 'Seinfeld,'" Bloomberg, https://www.bloomberg.com/politics/articles/2016-08-17/trump-campaign-ceo-s-r-sum-includes-goldman-and-seinfeld.

46. Anthony Zurcher, "Steve Bannon: The Downfall of Trump's Chief Strategist?" BBC News, February 6, 2017, http://www.bbc.com/news/election-us-2016-37971742.

47. "How Steve Bannon Became a Fixture in the White House," *PBS NewsHour*, http://www.pbs.org/newshour/rundown/steve-bannon-became-fixture-white-house/.

48. Domenico Montanaro, "Ambassadors: Do Patronage Picks Matter?" NBC News, last modified August 3, 2009, http://www.nbcnews.com/id/32268349/ns/politics-white_house/t/ambassadors-do-patronage-picks-matter/#.UczMtfmshzI.

49. Jones, *Passages to the Presidency*, 2.

50. Martha Joynt Kumar and Terry Sullivan, introduction to *The White House World*, ed. Kumar and Sullivan, xiii.

51. Doris Kearns Goodwin, *Team of Rivals: The Political Genius of Abraham Lincoln* (New York: Simon & Schuster, 2005).

52. "Founders Online: To Thomas Jefferson from George Washington, 23 August 1792," National Archives and Records Administration, https://founders.archives.gov/documents/Jefferson/01-24-02-0300.

53. Robert Dallek, *Camelot's Court: Inside the Kennedy White House* (New York: Harper Perennial, 2014).

54. Henry Kissinger, *White House Years* (New York: Simon & Schuster, 2011), 996.

55. "The Recession of 2007–2009," Bureau of Labor Statistics, 2012, http://www.bls.gov/spotlight/2012/recession/pdf/recession_bls_spotlight.pdf; Catherine Rampell, "Unemployment Today vs. the Great Depression," Economix (blog), *New York Times*, January 28, 2010, http://economix.blogs.nytimes.com/2010/01/28/unemployment-today-vs-the-great-depression/.

56. Clay Johnson, "The 2008–2009 Presidential Transition: Preparing Federal Agencies," *Presidential Studies Quarterly* 39, no. 4 (2009): 819–22.

57. Martha Joynt Kumar, "The 2008–2009 Presidential Transition through the Voices of Its Participants," *Presidential Studies Quarterly* 39, no. 4 (2009): 823–58.

58. Kumar and Sullivan, introduction, x.

59. John L. Helgerson, "Truman and Eisenhower: Launching the Process," from draft of *Getting to Know the President: CIA Briefings of Presidential Candidates from 1952 to 1992*, https://www.cia.gov/library/center-for-the-study-of-intelligence/csi-publications/csi-studies/studies/95unclass/Helgerson.html.

60. Helgerson, "Truman and Eisenhower."

61. Sheryl Gay Stolberg and Robert Pear, "Bush Warns of Vulnerability in a Transition," *New York Times*, November 6, 2008, A.23.

62. Peter Baker, "Bush Prepares Crisis Briefings to Aid Obama," *New York Times*, December 16, 2008, A.1.

63. "Remarks by President Obama and President-Elect Trump after Meeting," Barack Obama White House, November 10, 2016, https://obamawhitehouse.archives.gov/the-press-office/2016/11/10/remarks -president-obama-and-president-elect-trump-after-meeting.

64. Pfiffner, "Presidential Transitions," 91.

65. Carl M. Brauer, *Presidential Transitions: Eisenhower through Reagan* (New York: Oxford University Press, 1986), 258.

66. Kumar, "Like City Hall," 90–91.

67. *Recruiting Presidential Appointees: A Conference of Former Presidential Personnel Assistants* (Washington, DC: National Academy of Public Administration, 1984), 36, quoted in James P. Pfiffner, *The Strategic Presidency: Hitting the Ground Running*, 2nd rev. ed. (Lawrence: University Press of Kansas, 1996), 58.

68. Michelle Munn, "Clinton Transition Left $15,000 Damage, GAO Says," *Los Angeles Times*, June 12, 2002, http://articles.latimes.com/2002/jun/12/nation/na-clinton12.

69. Clinton and Lang, "Successful Presidential Transition," 43.

70. Whether mandates are real or merely imagined, it turns out, is a matter of substantial dispute. For examinations of the subject, see Patricia Conley, *Presidential Mandates: How Elections Shape the National Agenda* (Chicago: University of Chicago Press, 2001); and Julia Azari, *Delivering the People's Message: The Changing Politics of the Presidential Mandate* (Ithaca: Cornell University Press, 2014).

71. Clinton and Lang, "Successful Presidential Transition," 43.

72. Frederick C. Mosher, W. David Clinton, and Daniel G. Lang, "From Carter to Reagan," in Frederick C. Mosher, *Presidential Transitions and Foreign Affairs* (Baton Rouge: Louisiana State University Press, 1987), 224.

73. Mosher, Clinton, and Lang, "From Carter to Reagan," 226.

74. Clinton and Lang, "Successful Presidential Transition," 45.

75. Clinton and Lang, "Successful Presidential Transition," 45.

76. Robert A. Caro, *The Years of Lyndon Johnson: The Passage of Power* (New York: Alfred A. Knopf, 2012), ix.

77. Caro, *Years of Lyndon Johnson*, x.

78. Caro, *Years of Lyndon Johnson*, xii.

79. Quoted in Caro, *Years of Lyndon Johnson*, 354.

80. But for a critique of Johnson's legislative accomplishments, see Clay Risen, "The Shrinking of Lyndon Johnson," *New Republic*, February 9, 2014, https://newrepublic.com/article/116404/lbjs-civil-rights-act-arm -twisting-was-myth.

81. Quoted in Caro, *Years of Lyndon Johnson*, 430.

82. Matt Viser and Lisa Rein, "White House, Escalating Tensions, Orders Agencies to Rebuff Biden Transition Team," *Washington Post*, November 10, 2020, https://www.washingtonpost.com/politics/trump-transition -agencies-biden/2020/11/09/ad9f2ba2–22b7–11eb-952e-0c475972cfc0_story.html.

83. Brian Naylor, "Here's What GSA Approval Means for the Biden Transition," National Public Radio, November 24, 2020, https://www.npr.org/sections/biden-transition-updates/2020/11/24/938400849 /heres-what-gsa-approval-means-for-the-biden-transition.

84. "GSA Turns Over Transition HQ to New Administration," General Services Administration, Press Release, November 5, 2008, https://www.gsa.gov/about-us/newsroom/news-releases/gsa-turns-over -transition-hq-to-new-administration.

85. Denise Turner Roth, "Obama's GSA Administrator: Presidential Transition Is Too Important to Politicize," CNN, November 18, 2020, https://www.cnn.com/2020/11/18/opinions/obama-gsa-administrator -transition-turner-roth/index.html.

86. Roth, "Obama's GSA Administrator."

87. Bill Chappell, "'It's Dangerous to Delay' Transition, Democratic White House Veteran Podesta Says," National Public Radio, November 12, 2020, https://www.npr.org/sections/biden-transition-updates/2020/11 /12/934218529/its-dangerous-to-delay-transition-democratic-white-house-veteran-podesta-says.

88. Brian Naylor and Alana Wise, "President-Elect Biden to Begin Formal Transition Process after Agency OK," National Public Radio, November 23, 2020, https://www.npr.org/sections/biden-transition-updates /2020/11/23/937956178/trump-administration-to-begin-biden-transition-protocols.

89. Jim Rutenberg et al., "77 Days: Trump's Campaign to Subvert the Election," *New York Times*, February 1, 2021, A.1.

90. Nancy Cook, "Trump Budget Chief Hampers Biden Transition with Ban on Meetings," Bloomberg, December 31, 2020, https://www.bloomberg.com/news/articles/2020-12-31/trump-budget-chief-hampers -biden-transition-with-ban-on-meetings.

91. Cook, "Trump Budget Chief Hampers Biden Transition with Ban on Meetings."

92. Mike Memoli, "For Biden's Team, a Transition Many Months in the Making," NBC, January 19, 2021, https://www.nbcnews.com/politics/politics-news/biden-s-team-transition-many-months-making -n1254570.

PART III

Governance

8

Relations with Congress

UNDER THE CONSTITUTION, Congress, not the president, has the power to make law. If presidents want to achieve their policy goals, therefore, they must find ways to work with Congress. This is no easy task. Members of Congress, after all, have reasonably well-defined motivations for writing statutes and voting on legislation: partisan considerations, the drive to direct federal resources to local constituencies, and other ideological objectives, all of which can put them at odds with the president.

To make headway within Congress, presidents need to identify those policies that are likely to receive a favorable hearing from legislators and deploy institutional resources in order to advance them. The president's veto power is one such resource, and the president's expertise (particularly about foreign affairs) is another. The president can also draw upon the financial and informational resources of the executive branch.

But to really influence the production of legislation, say some, presidents must rely upon their abilities to persuade members of Congress that their interests are one and the same. Indeed, the famed presidency scholar Richard Neustadt went so far as to argue that presidential power *is* the power to persuade—that power and persuasion are synonymous. By bargaining and negotiating, Neustadt insisted, presidents seek to convince legislators to do things that they cannot accomplish on their own. Presidents' ability to persuade, in the end, defines the measure of their success.

For reasons we outline both in this chapter and the next, this particular line of reasoning is incomplete—if not outright mistaken. But however presidents engage Congress, the objectives are much the same: to advance their preferred policies through a long and difficult legislative process over which they exercise very little direct control; and to amend, delay, or block objectionable policies as best they're able.

8.1 Power through Persuasion

Persuasion can assume a variety of forms. Sometimes, presidents appeal to legislators' histories or worldviews to convince them to support a legislative initiative. Other times, presidents persuade by claiming to know essential facts about the state of the world (e.g., the nature of foreign threats, the long-term political implications of changes in public attitudes, or the status of new regulatory reforms) that bear upon ongoing policy debates.

Presidents can also promise political favors (campaigning on behalf of legislators, offering access to key donors, or supporting items that affect constituents) to sweeten a policy deal. When all else fails, presidents can swap sugar for salt and threaten to call out legislators publicly, support challengers against them in the next election, or shut them out of fund-raising opportunities.

8.1.1 An Archetypal Case: LBJ and the Civil Rights Act

Perhaps more than any modern president, Lyndon B. Johnson epitomizes the persuasive presidency. Before being elected vice president in 1960, Johnson served as a long-time Democratic senator who earned the nickname "Master of the Senate" for his vast knowledge of the legislative body's inner workings.* In 1963, President Kennedy's assassination thrust Johnson into the Oval Office, where, as discussed in chapter 7, he found few allies as he confronted a nation deep in mourning.

Johnson also faced a stalled policy program. During the Kennedy administration, legislative proposals for civil rights reform had remained bottled up in the House, and southern Democratic senators insisted that they would never come to a vote on the Senate floor. In the face of such daunting challenges, Johnson went to work on individual Congress members.

Recognizing the need to enlist the support of a leader in the Senate, Johnson turned to veteran Democratic senator (and future vice president) Hubert Humphrey. Humphrey had a reputation as a stalwart advocate for civil rights. Johnson worried, however, that the liberal Humphrey would be unwilling to compromise with moderate Republicans. As Humphrey later recalled, the president called him into his office and began his pitch. "You have got this opportunity now, Hubert, but you liberals will never deliver," Humphrey recalled Johnson saying. "You don't know the rules of the Senate, and your liberals will all be off making speeches when they ought to be present in the Senate. [Y]ou've got a great opportunity here, but I'm afraid it's going to fall between the boards." Later, Humphrey reflected on the effectiveness of the president's appeal: "[Johnson] sized me up; he knew very well that I would say, 'Damn you, I'll show you.'"[1] With this simple psychological tactic, Johnson managed to persuade one of the most important Democratic senators in the country to align himself with Republican leadership.

In addition to private appeals, Johnson used promises of support for senators' pet projects. One of Johnson's prime targets was Senator Carl Hayden of Arizona, who had long been a proponent of **states' rights** and was therefore philosophically opposed to federal civil rights legislation. Johnson, however, had a notion that political expediency might carry the day. The president authorized Secretary of the Interior Stewart Udall to offer Hayden a deal: if the senator agreed to support the civil rights legislation, the administra-

---

*During his twelve-year tenure in the Senate, Johnson shot up through the ranks of the party leadership, from whip to minority leader and finally to majority leader. For a masterful account of Johnson's ascendancy in Congress, see Robert Caro, *Master of the Senate: The Years of Lyndon Johnson* (New York: Vintage, 2003).

FIGURE 8.1. The Johnson Treatment. Lyndon Johnson squares off against the powerful southern Democrat, long-time supporter of racial segregation, and erstwhile mentor to the president, Richard Russell. *Source:* National Archives: Yoichi Okamoto.

tion would support the Central Arizona Water Project, a controversial plan that called for diverting water from the Colorado River to the water-deficient cities of Phoenix and Tucson. Upon hearing Johnson's proposal, Hayden quickly lent his support to the civil rights bill.[2]

Along with personal appeals and promises of political favors, not to mention his imposing physical stature, the president resorted to other forms of pressure. When Representative Howard Smith initially held up the civil rights bill in the House Rules Committee, Johnson called Katharine Graham, editor of the *Washington Post*, and hinted that she might consider pushing her staff to write more stories, "every day, front page," about how Smith and his allies were refusing to allow the House to even debate the bill.[3] Graham complied, and eventually Smith succumbed to mounting public pressure to bring the bill to a vote, which came out 11–4 in favor of passage.

Other times, Johnson directly threatened members, as for example when he told his former political mentor Senator Richard Russell, the southern Democrat leading the **filibuster** (a stalling tactic designed to block Senate action on a bill) against the civil rights bill, that the White House would not rally behind a single piece of legislation until civil rights came to a vote on the Senate floor (figure 8.1). "Dick, you've got to get out of my way," Johnson told Russell during an intimate chat in the White House. "I'm going to run you over. I don't intend to . . . compromise."[4] Though the southern Democrats did indeed mount a formidable filibuster that lasted eighty-three days, they eventually caved, due in no small part to Johnson's efforts. As the prominent civil rights activist James Farmer recalled, the president was constantly "calling senators, twisting their arms, threatening them, cajoling them, trying to line up votes for the Civil Rights Bill."[5] Ultimately, his efforts bore fruit. On June 2, 1964, Johnson signed the landmark Civil Rights Act into law.

8.1.2 The Limits of Persuasion

For all the purported success of the "Johnson Treatment," readers should refrain from judging today's presidents by their ability to wrangle and strong-arm senators. Numerous studies have shown that legislative success is primarily determined by factors that have very little to do with the personal qualities, psychological dispositions, or (in the case of Johnson) physical presence of individual presidents.[6] Presidents cannot meld circumstances to their liking, and they cannot bend politicians to their will. Rather, successful presidents learn to make the most of what Congress will allow.

PRESIDENTS AS FACILITATORS OF CHANGE

Presidency scholar George Edwards has written at length about the limited opportunities for political persuasion. Successful presidents do not induce members of Congress to become more compliant, more acquiescent. Rather, presidential accomplishments arise from the opportunities presidents inherit. Successful presidents, Edwards argues, act as "facilitators" of change. Though they cannot conjure support where it does not exist, facilitators "understand the opportunities for change in their environments" and work quickly to exploit them.[7]

To understand the role of the facilitator, let's look at the case of LBJ through a different lens. Though the tragic circumstances of Johnson's inauguration may not have seemed like "opportunities" at the time, they contributed to his negotiations with Congress. Entering office in the wake of President Kennedy's assassination, Johnson confronted a Congress that was eager to take actions that would honor Kennedy's legacy. One year later, Democrats secured large supermajorities in the House and Senate, which lent greater support for landmark civil rights legislation. And as we discussed in chapter 2, powerful social movements called upon the government to finally address the racism and social injustices born of slavery and Jim Crow. It was precisely this context—far more than the Johnson Treatment—that made possible the Civil Rights Act.

Political opportunities, however, constitute only half of Edwards's formulation for presidential success. As facilitators, presidents also must know how to exploit any opportunities for change that arise during their tenure. For Edwards, Johnson's success derived from his ability to recognize and then make the most of the opportunities before him. Immediately after his party's ascendance to power in 1964, Johnson laid out his Great Society agenda (ending poverty and racial inequality, reducing crime, and protecting the environment) and began flooding Congress with legislative proposals. "Every day, every hour it was drive, drive, drive," said one White House aide, describing the continuous cycle of legislative enactments and draft proposals.[8] Knowing that he would not always have 295 co-partisans in the House and another 68 in the Senate, and knowing, further, that "arithmetic is decisive," Johnson introduced all kinds of major domestic policy initiatives, of which the Civil Rights Act was only one.[9] Medicare, Medicaid, the Elementary and Secondary Education Act, the Equal Opportunity Act, the Voting Rights Act, and all kinds of other laws involving housing, poverty reduction, rural electrification, and a good deal more became law not because Johnson was especially persuasive. They became law because the public broadly supported change and the Democrats retained firm control over Congress.

Unlike Johnson, most presidents assume office at less opportune moments. And when they do, the challenges of passing landmark legislation are a good deal more formidable. President George W. Bush failed to capture a majority or even a plurality of votes in his 2000 campaign, with nearly a quarter of Americans believing that he "stole the election."[10] In the Senate, his party lost four seats—leaving the chamber evenly divided between fifty Democrats and fifty Republicans. In this context, the Bush administration clearly would not accomplish anything akin to Johnson's Great Society. Still, having been elected in the aftermath of consecutive federal budget surpluses, Bush confronted a Congress that was amenable to passing tax cuts. Not surprisingly, then, his first major legislative accomplishment was the Tax Relief Reconciliation Act of 2001, one of two tax cuts passed during Bush's tenure. Though the act was hardly revolutionary, its passage was achieved not through Bush's persuasive powers but by his understanding of the political landscape he occupied.

In ways both positive and negative for presidents, this landscape can change at any moment. The September 2001 terrorist attacks immediately reconstructed the one Bush confronted, instantly aligning the priorities of his administration, Congress, and the public. In the weeks and months that followed the attacks, Bush managed to secure approval for a war in Afghanistan and the creation of a new cabinet-level department. The attacks created new opportunities for the Bush administration, and ultimately a new legacy—one well beyond what the president could have anticipated.

PRESIDENTS AND POLITICAL TIME

Edwards is not the only scholar to recognize that events and circumstances shape a president's legislative performance. In one of the most influential books on executive politics of the last half century, political scientist Stephen Skowronek argues that a president's ability to advance policy change crucially depends upon the moment in "political time" they hold office.[11] Unlike secular time, which proceeds linearly, political time has cyclical qualities that relate to the "changing shape of the political regimes that have organized state-society relations for broad periods of American history."[12] In political time, regimes—defined broadly by dominant political party and the coalitions that support it—steadily erode as their claims are seen as outmoded and anachronistic and as the coalitions that support them become increasingly disenchanted and divided. When the claims of a regime become sufficiently tenuous, when its presumptions are broadly discredited, then an opponent can step in and altogether remake the normative understandings and coalitional alignments that define American politics. In these rare moments of political time, a new regime arises from the ashes of the old, and the same withering forces then set upon it until this new regime, too, is ultimately vanquished.

According to Skowronek, the definition and promise of presidential leadership crucially depends upon the moment in political time one inherits office. Presidents who are aligned to a discredited regime find it nearly impossible to pave a new pathway forward, whereas presidents who are opposed to a particularly strong regime run headlong into opposition at every turn. Now and again, though, a president assumes office at an especially propitious moment—one in which conventional understandings of the purposes of the state lose their sway, when party platforms are viewed as tired and irrelevant, and political coalitions have come entirely undone. In these instances—think Lincoln in 1860, McKinley in 1896, FDR in 1932, or Reagan in 1980—presidents can usher in an altogether new governing regime, one that reconstitutes the terms of party competition, coalitional arrangements, and public expectations of government—and one that is instantiated through the passage of landmark legislation.

Thereafter, the cycle repeats, and future presidents must work within the confines of the regimes that these "reconstructive" presidents built. More precisely, future presidents' ability to affect change—both within Congress and beyond—depends upon their relationship to the regime and its strength at the time they assume office. And each successive president, Skowronek explains, confronts profound challenges. For Truman, they involved repackaging New Deal orthodoxies as innovation; for Eisenhower, they involved carefully maneuvering around a robust New Deal coalition that looked skeptically upon the Republican Party; and for Carter, they involved piecing together a New Deal coalition that had frayed nearly beyond recognition. For all of these presidents, by virtue of where they stood in political time, the chances to advance meaningful political change were locked in the moment they assumed office.

In important respects, Skowronek and Edwards disagree about the nature and possibilities of presidential leadership. For Skowronek, presidential leadership is tethered to governing regimes, whereas for Edwards, leadership relates to the partisan composition of Congress and the content of public opinion. More crucially, Skowronek argues that at least some presidents really do transform their political environments, whereas Edwards sees little but facilitation. Still, both of these scholars are decidedly skeptical about the political returns from presidential persuasion. In place of the personal qualities, experiences, and assets that ostensibly allow presidents to persuade others to do their bidding, Skowronek and Edwards emphasize larger, more structural foundations of presidential leadership. In their view, when a president fails to curry the legislative support required to pass a bill in Congress, we need not resolve to elect a more competent, compelling, or skillful president. Rather, we may have to face the hard truth that some bills, sometimes, simply have no chance of enactment, no matter how gifted a persuader the president may be.

8.1.3 The Subjects of Persuasion

Persuasion may not take presidents especially far in terms of what they ultimately accomplish. But if presidents cannot dictate what politicians and constituents *think*, they have a tremendous amount of say over what constituents *think about*, which has important implications for what members of Congress debate, research, and eventually vote on. Presidents exercise remarkable agenda-setting powers, as nearly all of their significant legislative proposals eventually find a place on the congressional calendar.[13] They do not always secure a vote on the precise bill they would like to see enacted into law. Reliably, though, presidential initiatives attract notice—and with it, consideration—on Capitol Hill.

The president's agenda-setting influence derives in part from the Constitution itself. According to Article II, Section 3, the president is charged with giving "to Congress information of the State of the Union and recommend[ing] to their Consideration such measures as he shall judge necessary and expedient." What the Constitution required "from time to time" has become an annual ritual. Throughout much of the nineteenth century, presidents delivered a State of the Union document to Congress in writing. Since President Wilson's tenure from 1913 to 1921, however, nearly every president has appeared before Congress to deliver the State of the Union in person, and these presidents have taken this opportunity to lay out their domestic and foreign policy agenda for the coming year.

Presidents usually identify somewhere between ten and forty policy objectives in their annual speeches.[14] The majority of these objectives tend to be new policies, revealed to Congress and the public for the first time. By calling attention to such proposals in a highly public setting, it is thought, presidents can put pressure on legislators to adopt their agenda. Past scholarship on the State of the Union Address seems to justify this strategy: polls taken immediately after the address show elevated public concern for the issues identified by the president.[15] In this way, an address intended for communicating with Congress has allowed presidents to reshape the priorities of an entire country.

Over the course of the year, presidents have many more opportunities to promote their policy agendas. Whether appearing before Congress, visiting a naval base, or delivering a college commencement address, presidents are constantly delivering public remarks on a diverse array of subjects. Since every word a president utters is recorded and scrutinized, sometimes all it takes is a brief public statement to shift the subject—if not the terms—of a debate.

Making these various appearances, presidents can expect the media to shine a bright light on their agendas. In politics, after all, no one receives more media attention than presidents. What they say and do on any given day is, by definition, newsworthy. As one scholar noted, "Only the President can command simultaneous live coverage on all the television networks. Only the President can gather the nation at his feet, as if it were a family, and say, 'Dear friends, here is how I see things.'"[16] Repeatedly, presidents have used this power not just to share their opinions on the issues of the day but to declare which issues warrant public consideration. Even George Edwards—who earlier emphasized the limits of presidential persuasion—recognizes that "presidents operate as issue entrepreneurs, essentially creating attention where none exists."[17]

In certain policy domains, which we discuss at greater length later in this chapter, presidents enjoy powers to formally compel Congress to consider their policy recommendations. For instance, the Budget and Accounting Act of 1921 requires presidents to submit a draft budget proposal to Congress. Every year since, presidents have used their budget proposals to outline—for both Congress and the public—their funding priorities. And these priorities usually become the starting point for congressional negotiations. The president's agenda-setting authority in trade, meanwhile, is even stronger. There, members of Congress are statutorily required to vote on trade proposals that the president initiates under his "fast track" authority. According to the Trade Act of 1974, moreover, they must do so on an up-or-down basis—that is, they must vote yea or nay without amending or filibustering the proposal. This gives presidents a rare opportunity not only to set an agenda but also to pass it.[18]

More commonly, though, presidents look to allies within Congress to introduce bills on their behalf. Here persuasion comes into play with the presentation of policy initiatives that align with the president's agenda. Persuasive presidents are able to convince members of Congress to deliberate, and possibly even vote, on the things that matter most to them. But whether a favorable legislative outcome results? Well, that is another matter—one that ultimately depends upon factors that are beyond the president's control.

8.2 Predicting Legislative Success and Failure

Though the media fixate on the idiosyncratic and often highly personal dramas that accompany interbranch bargaining, the ability of presidents to advance policy initiatives within Congress often comes down to a handful of fundamentals. At what point during a presidential term is a policy being considered? Does the president's party control Congress? Does the policy under consideration concern foreign or domestic matters? Ideologically, do the two major parties within Congress share common ground?

8.2.1 Timing

When it comes, presidential success usually arrives early in a presidential term. Ever since FDR, presidents have sought to make the most of their "first 100 days" in office, often referred to as their "honeymoon period." As President Johnson once explained to a White House aide, "You've got to give it all you can that first year. I keep hitting hard because I know this honeymoon won't last."[19] The data in figure 8.2 underscore the accuracy of Johnson's assessment. Presidents generally enjoy their highest levels of support in Congress during their first year in office. As their terms progress, particularly during their second terms in office, Congress only becomes less receptive to presidents' legislative agendas.

The political scientist Paul Light refers to this trend as the "cycle of decreasing influence."[20] Put simply, presidents lose political capital—measured by public support and

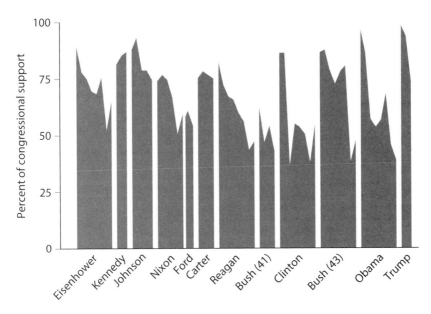

FIGURE 8.2. Presidential success in Congress. The figure presents the annual weighted average of bills endorsed by the president that are approved by the House and Senate. One factor that figures into a favorable vote from Congress is the timing of the endorsement (early versus late in the president's term). Presidents have more success in Congress early in their terms than they do later. Other factors include the partisan makeup of Congress and the nature of the legislation (foreign versus domestic). *Source:* Congressional Quarterly Almanacs, various years.

allies in Congress—as their elections fade from memory. The cycle has proven remarkably robust. As we will discuss in chapter 12, nearly every president since Truman has ended his term with less support in the polls than when he began. Similarly, the president's party almost always loses seats in the midterm elections. In the House, eighteen of the previous twenty midterm elections have resulted in losses for the president's party, making it all the more difficult for the president to pass an agenda.[21]

Light describes the cycle of decreasing influence as a natural consequence of occupying the Oval Office. Every day, presidents must make choices, few of which can please everyone. As an aide to President Ford remarked, "Each decision is bound to hurt somebody. . . . If [the president] doesn't make choices, he will be attacked for being indecisive. If he does, he will satisfy one group but anger three others."[22] And to complicate matters, Light points out that legislative success requires time and effort—resources that quickly dissipate after a president's first two years in office. As presidential primary campaigns have started earlier and earlier, presidents must spend an increasing amount of time planning their reelection campaigns. Even if the president wins reelection, however, there is little renewed enthusiasm in a second term. The president's second four years in office are simply a "continuation of the first" in the eyes of Congress. Thus, if newly elected presidents are to find any success with Congress, they must follow Johnson's advice and strike while the iron is hot.

8.2.2 Unified versus Divided Government

Presidents do not choose the partisan balance in Congress. Rather, they must work with legislators who have been independently elected. Because fellow partisans in Congress share many of their goals, presidents would prefer to have their party in control of both chambers of Congress. When the last five presidents (Clinton to Biden) first assumed office, their party held a majority of seats in both the House and Senate, a situation known as **unified government**. Early on, then, they all enjoyed relatively strong positions from which to pass legislation to their liking.* Within two years, though, four of these presidents lost control of one chamber (at the time of publication, 2022 midterms had not been held). Thereafter, **divided government** took hold, as the opposition party secured a majority of seats in either the House or the Senate. (In their second terms, Clinton, Bush, and Obama all lost control of both the House and Senate.)

When the opposition party controls both chambers, presidents typically face their most difficult challenges. To succeed, presidents need to curry the support of a significant number of members of the opposition party, though without alienating their fellow partisans. For both political and ideological reasons, the opposition party may want to deny the president policy victories. The leadership of the opposition party, as a consequence, may go out of its way to discourage its members from siding with the president even as the president makes concessions. The larger and more cohesive the opposition party, the more difficult the president's legislative challenges will be.

A substantial body of research within political science establishes a systematic relationship between divided government and legislative productivity.[23] When the president and majorities in Congress come from different parties, fewer landmark bills are enacted into laws. Though the two branches manage to coordinate on the mundane legislation required of everyday governance, they often come to loggerheads on the most significant policies.

8.2.3 Party Polarization

To pass, a president's proposed legislation must garner the support of a majority of both houses of Congress. In times of divided government, this requires winning over at least some members of the opposing party. Even in times of unified government, the threat of a Senate filibuster usually makes reaching across the aisle a practical necessity. Of late, however, bipartisanship has been in short supply.

One of the most striking trends in Congress during the past fifty years has been the increase in **party polarization**. As figure 8.3 shows, the levels of disagreement be-

---

* Even during periods of unified government, however, success is not certain. Party members do not always fall in line behind the president. In most years since 1953, fellow party members in the House voted against the president's position more than 20 percent of the time.

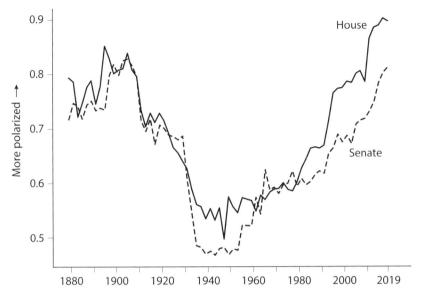

FIGURE 8.3. Party polarization in the House and Senate. The figure presents the yearly differences in each chamber's median Democratic and Republican member's NOMINATE score, which is a summary measure of legislators' ideologies based on their voting records. Larger values indicate higher levels of party polarization. The House is significantly more polarized than the Senate, but there too, polarization is higher than any year since the early 1900s. *Source:* Voteview: Congressional Roll-Call Votes Database, www.voteview.com.

tween the two parties have increased dramatically over the last half century—so much so, in fact, that contemporary differences in the Senate are now at historical highs not reached since the turn of the twentieth century; and they have broken records in the House.[*]

Greater polarization has, in general, made it increasingly difficult for presidents to advance their policy agendas in Congress. In the past, the White House was able to reach out to moderate members of Congress from the opposing party. Not so today. Moderates can hardly be found in the current, more polarized party system.[†]

---

[*] Northern congressional Democrats became slightly more liberal than their predecessors, and southern Democrats became much more liberal—largely because conservative southern Democrats, starting in the mid-1970s, switched parties and became Republicans.

[†] As some scholars have noted, polarization may not be the result of two parties moving with equal speed toward the ideological extremes. For more on how (and why) polarization proceeds unevenly between Republicans and Democrats, see Matthew Grossmann and David A. Hopkins, *Asymmetric Politics: Ideological Republicans and Group Interest Democrats* (New York: Oxford University Press, 2016).

Historical Transformations: Health Care Reform and Changes to Obama's Governing Strategy

The rising polarization of the two major parties within Congress and a profoundly cumbersome legislative process combine to affect not only what presidents attempt to accomplish but also how they seek to do so. Barack Obama assumed office with the promise of transcending the divisions that, in his view, impeded the federal government from solving social problems. In 2009, therefore, he sought to engage members of Congress in a conversation about the challenges that faced the nation. Over the course of his first term in office, however, he quickly came to appreciate the difficulties of the legislative process. The challenges of pushing through his greatest domestic policy achievement, the Affordable Care Act (ACA), helped convince the president to concentrate on maintaining Democratic solidarity rather than currying Republican support.

During the 2008 presidential campaign, Obama promised sweeping changes to the American health care system, an effort at which earlier U.S. presidents had failed. In a policy speech in 2007 he addressed the pessimistic view, prevalent in Washington, that enacting sweeping reform was politically impossible: "I know there's a cynicism out there about whether this can happen. . . . For too long, this debate has been stunted by what I call the smallness of our politics—the idea that there isn't much we can agree on or do about the major challenges facing our country."[24] Accepting the Democratic nomination at the national convention in August 2008, Obama reiterated his belief that bipartisan compromise was possible: "America, our work will not be easy. The challenges we face require tough choices, and Democrats as well as Republicans will need to cast off the worn-out ideas and politics of the past."[25]

Upon entering the Oval Office, Obama almost immediately followed up on his campaign promise by moving health care to the top of his domestic policy agenda. In March 2009, the newly seated president formally announced his intention to seek health care reform: "I will not accept the status quo as a solution. Not this time. Not now."[26] Moving into the legislative phase, Obama articulated some broad guidelines for reform, such as coverage for all Americans, but left the details to Congress. The president hoped that by actively soliciting Congress's involvement, he would avoid the perceived mistakes of the Clinton administration, which, critics charged, had failed to include key members of Congress in its efforts to reform health care. Obama urged Democratic lawmakers to focus on "those elements of the package that people agree on."[27]

Obama nevertheless met significant grassroots opposition from conservatives, most significantly from the **Tea Party movement**, which had emerged in 2009. The movement, which advocated fiscal responsibility, limited government, and the free market, gained national exposure through a series of local and national protests against the previous administration's bank bailouts and President Obama's $787 billion stimulus package, both responses to the economic crisis of 2008.

In response to the White House's push for universal health care, Tea Party members organized rallies throughout the country, pressured local representatives, and actively participated in political campaigns. For a time, it looked as though the Tea Party's efforts to defeat the plan might be successful. As 2009 drew to a close, Republicans and even moderate Democrats remained staunchly opposed to the legislation.

Faced with such stiff opposition, Obama changed course. Instead of focusing on winning over Republican legislators, he began to corral every Democratic vote in Congress. With the House and Senate in Democratic control, Obama knew he could pass a health care bill if his party voted as a solid bloc. To build public support for the bill, Obama launched small rallies all around the country. The president spoke at length about the responsibility that Democratic members of Congress had to bring about real change. "This is their moment, this is our moment, to live up to the trust that the American people have placed in us," Obama told reporters.[28] The president even called on liberal Internet bloggers to pressure their representatives to support health care reform. In a conference call, Obama told them, "It is important just to keep the pressure on members of Congress because . . . there is a default position of inertia here in Washington."[29]

When it came time for the House of Representatives to vote, Obama visited the chamber and made a rare personal appeal for lawmakers to support the bill. "Each and every one of you will be able to look back and say, 'This was my finest moment in politics,'" the president told the members of his party.[30]

Obama's lobbying paid off in the House. The bill narrowly passed with a vote of 220–215 but then moved on to an even tougher battle in the Senate. In an effort to rally the caucus, Obama met with Democratic senators behind closed doors. The final vote fell along party lines with a 60–39 vote.

In the aftermath of the ACA's enactment, Obama spent less time trying to forge productive ties with congressional Republicans and more time trying to maintain discipline within the ranks of his own party. The allure of bipartisanship rather quickly gave way to the imperatives of getting things done.

In the years ahead, the president also would not shy away from working around Congress altogether. Josh Earnest, the president's deputy press secretary, acknowledged that the administration would invoke "the image of a gridlocked, dysfunctional Congress and a president who is leaving no stone unturned to try to find solutions to the difficult . . . challenges facing the country."[31] The benefits and constraints of this strategy are explored at some length in chapter 9.

The ACA, then, mattered twice over: first, for the policy changes it instituted; and second, for the lessons the Obama administration drew about how best to exercise power in the policy debates that followed.

8.2.4 Nationalized Politics

Another factor in the president's legislative success—and one that interacts with the party polarization of recent decades—is the **nationalization of politics**.[32] To understand this trend, it may be helpful to recall what our elections used to look like. At the time of this nation's founding, local issues and institutions dominated political discourse. The Framers had designed a system in which voters' interest in their state governments was assumed; it was "beyond doubt," Madison wrote, "that the first and most natural attachment of the people will be to the governments of their respective States."[33]

Today, however, elections are determined less and less by local issues. Though ours is a federal government composed almost entirely of locally elected representatives, evidence indicates that these representatives are increasingly selected according to their stances on national issues. In other words, it is becoming less common for constituents to judge House and Senate candidates by their personalities or by the benefits they promise to deliver to their districts. Instead, these candidates are judged by their associations with a national party—and particularly with a party leader, the president.

In a study of thousands of voters and congressional elections from 2006 to 2012, researchers found that representatives' voting habits have almost no effect on constituents' support for their reelection.[34] Oppositely, in 2012, the strength of President Obama's support almost perfectly predicted the support of Democratic candidates for the House of Representatives. Together, these results suggest that the electoral fortunes of House members are tied to those of the most quintessentially national representative. This trend has fluctuated over time—dipping in the 1960s and rising again in the 1980s—but one thing is clear: voters' judgment of down-ballot candidates is linked to their views of the president or presidential candidate.

There are several potential contributors to this trend, such as the declining readership of local media outlets and the growing control of national interest groups over the two parties. For our purposes, though, the causes of nationalized politics matter less than its consequences.

Nationalized politics has the potential to bring the interests of the president and his congressional co-partisans into alignment. Unlike individual legislators, who are elected by small subsections of voters, the president is uniquely situated to pursue the interests of the entire country.[35] To pass legislation, the effects of which are both national and local, the president must convince legislators to prioritize what is good for their country over what is good for their home districts. This is no easy task, as it can mean imploring legislators to betray the voters who put them in office.

Under a system of nationalized politics, however, the distance between national and local concerns is diminished. As voters become less interested in local issues, and larger portions of congressional campaign contributions flow from sources outside legislators' home districts, legislators are freed to adopt the president's national outlook. Put another way, betraying one's local constituents becomes less costly than betraying the president, whose approval ratings shape voters' views of the party and its representatives.[36]

Still, legislators' local concerns have not entirely disappeared. Levels of "pork-barrel" spending—federal money sent back home to congressional districts—have remained stable despite constituents' declining interest in local issues.[37] Furthermore, presidents engage in their own kind of pork-barrel spending, in which they manipulate the federal budget to disproportionately favor co-partisan districts, often as a reward for important votes or as a way to boost electoral fortunes.[38] Presumably, if voters did not care at all about local conditions, such spending would not occur.

Of course, the nationalization of politics need not always play to the president's advantage. While this trend may help the president unify his own party's votes, the same is true for members of the opposition. That is, nationalized politics gives legislators outside the president's party fewer incentives to cooperate with the president's agenda. Traditionally, congressional Republicans who represented large elderly populations, for example, might have voted for a Democratic proposal to increase Medicare funding. Today, however, the calculus is different. If voters care more about partisanship and presidents than local issues, the same Republican legislator may decide to toe the party line. The result is deeper polarization of the sort we discussed earlier.

Though not determinate, the general effects of nationalized politics may be summarized as follows: under conditions of unified government, presidents can expect greater levels of party loyalty; under divided government, however, presidents have even less hope of delivering on their campaign promises.

8.2.5 Foreign versus Domestic Policy

A president's chances of legislative success also depend upon the kind of policy under consideration. In domestic policy, presidents can expect to run up against myriad organized interests, an attentive public, and a motivated assembly of legislators—all of which curtail the number of available policy options. In foreign policy, by contrast, presidents confront fewer interest groups, a sometimes-inattentive public, and a less-involved legislative body—a climate that gives presidents a freer hand at advancing their agenda. As a consequence, some political scientists have argued that for all practical purposes, there exist two presidencies, rather than one:

1. a domestic policy president, who must diligently cultivate public, interest-group, and congressional support to achieve objectives; and
2. a foreign policy president, who pursues policy objectives with considerable independence.

This **two-presidencies thesis** thus posits that presidents exert significantly more influence over foreign policy than they do over domestic policy.

Since Aaron Wildavsky wrote about it over half a century ago, the two-presidencies thesis has been the subject of an ongoing debate among empirically minded scholars.[39] The evidence has been mixed. One analysis, for instance, found that presidents can sway public opinion more easily in foreign than in domestic affairs. But presidents have not been consistently more successful in winning foreign policy votes than they have domestic policy votes in Congress.[40] Still, there appears to be a fair amount of evidence of heightened congressional deference to the president's foreign policy preferences. For instance, some research suggests that foreign policy appropriations better reflect presidential requests than do domestic policy appropriations and, moreover, that the structural designs of foreign policy agencies tend to be more amenable to presidential control than those of domestic policy agencies.[41]

Illustrations of these statistical trends are readily apparent in the real world. For example, in waging wars against governments in Afghanistan and Iraq and against terrorist networks worldwide, George W. Bush (and his successors) exerted considerable authority as commander in chief and challenged the applicability of some U.S. laws and international treaties. Where these efforts had domestic implications, however, such as in the detention and trial of terrorism suspects, Congress and the courts tended to resist the president's authority. Additionally, the stiffest legislative challenges to Bush's broader agenda were on domestic issues, particularly Social Security and immigration reform.

President Trump confronted a similar dichotomy. In the foreign arena, Congress consistently deferred to the president's authority, most notably in 2020 when Trump unilaterally authorized the killing of Qassem Soleimani, a major general in Iran. On the domestic policy front, however, the president's opponents in Congress eagerly attempted to stonewall almost every item on Trump's legislative agenda—including his sweeping tax reform bill, which did not receive a single Democratic vote in either the House or the Senate.

8.3 Veto Politics

Though presidents cannot usually introduce legislation directly, they can use their **veto** power to obtain legislation more to their liking.[42] When the president vetoes a bill, Congress can override the veto with a two-thirds majority of each chamber, but this step typically proves impossible to accomplish. Presidents have repeatedly used the veto to change the course of federal policy. For example, in 1971, in one of the more consequential displays of the veto power, Richard Nixon blocked the Comprehensive Child Development bill, which, if enacted, would have created a universal daycare system for American children. Because of Nixon's veto, it never came to be.

As we will soon see, however, the veto power does more than just block objectionable legislation; indeed, it need not even be deployed to be effective. Charles Cameron, in his groundbreaking book, *Veto Bargaining*, shows that merely threatening to veto a bill can lead Congress to alter its contents. Cameron's work is a classic institutional take on the president's "negative power." Before we can appreciate this work fully, however, let us take a moment to examine vetoes as they appear in the data—how often they are used and, just as importantly, how often they are overridden.

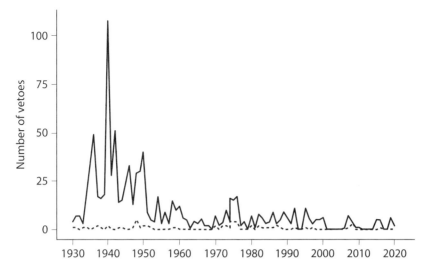

FIGURE 8.4. Annual number of presidential vetoes and congressional overrides. The solid line represents the total number of vetoes each year; the dotted line represents the annual number of successful veto overrides each year. Pocket vetoes are excluded. *Source:* United States Senate, https://www.senate.gov/legislative/vetoes/vetoCounts.htm.

8.3.1 Vetoes and Overrides

Presidents do not issue vetoes as frequently as one might assume. Indeed, early in the Republic, the veto was hardly used at all; and for much of the nineteenth century, it was considered appropriate only if the president believed a bill was unconstitutional. This expectation has clearly changed over time, and some presidents—in particular, Grover Cleveland and Franklin Roosevelt—saw fit to issue dozens of vetoes every year. Even so, presidents ultimately choose to sign—rather than veto—the vast majority of bills that come across their desk.

Figure 8.4 shows the annual number of presidential vetoes and congressional overrides from 1932 to 2020. There is a notable spike during the early part of this time series, when FDR and Truman issued roughly thirty vetoes per year. These vetoes, however, were not indicative of especially large policy differences on landmark legislation. Rather, most of these vetoes concerned personnel matters involving individual soldiers or groups of soldiers fighting in World War II. Thereafter, the annual number of presidential vetoes dropped dramatically.

Presidents George W. Bush and Barack Obama issued a total of twelve vetoes each during their two terms in office—an illustration, in part, of the anticipatory reactions of Congress as it contemplates the president's willingness to sign different versions of a bill and of presidents as they assess the likelihood of a veto being overridden. Donald Trump issued just ten formal vetoes during his time in office, but he made his willingness to exercise his veto power known, particularly after Democrats gained control of the House of Representatives in the 2018 midterm elections.*

Strictly speaking, the president's veto need not settle a legislative dispute once and for all. With two-thirds of both chambers voting in favor of a bill, Congress can pass laws without a presidential signature. For rather obvious reasons, though, overriding the president's veto is no easy task. Large majorities are increasingly rare in Congress; and as the parties have polarized, the prospects of securing support from the president's party have dimmed. In the case of a **pocket veto**, meanwhile, Congress does not even have the opportunity to override. (If Congress is not in session, presidents can kill a bill by not signing it for ten days and keeping it "in their pocket," with no override allowed.) All of this explains why, of the 1,450 vetoes issued from presidents FDR to Trump, only 62, or just 4 percent of the total, were successfully overridden. Nearly universally, the president's veto prevails.[43]

We should not infer from this, however, that Congress is powerless in these negotiations. Quite the contrary. The scarcity of vetoes in recent administrations may reflect, at least in part, the strategic behavior of presidents wary of issuing a veto they know will be overturned. If Congress has forged a two-thirds majority around a bill, presidents may think twice about issuing a veto. Because figure 8.4 does not show the vetoes presidents would have liked to issue, but were convinced by Congress not to, it conceals the larger influence of Congress's override power.

Even when Congress does not have the necessary votes to override a veto, it can still strike a powerful blow against the president.[44] In so-called **blame-game politics**, Congress attempts to make the president look ideologically extreme; members of Congress would rather put the president on record as having opposed a popular bill than enact a watered-down piece of legislation that secures the president's signature. In doing so, they forgo policy advancements in the hopes of eroding popular support for the sitting president or, better still, replacing him or her at the next election with someone more amenable to their policy goals.

In April 2012, for example, House Republicans passed the Interest Rate Reduction Act that would fund subsidies for student loans by making massive cuts to federal health care programs.[45] The bill was purely political in its calculations—in fact, Obama supported the subsidies for student loans while conservative groups such as Club for Growth opposed them. Congressional Republicans knew, however, that by taking the money from Obama's health care reforms, they were inviting the possibility of a presidential veto. In this way, Republicans hoped to corner Obama into taking a position against student loan reduc-

---

* For instance, Trump threatened to veto a bill that would extend U.S. foreign surveillance tools, resulting in a withdrawal of Republican support and, ultimately, the bill's defeat. Patricia Zengerle, "Bid to Extend U.S. Surveillance Tools Stalls after Trump Threatens Veto," Reuters, May 27, 2020, https://www.reuters.com/article /us-usa-surveillance-congress/bid-to-extend-u-s-surveillance-tools-stalls-after-trump-threatens-veto -idUSKBN2340C0.

tion—an important issue to middle-class families—in the middle of a contentious election season. Rather than try to pass a smaller, bipartisan loan subsidy bill, which the president could potentially take credit for on the campaign trail, Republicans chose instead to pass a bigger bill that they knew would trigger a veto. Fortunately—for the president, at least—the bill never came to a vote in the Senate.[46]

8.3.2 Veto Threats and Concessions

The veto is powerful not only when it is used but also when the president threatens its use. There are several ways presidents can make such a threat. Sometimes, they do so publicly in the middle of legislative negotiations, signaling to Congress and the media their opposition to a bill. Other times, presidents publicly threaten a veto before legislative negotiations have even begun. "Let them be forewarned," said Reagan to the Senate Budget Committee in 1985, "I have my veto pen drawn and ready for any tax increase that Congress might think of sending up. . . . Go ahead and make my day."[47] And still other times, presidents communicate their objections privately or enlist a staff member to send a written memo to Congress.

According to Cameron, these threats amount to more than just empty talk. Rather, they have the potential to exact important concessions from Congress. Whether such threats deliver on their promise, however, depends upon what Congress infers from them. It is possible, of course, that the president is being entirely truthful and that absent any revisions to the offending elements of the bill, the president will follow through on his threat and issue an actual veto. It is also possible, though, that the president secretly prefers Congress's bill over the status quo policy; but by issuing a veto threat, the president thinks, he can convince the enacting coalition to write a bill that conforms even more closely to his policy commitments. Given these two possibilities, members of Congress must gauge the probability that the president is bluffing and, when actually presented with a bill, will sign it into law. In this scenario, members who pass a bill without revisions risk running headlong into a presidential veto.

Should Congress lack the votes needed to override, its members then must decide whether to abandon the legislative effort altogether or to pass another bill that the president might sign into law. On the other hand, if members of Congress make revisions every time a veto threat is issued, they may unnecessarily capitulate to a president whose support they already enjoyed. The point of the veto threat, then, is straightforward enough to convince members of Congress to write a law that more closely abides the president's wishes. Whether these threats are effective, however, crucially depends on Congress's beliefs about the president's true policy preferences and the likelihood that the president's veto threat is sincere or, instead, a bluff aimed at extracting further concessions.

President George H. W. Bush put this tactic to good use during his negotiations over the Surface Transportation Efficiency Act of 1991, which reauthorized federal spending for transit programs. Bush did not outright oppose the bill. Nonetheless, he instructed Transportation Secretary Samuel Skinner to communicate three separate veto threats to the majority-Democratic Congress—one to push for the construction of a new National Highway system, another to oppose a gas-tax hike, and a third to protest the lax spending requirements for state governments. After the first two veto threats, Congress revised the bill to match Bush's preferences. After the third, Congress made no changes, and Bush—reneging on his veto threat—affixed his signature to the law. As is typical of these negotiations, Bush did not get everything he wanted, but the veto threat noticeably altered the legislation in his favor.

These veto threats are not purely anecdotal. During times of divided government, when communication between the branches is particularly fraught, Cameron estimates that 34 percent—more than a third—of the most significant legislation under consideration receives a veto threat from the president. Further, a whopping 90 percent of threatened bills provoke some sort of concession from Congress.* Understandably, when Congress does make concessions, presidents are far less likely to veto the offending bill, another potential reason for the relatively small number of vetoes issued annually in figure 8.4.

8.3.3 *The Line-Item Veto*

A veto is a big knife. Sometimes what the president really wants, though, is a scalpel. Presidents have long sought a more delicate device for fine-tuning bills in the form of the **line-item veto**, which would allow them to veto portions of bills rather than entire bills. (In the case of the Interest Rate Reduction Act, such a veto would have allowed Obama to preserve the bill's student loan subsidies while excising its health care cuts.) The 1996 Line Item Veto Act gave this power to presidents, but Clinton enjoyed it for only a short time. As discussed in greater length in chapter 11, in 1998 the Supreme Court ruled that the line-item veto unconstitutionally added to presidents' powers by, in effect, allowing them to amend proposed legislation—a task constitutionally reserved for Congress.

Since this setback, presidents have continued to pursue the line-item veto, though thus far they have done so entirely in vain. George W. Bush asked Congress to grant it outright, but Congress rebuffed him. In 2010, Obama requested a slight variation that would have allowed him to identify specific programs within the congressional budget and send them back to Congress for an up-or-down vote. Both Democrats and Republicans opposed the plan. In 2018, dissatisfied with the omnibus spending bill he had just signed, President Trump asked Congress for the line-item veto.[48] However, unlike President Obama's proposal, which received a vote in the House of Representatives, Trump's request failed to inspire any action on Capitol Hill.

---

*As Cameron's model predicts, veto threats are far less common during unified government, as Congress has reason to suspect that the president will accommodate any bill it puts forward.

Thinking Institutionally: Rules versus Norms

Alexander Hamilton wrote in *Federalist* 22 that "to give the minority a negative upon the majority is, in its tendency, to subject the sense of the greater number to that of the lesser number." Hamilton added that such a legislative rule would essentially create "an insignificant, turbulent or corrupt junto," which would inevitably "destroy the energy of government."

Despite Hamilton's warning, the idea of a minority wielding the power to negate majority rule has become a widely used legislative tactic in the U.S. Senate. The filibuster allows senators to speak for as long as they want in the lead-up to a vote over proposed legislation on the Senate floor.* As such, the rules permit the indefinite delay of a bill's formal consideration.

In order to stop such delays and force a vote on the bill, Senate rules require that a three-fifths majority—sixty out of one hundred total senators—must agree to end debate, a process known as invoking **cloture**.† If advocates for the bill cannot attract enough votes, the filibustering may continue all the way until the end of a congressional term, at which point the offending bill would need to be reintroduced and another filibuster could commence.

Though the filibuster has existed under Senate rules since nearly the body's founding, it was used sparingly in the 1800s and hardly at all in the first half of the twentieth century. During the 1950s and 1960s, several prominent pieces of civil rights legislation were filibustered by southern Democratic senators. Still, the number of cloture motions filed to end filibusters was consistently less than ten per year. By the early to mid-1970s, however, cloture filings jumped to over forty per year. Such filings have become increasingly frequent in the decades since, with totals measured in the hundreds rather than in the tens (see figure 8.5).

The filibuster has become a widely cited symbol of all that is wrong with partisan politics in Washington. Criticism of the practice has been vehement from liberals and conservatives alike, though it is usually directed at the opposing party. In 2010, for example, then–vice president (and former long-time senator) Joe Biden opined, "As long as I have served . . . I've never seen . . . the Constitution stood on its head as [Republicans] have done" with the filibuster.[49] Similarly, when George W. Bush was in the White House and Senate Republicans were in the majority, conservative Senate majority leader Mitch McConnell routinely lamented that his "Democratic colleagues want to change the rules" of the Senate.[50]

---

* Today, filibusters rarely involve such public performances. Instead, filibusters function much like holds, indefinitely stalling further consideration of a bill but without someone having to speak continuously from the floor.

† When cloture was created in 1917, it required the consent of two-thirds of the voting senators. In 1975, the rule was changed to require three-fifths of the entire Senate.

Continued on next page

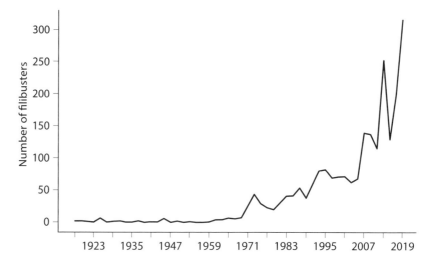

FIGURE 8.5. Annual number of filibusters. The figure presents the annual number of cloture motions filed within Congress, which corresponds to the annual number of filibusters. In explaining the increase in the use of the filibuster, we must remember to look at not only the rules governing such action but also the norms surrounding its use. *Source:* United States Senate, https://www.senate.gov /legislative/cloture/clotureCounts.htm.

The contention over the filibuster highlights two important factors when it comes to thinking institutionally. First, understanding institutional decision making requires careful attention to how the rules of a given institution create incentives for political actors to behave in one way or another. In this case, the Senate rules regarding debate over a piece of legislation allow for filibustering—that is, they allow for a minority of senators to block a bill favored by the majority. Despite all of the bluster by Democrats and Republicans over its "unconstitutional" nature, members of both parties put the rule to use when their party is in the minority. Formal changes in the administration of filibusters, moreover, may have contributed to their rise. In 1970, for example, the Senate moved to a "two-track" system, which allowed members to continue pursuing legislation while other items were being filibustered. In practice, the two-track system permitted senators to block legislation without delivering a speech; the "silent filibuster," as it has been called, is convenient, often anonymous, and considerably easier to deploy than its more public and more demanding predecessor.

More than just rules, however, political decisions also are motivated by **norms**— unwritten understandings of appropriate conduct. And changing norms also contributed to the rise of filibusters in the last several decades. The most striking changes to the filibuster occurred after Senator Mitch McConnell became the Republican minority leader in 2006. Whereas before McConnell's leadership, filibusters were used under exceptional circumstances, thereafter, they became de rigueur. McConnell and his fellow Republicans wielded the filibuster with abandon, blocking even mundane legislation that previous minorities would have approved. Without strictly changing Senate rules, McConnell pushed the chamber to the point of paralysis, a strategy his Democratic colleagues employed for their own purposes during the Trump presidency. Whereas only 39 of George W. Bush's judicial nominees were filibustered, 175 of Barack Obama's were. Under Trump, that number increased to more than 300.[51] Throughout this period, however, McConnell remained committed to the hyperactive use of the filibuster, promising the Democrats in 2021 that there would be "scorched earth" that nobody "can even begin to imagine" if the filibuster were reformed or eliminated.[52]

These changes have had a marked impact on the production of laws and appointments. They also have had downstream consequences for other long-standing norms and rules. As the filibuster became commonplace in the Senate, and sixty votes became the requirement for virtually all bills, senators increasingly relied on a process known as budget reconciliation to pass major legislation. Reconciliation requires only fifty votes, but as its name implies, it was designed only for changes to the budget. Wanting to avoid the filibuster, however, both parties have used reconciliation to pass large and controversial legislation, including the Trump tax cuts in 2017 and Biden's American Rescue Plan in 2021.

Changes in the norms surrounding filibusters also have triggered new rules about their usage. In 2013, with Republicans holding up Obama's judicial appointees, Senate Democrats exercised the so-called "nuclear option" and eliminated the filibuster for district and appellate judicial nominations. Four years later, in 2017, Republicans extended this rule to Supreme Court nominees, clearing the way for Trump to appoint Justices Neil Gorsuch, Brett Kavanaugh, and Amy Coney Barrett—none of whom secured anything close to the sixty votes previously needed to overcome a filibuster but all of whom secured the bare majority needed to ascend to the nation's highest court. Thus we see how changing rules and norms matter not only in their own right but also for the subsequent procedural changes they set in motion.[53]

8.4 Appropriations

As a constitutional matter, the power of the purse resides squarely with Congress. As a practical matter, however, the president has substantial opportunities to influence the federal budget.[54] Two of these avenues of influence stand out as especially important:

1. the *ex ante* influence that comes along with proposing a budget; and
2. the *ex post* influence associated with budgetary manipulations.

A third opportunity for presidents to influence the federal budget is through impoundment.

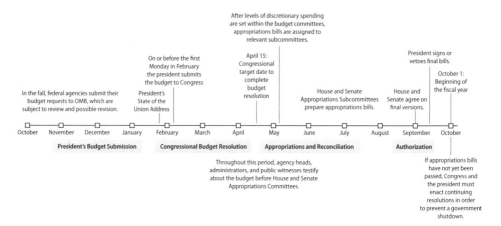

FIGURE 8.6. Budget timeline. Each year, the president and Congress are meant to follow a strict schedule in setting a federal budget. In practice, though, they rarely do.

8.4.1 Proposing a Budget: Ex Ante Influence

Since the enactment of the Budget and Accounting Act of 1921, the president has been responsible for composing a complete budget, which is supposed to be submitted to Congress in February of each year and which initiates the **authorization**, selection of agencies and programs eligible for federal funding in any given year, and appropriations processes. (See figure 8.6 for the complete schedule.) It is through these two processes that presidents exert *ex ante* influence—that is, they have an effect on an outcome, the budget, before the budget is passed.

Producing the budget is no trivial undertaking. In thousands of pages, the president's budget proposes funding not just for agencies but also for projects and employees within these agencies. The president supplements specific requests with extensive policy and legislative recommendations, detailed economic forecasts, and exhaustive accounts of the performance and finances of federal agencies and programs. When they approve a final budget, members of Congress usually rely on the president's proposal more than any other document for information.

The administration makes substantial efforts to ensure that the budget proposal reflects the president's policy priorities. To that end, rather than transmitting requests directly to Congress, agencies seeking federal funding must submit detailed reports to the Office of Management and Budget (OMB). Working at the behest of the president, the OMB then clears each of these reports to ensure that it reflects the chief executive's policy priorities. When reports reveal discrepancies, OMB officials either return them to the agencies for amendment or simply edit the documents themselves.

Upon submission of the president's budget, members of Congress may alter the fiscal blueprint in any number of ways. In doing so, though, they must contend with an actively engaged president. Coinciding with the State of the Union, the release of the president's budget is typically a highly public affair, wherein presidents and their surrogates make the case for their most important budget priorities, and agencies follow up with press releases and briefings of their own. During the appropriations process, numerous experts testify on behalf of their budget priorities. Concurrently, the president weighs in with direct solicitations to key members of Congress, public appeals, and ultimately the threat of a veto, all in an effort to shape the content of the final budget.

8.4.2 *Manipulating the Budget:* Ex Post *Influence*

After the budget's passage, the president has still more opportunities to influence how federal funds are spent—that is, he now has ***ex post* influence** on the budget. A substantial portion of the federal budget, after all, supports grants and programs that executive agencies administer. For example, consider the National Science Foundation (NSF). Though Congress decides how much the NSF can spend, bureaucrats within the agency decide where the money goes—who, for example, receives each of its doctoral dissertation grants. The same is true for research grants through the National Institutes of Health, disaster relief through the Federal Emergency Management Agency, financial assistance through the Small Business Administration, and so on. Decisions about agency expansion and personnel are also made within the executive branch.

Presidents have ample opportunities to redirect federal spending. Presidents can repurpose funds within certain budgetary accounts and, with Congress's approval, transfer funds between accounts. Contingency accounts, typically established for unforeseen disasters, give presidents a further opportunity to redirect federal funds. In addition, final budgets regularly leave presidents a fair amount of discretion to influence the geographic distribution of federal funds. For an artful president intent upon redirecting funds to a preferred constituency, notes one political observer, "the opportunity for mischief is substantial."[55]

EX POST INFLUENCE IN FOREIGN POLICY

Just as Congress grants the president broad legislative authority in foreign affairs, so, too, does Congress give the executive branch significant budgetary authority to direct foreign policy. Such was the case in 2001, in the wake of the September 11 attacks, when Congress authorized the Defense Emergency Response Fund (DERF). The fund was essentially a $15 billion (later $38 billion) slush fund for the Department of Defense (DoD). In theory, the department was meant to spend the money on "urgent and known needs" that it "would not normally incur"—mostly, rebuilding the Pentagon and waging the new War on Terror.[56] But Congress gave the DoD the money without any meaningful restrictions or clear guidelines on what to use it for.

Thus ensued a narrow but meaningful shift in the balance of power across the two branches of government. Article I of the Constitution grants Congress the ability to make appropriations for the military. By giving the military such a substantial and unrestricted sum of money, however, Congress limited its ability to force the administration to change course. As popular support for the War on Terror declined in 2003, Congress managed to regain its budgetary powers by ending unrestricted DERF funding. However, the experience left behind a precedent for Congress's divesting its own branch of a significant check on the executive's institutional authority.

EX POST INFLUENCE IN DOMESTIC POLICY

Broad delegations of budgetary authority to the president are not limited to the foreign policy arena. As part of the American Recovery and Reinvestment Act of 2009, for example, Congress allocated a whopping $100 billion in emergency funding to the Department of Education. This influx of money, which nearly doubled the department's operating budget, came with relatively few strings attached. As a result, President Obama and Secretary of Education Arne Duncan expanded and transformed the federal government's role in education reform. Perhaps most notably, Obama and Duncan used part of the money to create their Race to the Top program: a $4 billion contest, sponsored by the Department of Education, in which states compete for federal funding based on criteria set by the department.

Members of Congress, for their part, were not uniformly pleased with how Obama chose to use the education funding they had delegated. Several legislators voiced concerns that Race to the Top forced states to implement showy reforms at the expense of more substantive changes. Others worried that money and resources were being diverted away from school districts that desperately needed funds but happened to be in states that did not qualify. Still other members disagreed with the criteria upon which Race to the Top was being judged. As a result, Congress slashed nearly half of Race to the Top's budget for the 2011 fiscal year. By then, however, the course for education reform across the country had already been set.

8.4.3 Impoundment Authority

From Washington to Nixon, presidents exercised a peculiar kind of power called **impoundment**, which allowed them to block the disbursement of congressionally authorized funds. Like the veto and the filibuster, for most of the nation's history, this power was used prudently and without controversy. For example, in 1803, Thomas Jefferson refused to spend $50,000 that Congress had appropriated for gunboats to defend the Mississippi River from French attacks, which never materialized.* Nearly seventy-five years later, Ulysses Grant communicated to the House of Representatives that he would not spend money authorized for harbor and river improvements because some appropriations were

---

*In his annual message to Congress, Jefferson stated, "The sum of fifty thousand dollars appropriated by Congress for providing gunboats remains unexpended. The favorable and peaceable turn of affairs on the Mississippi rendered immediate execution of that law unnecessary." The full speech can be found in *Addresses and Messages of the Presidents of the United States* (New York: McClean and Taylor, 1839), 101–5.

for "works of purely private or local interest, in no sense national."[57] In neither instance did Congress object to the president's actions.

For Congress, the president's impoundment authority served as a useful check on its profligate ways. As the size of government grew, and as federal spending patterns increased, Congress opted to formalize this role with the Anti-Deficiency Acts of 1905 and 1906, which allowed presidents to temporarily withhold funds. In the decades that followed, FDR, Truman, Eisenhower, Kennedy, and Johnson all used impoundments to cut various forms of spending, particularly in defense. In almost all of these cases, impoundments were temporary, usually deferring funds until only the next fiscal year.

IMPOUNDMENT UNDER NIXON

Upon taking office, Nixon made it clear that he had no intention of keeping with precedent. Whereas previous administrations had wielded impoundment only occasionally, the Nixon White House resorted to it as a matter of course. On average, the Nixon administration impounded 17 to 20 percent of controllable funds appropriated by Congress every year he was in office.[58]

Nixon distinguished himself not merely by the frequency and size of his impoundments but also by the purposes to which impoundments were put. Rather than reducing waste or adjusting to unforeseen changes, Nixon used impoundments to promote his policy objectives. Under his administration, impoundments became an instrument in larger ideological and partisan battles between the branches of government.

As just one example, consider Nixon's haggling over the Federal Water Pollution Control Act. In 1972, Congress had passed the bill, Nixon had vetoed it, and Congress then overrode his veto. In response, Nixon temporarily impounded half of the $18 billion that had been allotted for the program for fiscal years 1972 to 1975. So doing, Nixon had turned impoundment into a kind of absolute veto.[59]

Neither the courts nor Congress looked kindly upon Nixon's actions.* Distressed beneficiaries filed suits to force the release of funds, and more than thirty lower court cases overturned impoundments. Eventually, the Supreme Court set matters straight. In *Train v. City of New York* (1975), a case that involved federal efforts to combat water pollution, the Court ruled that once funds had been appropriated by Congress, they could not be subsequently withheld by impoundment.[60]

---

*As Senator Edmund Muskie lamented: "How could we be clearer? We enacted that legislation by a unanimous vote in the Senate and by a unanimous vote in the House. The legislation went to the House-Senate Conference, came back to both houses and was overwhelmingly approved. The President vetoed it at midnight on one of the last days of the session. And within 24 hours, both the House and the Senate had overridden it. The President got only 12 votes in the Senate and 23 votes in the House to support his veto. How many times, may I ask, must Congress speak before our intention is clear?" See *The Advocates*, Public Broadcasting Service, WGBH-Boston (transcript), February 15, 1973; and N. Stanton, "History and Practice of Executive Impoundment of Appropriated Funds," *Nebraska Law Review* 53, no. 1 (1974): 1–30.

With the 1974 Budget and Impoundment Act, Congress also claimed for itself a new set of tools and resources for preventing presidential impoundments. One such tool was the **Congressional Budget Office** (CBO), a budgetary oversight office located exclusively within the legislative branch. Whereas before, Congress was beholden to the Office of Management and Budget for information about how budgets were being spent, Congress now had an agency of its own. Should a president attempt to impound funds, the act also empowered the comptroller general, who heads the Government Accountability Office, to bring suit against the executive in order to force their release.

The Budget and Impoundment Act, however, did not exclusively delimit the president's budgetary powers. The act also created two new procedures—**rescissions** and **deferrals**— by which presidents could *temporarily* override or delay the disbursement of congressional appropriations. Henceforth, presidents would not have the legal authority to unilaterally impound funds. If presidents wished to rescind appropriated funds, however, they would have to elicit from Congress a rescission bill permitting the cancellation of funds. If instead presidents wished to defer appropriated funds, they did not require permission from Congress, but the deferral would last only until the next fiscal year.*

With Nixon's resignation, Gerald Ford became the first president to work under the new procedures of the Budget and Impoundment Act. And rather quickly, Congress demonstrated little appetite for allowing the president to undo its budgetary handiwork. The Ford administration requested $9 billion in rescissions, of which Congress denied 86 percent. In the years that followed, Congress supported only half of rescission requests. Deferrals, however, were another matter. Congress upheld roughly 90 percent of deferrals issued by presidents after Ford.[61]

CONTEMPORARY IMPOUNDMENT POLITICS

In 2018, in the first formal rescission request since the Clinton administration, Donald Trump proposed $15 billion in cuts to a range of domestic programs, none of which were acted on by Congress.[62] Again, in the very last week of his presidency, Trump issued an even larger $27 billion rescission request, fulfilling his promise to send back a "redlined version" of the fiscal year 2021 budget with the "wasteful items" removed.[63] Congress did not authorize a single dollar in cuts.

Eager to test the limits of the post-Nixon spending powers, however, the Trump administration turned to budget deferrals.[64] Recall that, unlike rescissions, deferrals do not require immediate congressional approval. But whereas rescissions can be requested for any reason, including policy disagreements, deferrals are intended only for budget contingencies and to improve the efficiency of government spending. Flouting this requirement, the

---

*In 1983, the Supreme Court ruled that both chambers of Congress, rather than one or the other, had to vote to block the deferral of spending (*Immigration and Naturalization Service v. Chadha*, 462 U.S. 919). Today, to block the deferral of funds, both houses must pass a resolution via majority vote that the appropriated funds be spent immediately.

Trump administration instead enacted budget deferrals under the separate category of "programmatic delays"—temporary holds on funding "to determine the best way to run a program within the scope of the law."[65] Importantly, Trump's Office of Management and Budget (OMB) claimed that programmatic delays can be used for political reasons.

Given the tenuous distinction between deferrals and delays, the OMB granted itself the power to declare which actions fell into the latter category. In 2019, Trump used such a delay to withhold military aid to Ukraine—an entirely political maneuver that resulted in his first impeachment, which we will discuss later. Mark Paoletta, general counsel of the OMB, defended the decision by referencing the president's broad authority under both the take-care and commander-in-chief clauses. It was important, argued Paoletta, "to ensure that funds were not obligated prematurely in a manner that could conflict with the President's foreign policy."[66]

The following year, the Government Accountability Office (GAO) rejected the OMB's definition of programmatic delays and ruled that Trump's actions in Ukraine were in fact unlawful. Even after Trump's impeachment, however, the OMB maintained that the president's budgetary powers must be expanded beyond what the Budget and Impoundment Act allows for. Just two days before Trump left office, Paoletta sent a letter to the House budget chairman, arguing that the act has "plagued" the presidency and "is unworkable in practice and should be significantly reformed or repealed."[67]

As for programmatic delays, the category has survived into the Biden administration. Shortly after taking office, Biden delayed funding for Trump's border wall, citing the need to conduct environmental reviews and stakeholder conversations.[68] This time, the GAO upheld the decision—signaling its acceptance of programmatic delays, at least when used for plausibly apolitical reasons.

8.5 Battles over Institutional Power

We are accustomed to seeing presidents and members of Congress fight over public policy. Informing these debates, though, is a deeper struggle over the balance of power across the legislative and executive branches of government. In the long arc of American history, it is a struggle that members of Congress are losing—in part because they are ill-equipped to stand up for their institutional interests, and in part because they have made something of a habit of delegating broad authority to the president. In individual instances, though, members of Congress nonetheless manage to buck these trends and assert their will.

8.5.1 Congressional Delegations of Authority

When Congress alters the balance of power between the branches of government, it usually does so by ceding authority to the president. Sometimes Congress explicitly delegates policymaking tasks to the president. Other times, it writes vague statutes into which presidents can read their own policy preferences. These congressional delegations of authority can be broad, having few, if any, constraints, or narrow, containing any number of limits and restrictions. Regardless, presidents acquire a great deal of authority statutorily that, constitutionally at least, eludes them.

Political scientists have identified three distinct circumstances in which legislators are likely to expand the president's power through legislation. And in two of the situations, members of Congress cede authority knowing full well that it may be used to advance policy objectives with which they disagree.

The first situation is the most straightforward: when a legislator's ideal policy outcome is the same as or similar to the president's, the legislator strategically chooses to delegate authority to the president. This motivation for delegation is known as the **ally principle**. Usually, the ally principle reveals itself during unified government when members of Congress hope to empower the president to achieve shared policy goals. In certain circumstances, however, legislators from the opposing party may see the president as an ally. In the case of 2002's No Child Left Behind Act, liberal Democrats such as Senator Edward Kennedy were willing to delegate broad new powers to George W. Bush, a Republican, because they saw him as an ally in the fight to nationalize education reform.

The second circumstance that can result in Congress's delegating authority to the president is when they are faced with policy decisions involving significant technical complexity. If an issue is sufficiently complicated, legislators may have some general understanding of the goals they want to achieve, but identifying the means to realize these goals requires a far greater mastery of the subject. In these circumstances, members of Congress must rely on bureaucratic experts in the executive branch. For instance, most members of Congress have no technical understanding of the science behind carbon emissions. Thus, they delegate authority over regulating emission levels to the Environmental Protection Agency (EPA), whose staff includes environmental scientists. EPA officials, however, serve at the pleasure of the president. In this way, delegations of authority to bureaucratic experts have the (perhaps unintended) consequence of empowering presidents.

The final circumstance involves times of emergency. In moments of crisis, the government must act quickly. As a collective decision-making body, however, Congress is better suited to deliberation than action. Given the unitary nature of their office, presidents are better situated to handle emergencies. At such moments, even the president's most vocal opponents in Congress are frequently willing to delegate broad authority to the executive branch—though these opponents sometimes end up regretting this delegation once the crisis has passed. This, in fact, is exactly what happened in the wake of September 11, 2001.

ANATOMY OF A BROAD DELEGATION: THE 2001 AUTHORIZATION FOR USE OF MILITARY FORCE

In the immediate aftermath of September 11, 2001, the United States and its leaders were anxious to respond to the country's enemies with a decisive show of force. One newspaper described President George W. Bush as "eager to convey that he is in control and ready to take firm but unspecified action against the attackers."[69]

In the face of such uncertainty, Congress opted to delegate broad authority to the president. One week to the day after the attacks, Congress passed the Authorization for Use of Military Force (AUMF). The act, which took up less than a printed page, stated that "the President is authorized to use all necessary and appropriate force against those nations, organizations, or persons he determines planned, authorized, committed, or aided the terrorist attacks that occurred on September 11, 2001, or harbored such organizations or persons, in order to prevent any future acts of international terrorism against the United States by such nations, organizations or persons."[70]

At the time, the authorization was widely viewed as a necessary expansion of presidential power. Only one legislator, Representative Barbara Lee of California, voted against the bill. As she explained, "I believe we must make sure that Congress upholds its responsibilities and upholds checks and balances."[71] Lee's concerns were later emphasized by critics of the AUMF, who argued that "the checking and balancing functions of other institutions [Congress and the Supreme Court] have been marginalized" by such broad authorization.[72]

In fact, in the wake of the passage of the AUMF, the executive branch assumed the most sweeping and authoritative control over the nation's military and intelligence apparatuses since World War II. From the use of foreign extraditions, the trial of individuals suspected of terrorism in military tribunals, and the wiretapping of U.S. citizens to ground-level military operations, many of which were covertly conducted, Bush waged his War on Terror with very little congressional involvement.

In subsequent legal cases, Bush argued that the AUMF gave him broad authority to conduct operations that would have traditionally needed the approval of a court.[73] If Congress gave him the power without an expiration date or clear limitations, his argument went, then he did not require legislators' subsequent permission. Upon assuming office in 2009, Obama picked up where Bush left off, fiercely guarding his prerogatives over how to prosecute enemy combatants, calling for an even more aggressive campaign of drone strikes, and increasing U.S. military commitments in Afghanistan.

ANATOMY OF A NARROW DELEGATION:
FAA REAUTHORIZATION AND REFORM ACT OF 2012

Just because they are delegating authority to the president, members of Congress need not give away the store. Often, the authority that members of Congress grant a president is confined to a short period of time or a relatively limited collection of policy decisions. Delegation may also come with strings attached: reporting requirements, limits on permissible activities, or restrictions on the amount and use of public funds. Such requirements can help members of Congress regulate the activities of the executive branch and its agencies.

In February 2012, for example, Congress passed a bill that temporarily funded and reauthorized the mandate of the Federal Aviation Administration (FAA) to oversee all air travel in the United States. However, legislators were not willing to simply hand a blank check to the Obama administration. Instead, a bipartisan majority approved legislation that contained very specific conditions regarding how the money was to be spent. The FAA Reauthorization and Reform Act of 2012 provided the agency with a blueprint for modernizing air traffic control using the GPS-based NextGen system. It also stipulated exact milestones that the FAA had to meet in order to retain its funding.

In addition, Congress explicitly outlined actions from which the FAA was to refrain: the act ended ticket subsidies for small airports, added measures to increase transparency over regulations regarding labor relations, and required that airports be allowed to replace certain TSA officers with private security forces. These rules all overturned policies previously set by the Obama administration.

8.5.2 Congressional Oversight

Having delegated authority to the president, whether more or less, Congress does not automatically recede into the background. Its members can still monitor how this authority is put to use. And when they are troubled by what they find, members can either amend what the president does with the delegated authority or, as we shall see in the next section, attempt to curtail the president's ability to act.

It was not until the 1946 Legislative Reorganization Act that Congress formally assumed the responsibilities of **legislative oversight**, and it was not until the Government Performance and Results Act of 1993 that all bureaucratic agencies were required to consult annually with Congress.[74] Today, oversight is part of the daily life of both Congress and the bureaucracy.

Hearings, in which bureaucrats are called to testify about the performance and future plans of their department or agency, constitute the primary means by which members of Congress oversee activities within the executive branch. Typically, hearings are organized either by the relevant committee or subcommittee—for example, the Senate's Environment and Public Works Committee holds hearings about the Environmental Protection Agency—or by broader oversight committees.

Sometimes the end goal of hearings is clear: commonly, the gathering of data relevant to specific legislation. Other types of hearings, such as investigative hearings or oversight hearings, may be called with the more general goal of bringing to light important information concerning such things as suspected waste or malfeasance. If members of Congress feel that a specific executive branch official or agency has interpreted a statute in ways that clearly violate legislative intent, for example, they may recommend that a committee hold oversight hearings and call the parties in question to testify. These calls usually come as invitations to appear before the committee. If necessary, though, a committee may subpoena officials to demand their testimony—a tactic, of late, that has met with mixed success.

The vast majority of oversight hearings are predictable affairs: bureaucrats anticipate what the politicians will ask, and the politicians anticipate how the bureaucrats will respond.[75] Political scientist David Truman famously described oversight hearings as a "propaganda channel"[76]—a carefully scripted, made-for-television show in which politicians attempt to turn their political talking points into media headlines.[77] Despite being choreographed, however, the hearings facilitate the efforts of Congress to shape, and shake up, the executive branch, especially in times of divided government. In these instances, hearings may indeed be propaganda channels—but when the party in charge of Congress does not occupy the White House, they can be too alluring to pass up.[78]

Consider the 2013 congressional investigation into allegations that the Internal Revenue Service (IRS) singled out Tea Party groups for special scrutiny. The hearings were spearheaded by Darrell Issa, the Republican chair of the House Oversight and Government Reform Committee, who intimated that the Obama White House itself may have been responsible for the IRS's alleged misdeeds. The hearings were highly theatrical. Elijah Cummings, the top Democrat on the committee, accused Issa of peddling "unsubstantiated nonsense." Issa responded by calling Cummings a "little boy."[79]

The IRS eventually admitted wrongdoing.[80] Thanks in no small part to the scandal, by the end of 2013 the president's approval ratings had fallen to the low 40s.[81] At the same time, the hearings significantly increased Issa's public profile. At the scandal's peak, he was publishing editorials in multiple newspapers and appearing on cable television to talk about the scandal.[82] For both Congress and the bureaucracy, then, the hearings served a valuable purpose. The IRS was forced to confront its own misbehavior, and a member of Congress nourished his professional ambitions.*

8.5.3 *Attempting to Dismantle Presidential Power: The Bricker Amendment*

Over the years, Congress and the courts have delegated to the president significant powers over the domestic economy, the exercise of military force, the budget, state emergencies, foreign trade, and so on. Once such powers are granted, they are rarely retracted. Sitting on the books at any time are sweeping delegations of authority, many of which were made decades prior, for presidents to use in justifying their policy initiatives.

Just as crucially, members of Congress and the courts regularly turn a blind eye to the power-grabs of sitting presidents. Whereas power considerations "only weakly motivate" the behavior of congressional representatives, as political scientist Terry Moe has pointed out, they preoccupy presidents.[83]

Nonetheless, the balance of power between the legislative and executive branches involves a constant give-and-take. Typically, Congress checks the president by placing limits on presidential action. Occasionally, however, Congress passes legislation that explicitly strips presidents of powers that they have acquired through years of institutional expansion.

---

* In October 2015, the Justice Department announced that it would not bring any criminal charges against IRS employees connected to the scandal.

In the years after World War II, for example, the president steadily gained more and more influence over U.S. foreign policy. Constitutionally, treaties negotiated by the executive branch require ratification by a two-thirds vote in the Senate. To avoid this check on presidential authority, Presidents Truman and Eisenhower, began cementing agreements with foreign countries by signing executive agreements instead. Like a formal treaty, an executive agreement signals a mutual accord between the United States and a foreign power. Unlike a treaty, however, executive agreements are made solely under the president's authority.[84] (Executive agreements will be discussed in more detail in chapter 9.)

The concept of executive agreements deeply worried some senators, especially Senator John Bricker of Ohio. In 1952, Bricker proposed an amendment to the Constitution that would effectively abolish the use of executive agreements.[85] Eisenhower, as any president might, resented Bricker's power play. The president therefore took his message to the public, telling the press that Bricker's amendment could make the country unsafe by limiting the president's ability to conduct diplomacy. Several congressmen echoed his concerns. Senate Foreign Relations chairman Alexander Wiley, for example, wrote that the amendment would make the president "the serf of Congress" and that it would "break checks and balances."[86]

The Bricker Amendment nonetheless received support from more than a few senators, who found the prospect of losing control over the treaty-making process more frightening than the specter of ineffective diplomacy. Eisenhower attempted to reach a compromise by endorsing a competing amendment from Senator William F. Knowland, which stated that executive agreements would only become law after the Senate ratified them and that no agreement could conflict with the Constitution.[87] Republicans still strongly supported the Bricker Amendment, however, so Eisenhower engineered another competing amendment from Walter George of Georgia to draw away votes. These amendments, combined with heavy pressure from the White House and a protracted battle in the press, enabled Eisenhower to defeat the Bricker Amendment by one vote in the Senate.*

Despite Eisenhower's victory, subsequent presidents were put on notice. In ongoing disputes over policy, presidential power claims might be met with congressional resistance. What presidents seek to build, Congress may try to dismantle.

8.6 Removing the President from Office

Routinely, members of Congress stand in the president's way. Occasionally, though, Congress ratchets up the confrontation and seeks to actually remove a president from office. (Recall from chapter 1 that the Framers of the Constitution granted the power of impeachment to the legislative branch as a check against presidential tyranny.) The House of Rep-

---

*In the half century since Congress failed to pass the Bricker Amendment, presidents have relied upon executive agreements with rising frequency. Whereas treaties outnumbered executive agreements for the first 150 years of the nation's history, today, more than ten executive agreements are issued for every treaty signed. (For more specifics on these historical trends, see figure 9.3.)

resentatives has impeached a sitting president four times, though in all instances the Senate opted not to convict.*

The history of these four impeachments is both short enough to permit a full retelling and significant enough to compel one. There is no more radical action Congress can take than to remove a sitting president from office. Thus, in this section, we will discuss the purposes of impeachment and then tell the story of each, beginning with Andrew Johnson and continuing most recently through Donald Trump. As we will see, these impeachments had lasting consequences for the legacies of impeached presidents and the contours of presidential power.

8.6.1 The Purposes of Impeachment

Charged with "high crimes and misdemeanors" in the House, a president can be im- peached with a simple majority of votes. To be convicted, however, a two-thirds majority of the Senate must vote against the president (see chapter 1). If this latter condition is met—a yet unseen occurrence in American politics—the president faces two conse- quences. First, of course, is a forced removal from office. But no less important is the second consequence: a lifetime ban from holding the office again. According to Article I, Section 3, a Senate conviction results in a "disqualification to hold and enjoy any Office of honor, Trust, or Profit under the United States."

Since the Senate has never voted to convict, neither of these consequences has been visited upon a president. It would be a mistake, however, to conclude that impeached presidents have emerged entirely unscathed from their ordeals or that the political signifi- cance of impeachment is confined to those purposes expressly recognized in the Constitution.

More than any other tool at Congress's disposal, impeachment represents a formal and lasting rebuke of presidential conduct.[88] With or without conviction, impeachment sends a message to both the president and the public about what does *not* qualify as acceptable behavior from the commander in chief. Writer and philosopher Edmund Burke believed that impeachment was more important than the verdict it invites, because it affirms "the substantial excellence of our constitution . . . [that] no man, in no circumstance, can es- cape the account, which he owes to the laws of his country."[89]

Impeachment leaves an unmistakable stain on a president's historical legacy. "One hun- dred years from now, no one's going to remember what speech Pelosi is going to give about Trump's behavior," said Jens David Ohlin, vice dean at Cornell Law School. "But historians

---

* Additionally, in 1974, the House Judiciary Committee proposed that the full House impeach President Richard Nixon for obstruction of justice, for abuse of power, and for disobeying congressional subpoenas. Before the House could vote, though, Nixon became the first and only president to resign from office. Valerie Strauss, "Analysis | History Lesson: Richard Nixon Was Not Impeached," *Washington Post*, May 29, 2017, https://www.washingtonpost.com/news/answer-sheet/wp/2017/05/29/richard-nixon-was-not-impeached -despite-what-hillary-clinton-and-others-say/.

are certainly going to remember that Trump [was] impeached by the House."[90] Part of the power of this stain comes from its sparing use. For each successful House impeachment, there are plenty of instances in which Congress opted *not* to impeach. Reagan was not impeached for the Iran-Contra affair, nor was Kennedy impeached for his many extramarital affairs. Reserving impeachment for presidents whose conduct truly threatens the constitutional order, Congress preserves the measure's historical significance.

Of course, there are other ways Congress can publicly repudiate presidents. Among the formal mechanisms at Congress's disposal, a **censure** is the most obvious alternative. Through a simple majority vote, Congress can formally reprimand the president or any other members of government. On paper, censure looks very much like impeachment without conviction; the president is denounced, yet remains in the White House. But in reality, censure does not hold the same historical weight as impeachment. In 1834, President Andrew Jackson became the only president to be successfully censured by Congress, an event few people could recall today. By withdrawing even the *threat* of removal, Jackson's censure communicated to the public that his actions—withholding documents from Congress—would be rhetorically condemned, yet formally tolerated. And sure enough, Jackson's censure was later reversed, and he became the face of the twenty-dollar bill.

Impeachment, by contrast, hangs heavily on the legacies of Johnson, Clinton, and Trump, just as resignation hangs heavily on Nixon's. More importantly still, these impeachments communicate enduring lessons about what members of Congress, and by extension the public, expect of their presidents: the actions they deem appropriate, the ethical standards they want to see upheld, the democratic commitments they wish to preserve. A substantial body of political science underscores the fragility of democracy, which ultimately is maintained not through the regular application of force but through mutually reinforcing expectations.[91] The content of these expectations, of course, remains contested and evolving. Through their actions and public declarations, presidents participate in their construction. But Congress, too, has a vital say in the matter. And when presidents reach too far or offend too much, impeachments allow for a formal rebuttal, one that helps set the boundaries of presidential power and the precepts of democratic governance.

What kinds of presidential actions should disqualify someone from office? The Constitution remains unavoidably ambiguous. As a result, we again see how constitutional meanings are clarified not through close textual readings but through the practice of politics—the judgments that Congress renders over the president, the construction of presidential legacies, and the evolving understandings of the politics that presidents make.

8.6.2 Johnson's Impeachment

In the aftermath of the Civil War, the national government had to figure out how to reincorporate the South into the Union and extend new rights and privileges to recently freed slaves. Republican majorities within Congress were inclined to intervene aggressively in the governing affairs of their former adversaries, set clear conditions for their ability to secure political representation in Washington, and accelerate the enfranchisement of African Americans. President Andrew Johnson, by contrast, looked skeptically upon these efforts. As a Democrat from Tennessee, Johnson assumed a more accommodating posture toward his white, Southern brethren. Rather than cooperate with Republicans, therefore, he stood squarely in their way.

At the time, Northern Republican legislators were not especially keen on allowing Southern legislators back into Congress. Doing so, they feared, would enable Democrats to block any legislation that aided newly freed African Americans and, worse still, return them to a position of base servitude.[92] Republicans worked hurriedly to pass a series of bills that explicitly recognized and then protected the welfare and rights of former slaves. Many of these bills died on the president's desk, where Johnson vetoed them.

Secretary of War Edwin Stanton, appointed under President Lincoln, was an ally of congressional Republicans. While in office, he spearheaded a number of federal initiatives to assist African Americans in the South. He also advocated for the South's continued military occupation in order to oversee Reconstruction and enforce the Thirteenth Amendment. Struggling to curtail Stanton, Johnson finally decided to fire him.

The dismissal generated an uproar in Congress. Congressional Republicans argued that Johnson's action violated the 1867 Tenure of Office Act, which stated that the president could not remove certain, high-level officials from office without the Senate's approval. Though it later repealed the act, the House voted along party lines in favor of impeachment. In the Senate, which must either convict or acquit the president following an impeachment, thirty-five senators voted "guilty" and nineteen senators voted "not guilty." Republicans fell just one vote shy of the necessary supermajority for successful removal.

As discussed in chapter 1, presidents are meant to be impeached when they have committed "high crimes and misdemeanors." It's difficult to see how Johnson's actions qualify as such. In this instance, impeachment proceedings grew out of pressing fights over the legacies of slavery and the civil war. Unable to persuade the president about the merits of their worldview, and worried about the imminent erosion of their power, Republicans escalated the interbranch conflict and exercised their removal powers where their legislative authority had failed them. Impeachment, in this case, was not an interruption of ongoing political disagreement. Impeachment was its logical extension.

8.6.3 Nixon's Resignation

Ironically, the nation's most notorious impeachment is one that never came to pass. In June 1972, while President Richard Nixon was running for reelection, five men were caught breaking into the Watergate Hotel, the site of the Democratic National Committee Headquarters in Washington, D.C. Charged with burglary and "possession of implements of crime,"[93] the men were soon revealed as paid affiliates of Nixon's reelection committee. Controversy spread hot and quick. By September, *Washington Post* reporters Carl Bernstein and Bob Woodward had uncovered evidence of illegal espionage coming from Nixon's White House. By May 1973, Attorney General-designate Elliot Richardson had appointed Archibald Cox to investigate Nixon's role in the so-called "Watergate Scandal."[94] As Nixon pleaded innocence to the press, he tried desperately to cover up his crimes by destroying evidence, tampering with witnesses, and more. But in the long run, Nixon's cover-up attempts proved far less valuable than the loyalty of his Republican allies in Congress.

Throughout the investigation, House and Senate Republicans were stalwart defenders of the president. Some—believing the investigation a partisan witch hunt—acted out of a sincere belief that Nixon was innocent. Others sought to avoid alienating Nixon's enthusiastic base of supporters. Whatever their motives, their unified support kept Nixon not only safe but *popular*. Nixon went on to win his reelection bid with more than 60 percent of the vote. And even as more details of his misdeeds came to light, his approval rating among Republicans maintained an upward trend for several months.[95]

Behind this unified front, however, small tensions were rising between Nixon and congressional Republicans. As the Watergate trials progressed, District Judge John Sirica applied pressure on the five burglars to turn on their co-conspirators.[96] The first to do so was James McCord, a former CIA officer and an employee of Nixon's reelection committee. McCord revealed not only that the White House knew about the burglary attempt but that its top officials were directly involved.[97] For the first time, Republicans in Congress began to worry about how the trials might end. But still they declined to speak out against the president. Even though doubts were growing among some Republican donors, Nixon maintained strong support from most GOP voters.

The investigations continued, and word spread about the existence of White House tapes that could prove Nixon's guilt. When Nixon cited executive privilege to block access to the tapes, Archibald Cox, the special prosecutor, had them subpoenaed. By now, these tapes had become central to the investigation and to voters' assessments of Nixon's innocence. Determined to prevent their release, Nixon brazenly ordered his attorney general to fire Cox on October 20, 1973—an event subsequently referred to as the "Saturday Night Massacre." When the attorney general refused and resigned, Nixon gave the same order to his assistant attorney general, who also refused and was fired. Finally, Nixon appointed Robert Bork as acting attorney general, and Bork complied. In a single night, Nixon had fired two of the highest-ranking officials in the Justice Department as well as Archibald Cox, the man responsible for determining his guilt or innocence.

Public support for Nixon plummeted overnight. Support for his removal doubled, from 20 to nearly 40 percent.[98] Meanwhile, congressional Republicans were caught unprepared. Privately, they were furious that Nixon had not warned them about his plans to fire officials at the Justice Department. Publicly, however, they said only that Nixon had "mishandled" the situation but that impeachment was unwarranted.[99] Conservative leader Barry Goldwater, for example, maintained that the investigation was "political" and that Nixon had not committed an impeachable offense.[100]

Despite statements like these, fissures within the Republican Party began to surface. Nixon's misdeeds were having real consequences for the party's image—leading some to seriously consider impeachment. Their allegiance to the president had cost them several House seats in Pennsylvania, Michigan, Ohio, and California, all of which they had held for upwards of thirty years. Republicans were described as "walking Gallup Poll[s]"—constantly gauging the public's views on impeachment, struggling to maintain the support of core GOP voters without upsetting everyone else.[101]

In April 1974, Nixon finally acquiesced to public pressure and released transcripts for all the White House tapes. Immediately, the public understood why he had fought so hard to keep them concealed. The tapes revealed a "profane, crude, and cynical" side of Nixon's personality—which, although irrelevant to the law, eroded his support among the broader public.[102] Even the *Chicago Tribune*, then a conservative media outlet, began calling for his removal.[103] Privately, many congressional Republicans wished that Nixon would resign, but they needed more evidence before they could demand as much in public.

The first article of impeachment was filed by a Democratic representative on July 26, 1974. It focused on obstruction of justice, a charge that accounted for Nixon's several cover-up schemes, attempts to halt the investigation, and refusal to comply with House subpoenas.[104] Additionally, Nixon was charged with "violating the constitutional rights of citizens" by interfering with FBI and CIA Watergate investigations and obtaining confidential tax data from the IRS. On July 27, six Republicans joined twenty-one Democrats in the House Judiciary Committee to advance the first articles of impeachment to a floor vote.[105] Despite this bipartisan action, the articles still seemed unlikely to make it through the Senate, where Republicans like Goldwater continued to doubt the political merits of defying the president.

Meanwhile, the Supreme Court ruled in *United States v. Nixon*—covered at length in chapter 11—that a new batch of Nixon's private tapes should be released. They included evidence that conclusively demonstrated Nixon's involvement in the cover-up of Watergate.[106] In a meeting with his chief of staff, Nixon was heard agreeing to approach the CIA and FBI to halt the investigation, a clear obstruction of justice. So definitive was this evidence that congressional Republicans promptly renounced their political obligations to Nixon. Every Republican member of the House Judiciary Committee that had voted against the articles of impeachment pledged that they would vote for it on the floor. In the Senate, Goldwater swore that "[Nixon] had lied to me for the last time" and led a delegation of like-minded Republicans.[107] According to Republican leadership estimates, no more than twenty-five members of the combined House and Senate were going to vote in favor of the president—a fact that, undoubtedly, made its way to the White House.

On August 8, 1974, Nixon became the first president in the nation's history to resign from office. In a speech two days later, Nixon refused to admit any wrongdoing or guilt but simply stated that he "no longer had a strong enough political base in Congress."[108] However deceiving this claim may be, it does point to a larger truth about the Watergate scandal: Nixon's decision to resign was driven by—and indeed may not have happened without—a loss of Republican support in Congress. As we will see, it is this loss that distinguishes Nixon from the modern impeachments of Bill Clinton and Donald Trump.

8.6.4 Clinton's Impeachment

In 1998, President Bill Clinton was impeached by the House under the auspices of perjury and obstruction of justice. Subsequently, he was acquitted by the Senate. Like the Johnson case, votes were cast along party lines. Unlike Johnson's impeachment, though, the immediate impetus for removal was not about public policy. Rather, it was about sex, lies, and a compendium of lawsuits and investigations.

Starting in 1995, Clinton began a year-and-a-half affair with White House intern Monica Lewinsky. Later, when Lewinsky was transferred to the Pentagon, she revealed the details of her affair to a coworker, who secretly recorded her account. In 1998, Lewinsky was subpoenaed by the lawyers of another woman, Paula Jones, who claimed that Clinton had sexually harassed her when he was the governor of Arkansas. At the president's behest, Lewinsky denied the affair. Five days after she filed the false affidavit, though, Linda Tripp, Lewinsky's coworker who had recorded their conversations, sent the tapes to Independent Counsel Kenneth Starr, who was investigating Clinton for past financial misdeeds. Tripp was wired and sent to talk to Lewinsky, after which the FBI questioned Lewinsky and offered her and her family immunity in exchange for her cooperation. At the time, Clinton publicly denied the affair, rather famously insisting, "I did not have sexual relations with that woman."[109]

Over the ensuing months, Lewinsky and Clinton testified before a grand jury, and Starr submitted a report to the House of Representatives that outlined eleven grounds for impeachment, including perjury, obstruction of justice, witness tampering, and abuse of power. In an attempt to cover up his affair, the report argued, Clinton had convinced Lewinsky to give false testimony, perjured himself, and obstructed the investigation into his misconduct. The House Judiciary Committee proposed impeaching Clinton on three of the articles outlined in the report, and the full House approved. The case went to the Senate and Chief Justice William Rehnquist presided over the trial. The Senate, however, opted not to convict, voting 55–45 "not guilty" on the perjury charge and 50–50 on the obstruction-of-justice charge. As a consequence, President Clinton served out the remainder of his term in office.

What are we to make of this series of events? On the facts, a strong case can be made in favor of Starr's report. At the time of Clinton's impeachment, however, the public looked favorably upon his performance.[110] Indeed, much of the public and virtually all of the Democrats in Congress believed that Clinton's actions and misjudgment, though morally dubious, did not justify his early removal from office. For them, the central issue was not about perjury or obstruction of justice. Rather, it was about the government's unwarranted intervention into the private life of an elected official—something that they were reluctant to endorse then but that today, in the aftermath of the #MeToo awakening, might render a different verdict.

8.6.5 Trump's First Impeachment

Donald Trump was first impeached on December 18, 2019, but calls for his impeachment began much earlier. Soon after his inauguration, the president's critics cited his personal business entanglements, alleged collusion with Russia during the 2016 election, his firing of FBI director James Comey and threats against Special Counsel Robert Mueller, previous allegations of sexual misconduct, attacks on the press, and a slew of other issues as potential grounds for his removal from office. As one House Democrat put it, "There's a growing realization in the caucus that impeachment is inevitable. It's not a question of if but when."[111] However, official proceedings could not begin without the approval of Democratic House Speaker Nancy Pelosi, who then believed that impeachment was divisive and potentially helpful to Trump's reelection campaign.

When new allegations implicated Trump in an international plot to secure his reelection, Pelosi reversed her position in September 2019. According to a whistleblower complaint submitted by an anonymous intelligence official, Trump withheld $391 million of military aid that Congress had allocated for Ukraine. In exchange for these funds, Trump requested the newly elected Ukrainian president Volodymyr Zelenskyy announce an investigation into his political rival, Joe Biden. Trump insisted there was nothing illegal about his dealings with Ukraine and soon released a partial transcript of one of his phone calls with the foreign leader. Trump also attempted to deflect attention to Joe Biden and his son Hunter, who sat on the board of a Ukrainian energy company while his father was vice president.

Nonetheless, energized by the allegations, Democrats pressed forward with impeachment proceedings. After two months of televised hearings, Pelosi drafted and unveiled two articles of impeachment: one for abuse of power and the other for obstruction of Congress. The former article related specifically to the withholding of military aid; the latter admonished Trump for his defiance of subpoenas related to the impeachment proceedings. The actions listed in these articles constituted "high crimes and misdemeanors" necessary for impeachment—at least according to Democrats.

In the House, all but four Democrats voted in favor of the articles, whereas not a single Republican did. The articles passed and were sent to the Republican-held Senate, where an acquittal was expected. Unlike the Clinton impeachment, Republican senators were openly working with the White House to coordinate their impeachment strategy. Senate majority leader Mitch McConnell said: "Everything I do during this, I am coordinating with White House counsel. There will be no difference between the president's position and our position."[112] With Chief Justice John Roberts presiding over his trial, Trump was acquitted on a party-line vote.*

8.6.6 Trump's Second Impeachment

Shortly before noon on January 6, 2021, thousands of protestors gathered at the Ellipse, a park just south of the White House. They were guests of the president. "Big protest in D.C. on January 6th," Donald Trump tweeted to his online followers.[113] "Be there, will be wild!" For weeks he promoted the event, which had been dubbed the "March to Save America"—a march to contest the legitimate results of the 2020 election. "Washington is being inundated with people who don't want to see an election victory stolen by

---

* Only one Republican joined Democrats in voting to remove Trump from office: Utah senator Mitt Romney, who was the Republican presidential nominee in 2012.

emboldened Radical Left Democrats," the president tweeted. "Our Country has had enough, they won't take it anymore!"[114] Trump was so enthusiastic about the event, in fact, that he is said to have spent time in the Oval Office planning the speaker lineup and selecting his entrance music.

Trump spoke to the crowd for over an hour, but hardly anything new was said. He repeated the same list of lies and baseless accusations that had occupied his Twitter feed since election night—that duffel bags full of unsecure ballots had been delivered to polling locations, that state voting procedures had been illegally modified, that the electronic voting system used to count ballots had been manipulated, and more.

Trump encouraged the crowd to march to the Capitol, where Congress was voting to certify the results of the election. What was historically a ceremonial vote had become, as with many things in Washington, bitterly polarized. Fifteen Republican members of the Senate and 139 Republican members of the House planned to reject certain states' Electoral College results. The goal of Trump's protest, therefore, was to give the remaining "weak Republicans" the "boldness" they needed to switch sides.[115]

By now, most readers will know how this story ended. Many have seen the footage. Trump's supporters not only marched to the Capitol; some brought bear spray, zip ties, and tactical equipment. Rioters quickly overwhelmed the Capitol Police as members of Congress and the vice president were evacuated. The mob destroyed property and waved the Confederate flag inside the Capitol—a feat even the Confederate Army failed to accomplish. Clashes between rioters and Capitol Police resulted in the deaths of five Americans.

Condemnation of the president was swift and decisive, with little time wasted in drafting articles of impeachment. Speaker Pelosi announced a formal inquiry just two days after the uprising, and on January 11, a resolution was submitted to the House. It alleged that by knowingly spreading false information about the election, and by warning his supporters on January 6 that "if you don't fight like hell, you're not going to have a country anymore," Trump had incited an insurrection against the United States government.[116] The article passed with unanimous support among Democrats, joined by ten Republicans—which was ten more than had crossed party lines for Trump's first impeachment vote, just thirteen months prior.

Meanwhile in the Senate, battle lines were still being drawn. The trial did not formally begin until Trump had left office, and even then, some Republicans questioned whether it was legal to proceed. "I think the ex-president's rhetoric on the day was inflammatory," said Josh Hawley, the first senator to question states' Electoral College results. "But I think that this impeachment effort is, I mean, I think it's blatantly unconstitutional. It's a really, really, really dangerous precedent."[117]

At issue was whether the Senate could legally impeach a former president. In the words of one Republican senator, "The Founders designed the impeachment process as a way to remove officeholders from public office—not an inquest against private citizens."[118] This argument is not without its appeal; after all, Article II mentions only that the "President, Vice President, and all civil officers of the United States" may be impeached and removed. Should we assume the founders meant this as an incomplete list?

Moreover, the implications of impeaching ex-presidents do seem dangerous. Political grievances do not expire when presidents leave office; many politicians still lament George W. Bush's decision—made decades ago—to initiate a war in Iraq. Many others decry Obama's 2010 health care reform bill. In this way, it is easy to imagine an ex-president's impeachment as a kind of open season on political rivals.

Democrats, however, raised concerns about the implications of *not* allowing the impeachment of former presidents. If Trump was not impeachable, they warned, there will be a "January exception" in which presidents cannot be held accountable for actions taken in the last month of their term. Additionally, they reminded Republicans that the United States had impeached retired officials before. In 1876, Secretary of War William Belknap was impeached after leaving office, and most senators voted that they did indeed have the power to convict. Why the precedent should be overturned for a retired president, rather than a cabinet secretary, remained a mystery.

Nonetheless, most Republicans maintained their constitutionality defense until the bitter end. Once again, Trump was acquitted—this time with seven Republican senators voting for conviction.

That he was acquitted, of course, does not mean that Trump was innocent; and the verdict certainly did not reflect the Republican Party's confidence in his leadership. Following the final vote, Minority Leader Mitch McConnell delivered a scathing speech on the Senate floor. "There's no question, none, that President Trump is practically and morally responsible for provoking the events of the day."[119] McConnell also assured Americans that Trump "didn't get away with anything yet" and that the former president was still liable for criminal actions taken while in the White House. Thus, McConnell and like-minded Republicans did not dispute the need for justice but rather its ideal source.

8.6.7 *The Politics of Impeachment*

When it comes to impeachment, members of Congress routinely situate themselves within the Republic's constitutional order and the historical traditions that define it. Announcing Trump's first impeachment inquiry, Speaker Pelosi observed that "the times have found us"—a reference to Thomas Paine's call for independence from Great Britain.[120] The impeachment proceedings of Bill Clinton were similarly awash in references to the founders, the Constitution, and Congress's sacred duty to uphold the rule of law. Don't be fooled. For most members of Congress, such incantations belie partisan motivations.

The political factors that shape a president's legislative outcomes—timing, divided government, and polarization—do not disappear when members of Congress contemplate removing a president from office. Impeachment efforts tend to occur during a president's final term in office, a pattern that aligns with what we have said about timing: that presidents enjoy their greatest support early in their tenure. Partisan considerations also undergird nearly every aspect of these politics. It is no coincidence that the impeachments we examined all occurred during periods of divided government. In every case, calls for removal emanated from the opposition, while co-partisans nearly unanimously rose to the president's defense.

Polarization between the two parties also bears upon impeachment proceedings. As the parties have drifted apart, calls for a president's removal have become more frequent. Meanwhile the prospects for conviction, which typically requires at least some senators to break with their party, have grown dimmer. As many historians and political scientists have observed, "It is abundantly clear that the most likely context for a presidential impeachment has never been overt criminal behavior, but instead has been a hostile partisan division between the president and Congress."[121]

These partisan dynamics, it bears emphasizing, are not confined to impeachments. As we have seen, they affect *every* institutional interaction between the president and Congress. Members of Congress are much more willing to delegate authority to the president when one of their own occupies the White House. During times of unified government, presidents are far more likely to see their policy priorities enacted into law and reflected in the federal budget. When government is divided, however, the president's fortunes quickly shift course. Then, their policy proposals die on arrival, their actions are the subject of public hearings, and the flow of delegated authority dries up.

Battles over institutional power cannot be easily disentangled from battles over partisan power. Presidents exercise the veto—a basic constitutional provision—far more often when the opposition party controls Congress. Members of Congress exercise the filibuster—an extraconstitutional provision—when their political opponents control the Senate. And so it is that the president's partisan opponents are most likely to draw up letters of impeachment.

That Congress has the authority to act against the president does not mean that it reliably will—even when an objective reading of the facts provides ample cause for doing so. Constitutional ambiguities certainly are clarified in the practice of politics. These politics, however, are riven with ideological and partisan considerations that often have very little to do with a faithful reading of Article II.

Conclusion

To advance an agenda, presidents often must work with Congress. They do so in many different ways—through persuading, negotiating, and sometimes vetoing legislation. For their parts, members of Congress like to think that the president cannot accomplish anything without them. And in some policy domains, they are exactly right. To advance landmark policy change, the president usually has no choice but to work closely with allies in Congress.

But this isn't the be-all and end-all of public policymaking. Presidents regularly rely upon their unilateral powers to effect policy change, a topic we take up in earnest in chapter 9. Certain policy domains, foreign policy for example, offer built-in advantages to presidents. Others that would appear to privilege Congress, such as budgets, still afford presidents opportunities to exercise independent influence over decision making. And coursing through these politics are ongoing struggles over the allocation of authority across the two branches of government and political calculations about when to delegate authority, when to retract it, and when to try to remove the individual occupying the nation's highest office.

Notice, then, that presidents' chances at success derive primarily from factors that have nothing to do with their personal history, personality, or political skills. Rather, they concern features of the Constitution's Article II powers (e.g., the veto), the presidency's institutional evolution (e.g., the obligation to propose the federal budget), and the most recent electoral returns (which may yield a greater or lesser number of seats held by co-partisans on Capitol Hill). To make sense of each president's dealings with Congress, as with any political actor, we would do well to think in institutional terms.

Key Terms

states' rights	norms
filibuster	authorization
unified government	*ex ante* influence
divided government	*ex post* influence
party polarization	impoundment
Tea Party movement	Congressional Budget Office
nationalization of politics	rescissions
two-presidencies thesis	deferrals
veto	ally principle
pocket veto	legislative oversight
blame-game politics	hearings
line-item veto	censure
cloture	

Questions for Discussion

1. Some scholars believe that a successful presidency depends on a president's power of persuasion. Others argue that persuasion has little to do with presidential success. Explain the institutional contexts within each scholar's theory of presidential success.

2. What are some of the institutional reasons that presidents enjoy a greater measure of success when bargaining with Congress over foreign policy than over domestic policy?

3. Is it an oxymoron to say that we can have norms about the use of formal rules?

4. How do norms and rules interact with one another?

5. If Congress holds the power of the purse, must the president acquiesce to its members' wishes whenever political debates turn to money?

6. In what ways do interbranch political struggles over policy differ from those over institutional power?

Suggested Readings

Beckman, Matthew. *Pushing the Agenda: Presidential Leadership in U.S. Lawmaking, 1953–2004*. New York: Cambridge University Press, 2010.

Binder, Sarah. *Stalemate: Causes and Consequences of Legislative Gridlock*. Washington, DC: Brookings Institution Press, 2003.

Bond, Jon, and Richard Fleisher. *The President in the Legislative Arena*. Chicago: University of Chicago Press, 1992.

Cameron, Charles M. *Veto Bargaining: Presidents and the Politics of Negative Power*. New York: Cambridge University Press, 2000.

Cohen, Jeffrey. *The President's Legislative Policy Agenda, 1789–2002*. New York: Cambridge University Press, 2012.

Dearborn, John. *Power Shifts: Congress and Presidential Representation*. Chicago: University of Chicago Press, 2021.

Edwards, George C. *The Strategic President: Persuasion and Opportunity in Presidential Leadership*. Princeton: Princeton University Press, 2009.

Fisher, Louis. *The Politics of Shared Power: Congress and the Executive*. 4th ed. College Station: Texas A&M University Press, 1998.

Gerhardt, Michael. *The Federal Impeachment Process: A Constitutional and Historical Analysis*. 3rd ed. Chicago: University of Chicago Press, 2019.

Kriner, Douglas L., and Eric Schickler. *Investigating the President: Congressional Checks on Presidential Power*. Princeton: Princeton University Press, 2016.

Lee, Frances. *Insecure Majorities: Congress and the Perpetual Campaign*. Chicago: University of Chicago Press, 2016.

Sinclair, Barbara. *Unorthodox Lawmaking: New Legislative Processes in the U.S. Congress*. 5th ed. Washington, DC: Congressional Quarterly Press, 2016.

Notes

1. Ted Gittinger and Allen Fisher, "LBJ Champions the Civil Rights Act of 1964, Part 2," *Prologue Magazine* 36, no. 2 (2004), https://www.archives.gov/publications/prologue/2004/summer/civil-rights-act-2.html.

2. Randall B. Woods, *LBJ: Architect of American Ambition* (New York: Free Press, 2006), 477.

3. Gittinger and Fisher, "LBJ Champions the Civil Rights Act."

4. Woods, *LBJ*, 473.

5. Quoted in George Packer, "LBJ's Moment," *New Yorker*, August 24, 2008, https://www.newyorker.com/news/george-packer/l-b-j-s-moment.

6. Bert A. Rockman et al., "Which Presidents Are Uncommonly Successful in Congress?" in Bert A. Rockman and Richard W. Waterman, *Presidential Leadership: The Vortex of Power* (New York: Oxford University Press, 2008), 191–214.

7. George C. Edwards, *The Strategic President: Persuasion and Opportunity in Presidential Leadership* (Princeton: Princeton University Press, 2009), 27.

8. Quoted in Edwards, *The Strategic President*, 136.

9. Quoted in Edwards, *The Strategic President*, 139.

10. Joseph Carroll, "Seven out of 10 Americans Accept Bush as Legitimate President," Gallup, July 17, 2001, https://news.gallup.com/poll/4687/seven-americans-accept-bush-legitimate-president.aspx.

11. Stephen Skowronek, *The Politics Presidents Make: Leadership from John Adams to Bill Clinton*, 2nd ed. (Cambridge, MA: Belknap Press, 1997).

12. Stephen Skowronek, "Presidents in Political Time," in *The Presidency in the Political System*, 5th ed., ed. Michael Nelson (Washington, DC: Congressional Quarterly Press, 1998), 125.

13. George C. Edwards and Andrew Barrett, "Presidential Agenda Setting in Congress," in *Polarized Politics: Congress and the President in a Partisan Era*, ed. Jon R. Bond and Richard Fleisher (Washington, DC: Congressional Quarterly Press, 2004), 109–33.

14. Lyn Ragsdale, *Vital Statistics on the Presidency*, 4th ed. (Washington, DC: Congressional Quarterly Press, 2014), table 9–3.

15. Jeffrey E. Cohen, *Presidential Responsiveness and Public Policy-Making: The Public and the Policies That Presidents Choose* (Ann Arbor: University of Michigan Press, 2014).

16. David S. Broder, *Behind the Front Page: A Candid Look at How the News Is Made* (New York: Simon & Schuster, 2000), 4.

17. George C. Edwards and B. Dan Wood, "Who Influences Whom? The President, Congress, and the Media," *American Political Science Review* 93, no. 2 (1999): 327–44.

18. "Trade Promotion Authority (TPA): Frequently Asked Questions," CRS Report R43491 (Washington, DC: Congressional Research Service, 2019), https://fas.org/sgp/crs/misc/R43491.pdf.

19. Quoted in Edwards, *Strategic President*, 135.

20. Paul C. Light, *The President's Agenda: Domestic Policy Choice from Kennedy to Clinton*, 3rd ed. (Baltimore: Johns Hopkins University Press, 1999).

21. "Seats in Congress Gained/Lost by the President's Party in Mid-Term Elections," American Presidency Project, https://www.presidency.ucsb.edu/node/332343/.

22. Light, *The President's Agenda*, 36.

23. For an overview of literature on lawmaking during unified and divided governments, see John J. Coleman, "Unified Government, Divided Government, and Party Responsiveness," *American Political Science Review* 93, no. 4 (1999): 821–35.

24. Barack Obama, "The Time Has Come for Universal Health Care" (speech, Families USA Conference, Washington, DC, January 25, 2007).

25. Barack Obama, "The American Promise" (speech, Democratic National Convention, Denver, CO, August 28, 2008).

26. "Remarks by the President to a Joint Session of Congress on Health Care," Barack Obama White House Office of the Press Secretary, September 9, 2009, https://obamawhitehouse.archives.gov/the-press-office/remarks-president-a-joint-session-congress-health-care.

27. "Obama Urges Pared-Back Health Care Bill," ABC, January 20, 2010, https://abc13.com/archive/7229776/.

28. "House Passes Health Care Reform Bill," CNN, November 8, 2009, http://www.cnn.com/2009/POLITICS/11/07/health.care/index.html.

29. Sam Stein, "Obama Calls on Bloggers to Keep Health Care Pressure on Congress," *Huffington Post*, July 20, 2009, http://www.huffingtonpost.com/2009/07/20/obama-calls-on-bloggers-t_n_241570.html.

30. David M. Herszenhorn and Sheryl G. Stolberg, "Obama Rallies House Democrats," Prescriptions (blog), *New York Times*, November 7, 2009, https://prescriptions.blogs.nytimes.com/2009/11/07/obamas-in-the-house/.

31. Quoted in Mark Landler, "Obama to Turn Up Attacks on Congress in Campaign," *New York Times*, January 1, 2012, A.1.

32. Much of the information in this section was derived from Daniel J. Hopkins, *The Increasingly United States: How and Why American Political Behavior Nationalized* (Chicago: University of Chicago Press, 2018).

33. James Madison, "Federalist No. 46," in *The Federalist Papers*, ed. Clinton Rossiter, intro. Charles R. Kessler (New York: Penguin Putnam, 1961; Signet, 2003).

34. Hopkins, *The Increasingly United States*, 41.

35. William G. Howell, Saul P. Jackman, and Jon C. Rogowski, *The Wartime President: Executive Influence and the Nationalizing Politics of Threat* (Chicago: University of Chicago Press, 2013).

36. Gary C. Jacobson, "The President's Effect on Partisan Attitudes," *Presidential Studies Quarterly* 42, no. 4 (2012): 683–718.

37. Craig Volden and Alan E. Wiseman, "Bargaining in Legislatures over Particularistic and Collective Goods," *American Political Science Review* 101, no. 1 (2007): 79–92.

38. Christopher R. Berry, Barry C. Burden, and William G. Howell, "The President and the Distribution of Federal Spending," *American Political Science Review* 104, no. 4 (2010): 783–99.

39. Aaron Wildavsky, "The Two Presidencies," *Trans-Action/Society* 4 (December 1966): 7–14.

40. See, for example, George Edwards, "The Two Presidencies: A Reevaluation," *American Politics Quarterly* 14, no. 3 (1986): 247–63; Duane Oldfield and Aaron Wildavsky, "Reconsidering the Two Presidencies," *Society* 26, no. 5 (1989): 54–59; and Lee Sigelman, "A Reassessment of the Two Presidencies Thesis," *Journal of Politics* 41, no. 4 (1979): 1195–1205.

41. Brandice Canes-Wrone, William G. Howell, and David Lewis, "Executive Influence in Foreign versus Domestic Policy Making: Toward a Broader Understanding of Presidential Power," *Journal of Politics* 70, no. 1 (2008): 1–16.

42. Charles M. Cameron, *Veto Bargaining: Presidents and the Politics of Negative Power* (New York: Cambridge University Press, 2000).

43. "Summary of Bills Vetoed, 1789–Present," United States Senate, http://www.senate.gov/reference /Legislation/Vetoes/vetoCounts.htm.

44. See, for example, Timothy Groseclose and Nolan McCarty, "The Politics of Blame: Bargaining before an Audience," *American Journal of Political Science* 45, no. 1 (2000): 100–119.

45. Jennifer Steinhauer, "House Passes Student Loan Bill Despite Veto Threat," *New York Times*, April 27, 2012, A.11.

46. "H.R. 4628 (112th): Interest Rate Reduction Act," *GovTrack.us*, https://www.govtrack.us/congress/bills /112/hr4628.

47. Quoted in Cameron, *Veto Bargaining*, 178.

48. Louis Nelson, "Trump, Unhappy with Omnibus Bill, Calls on Congress to Reinstate Line-Item Veto," *POLITICO*, March 23, 2018, https://www.politico.com/story/2018/03/23/trump-line-item-veto-482192.

49. "Barney Frank: 'God Didn't Create the Filibuster,'" *Huffington Post*, March 21, 2010, http://www .huffingtonpost.com/2010/01/19/barney-frank-god-didnt-cr_n_428408.html; Alexander Burns, "Biden Slams Filibuster; VP: Constitution 'on Its Head,'" *POLITICO*, January 18, 2010, http://www.politico.com /politico44/perm/0110/biden_slams_filibuster_fe40df44-9045-4c26-a715-51c427035eae.html.

50. Ian Millhiser, "After Calling Judicial Filibusters Unconstitutional, Republican Senators Line Up behind Judicial Filibuster," *ThinkProgress*, May 19, 2011, https://thinkprogress.org/after-calling-judicial-filibusters -unconstitutional-republican-senators-line-up-behind-judicial-afd49e2b95b4/.

51. Burgess Everett and Marianne Levine, "The Senate's Record-Breaking Gridlock under Trump," *POLITICO*, June 8, 2020, https://www.politico.com/news/2020/06/08/senate-record-breaking -gridlocktrump-303811.

52. Lisa Mascaro, "McConnell Vows 'Scorched Earth' If Senate Ends Filibuster," Associated Press, March 16, 2021, https://apnews.com/article/joe-biden-politics-mitch-mcconnell-legislation-filibusters-cdceb62f3a4c8 ba933deb246c43de50d.

53. For more on this point, see Julia R. Azari and Jennifer K. Smith, "Unwritten Rules: Informal Institutions in Established Democracies," *Perspectives on Politics* 10, no. 1 (2012): 37–55.

54. Elements of this section draw from Christopher R. Berry, Barry C. Burden, and William G. Howell, "The President and the Distribution of Federal Spending," *American Political Science Review* 104, no. 4 (2011): 783–99.

55. Louis Fisher, *Presidential Spending Power* (Princeton: Princeton University Press, 1975), 88.

56. "Defense Budget: Tracking of Emergency Response Funds for the War on Terrorism," Report to the Subcommittee on Defense, GAO-03–346 (Washington, DC: Government Accountability Office, 2003), https://www.gao.gov/products/gao-03-346.

57. 4 Cong. Rec. 5268 (1986).

58. Christopher Wlezien, "The Politics of Impoundments," *Political Research Quarterly* 47, no. 1 (1994): 59.

59. Dennis S. Ippolito, *The Budget and National Politics* (San Francisco: Freeman, 1978), 138–39.

60. *Train v. City of New York*, 420 U.S. 35 (1975).

61. John W. Ellwood and James A. Thurber, "The Congressional Budget Process Re-examined," in *Congress Reconsidered*, 2nd ed., ed. Lawrence C. Dodd and Bruce I. Oppenheimer (Washington, DC: Congressional Quarterly Press, 1981), 226.

62. "Updated Rescission Statistics, Fiscal Years 1974–2020," U.S. Government Accountability Office, July 16, 2020, https://www.gao.gov/products/b-330828.

63. Joseph Choi and Niv Elis, "Trump Seeks to Freeze $27.4 Billion of Programs in Final Week of Presidency," *The Hill*, January 21, 2021, https://thehill.com/homenews/administration/534355-trump-asks-congress-for-274-billion-in-spending-cuts-days-before?rl=1.

64. Meena Bose, Andrew Rudalevige, and Eloise Pasachoff, "The President's Budget Powers in the Trump Era," in *Executive Policymaking: The Role of the OMB in the Presidency*, ed. Meena Bose and Andrew Rudalevige (Washington, DC: Brookings Institution Press, 2020), 69–98.

65. Russell T. Vought, Director, OMB, and Mark R. Paoletta, General Counsel, OMB, to John Yarmuth, Chairman, House Committee on the Budget, January 19, 2021, 4.

66. Quoted in Bose, Rudalevige, and Pasachoff, "The President's Budget Powers in the Trump Era," 76.

67. Vought and Paoletta to Yarmuth, January 19, 2021, 1.

68. David Higgins, "Biden's Holdup of Border Wall Funding Didn't Violate Law, GAO Rules," *Roll Call*, June 16, 2021, https://www.rollcall.com/2021/06/15/bidens-holdup-of-border-wall-funding-didnt-violate-law-gao-rules/.

69. Jena Heath, "Bush Airs Anger, Resolve, Sadness," *Austin American-Statesman*, September 13, 2001, A.6.

70. Authorization for Use of Military Force, S.J. Res. 23, 107th Cong. (2001).

71. Peter Carlson, "The Solitary Vote of Barbara Lee," *Washington Post*, September 19, 2011, C.1.

72. Nancy Kassop, "The War Power and Its Limits," *Presidential Studies Quarterly* 33, no. 3 (2003): 509–29.

73. David Cole, "Reviving the Nixon Doctrine: NSA Spying, the Commander-in-Chief, and Executive Power in the War on Terror," *Washington and Lee Journal of Civil Rights and Social Justice* 13, no. 1 (2006): 17–40.

74. Frederick M. Kaiser, "Congressional Oversight," CRS Report No. 97–936 GOV (Washington, DC: Congressional Research Service, 2001), https://www.everycrsreport.com/files/20010102_97-936GOV_871 70403be2100ac2121e6d725830203dcc65946.pdf.

75. Walter J. Oleszek, *Congressional Procedures and the Policy Process* (Washington, DC: Congressional Quarterly Press, 1989).

76. David Truman, *The Governmental Process* (New York: Alfred A. Knopf, 1951).

77. For a review of related literature, as well as an innovative look at the role of information in congressional hearings, see Daniel Diermeier and Timothy J. Feddersen, "Information and Congressional Hearings," *American Journal of Political Science* 44, no. 1 (2000): 51–65.

78. Douglas L. Kriner and Eric Schickler, *Investigating the President: Congressional Checks on Presidential Power* (Princeton: Princeton University Press, 2016).

79. Aliyah Frumin, "Issa to Cummings at Testy IRS Hearing: You're Acting like a 'Little Boy,'" MSNBC, September 12, 2013, http://www.msnbc.com/hardball/issa-cummings-testy-irs-hearing-youre.

80. "Inappropriate Criteria Were Used to Identify Tax-Exempt Applications for Review," Treasury Secretary General for Tax Administration, May 14, 2013, http://www.treasury.gov/tigta/auditreports/2013reports/201310053fr.pdf.

81. Ashley Killough, "Poll: Obama's Approval Ratings Drop, Americans Say He's Not Trustworthy," Political Ticker (blog), CNN, November 12, 2013, http://politicalticker.blogs.cnn.com/2013/11/12/poll-obama-approval-ratings-drop-americans-say-hes-not-trustworthy/.

82. David Weigel, "Darrell Issa's Big New IRS Revelation about the White House Was Actually Reported Months Ago," *Slate*, July 18, 2013, http://www.slate.com/blogs/weigel/2013/07/18/darrell_issa_s_big_irs _revelation_about_the_white_house_was_reve aled_two.html.

83. Terry Moe, "The Presidency and the Bureaucracy: The Presidential Advantage," in *The Presidency and the Political System*, 6th ed., ed. Michael Nelson (Washington, DC: Congressional Quarterly Press 2000), 416.

84. "Treaty vs. Executive Agreement," U.S. Department of State, https://2009-2017.state.gov/s/l/treaty /faqs/70133.htm.

85. Arthur H. Dean, "The Bricker Amendment and Authority over Foreign Affairs," *Foreign Affairs* 32, no. 1 (1953): 1–19.

86. William Theis, "Wiley's Stand on Bricker Plan Rapped," *Milwaukee Sentinel*, June 27, 1953.

87. Dean, "The Bricker Amendment and Authority over Foreign Affairs."

88. Jonathan Turley, "Congress as Grand Jury: The Role of the House of Representatives in the Impeachment of an American President," *George Washington Law Review* 67, no. 3 (1999): 735–90.

89. Quoted in Turley, "Congress as Grand Jury," 736.

90. Amber Phillips, "'We All Have to Answer for What We Did': A Compelling Argument for Impeachment, Explained," *Washington Post*, June 10, 2019, https://www.washingtonpost.com/politics/2019/06/10/we -all-have-answer-what-we-did-compelling-argument-impeachment-explained/.

91. See, for example, Adam Przeworski, *Democracy and the Limits of Self-Government* (New York: Cambridge University Press, 2011); and James Fearon, "Self-Enforcing Democracy," *Quarterly Journal of Economics* 126, no. 4 (2011): 1661–1708.

92. Raoul Berger, *Impeachment: The Constitutional Problems*, enlarged ed. (Cambridge, MA: Harvard University Press, 1999).

93. "Watergate Burglars Arrested," *History.com* (A&E Television Networks, February 9, 2010), https://www .history.com/this-day-in-history/watergate-burglars-arrested-2.

94. George Lardner, "Cox Is Chosen as Special Prosecutor," *Washington Post*, May 19, 1973, https://www .washingtonpost.com/wp-srv/national/longterm/watergate/articles/051973-1.htm.

95. Shayanne Gal and James Pasley, "Impeachment Crushed Nixon's Approval Ratings, but Clinton Emerged Unscathed; Here's How Trump Could Survive, Too," *Business Insider*, November 27, 2019, https:// www.businessinsider.in/politics/news/impeachment-crushed-nixons-approval-ratings-but-clinton-emerged -unscathed-heres-how-trump-could-survive-too-/articleshow/72249747.cms.

96. John A. Farrell, "James McCord: The Watergate Burglar Who Cracked," *POLITICO*, December 29, 2019, https://www.politico.com/news/magazine/2019/12/29/james-mccord-watergate-burglar-obituary -086480.

97. Mark Nevin, "Nixon Loyalists, Barry Goldwater, and Republican Support for President Nixon during Watergate," *Journal of Policy History* 29, no. 3 (2017): 403–4.

98. Mark Mellman, "Learning from Impeachments Past," *The Hill*, October 8, 2019, https://thehill.com /opinion/columnists/464934-mellman-learning-from-impeachments-past.

99. Nevin, "Nixon Loyalists, Barry Goldwater, and Republican Support for President Nixon during Watergate," 403–4.

100. Mark Mellman, "Watergate Republicans vs. Trump Republicans," *The Hill*, November 12, 2019, https:// thehill.com/opinion/columnists/470169-mark-mellman-watergate-republicans-vs-trump-republicans.

101. Nevin, "Nixon Loyalists, Barry Goldwater, and Republican Support for President Nixon during Watergate," 403–4.

102. Nevin, "Nixon Loyalists, Barry Goldwater, and Republican Support for President Nixon during Watergate," 403–4.

103. Editorial Board, "Listen, Mr. Nixon . . . ," *Chicago Tribune*, May 9, 1974, https://www.chicagotribune .com/opinion/ct-opinion-richard-nixon-impeach-1974-editorial-20191003-mzcdixaq3fetbg5zz3y6muvu4q -story.html.

104. U.S. Congress, House Judiciary Committee, Articles of Impeachment against President Richard Nixon, July 27, 1974, https://watergate.info/impeachment/articles-of-impeachment.

105. Nevin, "Nixon Loyalists, Barry Goldwater, and Republican Support for President Nixon during Watergate," 403–4.

106. Nevin, "Nixon Loyalists, Barry Goldwater, and Republican Support for President Nixon during Watergate," 403–4.

107. Andrew Glass and Alex Isenstadt, "Watergate 'Smoking Gun' Tape Released, Aug. 5, 1974," *POLITICO*, August 5, 2018, https://www.politico.com/story/2018/08/05/watergate-smoking-gun-tape-released-aug-5 -1974-753086.

108. Patrick Horst, "The Politics of Removal: The Impeachment of a President," in *Mobilization, Representation, and Responsiveness in the American Democracy*, ed. Michael T. Oswald (Cham, Switzerland: Palgrave Macmillan, 2020), 63–104.

109. History.com Editors, "This Day in History | December 19, 1998: President Clinton Impeached," *History*, August 21, 2018, https://www.history.com/this-day-in-history/president-clinton-impeached.

110. "Presidential Approval Ratings—Bill Clinton," Gallup, http://news.gallup.com/poll/116584 /Presidential-Approval-Ratings-Bill-Clinton.aspx.

111. Susan Davis and Kelsey Snell, "Democrats' Impeachment Divide Tests Pelosi," National Public Radio, https://www.npr.org/2019/05/21/725356771/democrats-impeachment-divide-tests-pelosi.

112. Jordain Carney, "McConnell Says He'll Be in 'Total Coordination' with White House on Impeachment Trial Strategy," *The Hill*, December 12, 2019, https://thehill.com/homenews/senate/474399-mcconnell-says -hell-be-in-total-coordination-with-white-house-on-impeachment.

113. Donald Trump, Twitter post, December 19, 2020, 1:42:42 a.m.

114. Donald Trump, Twitter post, January 5, 2021, 5:05:56 p.m.

115. The full transcript of Trump's speech is available at https://www.npr.org/2021/02/10/966396848 /read-trumps-jan-6-speech-a-key-part-of-impeachment-trial.

116. U.S. Congress, House, *Impeaching Donald John Trump, President of the United States, for High Crimes and Misdemeanors*, H.Res.24, 117th Cong., introduced January 11, 2021.

117. Domenico Montanaro, "There Is Precedent for Trying a Former Government Official, Established 145 Years Ago," National Public Radio, January 29, 2021, https://www.npr.org/2021/01/29/961330810/there -is-precedent-for-trying-a-former-government-official-established-145-years.

118. Tom Cotton, "Cotton Statement on Senate Impeachment Proceedings," January 12, 2021, https://www .cotton.senate.gov/news/press-releases/cotton-statement-on-senate-impeachment-proceedings.

119. Mitch McConnell, Remarks on Donald Trump's Second Impeachment Trial, February 13, 2021.

120. Heidi Przybyla and Adam Edelman, "Nancy Pelosi Announces Formal Impeachment Inquiry of Trump," NBC News, September 25, 2019, https://www.nbcnews.com/politics/trump-impeachment-inquiry /pelosi-announce-formal-impeachment-inquiry-trump-n1058251.

121. Daniel P. Franklin et al., *The Politics of Presidential Impeachment* (Albany: State University of New York Press, 2020), 20.

9

Unilateral Powers

WITH THE OUTBREAK of the Civil War, President Lincoln issued a proclamation "directing trial by court martial or military commissions of all persons who impeded the draft, discouraged enlistments or committed other disloyal acts."[1] As a result of this unilateral action, nearly forty thousand people were jailed and denied habeas corpus. Thereafter, Lincoln proceeded further along this course. Much of the Civil War would be waged through **unilateral directives** rather than statutes. Famously, the edict freeing Southern slaves came in the form of a proclamation rather than a law. And in the wake of the Civil War, President Lincoln unilaterally pardoned numerous deserters and Confederates who agreed to swear allegiance to the Constitution.

Lincoln's decisions to act without consulting Congress highlight the two options all presidents have to advance their policy agendas:

1. Submit proposals to Congress and hope its members faithfully shepherd them into law (a process investigated in chapter 8).
2. Exercise their unilateral powers to create policies that assume the weight of law without the formal endorsement of Congress.

To pursue a unilateral strategy, of course, presidents must be able to justify their actions on the basis of some blend of statutory and constitutional powers. When it comes to the pardon, the president operates on the strongest possible grounds, as the Constitution explicitly recognizes its existence in Article II. Still, the ambiguity of other executive powers and the massive corpus of law that presidents can draw upon provide ample opportunities for presidents to issue unilateral directives with wide-ranging policy content.[2] And since Lincoln's time in office, presidents have made the most of them.

9.1 Power without Persuasion

In his seminal book *Presidential Power*, originally published in 1960, Richard Neustadt argued that when thinking about the presidency, "weak remains the word with which to start."[3] In Neustadt's view, modern presidents are more clerk than leader, struggling to stay atop world events, congressional dealings, media cycles, and dissension within their party,

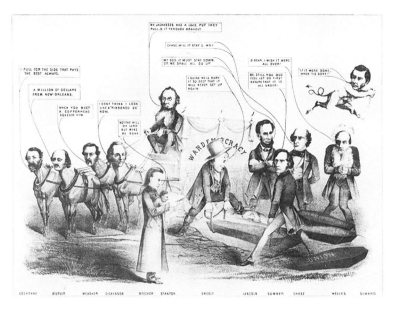

FIGURE 9.1. The first in a series of four anti-Lincoln satires published in 1864, this cartoon dream of Jack Downing (a character created in the 1830s) portrays Lincoln, his supporters, and cabinet members acting as undertakers about to bury the Constitution. *Source:* Library of Congress Prints and Photographs Division [LC-USZ62–8876].

cabinet, and the White House. Though held responsible for just about everything, presidents control almost nothing. Congress, after all, enacts laws, and the bureaucracy implements them, placing presidents at the periphery of government action. The pursuit of their policy agenda is marked more by compromise than conviction, and their eventual success ultimately depends upon the willingness of others to do things that they cannot possibly accomplish on their own.

Neustadt identified the basic dilemma facing all modern presidents, and the one that motivated much of the discussion in chapter 4: the public expects them to accomplish far more than their formal powers alone permit. This has been especially true since the New Deal, when the federal government assumed responsibility for the nation's economy and social welfare. Today, presidents must address almost every conceivable social and economic problem, from the proliferation of terrorist activities around the globe to the oversight of a sprawling and increasingly complex financial industry.

Armed with little more than the powers to propose and veto legislation and recommend the appointment of bureaucrats and judges, modern presidents appear doomed to failure from the very start. For presidents to enjoy any measure of success, Neustadt argued, they must master the art of persuasion. Power, in his view, is about bargaining and negotiating; about brokering deals and trading promises; and about cajoling legislators, bureaucrats, and justices to do the president's bidding.* Presidents wield influence when they manage to enhance their own bargaining positions by drawing upon the experiences, skills, and reputations that they bring to the office.†

Persuasion, however, is not all there is to power. Indeed, scholarship that equates the two fails to explain presidents who have struck out on their own to conduct a war on terrorism, or revamp civil rights policies, or reconstruct the federal bureaucracy. George W. Bush did not stand idly by while committee chairs debated whether to introduce legislation on his behalf. Instead, in conducting a secret war on terrorism, dismantling international treaties brokered by previous administrations, and performing end runs around some of the most important environmental laws enacted during the past half century, he seized the initiative, acted boldly (some would say irresponsibly or even unconstitutionally), and then dared his political adversaries to defy him. Having issued a directive, Bush sought not so much to cultivate Congress's support as to neutralize its criticism. And so have all modern presidents, before and since.

The unilateral actions that modern presidents have taken turn the central precepts of Neustadt's argument upside down: unilateral action has little to do with persuasion; presidential power does not hinge upon a capacity to "convince [political actors] that what the White House wants of them is what they ought to do for their sake and for their authority."[4] Rather, through unilateral directives, presidents set public policy and wait for Congress and the courts to counter. If Congress and the courts choose not to do so, through either law or opinion, then the order stands. In this view, when presidents act unilaterally, they play from strength and act alone. They need not rally majorities, compromise with adversaries, or wait for an interest group to bring a case to court. Instead, modern presidents lead by breaking through the stasis that pervades the federal government and imposing their will in new areas of governance.

9.1.1 Unilateral Directives

Presidents have at their disposal a wide variety of tools by which to exercise their unilateral powers. The most significant unilateral directives, and the best documented in contemporary scholarship, include executive orders, proclamations, national security directives (NSDs), and executive agreements. Though there are no hard-and-fast rules regarding their

---

*Neustadt certainly was not the only scholar to equate power with persuasion. Some seven years before Neustadt published his seminal tract on presidential power, Robert Dahl and Charles Lindblom observed that "like everyone else in the American policy process, the president must bargain constantly—with Congressional leaders, individual Congressmen, his department heads, bureau chiefs, and leaders of nongovernmental organizations." See Robert A. Dahl and Charles E. Lindblom, *Politics, Economics, and Welfare* (Chicago: University of Chicago Press, 1953), 333.

†A number of scholars have challenged this last claim, namely that power is personal and depends upon a president's reputation and prestige. For one of the more trenchant critiques, see Terry M. Moe, "Presidents, Institutions, and Theory," in *Researching the Presidency: Vital Questions, New Approaches*, ed. George C. Edwards, John H. Kessel, and Bert A. Rockman (Pittsburgh: University of Pittsburgh Press, 1993).

TABLE 9.1. The President's Policy Tool Kit

Policy Tool	Scope of Policy Content	Audience	Publicly Available?
Executive Orders	Alter foreign or domestic policies	Executive branch officials	Published in the *Federal Register*
Proclamations	Alter foreign or domestic policies	Private citizens	Published in the *Federal Register*
National Security Directives	Alter national security policies	Executive branch officials	Available only upon declassification
Executive Agreements	Negotiate and commit to deals with foreign leaders	Executive branch officials and foreign governments	Must be reported to Congress
Memoranda	Alter foreign or domestic policies	Executive branch officials	No publishing requirement
Departmental and Secretarial Orders	Restructure the federal bureaucracy	Executive branch officials	No publishing requirement

Note: The most significant unilateral tools at the president's disposal differ in a few key respects. Only with national security directives, for example, can presidents count on their actions being kept secret. And only proclamations are (more often than not) directed exclusively to private citizens.

use, and though presidents have shown remarkable dexterity in redefining and adapting their usage to suit their particular purposes, some guidelines help distinguish these tools.

As table 9.1 shows, these tools vary with regard to their policy content, whom they are addressed to, and the secrecy they lend to the president's actions. Among the options listed, executive orders are by far the most versatile and popular, and it is fitting that we should start our inventory of the president's unilateral powers with these. But as will be explained in the sections below, if presidents want to avoid attention, or direct their orders to different groups, other tools may be preferred.

EXECUTIVE ORDERS

Among all unilateral directives, **executive orders** "combine the highest levels of substance, discretion, and direct presidential involvement"[5] and are probably the closest substitute for a legislative enactment. Generally, executive orders instruct government officials and administrative agencies to take specific actions with regard to domestic and foreign affairs. Executive orders are, according to Phillip Cooper, "directives issued by the president to officers of the executive branch, requiring them to take an action, stop a certain type of activity, alter policy, change management practices, or accept a delegation of authority under which they will henceforth be responsible for the implementation of law."[6]

While presidents direct executive orders to subordinates within the executive branch, the impact of these orders is felt well beyond the boundaries of the federal government.

Terry Eastland, who worked in the Justice Department during the Reagan administration, cautions, "In theory executive orders are directed to those who enforce the laws but often they have at least as much impact on the governed as the governors."[7] Through executive orders, presidents have dictated the terms by which government contractors hire and fire their employees, set restrictions on where American citizens can travel abroad, frozen the financial holdings of private parties, reset trade tariffs, and determined the kinds of recreational activities that are allowed on public lands.

PROCLAMATIONS

While executive orders are typically directed to officials *within* the federal government, presidential **proclamations** almost always target individuals and groups *outside* of the government. Because Article II of the Constitution does not endow the president with clear and immediate authority over private parties, it is not surprising that proclamations mostly involve ceremonial and commemorative affairs. For example, in the first months of his presidency, Biden used proclamations to announce a national day of unity, American Heart Month, National Black History Month, and Irish-American Heritage Month, among others. Presidents also use proclamations to order flags flown at half-staff in the wake of national tragedies.

Historically, though, proclamations occupied a prominent role in presidential policy-making. Before 1945, the preponderance of proclamations contained significant policy content to, among other things, change trade policy, designate public lands and national monuments, and, especially, mobilize war efforts.[8] While the number of ceremonial proclamations has maintained an upward trajectory, the end of World War II greatly reduced the number of policy-based proclamations. There are, however, important exceptions, such as Nixon's 1971 proclamations temporarily freezing all wages, rents, and prices as part of the national economic stabilization program; Ford's 1973 proclamation granting pardons to draft evaders; Carter's 1980 proclamations imposing new surcharges on imported oil; and Trump's and Biden's 2020 and 2021 proclamations aimed at stemming the flow of immigrants into the United States from regions of the world with high Covid-19 rates.

NATIONAL SECURITY DIRECTIVES

Beyond the 1935 Federal Register Act's publication requirements, which are discussed in depth in section 9.3.1, presidents need not abide by any fixed rules when developing, issuing, or circulating either an executive order or a proclamation. There are occasions, however, when presidents would prefer to entirely conceal their actions from Congress, the courts, and the public. In these cases, presidents can turn to **national security directives** (also known as *national security decision directives* or *presidential decision directives*). Issued through the National Security Council, national security directives are typically classified upon issuance; and only years, and often decades, later are they declassified. While, in theory, presidents use these directives only to safeguard the nation's security, in practice presidents may repackage a particularly controversial executive order as a national security directive and thereby avoid public scrutiny.*

Though precise figures are hard to come by, the General Accounting Office (GAO) estimated that from 1961 to 1988 presidents issued over a thousand national security directives. Of those the GAO was able to review, 41 percent directly affected military policy, 63 percent foreign policy, and 22 percent domestic policy.[9] A sample of recently declassified national security directives includes orders to the CIA to support and recruit Nicaraguan Contras, the funding of covert operations to prevent the spread of communism, the authorization to execute preemptive and retaliatory strikes against confirmed and suspected terrorists, the establishment of new classified information rules for the National Security Agency, and the approval of the invasion of Grenada in 1983. According to Harold Relyea, the content of national security directives "is not only imaginatively diverse, but also often highly controversial, if not dangerous."[10]

EXECUTIVE AGREEMENTS

While executive orders, proclamations, and (to a lesser degree) national security directives all are unilateral counterparts to legislation, **executive agreements** provide presidents with an alternative to the treaty ratification process. Rather than having to secure the consent of two-thirds of the Senate, presidents can use executive agreements to unilaterally commit the United States to deals involving international trade, ocean fishing rights, open air space, environmental standards, or immigration patterns. While most of these agreements concern specific and often technical matters, the number issued during the modern era has increased at such an astronomical rate that collectively they now constitute a vital means by which presidents conduct foreign diplomacy.

Though far more accessible than treaties, executive agreements are no less effectual. In its 1937 decision *United States v. Belmont*, the Supreme Court affirmed that the president has "the authority to speak as the sole organ" of the government when conducting foreign affairs, thus granting executive agreements the same binding status as treaties.[11] After this decision, and propelled by the onset of World War II, executive agreements became increasingly popular in the White House. In 1940, FDR used an executive agreement to give fifty battleships to Great Britain in exchange for the right to construct military bases on English islands. Despite pushback from Congress and claims that it violated America's isolationist stance, the agreement nonetheless took on the full force of law.

---

* As Phillip Cooper notes, "It is tempting to employ NSDs because they cloud actions the president wishes to take with the mantle of national security and hold out the threat of security laws for violation. Although it happens, it is more dangerous for employees to leak or discuss these devices, and Congress has difficulty getting into documents it cannot see. It is even tempting to use NSDs in ways that help the president domestically." Phillip Cooper, "Power Tools for an Effective and Responsible Presidency," *Administration & Society* 29, no. 5 (1997): 547.

MEMORANDA

Through still other means, presidents have managed to perform end runs around the legislative process. Presidents can package their policy directives as **memoranda**, which function like executive orders but with fewer legal requirements for their use. Unlike executive orders, memoranda need not be published in the *Federal Register*. Also unlike executive orders, memoranda need not cite any statutory or constitutional authority to take effect. Thus, even though the Justice Department has said that "there is no substantive difference in the legal effectiveness of an executive order and a presidential directive that is styled other than as an executive order," there are clear advantages to signing directives as memoranda.[12]

Barack Obama made something of a habit of doing so. With memoranda, Obama imposed economic sanctions on foreign nations, altered immigration and labor regulations, and determined which public lands are available for oil exploration.[13] Most famously, after Congress failed for several years to pass immigration reform, Obama instructed Secretary of Homeland Security Janet Napolitano to issue a memorandum halting deportation of young undocumented immigrants, a policy that immediately affected over eight hundred thousand people.[14]

DEPARTMENTAL AND SECRETARIAL ORDERS

In some instances, unilateral directives do not come straight from the president's desk. Rather, a department secretary or undersecretary acting on the president's behalf signs the actual order. Relative to executive orders, these **departmental orders** and **secretarial orders** are somewhat limited in scope. Rather than make sweeping changes to foreign or domestic policy, these orders usually reshape the administrative structure of the federal bureaucracy, often with the aim of creating a new agency. This does not mean, however, that departmental and secretarial orders are unimportant. As we discuss at greater length in chapter 10, the politics of bureaucratic structure have tremendous implications for the president's ability to advance his policy agenda both at home and abroad.

When setting public policy, presidents frequently issue combinations of these various policy directives. To force the integration of schools in Little Rock, Arkansas, for example, President Eisenhower simultaneously issued a proclamation and an executive order. Carter relied upon a series of executive orders and executive agreements to negotiate the Iran Hostage Crisis. Presiding over World War II, the Korean War, and the Vietnam War, FDR, Truman, Johnson, and Nixon all issued a wide array of national security directives. Presidents frequently use executive orders and other related tools (including secretarial orders and reorganization plans, which focus exclusively on matters of institutional design) to create and oversee administrative agencies. Presidents can mix and match these unilateral directives to advance their policy goals with considerable ease.

Historical Transformations: National Security Directives as a Policy Tool

Some institutional transformations take place rather suddenly; others develop over decades. The story of the national security directive (NSD) falls into the latter category. The NSD is a policy instrument that emerged in the short window between World War II and the beginning of the Cold War. For many in Washington, the surprise attack on Pearl Harbor in 1941 could be attributed, at least in part, to the lack of coordination among the different branches of the U.S. Armed Forces.

After the war, as tensions with the Soviet Union intensified, President Truman and other policymakers sought to centralize and expand the scope of the military and intelligence-gathering agencies within the federal government. In 1947 Congress passed the National Security Act, which brought the Department of War and the Department of the Navy under the aegis of the secretary of defense and established both the National Security Council (NSC) and the Central Intelligence Agency. According to the act, the mission of the NSC was to "advise the President with respect to the integration of domestic, foreign, and military policies relating to the national security so as to enable the military services and the other departments and agencies of the Government to cooperate more effectively in matters involving the national security." Among its duties, the NSC was "from time to time" to "make such recommendations, and such other reports to the President as it deems appropriate or as the President may require."[15] It was this clause that opened the way for the national security directive, a tool that allows the president to create secret policy.

While some members of Congress worried that the NSC lacked sufficient congressional oversight, most were in favor of creating a tight, impermeable link between the NSC and the president in order to keep a lid on sensitive classified information. In the final legislation, after rejecting a proposal that would have required all NSC reports to be made available to congressional leaders, Congress chose secrecy over transparency. To send NSC reports to Congress would be the equivalent of "reporting to the entire world," according to Representative James Wadsworth.[16] Moreover, supporters of the act were convinced that the American system of government already provided the checks on executive power necessary to prevent any presidential overreach.

The law had unintended consequences, however. Truman began using NSC policy reports as a means of issuing formal orders. After receiving an NSC paper—often commissioned by Truman himself—and deeming its recommendations to be the best course of action, Truman would sign off on the report and thereby turn a proposal into an official policy statement. By transforming a report into a presidential order, Truman invented the national security directive.

Truman's successors formalized the use of national security directives. After using the first of his NSC papers to announce that all existing presidential directives would remain active unless otherwise specified, Eisenhower began issuing national security

Continued on next page

directives to overturn or modify entrenched policies that he disliked. For instance, NSC 162/2 introduced his "New Look" policy on foreign affairs, which aimed to stabilize defense spending and emphasized the use of strategic nuclear weapons over conventional military buildup. This was in many ways a rejection of Truman's NSC 68, which had called for a massive expansion of the entire military.

President Kennedy, too, used national security directives to suit his own purposes. To wit, he began calling them by a new name: National Security Action Memoranda (NSAM).* Kennedy then expanded the use of security directives to include issues not directly related to national security. His administration issued 272 NSAMs that, among other things, formulated policy on sugar quotas in Latin America, U.S. investment in Europe, and development loans for the U.S. Agency for International Development.

By the late 1980s national security directives were under increasing scrutiny. In what would eventually become one of the most notorious political scandals of the era, Reagan used an NSD to support anticommunist forces in Nicaragua, known as the Contras, in overthrowing the ruling Sandinista government. When Congress learned from the press that Reagan had authorized military action without its approval, it promptly passed the Boland Amendment, which explicitly prohibited the executive branch from using military funds in Nicaragua. Intent upon continuing U.S. involvement in Nicaragua, the Reagan administration turned again to an NSD to realize its goals through clandestine means. Instead of tapping military funds to aid the Contras, it negotiated the sale of arms to the Iranian government (violating a U.S. arms embargo on Iran) and passed on the revenues to its Nicaraguan allies.

In the years after the Iran-Contra scandal became public in 1986, Congress attempted to exert some measure of oversight over national security directives. A congressional subcommittee report found that security directives constituted a form of "foreign and military policy-making" that did "not appear to be issued under statutory authority conferred by Congress and thus do not have the force and effect of law."[17] But the administration of George H. W. Bush, in power at the time, would not cooperate with Congress's investigation and refused to provide information on its use of NSDs.

Presidents continue to issue NSDs, but their policy content is neither publicly released nor subject to Freedom of Information Act requests. Even when certain directives are declassified, it is only at the discretion of the presidents who issued them, and usually long after they have left office. Whatever its intentions in 1947, Congress today does very little to oversee the issuance of these unilateral directives.

---

*Under Truman and Eisenhower, security directives were called National Security Council policy papers (NSCs). Kennedy and Johnson dubbed them National Security Action Memoranda (NSAM); Nixon and Ford called them National Security Decision Memorandums (NSDMs); and so on, all the way to the Obama administration's Presidential Policy Directives (PPDs).

9.1.2 *Unilateral Decisions*

For the most part, academic surveys of the presidency's unilateral powers begin and end with the above list of directives—executive orders, proclamations, NSDs, executive agreements, memoranda, and departmental and secretarial orders. However, presidents' unilateral activity is not limited to just these formal mechanisms. In addition to unilateral directives, presidents are empowered to make all sorts of **unilateral decisions** that, even if they don't directly change public policy, nonetheless alter the doings of government in interesting and important ways.

What follows is not an exhaustive list of the unilateral decisions available to presidents but rather a close look at some of the most important—beginning with the pardon power, the only unilateral action mentioned in the Constitution.

PARDONS

The Constitution states that the president "shall have Power to grant Reprieves and Pardons for Offences against the United States, except in Cases of Impeachment."[18] Much like the veto, which presidents use to reject *legislative* actions, **pardons** allow presidents to reject *judicial* actions they deem unfair or contrary to the public interest. Unlike the veto, however, pardons are not subject to legislative review, nor are they subject to judicial review. Absent impeachment and electoral defeat, there is no official recourse to presidents who abuse the pardon power. Once granted, a pardon cannot be revoked.[19]

The Constitution places only two limits on this power. First, the president cannot intervene in civil or state-level proceedings, as pardonable offenses must be "against the United States." Second, the president cannot intervene in impeachments. Beyond these, however, the limitations on presidential pardons have been the subject of continuous debate. Can presidents pardon themselves? Though such a pardon has never been attempted, several legal scholars contend that, by prohibiting pardons in cases of impeachment, the Constitution implies additional restraints, including one against a self-pardon. Others disagree.[20] The legal teams of both Richard Nixon and George H. W. Bush concluded that, because the Constitution does not explicitly state otherwise, self-pardons are in fact legal. Notably, this argument leaves the door open for other controversial pardons, including pardons of the president's friends and family.

The courts have rejected numerous efforts to rein in the pardon power. In *Ex parte Garland* (1866), for example, the Supreme Court ruled that a pardon can be granted any time after an offense is committed—even before legal proceedings—and "Congress can neither limit the effect of his pardon, nor exclude from its exercise any class of offenders."[21] This decision was echoed by the justices in *Schick v. Reed* (1977), who ruled that the pardon power "flows from the Constitution alone" and "cannot be modified, abridged, or diminished by the Congress."[22] A constitutional amendment could effectively circumvent these rulings, but Congress has yet to seriously consider such a proposal.[23]

NATIONAL SECURITY CLASSIFICATIONS

For most of American history, decisions about what information to keep secret, from whom, and for how long were left to the military.[24] Shortly before the U.S. entry into World War II, however, President Roosevelt formalized White House control over national security classifications. Executive Order 8381 asserted the president's obligation to "[protect] against the general dissemination of information" pertaining to sensitive military operations.[25] So doing, the order established standards for military and executive branch officials to follow when protecting information, standards that would be revised and expanded by subsequent administrations. The most recent guidelines, created by President Obama in Executive Order 13526, mention eight broad categories of classifiable information, including, among others, "foreign government information" and "scientific, technological, or economic matters relating to the national security." Information can only be classified by authorized individuals, which the order specifies as the president, vice president, and "agency heads and officials designated by the President."[26]

Congress has occasionally sought to qualify—but never fully curtail—presidents' classification authority. In 2010, for example, Congress enacted the Reducing Over-Classification Act, which required executive branch inspectors general to assess their agencies' compliance with classification policies and determine whether information was being kept at a "more restricted level than is warranted."[27] If Congress wants to declassify specific documents, it can do so through a vote in the House or Senate intelligence committee. But more often, since members of Congress do not know whether desired documents exist, members opt to request—but not require—the president or a relevant agency to undergo a "declassification review," in which all documents pertaining to a particular subject are surveyed and made public to the maximum extent possible.[28]

Typically, presidents wait considerable amounts of time to declassify information; and then, they do so only after careful deliberation. In 1999, for example, the Clinton administration agreed to declassify thousands of documents on U.S. involvement in Augusto Pinochet's 1973 military coup in Chile.[29] Under normal circumstances, Clinton would have preferred the documents—detailing numerous human rights abuses sponsored by the U.S. government—remain concealed. Under increased pressure from international groups who wanted to see Pinochet convicted, however, Clinton was ultimately persuaded to make them public.[30]

COMPLIANCE DECISIONS

When members of Congress want something from the executive branch—whether it be information, sworn testimony, or influence over policy implementation—the president has the final say over whether to grant or deny their request. In most instances, presidents opt to comply, particularly when the stakes are low and the request comes from co-partisans. Occasionally, though, presidents instruct their administrations to ignore or disobey the demands of Congress.

One such example occurred in 2001, when Congress launched an investigation into an energy task force assembled by the George W. Bush administration, alleging that Bush's supporters in the oil industry had unfairly influenced the task force's deliberations. Ordered to disclose documents about task force meetings, the Bush administration flatly refused, explaining that the executive branch could not function without "confidentiality of communication among a president, a vice president, the president's other senior advisers and others."[31] Congress sued for the documents, but a federal court denied their request in December 2002. Unable to obtain information from the White House, the General Accounting Office (GAO) suspended the investigation in 2003. "This is the first and only time that we have not been able to work out a reasoned and reasonable accommodation to get information that we need to do our job," said the head of the GAO. "We hope and expect that this is an isolated instance, but only time will tell."[32]

It was certainly not an isolated instance. In fact, this sort of defiance was routinized during the Trump administration. In 2019, Trump ordered all senior members of his administration, current and former, to defy congressional subpoenas related to his first impeachment inquiry. "We're fighting all the subpoenas," said Trump. "These aren't, like, impartial people. The Democrats are trying to win in 2020."[33] Trump, of course, was eventually impeached, and the testimony of some career civil servants who refused to abide Trump's orders played an important role. Still, many other career appointees working within the Trump administration who had critical information about Trump's dealings in Ukraine followed Trump's orders, refused to come before Congress, and thereby weakened the Democrats' case for conviction, which the Senate refused to deliver.

The president's unilateral decisions regarding compliance, of course, are not absolute. The Constitution does not grant the president the authority to ignore congressional oversight, and compliance can be mandated by the courts. Nevertheless, when presidents decide not to comply, their refusal can complicate congressional oversight efforts (as in the case of Trump's impeachment) or altogether defeat them (as in the case of Bush's energy commission).

MILITARY DECISIONS

Presidents enjoy considerable independence when conducting foreign policy, especially as it pertains to their role as commander in chief of the military. Though Congress has substantial constitutional authority over war-making, military deployments are strategized within the White House. And through successive delegations of authority like the 2001 Authorization for Use of Military Force (see chapter 8), Congress has expanded the range of unilateral decisions available to the commander in chief.

In the conduct of war, presidents exercise their unilateral powers with abandon. Without prior sanction from either Congress or the courts, presidents decide whether to launch new strikes against foreign countries, to escalate ongoing military ventures abroad, or to draw down existing troop deployments. As we discuss at length in chapter 15, presidents must navigate a thicket of international and domestic constraints when contemplating military action abroad. Still, the ultimate decision—or more exactly, the confluence of many decisions—to either send troops to fight and die or bring them home rests with the president.

Consider the actions taken by Biden during his first year in office. Following through on a campaign promise, he brought the nation's twenty-year war in Afghanistan to a close without ever securing Congress's formal consent. He simply issued the necessary orders and left it to the adjoining branches of government to try to fashion a response. Biden's unilateral activities also concerned matters of ongoing military policy, as when he decided on new standards for how and whether strikes should occur. Whereas President Trump had vowed to launch counterattacks against any nation or group that killed U.S. personnel, Biden set a lower standard, instead launching counterstrikes against both lethal *and nonlethal* attacks. Such a standard, the Biden administration believed, would more effectively deter assaults on American military facilities abroad.[34]

Actions like these are not catalogued and counted like executive orders or proclamations. Nor are they subject to the same sorts of formal reporting requirements. Still, presidents regularly command the military to do things without Congress's formal approval. And often, these commands yield changes in practice and policy that Congress, left to its devices, would not legislate. Presidential decisions over military action, much like their other decisions over whom to pardon, which secrets to reveal, and when to comply with Congress, populate a domain of unilateral activity that is a good deal more capacious than the existing scholarship of the subject supposes and that, in an era of partisan polarization and congressional gridlock, plays an increasingly important role in redefining the doings of government.

9.1.3 Trends in Unilateral Activity

A defining feature of presidential powers during the modern era is a propensity, and a capacity, to go it alone. Presidents have used unilateral directives to intervene in a whole host of policy arenas. In domestic affairs, for example, decades before the passage of the landmark 1964 Civil Rights Act and 1965 Voting Rights Act, presidents initiated the federal government's involvement in civil rights by creating the Fair Employment Practices Committee (and its subsequent incarnations) and by desegregating the military—a history surveyed in some detail in chapter 2. In foreign policy, without any prior congressional authorization, recent presidents have launched military strikes against Bosnia, Grenada, Haiti, Iran, Libya, Lebanon, Panama, Somalia, and Syria.

It may seem puzzling, then, that the trend line for the issuance of executive orders—the most well-known of presidents' unilateral directives—points downward. Partly, this is an artifact of what counts as an executive order. During the first half of the twentieth century, all sorts of executive orders were issued that attended to decidedly mundane administrative tasks, such as allowing individual bureaucrats to delay their mandatory retirement. Still, when considering the subset of executive orders that advance substantively important policy, a similar downward trend carries through most of the modern era.

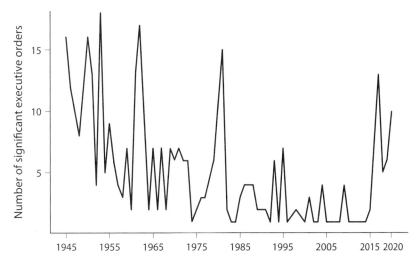

FIGURE 9.2. Significant executive orders, 1945–2020. The figure presents the number of executive orders issued each year that received coverage in the *New York Times*. Scholars use coverage in the *Times* to distinguish executive orders with policy import. While the total number of orders varies greatly, the overall trend is slightly downward.

Figure 9.2 plots the total number of executive orders issued each year that appeared in the *New York Times*, a rough measure of their policy import. Throughout this seventy-five-year period, we see presidents issuing fewer than twenty significant executive orders each year, the exact number varying greatly between newly elected and lame-duck administrations. Nonetheless, a slight decline can be detected over the time period as presidents issue fewer significant orders later in the series than they do earlier in the series.

None of this is evidence, however, that presidents are less likely to act unilaterally than they used to. Quite the opposite. For one reason, the size of the *New York Times* news section has shrunk noticeably over the past half century—decreasing the odds that more recent executive orders will be included in the newspaper. More importantly, though, executive orders are just one of the many options presidents have when crafting a unilateral directive. Tasks once carried out via executive order might be labeled differently today, but they have no less policy significance.

As we've seen, naming conventions make it difficult to use executive orders as a metric for evaluating presidential use of unilateral directives. President George W. Bush, for example, relied heavily upon his unilateral powers in virtually all facets of his War on Terror. In one unprecedented move, Bush issued a "military order"—a unilateral directive to the armed forces—that created military tribunals to try noncitizens suspected of terrorism. Suspects were charged, prosecuted, judged, and sentenced not by judges and juries but by military officials. Though the two are technically distinct, the "military order" was listed as an "executive order" on the Bush White House website and likewise published in the

Federal Register.[35] But, because of the particular form it took, the order was not included in figure 9.2 nor any similar compilation of significant executive orders.

Sometimes, presidents' unilateral actions are so distinctive as to defy categorization altogether. Obama's work on education policy constitutes one of the most creative—and brazen—efforts to bypass Congress. When he assumed office, he expressed interest in dramatically revising the 2001 No Child Left Behind Act, the signature policy achievement of his predecessor. Rather than work with Congress to reauthorize it, however, Obama exploited a loophole in the existing law, allowing him to dismantle it and rebuild education policy not through Congress but through state governments across the nation. By the end of his presidency, Obama had unilaterally issued waivers to nearly every state and the District of Columbia, thereby exempting them from their obligation to meet goals under the act.* Rather than simply grant unconditional relief to states, however, Obama used the waivers as leverage to encourage—some would say blackmail—state governments to adopt education policies more to the president's liking. In so doing, states all around the country committed themselves to Obama's education initiatives, such as teacher evaluations based on student performance.[36]

Needless to say, actions like these are difficult to explain using numbers alone. For a more expansive display of unilateral trends, however, we can turn to executive agreements, which are more emblematic of presidents' unilateral activity in the last half century. During the first 50 years of the nation's history, treaties (which require Senate ratification) outnumbered executive agreements (which do not) by two to one: between 1789 and 1839, presidents signed 60 treaties but issued just 27 executive agreements. Over the next 50 years, presidents signed 215 treaties and issued 238 executive agreements. And between 1889 and 1933, presidents signed 431 treaties and issued 804 executive agreements.

In the 90 years that followed, executive agreements vastly outnumbered treaties. Figure 9.3 shows the total number of times each foreign policy tool was used under each president since FDR.[37] During his two terms in office, for example, President Obama negotiated over a thousand executive agreements but only several dozen treaties. During his two presidential terms, President George W. Bush signed almost 2,000 executive agreements but only 136 treaties. In keeping with his inward-looking worldview, Trump signed hardly any international trade agreements during the first two years of his presidency. Still, like all of his predecessors, nearly all of those that he did successfully negotiate took the form of executive agreements rather than treaties.

Recent empirical scholarship has attempted to build a more comprehensive measure of the many ways in which presidents exercise their unilateral powers. One such study collates

---

* The Heritage Foundation blasted the waivers, saying they "pose serious legal questions, circumvent the normal legislative process, significantly grow federal intervention in local school policy, and fail to offer genuine relief to states." Conservative groups were especially angered by the waivers because several drafts of a revised No Child Left Behind law were under consideration in Congress at the time. See Lindsey Burke, "No Child Left Behind Waivers: Bogus Relief, Genuine Overreach," *Heritage Foundation*, September 5, 2012, http://www.heritage.org/research/reports/2012/09/no-child-left-behind-waivers-bogus-relief-genuine-overreach.

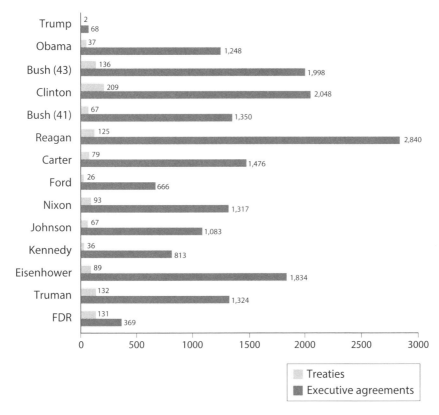

FIGURE 9.3. U.S. treaties and executive agreements, 1933–2018. The number of treaties includes those concluded during the indicated span of years. Some of these treaties did not receive the consent of the Senate. Because of varying definitions of what comprises an executive agreement, the numbers in the table are approximate. *Sources:* 1933–2008: Harold W. Stanley and Richard G. Niemi, *Vital Statistics on American Politics, 2015–2016* (Washington, DC: Congressional Quarterly Press, 2015), table 9–1, 326; 2009–18: Jeffrey S. Peake, "The Decline of Treaties? Obama, Trump, and the Politics of International Agreements," April 17, 2018, https://papers.ssrn.com/sol3/papers.cfm?abstract_id=3153840.

nearly 34,000 executive orders, proclamations, memoranda, public land orders, executive agreements, and agency directives issued by presidents between 1946 and 2020. After accounting for the policy significance of these directives, the resulting trend lines point upward. "Prior to 1990," the authors report, "presidents issued an average of 50 significant directives per year; since then, the annual average more than doubled to about 123."[38]

Pardons, meanwhile, are an odd exception to presidents' growing reliance on unilateral powers. Whereas early presidents frequently issued pardons as displays of mercy toward political and military enemies, modern presidents are far less likely to do so. The first series of pardons was granted by George Washington, who forgave the violent protestors involved in the Whiskey Rebellion in 1794.[39] Similarly, as mentioned in the introduction to this chapter, Abraham Lincoln offered pardons to Confederate soldiers following the end

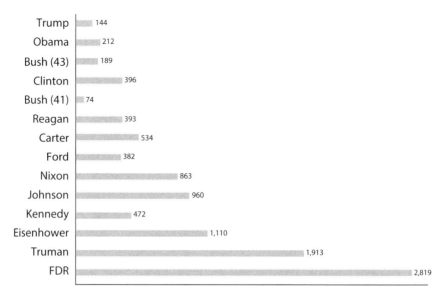

FIGURE 9.4. Presidential pardons, FDR to Trump. Some presidents were prolific with their pardons. More recent presidents issued them sparingly. The majority of pardons issued by FDR, Truman, and Carter involved individuals who committed wartime offenses. *Source:* U.S. Department of Justice.

of the Civil War. FDR pardoned everyone convicted of sedition and other violations of the Espionage Act during World War I,[40] and Truman pardoned more than 1,500 convicts who served in World War II.[41] Similarly, Jimmy Carter spent his first day in office pardoning individuals who evaded the Vietnam War draft and who were convicted under the Selective Service Act.[42]

But as Figure 9.4 shows, the decline in presidential pardons has been steep. In large part, this trend can be explained by the end of the twentieth century's major wars and the move to an all-volunteer military. It is also true, however, that presidents fulfill a much smaller fraction of pardon requests than they once did—a remnant, some argue, of the politics of the war on crime in the 1980s, during which time the perception of being "soft on crime" could damage a president's reputation.[43]

Ironically, while presidential pardons have fallen out of use for most individuals convicted of a crime, they have become far more popular for a different set of criminal offenders: the president's friends and political allies. Beginning in the Nixon administration, and continuing for presidents in both parties, a new trend of "back-door" pardons took shape. Pardons have been routinely granted to individuals associated with the president's administration—such as George H. W. Bush's 1992 pardons of several men involved in the Iran-Contra affair—or with the president's campaign—such as Bill Clinton's pardon of Marc Rich, an international commodities trader charged with tax fraud, whose wife had contributed almost half a million dollars to Clinton's presidential library. Often, presidents issue these pardons at the very end of their terms, hoping to attract as little attention as possible. Clinton's pardon of Marc Rich, for example, took place the day of his successor's inauguration.[44]

The Trump administration was no exception to this new trend. Despite receiving thousands of pardon requests in his single term in office, Trump issued 144 pardons—116 of which took place in the final month of his presidency.[45] In addition to these pardons, Trump also commuted the sentences of 94 individuals. Among the most controversial actions was the commutation he granted to Roger Stone, his long-time friend and campaign operative. Stone was found guilty of obstructing justice, lying to Congress, and witness tampering in relation to the investigation of the Trump campaign's ties to Russia. In an official statement, Trump called Stone "a victim of the Russia Hoax that the Left and its allies in the media perpetrated."[46] Stone's commutation was largely viewed as a reward for not cooperating with the investigation. Despite the obvious opportunities for corruption the pardon power creates, however, its placement in the Constitution makes it nearly impossible to reform or revoke.

9.2 The Legal Basis for Unilateral Action

Unilaterally, presidents can essentially write and implement their own laws. Who gave them this power? Why do the courts allow presidents to exercise powers clearly reserved for Congress in Article I? To answer these questions, recall from chapter 1 that ours is a system of both separated and shared powers; though Congress has lawmaking abilities, no branch of government is truly independent in its sphere of influence. Recall too that the Constitution, though precise in some ways, is remarkably ambiguous in others. The vesting clause of Article II states that "the executive Power shall be vested in a President of the United States of America." What exactly is the executive power? Does it grant the president specific abilities, or is it merely a descriptive title of the office? Presidents have flourished amid this ambiguity, using it to claim the possession of "inherent powers" mentioned nowhere in the Constitution.

Though executive authority has undergone decades of reinterpretation and expansion, it is not unlimited. From the earliest days of the Union, this authority has been subject to the same primary constraints. In the words of Associate Supreme Court Justice Hugo Black, "The President's power, if any . . . must stem either from an act of Congress or from the Constitution itself."[47] Understanding the legal basis for unilateral action, then, requires us to look to the Constitution and Congress for authorizing language that sometimes applies in the regular course of governing and other times, we shall see, applies uniquely during periods of national emergency.*

---

*To clarify, this section considers whether unilateral actions are "legal" in the sense that they will (or won't) survive in court. Unilateral actions are not "legal" in the same way that laws and the Constitution are, as they do not confer rights or responsibilities that presidents are compelled to uphold.

9.2.1 Constitutional Authority

Three clauses in Article II establish the legal basis of many unilateral actions (see chapter 1). The first is the vesting clause, which grants "executive power" to the president. The Constitution further stipulates that "The President shall be Commander-in-Chief of the Army and Navy of the United States." Finally, the president "shall take Care that the Laws be faithfully executed."

To some readers, these clauses may not confer broad authority to the president. In particular, the take-care clause seems to relegate the president to the role of congressional clerk, faithfully administering the actions of the legislative branch. But to other readers—particularly those with an incentive to bolster the presidency—these clauses form the foundation of the president's inherent powers. President Lincoln believed that the commander-in-chief clause, combined with the take-care clause, granted a "War Power" which he used to suspend habeas corpus and seize merchant ships during the Civil War. Just two months after the bombing of Pearl Harbor, President Franklin D. Roosevelt invoked the commander-in-chief clause to relocate and intern approximately 110,000 people of Japanese ancestry, more than half of whom were American citizens. President Truman signed Executive Order 10340 to take possession of steel mills amid a wartime labor dispute; his solicitor general attempted to defend the order in court using a combination of the vesting clause, the commander-in-chief clause, and the take-care clause.

Of course, these sorts of claims are only as persuasive as the courts are willing to admit. One of the earliest examples of the Supreme Court recognizing a president's unilateral power comes from the *Prize* cases. In 1861, shortly after the surrender of Fort Sumter, President Lincoln placed a naval blockade on Confederate states. The blockades were announced and enforced without assistance from Congress, which had yet to formally declare war on the Confederacy. In the absence of such a declaration, the legality of the blockade was questioned, and the Supreme Court was forced to intervene. Ultimately, the Court sided with Lincoln on the grounds that "the President was bound to meet [the war] in the shape it presented itself, without waiting for Congress to baptize it with a name."[48] This decision relied heavily on the commander-in-chief clause, which the justices recognized not just as a title but as a legitimate and compelling source of presidential authority.

In *United States v. Curtiss-Wright* (1936), the Supreme Court similarly upheld the president's unilateral authority in foreign affairs. At issue was the Curtiss-Wright Export Corporation's violation of one of President Franklin Roosevelt's proclamations that barred the sale of munitions to countries engaged in armed conflict. Curtiss-Wright challenged the proclamation and claimed that Congress had delegated too much of its authority to the president. The Court disagreed. According to seven of the deciding justices, the Constitution made the president "the sole organ of the federal government in the field of international relations";[49] and on this basis, they deemed the proclamation constitutional.

This sort of logic applies not only to executive orders and proclamations but to executive agreements as well. In *United States v. Pink* (1942), the Court upheld President Roosevelt's authority to transfer funds from Soviet Russia to the United States. (The transfer was part of a larger set of agreements known as the Litvinov Assignment, in which the United States recognized the legitimacy of the Soviet Union.) In siding with Roosevelt, the Court acknowledged that executive agreements have the full force of treaties ratified by the Senate.

These rulings—*Prize*, *Curtiss-Wright*, and *Pink*—describe unilateral authority, at least in the realm of foreign affairs, as an integral part of the institutional presidency. This authority does not derive straightforwardly from congressional action. Rather, it comes from a combination of presidential initiative and judicial readings of Article II powers and responsibilities.

9.2.2 Statutory Authority

The Constitution, however, is not the only source of power for presidents. Unilateral actions are strongest—that is, most likely to survive legal challenges—when combined with congressional delegations of authority. This combination also allows presidents to reinterpret and transform existing laws into sweeping assertions of executive power. Thus, it is common for presidents to cite existing laws when acting unilaterally.

Consider President FDR's Executive Order 6102, which instructed the government to confiscate large amounts of gold coin held by private individuals. The order was a bold response to the Great Depression, at which time the government could not print paper money without holding an equal supply of gold. As justification, the order's first line cited "the authority vested in [the president] by Section 5(b)" of the amended Trading with the Enemy Act of 1917, which allowed him to regulate the "hoarding, melting, or earmarking of gold or silver coin."[50] However unprecedented the order may have seemed, it derived its authority from an act of Congress.

When presidents do not cite Congress in their unilateral actions, they put themselves at a higher risk of being challenged in court. Thankfully for presidents' agendas, however, the courts have proven themselves reliable defenders of executive power. For example, in Executive Order 10925—ordering government contractors to take "affirmative action" in hiring and promoting minorities—Kennedy cited only the authority given to him "by the Constitution and statutes of the United States." He failed to mention any particular statutes. The Civil Rights Act, of course, would not be passed until 1964, and Kennedy could not cite it in his 1961 order. Fortunately for Kennedy, the Supreme Court upheld order 10925 using, of all things, the Federal Property and Administrative Services Act. Congress passed this law in 1949 to establish the General Services Administration and improve the efficiency of government operations. In the law's text, Congress allowed the president to "prescribe such policies and directives . . . as he shall deem necessary to effectuate the provisions of said Act." According to the Court, affirmative action qualified as such a policy, and Kennedy's order was upheld.

In other cases, members of the Court went even further out of their way to uphold the president's unilateral powers. In *United States v. Midwest Oil Company* (1915), the Court affirmed the president's ability to withdraw public lands from private acquisition without citing any congressional delegation of authority. The Court decided that "the long acquiescence in a governmental practice raises a presumption of authority."[51] In other words, because Congress knew about similar unilateral actions taken by other presidents, its continued inaction was a sign of tacit consent. Under what is known as the "**doctrine of acquiescence**," Congress need not always give the president express approval to act. Sometimes, it need only remain silent.

When contemplating the legality of unilateral actions, it may be best to ask what presidents cannot do, rather than what they can. Combining ambiguous constitutional language with broad delegations of power obtained over time, some have concluded that the only obvious power "which the president lacks is that of dissolving Congress entirely and calling new elections."[52]

9.2.3 Emergency Powers

Presidents are most powerful during times of national crisis or emergency. Confronted with imminent danger—war, for example—the public judges its leaders by the strength and resolve they display. All too often, national crises increase the public's tolerance for executive overreach, and leaders are given permission to act in ways which, under normal conditions, would not be tolerated.

Throughout history, American presidents have used emergency powers to act decisively when it matters most. The first president to issue a formal emergency proclamation was Woodrow Wilson, who was concerned about water transportation policy during World War I. Wilson was scrupulous about obtaining congressional approval for his actions; in April 1918, Congress passed the Overman Act to expand his control over the wartime economy. When the war was over, Wilson instructed Congress to repeal the authority it had granted.

Presidents since Wilson, however, have been less conservative in their exercise of emergency powers. The second emergency proclamation came from Franklin D. Roosevelt, who relied on the Trading with the Enemy Act of 1917 to temporarily shut down the banking system during the Great Depression. This proclamation was unprecedented in two ways. First, the Trading with the Enemy Act was designed specifically for wartime crises, which the Depression certainly was not. By citing it, Roosevelt had unknowingly created a precedent in which presidents could rely on any statutory authority to meet the needs of any crisis. Second, Roosevelt did not relinquish any authority once the crisis was over, and his proclamation remained in effect for more than forty years after it was signed.

Presidents since have declared numerous more emergencies and thereby laid claim to new statutory powers. Several laws were passed in response to the legitimate crises of World War II, the Korean War, and the Gulf of Tonkin incident, each of which augmented presidential powers. The Defense Production Act (DPA), for example, was passed in 1950 as a response to the Korean War. During an emergency, whether war-related or not, it allows the president to require American manufacturers to produce certain necessary goods, including weapons and ammunition. Statutes such as these began to accumulate throughout the 1950s and 1960s. By 1973, the list of emergency statutes available to the president exceeded 470.[53]

Recognizing this startling growth in presidential emergency powers, in 1976 Congress passed the National Emergencies Act (NEA), which formalized the emergency declaration process without hampering the president's ability to act deliberately in a crisis. It did so, first, by deactivating some of the president's emergency powers and returning most to a dormant status. (Since its passage, the number of available emergency powers has diminished from 470 to 123.)[54] Under the law, presidents also were required to state which specific statutes they intend to use before the statutes would be reactivated. Further, the law stated that emergency declarations will automatically expire after one year unless renewed by the president. Finally, the NEA granted Congress the power to overturn an emergency declaration with simple majorities in both chambers.

Though the office's emergency powers are smaller in scope than they were before the NEA, modern presidents have proven quite capable of utilizing and even politicizing the remaining 123 statutes. In 2019, President Trump declared a national emergency concerning immigration across the U.S.-Mexico border, calling it a "humanitarian crisis that threatens core national security interests."[55] He then made the unprecedented move of issuing Proclamation 9844, "Declaring a National Emergency Concerning the Southern Border of the United States." The proclamation specifically cited 10 U.S.C. 2808 (a): "Construction authority in the event of a declaration of war or national emergency." This statute allows presidents to "authorize Secretaries of the military departments to undertake military construction projects . . . within the total amount of funds that have been appropriated for military construction."[56] Thus, Trump was empowered to divert more than $15 billion of government funds, most of which Congress had authorized for the Department of Defense, to instead support the president's border wall.

The declaration and proclamation came in the aftermath of Trump's failure to convince Congress to pay the $25 billion necessary for border wall construction. In his campaign announcement speech, Trump had promised to "build a great wall," saying of Mexican immigrants: "They're bringing drugs. They're bringing crime. They're rapists." After his election, however, Democrats took a clear stance against the wall; House Speaker Nancy Pelosi called it "immoral, expensive, [and] unwise."[57]

Tensions between Trump and Congress peaked when, in December 2018, Trump refused to sign an appropriations bill without adequate funding for his border wall, and the government shut down. A government shutdown occurs when Congress fails to pass a federal budget for the upcoming fiscal year, and all nonessential federal employees are furloughed until Congress reaches an agreement. The 2018 shutdown affected more than 800,000 federal employees and lasted 34 days—making it the longest shutdown in American history. Trump, meanwhile, seemed willing to extend the shutdown indefinitely, or until he received funding for his wall. "We are totally prepared for a very long shutdown," Trump said, "and this is our only chance that we'll ever have, in our opinion . . . to get great border security."[58] After 34 days, on January 25, 2019, the government reopened with a spending bill that included just $1.375 billion for border security—far from the $25 billion Trump wanted. He responded by issuing Proclamation 9844.

Of all the national emergencies declared since the NEA, Trump's was the only one to obtain funding for an initiative which Congress had explicitly weighed and rejected.[59] Through emergency powers, Trump circumvented the will of Congress and left what appears to be a permanent mark on the southern border. But though Trump's actions were unprecedented, focusing only on his presidency ignores larger, unsettling trends in emergency powers. From 1976 to 2020, 69 national emergencies have been declared. And— completely unknown to most Americans—over half of these emergencies have been renewed annually and thus remain in effect.[60] The oldest of these emergencies originated with President Carter and his response to the Iran Hostage Crisis. Two emergencies were declared after the terrorist attacks on September 11, 2001, and both persist.

Why have presidents continued to renew these emergencies for so long? Given the statutory powers that emergencies grant, a better question might be: Why would presidents voluntarily let emergencies expire? Once emergency powers have been legally obtained, presidents have little incentive to relinquish them. It should be emphasized that, as Franklin Roosevelt discovered, the delegated emergency powers need not match the emergency at hand. Once a president declares an emergency (and states which powers he intends to use), the floodgates open. So long as the declaration remains in effect, the accompanying powers belong to the presidency.

It seems, then, that the very problem that inspired the NEA—namely, the unchecked growth of the president's emergency powers—has become problematic once again. Why has Congress failed to terminate or overturn existing national emergencies? One provision of the NEA requires Congress to meet every six months to discuss and vote on existing emergencies. In the more than forty years since the law was signed, Congress has never met for this purpose. Presidents, meanwhile, can repel congressional efforts to roll back their emergency powers. Though Congress can terminate an emergency declaration with a majority vote in both houses, it requires significantly more votes to overturn a presidential veto (see chapter 8). Hence, in 2019, Congress passed two resolutions to overturn Trump's border wall proclamations. Trump vetoed both resolutions, and Congress failed to achieve the two-thirds majority necessary to override.

What about the courts? For reasons that will be properly examined in chapter 11, courts tend to be surprisingly deferential to executive power. In *INS v. Chadha* (1983), the Supreme Court weakened Congress's ability to oversee and overturn emergency declarations.[61] Originally, the NEA allowed Congress to overturn an emergency declaration using a concurrent resolution—which presidents cannot veto. Thus, Congress would have a "legislative veto" over emergency powers with a simple majority of votes. In a 7–2 decision, however, the justices in *INS* stripped Congress of the legislative veto, arguing that it violated constitutional separation of powers. Since then, the courts have done little to challenge presidents' emergency declarations. In 2019, the Supreme Court upheld Trump's border wall emergency on the grounds that the plaintiff—the Sierra Club—lacked "cause of action" to challenge it. It was not until Biden assumed office that the construction of the border wall finally ended.

9.3 Institutional Checks on Unilateral Action

Presidents cannot advance every aspect of their policy agenda by decree. Should they proceed without statutory or constitutional authority, the checks and balances that define our system of governance can come into play. The courts can overturn the president's actions, just as Congress can amend them, cut funding for their operations, or eliminate them outright. Even in those moments when presidential power reaches its zenith— namely, during times of national crisis—judicial and congressional prerogatives may be asserted.[62] In important respects, the politics of unilateral action are informed by inter- and intrabranch struggles over information, money, bureaucratic compliance, succession, and public support. Let's consider each in turn.

9.3.1 Reporting Requirements

In foreign affairs, the president enjoys important informational advantages over Congress and the general public. This is especially true in foreign affairs, where a massive network of national security advisors, an entire intelligence community, and diplomats and ambassadors stationed all over the globe report more or less directly to the president. Members of Congress, on the other hand, rely on presidents and those within their administrations to share information. Recognizing that presidents are not always forthcoming, Congress has established numerous reporting requirements.[63] Though intended to mitigate Congress's information deficits, these requirements have not restored a level playing field between the two branches of government.

For stretches of American history, Congress lacked basic information on what presidents had even done. Before FDR's first term, Congress could not take for granted that presidents would publicly release the contents of their policy directives. Though presidents issued literally thousands of executive orders, proclamations, and rules and regulations, they were not required to publish them, and no central clearinghouse existed for lawmakers to review them. With the growth of the federal government came considerable confusion, as legislative enactments conflicted with unilateral directives, judges and bureaucrats wondered what the law of the day was, and executive departments struggled to keep track of one another's doings.

Recognizing that the "number and importance of administrative regulations [had] enormously increased" and that no system was in place to classify or catalogue them, Harvard Law dean Erwin Griswold warned at the time that the very principles of limited government and checks and balances were imperiled. "It might well be said that our government is not wholly free from Bentham's censure of the tyrant who punishes men for disobedience to laws or orders which he had kept them from the knowledge of."[64]

To correct this state of affairs, in 1935 Congress enacted the **Federal Register Act**, which required the Government Printing Office, in collaboration with the National Archives, to publish all executive orders, proclamations, agency rules, and regulations; later, notices and proposed rules were added to the list. The act offered a pragmatic solution to a growing administrative problem. The act also had important consequences for the workings of the nation's system of separated powers: by promptly publishing and cataloguing unilateral directives, the act at last established a system for members of Congress to oversee—and to check—presidential policymaking.

Almost forty years later Congress revisited these issues, this time addressing the issuance of executive agreements. As the Federal Register Act does not require presidents to publish accords reached with foreign countries, Congress often was left in the dark about new trade or security agreements brokered by presidents.* During the 1950s and 1960s, for example, the Eisenhower, Kennedy, and Johnson administrations negotiated a series of executive agreements with the government of South Vietnam, but Congress did not learn of their existence until Nixon assumed office.

To address this situation, in 1972 Congress passed the **Case Act**, requiring presidents to report every "international agreement, other than a treaty," within sixty days. In 1977, and again in 1979, Congress passed additional legislation that reduced the reporting period to twenty days and expanded the scope of the Case Act to include international agreements brokered by executive agencies and departments. Unlike executive orders and proclamations, however, executive agreements still do not have a uniform classification or numbering scheme, making it difficult for politicians (not to mention scholars) to track them.

Congress has also passed laws that impose reporting requirements on military actions. The most famous of these, the 1973 **War Powers Resolution**, attempted to limit the president's ability to freely decide when, and for how long, troops would be sent abroad. The resolution required presidents to consult with Congress "in every possible instance" before introducing military forces into foreign hostilities and required that troops be withdrawn if Congress did not authorize the action within sixty or ninety days. Having to obtain congressional authorization, it was supposed, would induce presidents to supply members of Congress with information about the costs and benefits of military action; should members disagree with the president's decision to enter into the conflict, Congress could then force an end to the military campaign.

Though the Federal Register Act, the Case Act, and the War Powers Resolution have helped Congress monitor the exercise of a president's unilateral powers, problems nonetheless persist. Presidents regularly ignore the War Powers reporting requirements;[65] they relabel executive agreements as "arrangements" or "accords" in order to circumvent the Case Act;[66] and they declare **executive privilege**—the claim of immunity from subpoenas

---

* For more on the conditions under which presidents issue executive agreements versus treaties, see Glen Krutz and Jeffrey Peake, *Treaty Politics and the Rise of Executive Agreements: International Commitments in a System of Shared Powers* (Ann Arbor: University of Michigan Press, 2011).

and other informational requests made by the legislative and judicial branches—to conceal their efforts to construct and implement public policy.[67] Having been told that they have a legal obligation to formally report all "binding" executive agreements, presidents and their underlings now regularly classify these agreements as "nonbinding"—despite the fact that roughly equivalent enforcement mechanisms apply—in order to guard their activities from congressional oversight.[68]

Meanwhile, one of the most striking examples of executive secrecy continues unchecked: national security directives, which are kept confidential and are nearly impossible for members of Congress to regulate. In the past several decades, presidents have used national security directives to escalate the war in Vietnam, commission studies on the Star Wars missile defense system, direct the nation's efforts to combat the international drug trade, develop national policy on telecommunications security, and define the nation's relationship with the former Soviet Union. Moreover, we only know about these particular actions because presidents, on their own accord, declassified them.

Presidents can also use the pretext of war to avoid sharing information with the other branches of government. On November 13, 2001, Bush announced that his administration had the authority to try any non-American citizen determined to be a member of Al-Qaeda or involved in international terrorism using military courts. This Presidential Military Order empowered the secretary of defense to decide where suspected terrorists and their tribunals would be held. The order also forbade suspected terrorists from seeking redress in international or domestic courts. By holding and prosecuting suspected terrorists in military commissions, Bush restricted the amount of information Congress, the courts, and the public received about detainees' charges and treatment.

Detainees have challenged their status as "enemy combatants" in court several times, leading to cases such as *Hamdan v. Rumsfeld* (2006), in which the U.S. Supreme Court ruled that military commissions at Guantánamo Bay under the military order were illegal under the Uniform Code of Military Justice.[69] The Bush administration, however, continued to use military commissions to try suspected terrorists. Upon assuming office, Obama did not change course. In February 2009, he filed papers declaring that detainees then held in Afghanistan were "enemy combatants" and could not use U.S. courts to seek release. A few weeks later, Obama announced that the Justice Department would no longer use the term "enemy combatants" but would continue the policy of detaining people affiliated with terrorist organizations.

Obviously, to check executive power, legislators and judges must know what presidents have done. It is of considerable consequence and concern, then, when presidents conceal information from Congress, citing national security concerns or executive privilege.

9.3.2 Budgets

In the politics of unilateral action, Congress holds an ace up its sleeve: appropriations. When a unilateral action requires funding, a president's directive requires positive action by Congress. After issuing a unilateral directive, then, presidents must build and sustain coalitions that will deliver the needed financial support. Should they fail, orders may not translate into action.

A failure to secure congressional appropriations can spell the demise of a presidential initiative, very much including overseas military operations. In 1976, attempting to restore America's international reputation after the collapse of South Vietnam, President Gerald Ford began covert operations to shape the outcome of the Angolan Civil War. Wary of another foreign entanglement, however, Congress passed an appropriations act stipulating that no funds would be used "for any activities involving Angola other than intelligence gathering."[70] Four months later, when Congress made the appropriations ban permanent, President Ford was forced to suspend all military action in and aid to the country.

In other instances, the need to secure congressional appropriations forces presidents to scale back their policy ambitions. A decade after Ford's failure in Angola, President Ronald Reagan sought to deliver military aid to the Nicaraguan Contras in their guerrilla war against their socialist Sandinista government. As previously discussed in this chapter's Historical Transformations feature, Reagan was only able to do so by issuing a national security directive that diverted funds illegally obtained from an Iranian arms deal. The reason for Reagan's backdoor dealing was simple: Congress had passed an appropriations bill that forbade "supporting, directly or indirectly, military or paramilitary operations in Nicaragua."[71] Had Congress not stood in his way, it is likely Reagan would have sought direct intervention in Nicaragua, or at least substantially more aid than he obtained from Iran.

For at least three reasons, however, Congress's grip on the purse strings does not altogether erase the influence that presidents wield through their unilateral powers. First, and most obviously, not all unilateral directives require appropriations. For instance, George W. Bush's orders took immediate effect when he decided to include farm-raised salmon in federal counts under the Endangered Species Act, removing twenty-three of twenty-seven salmon species from the list of endangered species and thereby opening vast tracts of federal waters to public development.[72] When presidents create a rule or revise an existing law, their orders are, to borrow Neustadt's term, "self-executing," and the appropriations process no longer binds.

Second, as discussed in chapter 8, the appropriations process is a good deal more streamlined than the legislative process. It has to be, for Congress must pass a continually expanding federal budget every year, which would be impossible if the support of supermajorities were required. By lowering the bar to clear appropriations, Congress relaxes the check it places on the president's unilateral powers. A host of programs and agencies that lack the supermajorities needed to create them legislatively still manage to muster the support of majorities needed to fund them.

Third, and finally, given the size of the overall budget and the availability of discretionary funds, presidents occasionally find ways to secure funding for agencies and programs that even a majority of members of Congress oppose. Presidents may request funds for popular initiatives and then, once these have been secured, siphon off portions to unilaterally jump-start more controversial programs and agencies. Presidents can reprogram funds within budgetary accounts, draw from contingency accounts, or, when Congress assents, even transfer funds between accounts.

As evidence of this last scenario, consider Kennedy's 1961 Executive Order 10924, creating the Peace Corps. For several years prior, Congress had considered—and rejected—the idea of creating an agency that would send volunteers abroad to perform public works. Republicans in Congress were not exactly thrilled with the idea of spending millions on a "juvenile experiment" whose principal purpose, in their view, was to "help volunteers escape the draft." Democrats, for their part, refused to put the weight of their party behind the proposal.[73]

Kennedy chose to unilaterally create the Peace Corps and then use contingency accounts to fund it during its first year. When Congress was faced with financing it in 1962, the landscape had changed dramatically: the program had almost four hundred Washington employees and six hundred volunteers at work in eight countries. If Congress withheld funding, it would eliminate personnel who had already been hired and facilities that had already been purchased. Not surprisingly, Congress chose instead to appropriate the funds Kennedy requested.

Notice the similarities between this outcome and Trump's fight to secure border wall funds. Using emergency powers, Trump obtained billions of dollars that Congress would not have otherwise granted—proving that, when the politics of unilateral action and appropriations intersect, presidents have more than one way to get what they want.

9.3.3 Bureaucratic Resistance

This chapter's title notwithstanding, it is important to consider the ways in which the president's unilateral powers are not, in fact, exercised unilaterally. Alone, presidents and their White House staff lack the institutional capacity to prepare, draft, and implement their own executive orders. In need of manpower and technical expertise, presidents delegate much of this work to executive departments and agencies. This delegation often takes place across multiple administrative units, with more or less input from the White House. Before the president signs an executive order, numerous bureaucrats and department heads have likely negotiated and altered its terms. According to Andrew Rudalevige, nearly half of executive orders are "fully decentralized"—meaning that they were not only drafted but also proposed by individuals working outside the White House.[74] Another 30 percent are the result of negotiations between agencies and the Executive Office of the President (EOP).

Through their expertise and involvement, agencies can stand in the way of presidents who seek to deploy their unilateral powers for various purposes. Consider President Jimmy Carter, who, in 1977, wanted to sign an order requiring government officials to keep a log of their work-related interactions. Rather promptly, he confronted all sorts of administrative resistance. The order—a wish-list item for government accountability organizations—was considered a nuisance by federal agencies, which registered views that were "overwhelmingly opposed to the issuance of the proposed order."[75] After a year of continuous talks, President Carter abandoned the idea.

Or consider another example from President Reagan's tenure in office. When seeking reelection in 1984, Reagan hoped to unilaterally end the federal government's use of affirmative action hiring policies. At the time, Reagan was a popular president whose party controlled the Senate. Still, his proposed executive order met strict opposition in the Department of Labor, which insisted that the business community did not want to revise its hiring practices. Reagan assembled a working group to craft compromise language, but he eventually relinquished, and the threatened affirmative action policies persisted into his second term.

Of course, executive agencies do not have the formal power to veto a president's unilateral agenda. That said, agencies can deliver information to the president to make the order seem less worthwhile. They can sue, resign in protest, or leak unsavory details to the press. Most importantly, they can drag their feet and delay negotiations.

Analyzing a sample of more than five hundred orders signed between 1937 and 2004, Rudalevige sees significant variation in the time it takes to create an order. Though some take only a day, many take much longer. A variety of factors contribute to these delays. Orders drafted in response to national crises, for example, are completed more quickly than mundane, procedural orders. But delays also reflect the cost of negotiating with a fragmented bureaucracy. Notably, Rudalevige found that the addition of a single new agency to an order's review process delayed the order's signing by five days.

When negotiations are especially contentious, executive orders can take years to sign. Shortly after his inauguration in 2009, President Obama proposed an executive order that reviewed detainees in Guantánamo Bay (a military prison Obama had campaigned on closing). Hampered by "'fits and starts' in the interagency review process," however, the order would not be signed for two years. Similarly, President Trump's attempt to unilaterally revoke Obama's order and protect Guantánamo was delayed a year as executive agencies debated its finer details. "We tend to think of EOs as mechanisms for rapid response," Rudalevige reports, "but in fact a lot of waiting lurks behind even headline-level policymaking."[76]

Meanwhile, some orders do not pass at all. In Rudalevige's analysis, roughly 20 percent of proposed executive orders were abandoned. Some orders are abandoned because they are incomplete when presidents leave office, or they are rewritten as proclamations or NSDs. The leading cause of abandonment, however, is bureaucratic resistance: agency opposition was responsible for the defeat of 25 percent of the abandoned orders examined by Rudalevige. In the words of one Office of Management and Budget staffer who sought to allay concerns about the Trump administration's flurry of post-inauguration executive orders: they "should see what we stopped."[77]

Executive branch agencies play a vital role in the crafting of unilateral directives. But this role should not be overstated. Though presidents sometimes abandon their proposed orders—or sign orders proposed by other government officials—they cannot be coerced into signing orders with which they do not agree. Similarly, relationships between the White House and the executive branch are not always adversarial. As was mentioned earlier, executive agencies vary in their ideology and proximity to the president. With some agencies—especially those sympathetic to the president's agenda—intense negotiation and oversight are not required. This point is emphasized by recent research demonstrating that some agencies are more loyal to presidents than others and are more faithful in executing their orders.[78] (For more about factors affecting bureaucratic responsiveness, see section 10.2.)

Still, enduring lessons flow from Rudalevige's work. "Unilateral action," we see, does not imply that presidents "act alone." For even when presidents forgo the legislative process, they still operate in a dense network of government offices and agency heads that, in all sorts of ways, contribute to the production of unilateral directives; and they may do so in ways that diverge from the separate interests of presidents.

9.3.4 Presidents Checking Presidents

At a 2016 campaign rally in Burlington, Vermont, Donald Trump said to a roomful of supporters: "I'll tell you, the one good thing about an executive order is that the new president [can] come in and with just a signature, they're all gone."[79]

Trump was not entirely wrong. Incoming presidents can revise or overturn executive orders issued by their predecessors. And they often do. When incumbent presidents lose their reelection bids, or when their party's standard-bearer is defeated, they can expect a significant portion of their unilateral directives to be revoked by the next administration. In this respect, it would seem that the influence sitting presidents wield is limited by the anticipated actions of their successors.

For an illustrative example, consider Ronald Reagan's 1984 "Mexico City Policy." Reagan first announced the policy—a reinterpretation of his responsibilities under the 1961 Foreign Assistance Act—to unilaterally prohibit funding for foreign NGOs that provide abortion counseling or services. The policy was upheld by the administration of George H. W. Bush, who had served as Reagan's vice president. When Democrat Bill Clinton took office in 1993, however, the policy was promptly revoked via presidential memorandum. Thereafter, the funding ban was restored by Republican administrations and eliminated by Democratic ones. After Clinton, George W. Bush reinstated the ban, Obama revoked it, Trump reinstated it, and Biden revoked it. The next time a Republican enters the White House, it seems a safe bet that the ban will be reinstated yet again.

So we see how presidential turnover gives way to volatility in unilateral policymaking. And in this regard, the Mexico City Policy is hardly exceptional. According to an analysis of all executive orders signed between 1937 and 2013, more than 15 percent were revoked by subsequent administrations. Another 26 percent were modified in some way.[80] For obvious reasons, presidents would prefer that their policies persist long after they leave office. Alas, there are no guarantees that unilateral directives will result in lasting change.

Still, these dynamics do not mean that presidents' unilateral directives are necessarily doomed the moment they leave office. Research suggests that when directives are ideologically moderate, are issued by popular presidents, or are firmly rooted in statutory or constitutional authority, they are far less likely to be revoked.[81]

Politics also can play to a directive's advantage. Even when presidents enjoy broad legal authority to amend or overturn an executive order or proclamation, they cannot always do so without paying a political price.[82] In 2001, Bush learned this lesson when he attempted to delay implementation of an environmental rule change that Clinton made in the final days of his administration. Issued by the Environmental Protection Agency, the rule would have cut the amount of arsenic allowed in drinking water by 80 percent. According to the Bush administration, however, the rule's benefits did not outweigh its costs, as it would have forced thousands of communities to update their water systems. Most Americans disagreed with Bush's quantitative analysis, though, and the Democrats capitalized on the ordeal. In one Democrat-sponsored television ad, a toddler was shown asking, "Can I please have some more arsenic in my water, Mommy?"[83] Having dramatically reduced the amount of allowable arsenic in drinking water, Clinton's order enjoyed staying power not because it was illegal to change it but because it was politically costly to do so.

Such calculations are not confined to domestic policy orders. Consider executive agreements, which presidents are free to abandon without securing Congress's formal consent. Doing so, though, can also come at a cost. Ignoring an established international commitment, after all, can harm the nation's credibility and hinder future agreements, causing some presidents to consign themselves to the status quo.

There also are times when, no matter how hard the incoming president might try, unilateral actions simply cannot be undone. Pardons are one example. Just as they cannot be overturned by Congress or the courts, pardons cannot be retracted by future presidents. This is also true when presidents unilaterally establish national monuments, which can only be reversed by an act of law. President Clinton relied on this strategy to permanently protect several areas from domestic drilling operations during the Bush administration and beyond—demonstrating yet again that unilateral actions, though susceptible to change by future presidents, are more durable than they might appear.

9.3.5 The Public as a Final Line of Defense?

A burgeoning body of recent research examines the public's views about presidential power, nearly all of which suggests that Americans look rather dimly on unilateral activity. Presidents who bypass the legislative process in favor of executive orders and other kinds of unilateral directives risk running afoul of a public that stands as a final line of defense against an imperial presidency. Where Congress, the courts, and the bureaucracy fail, it is supposed, the public promises to deliver the necessary corrective—and thereby ensure that presidents broadly comport with not only legal and constitutional strictures but also the best interests of the nation.

Why does the public look so skeptically upon the president's unilateral powers? Here, scholars offer differing accounts. According to political scientists Dino Christenson and Doug Kriner,[84] Americans' attitudes about unilateral activity routinely betray their partisan allegiances. Republicans are perfectly happy when the president issues executive orders just so long as a Republican occupies the White House. And so it is with Democrats. Members of both parties, meanwhile, scream and holler about the gross abuses of the Constitution and statutory law when the opposition holds power. Theirs, though, are ultimately arguments of convenience. For just as soon as one of their own assumes office, the mode of delivering policy change no longer seems quite so important, just so long as it is delivered. Stalwart constitutionalists and tireless defenders of democracy, it would seem, are to be found nearly exclusively from the ranks of the opposition party.

Andrew Reeves and Jon Rogowski offer a more optimistic portrait of the American public.[85] According to these two scholars, there is a more principled basis for public opposition to unilateral activity. Americans ascribe to enduring political values that, quite apart from their political allegiances, yield a deep ambivalence about presidential power. To be sure, Americans celebrate presidents who use their powers to rack up policy accomplishments. But Americans also retain an abiding aversion to concentrations of power and, concomitantly, a profound commitment to the rule of law. Wary of any individual using the powers of the office for personal gain, and skeptical of perceived end runs around established legislative procedures, Americans routinely disavow the exercise of unilateral powers. Again and again, Reeves and Rogowski report, the public expresses a preference for policy change through legislative rather than administrative channels. And when forced to choose between unilateral action and no action at all, Americans often profess a willingness to settle for the status quo.

On one matter, though, these two teams of scholars agree with one another: quite apart from the formal institutions that limit unilateral activity, Americans stand to punish presidents who push too far; and as a consequence, the public can be viewed as the ultimate guardrail on unilateral activity. Presidents have plenty of reasons not to crash through it. Should they alienate the public, after all, presidents may imperil their (or their party's) chances at reelection; they may embolden their political opponents in Congress, who may launch hearings and investigations; and they may undermine other aspects of their legislative agenda. As a consequence, Christenson and Kriner note, presidents "consider the political costs of acting alone and often forgo executive action when they lack broad support among the public."[86]

It is an interesting thought. And as Christenson and Kriner go on to show, there is a remarkable correspondence between the content of public opinion and the exercise of unilateral powers. But should we think about the public, strictly speaking, as a constraint on presidential power? At least two lines of thinking suggest that there is more to the story. First, the public's demand for action often propels presidents to exercise their unilateral powers; it does not inhibit them from doing so. This is true within specific policies, when presidents issue orders at the behest of organized interests and changing public opinion. (Here, recall FDR's decision to unilaterally create the Fair Employment Practices Commission not because it was especially important to him but because he wanted to avert a march on Washington by civil rights organizers.) But public opinion also has served as an important impetus for building the various tools of unilateral action themselves. As discussed at length in chapter 4, the public expects presidents to accomplish far more than their enumerated powers will allow; and as the earlier discussion on national security directives well illustrates, presidents develop and then deploy their unilateral powers in no small part to meet these outsized public expectations.

Notice, too, that the public lacks any means by which to directly block, amend, or overturn a unilateral directive issued by the president. Congress, the judiciary, and bureaucrats themselves all have formal powers that enable them to immediately affect the production and implementation of unilateral directives. The public, by contrast, can only voice its displeasure at actions that the president takes (or, just as importantly, fails to take). And though the public can certainly make its views known on Election Day, it must then weigh its concerns about an objectionable executive order against the many other issues and actions that define presidential elections.

Public opinion certainly informs the willingness of politicians to support or oppose the president's unilateral actions. But to conceive of the public as a final line of defense against the improper use of unilateral powers, we need to evaluate its direct influence on presidents. When Congress, the courts, and the federal bureaucracy all support the president, can the public be expected to stand in the president's way? Not usually. And so, while public support is certainly a currency that presidents covet, the public itself, at least in the regular course of governing, may not function as an especially reliable or independent check on unilateral activity.

9.4 The Demonstration of Presidential Influence

That presidents use their unilateral powers with rising frequency does not necessarily imply that they are getting more of what they want. Richard Neustadt fairly warns that one must distinguish the exercise of powers (plural) from the demonstration of power (singular), for one hardly guarantees the other. As *powers*, Neustadt would surely concede that unilateral directives are an integral part of the president's arsenal. His skepticism lies in whether these powers yield *power*, and he outright rejects the notion that such directives enable presidents to meaningfully address the awesome responsibilities laid at their feet. For Neustadt, the exercise of unilateral powers, as with virtually all formal powers, represents a "painful last resort, a forced response to the exhaustion of other remedies, suggestive less of mastery than of failure—the failure of attempts to gain an end by softer means."[87]

Neustadt's distinction between *powers* and *power* is useful.[88] Obviously, presidents do not gain power simply by producing more executive orders, any more than they do by issuing additional vetoes or proposing more legislation. The frequency with which formal *powers* are asserted says little, if anything, about the *power* presidents wield, especially in a system of governance where numerous other political actors have their own authority and means to resist. If executive orders merely institute policies that Congress, left to its own devices, would have enacted as law, then unilateral powers cannot be said to augment executive power. Likewise, if statutory and constitutional provisions only allow presidents to issue the most trivial of orders, then unilateral directives hardly constitute a boon to presidential influence.

To demonstrate power, the president's actions must leave a distinct imprint on the law and, ultimately, on the doings of government. To measure this imprint, the proper comparison is not between the world that is and the world that the president might prefer, nor is it between the worlds that exist before and after an action has been taken. As discussed in chapter 4, the apt comparison, instead, is between the state of the world that exists in the aftermath of an actual or threatened presidential order and the one that would exist if the president could not act unilaterally at all.

If the president is merely doing things that other political actors would have done themselves, and if the president's mere ability to act unilaterally does not weigh upon other political actors, then no difference between this observed and this imagined world will appear. Similarly, if members of Congress immediately undo every presidential order that does not perfectly reflect their own interests then, again, these two worlds probably will look much alike. But if presidents use unilateral powers to institute policies that would not survive the legislative process, or to issue policies that look substantially different from those that members of Congress might prefer, then their unique imprints are revealed.

9.4.1 The Strategic Exercise of Unilateral Powers

When do presidents tend to exercise their unilateral powers, and how much influence do they gain from doing so? Presidents have strong incentives to issue unilateral directives in two circumstances, and in both, they create policies that differ from those that other branches of government would produce, were they left to their own devices.*

First, when Congress is poised to enact sweeping policy changes that the president opposes, the president can occasionally preempt the legislative process with more moderate policy shifts. To see the logic of this claim, consider the weak Occupational Safety and Health Administration created under Nixon, the modest sanctions levied by Reagan against South Africa's apartheid regime, and the narrow focus, and minimal powers, that George W. Bush originally assigned to the independent commission investigating intelligence failures on Iraq and weapons proliferation. In each of these cases, Congress stood poised to create either a stronger agency or more robust public policy, and the president lacked the support required to kill these initiatives with a veto. In each case, executive influence was revealed by the president's ability to derail congressional efforts by issuing weaker versions of proposed legislation.

Second, presidents use their unilateral powers to determine policy when Congress exhibits **gridlock**, a condition in which Congress is incapable of changing the status quo. In this instance, the defining stamp of power is not the amendment of an existing policy but instead the enactment of an altogether new one. For example, as Congress failed to deal in any substantive way with civil rights issues during the 1940s and 1950s, the classification

---

* These situations are characterized formally in William G. Howell, *Power without Persuasion: The Politics of Direct Presidential Action* (Princeton: Princeton University Press, 2003). For a useful summary of the theoretical literature on unilateral powers, see Kenneth Lowande and Jon Rogowski, "Presidential Unilateral Power," *Annual Review of Political Science* 24 (2021): 21–43.

of intelligence during much of the post–World War II era, or terrorism in the aftermath of September 11, presidents stepped in and unilaterally defined the government's involvement in these policy arenas.[89] As Justice Robert Jackson recognized in his famous concurring opinion in *Youngstown Sheet & Tube Co. v. Sawyer* (1952), "Congressional inertia, indifference, or quiescence may sometimes, at least as a practical matter, enable, if not invite, measures of independent presidential responsibility."[90]

In both of these scenarios, the contours of executive influence are readily discernible. In the first, were it not for the president's actions, coalitions supporting dramatic policy change in Congress would retain the votes of their more moderate members. With the president's unilateral directive in place, though, these moderate legislators break away and the votes needed for sweeping policy change are lost. In the second instance, the mark of presidential influence is not a public policy that is weaker than what Congress would pass on its own—rather, it is the unilateral creation of a policy that otherwise would not exist at all.

Thinking Institutionally: Explaining Trump's Many Defeats

Acting strategically, presidents routinely survey the political landscape before exercising their unilateral powers. Recognizing an opportunity to press forward undeterred, presidents may issue a directive. But anticipating a rebuke by either Congress or the courts, presidents either scale back or delay their policy initiatives. As a consequence, the very real institutional constraints that define the boundaries of presidential power often lay dormant.

Not so under the Trump administration. Many of Trump's key campaign promises were attempted unilaterally, only to be struck down by the courts. On immigration, perhaps the centerpiece of his candidacy, Trump ordered his Justice Department to terminate the Deferred Action for Childhood Arrivals program, also known as DACA. The Obama-era program was designed to prevent deportations of immigrants brought to the United States as children. In a stunning 5–4 decision, however, the Supreme Court ruled that the move violated the Administrative Procedure Act, which governs the ways in which the government can and cannot alter regulations. Similar legal defeats, in the Supreme Court and throughout the federal judiciary, would come to define the Trump administration. Attempts to add a citizenship question to the 2020 Census, prohibit diversity training in federal agencies, ban the popular social media platform TikTok, and cut funding for "sanctuary cities" were either stalled or shut down in court. All told, Trump administration regulations received more than 140 unfavorable rulings in just four years.[91]

What explains these many defeats? Part of the answer, surely, concerns the characteristics of the president himself. His inexperience, volatility, and impulsiveness all may have played a part. In fact, several of his legal defeats were prompted by his

FIGURE 9.5. Repeatedly, the federal judiciary struck down unilateral actions taken by the Trump administration for having violated either the Constitution or statutory law, most commonly the Administrative Procedures Act. *Source:* Drew Sheneman/ The Newark Star-Ledger/TCA.

own actions. Shortly after Trump referred to African nations as "shithole countries," for example, a San Francisco judge cited the administration's apparent racial bias in ruling against one of its immigration policies.[92] His brash persona also may have led him to issue unilateral directives without contemplating how others, with political authority all of their own, might respond. "Let's remember, this man does not read, does not listen," wrote Michael Wolff, a journalist who spent several months inside the Trump White House. "He's like a pinball, just shooting off the sides."[93]

Two other factors, however, suggest that there may have been some method to Trump's madness. The first concerns the uncertainty about what the adjoining branches of government would actually permit. Historically, we usually witness presidents unilaterally issuing modest renditions of their policy objectives; then, upon securing the approval of Congress and the courts, these presidents build upon their earlier successes in order to make the most of what the adjoining branches of government will allow. Trump, by contrast, worked in reverse. From the outset, he issued orders that strained legal credulity and legislative will; and only upon being defeated did he trim the offending portions of a policy initiative before testing the political waters once again.

Perhaps nowhere was this reverse-engineered unilateralism more apparent than in Trump's repeated attempts to impose a "Muslim ban" on the U.S. immigration system. Just one week after entering office, Trump signed the first of three executive orders to ban the entry of foreign nationals from seven majority-Muslim countries—Iran, Iraq,

Continued on next page

Libya, Somalia, Sudan, Syria, and Yemen. The order was almost immediately blocked by judges in New York and Massachusetts before its ultimate defeat in the Ninth Circuit Court of Appeals in February 2017. In response, Trump reissued the order—this time excluding Iraq from the list of affected countries—but once again it was struck down. On his third and final attempt, Trump softened the order by adding a phase-in period and including the non-Muslim-majority countries of Venezuela and North Korea. After a series of trials and errors, this latest—and weakest—version was upheld by the Supreme Court in 2018. It's possible, of course, that the president would ultimately have secured a different policy outcome had he started small and then added incremental enhancements to the policy. But there is at least a discernible logic to his chosen strategy of aiming high and then scaling back only when compelled to do so.

The second rationale points to the logic of Trump's political appeal. In 2016, Trump distinguished himself from a crowded field of Republican stalwarts vying for the party's nomination by assuming the mantle of populism. The government had failed the people, Trump insisted; and he, as an outsider with no previous political experience, stood to set things right. The administrative state was a swamp. Elections were rigged. So-called experts didn't care a lick about the needs and interests of true Americans. But rest assured, Trump argued, he would take the fight to the Washington establishment.

And so he did. From the moment he assumed office, Trump upset all kinds of norms of presidential behavior. In his actions, speech, and modes of public presentation, he distinguished himself from the politicians who, for too long, had sold the country a bill of goods; and he lashed out against anyone who stood in his way. He labeled his enemies—including those in his own party and administration—as "liars," "lapdogs," and "losers." He sought to align himself with the public, describing any individual or institution who opposed him (especially the media) as the "Enemy of the People."[94]

Within this setting, legislative and judicial defeats served distinct political purposes. First, they served as proof positive that the president was, in fact, taking on the organized interests, parties, and cabals that for too long had failed the American people. Rejections in Congress and the judiciary were not solemn occasions that called for apology or regret. They were badges of honor. And second, these many defeats underscored the central narrative that justified Trump's rise to power: namely, that the established centers of political power were out of touch with the American people. That Congress wouldn't fund a "desperately needed" wall on its southern border and that the judiciary wouldn't uphold his immigration ban revealed just how insulated they were from the "dire threat" that immigrants presented to our country's safety and well-being. For the president's political base, then, these defeats underscored just how important it was to keep Trump in power, to rally to his populist cause, and to continue the fight against a corrupt political system.

9.4.2 Implementing Public Policy

Presidential orders do not always translate into action. When presidents set new mandates that require the active cooperation of other political actors, they can face difficulties. As we have seen, bureaucrats may read their mandates selectively, insert their own preferences when they think they can get away with it, and report incomplete, and sometimes false, information about the policy's successes and failures. (In chapter 10, we investigate these and other challenges associated with governing the federal bureaucracy.)

Having issued a directive, however, presidents do not sit idly by and hope that bureaucrats will step forward and advance their policy goals. Instead, presidents often follow up with additional orders and rule changes that direct specific personnel to fulfill specific tasks. Recall, for example, George W. Bush's faith-based initiatives. From the moment he took office, Bush set out to expand the role of religious organizations in state affairs and to open the government's coffers to churches and synagogues. On January 29, 2001, he issued an executive order that established the White House Office of Faith-Based and Community Initiatives, which was directed to "identify and remove needless barriers that thwart the heroic work of faith-based groups" and "enlist, equip, enable, empower, and expand" the work of faith-based organizations nationwide.

Bush's reliance on unilateral powers did not cease once his broad objectives were achieved. Instead, in the following months and years he issued additional rules, directives, and executive orders that served to advance the specifics of his policy goals throughout the federal bureaucracy. In August 2001, for example, Bush ordered an internal audit of department regulations, policies, and practices that discouraged (or forbade) faith-based organizations from receiving federal grants and delivering social services. He set up offices whose job it was to promote government partnerships with faith-based organizations and placed them in outposts throughout the federal government, including the departments of Housing and Urban Development, Labor, Education, Justice, Agriculture, Veterans Affairs, and Commerce, as well as in such agencies as the Environmental Protection Agency, the Small Business Administration, Fannie Mae, and Freddie Mac.

The administration conducted dozens of workshops and conferences that advised religious organizations about new funding opportunities. It opened a Compassion Capital Fund and resource centers around the nation to provide technical assistance with grant writing, staff development, and management. For smaller faith-based organizations, agencies simplified application processes, developed networking opportunities, and provided specialized training seminars.

The results of these efforts were remarkable. The Faith-Based Initiative tore down previous restrictions on the religious organizations' hiring practices, displays of religious symbols, eligibility requirements for federal grants, and opportunities to obtain government-forfeited properties. Religious institutions could now apply for federal funds to renovate their places of worship, just as they could hire and fire people on the basis of their religious beliefs. Billions of dollars flowed to religious institutions, which used them to serve such varied tasks as tutoring children in underperforming public schools, promoting drug prevention, abstinence, and marriage, and providing childcare, job training, and literacy programs both domestically and abroad.[95] Some of these funds were channeled through previously existing programs, for which religious organizations could now compete; other funds—for example, those involving building construction and restoration—were specifically intended to support religious organizations.

In this instance, a single executive order launched the president's core initiative, but numerous unilateral directives soon followed, each designed to ensure that departments and agencies would implement its key provisions. As Anne Farris, Richard Nathan, and David Wright report in their comprehensive review of Bush's Faith-Based Initiative, "in the absence of new legislative authority, the President has used executive orders, rule changes, managerial realignment in federal agencies, and other prerogatives of his office to aggressively implement the initiative."[96] Note the language here: the president used these powers not just to *write* the initiative but to *implement* it.

Unilateral powers do have limits, for which any evaluation of unilateral action must account. As the success of Bush's faith-based initiatives suggests, however, even within these limits presidents can shape both the content and implementation of important policies that stand little chance of enactment within Congress.

9.4.3 Enhanced Control over the Bureaucracy

Presidents can use their unilateral powers not only to craft specific policies but also to exert influence over the federal bureaucracy. In these instances, presidents use their unilateral powers to create oversight and rulemaking procedures that enhance their control over the administrative state.

One illustrative case involves the evolution of the Office of Information and Regulatory Affairs (OIRA), housed within the Office of Management and Budget (OMB). Created by the Paperwork Reduction Act in 1980, the final year of Jimmy Carter's presidency, OIRA was originally intended to coordinate the efforts of other federal agencies to collect information from the general public. But with the signing of Executive Order 12291 one year later, President Reagan invested OIRA with tremendous new power: all federal regulatory agencies, such as the Environmental Protection Agency (EPA) and the Food and Drug Administration (FDA), were now legally required to submit any proposed rule to OIRA for review. Not only that, but all submissions had to include a cost-benefit analysis, and only rules whose benefits to society could be proven to outweigh the costs would be approved. Additionally, OIRA could delay the enactment of new rules indefinitely while they were under review. With one stroke of the pen, Reagan created a kind of über-regulator to oversee all other regulators—albeit one whose job was to curtail regulation—and its authority was deliberately set in the Executive Office of the President.

From the New Deal onward, the size and responsibilities of the federal government increased dramatically. And as they did, the federal bureaucracy produced more and more regulations. By the late 1960s a wellspring of new environmental and consumer advocacy groups was fueling a movement to hold private businesses accountable for practices that threatened public safety or the environment. The early 1970s were consequently a period of regulatory growth in the United States. Together with the EPA, which Nixon created in 1970 through executive order, the Occupational Safety and Health Administration (1971) and the Consumer Product Safety Commission (1972) were founded in this period. In addition, Congress invested other government bodies with new regulatory mandates. Overall, between 1970 and 1974, some twenty-nine new federal regulatory statutes were passed. But the 1970s also marked the last decade of the twentieth century in which a major federal regulatory agency was created.

Increasingly, businesses fought against the regulatory tide and won the support of presidents and other policymakers. In 1971, Nixon created a Quality of Life Review process to rein in the EPA, which had begun issuing antipollution regulations that threatened to impose huge costs on industry. As the U.S. economy entered a period of decline, Nixon sought to make the EPA more business friendly by requiring the agency to submit its proposed rules to the OMB, which would send them to the Department of Commerce and other agencies for their comments.

Like his predecessor Nixon, President Ford also sought to circumscribe the power of regulatory agencies by forcing them to report to the Executive Office of the President on the economic impact of their proposed rules. President Carter, too, mandated that the agencies produce reams of analysis for any rule that might hamper business growth.

Still, it was Reagan who dealt the final blow to the regulatory era, with Executive Order 12291. Reagan's co-option of OIRA represented a forceful maneuver to ensure the triumph of his policy agenda in the face of an often-hostile Congress. Congress managed to only chip away at OIRA's influence over regulatory agencies, in particular the EPA. According to some observers, this "piecemeal and fragmented" approach only resulted in "burying the EPA in more bureaucracy."[97] Meanwhile, OIRA lives on.

9.4.4 Getting onto the Legislative Agenda

Given the sheer number of problems that Congress must cope with, and the limited amount of time and resources available to legislators, it can be difficult just to place an issue on the public agenda. More than most politicians, however, presidents command the larger polity. By going public, introducing their annual budget proposals, and leaning on key committee members, presidents can train the attention of legislators on key issues of national importance.

When they hold a summit or announce a policy initiative in the annual State of the Union Address, presidents often succeed in launching public debate on their agendas. But on smaller matters, members of Congress can check presidential influence not so much by mobilizing opposition but rather by letting presidential proposals languish. As a consequence, congressional inaction is at times the preferred response to White House entreaties—and the bane of presidents banking their legacies on legislative victories.

Fortunately, from the president's perspective, unilateral directives provide a way out. With the stroke of a pen, presidents can instantly make regulatory relief or military tribunals the news of the day. If its members hope to affect the course of policymaking, Congress had better spring into action, for an executive order retains the weight of law unless and until someone else overturns it. The strategy of inaction is thus turned against Congress; indeed, once a president has issued a unilateral directive, congressional inaction often is functionally equivalent to support.

By issuing a unilateral directive, however, presidents do more than capture the attention of members of Congress: they also reshape the nature of the discussions that ensue. When members of Congress consider whether or not to fund a unilaterally created agency or to amend a newly issued order or to codify a president's action into law, discussions do not percolate around a batch of hypotheticals and forecasts. Instead, they grapple with the specific policies that presidents themselves previously issued and that retain legally binding force until Congress or the courts do something about it.

This fact is made abundantly clear when presidents send troops abroad. Though Obama faced a fair measure of opposition to his plans to intervene in Libya—as Clinton did when he planned for operations in Haiti and Bosnia, as George H. W. Bush did when he tried to make the case for invading Panama, and as Reagan did when he considered action in Lebanon and Grenada—the terms of debate irrevocably changed the moment these presidents launched the military ventures.

The moment that troops were deployed, the conversation shifted away from the general merits of military actions and toward the imperatives of protecting the lives of young men and women fighting for their country. Though Congress retained important avenues of influence over the conduct of these military campaigns, opponents of the president, at least initially, were put on the defensive. By using force unilaterally, these presidents effectively remade the political universe, pushing their policy initiatives to the top of Congress's agenda and ensuring that they received a fuller hearing than they would have during the weeks and months that preceded the actions.

None of this is to say that presidents reliably get exactly what they want. On all sorts of important policy matters, presidents lack the requisite authority to act unilaterally, and in these instances, their only option is to engage Congress. Moreover, even when they retain the option of an administrative strategy, presidents cannot be sure that Congress will abstain from amending or overturning their actions. The basic point, however, remains: unilateral directives can instill subsequent discussions with a sense of urgency and alter the terms of debate in ways that are favorable to the president. And with that, we come full circle. Having bypassed the legislative process in one moment, presidents resurrect their chances of success within it the next. Viewed this way, unilateral directives are not mere substitutes for legislative proposals. In some instances, they are clear complements.

Conclusion

The legislative arena is hardly the only venue in which presidents exercise power. Increasingly, presidents pursue their policy agendas not through laws but instead through some combination of executive orders, executive agreements, proclamations, memoranda, and other unilateral directives. Until we account for the trade-offs associated with administrative and legislative strategies—and more fully document the regularity with which presidents pursue one or the other—our understanding of presidential power will remain incomplete.

Two facts about the politics of unilateral action are especially important. First, *the insights and lessons about presidential success* within *Congress may not accurately explain presidential success* outside *of Congress*. Theories of lawmaking and theories of unilateral action generate different expectations about the conditions under which policy change occurs. For instance, our discussion in chapter 8 suggests that Congress and the president should produce more laws when the preferences within and across the two respective branches are relatively cohesive. As we have seen, however, the production of unilateral directives follows a very different logic. When members of Congress are unified and strong, unilateral activity declines, but when gridlock reigns, presidents seize the opportunity to issue policies through unilateral directives that could not survive the legislative process.

Second, *when presidents contemplate unilateral action in lieu of legislation, their relationship with the adjoining branches of government shifts in important ways*. When unilateral powers are exercised, legislators, judges, and the executive do not work collectively to effect meaningful policy change, and opportunities for change do not depend upon the willingness and capacity of different branches of government to cooperate with one another. Quite the contrary: as presidents issue unilateral directives, they struggle to protect their integrity and to undermine the efforts of adjoining branches of government to amend or overturn them.

Key Terms

unilateral directives	unilateral decisions
executive orders	pardon
proclamations	doctrine of acquiescence
national security directives	Federal Register Act
executive agreements	Case Act
memoranda	War Powers Resolution
departmental order	executive privilege
secretarial order	gridlock

Questions for Discussion

1. Are unilateral powers manufactured or inherited?
2. How does the institutional logic of persuasion differ from that of unilateral action?
3. What defines the institutional constraints on the president's unilateral powers?
4. In what ways might bureaucratic agencies resist the president's efforts to control them? In what ways might the president's unilateral powers provide a response?

5. When might a president's capacity for unilateral action encourage compromise with Congress? When might it prevent compromise?

Suggested Readings

Bolton, Alexander, and Sharece Thrower. *Checks in the Balance: Legislative Capacity and the Dynamics of Executive Power*. Princeton: Princeton University Press, 2021.

Chiou, Fang-Yi, and Lawrence Rothenberg. *The Enigma of Presidential Power: Parties, Policies, and Strategic Uses of Unilateral Action*. New York: Cambridge University Press, 2017.

Christenson, Dino, and Douglas Kriner. *The Myth of the Imperial Presidency: How Public Opinion Checks the Unilateral Executive*. Chicago: University of Chicago Press, 2020.

Cooper, Phillip. *By Order of the President: The Use and Abuse of Executive Direct Action*. 2nd ed. Lawrence: University Press of Kansas, 2014.

Crouch, Jeffrey. *The Presidential Pardon Power*. Lawrence: University Press of Kansas, 2009.

Howell, William G. *Power without Persuasion: The Politics of Direct Presidential Action*. Princeton: Princeton University Press, 2003.

Krutz, Glen, and Jeffrey Peake. *Treaty Politics and the Rise of Executive Agreements: International Commitments in a System of Shared Powers*. Ann Arbor: University of Michigan Press, 2011.

Martin, Lisa. *Democratic Commitments: Legislatures and International Cooperation*. Princeton: Princeton University Press, 2000.

Mayer, Kenneth. *With the Stroke of a Pen: Executive Orders and Presidential Power*. Princeton: Princeton University Press, 2001.

Reeves, Andrew, and Jon Rogowski. *No Blank Check: Public Opinion and Presidential Power*. New York: Cambridge University Press, 2022.

Rudalevige, Andrew. *By Executive Order: Bureaucratic Management and the Limits of Presidential Power*. Princeton: Princeton University Press, 2021.

Notes

1. Mary M. Cronin, *An Indispensable Liberty: The Fight for Free Speech in Nineteenth-Century America* (Carbondale: Southern Illinois University Press, 2016), 55.

2. Portions of this chapter draw from William G. Howell, *Power without Persuasion: The Politics of Direct Presidential Action* (Princeton: Princeton University Press, 2003); William G. Howell, "Unilateral Politics: A Brief Overview," *Presidential Studies Quarterly* 35, no. 3 (2005): 417–35; and William G. Howell and Douglas Kriner, "Power without Persuasion: Identifying Executive Influence," in Bert A. Rockman and Richard W. Waterman, *Presidential Leadership: The Vortex of Power* (New York: Oxford University Press, 2007).

3. Richard E. Neustadt, *Presidential Power and the Modern Presidents: The Politics of Leadership from Roosevelt to Reagan* (New York: Free Press, 1991), xix.

4. Neustadt, *Presidential Power*, 30.

5. Kenneth Mayer, *With the Stroke of a Pen: Executive Orders and Presidential Power* (Princeton: Princeton University Press, 2001), 35.

6. Phillip Cooper, *By Order of the President: The Use and Abuse of Executive Direct Action* (Lawrence: University Press of Kansas, 2002), 16.

7. Terry Eastland, *Energy in the Executive: The Case for the Strong Presidency* (New York: Free Press, 1992), 351.

8. Michelle Belco and Brandon Rottinghaus, *The Dual Executive: Unilateral Orders in a Separated and Shared Power System* (Stanford: Stanford University Press, 2017).

9. "The Use of Presidential Directives to Make and Implement U.S. Policy," Report to the Chairman, Committee on Government Operations, House of Representatives, GAO/NSIAD-89–31 (Washington, DC: General Accounting Office, 1988), https://www.gao.gov/assets/nsiad-89-31.pdf.

10. Harold Relyea, "The Coming of Secret Law," *Government Information Quarterly* 5, no. 2 (1988): 108.

11. *United States v. Belmont*, 301 U.S. 324.

12. Cited in "Executive Orders: An Introduction," *Congressional Research Service*, March 29, 2021, p. 21, https://crsreports.congress.gov/product/pdf/R/R46738.

13. Gregory Korte, "Obama Issues 'Executive Orders by Another Name,'" *USA Today*, December 17, 2014, https://www.usatoday.com/story/news/politics/2014/12/16/obama-presidential-memoranda-executive-orders/20191805/.

14. "Obama Suspends Deportation for Thousands of Illegals, Tells GOP to Pass DREAM Act," FoxNews.com, June 15, 2012, http://www.foxnews.com/politics/2012/06/15/obama-administration-to-offer-immunity-to-younger-immigrants/.

15. National Security Act of 1947, P.L. 80–253.

16. Cong. Rec., 80th Cong., 1st Sess. (1947), 9939.

17. "The Use of Presidential Directives to Make and Implement U.S. Policy," Report to the Chairman, Legislation and National Security Subcommittee, Committee on Government Operations, House of Representatives, GAO/NSIAD-92–72 (Washington, DC: General Accounting Office, 1992), http://www.fas.org/irp/offdocs/gao-nsiad-92–72.pdf.

18. U.S. Const., art. II, § 2.

19. "An Overview of the Presidential Pardon Power," *Congressional Research Service*, January 7, 2009, https://www.everycrsreport.com/files/20090107_R40128_56d9bc830b6a3ba9f7120a528fd8296b1929c1f8.pdf.

20. Robert Nida and Rebecca L. Spiro, "The President as His Own Judge and Jury: A Legal Analysis of the Presidential Self-Pardon Power," *Oklahoma Law Review* 52, no. 2 (1999): 197–226.

21. *Ex parte Garland*, 71 U.S. (4 Wall.) 333 (1866).

22. *Schick v. Reed*, 419 U.S. 256 (1974).

23. See, for example, H.J. Res. 48, 110th Cong. (2007), https://www.congress.gov/bill/110th-congress/house-joint-resolution/48/actions?q=%7B%22search%22%3A%5B%22Hjr48%22%5D%7D&r=1&s=4.

24. Harold C. Relyea, "Security Classified and Controlled Information: History, Status, and Emerging Management Issues" (Congressional Research Service, February 11, 2008), https://fas.org/sgp/crs/secrecy/RL33494.pdf.

25. 5 F.R. 1147 (March 26, 1940).

26. 75 F.R. 707 (January 5, 2010).

27. Quoted in Kevin R. Kosar, "Classified Information Policy and Executive Order 13526" (Congressional Research Service, December 10, 2010), 5.

28. Jennifer K. Elsea, "The Protection of Classified Information: The Legal Framework" (Congressional Research Service, May 18, 2017), https://fas.org/sgp/crs/secrecy/RS21900.pdf.

29. Peter Kornbluh, "The Declassified Pinochet File: Delivering the Verdict of History," *Radical History Review* 2016, no. 124 (January 2016): 203–16.

30. Notably, few consequences follow for presidents who casually or accidentally reveal national secrets, as President Trump reportedly did in a private meeting with representatives of the Russian government. See Greg Miller and Greg Jaffe, "Trump Revealed Highly Classified Information to Russian Foreign Minister and Ambassador," *Washington Post*, May 15, 2017.

31. Joseph Kahn, "Cheney Refuses to Release Energy Task Force Records," *New York Times*, August 4, 2001, https://www.nytimes.com/2001/08/04/us/cheney-refuses-to-release-energy-task-force-records.html.

32. Richard Simon, "Probe of Energy Task Force Ends," *Los Angeles Times*, August 26, 2003, https://www.latimes.com/archives/la-xpm-2003-aug-26-na-cheney26-story.html.

33. Charlie Savage, "Trump Vows Stonewall of 'All' House Subpoenas, Setting up Fight over Powers," *New York Times*, April 25, 2019, https://www.nytimes.com/2019/04/24/us/politics/donald-trump-subpoenas.html.

34. John Hudson and Louisa Loveluck, "In Launching Airstrikes in Syria and Iraq, Biden Lowers Bar for Use of Military Force," *Washington Post*, July 2, 2021, https://www.washingtonpost.com/national-security/biden-military-strikes-policy/2021/07/01/9ab7d7d0-da60–11eb-ae62–2d07d7df83bd_story.html.

35. "Executive Orders Issued by President George W. Bush," George W. Bush White House, https://georgewbush-whitehouse.archives.gov/news/orders/.

36. Motoko Rich, "Holding States and Schools Accountable," *New York Times*, February 9, 2013, A.25.

37. Lawrence Margolis, *Executive Agreements and Presidential Power in Foreign Policy* (New York: Praeger, 1986); Terry M. Moe and William G. Howell, "Unilateral Action and Presidential Power: A Theory," *Presidential Studies Quarterly* 29 no. 4 (1999): 850–73.

38. Aaron R. Kaufman and Jon C. Rogowski, "Divided Government and Presidential Unilateralism" (University of Chicago Mimeo, 2021), 6. See also Aaron R. Kaufman and Jon C. Rogowski, "Presidential Policymaking, 1877–2020" (University of Chicago Mimeo, 2022).

39. Outraged by a federal tax on whiskey, over three years farmers and distillers from western Pennsylvania engaged in a variety of protests and violent acts that collectively came to be known as the Whiskey Rebellion. To quell the insurrection, President George Washington in 1794 deployed a militia of troops from surrounding states and regions. The rebellion is broadly recognized as an early test of the newly formed federal government and the powers of the presidency. For more on the subject, see Thomas Slaughter, *The Whiskey Rebellion: Frontier Epilogue to the American Revolution* (New York: Oxford University Press, 1988).

40. "Granting Pardon to Persons Convicted of Certain War-Time Offenses," FDR Presidential Library, 1933.

41. Margaret Love, "The Twilight of the Pardon Power," *Journal of Criminal Law and Criminology* 100, no. 3 (2010): 1174.

42. "Granting Pardon for Violations of the Selective Service Act," National Archives (1973), https://www.archives.gov/federal-register/codification/proclamations/04483.html.

43. Love, "The Twilight of the Pardon Power."

44. Jeffrey Crouch, "The Law: Presidential Misuse of the Pardon Power," *Presidential Studies Quarterly* 38, no. 4 (2008): 722–34.

45. "Pardons Granted by President Donald J. Trump (2017–2021)," United States Department of Justice, April 28, 2021, https://www.justice.gov/pardon/pardons-granted-president-donald-j-trump-2017-2021.

46. "Statement from the Press Secretary Regarding Executive Grant of Clemency for Roger Stone, Jr.," Trump White House, July 10, 2020, https://trumpwhitehouse.archives.gov/briefings-statements/statement-press-secretary-regarding-executive-grant-clemency-roger-stone-jr/.

47. *Youngstown Sheet & Tube Co. v. Sawyer*, 343 U.S. 585 (1952).

48. *Prize Cases*, 67 U.S. 635 (1862).

49. *United States v. Curtiss-Wright Export Corp.*, 299 U.S. 304 (1936).

50. Trading with the Enemy Act of 1917, 50a U.S.C. §§ 3–30 (Suppl. 2 1940).

51. *United States v. Midwest Oil Co.*, 236 U.S. 459 (1915).

52. Joel L. Fleishman and Arthur H. Aufses, "Law and Orders: The Problem of Presidential Legislation," *Law and Contemporary Problems* 40, no. 3 (1976): 4–5.

53. U.S. Congress, Senate, Special Committee on the Termination of the National Emergency, *Emergency Powers Statutes*, 93rd Cong., 1st sess., 1973, http://www.ncrepublic.org/images/lib/SenateReport93_549.pdf.

54. "A Guide to Emergency Powers and Their Use," Brennan Center for Justice, December 5, 2018, https://www.brennancenter.org/our-work/research-reports/guide-emergency-powers-and-their-use.

55. President Donald Trump, "Declaring a National Emergency Concerning the Southern Border of the United States, Proclamation 9844 of February 15, 2019," *Federal Register* 84, no. 34 (February 20, 2019): 4949–50.

56. 10 U.S. Code § 2808.

57. Kailani Koenig, "Nancy Pelosi: Border Wall Is 'Immoral, Expensive, Unwise,'" NBC News, April 23, 2017, https://www.nbcnews.com/politics/congress/nancy-pelosi-border-wall-immoral-expensive-unwise -n749841.

58. Chris Mills Rodrigo, "Trump: 'We're Totally Prepared for a Very Long Shutdown,'" *The Hill*, December 21, 2018, https://thehill.com/homenews/administration/422492-trump-were-totally-prepared-for-a-very -long-shutdown/.

59. Charlie Savage, "Presidents Have Declared Dozens of Emergencies, but None Like Trump's," *New York Times*, February 16, 2019, A.1.

60. "Declared National Emergencies under the National Emergencies Act," Brennan Center for Justice, May 17, 2019, https://www.brennancenter.org/our-work/research-reports/declared-national-emergencies -under-national-emergencies-act, "Declarations under the National Emergencies Act, Part 1: Declarations Currently in Effect."

61. *INS v. Chadha*, 462 U.S. 919 (1983).

62. William G. Howell and Jon C. Pevehouse, *While Dangers Gather: Congressional Checks on Presidential War Powers* (Princeton: Princeton University Press, 2007); Doug Kriner, *After the Rubicon: Congress, Presidents, and the Politics of Waging War* (Chicago: University of Chicago Press, 2010).

63. D. Roderick Kiewiet and Mathew McCubbins, *The Logic of Delegation: Congressional Parties and the Appropriations Process* (Chicago: University of Chicago Press, 1991).

64. E. N. Griswold, "Government in Ignorance of the Law: A Plea for Better Publication of Executive Legislation," *Harvard Law Review* 48, no. 2 (1934): 213.

65. Louis Fisher, *Congressional Abdication on War and Spending* (College Station: Texas A&M University Press, 2000).

66. Quoted in Richard Hall, *Participation in Congress* (New Haven: Yale University Press, 1996), 267.

67. Mark Rozell, *Executive Privilege: Presidential Power, Secrecy, and Accountability* (Lawrence: University of Kansas Press, 2002).

68. Curtis Bradley, Jack Goldsmith, and Oona Hathaway, "The Failed Transparency Regime for Executive Agreements: An Empirical and Normative Analysis," *Harvard Law Review* 133 (2020): 629–725.

69. *Hamdan v. Rumsfeld*, 548 U.S. 557 (2006).

70. P.L. 94–212.

71. P.L. 98–473.

72. Timothy Egan, "Shift on Salmon Reignites Fight on Species Law," *New York Times*, May 8, 2004, A.1.

73. Donald R. Whitnah, *Government Agencies* (Westport, CT: Greenwood Press, 1983).

74. Andrew Rudalevige, *By Executive Order: Bureaucratic Management and the Limits of Presidential Power* (Princeton: Princeton University Press, 2021).

75. As quoted in Rudalevige, *By Executive Order*, 8.

76. Rudalevige, *By Executive Order*, 140.

77. As quoted in Rudalevige, *By Executive Order*, 187.

78. Joshua B. Kennedy, "'Do This! Do That!' and Nothing Will Happen," *American Politics Research* 43, no. 1 (2014): 59–82.

79. Meredith Conroy, "Why Revoking Trump's Executive Orders Isn't Enough to Undo Their Effects," *FiveThirtyEight*, February 11, 2021, https://fivethirtyeight.com/features/why-revoking-trumps-executive-orders -isnt-enough-to-undo-their-effects/.

80. Sharece Thrower, "To Revoke or Not Revoke? The Political Determinants of Executive Order Longevity," *American Journal of Political Science* 61, no. 3 (2017): 642–56, https://doi.org/10.1111/ajps.12294.

81. Thrower, "To Revoke or Not Revoke?"

82. William G. Howell and Kenneth R. Mayer, "The Last One Hundred Days," *Presidential Studies Quarterly* 35, no. 3 (2005): 533–53.

83. Quoted in Howell and Mayer, "The Last One Hundred Days," 544.

84. Dino Christenson and Douglas Kriner, *The Myth of the Imperial Presidency: How Public Opinion Checks the Unilateral Executive* (Chicago: University of Chicago Press, 2020).

85. Andrew Reeves and Jon Rogowski, *No Blank Check: Public Opinion and Presidential Power* (New York: Cambridge University Press, 2022).

86. Dino Christenson and Douglas Kriner, "Does Public Opinion Constrain Presidential Unilateralism?" *American Political Science Review* 113, no. 4 (2019): 1071.

87. Neustadt, *Presidential Power*, 24.

88. Howell, "Unilateral Politics."

89. Cooper, *Order of the President*; Mayer, *Stroke of a Pen*.

90. *Youngstown Sheet & Tube Co. v. Sawyer*, 343 U.S. 579 (1952), 637.

91. "Roundup: Trump-Era Agency Policy in the Courts," Institute for Policy Integrity, NYU School of Law, https://policyintegrity.org/trump-court-roundup.

92. Fred Barbash and Deanna Paul, "The Real Reason the Trump Administration Is Constantly Losing in Court," *Washington Post*, March 19, 2019, https://www.washingtonpost.com/world/national-security/the-real-reason-president-trump-is-constantly-losing-in-court/2019/03/19/f5ffb056-33a8-11e9-af5b-b51b7ff322e9_story.html.

93. Adam Edelman, "'Fire and Fury' Author Wolff Calls Trump Least Credible Person Who Has Ever Walked on Earth," NBC News, January 5, 2018, https://www.nbcnews.com/politics/donald-trump/michael-wolff-says-donald-trump-least-credible-person-who-has-n834921.

94. Jasmine C. Lee and Kevin Quealy, "The 598 People, Places and Things Donald Trump Has Insulted on Twitter: A Complete List," *New York Times*, updated May 24, 2019, https://www.nytimes.com/interactive/2016/01/28/upshot/donald-trump-twitter-insults.html.

95. Anne Farris, Richard P. Nathan, and David J. Wright, *The Expanding Administrative Presidency: George W. Bush and the Faith-Based Initiative* (Washington, DC: Roundtable on Religion and Social Policy, 2004).

96. Farris, Nathan, and Wright, *Expanding Administrative Presidency*, 1.

97. Terry M. Moe and Scott A. Wilson, "Presidents and the Politics of Structure," *Law and Contemporary Problems* 57 (1994): 39.

10

Control of the Bureaucracy

THE PRESIDENT HOLDS THE PRIMARY—some would say exclusive—constitutional authority to execute the law. To actualize this authority, however, presidents must harness the federal bureaucracy, with its myriad agencies, departments, bureaus, and offices. Bureaucrats—not presidents themselves—do the work of converting laws and unilateral directives into government action.

In their interactions with the bureaucracy, presidents must wade through a slew of administrative and political challenges. There are no guarantees, after all, that bureaucrats will abide the interests of presidents. Left to their own devices, bureaucrats instead may write environmental regulations, draft worker safety rules, make infrastructure investments, and engage in foreign diplomacy in ways that reflect congressional, judicial, public, or even their own independent interests and priorities.

To mitigate these problems, presidents—all presidents—seek to control the bureaucracy. In important respects, struggles for control are the essence of bureaucratic politics. But as nearly all presidents have learned, opportunities for exercising control are limited; and the control presidents wield is invariably partial. The sheer magnitude of the executive branch, comprised mainly of employees who worked there before the president took office and will continue to work there long after the president leaves, makes the challenge nearly impossible to solve.

Hence, and as we shall see, presidents rely upon multiple strategies to wrest some modicum of influence over the administrative state.

10.1 Administrative and Political Problems

To some Americans, the very word "bureaucracy" implies inefficiency, waste, and red tape—problems in need of solutions. And so, president after president has pledged to fix the bureaucracy, to bring it more in line with the supposedly more efficient practices of the private sector. But for all the resources spent on reform initiatives over the last eighty years, administrative challenges continue to vex presidents.[1] As we shall see, the inextricably political nature of administrative reform has been responsible for the failure of numerous reform initiatives.

10.1.1 The Long History of Administrative Reform

We tend to think about reforms associated with the federal bureaucracy in purely administrative terms: minimizing financial waste, increasing expertise and efficiency, and promoting good governance. Calls for reforms come about when bureaucratic agencies make headlines for misspending taxpayer dollars. Occasionally, presidents themselves promote administrative reforms that are intended to increase efficiency by, for example, drawing on impartial experts to apply the principles of scientific management.

References to neutral competence, efficiency, and standardization figured prominently in President Franklin Delano Roosevelt's Brownlow Committee, an early effort to expand the president's control over the administrative state. (See chapter 2 for a discussion of scientific management and the Brownlow Committee.) The work of this committee, though, harkened back to even earlier presidential initiatives to impose some order on an expanding bureaucratic apparatus. Some thirty years prior, FDR's distant cousin Theodore Roosevelt launched his own initiative "to investigate and find out what changes are needed to place the conduct of the executive business of the Government in all its branches on the most economical and effective basis in the light of the best modern business practice."[2] According to both Roosevelts, the federal administration should be understood as an organization like any other and should thus be expected to maximize efficiency and improve the quality of outputs. But FDR also thought that the president, as chief administrator, held a special place in this expanding bureaucracy.[3] It was the president, after all, who would stand atop the bureaucratic hierarchy, oversee the interactions between the various components of the administrative state, and ensure that government responsibilities were appropriately divided and distributed across agencies, departments, and bureaus.

Not long after Brownlow, the Republican Congress in 1947 proposed the establishment of the Commission on Organization of the Executive Branch of Government, in large part to counter the expansion of the federal government that had arisen in the wake of FDR's New Deal.[4] Republicans intended for the commission to advise the next president (whom they expected to be a Republican), but the Truman administration effectively co-opted it after the 1948 election. One commentator noted, "Big Government is with us and is likely to stay," despite the fact that chairman (and former president) Herbert Hoover's "social philosophy and outlook were notoriously unsympathetic with recent trends toward a Welfare State."[5] Hoover himself remarked, "Our job is to make every Government activity that now exists work efficiently. It is not our function to say whether it should exist or not, but it is our function to see if we cannot make it work better."[6] The recommendations of the Hoover Commission, as it came to be known, embraced the managerial presidency, rationalized the bureaucracy, and lent organizational support to the expanding government.[7]

Not long after he took office in 1953, President Eisenhower convened a second Hoover Commission, also chaired by the former president. Though he had criticized the "big government" programs of Truman's Fair Deal during his first campaign, Eisenhower never reverted to the goals of Republican congressmen from the 1940s. As he put it in a letter to his brother, "Should any political party attempt to abolish social security and unemployment insurance, and eliminate labor laws and farm programs, you would not hear of that party again in our political history."[8] Therefore, this second commission, like the first, focused on bureaucratic organization and efficiency rather than political change.[9]

More recent presidents have continued to build on FDR's efforts to rationalize the federal bureaucracy. In launching one such reform initiative, President Bill Clinton declared, "Our goal is to make the entire federal government less expensive and more efficient, and to change the culture of our national bureaucracy away from complacency and entitlement toward initiative and empowerment."[10] The project, headed by Vice President Al Gore and named the National Performance Review (NPR), scrutinized the internal operations of individual agencies, all with an eye toward eliminating waste and improving the operations of the federal government. Across Clinton's two terms in office, NPR cut hundreds of thousands of government jobs and closed thousands of federal field offices—leading Gore to declare, with some pride, that the federal government workforce of 1996 was "the smallest it [had] been in more than 30 years."[11]

Clinton's successors, both Democrats and Republicans, continued these efforts to reorganize and consolidate the executive branch. Their initiatives combined objective evaluation—such as George W. Bush's "green-yellow-red" stoplight scorecard to track the effectiveness of major agencies and departments—and subjective assessments—such as Obama's solicitation of personal feedback from federal employees.

All of these good government initiatives were couched in the language of efficiency and effectiveness. No matter how prudent or sincere, however, they could not keep politics at bay.

10.1.2 Enter Politics

President Woodrow Wilson, an academic and political scientist by trade, famously argued that the work of public administration should be shielded from the nefarious influence of politics. "Most important to be observed," Wilson wrote, "is the truth already so much and so fortunately insisted upon by our civil-service reformers; namely, that administration lies outside the proper sphere of politics. Administrative questions are not political questions."[12] This division between administration and politics has rhetorical appeal, to be sure, but drawing such a line, in reality, is nearly impossible.

Calls for cost-saving measures, transparency, improved customer service, and good management obscure the federal bureaucracy's inherently political nature. A fundamentally different logic applies to government administration than to corporate management. The very purposes of government are deeply contested by parties, politicians, and the public at large. As a result, questions about *how* best to perform a specific action are inextricably tied to prior and inherently political questions about *what* actions should be performed.

For all they do to impose order and rationality on the bureaucracy, presidents also play an important part in its politicization. Presidents do not want the bureaucracy to perform mandated functions efficiently, per se. Rather, they want the bureaucracy to perform the specific functions that matter most to them. Presidents certainly see the value of streamlining and consolidating the bureaucracy, but first they must control it.

10.1.3 Whose Bureaucracy?

The bureaucratic apparatus is hardly a neutral entity that faithfully and efficiently serves well-defined public purposes. Rather, it is the site of political contestation over the production and implementation of public policy. Thus, control over the bureaucracy does not come easily to presidents, who must overcome impediments from Congress, interest groups, and bureaucrats, all with agendas of their own.

CONGRESS

Through hearings, investigations, and budgetary adjustments, members of Congress can interrupt—and, in some cases, impede—presidential efforts to control the bureaucracy. For the most part, members of Congress want to see the legislation they pass enacted in a manner consistent with their intent. Thus, they may pass laws specifically aimed at making bureaucratic actions more transparent and insulating agencies from presidential control. Frequently, Congress and the president will try to set different agendas for the bureaucracy, which makes it nearly impossible for bureaucrats to realize the efficient and effective outcomes that the public expects.

The persistent debate over federal education policy provides a case in point. In 2001, President George W. Bush and a bipartisan group of congressional members worked together to pass the No Child Left Behind Act (NCLB), a new law that completely overhauled and expanded the federal government's role in education. The changes, which included the development of new tests, new standards for evaluating student learning, and an array of punitive measures for schools that failed to meet the standards, placed a heavy burden on bureaucrats charged with interpreting and implementing the law.

Upon taking office in 2009, President Obama sought to revise the standards set by NCLB. In 2011, he announced that he would give states the ability to waive certain constraints imposed by the original legislation. In exchange, the president said he expected state officials to adopt his administration's education agenda. (For more on Obama's efforts here, see chapters 4 and 9). Even as bureaucrats worked to implement NCLB, therefore, they had to respond to Obama's new directives and plan for the possibility of future congressional legislation. Sure enough, in December 2015, Congress passed an updated version of NCLB, the Every Student Succeeds Act, with yet another round of changes for national education policy.[13] Just keeping pace with the policy, born of political strategizing and compromise, proved to be a challenge for the bureaucracy.

INTEREST GROUPS

In addition to Congress, interest groups may interfere with the president's ability to influence agency agendas. Some critics, for instance, have argued that the Food and Drug Administration (FDA) has been co-opted by pharmaceutical companies, which stand to make massive amounts of money when a drug is approved for public consumption, when costly regulations are eased, or when the opportunities for new, competing medical products to enter the market are foreclosed.* These companies, which have profited trillions of dollars in recent years,[14] lobby members of Congress and launch major public relations campaigns intended to influence the FDA agenda.[15] To be fair, the FDA is often placed in a difficult position. If it does not approve products quickly enough, it invites charges of ignoring citizens in need of new treatments, but if it does so hastily, it risks endangering the public's health. Trying to weigh these competing imperatives, the FDA sometimes takes its cues from the very companies it is supposed to regulate.

BUREAUCRATS' AGENDAS

Possibly the biggest impediment to presidential control is bureaucrats' own agendas. Bureaucrats enjoy substantial discretion by virtue of their expertise about policy matters, their networks of relationships with interest groups and politicians, and the fact that much of their labor takes place well beyond the watchful eyes of elected officials. Some bureaucrats may not work as hard as the president would like them to—a phenomenon that social scientists call **slack**. Other times, bureaucrats may be perfectly willing to work hard, but they choose to do so in the service of objectives that do not align with the president's, which social scientists call **drift**. In either instance, the president's policy goals can founder on the rocks of a recalcitrant bureaucracy.

For all parties involved, the stakes of bureaucratic politics are high. But they are especially so for the chief executive, who, more than anyone else, can expect to reap the blame or praise for the federal bureaucracy's performance. How do presidents stack the odds in their favor? Control is of the essence, and presidents have developed strategies for acquiring it. In the sections that follow, we examine three strategies: politicization, centralization, and bureaucratic redesign.

---

* The FDA, for instance, tried for years to get sunscreen manufacturers to change labels advertising improbably high SPFs, as well as "waterproof" or "sweat-proof" sunblock. (Sunscreen falls into the category of a drug, according to FDA rules.) Pharmaceutical companies that manufacture sunscreen eventually convinced the FDA to delay these regulations, leaving consumers to navigate products on their own at a time when skin cancer rates are at their highest. See Scott Hensley, "FDA Delays Sunscreen Label Redo," National Public Radio, May 16, 2012, http://www.npr.org/blogs/health/2012/05/16/152822423/fda-delays-sunscreen-label-redo; and "FDA Delays Sunscreen Label Changes by 6 Months," CBS News, May 15, 2012, http://www.cbsnews.com/news/fda-delays-sunscreen-label-changes-by-6-months/.

10.2 Politicization

One way presidents aim to exert control over the more than two million employees who make up the executive branch is through **politicization**—that is, the appointment of loyal and like-minded personnel. By hiring staff who are directly accountable to them, presidents intend to reorient the bureaucracy around their objectives, their priorities, and their worldviews. They fill high-level staff positions with people who share their own commitments and who will work toward aligning the rest of the federal bureaucracy accordingly. **Political appointees** can be expected to do this more reliably than can **career bureaucrats**.

10.2.1 What Politicization Looks Like

Major attempts to reform the federal bureaucracy are usually politically motivated, with Congress and the president closely monitoring agencies whose activities they would just as soon reduce, or even eliminate. There are other instances, however, when presidents want to extend the reach of an agency or department. High-level appointments and firings within these agencies are often made on the basis of ideology rather than competence. And sometimes a president's interests are best served by leaving a position vacant.

HIRING

James Watt's tenure as secretary of the interior under President Ronald Reagan and Gale Norton's time in the same office under President George W. Bush illustrate the phenomenon of ideological appointments. Both Watt and Norton had been attorneys for the Mountain States Legal Foundation, an advocacy organization that fights against environmental regulation.[16] During both of their tenures at the Department of the Interior, critics charged that the presidents who appointed them were less interested in protecting federal lands than they were in developing them.

Certainly, these presidents chose secretaries they knew would take a limited (or, some would argue, appropriately balanced) view of their duties to secure the well-being of the nation's parks and lands. The public should probably not have expected anything different. Neither Reagan nor Bush made any effort to hide his views about environmental regulation when campaigning for office. It would not have been in either's interest to appoint a secretary who fundamentally disagreed with his public position.

Reagan's appointment of Anne Gorsuch (whose son would become a Supreme Court justice under Trump) to head the Environmental Protection Agency (EPA) also invited controversy. An ideological ally of Reagan, Gorsuch aimed to limit the size and scope of the EPA—in direct violation of legislative intent.[17] Her short-lived tenure at the EPA was rife with budget cuts, conflicts with long-serving employees, and mismanagement of the Superfund cleanup initiative, which ultimately led to her resignation.[18] Seeking to restore trust in the agency—and more importantly, his administration's leadership of it—Reagan replaced Gorsuch with William Ruckelshaus, the EPA's original administrator and a strong advocate for environmental regulation.[19] Thus, in this particular instance the president's attempt to politicize the EPA produced an agency more committed to the environmentalist cause than the president initially intended. (For more on scandals like these, see section 10.5.3.)

President Trump followed the example of Reagan and Bush in making ideologically motivated cabinet appointments, some of which resulted in secretaries who opposed the existence of the very agency they were tasked to run. For example, Trump nominated former Texas governor Rick Perry to head up the Department of Energy. Though he had a long résumé of government experience, Perry famously called for the complete elimination of several departments and agencies in his bid for president in 2011, including the very one he ran.[20] Similarly, Trump appointed billionaire Republican donor Betsy DeVos, a strong advocate for charter schools and private-school vouchers, as secretary of education. A long-time critic of public schools, DeVos was placed in charge of the single most important federal agency for education policy.

Politicization, however, does not always impede bureaucratic initiative or undermine an agency's or department's mandate. Sometimes, political appointments instead are used to accelerate the pace of bureaucratic policymaking. Take, for instance, Obama's appointment of Steven Chu as secretary of energy. Chu hoped to ratchet up the Energy Department's efforts to combat climate change. In a statement prepared for his Senate confirmation committee hearing, Chu said, "Climate change is a growing and pressing problem. It is clear now that if we continue on our current path, we run the risk of dramatic, disruptive changes to our climate system in the lifetimes of our children and grandchildren."[21] He later asserted the overwhelming scientific consensus that human activity has played a "significant and likely dominant role in climate change."[22]

Such declarations foretold aggressive policy initiatives. During his four-year tenure, Chu worked to address climate change, amplify green energy efforts, and decrease dependence on foreign energy sources—all goals compatible with the president's own climate commitments. To be sure, some of the programs Chu spearheaded failed, most notably the financial backing of the solar firm Solyndra, which brought on harsh criticism of him, his department, and Obama. Much of the criticism throughout his tenure, however, came from Republicans in Congress, highlighting just how *political* political appointments can be.

FIRING

The politicization of the bureaucracy involves more than just the decision to hire individuals: it also relates to the decision to fire them. Presidents can and do release their own appointees when their interests diverge. One example is provided by Paul O'Neill, who had a relatively brief tenure as secretary of the treasury for the George W. Bush administration. Even before his appointment, O'Neill made a habit of expressing opposition to Bush's policies, from tax cuts to the decision to invade Iraq; once in office, his failure to toe the party line, or the president's line, ultimately resulted in his firing. Journalist Ron Suskind describes O'Neill's experience in *The Price of Loyalty*, beginning with the following quote from Hannah Arendt: "Total loyalty is possible only when fidelity is emptied of all concrete content, from which changes of mind might naturally arise."[23]

LEAVING POSITIONS VACANT

Relatedly, presidents may politicize by simply refusing to fill certain positions. By leaving vacancies unfilled, argues Christina Kinane, presidents can limit the reach of an agency while avoiding potentially costly nomination fights.[24] Notice, moreover, that Congress is ill-equipped to counter this strategy: Congress cannot nominate its own department heads, nor can it compel the president to do so. And so, when Trump inherited a federal bureaucracy engaged in policy activities with which he disagreed, he did not simply appoint loyalists to key positions of power. He also left vast swaths of the administrative state—in some departments and agencies, as much as 40 to 50 percent of political appointments—entirely empty.

10.2.2 *Opportunities for Politicization*

Over the course of their administrations, contemporary presidents make between 3,000 and 4,000 appointments.[25] Although comprising less than 2 percent of the total civilian workforce within the federal bureaucracy, these partisan appointees dominate the highest echelons of management. More than half of the 2.5 million American civil servants are "excepted" from traditional merit-based guidelines for employment. The majority of these serve in agency-specific personnel systems that officially operate under the merit scheme but give flexibility to managers, making it easier to circumvent rules in hiring and promotion. The rest are top-level positions that are even more susceptible to politicization. While relatively small in number, these positions are filled outside of the traditional merit system, receive the highest salaries, and have the most responsibility in all of the federal civilian personnel system.

Three main classes of positions are susceptible to politicization (figure 10.1):

1. **Presidential Appointments with Senate confirmation** (PAS), which include department secretaries and undersecretaries, heads of major bureaus, and ambassadors, have the greatest authority. Within this class, presidents also select the individuals and boards that govern independent federal agencies, regulatory commissions, and government corporations, although these appointees often must satisfy various rules and restrictions.

2. **Senior Executive Service (SES) personnel** are charged with implementing the president's agenda across the bureaucracy. These senior staff often work in the offices of cabinet secretaries, deputy secretaries, and agency heads. SES positions were a creation of the Civil Service Reform Act of 1978, which was intended to provide presidents with more control over positions most relevant for the implementation of their agendas. Presidents or their subordinates can choose an

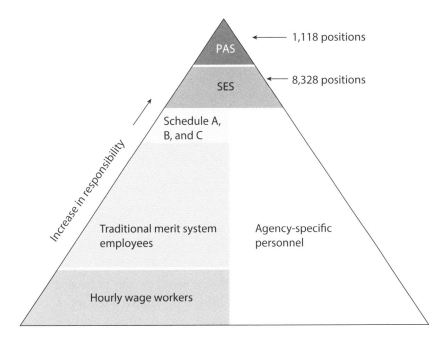

FIGURE 10.1. Personnel system in the federal bureaucracy. The vast majority of employees in the executive branch are hired without any input from the White House. Those employees whom the president does appoint, however, sit at the very top of the bureaucratic hierarchy, enjoying the highest pay and greatest responsibility. These are the positions that are susceptible to politicization. Shades of gray indicate positions that are not politicized. Numbers of PAS and SES positions listed as of December 2020. *Source:* Committee on Oversight and Reform, U.S. House of Representatives, December 2020, https://www.govinfo.gov/content/pkg/GPO-PLUMBOOK-2020/pdf/GPO-PLUMBOOK-2020.pdf.

existing (career) member of the SES or a political appointee from outside the SES to fill a position. By law, however, political appointees in SES positions cannot exceed 10 percent of the entire SES workforce, nor can they account for more than 25 percent of the SES positions within a single agency. According to one study, politically appointed SES bureaucrats, like bureaucrats generally, are most likely to be added to agencies that share the president's policy views.[26]

3. Lastly, federal agencies use the **excepted service** to bypass competitive, merit-based hiring practices. This category helps streamline the employment process in certain circumstances—for example, when trying to hire people with disabilities or students and recent graduates. Within the excepted service, a subset known as "Schedule C" has found its way under presidential control. According to the Office of Personnel Management (OPM), Schedule C positions "are for political appointments to confidential or policy-setting positions."[27] Most (but not all) of these positions fall just below SES personnel, working as policy experts or assistants to PAS employees. The president appoints Schedule C employees with

OPM authorization—sometimes for the express purpose of advancing specific policy objectives but often just to reward political supporters.

Within certain segments of the bureaucracy, the president has ample opportunities to appoint like-minded personnel. That these opportunities exist, however, does not mean that they will be taken.

10.2.3 When Do Presidents Politicize?

Upon taking office, presidents set to work on politicizing the bureaucracy. The task may assume a sense of particular urgency when presidents seek control over agencies serving purposes aligned with their political opponents. Nearly all political appointees, however, can expect their tenures in office to come to a close when the president who appointed them leaves office.

Notably, historical politicization trends do not reveal steadily increasing attempts at presidential control over time. Rather, presidents make varying numbers of political appointments in different agencies and at different times.[28] Just how many depends, among other things, on the levels of support that presidents can expect to find in agencies, Congress, and the polity more generally. Politicization thus functions as a sort of antidote to opposition: the more support presidents enjoy in office, the less they need to politicize.

At any given moment, decisions about whether to politicize an agency hinge, in large part, on a perceived trade-off between responsiveness and competence.[29] When confronting an agency that is either pursuing a mandate that the president opposes or filled with bureaucrats who oppose the president's policy commitments, the president has strong incentives to politicize. It is precisely for this reason that Republican presidents have politicized the EPA and Department of the Interior, while Democratic presidents have politicized significant portions of the foreign policy apparatus.[30]

What they gain in loyalty, however, presidents may lose in competence. By its very nature, politicization privileges ideology over expertise. Recognizing that their time in office may be short, some political appointees spend less effort acquiring new knowledge and more time advancing, as best they can, specific policy directives. Accordingly, when the tasks that an agency performs are particularly complex, or when the costs of administrative errors are particularly high, presidents may assign greater value to neutral competence and shy away from taking full advantage of their opportunities to politicize.

10.2.4 Politicization's Close Cousin: Patronage

With politicization, presidents appoint like-minded bureaucrats in order to assert their policy influence over an agency or department. Occasionally, however, presidents use appointments for purposes of **political patronage**—that is, the rewarding of people for their past political support.

U.S. ambassadorships often satisfy the president's need for patronage appointments. Making large donations to a president's campaign does not guarantee a donor a plush ambassadorship, but it certainly doesn't hurt. Though the 1980 Foreign Service Act mandates that "contributions to political campaigns should not be a factor in the appointment of an individual as a chief of mission," presidents since then have generally followed a 70/30 rule when it comes to such appointments: they nominate career foreign service officers for roughly 70 percent of them and reserve the rest for political supporters. For one example of patronage, note Obama's appointment of Colleen Bell, a producer of *The Bold and the Beautiful* soap opera who donated hundreds of thousands of dollars to the president's last election and raised considerably more, as ambassador to Hungary. In her confirmation hearings, Bell stumbled badly during testimony about U.S. strategic interests in the country, but she was appointed just the same.[31]

Figure 10.2 plots the backgrounds of U.S. ambassadors appointed by Donald Trump against the standards of living in the countries to which they were assigned. Overwhelmingly, political appointees (who appear in gray) made their way to countries with higher standards of living than did career officers (who appear in black). Moreover, ambassadorships at many of the countries with the very highest standards of living were reserved for political appointees who made especially large political donations.

Trump, of course, was not the only president to behave in this way. Past presidents made just as many political appointments to ambassadorships around the globe, and, like Trump, these presidents reserved the choicest positions for people who raised large amounts for their political campaigns.[32]

Notice, though, that the point of patronage appointments is slightly different from that of political appointments. Whereas political appointments are primarily intended to align the operations of an agency with the president's policy preferences and commitments, patronage appointments are intended to reward individuals for their past and ongoing political support. Presidents, as such, use these appointments not only to control the bureaucracy but also to shore up their—and, by extension, their party's—electoral fortunes.

Presidents aren't limited to ambassadorships when rewarding loyal and wealthy supporters. In principle, presidents can make patronage appointments to any agency. In making such appointments, however, presidents again must assess the trade-off between responsiveness and competence. Patronage appointees, like political appointees, are not chosen on the basis of their neutral expertise. Rather, they are selected because of their demonstrated willingness to lend political support to the president. As a result, they are usually less adept at their jobs than are civil servants and working professionals who have devoted their lives to studying a particular policy problem.

Not surprisingly, then, presidents tend to reward their political supporters with patronage jobs that require less skill, that focus on policy issues that are less important to the president, that are less disruptive to an agency's ongoing operations, and that operate in administrative units that already are aligned with the president's policy objectives.[33] So

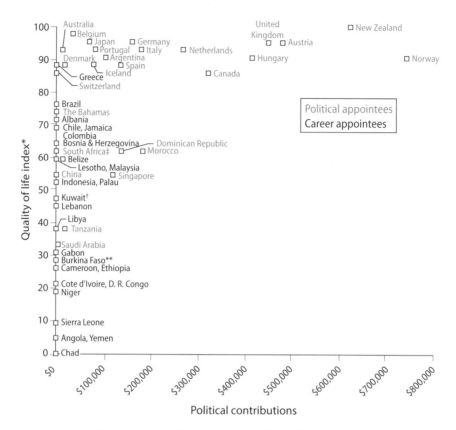

FIGURE 10.2. Patronage and the president's ambassadors. Ambassadorships in gray are patronage appointees. These posts are usually a reward for political contributions. "Political contributions" is the sum of political contributions to Donald Trump and the Republican National Committee after June 2015. *Sources:* "Appointments—Donald J. Trump," American Foreign Service Association, http://www.afsa.org/appointments-donald-j-trump; https://www.opensecrets.org/donor-lookup/; "Human Development Data (1990–2017)," United Nations Development Programme, Human Development Reports, n.d., http://hdr.undp.org/en/data#.

doing, presidents manage to reward the political loyalties of their supporters without causing irreparable damage to government operations.

10.3 Centralization

If politicization involves sending the president's allies out into the bureaucracy, then an alternative strategy—called **centralization**—involves bringing the bureaucracy closer to the president. Throughout the White House, officials directly tied to the president perform tasks that mirror, supplement, or coordinate the work of bureaucrats in outer agencies or departments. Keeping this work close by—and in many cases, just down the hall—presidents can be sure that these agencies are advancing their core interests.

10.3.1 White House Staff

Centralization is not like a light switch with on and off positions; it's more like a dimmer. Presidents can centralize to a greater or lesser degree, shifting decision-making authority from the far reaches of government bureaucracy into the Executive Office of the President (EOP). Within the EOP, different administrative units allow the president greater or lesser degrees of oversight. But short of presidents just performing tasks themselves, the apex of centralization resides in the White House staff.

Though the president has always had advisors and aides, the White House Office (WHO) was a twentieth-century invention. In chapter 3, we briefly examined the WHO's various political and policy offices, which host a range of employees from the president's daily schedulers to the advisors at the National Space Council. What unifies these offices, however, is their proximity to the president. The WHO staff are closest to the president, both physically—as the name suggests, many are housed in the White House—and organizationally, as they oversee the president's highest priorities. In large part, the WHO's very reason for existing is to attend to immediate requests and demands of the president.

The White House staff direct the flows of communication both to and from the president. Consequently, they are crucial allies in the president's efforts to control the bureaucracy. On the incoming side, they field suggestions, requests, and data; reprocess this information to fit the president's preferences; and prioritize what should move on to the Oval Office. On the outgoing side, they inform other governmental bodies of the president's priorities and oversee the agencies that are entrusted with implementing the president's policies.

Currently, administrative units within the WHO help the president monitor and manage government offices outside the White House (see figure 3.2). Key components of the WHO staff include:

- the Domestic Policy Council, which supervises the development and execution of domestic policy across the entire government, including presenting the president's priorities to Congress;
- the National Economic Council, which coordinates economic policymaking across agencies, advises the president on current issues, and monitors the implementation of policy throughout the government;
- the Office of Legislative Affairs, which works with Congress to write legislation and set policy priorities, even going so far as to help congressional staff write briefs and fact sheets; and
- the Office of Public Engagement, which interacts and builds relationships with advocacy groups, nongovernmental organizations, and state governments.

In addition to these larger administrative units, various subcomponents of the WHO answer the president's mail, schedule public appearances, prioritize and research policy positions, and communicate with Congress, other governmental agencies, and lobbying groups. In addition to organizational assistance, WHO staff offer political advice and policy expertise. Many of the president's closest confidants are among its ranks. And as the Thinking Institutionally feature of this chapter shows, all presidents consider a host of institutional factors when thinking about how best to build their WHO staff.

Thinking Institutionally: White House Staffing Trends

Just how many policy advisors should a president hire? In recent decades, presidents have answered, "More than my predecessors." Some scholars have pointed to the Nixon administration as marking a definitive break from previous staffing trends, insofar as it developed a much larger staff with a more elaborate hierarchy than had previous administrations.[34] By 2020, over four hundred staff worked in the WHO, including an official—and handsomely paid—calligrapher, as well as numerous administrators boasting vague titles such as "vetter" and "analyst."[35]

Of course, presidents' staffing decisions depend upon their policy agendas, leadership styles, prior experience in office, and the like. Yet there is also an important institutional dimension to this calculus. Political scientist Matthew Dickinson has argued that the historical growth of the White House staff is principally driven by "changes in presidents' bargaining relations with Congress, the media, and the public, and only secondarily by the general growth in government's responsibilities."[36] In other words, presidents build up staffs to counter rising uncertainty about their power vis-à-vis other actors.

To be sure, political outcomes are always uncertain in our system of government, but of late, Dickinson argues, this uncertainty has intensified. The polarization of the two major parties (see section 8.2.3), the withering of party discipline, and the rise of subcommittees have degraded traditional bargaining processes. In order to accommodate these changing political realities, wherein power is increasingly decentralized and dispersed, presidents have worked to fortify their own institution.

To empirically evaluate such claims, Dickinson tracked the total number of employees in the White House and total expenditures within the EOP and then related changes in these two quantities to measures of the president's bargaining relationship with Congress, the public, and the media. Dickinson concluded that presidents rely upon larger staff when the opposition party holds a greater number of seats within Congress, when the president's popularity is low, and when the size of the press corps increases. In all of these instances, Dickinson argues, the president's ability to advance a policy agenda is compromised, and presidents attempt to fortify their position by hiring staff members.

Beyond short-term political imperatives, the growth of presidential staff also reflects the rising expectations placed upon presidents. Increasingly, presidents are expected to solve tasks that they would have had no business meddling in a century ago. They are expected to "run the world" abroad while shepherding the economy at home and commanding a sprawling bureaucracy—all this while Congress and the

Supreme Court bite at their heels.[37] Individual presidents have personal preferences about whom to hire and how best to organize them within the WHO. But all presidents must respond to an avalanche of public expectations, which requires them to invest in a deep bench of White House staff.

10.3.2 Policy Czars

Another way in which presidents have enhanced centralization and augmented their political control of the federal bureaucracy is through the designation of so-called **czars**—policy advisors whose job is to coordinate and centralize the activities of multiple units of the executive branch. Unlike traditional public ministers, consultants, and public officers, the Constitution does not mention czars. Their appointments, moreover, do not require congressional oversight. Both in the creation of these positions and the selection of individuals to fill them, presidents exert unparalleled influence.

The term "czar" has its origins in the nineteenth century, when it was usually used derisively to refer to presidential advisors who were seen as overstepping their authority. By the middle of the twentieth century, however, the once-derogatory nomenclature and the kind of position it referenced had been embraced by presidential administrations. When Nixon first created the position of drug czar to oversee the enforcement of drug prohibition laws, the term conveyed a take-charge approach to a national crisis that could not be solved through the usual bureaucratic channels. Subsequent presidents appointed czars with rising frequency, and by the beginning of the twenty-first century, czars were widely accepted in American political culture.[38] Under the presidency of George W. Bush, the use of czars reached new heights, jumping to a remarkable fifty-five from seventeen under Clinton. Obama took this precedent and ran with it, appointing fifty-four policy czars during his first three years in office.

To understand the usefulness of czars in the policymaking process, take a look at figure 10.3, which depicts the configuration of agencies focusing on drug policy under the Obama administration. Within this single domain the president sits atop a nearly inscrutable web of agencies, subagencies, and intergovernmental departments. Meanwhile, the drug czar's department, the Office of National Drug Control Policy (ONDCP), operates right at the center: below the president's cabinet-level positions but above the various subagencies that carry out the day-to-day work of drug enforcement.

The centrality of the ONDCP is no coincidence. Indeed, it is the key to the drug czar's success. On one side, the ONDCP coordinates with the Centers for Disease Control and Prevention (CDC), which focuses on public health and disease prevention. On the other, it coordinates with the Drug Enforcement Administration (DEA), which combats drug trafficking and distribution. Representing functionally opposite approaches to drug policy—medical and legal enforcement—the CDC and DEA seldom collaborate, communicate, or otherwise work together. The gap between their areas of operation is simply too large. But the drug czar's domain (shown in dark grey) bridges the divide.

FIGURE 10.3. The drug czar in the administrative state. Responding directly to the president, the drug czar oversees the ONDCP, through which partial approaches to an issue are made whole. Lines denote a regular and formal working relationship between two administrative units. Agencies under the immediate purview of the drug czar are coded in dark gray; all other agencies are coded in light gray.

Thus, the czar serves to unite, coordinate, and provide administrative oversight to an entire field of policymaking. For the president, communicating with the bureaucracy is difficult enough; encouraging bureaucratic agencies to communicate *with each other* is an entirely separate task. Such is the usefulness of policy czars: they can facilitate coordination and communication within the bureaucracy, just as they improve the president's oversight and control over it.

Still, not every president has been so quick to embrace the role of policy czars. In February 2020, with the global coronavirus pandemic looming in the United States, national leaders called on President Trump to appoint a "coronavirus czar," just as Obama had done for the Ebola outbreak in 2014. "The Trump administration must appoint a point-person—a czar—to implement a real plan to manage the coronavirus: an independent, non-partisan, global health expert," declared Senate minority leader Chuck Schumer.[39]

Trump went in a different direction. Rather than a single individual, Trump assembled the White House Coronavirus Task Force, a twenty-eight-member team of scientists, cabinet secretaries, lawyers, and administrators. Though some of its members were colloquially referred to as "czars," their job descriptions differed in important ways. Moreover, because of the sprawling nature of the task force, it was never clear who was in charge. While the team was chaired by Vice President Mike Pence, it was Dr. Deborah Birx—formerly the U.S. Global AIDS Coordinator—who wore the title "Coronavirus Response Coordinator." Birx, however, frequently took a back seat to Trump himself, and particularly so during daily coronavirus press briefings when Trump informed the public about the administration's efforts.

At these briefings, Trump would often contradict members of his own task force. For example, despite "Testing Czar" Adm. Brett Giroir's repeated claims to the contrary, Trump maintained that surges in coronavirus cases were due to increases in testing.[40] Once, Trump suggested—to Birx's visible dismay—that disinfectant be injected into patients' bodies to kill the virus.[41] Meanwhile, deaths from the coronavirus continued to climb throughout Trump's time in office. The ultimate failure of his administration's coronavirus response speaks, at least in part, to the importance of unified leadership in the face of national crises— leadership that some presidents seek in the appointment of a policy czar.

10.3.3 When Do Presidents Centralize?

When do presidents rely on individuals within the EOP for policy advice, and when do they turn to bureaucrats outside of it? Individuals within the EOP are more likely to follow the president's lead, but they tend to know less about the technicalities of public policy. Employees outside the EOP who have more expertise about policy cannot so easily be trusted to serve the president's interests. The challenge for the president, therefore, is to figure out how best to weigh these competing considerations.

As we saw with politicization, the tendency toward centralization can vary from one issue to the next.[42] Presidents are more likely to centralize when the policy consequences of forgoing expertise are less severe. By contrast, presidents tend to worry more about the importance of expertise when an issue is highly complex or technical; in these instances, presidents turn to department bureaucrats when developing a policy agenda, particularly when the costs of acquiring reliable information from departments are low.

According to one study, the three strongest predictors of centralization are the relative newness of a policy issue, the likely involvement of a large number of agencies in its handling, and the need for an agency's reorganization.[43] When a president wants quick action to address an emerging issue, centralization is more likely. When there are a number of agencies interested in a given policy, centralization can satisfy a demand for coordination and control across invested departments. Finally, proposals to reorganize agencies are more likely to be hashed out within the EOP than in the agencies that could be affected by the restructuring.

Historical Transformations: The National Intelligence Bureaucracy and 9/11

Consider for a moment the numerous executive agencies tasked with providing intelligence services. While the Central Intelligence Agency (CIA) is the organization best known for collecting and analyzing foreign intelligence, it is not the only arm of the executive branch with such responsibilities. The National Security Agency (NSA) is far larger than the CIA, and the State and Defense Departments have their own intelligence arms, each boasting a significant staff and budget. Additionally, each military service branch—the U.S. Army, Navy, Air Force, Marines, Coast Guard, and Space Force—conducts its own intelligence activities and contributes to the development of foreign policy strategies. Even the Federal Bureau of Investigation (FBI), which

Continued on next page

ostensibly focuses on domestic security issues, tracks international terrorism suspects who travel to the United States and keeps close tabs on any terrorist group that may operate within the nation's borders.

When agencies work at cross-purposes, the foreign policy bureaucracy is not nearly as efficient or as effective as it might be. Sometimes, bureaucratic inefficiency is just a costly nuisance. In matters involving national intelligence, however, the stakes are much higher. Presidents are inundated with multiple, often conflicting sources of intelligence; failing to use them wisely can lead to incalculable harm, for their own legacies and for the nation's security. Faced with this dilemma, a chief executive needs to find ways to rationalize the information pouring in from across the bureaucracy.

In the aftermath of the September 11, 2001, terrorist attacks, the challenge of coordinating and overseeing the many intelligence agencies in the federal government became more pressing than ever. In 2002, the National Commission on Terrorist Attacks Upon the United States (better known as the 9/11 Commission) recommended the creation of the Office of the Director of National Intelligence (ODNI) to serve as a central clearinghouse for national security intelligence, which, it was thought, would reduce the chances of another major terrorist attack.

Centralizing intelligence can bring its own costs, however. After 9/11, the president and vice president demanded access to even more intelligence than they had previously received. Senior White House staff, most of whom had no background in intelligence, were presented with a daily Threat Matrix detailing potential domestic attacks. On a single day in October 2001, this document included intelligence on approximately one hundred threats.[44] One member of the NSC later said that the chief mistake of the post-9/11 Bush presidency was showing too much information to the president directly—in other words, *excessively* centralizing. Officials suffered "sensory overload" and became "paranoid."[45]

As the response to 9/11 demonstrates, presidents are sometimes forced to choose between bad options. Bush could either centralize intelligence efforts or defer to others. The first option would increase his level of control, while requiring expertise that he and his senior officials lacked. The second would allow him to delegate decision making to others, thereby increasing his chances of being blamed for "falling asleep at the switch," should another attack occur.

Looking back, it seems Bush chose the former, opting to overwhelm himself and his administration rather than be painted as a disinterested president. Note that this decision was in line with what we predicted of presidents in chapter 4—that, whatever the situation, presidents will pursue power wherever they can find it. When confronting whether to centralize or politicize part of the bureaucracy, the single-minded pursuit of power continues to guide presidential decision making.

10.4 Bureaucratic Redesign: Cutting, Restructuring, and Creating Anew

Presidents do not need to take the existing bureaucracy as given. Rather, when they so choose, presidents can dismantle or restructure existing agencies, departments, and positions; or, alternatively, they can create new ones that are directly beholden to their influence. So doing, presidents attempt to fashion a bureaucracy more in line with their policy objectives and more attentive to their political needs.

More than four hundred agencies were created in the second half of the twentieth century. Of these, over half were established through the kinds of unilateral presidential actions that were discussed in chapter 9.[46] In addition, presidents frequently exercised their authority to eliminate existing agencies. When Nixon took office, he promptly set about dismantling the institutional centerpiece of Johnson's Great Society program, the Office of Economic Opportunity. Similarly, in an effort to restrict the power of the EPA to regulate industry, Reagan eliminated the Office of Enforcement. According to one analysis, fully 60 percent of all agencies created between 1946 and 1997 had been eliminated by 2000.[47]

Different kinds of agencies tend to survive for different lengths of time. Government corporations and independent agencies and commissions, which are intentionally given more autonomy, tend to live longer than agencies located within the EOP, which are subject to more presidential control. Presidents also have a more difficult time eliminating agencies whose heads serve for fixed terms and/or satisfy certain party balancing requirements.

Politics also appears to contribute to the life span of different agencies. Presidents are more likely to eliminate agencies created under the administration of presidents from the opposite party.* Take, for example, the USA Freedom Corps, a WHO policy council founded under President Bush that was meant to encourage volunteer participation in domestic security in the aftermath of the September 11 attacks. When he took office in 2009, Obama dramatically reorganized the corps, restoring some of its subunits to the agencies in which they resided before Bush consolidated them into the corps, while relocating others to the offices of the Surgeon General, Department of Homeland Security, and the Bureau of Justice Assistance.

When presidents are unable to eliminate or restructure objectionable agencies, they may set about creating new ones more to their liking. Imagine the challenge faced by a president who assumes office after an extended period of control by the opposition party.

---

* This finding can be interpreted in a number of ways. It is possible that presidents target programs created by the opposition party simply because they oppose them. Alternatively, partisan turnover in the White House may reflect broader changes in the public's spending priorities. If so, then the fact that agencies tend to die when a new party assumes the presidency has less to do with the powers wielded by the new president and more to do with the general efforts of elected politicians to keep pace with public opinion.

Rather than relying on individuals appointed under the former administrations to carry out a new agenda, presidents may decide to create altogether new agencies. In so doing, the new president contributes to the inefficiency often associated with bureaucracy. Presidents do so, though, with cause. Redundancy may simply be the cost of successive presidents' creating agencies best suited to their policy and political needs.

10.5 Downsides, Limitations, and Scandal

Presidents use the strategies of politicization, centralization, and bureaucratic redesign at different times and under different circumstances. Each strategy, however, comes with its own costs and limitations. When they are especially acute, presidents may temper their efforts to control the bureaucracy, preferring, instead, to allow civil servants to work more independently.

10.5.1 Downsides

Political scientist David Lewis has conducted some of the most comprehensive and careful evaluations of presidential efforts to politicize the federal bureaucracy.[48] In addition to documenting the particular conditions under which presidents politicize, Lewis investigates the impact of politicization on agency performance. His findings are sobering. Those agencies that employ a greater proportion of political employees, Lewis shows, function much less effectively than others. More-politicized agencies have trouble clarifying their goals, reconciling short- and long-term planning, maintaining adequate management, and producing desirable results.

Entirely consistent with Lewis's empirical research, a significant body of theoretical work reveals a basic—and by now familiar—trade-off between responsiveness and competence.[49] What presidents gain in control by politicizing an administrative unit, this literature shows, they invariably lose in expertise.[50] The willingness of bureaucrats to invest in expertise, after all, crucially depends upon their ability to act upon it and to help draft rules and implement policies that are consistent with what they learn and know. The entire point of politicizing an agency, though, is to constrain the actions an agency might take, particularly when its employees object to elements of a president's agenda. As a result, expertise becomes less valuable and bureaucrats, all else equal, become less likely to make costly investments in it, yielding a less capable, less effective administrative agency.

Other aspects of political appointments help explain why politicization is not especially conducive to an effective or efficient bureaucracy. The relatively short tenures of political appointees, most obviously, can compromise their ability to learn the culture of their agencies, secure the trust of their subordinates, and implement lasting policy change. Sometimes, too, a change in culture at the top can cause lower-level administrators to leave their posts and seek other employment in the public or private sector. According to some surveys, about 25 percent of career executives claimed that they intended to leave their position within the year.[51] Forty percent had job opportunities presented to them outside the federal government and 43 percent were eligible to retire. Such turnover may erode an agency's **institutional memory**—that is, employees' accumulated knowledge about an agency's operations. Compounding this problem is the regular difficulty in replacing employees. With partisanship on the rise and many presidential appointments requiring Senate confirmation, in any given year over the past several decades an average of 20 percent of such positions have been unfilled.

Centralization also can exacerbate political tensions between the White House and Congress and other political actors. Members of Congress often publicly decry the president's use of czars in lieu of cabinet members, for example, as a means of circumventing the Senate confirmation process, and cabinet members, federal agencies, and the career bureaucracy can all take issue with such a strategy if it is viewed as an attempt to displace them from the decision-making process.[52] The president may face political pushback on all fronts, including congressional attempts at oversight or the imposition of funding constraints.

10.5.2 Limitations

For all their side effects, the available remedies for bureaucratic intransigence may not offer a complete cure. If an agency has a mission or agenda that is inconsistent with the president's, a single political appointee, even in a position of influence, may have little success in aligning the agency with the president's priorities.[53] Nor is the decision about whether to politicize up to the president alone. Many political appointments require Senate confirmation, which can impede the president's efforts to politicize the bureaucracy.

When the Senate refuses to confirm a president's appointment, the president can either withdraw the nomination and offer up a new candidate or make a **recess appointment** after the Senate term ends. Discussed at greater length in chapter 11, recess appointments were originally designed to ensure that the government continued to function when the Senate adjourned for long periods of time. Increasingly, however, presidents turn to them to circumvent political opposition within Congress.*

But recess appointments do not make for a perfect end run around Congress, as its members have a variety of parliamentary tricks up their own sleeves. In 2007, for example, Senate majority leader Harry Reid was able to keep the Democrat-controlled Senate in perpetual session in order to prevent controversial appointments by Bush during recess.[54] In 2012, during what would otherwise have been a recess, Senate Republicans similarly attempted to block President Obama from making appointments without Senate confirmation by gaveling in for a few minutes or even seconds at a time when most members were scattered across the country.[55]

---

*According to one study, presidents are more likely to make recess appointments when they lack partisan support in the Senate, such as during times of divided government, and when they have high public approval. See Pamela C. Corley, "Avoiding Advice and Consent: Recess Appointments and Presidential Power," *Presidential Studies Quarterly* 36, no. 4 (2006): 670–80.

FIGURE 10.4. Recess appointments are not always successful. Obama was hardly the first president to rely upon recess appointments. Still, his efforts to circumvent Congress ran into trouble within the federal judiciary, which ruled his actions unconstitutional. Copyright 2012 Jimmy Margulies. Reproduced by permission of Cagle Cartoons.

When Obama proceeded with his appointments to the National Labor Relations Board (NLRB) and Consumer Financial Protection Bureau (CFPB) anyway, the interbranch fight shifted to the judiciary (figure 10.4). Companies affected by the decisions of these agencies sued, claiming that NLRB and CFPB officials had been appointed unconstitutionally. In their unanimous 2014 decision on *National Labor Relations Board v. Noel Canning*, the Supreme Court ruled 9–0 that the Constitution's recess appointments clause gives Congress the power to decide when it is in session and that Obama's recess appointments were therefore unconstitutional.

To avoid fights like these, some presidents have given up on the Senate confirmation process for certain appointments. Instead, these presidents install so-called "acting" or "interim" officials—temporary officeholders who do not require congressional approval. According to the Federal Vacancies Reform Act of 1998, the president can promote individuals to these positions for a period of at least 210 days, and sometimes much longer.* Alternatively, the president can simply delegate a vacant position's duties to lower-level officials, an option that does not come with clearly defined time limits.

* According to one scholar, the time limits laid out in the Federal Vacancies Reform Act are "a puzzle fit for a math class." The tenure of acting officials depends on whether the vacancy existed when the president took office as well as whether the president is actively trying to nominate a replacement. For more information, see Anne Joseph O'Connell, "Actings," *Columbia Law Review* (April 2020): 630.

Recent presidents have relied on acting officials to fill high-level jobs. In fact, of all the cabinet secretaries to serve from 1981 to 2020, nearly half served in an acting capacity. The Trump administration seemed to relish the opportunity to appoint individuals in an acting capacity. Unlike past presidents, in fact, Trump's acting cabinet secretaries outnumbered those confirmed by the Senate. Moreover, whereas Bush and Obama typically filled vacancies with deputies whose previous positions required congressional approval, Trump was far more likely to pull from political, non-Senate-confirmed positions such as chief of staff.[56]

While acting officials might seem like flexible alternatives to Senate confirmation, they suffer from what some have dubbed the "substitute teacher" problem.[57] Like substitute teachers working in classrooms, acting officials have considerably less sway over their departments than Senate-confirmed officials, even if they technically have the same powers. This much is evident in their official titles; rather than, say, "Director of the National Park Service," an acting official might be called "Deputy Director Exercising the Authority of Director of the National Park."[58] Such designations can degrade officials' ability to carry out the president's orders.

Meanwhile, a president who succeeds at bureaucratic centralization may clash with Congress. According to one study, the president's legislative initiatives are less likely to be enacted when the president centralizes authority.[59] The reasons for this, however, are not entirely clear. Members of Congress may look skeptically upon policy proposals coming from White House insiders rather than departmental experts. Alternatively, presidents may choose to centralize when they anticipate a difficult legislative road ahead. If so, then causality would appear to be reversed—expectations about legislative failure may encourage centralization, rather than centralization leading to legislative breakdown.

Presidents employ all three strategies—politicization, centralization, and bureaucratic restructuring—to deal with the problems of an unresponsive bureaucracy. Although increasing numbers of individuals and organizations work on a single policy issue, lines of responsibility can begin to blur and presidents can inadvertently create "an unwieldy, tower hierarchy in which accountability is diffuse at best and the president is sometimes the last to know."[60] The bureaucratization of staff within the White House, in other words, can create anew the same challenges that the system was initially designed to guard against.[61]

10.5.3 Scandal

Political appointees can cause all manner of political problems for their presidents. For when an unqualified lackey of the president bungles a job, recriminations may quickly fall upon his political superior. Consider Michael Brown's tenure as head of the Federal Emergency Management Agency (FEMA). Many argued that President George W. Bush appointed Brown, a former commissioner for the International Arabian Horse Association who had no experience running a major disaster relief organization, purely because of his political allegiance to the president. When Brown failed to demonstrate clear leadership of FEMA during the lead-up to and aftermath of Hurricane Katrina in 2005, many called for his resignation—which was promptly tendered—and railed against the Bush administration for having placed a political appointee in a position of such responsibility.

The Michael Brown scandal, however, pales in comparison to the one visited upon another Republican president nearly a century earlier. In the 1920s, an obscure geological formation called Teapot Dome came to symbolize government corruption in President Warren G. Harding's administration. The site of a Wyoming oil field that the government depended upon to fuel the navy in wartime, Teapot Dome was the subject of at least two controversies, the first of which involved private industries that wanted to exploit the oil reserves, and the second of which concerned private wells that surrounded the naval reserve fields and siphoned off their deposits.[62]

At the epicenter of these controversies was Albert Fall, a personal friend of Harding who was appointed secretary of the interior in 1921. Early in his term, Fall convinced Harding and Secretary of the Navy Edwin Denby to transfer the naval oil reserves at Teapot Dome to the Department of the Interior. He then secretly leased oil rights to Teapot Dome and other reserves under the control of the Department of the Interior to his friends Harry Sinclair (of the Mammoth Oil Corporation) and Edward Doheny (of Pan-American Petroleum and Transport).

When news of this deal broke in April 1922, Senator Robert La Follette called for a Senate investigation, which got underway in October that same year. Both men acknowledged giving Fall gifts, but both denied that the gifts had anything to do with their shared oil interests. With these early findings in hand, the Senate asked the president to cancel the leases and select special counsel to investigate the matter more fully.[63]

Throughout this period, Fall insisted that his actions were in the public's interest, since private wells at the field's perimeter threatened to drain the navy's oil reserves. Fall further argued that secrecy was of the essence, since the storage facilities were potential targets in a war. Neither claim advanced his cause, and Fall resigned from office in January 1923, less than two years after his original appointment.

When Harding died in August 1923, Vice President Calvin Coolidge succeeded him as president. Coolidge then appointed two special prosecutors to take over the investigation. Under the leadership of Owen J. Roberts (a Republican) and Atlee Pomerene (a Democrat), the investigation revealed that one of Sinclair's companies had transferred hundreds of thousands of dollars to Fall and his family, and that Sinclair had also donated substantial sums of money to the Republican Party. Fall was sentenced to a year in jail—the first such sentence for a former cabinet member stemming from his official conduct in office. Harding had died before his involvement was established, but, when all was said and done, numerous bribes, embezzlement, and fraud were exposed, and Harding's political legacy was permanently ruined.

Conclusion

Presidents confront all sorts of trade-offs and political costs when they politicize, centralize, and remake the federal bureaucracy. Given their druthers, presidents would like to have both expertise and loyalty within the bureaucracy. Often, though, they must choose one or the other, as it is difficult, if not impossible, to combine political responsiveness and technical competence within a single agency. Moreover, numerous political actors can obstruct a president who jostles to oversee and redirect agencies. Congress and the courts can throw any number of obstacles in a president's way, and bureaucrats will fight to preserve their administrative autonomy. Such is the nature of our politics—not just when it comes to the bureaucracy but in all matters of governance. No political actor has the final say; all influence is fettered; all power is provisional. Presidents who hope to achieve anything meaningful had better be ready for a fight.

That there are downsides to politicizing appointments, centralizing authority, and eliminating or creating administrative agencies does not mean that presidents should abandon these efforts. Rather, presidents must carefully weigh the benefits and costs of political control. They must proceed cautiously and strategically and be constantly mindful of the larger political environment. To do otherwise is to court political disaster, whether in the form of policy failure, administrative insurrection, or scandal. But not to act at all, to set adrift the massive bureaucratic apparatus that defines the modern state, is to forsake the central challenge that all presidents face: namely, how to meet the public's extraordinary expectations and secure a legacy of policy achievements in a system of separate powers that is in so many ways stacked against chief executives.

Key Terms

slack	Senior Executive Service (SES) personnel
drift	excepted service
politicization	political patronage
political appointees	centralization
career bureaucrats	czars
Presidential Appointments with	institutional memory
Senate confirmation (PAS)	recess appointment

Questions for Discussion

1. Are the goals of public administration necessarily at odds with those of political control?
2. Is centralization a short-term or long-term strategy? Why?
3. What are the costs of vigorously pursuing a strategy of politicization or centralization?

4. In midterm elections, the president's party often loses seats in Congress and sometimes loses majority control of at least one of its chambers. What implications does this have for WHO staffing trends during the course of a presidential administration?

5. Instead of merely appointing loyalists, Donald Trump left vacancies across the federal government. What effects might this strategy have on bureaucratic operations? Why may future presidents follow a similar course—or avoid it?

Suggested Readings

Gailmard, Sean, and John Patty. *Learning while Governing: Expertise and Accountability in the Executive Branch.* Chicago: University of Chicago Press, 2012.

Hess, Stephen. *Organizing the Presidency.* 3rd ed. Washington, DC: Brookings Institution Press, 2002.

Lewis, David E. *The Politics of Presidential Appointments: Political Control and Bureaucratic Performance.* Princeton: Princeton University Press, 2008.

Miller, Gary, and Andrew Whitford. *Above Politics: Bureaucratic Discretion and Credible Commitment.* New York: Cambridge University Press, 2016.

Potter, Rachel. *Bending the Rules: Procedural Politicking in the Bureaucracy.* Chicago: University of Chicago Press, 2019.

Rudalevige, Andrew. *Managing the President's Program: Presidential Leadership and Legislative Policy Formation.* Princeton: Princeton University Press, 2002.

Skowronek, Stephen, John A. Dearborn, and Desmond King. *Phantoms of a Beleaguered Republic: The Deep State and the Unitary Executive.* New York: Oxford University Press, 2021.

Warshaw, Shirley Anne. *Powersharing: White House-Cabinet Relations in the Modern Presidency.* Albany: State University of New York Press, 1996.

Weko, Thomas. *The Politicizing Presidency: The White House Personnel Office, 1948–1994.* Lawrence: University Press of Kansas, 1995.

Notes

1. Beryl Radin, *Federal Management Reform in a World of Contradictions* (Washington, DC: Georgetown University Press, 2012).

2. Quoted in Harold T. Pinkett, "The Keep Commission, 1905–1909: A Rooseveltian Effort for Administrative Reform," *Journal of American History* 52, no. 2 (1965): 300.

3. Pinkett, "The Keep Commission," 312.

4. James P. Pfiffner, "The American Tradition of Administrative Reform," in *The White House and the Blue House: Government Reform in the United States and Korea*, ed. Yong Hyo Cho and H. George Frederickson (Lanham, MD: University Press of America, 1997).

5. John W. Lederle, "The Hoover Commission Reports on Federal Reorganization," *Marquette Law Review* 33, no. 2 (1949): 90–91.

6. Quoted in William E. Pemberton, "Truman and the Hoover Commission," *Whistle Stop* 19, no. 1 (1991).

7. William E. Pemberton, "Struggle for the New Deal: Truman and the Hoover Commission," *Presidential Studies Quarterly* 16, no. 3 (1986): 511–22; Peri E. Arnold, "The First Hoover Commission and the Managerial Presidency," *Journal of Politics* 38, no. 1 (1976): 46–70.

8. Dwight Eisenhower to Edgar Eisenhower, November 8, 1954, "Personal and Confidential to Edgar Newton Eisenhower," in *The Papers of Dwight David Eisenhower*, ed. L. Galambos and D. van Ee (Baltimore: Johns Hopkins University Press, 1996).

9. John D. Millett, "Another Hoover Commission?" *Public Administration Review* 28, no. 2 (1968): 201–3.

10. Bill Clinton, "Remarks by President Clinton Announcing the Initiative to Streamline Government," March 3, 1993, http://govinfo.library.unt.edu/npr/library/speeches/030393.html.

11. Al Gore, "The Best Kept Secrets in Washington: A Report to President Bill Clinton," National Performance Review (Washington, DC: Government Printing Office, 1996), 1, 5, http://govinfo.library.unt.edu/npr/library/nprrpt/annrpt/vp-rpt96/npr1.pdf.

12. Woodrow Wilson, "The Study of Administration," *Political Science Quarterly* 2, no. 2 (1887): 210.

13. Lyndsey Layton, "Senate Overwhelmingly Passes New National Education Legislation," *Washington Post*, December 9, 2015, https://www.washingtonpost.com/local/education/senate-overwhelmingly-passes-new-national-education-legislation/2015/12/09/be1b1f94–9d2a-11e5-a3c5-c77f2cc5a43c_story.html.

14. Rosie McCall, "Big Pharma Companies Earn More Profits than Most Other Industries, Study Suggests," *Newsweek*, March 4, 2020, https://www.newsweek.com/big-pharma-companies-profits-industries-study-1490407#:~:text=Big%20Pharma%20Companies%20Earn%20More%20Profits%20Than%20Most%20Other%20In dustries%2C%20Study%20Suggests,-By%20Rosie%20McCall&text=Big%20pharmaceutical%20companies%20appear%20to,according%20to%20a%20 new%20study.

15. "Medicine Use and Spending in the U.S.," IQVIA Institute, May 9, 2019, https://www.iqvia.com/insights/the-iqvia-institute/reports/medicine-use-and-spending-in-the-us-a-review-of-2018-and-outlook-to-2023.

16. See "About Us," Mountain States Legal Foundation, https://mslegal.org/about/.

17. Brady Dennis and Chris Mooney, "Neil Gorsuch's Mother Once Ran the EPA; It Didn't Go Well," *Washington Post*, February 1, 2017, https://www.washingtonpost.com/news/energy-environment/wp/2017/02/01/neil-gorsuchs-mother-once-ran-the-epa-it-was-a-disaster/.

18. Gorsuch also ran into trouble with Congress by refusing to turn over documents associated with hazardous waste sites, arguing that they were "enforcement-sensitive." As a result of these actions, Congress held her in contempt, though it never authorized her arrest. Members of Congress insisted that they had a right to oversee the programs they legislated, though Gorsuch claimed she was obligated to follow the instructions of the president who appointed her. D. V. Feliciano, "Gorsuch Cited for Contempt of Congress," *Journal (Water Pollution Control Federation)* 55, no. 2 (1983): 119–22.

19. Steven R. Weisman, "President Names Ruckelshaus Head of Troubled EPA," *New York Times*, March 22, 1983, A.1.

20. Russell Berman, "The Donald Trump Cabinet Tracker," *The Atlantic*, November 7, 2018, https://www.theatlantic.com/politics/archive/2018/11/trump-cabinet-tracker/510527/.

21. Steven Chu, "Statement of Steven Chu, Secretary of Energy-Designate before the Committee on Energy and National Resources U.S. Senate," January 13, 2009, https://www.energy.gov/sites/default/files/ciprod/documents/SENR_Chu_testimony_Jan_09.pdf.

22. Steven Chu, "Letter from Secretary Steven Chu to Energy Department Employees Announcing His Decision Not to Serve a Second Term," February 1, 2013, https://www.energy.gov/articles/letter-secretary-steven-chu-energy-department-employees.

23. Ron Suskind, *The Price of Loyalty: George W. Bush, the White House, and the Education of Paul O'Neill* (New York: Simon & Schuster, 2004).

24. Christina Kinane, "Control without Confirmation: The Politics of Vacancies in Presidential Appointments," *American Political Science Review* 115, no. 2 (2021): 599–614.

25. David E. Lewis, "The Contemporary Presidency: The Personnel Process in the Modern Presidency," *Presidential Studies Quarterly* 42, no. 3 (2012): 578; Robert F. Durant and William G. Resh, "Presidential Agendas, Administrative Strategies, and the Bureaucracy," in *The Oxford Handbook of the American Presidency*, ed. George C. Edwards and William G. Howell (New York: Oxford University Press, 2009), 586.

26. David E. Lewis, *The Politics of Presidential Appointments: Political Control and Bureaucratic Performance* (Princeton: Princeton University Press, 2008).

27. United States Office of Personnel Management, "Excepted Service Hiring Authorities: Their Use and Effectiveness in the Executive Branch," July 2018, https://www.opm.gov/policy-data-oversight/hiring-information/excepted-service/excepted-service-study-report.pdf.

28. Lewis, *Politics of Presidential Appointments*, 54.

29. Lewis, *Politics of Presidential Appointments*, 68.

30. For a critique of Obama's record in this regard, see Secretary of Defense Robert Gates's memoir, *Duty: Memoirs of a Secretary at War* (New York: Knopf, 2014).

31. Juliet Eilperin, "Obama Ambassador Nominees Prompt an Uproar with Bungled Answers, Lack of Ties," *Washington Post*, February 14, 2014, https://www.washingtonpost.com/politics/obama-ambassador-nominees-prompt-an-uproar-with-bungled-answers-lack-of-ties/2014/02/14/20fb0fe4-94b2-11e3-83b9-1f024193bb84_story.html.

32. "AFSA Statement on Ambassadors," American Foreign Service Association, http://www.afsa.org/ambassadors.aspx.

33. Gary E. Hollibaugh Jr., Gabriel Horton, and David E. Lewis, "Presidents and Patronage," *American Journal of Political Science* 58, no. 4 (2014): 1024–42.

34. Karen Hult and Charles Walcott, *Empowering the White House: Governance under Nixon, Ford and Carter* (Lawrence: University Press of Kansas, 2004).

35. "Annual Report to Congress on White House Office Personnel," Executive Office of the President, Trump White House, June 26, 2020, https://trumpwhitehouse.archives.gov/wp-content/uploads/2020/06/July-1-2020-Report-FINAL.pdf.

36. Matthew Dickinson and Matthew Lebo, "Reexamining the Growth of the Institutional Presidency, 1940–2000," *Journal of Politics* 69, no. 1 (2007): 206–19. See also Matthew Dickinson, "Bargaining, Uncertainty, and the Growth of the White House Staff, 1940–2000," in *Uncertainty in American Politics*, ed. Barry C. Burden (New York: Cambridge University Press, 2003); and Matthew Dickinson, *Bitter Harvest: FDR, Presidential Power and the Growth of the Presidential Branch* (New York: Cambridge University Press, 1999).

37. For an eloquent articulation of this argument, see Theodore J. Lowi, *The Personal President: Power Invested, Promise Unfulfilled* (Ithaca: Cornell University Press, 1985).

38. Mitchel A. Sollenberger and Mark J. Rozell, *The President's Czars: Undermining Congress and the Constitution* (Lawrence: University Press of Kansas, 2012).

39. David Welna, "Trump White House Resists Calls to Appoint a Coronavirus Czar," National Public Radio, February 26, 2020, https://www.npr.org/2020/02/26/809726490/trump-white-house-resists-calls-to-appoint-a-coronavirus-czar.

40. Quint Forgey, "Giroir Breaks with Trump, Says Surge in Coronavirus Cases 'Not Just a Function of Testing,'" *POLITICO*, October 28, 2020, https://www.politico.com/news/2020/10/28/brett-giroir-trump-coronavirus-surge-testing-433187.

41. Dartunorro Clark, "Trump Suggests 'Injection' of Disinfectant to Beat Coronavirus and 'Clean' the Lungs," NBC News, April 23, 2020, https://www.nbcnews.com/politics/donald-trump/trump-suggests-injection-disinfectant-beat-coronavirus-clean-lungs-n1191216.

42. John P. Burke, "Organizational Structure and Presidential Decision-Making," in *The Oxford Handbook of the American Presidency*, ed. Edwards and Howell, 512; Daniel E. Ponder, *Good Advice: Information and Policy Making in the White House* (College Station: Texas A&M University Press, 2000).

43. Andrew Rudalevige, *Managing the President's Program: Presidential Leadership and Legislative Policy Formation* (Princeton: Princeton University Press, 2002).

44. Bob Woodward, "CIA Told to Do 'Whatever Is Necessary' to Kill Bin Laden," *Washington Post*, October 21, 2001, A.1.

45. Jane Mayer, *The Dark Side* (New York: Random House, 2008), 5.

46. William G. Howell and David E. Lewis, "Agencies by Presidential Design," *Journal of Politics* 64, no. 4 (2002): 1095.

47. David E. Lewis, *Presidents and the Politics of Agency Design: Political Insulation in the United States Government Bureaucracy, 1946–1997* (Stanford: Stanford University Press, 2003); David E. Lewis, "The Adverse Consequences of the Politics of Agency Design for Presidential Management in the United States: The Relative Durability of Insulated Agencies," *British Journal of Political Science* 34, no. 3 (2004): 377–404.

48. Lewis, *The Politics of Presidential Appointments*.

49. For a nice review of this literature, see Sean Gailmard and John W. Patty, "Formal Models of Bureaucracy," *Annual Review of Political Science* 15 (2012): 353–77.

50. For a formal model of this trade-off, see Sean Gailmard and John W. Patty, "Slackers and Zealots: Civil Service, Policy Discretion, and Bureaucratic Expertise," *American Journal of Political Science* 51, no. 4 (2007): 873–89.

51. David E. Lewis, "Deconstructing the Administrative State," *Journal of Politics* 81, no. 3 (2019): 767–89.

52. Durant and Resh, "Presidential Agendas, Administrative Strategies," 580.

53. Durant and Resh, "Presidential Agendas, Administrative Strategies," 586.

54. Ryan C. Black et al., "Assessing Congressional Responses to Growing Presidential Powers: The Case of Recess Appointments," *Presidential Studies Quarterly* 41, no. 3 (2011): 571.

55. Helene Cooper and Jennifer Steinhauer, "Bucking Senate, Obama Appoints Consumer Chief," *New York Times*, January 5, 2012, A.1.

56. Anne Joseph O'Connell, "Actings," *Columbia Law Review* (April 2020): 613–728.

57. Anne Joseph O'Connell, "Acting Leaders: Recent Practices, Consequences, and Reforms," *Brookings*, July 29, 2019, https://www.brookings.edu/research/acting-leaders/.

58. Joel Rose, "How Trump Has Filled High-Level Jobs without Senate Confirmation Votes," National Public Radio, March 9, 2020, https://www.npr.org/2020/03/09/813577462/how-trump-has-filled-high-level-jobs-without-senate-confirmation.

59. Rudalevige, *Managing the President's Program*, 149.

60. Paul Light, *Thickening Government: Federal Hierarchy and the Diffusion of Accountability* (Washington, DC: Brookings Institution, 1995), 1.

61. Burke, "Organizational Structure and Presidential Decision-Making," 513–14; John P. Burke, *The Institutional Presidency: Organizing and Managing the White House from FDR to Clinton* (Baltimore: Johns Hopkins University Press, 2000).

62. Laton McCartney, *The Teapot Dome Scandal: How Big Oil Bought the Harding White House and Tried to Steal the Country* (New York: Random House, 2008).

63. David H. Stratton, *Tempest Over Teapot Dome* (Norman: University of Oklahoma Press, 1998).

11

Relations with the Federal Judiciary

IF ARTICLE I OF THE CONSTITUTION establishes Congress as the first branch of government, Article III relegates the judiciary to third place. As described by Alexander Hamilton, the judiciary is "beyond comparison the weakest of the three departments of power"[1]— equipped only with the power to observe and pass judgment on the actions of the other two.

Of course, judges can—and frequently do—constrain presidents by ruling that their initiatives are either unconstitutional or lack statutory authority. But in situations like these, presidents do not sit idly by as their authority is diminished. Rather, they pursue legal interpretations and arguments of their own, and through appointments, they seek to remake the judiciary to match their preferences. As we will see in this chapter, presidents not only enjoy a number of important institutional advantages over the judiciary; they use them to their considerable advantage.

11.1 Foundations of Judicial Decision Making

The federal judiciary is made up of district courts, courts of appeals, and the U.S. Supreme Court (figure 11.1). The judges who serve on district and appellate courts and the justices who serve on the Supreme Court all have lifetime appointments. Unlike legislators who must weigh the electoral consequences of their decisions, federal judges and justices would appear to be entirely free to decide cases however they choose.

They are not. Though scholars continue to disagree about their relative importance, at least three broad classes of consideration weigh on judges and justices as they render opinions and adjudicate disputes involving the president. They are:

- legal norms and principles;
- ideological convictions; and
- concerns about their institution's legitimacy.

In this section, we briefly characterize each of these foundations of judicial decision making, and we then analyze their separate and sometimes competing influences in any single case. In the section that follows, we evaluate their collective implications for cases that involve the presidency.

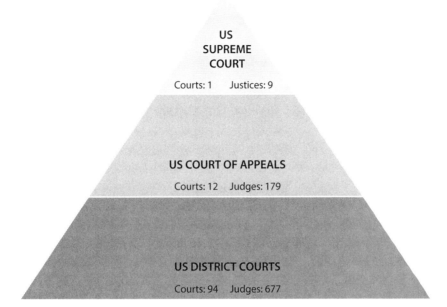

FIGURE 11.1. The federal judiciary. There are three main levels of the federal court system: district courts, courts of appeals, and the U.S. Supreme Court. The judges of the district courts and courts of appeals and the justices of the Supreme Court are all chosen by the president and confirmed by the Senate. Figures current as of 2021.

11.1.1 Applying Legal Norms and Principles

According to some constitutional law scholars, judges follow a three-step process in rendering decisions regarding constitutionality:

1. They rely upon their legal expertise to interpret a law, policy, or practice.
2. They determine the relevant portions of the Constitution to which it applies.
3. They decide whether there is any conflict between the two.[2]

This basic understanding of judicial review is known as the **legal model**.

In the legal model, different judges interpret the Constitution according to different judicial philosophies. As discussed in chapter 1, some judges—so-called originalists—pay careful attention to the intentions of the Framers who wrote and ratified the document. For them, the Constitution's text, as it was understood at the time of its creation, is the sine qua non of judicial reasoning. Others—advocates of a Living Constitution—make much of the fact that Article II is highly ambiguous and insist that its meanings crucially depend upon the historical contexts in which it is interpreted and applied.*

---

*These, of course, do not exhaust all of the types of constitutional interpretation. In addition to originalists and advocates of a Living Constitution, there are "textualists," "functionalists," "structuralists," and a good deal

Despite their considerable disagreements, the characterizations of both of these camps are consistent with the legal model. Though they rely upon different philosophies for interpreting the Constitution, originalists and advocates of a Living Constitution try to apply the same basic principles of jurisprudence. The most important of these is **stare decisis**—literally, "to stand by things already decided." According to this principle, judges must carefully weigh the decisions made by their predecessors in similar cases. If the basic elements of the case are the same, judges are meant to render the same decision about a law's constitutionality.

Beyond stare decisis, judges have at their disposal many other principles for deciding cases that come before them. Some, such as **standing** (the principle that only parties with a sufficient connection to a harm may bring a suit) and **ripeness** (the principle that the judiciary should only hear cases that constitute actual disputes that are ready for litigation) concern decisions about whether to hear a particular case. Others are developed to facilitate judicial decision making in particular areas of the law, such as employment, contracts, or copyright.

The purpose of these principles is to guide judges in different policy contexts and historical periods, so that the sum total of their decisions makes sense. Judges worry a great deal about the principled connections that bind different cases together, as well as the internal logic of any single ruling. Unlike statutes or executive orders, judicial rulings contain not only the final decision about a policy matter but also the reasoning that supports the decision. Judges cite legal principles to explain how their decision on a specific case relates to past and future cases.

Evidence in support of the legal model would appear to be plentiful. Judges, after all, routinely cite legal principles and relevant **case law** (interpretations of statutory and constitutional law by past courts) when making their arguments. It is extremely difficult, however, to show that these principles and case law are what actually lead judges to rule as they do. Judges have a tremendous amount of discretion to choose which prior cases they want to cite and how they want to cite them. It is possible, then, that judges, after figuring out how they want to rule on a case, search through the existing case law to select those cases that best support their position. And it is precisely this discretion that convinces many court observers that other, nonlegal factors contribute to judicial decision making.

11.1.2 Ideological Convictions

Many scholars, especially political scientists, argue that the legal principles that judges use to justify their rulings constitute little more than convenient fiction. Though judges try to project an image of neutrality, these scholars say, they actually use their powers in the service of their policy preferences. According to this **attitudinal model**, judicial decisions are made in much the same way that elected politicians decide which policies to adopt: they are based on judges' own ideological convictions. Arguments in favor of the

---

more besides. For our purposes, however, the most important distinction lies between originalists and advocates of a Living Constitution.

attitudinal model tend to focus on Supreme Court justices and, to a lesser extent, appellate court judges. Because they reside at the bottom of the judicial hierarchy and their decisions are subject to review from higher courts, district-level judges do not have much discretion to indulge their ideological preferences.

Political scientists favoring the attitudinal model have developed a variety of ways to empirically gauge judges' policy preferences. The most common of these is the party affiliation of the president who appointed the judge. Judges appointed by Republicans tend to be conservative and judges appointed by Democrats tend to be liberal. And, as discussed at greater length later in this chapter, the overwhelming majority of judicial appointees identify with the same political party as the president who nominated them: over the past thirty years, roughly 90 percent of district and appellate court appointees were registered members of the president's party. These judicial nominees, moreover, have not been passive party members. Most of them actively supported their preferred political party before becoming judges. Between 1970 and 2016, an average of 56 percent of federal court appointees had prior records of party activism.[3] Under Trump's presidency, the numbers were even higher. By one count, over 90 percent of Trump's appellate court appointees were politically active before taking the bench.[4]

In the attitudinal model, judges are political creatures, and their politics inform their official conduct.[5] Consistent with this model, scholars have found that the ideologies of judges strongly correspond with the decisions that they render.[6] Even after accounting for a wide range of other influences, judges' personal ideologies appear to be far and away the most important determinant of decisions.[7] According to one study, judges rule on civil liberties cases in ways that are consistent with their ideological preferences roughly 80 percent of the time. As one political scientist notes, "even critics of the attitudinal model have conceded [the] exceptional explanatory ability" of justices' policy preferences.[8]

The fact that judges' ideologies appear to be such a powerful predictor of case outcomes, however, does not mean that ideology is the primary factor in every case. Political scientists generally concede, for instance, that ideology plays a smaller role in determining the outcome of criminal cases, and that even when deciding civil cases, a judge's ideology may not be the only relevant consideration. For instance, if public opinion strongly leans in one direction or another, or if the nation is at war, or if the president indicates that he or she will ignore an objectionable court ruling, then judges may set aside their own policy preferences when formulating a decision.

Thinking Institutionally: The Ideological Foundations of *Bush v. Gore*

When thinking institutionally, we must take stock of the incentives and resources available to political actors. Often, this requires interrogating what politicians and government officials say in order to understand what truly motivates their decisions. Ask judges, for instance, about the process by which they make decisions, and you can

Continued on next page

expect to hear a great deal about the importance of the Constitution, the rule of law, the constraint of precedents, and the like. In cases such as the landmark Supreme Court rulings in *Bush v. Gore* (2000), however, it is important to resist the temptation to treat judges' testimony as if it were gospel.

In 2000, the Supreme Court had the opportunity to effectively decide who would be the next president of the United States. As election night came to a close, Republican candidate George W. Bush had 246 electoral votes while Democrat Al Gore had 266, with 270 votes needed to win. Florida, which was worth 25 electoral votes, remained "too close to call." Two days after the election, Bush was announced the victor, by 1,784 votes—less than one-half of 1 percent of the votes cast in that state.[9] The close margin triggered an automatic, machine-based recount in all Florida counties. The next day, with only one county still tallying, Bush's lead had shrunk to 327 votes.

Given the narrow gap, Democrats began requesting that recounts be done by hand in major counties where ballots were disputed.* Meanwhile, Florida secretary of state Katherine Harris, a Republican, attempted to certify Bush as the winner of the Florida election. In response, the Florida Supreme Court blocked the certification and ordered a manual recount of every ballot that had been machine recorded as not choosing a candidate—about 45,000 ballots in all. Bush appealed this ruling to the U.S. Supreme Court, thereby halting the recount while the justices decided the issue.

The Bush legal team put forth two main claims. First, it argued that the manual recount violated the Equal Protection Clause of the Fourteenth Amendment, which previous Supreme Court decisions had interpreted as "forbid[ding] the state from treating similarly situated voters differently based merely on where they live."[10] (When it ordered the recount, the Florida Supreme Court had not established a standard method for counting votes, which allowed for the possibility that voters from different locales would be treated differently.) In addition, the Bush team claimed that the Florida court had violated Article II of the Constitution, which states that "Each State shall appoint, in such Manner as the Legislature thereof may direct, a Number of Electors" who choose the president. The Bush team argued that, because the Florida Supreme Court had established "new standards for resolving" disputes in a presidential election, the court had overridden the state legislature. The Gore legal team disputed both of these claims.

In a 5–4 ruling, the Supreme Court ruled in favor of Bush and thereby handed him the presidency. The justices were split evenly along ideological lines. Writing for the majority (comprised of moderate-to-conservative Justices O'Connor, Kennedy, Rehnquist, Scalia, and Thomas), Chief Justice William Rehnquist argued that the Equal Protection Clause had indeed been violated, because the state had "by later arbitrary and disparate treatment, value[d] one person's vote over that of another."[11] The majority also took the unorthodox step of "revers[ing] the judgment of the Supreme

---

*Election observers are allowed to dispute ballots that they believe are being inaccurately counted—for instance, if they believe a stray mark is erroneously being counted as a vote or if they believe an attempt to vote is being improperly disregarded.

FIGURE 11.2. The lead attorney for George W. Bush, Theodore Olson, speaks to a gaggle of reporters outside the Supreme Court following oral arguments in *Bush v. Gore*. Copyright 2000 Alex Wong/Hulton Archive-Getty Images. Reproduced with permission.

Court of Florida ordering a recount to proceed," effectively stopping the state court's desired remedy for addressing the violation.[12] This exercise in judicial intervention was particularly surprising, given that Chief Justice Rehnquist had previously described himself as an "apostle of judicial restraint" who attempted to leave decision making in local hands whenever possible.[13]

The more liberal justices making up the minority did not appear any less ideologically motivated. For example, Justices Ginsburg and Stevens argued in a dissent written by Ginsburg that the Florida Supreme Court justices had done "their mortal best to discharge their oath of office," and therefore there was "no cause to upset their reasoned interpretation of Florida law."[14]* Moreover, Ginsburg and Stevens argued that the Supreme Court must be "mindful of the full measure of respect we owe to interpretations of state law by a State's highest court."[15] This states' rights argument appeared to contradict the legal philosophies of these two liberal judges, who had previously been perfectly willing to overrule state laws and state court decisions, especially when a constitutional right was potentially being violated.

Five days after the ruling, the *Los Angeles Times* ran an article titled "Supreme Court: Should We Trust Judges?" which argued that the "George W. Bush Court" had ruled erroneously.[16] Others charged that the Court had become unduly politicized, with justices showing more loyalty to their political party than to the law. In a stinging

---

* Ironically, the ruling cited by Ginsburg to justify their argument had been authored by conservative Rehnquist almost two decades earlier—and Stevens had originally dissented from it.

Continued on next page

rebuke published in the *New Republic*, legal analyst Jeffrey Rosen argued that the ruling in *Bush v. Gore* brought nothing less than "disgrace" upon the institution that delivered it. In his view, with this decision, a Supreme Court that prides itself on objectivity dove headlong into the muddy waters of politics.[17]

11.1.3 Concerns about Institutional Legitimacy

If legal precedent and policy preferences inform judges' rulings, so too does an abiding concern for their institutional legitimacy. This concern is no idle matter. The judiciary, after all, can only render judgments; it cannot command the army, negotiate deals, or re-direct federal spending. As Alexander Hamilton recognized in *Federalist* 78, the courts "have neither FORCE nor WILL but merely judgment; and must ultimately depend upon the aid of the executive arm even for the efficacy of its judgments."[18] This dependency, we shall see, distinguishes the judiciary from both of the elected branches; and in cases involving executive power, it instills in judges a measure of deference to presidential interests.

In his influential book *The Hollow Hope*, Gerald Rosenberg described the inherent weakness of the judiciary and wrote that "court decisions, requiring people to act, are not self-executing."[19] For expenditures, the courts rely on Congress. For enforcement, they rely on the executive. Without any formal, independent means of financial support or enforcement, the weight of judicial opinion derives in large part from the institution's public standing. The rituals of court proceedings, the formal titles bestowed upon judges and justices, the reflexive homage paid to timeless legal principles, and even the robes worn by judges all serve to publicly affirm that these unelected officials transcend politics. The **cult of the robe**—the view that the legal decisions of judges and justices are inviolable—requires that judges insist, against all facts to the contrary, that they remain independent and impartial interpreters of the Constitution.[20]

The judiciary's perceived legitimacy derives from, as much as it contributes to, the willingness of other political actors to heed court rulings. Though outright defiance is rare, past presidents have taken advantage of the judiciary's lack of formal powers. Following an unfavorable decision for his administration in 1832, President Jackson allegedly remarked: "[Chief Justice] John Marshall has made his decision. Now let him enforce it."[21] Situations like this, in which other actors reject a court decision, can call into question the legitimacy of the ruling—and, by implication, the legitimacy of the institution that delivered it.

To avoid defiance of or disregard for their rulings, judges strategically position themselves on the side of public opinion. "Courts are wary of stepping too far out of the political mainstream," Rosenberg writes, for doing so may invite a political backlash that the courts are ill-equipped to handle.[22] In line with this theory, a body of evidence demonstrates that Supreme Court justices tend to side with public opinion in especially high-profile cases.[23] Of course, it is unlikely that justices consult polling data before rendering their decisions.

Moreover, legal norms and ideological commitments remain essential factors in shaping their rulings. Still, the evidence on offer suggests that public opinion—however construed—is one of several elements that inform judicial decision making.

In most cases, judges can rely upon the backing of the executive branch. When opposition is mobilized against the judiciary, however, and executive enforcement is uncertain, judges may temporarily decline to render a decision.* Indeed, some scholars believe that courts will *never* issue a ruling unless they are reasonably certain that other actors will enforce it. For should aggrieved parties ignore a court ruling and get away with it, the institutional weaknesses of the judiciary will be made plain for all to see, which will invite further defiance, and with it, continued erosion of the third branch of government. But as the judiciary has grown institutionally and established its powers of judicial review, the political costs of ignoring a court ruling may have escalated; thus, this particular threat to the judiciary's legitimacy may well have diminished.

11.1.4 In Practice, More than One Motivation

The three foundations of judicial decision making—legal principles, ideological convictions, and concerns about institutional legitimacy—are not mutually exclusive. Principles of jurisprudence like stare decisis, for example, can be developed and applied in ways that advance a judge's ideological and institutional interests. In virtually any given case, we can find traces of legal, ideological, and institutional considerations bearing on court rulings. The Supreme Court's 2012 ruling on the Affordable Care Act (ACA), Obama's health care policy, in *National Federation of Independent Businesses v. Sebelius* provides an illustrative example.[24]

The Court's decision on the constitutionality of the ACA clearly shows the justices critically engaging with a complex set of legal rules and principles. At stake were two key portions of the ACA: the individual mandate, which required every uninsured citizen to buy health insurance or else pay a penalty to the federal government, and the expansion of Medicaid, which required states to grow the program or lose access to existing federal funding. The four justices in the dissenting minority (Antonin Scalia, Clarence Thomas, Samuel Alito, and Anthony Kennedy) were unanimous in their belief that both the mandate and the expansion were unconstitutional, thereby making the law as a whole invalid.

Even among the five justices in the majority there was a great deal of disagreement concerning which portions of the ACA were legal and why. Writing for the majority, and

---

* For this reason, federal judges expressed deep ambivalence about deciding cases pertaining to slavery and Native American lands in the nineteenth century, and reapportionment and integration in the twentieth century. On these matters, resistance from state governments was probable and executive backing uncertain. See, for example, *Texas v. White*, 7 Wall. 700, 729 (1866); *Mississippi v. Johnson*, 4 Wall. 475 (1866); and *Georgia v. Stanton*, 6 Wall. 50 (1867).

quoting from an 1895 Court case,[25] Chief Justice John Roberts insisted that "every reasonable construction must be resorted to, in order to save a statute from unconstitutionality." Roberts insisted that the mandate was *not* supported by the Commerce Clause or the Necessary and Proper Clause, a claim that affirmed the minority's argument. The Chief Justice—joined by all four of his liberal colleagues—then held that the individual mandate was constitutional because the penalty on individuals was akin to a tax, which the federal government was legally allowed to levy.

In the majority opinion, Roberts also claimed that the Medicaid expansion was unconstitutionally coercive. The federal government could encourage state expansion of the program, but it could not punish states for failing to do so. This part of the decision was supported by Stephen Breyer and Elena Kagan, as well as the entire minority, but it earned an additional dissent from Ruth Bader Ginsburg and Sonia Sotomayor. That the majority ruling was so fractious and contentious implies that the justices were sincerely invested in the case's legal questions, as opposed to blindly upholding their ideological convictions.

At the same time, the political ramifications of the justices' actions are readily apparent. The ACA was the crowning policy achievement of Obama's first term in office, the biggest overhaul of the health care system since President Johnson created Medicare and Medicaid in the 1960s. The Court's decision was handed down mere months before the presidential election, at a time when Republicans, including presidential candidate Mitt Romney, were running against what they perceived to be the egregious government overreach of "Obamacare."

Tellingly, the four liberal Supreme Court justices all voted to uphold the ACA, while four of the five more conservative justices voted to strike it down. Court observers at the time expressed shock that Chief Justice Roberts, a conservative appointed by George W. Bush, upheld the law; no commentators, in contrast, seemed at all surprised that the remaining eight justices all broke along ideological lines. Especially in cases with obvious political consequences, such as *Bush v. Gore*, pundits tend to just assume that justices will vote in line with their ideological preferences.[26]

In the aftermath of the decision, it became a popular parlor game in Washington to guess what had motivated the Chief Justice's actions. Had Roberts merely taken a courageous stand in favor of what he believed to be the correct legal doctrine? Or was he concerned that a ruling strictly along ideological lines would cement the notion, popular among political scientists and ordinary citizens alike, that the Supreme Court was a mere political body, and an unelected one at that?

Most pundits at the time emphasized the latter. One reporter even quoted an anonymous source within the Court itself who claimed that Roberts had initially been inclined to rule against the health care bill but had switched sides at the last minute upon realizing that the ruling would fall along political lines. Others speculated that Roberts, the public face of the Court and someone with a keen understanding of its place in the long arc of history, was worried that the Court's striking down such major legislation would be seen as another example of judicial overreach. Whether the issue was one of politicization or overreach in Roberts's mind, it does seem likely that the Chief Justice was motivated at least in part by institutional concerns.[27]

Ultimately, the Court's decision on the ACA illustrates how difficult it can be to parse the possible motivations for justices' actions. All the justices but Roberts voted in accordance with their ideological convictions. Were they merely voting their political preferences, or were they motivated by deeper legal philosophies or institutional considerations? It is difficult to know for sure.

11.2 Implications for Cases Involving the President

More often than not, judges' legal, ideological, and institutional concerns bode well for the president. Even when most sitting Supreme Court justices do not share a president's partisan preferences, their reluctance to challenge the elected branches might prevent them from ruling against the president—or issuing a ruling at all.

Over the years, these concerns have been codified in a set of principles meant to structure deliberations in cases involving the presidency. Some of them establish a principled rationale for the judiciary to withdraw from challenges to the president; others offer guidance on how judges ought to evaluate the statutory authority of presidential actions; still others counsel broad deference to the administrative agencies the president oversees. These principles do not guarantee that presidents will always win in the courts, but they do reveal the president's distinct institutional advantages.

11.2.1 Political Question Doctrine

The **political question doctrine** establishes limits on the kinds of claims and disputes that justifiably come before the courts.[28] This doctrine traces back to *Marbury v. Madison*, a case from 1803 that centered on a minor political dispute about a handful of last-hour judicial appointments issued by an outgoing presidential administration. Its landmark status in the pantheon of Supreme Court cases comes from its establishment of the concept of **judicial review**, whereby federal courts may void legislative acts of Congress (and policy acts of the president) that they deem unconstitutional.

While carving out this judicial power, the justices in *Marbury v. Madison* also demarcated boundaries around disputes that were *not* subject to judicial review. In the majority opinion, Chief Justice John Marshall wrote, "Questions in their nature political or which are, by the Constitution and laws, submitted to the Executive, can never be made in this court."[29] In other words, it was up to Congress, not the judiciary, to review the inner workings of agencies overseen by the president.

Over the next century and a half, the Court continued to apply the political question doctrine. In 1863, the Court relied on the doctrine when it supported President Lincoln's decision to order a blockade of Confederate ports and seizure of enemy vessels.[30] Similarly, in *Oetjen v. Central Leather Co.* (1918), the Court affirmed that foreign relations (in this case, recognizing another state) were the exclusive domain of Congress and the president.

As the Court wrote, "The conduct of our foreign relations is committed by the Constitution to the executive and legislative—the political—departments of the government, and the propriety of what may be done in the exercise of this political power is not subject to judicial inquiry or decision."[31]

The contours of what counts as a political question were clarified further in *Baker v. Carr* (1962). Writing for the majority, Justice William Brennan outlined key factors that identify political questions, including "the potentiality of embarrassment from multifarious pronouncements by various departments on one question" and "the impossibility of a court's undertaking independent resolution without expressing lack of the respect due coordinate branches of government."[32]

For the most part, the political question doctrine plays to the president's advantage. In *Goldwater v. Carter* (1979), for example, Senator Barry Goldwater sued to prevent President Carter from breaking an existing treaty with the Republic of China. The Court dismissed the case against Carter, stating that treaties were a political issue that had to be resolved between the president and Congress: "The Judicial Branch should not decide issues affecting the allocation of power between the President and Congress," wrote Justice Lewis Powell, "until the political branches reach a constitutional impasse."[33] The lesson was plain: Congress should not count on the judiciary to come to its defense when it fails to exercise its own powers to constrain the president.

11.2.2 *The "Zone of Twilight"*

The political question doctrine makes it clear that the judiciary will not intervene in disputes between the other two branches when the issue at stake is essentially political. But what happens when a dispute between Congress and the president centers on an interpretation of a law or statute? In these instances, the Supreme Court has laid out a different test for evaluating the powers conferred upon a president.

The Court established this test in a 1952 ruling, *Youngstown Sheet & Tube Co. v. Sawyer*, which arose from a labor-management dispute in the steel industry. In April 1952, the United Steel Workers of America announced its intention to launch a nationwide strike. Such an action would have had significant repercussions for the U.S. economy at any time, but in 1952 the country was fighting the Korean War. A sudden halt in steel production, the White House believed, would have real and dangerous consequences for the war effort.

In response to the strike, President Truman issued Executive Order 10340, which directed Secretary of Commerce Charles Sawyer to seize the steel mills and thereby ensure their continued operation. The owners of the mills promptly challenged the constitutionality of Truman's executive order. In less than a month, the Supreme Court heard oral arguments in the case.

Lawyers for the steel mills argued that the president's order amounted to an unconstitutional commandeering of private property and a usurpation of Congress's legislative authority. Moreover, the president's actions violated the basic procedures laid out by Congress for reconciling labor-management disputes in the 1947 Labor Management Relations Act, more popularly known as the Taft-Hartley Act. Truman's counsel responded that the order, though not expressly authorized by congressional statute or the Constitution itself, was nevertheless needed in order to avert a national catastrophe.

In a 6–3 ruling, the Court found in favor of the mill owners. Each of the justices in the majority wrote a separate concurring opinion, underscoring the lack of consensus on the bench. For many of the justices, though, one central fact proved crucial: the legislative history of Taft-Hartley, a law enacted over Truman's veto that significantly limited the rights of labor unions to engage in strikes and other collective bargaining strategies. When they were debating the bill before its passage, members of Congress had considered, and rejected, an amendment that would have granted the president the power to intervene directly in labor-management disputes when the nation was at war. Because the "will of Congress" figures prominently in judicial reasoning involving the justification for presidential actions, the Court saw fit to overturn Truman's seizure.

The historical significance of *Youngstown* has less to do with the immediate policy dispute at hand and more to do with subsequent jurisprudence on separation of powers issues. While the majority decision served in this instance to limit presidential power, *Youngstown* also laid out a general test for when presidents *were* within their rights when interpreting a statute. Justice Robert Jackson's concurring opinion established a framework within which judges and justices can evaluate challenges to the president's authority. His opinion stands as one of the most historically important statements about separation of powers issues generally, and presidential powers particularly.[34]

Jackson's three-pronged test is as follows: when Congress has explicitly prohibited certain acts, the president's powers are at their weakest; inversely, when the president follows the expressed or implied authorization of Congress, the president's authority is greatest. When presidents act without authorization from Congress, however, they enter a "zone of twilight" where their actions are subject to judicial review. According to Jackson's simple test, where a case falls within these three categories dictates how judges should evaluate the president's actions.

Whether he meant to or not, Jackson's test tended to expand presidential power rather than contract it. In theory, the "zone of twilight" merely demarcated a gray area in which judicial scrutiny was required. In its application, however, judges usually defer to the executive branch's interpretations in cases falling into this gray area. Since *Youngstown*, the absence of any explicit congressional opinion on an issue has come to imply consent, and the Court usually upholds presidents even when they wander well into the twilight zone.[35]

Under Jackson's scheme, there remains just one category of cases in which the courts will reliably overturn the president. Ironically, it is precisely the category in which the courts are needed least.

11.2.3 Chevron *Deference*

Typically, presidents do not implement policy: rather, they execute laws through the federal bureaucracy. As a result, many confrontations between the judiciary and the president arise out of cases in which a particular agency's interpretation of a law is called into dispute. In these cases, too, the Supreme Court tends to defer to the executive branch.

The principled basis for administrative deference dates to the 1984 case *Chevron U.S.A., Inc. v. National Resources Defense Council, Inc.* At issue was an interpretation of the Clean Air Act Amendments, a set of rules passed in 1977 that set pollution limits for states. Upon being elected in 1981, President Ronald Reagan sought to downplay the amendments' restrictions, which he felt encroached on the right of states to decide local issues. Under Reagan's leadership, the Environmental Protection Agency (EPA) redefined what it considered to be a "stationary source" of pollution under the Clean Air Act. According to the new interpretation, an entire factory or plant was considered to be one source, which meant business owners could add new machinery without having to get a permit, as long as the factory's overall emissions stayed consistent.[36]

Environmental groups led by the National Resources Defense Council sought to block the new interpretation. They argued that the EPA's policy would allow business owners to purchase equipment that created more pollution than was allowed under the Clean Air Act amendments. On the other side of the case, private businesses led by the oil company Chevron argued that the EPA was allowed to interpret the Clean Air Act in such a manner.

The dispute went all the way to the Supreme Court, which ultimately decided in favor of Chevron and the EPA. In its ruling, the Court articulated the principle of **administrative deference**, which lays out a simple two-part test for the Court to decide whether an agency's interpretation of a statute ought to be upheld. The judiciary must defer to an agency, first, when Congress has not "directly spoken to the precise question at issue." (In *Chevron*, there was no definition within the statute of what a "stationary source" of pollution was.) If this part of the test is passed, then the Court moves to the second part, which concerns whether the agency's interpretation "is based on a permissible construction of the statute." This test rules out any agency interpretation that obviously contradicts the law in question. If both of these criteria are met, according to the *Chevron* ruling, the Court should not intervene.

The Court's primary justification for this deference rests on a simple proposition: agencies tend to have more information about the issues they oversee than does the Supreme Court. In his majority opinion in *Chevron*, Justice John Paul Stevens noted that justices are not "experts in the field," so deference is owed in cases where the "regulatory scheme is technical and complex." According to this line of reasoning, judges must uphold executive agency policies when they lack the technical training necessary to make an independent judgment about a regulation and its effects. Since *Chevron*, that is exactly what the Supreme Court has done. The Court has sided with agencies such as the Department of Defense and the U.S. International Trade Commission in cases specifically related to their areas of competence, and it has also deferred to specialized judges such as those on the Court of Federal Claims.[37]

11.3 Taking on the President

When the Supreme Court accepts a case involving presidential power, its rulings often come out in the president's favor—but not always. In a variety of instances, the Court has rejected a president's claims to special privilege, newly acquired powers, and immunity to civil prosecution. The Court also has shot down provisions of a sitting president's policies. In this section, we recount examples of each of these kinds of judicial defeats.

11.3.1 Challenging an Executive's Special Privileges

As we have seen, judges and justices have developed principled rationales that allow them to defer to the executive branch when it is politically expedient to do so. Occasionally, though, they do strike out against the president. Such was the case in *United States v. Nixon*, a landmark 1974 ruling that curtailed the president's discretionary authority.

The *Nixon* case originates from one of the most infamous political scandals in the nation's history. On June 17, 1972, five men were arrested for breaking into the Democratic National Committee (DNC) headquarters in Washington, D.C.'s Watergate office complex. Suspicion quickly fell on Nixon's administration, and it intensified when reporters from the *Washington Post* suggested that the burglary had been ordered by high-level Republican officials in the White House.[38] The Oval Office first attempted to conceal its involvement, then downplayed the events and sometimes outright lied to the press.

The Senate established a special Watergate Committee in May 1973 to investigate the incident and ensuing cover-up. Nixon came under the spotlight in June, when former advisor John Dean, declaring that he would not be a "scapegoat," stated that Nixon had been personally involved in concealing the burglary and that Nixon had tape-recorded conversations that established his complicity (Figure 11.3).[39] The Senate committee and Archibald Cox, the special prosecutor who had been appointed by the attorney general, demanded Nixon turn over the recordings. Nixon refused, even though Cox issued a formal subpoena. Instead, on October 20, 1973, Nixon ordered that Cox be fired, prompting both the attorney general and deputy attorney general to resign in protest. In 1974, the new special prosecutor in the case, Leon Jaworski, sued to have the full tapes handed over. The district court ordered Nixon to comply.

Nixon still refused to relinquish the tapes, citing two justifications. First, he claimed that the courts could not order him to produce the evidence, since the special prosecutor was headquartered within the Department of Justice, an executive department, and the dispute over the tapes was therefore within the executive branch. Second, Nixon claimed he had the right of executive privilege, which meant he could refuse to disclose confidential information. The concept of executive privilege goes all the way back to George Washington, who at first refused to give Congress sensitive information about a military campaign against Native Americans (although Washington eventually recanted and released that information). It also has been invoked by modern presidents such as Eisenhower, who used it to prevent aides from testifying about possible preferential treatment in the army.[40]

The Supreme Court rejected both of these lines of defense. On the first count, the Court declared that "it is emphatically the province and duty of the judicial department to say what the law is," which means that the Court had final say over what is or is not legal.[41] In fact, the Court argued, it would be illegal under Article III of the Constitution for the president, rather than the judiciary, to decide whether or not a specific action is

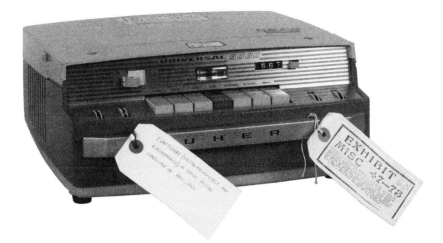

FIGURE 11.3. The tapes that brought down a presidency. One of the actual White House tape recorders that captured conversations that firmly established Richard Nixon's complicity in the Watergate scandal and led to the president's ouster from office. *Source:* National Archives.

legal. The Court also cited the early decision of *Marbury v. Madison*, which established that the Supreme Court can overrule actions by the other branches that violate the Constitution.

Having decided that Nixon's first defense was invalid, the Court moved on to his second defense, the invocation of executive privilege. The Court acknowledged that, in some circumstances, the president was entitled to the privacy that executive privilege promises. For example, Chief Justice Burger wrote that "the need for confidentiality even as to idle conversations with associates in which casual reference might be made concerning political leaders within the country or foreign statesmen is too obvious to call for further treatment." The justices had no doubt that presidents ought to be able to discuss policy without worrying that their conversations would become public.

The subpoena had not requested that the tapes be made public, however. Rather, the subpoena had requested that the tapes be turned over to the special prosecutor who worked in the president's own Department of Justice. The justices recognized that presidents might legitimately prefer to keep information secret, even from people within their own administration, if it presented "a claim of need to protect military, diplomatic, or sensitive national security secrets." In these most delicate of state affairs, it might be more important to public safety that information be kept secret. Yet if the case did not compromise the nation's safety—and releasing the Nixon tapes did not—then executive privilege did not extend to a Department of Justice investigation. Thus, the Court ordered the president to hand the tapes over, which Nixon finally did. Soon thereafter, he resigned from office.

United States v. Nixon made it clear that the Supreme Court could—and would—adjudicate disputes between departments within the executive branch and the president.

So doing, it also restricted the circumstances under which the president could withhold information from other parts of the executive branch.*

11.3.2 Challenging an Executive's Newly Acquired Powers

As we have seen, the judiciary is generally reluctant to get between Congress and the president. Judges and justices recognize the need for Congress to delegate authority to the president both to interpret existing policy and, when necessary, to create new policy. When fights erupt over how this delegated authority is put to use, the courts usually leave it to the elected branches of government to sort things out.

In rare instances, though, the courts do intervene, particularly when they determine that Congress has allocated too much power to the executive branch. The **nondelegation doctrine** dictates that Congress cannot relinquish its core legislative power to executive agencies. Though infrequently deployed, the handful of times that the federal courts have put the nondelegation doctrine to use, they have struck down important presidential powers newly bestowed on the president by Congress.

In three cases over a two-year span, the Supreme Court invoked the nondelegation doctrine in order to retract legislative powers bestowed on the executive branch:

- In *Panama Refining Co. v. Ryan* (1935), the Court found that the 1933 National Industrial Recovery Act (NIRA) was unconstitutional because it allowed the president to prohibit interstate trade of excess petroleum without adequately defining the criteria for the president's oversight responsibilities.[42]
- In *A. L. A. Schechter Poultry Corp. v. United States* (1935), the Court stipulated that the NIRA violated the nondelegation doctrine because Congress had failed to define the "codes of fair competition" that the president was charged with implementing. From the Court's vantage point, regulation of the poultry industry under the NIRA delegated too much unfettered legislative power to the executive branch.[43]
- In *Carter v. Carter Coal Company* (1936), the Court struck down the Bituminous Coal Conservation Act of 1935, which created the Bituminous Coal Commission to set the price of coal and ensure fair competition in the coal industry.[44] Here again, the Court ruled that it was unconstitutional for Congress to hand over to the president the power to set wages and hours for the coal industry.

---

* Nonetheless, controversy persists over when and from whom presidents can withhold information. For example, President George W. Bush refused a congressional subpoena to produce evidence related to the December 2006 firing of eight federal prosecutors, citing his right to executive privilege ("White House Refuses Congressional Subpoenas," National Public Radio, June 28, 2007, http://www.npr.org/templates/story/story.php?storyId=11502745&ps=rs). The extent of executive privilege is also unclear when it involves disputes between branches of government. In *Nixon* one of the reasons the Supreme Court found that the need for secrecy was not compelling was that the information only needed to be shared with one individual within the executive branch. The ruling does not speak to how the Court might view, for example, the executive's refusal to provide potentially sensitive security information to Congress.

Such is the short history of cases that explicitly recognize the nondelegation doctrine. In the vast majority of subsequent cases involving the president's statutory authority to exercise one power or another, the crux of debate has centered on the meaning of delegated authority, not on whether Congress has the explicit right to delegate authority—lawmaking or otherwise—in the first place. But still, the Court has occasionally ruled that Congress has gone too far when empowering the president. *Clinton v. City of New York* (1998) is one of the more consequential of such rulings.

In 1996, Congress passed the Line Item Veto Act, fulfilling over twenty years of campaign promises by fiscal conservatives. The act allowed the president to remove any new expenditure or tax credit from a bill and send the bill back to Congress without vetoing it entirely. Given the prominence of "logrolling" within Congress—that is, the trading of votes and favors—laws regularly include funding for projects that have little or nothing to do with the larger purpose of that legislation. Advocates believed that the line-item veto would allow the president to eliminate wasteful spending without fundamentally corrupting the legislative process. Indeed, the whole point of the line-item veto was to recover a measure of discipline and order on a legislative process that, many thought, had become a feeding ground for special-interest lobbyists.

In the year after the passage of the Line Item Veto Act, President Clinton used the line-item veto eighty-two times to cut roughly $600 million worth of projects, including a $600,000 solar wastewater treatment project in Vermont, a $2 million dredging project slated to benefit a single tour boat operator in Fairbanks, Alaska, and a $900,000 cemetery for veterans that the Department of Veterans Affairs insisted it did not need.[45]

In 1998, however, a group of organizations that included a farmer's cooperative, a hospital, and a health care union sued the government after President Clinton removed several tax provisions from the 1997 budget from which they had stood to benefit. These groups alleged that the president lacked the constitutional authority to make such changes. The Supreme Court agreed, finding in a 6–3 decision that the Line Item Veto Act violated the Constitution.

Writing for the majority, Justice John Paul Stevens insisted that there was only one way to pass a law: through the "single, finely wrought and exhaustively considered procedure" outlined in Article I. The Court viewed the president's power to remove spending provisions from a bill as a means of "amending" rather than "executing" it, thereby violating the Article I provision that all "legislative powers" lie with Congress.[46] After the ruling, Republican senators Dan Coats and John McCain attempted to pass a replacement bill that would break appropriations bills into thousands of one-item miniature bills so that each could be signed or vetoed by the president. Their proposal did not pass. As a consequence, even though all but a handful of state governors around the nation retain some form of line-item veto power, to this day the president has none.

11.3.3 Suing the President

Presidents are frequently forced to make difficult, and sometimes unpopular, choices. Some of those decisions incite aggrieved parties to fight back in court. How can the judiciary protect presidents from vindictive legal actions that would impede their ability to govern, while still holding these same presidents broadly accountable to the law?

The Supreme Court has struggled to find this balance, especially in the last fifty years. Over time, justices have developed a qualified doctrine of **presidential immunity**, whereby presidents are protected from civil suits resulting from actions taken while president but are not protected from either criminal cases or civil cases that were initiated before they entered office.

In *Nixon v. Fitzgerald*, the Supreme Court recognized the president's immunity from some civil cases.[47] In this 1982 case, government employee A. Ernest Fitzgerald sued former president Nixon for his firing from the Department of the Air Force, which he alleged was a result of his 1968 testimony to Congress on massive financial waste in the department's aircraft development program. At a 1973 press conference, Nixon had publicly claimed responsibility for firing Fitzgerald, saying he was "totally aware that Mr. Fitzgerald would be fired or discharged or urged to resign. I approved it. . . . It was a decision . . . I made and I stick by it."[48]

Under normal circumstances, Fitzgerald would have a strong claim to civil remedy against the man who fired him. Since that man was president of the United States, however, the Supreme Court ruled that Nixon was "entitled to absolute immunity from damages liability predicated on his official acts." The Court reasoned that certain individuals, like judges and presidents, must be able to make decisions without fear of judicial reprisals. Opening the president up to lawsuits from individuals, Justice Powell wrote in the majority decision, would pose "unique risks to the effective functioning of government."

According to Powell, this did not mean presidents could flout the law entirely. The other branches of government were certainly entitled to oversee their actions, and there existed "the constitutional remedy of impeachment" to punish presidents who overstep. Furthermore, the Court argued, there are other forces restraining presidents, such as "constant scrutiny by the press and vigilant oversight by Congress" as well as "a desire to earn reelection, the need to maintain prestige as an element of Presidential influence, and a President's traditional concern for his historical stature."

Despite the explicitly limited nature of presidential immunity established in *Nixon v. Fitzgerald*, the notion still evoked criticism from the public and press. The *Spokane Chronicle* ran the headline "Supreme Court Colors White House Infallible," while the *Toledo Blade*'s Mary McGrory wrote that the Framers were "turning over in their graves."[49] It was not only unethical to give presidents carte blanche in their public duties, these observers argued, but it also invited the sort of tyranny the Framers sought to prevent. Impeachment proceedings are slow and difficult to carry out. Furthermore, a politically friendly Congress would have little incentive to impeach a president who, for instance, fired several employees for being members of a widely disliked group. For these reasons, a number of legal scholars argued that removing the threat of lawsuits placed presidents above the law.[50]

Since the *Nixon* ruling, the Court has clarified some of the limits of presidential immunity. For example, in the case of *Clinton v. Jones* (1997), President Bill Clinton faced charges of having sexually harassed a subordinate during his time as governor of Arkansas.[51] Clinton argued that the civil trial could not move forward while he was president, because he had immunity under *Nixon v. Fitzgerald*. Even though he was only seeking to delay the trial, the Supreme Court refused to accommodate the president's request because the allegations stemmed from actions taken before he was president. The Court further explained that the purpose of presidential immunity was "to enable [presidents] to perform their designated functions effectively without fear that a particular decision may give rise to personal liability."

This more restricted view of presidential immunity was later upheld in the 2020 Supreme Court case *Trump v. Vance*.[52] In 2019, as part of the investigation into President Donald Trump's illegal "hush money" payments for extramarital affairs, his tax returns were subpoenaed by the district attorney of Manhattan. Trump ordered that the subpoena be blocked, arguing that the president enjoys "absolute immunity from criminal process of any kind" while in office.[53] Ultimately, the Court rejected this argument, ruling instead that no citizen—including the president—is exempt from the duty to produce evidence when requested during criminal proceedings.

11.3.4 Striking Down a President's Policy

Sometimes the Supreme Court confronts presidents head-on and overturns their policy decisions. We have already discussed the most famous example of such a confrontation, *Youngstown v. Sawyer*, in which the justices overturned Truman's order to seize the steel mills. More recently, the 5–4 ruling in *Department of Homeland Security v. Regents of the University of California* (2020) struck down Trump's rescission of an Obama-era immigration program.

Plenty of other examples populate the history of the Supreme Court—a history that extends far earlier than *Youngstown*. Throughout this chapter, we have focused primarily on cases from the twentieth and twenty-first centuries. But a notorious case from the nineteenth century, *Ex parte Milligan* (1866), reveals the Court's willingness to overturn presidential policies even during wartime, when, as we will see in chapter 16, the adjoining branches of government typically defer to the president's judgment. When it strikes down decisions rendered by the commander in chief, and thereby restores limits on the extraordinary powers wielded by a wartime president, the Supreme Court reasserts its relevance in all domains of presidential action.

In *Ex parte Milligan*, the federal judiciary attempted to reclaim powers that a wartime president had seized by fiat.[54] The case centered on Lambdin P. Milligan, who had been arrested at his home in Indiana in 1864 and charged with conspiracy against the government, inciting insurrection, and giving aid and comfort to the enemy. According to the

U.S. military commandant of the District of Indiana, Milligan had been participating in a plot to liberate Confederate prisoners of war and overthrow the state governments of Indiana, Ohio, and Michigan. For these crimes, Milligan was tried within a system of military courts that Lincoln had unilaterally created in 1862. The military court found Milligan guilty and sentenced him to death.

Luckily for Milligan, the Civil War ended just before his scheduled hanging on May 19, 1865, and Milligan's lawyers promptly appealed his sentence. The appellate court's two-judge panel, however, could not come to any resolution about the essential issues of the case: whether an 1863 congressional statute gave the president the necessary authority to suspend the writ of **habeas corpus** and try citizens in military rather than civilian courts, whether a civilian court had jurisdiction to hear an appeal from a military court, and whether a civilian court could discharge a defendant from military custody.

In 1866, the case came before the Supreme Court, which sided with Milligan. According to the Court, neither the 1863 statute nor conditions in Indiana justified the imposition of martial law or the creation of military tribunals. The Court further ruled that, as a U.S. civilian and resident of a Northern state, Milligan retained the right to be tried in a civilian court. The Court then found the allegations against Milligan sufficiently weak that they warranted his immediate release from custody.

For many, *Milligan* would emerge as a monument to judicial checks on presidential war powers and as a rejection of the notion that there exists, as John Quincy Adams argued in 1831, a "war power" that is limited "only by the laws and usages of nations," as distinct from a "peace power" that is "limited by regulation and restricted by provision in the Constitution."[55] In their arguments before the Supreme Court, all three of Milligan's attorneys insisted that his case had more to do with presidential war powers than it did with a single man's fate (though Milligan surely felt otherwise). According to attorney David Field, constitutional checks on presidential power "were made for a state of war as well as a state of peace." James Garfield, who would assume the presidency fifteen years later, pleaded with the Court not to let the Constitution be "lost in war." And if the British king lacked the power to "stretch the royal authority far enough to justify military trials," as Jeremiah Black argued, then surely the president could not assume the authority to do so. After all, Black famously argued, the Constitution does "not carry the seeds of destruction in its own bosom."[56]

A closer look at the Court's majority opinion suggests that *Milligan*, in fact, represents a limited defeat for the president. The opinion hints that if the Court had rendered its opinion while the war still raged, then Milligan might well have been executed. The opening lines of Justice Davis's opinion admitted that "during the late wicked Rebellion, the temper of the times did not allow that calmness in deliberation and discussion so necessary to a correct conclusion of a purely judicial question." With the return of peace, though, "considerations of safety" need not be intermingled with "the exercise of power," and at long last the Court could review a case without "the admixture of any element not required to form a legal opinion."

Davis's majority opinion does contain strong language in support of constitutional limits on presidential power, and it expresses strong distrust of any president who would use war as a pretext for aggrandizing his or her own authority. But the opinion also contains repeated references to the allowances the Court ought to grant the president in wartime. Moreover, Chief Justice Chase reiterated that the Constitution affords greater powers to the government during times of war. When national security concerns are sufficiently acute, the Court may grant the adjoining branches of government allowances that it would promptly retract during peacetime.

The historical significance of *Milligan*, then, is mixed. On the one hand, it signals a willingness on the Supreme Court's part to overturn a presidential order issued at the very height of his or her power—namely, when the nation is at war. On the other hand, the timing of the Court's ruling and the careful hedges offered in the concurring opinions hint at the general reluctance of Supreme Court justices to rule against the nation's commander in chief. The Court may well stand in the president's way. But when the nation is at war, it tends to do so only reluctantly.

11.4 All the President's Lawyers

Presidents do not sit alone, unguarded in the judiciary's spotlight. Rather, presidents have at their disposal a bevy of lawyers who offer legal counsel, who write opinions about the constitutionality and statutory authority underpinning presidential orders, and who represent the president before the courts. To be sure, these lawyers are not hired guns for the president. They enjoy a measure of discretion and professional independence of their own. Even so, and in some instances precisely because of this independence, these lawyers perform a whole host of functions that aid presidents in the courts.

11.4.1 Lending Advice and Legal Cover

For a variety of institutional reasons, Supreme Court justices often refuse to wade into political disputes between Congress and the president. To clarify these matters, and to clarify them in ways that are distinctly advantageous, presidents can instead turn to the Department of Justice's **Office of Legal Counsel** (OLC), whose legal opinions can help legitimize the president's actions.

Headed by an assistant attorney general—presidentially appointed with consent of the Senate—the OLC serves as a centralized legal authority in the executive branch. The primary function of its roughly two dozen lawyers is to produce legal opinions that guide the president and other executive branch officials. Though these opinions can be requested at any time by the heads of executive branch agencies, the OLC's most important client is the president.[57]

In many ways, the OLC operates like a quasi-judicial body. If an OLC opinion conflicts with a judicial ruling, the ruling will take precedence. Rarely, though, does this happen, since matters handled by the OLC (such as separation-of-powers arguments) often are disregarded by the courts. Meanwhile, the OLC's legal opinions are typically treated as legally binding on the bureaucracy, even though there are no institutional mechanisms by which the office can ensure compliance.[58] The OLC also maintains a commitment to stare decisis. As a result, OLC opinions issued during one administration will likely be cited and upheld by future OLC lawyers, no matter which party the new administration belongs to. In the words of former assistant attorney general Jack Goldsmith, who headed the OLC from 2003 to 2004, the office adheres to its past decisions "even when the head of the office concludes that they [the past decisions] are wrong."[59] For many, this tradition establishes the OLC's reputation as an independent arbiter of inter- and intrabranch disputes.

Other facts, however, point toward very different conclusions. The OLC is located squarely within the executive branch, its members are appointed by the president himself, and they, unlike federal judges, serve at the president's pleasure. As a consequence, the OLC tends to maintain a solidly pro-presidential outlook. The OLC has itself claimed to have "a constitutional obligation . . . to assert and maintain the legitimate powers and privileges of the President against inadvertent or intentional congressional intrusion."[60] When presidents ask the OLC whether their actions or initiatives are constitutionally permissible, its lawyers have strong incentives to say yes.

Much of the OLC's compliance derives from the fact that its lawyers are both hired and promoted by the president. Goldsmith, for example, recalls being hired by the George W. Bush administration "in large part because I shared the basic assumptions, outlook, and goals of top administration officials."[61] It is natural for presidential appointees to feel indebted to the president. For this reason, Goldsmith admits that he "work[ed] hard to find a way for the President to achieve his ends."[62] Meanwhile, presidents may influence OLC lawyers through the promise of further promotions. As one constitutional law scholar put it, the president "hold[s] the keys to some of the most desirable appointments to which lawyers aspire."[63] Advancements within the Justice Department and appointments to the federal judiciary may entice OLC lawyers to craft opinions that lend support to the president's policy goals.

For their part, presidents have much to gain by keeping the OLC in their corner. The OLC's reputation as an impartial, court-like institution—deserved or not—generates widespread deference to its opinions. When the office greenlights a contentious White House initiative, it "enables the executive to make aggressive claims that the law is on his side."[64]

OLC opinions also help tighten the president's grip on the bureaucracy. Goldsmith equates these opinions with "advance pardons" or "get-out-of-jail-free cards."[65] Wary of following a president's controversial orders, especially if those orders could invite reprimand from Congress or a future administration's Department of Justice, executive branch officials are put at ease when the OLC affirms their constitutionality. Bureaucratic compliance, as such, flows from the legal cover that OLC lawyers provide.

Because of the OLC's commitment to stare decisis, opinions that empower one president will likely empower future presidents as well. During an investigation into its ties to the Russian government, for example, the Trump administration benefited from the "longstanding Department [of Justice] policy" that a sitting president cannot be charged with a federal crime.[66] This policy originated with a 1973 OLC memo, clarified and upheld by the office in 2000, which stated that an indictment "would impermissibly undermine the capacity of the executive" to perform its duties.[67] As opinions like these get older, their findings become entrenched; subsequent scholars cite them as categorical precedent, dispensing any uncertainty that the original authors might have harbored.

Having cautioned against reading too much into claims about the OLC's fidelity to neutral competence and the Constitution, however, we also should be wary of overstating the politics that undergird this body's work. The OLC, after all, hardly amounts to a cabal of presidential cronies and political apologists. Nor do presidents want it to become one. When trying to determine how the federal judiciary is likely to rule on their orders, after all, presidents benefit from the neutral expertise of experienced and knowledgeable OLC lawyers. And the legal cover that OLC opinions provide crucially depends upon the office's reputation for independence. Should the OLC function as a mere rubber stamp for presidential policy ambitions, the chief executive receives neither the advice needed to avoid an embarrassing defeat in the judiciary nor the approval needed to curry support within the administrative state.*

The result, then, is an OLC that remains suspended in a state of persistent tension. In any given moment, presidents might prefer that the OLC affirm their immediate wants and wishes. But a political world in which the office routinely does so, ultimately, redounds to presidents' disadvantage. When lawyers at the OLC weigh in on a matter, therefore, their advice is reasonably candid, well-informed, and, more often than not, favorable to the president.

11.4.2 Representing the President in the Federal Judiciary

The Office of the **Solicitor General,** also located within the Department of Justice, manages the government's interactions with the Supreme Court. Because the solicitor general is appointed by the president, this office plays an integral role in representing and defending the president's interests within the judiciary.

Whenever a citizen, company, or organization challenges a federal law in lower courts and wins, the Office of the Solicitor General determines whether an appeal is warranted. In cases in which the government is not a named party, but in which an important federal law is called into question, the solicitor general may file an **amicus curiae** brief—a brief containing information directly pertinent to the case in hand—that the Supreme Court may consult in its deliberations. When a government case comes before the Supreme

---

*As evidence, recall the controversy surrounding the OLC's "Torture Memos," which provided a thin legal gloss to the George W. Bush administration's use of waterboarding, sleep deprivation, starvation, and other interrogation tactics against prisoners of the War on Terror. These opinions, which relied upon dubious interpretations of the Constitution's commander-in-chief clause, were later criticized by Justice Department officials and called "an unfortunate chapter" in the history of the OLC. Trevor W. Morrison, "Stare Decisis in the Office of Legal Counsel," *Columbia Law Review* 110 (2010): 1524.

TABLE 11.1. Percentage of Cases Won by the Solicitor General in the Supreme Court, 1946–2019

	Petitioner Win (%)	Respondent Win (%)
Solicitor General	71	50
Other Litigants	62	35

Court, particularly one that concerns the president, the solicitor general formulates strategy and argues the case on the floor.

The solicitor general's office has historically been highly successful in its advocacy for the federal government. The Supreme Court agrees to hear 70 percent of the cases brought by the solicitor general, in contrast to only 3 percent of the petitions brought from other litigants,[68] and the Court agrees with amicus briefs filed by the solicitor general over 75 percent of the time.* As table 11.1 shows, the solicitor general also does remarkably well when arguing cases before the Court. Depending on whether the solicitor general is the petitioner (who brings the case to the Court) or respondent (who is being accused, similar to a defendant), the solicitor general wins either 9 or 15 percentage points more often than do other litigants before the Court.

In theory, solicitors general act independently of the president, making their own decisions about which laws to appeal and how to appeal them. However, a substantial body of empirical research shows that in practice, the president and solicitor general almost always share the same ideological convictions.[69] Moreover, where differences in ideology do emerge, the president can be expected to prevail. The solicitor general serves at the president's pleasure, and it is the solicitor general's job to present the viewpoint of the executive branch generally, and the president in particular. Solicitor General Francis Biddle, who served under FDR, went so far as to argue that the solicitor general is a "direct agent of the president."[70]

Solicitors general sometimes publicly recognize their place in the executive pecking order. Former solicitor general Erwin Griswold candidly observed that it is "unwise to lose sight of the reality that a Solicitor General is not an ombudsman with a roving commission to do justice as he sees it. He is a lawyer who must render conscientious representation to his client's interests."[71] Subsequent solicitors general have made similar observations. Reagan's first solicitor general, Rex E. Lee, plainly declared that representing the administration's policies is "part of [the] job."[72] Reflecting upon his own experience as solicitor general under George H. W. Bush, Kenneth Starr recognized that "[he] was an 'inferior' or 'subordinate' officer in the executive branch. If [he] could not in conscience abide by the president's judgment, then [he] should resign."[73]

---

* In fact, the Supreme Court values the opinion of the solicitor general so highly that the solicitor general is the only party with a special formatting for its memos, which are submitted in gray so that the justices can easily find and read them.

This perspective contradicts the common view of the solicitor general as the "Tenth Justice," someone who is equally beholden to the Supreme Court and the president.[74] To effectively perform the job, of course, the solicitor general needs to cultivate a professional reputation and positive relationship with the judges and justices. The purpose of this reputation and relationship, however, is not to improve the solicitor general's professional standing or to ingratiate him or her with the Supreme Court. Rather, in the final analysis, it is to more effectively promote and protect the president's interests.

Historical Transformations: Roosevelt's Court-Packing Scheme

In his 1933 inauguration speech, FDR declared, "This nation asks for action, and action now" in order to combat the worst economic depression the nation had ever seen. In the weeks to follow, the president pushed for a flurry of legislation.[75] Roosevelt employed a try-anything attitude toward bringing down the 25 percent national unemployment rate. Crucial to the effort was the prompt creation of agencies and programs, including the Federal Emergency Relief Administration, Civil Works Administration, Works Progress Administration, Public Works Administration, Farm Credit Act, and National Industrial Recovery Act (NIRA).[76]

Critics attacked many of these programs, but especially the NIRA. The NIRA aimed to increase employment by creating "alliances" of industries and letting them decide on production quotas, fixed prices, fixed wages, and work hours. FDR declared that these industry alliances could make these decisions even if they violated existing laws, including antitrust laws, which had long before prohibited the setting of fixed prices or wages by groups of large companies. Early challengers of the NIRA protested against what they believed were unfair regulations of private industry. In 1934, the Supreme Court upheld existing state economic regulations in *Home Building and Loan Association v. Blaisdell* and *Nebbia v. New York*. Over the following year, however, the result of federal litigation was mixed, with some positive for FDR (e.g., the *Gold Clause Cases*) and some negative (e.g., *Panama Refining Co. v. Ryan*).

On May 27, 1935, FDR's relationship with the courts, already tenuous, took a sharp turn for the worse. On "Black Monday," the Supreme Court announced three major decisions, all against the administration. In the last case to be announced, *Schechter Poultry Corp. v. United States*, the Court invalidated the entirety of the NIRA on the grounds that it unconstitutionally delegated to the president legislative authority that properly belonged to Congress. Furthermore, the Court insisted that the NIRA was unconstitutional "because it exceeds the power of Congress to regulate interstate commerce and invades the power reserved exclusively to the States."

FDR balked at this deep cut to his powers and ridiculed the Supreme Court for using a "horse and buggy definition of interstate commerce."[77] The president had already chafed at the Supreme Court's willingness to undermine his agenda. Now, he sought to challenge the Supreme Court's authority.

FIGURE 11.4. After the Supreme Court ruled unconstitutional a number of his New Deal laws, FDR moved to increase the number of sitting justices, which would have allowed him to appoint a batch of allies—or, as this cartoon suggests, clones—who could be counted on to uphold his agenda. *Source:* AP Images.

In 1937, FDR proposed the Judicial Procedures Reform Bill of 1937. No Supreme Court justice had retired since 1932, when Oliver Wendell Holmes left the Supreme Court, in part because FDR's Economy Act had cut the Supreme Court's pensions in half (from $20,000 to $10,000). The Judicial Procedures Reform Bill would have enabled FDR to appoint an additional judge for every federal justice on the bench over the age of seventy, when full retirement became available, with an upper limit of six justices on the Supreme Court and two on each federal court bench. As most prior Supreme Court decisions had broken 5–4, the additional justices would have given FDR a comfortable margin against future challenges.

Continued on next page

FDR was not secretive about his intentions. In his March 1937 "Fireside Chat," FDR stated that "the Court has more and more often and more and more boldly asserted a power to veto laws passed by the Congress and State Legislatures," and so doing, it had become "a policy-making body."[78] He also portrayed a spate of recent 5–4 decisions as resting on volatile, dangerous margins where a "change of one vote" could create "chaos." To avoid the appearance of purely political motivations, FDR also emphasized the need to relieve elderly judges and bring "new blood" into the courts.[79] FDR argued that these new judges would have different life experiences, particularly when it came to recent economic and social conditions. Younger judges, he argued, might understand the impact of his New Deal legislation better than the older, sitting justices.

Despite FDR's appeals to the public, his "court-packing" plan, as it came to be known, promptly sparked a public and congressional backlash. A 1937 Gallup poll found that 44 percent of Americans disapproved of FDR's plan to make the Court "more liberal" by adding more justices, even though FDR had enjoyed high personal approval ratings throughout his presidency.[80] The House of Representatives refused to even take up the bill.

The Supreme Court itself also helped foil FDR's plan, albeit in a conciliatory manner: on March 29, 1937 ("White Monday"), just two months after FDR announced his strategy, the Court issued three pro-administration decisions in quick succession. In these decisions, Justice Owen Roberts, one of the Court's two swing votes, sided with the administration. Roberts's shift in position and the Court's liberal rulings for the remainder of that year became known as "the switch in time that saved nine."[81]

A variety of institutional lessons can be drawn from this historical interlude. According to some, the debacle served as proof that presidential overreach will lead to a sharp rebuke. Years later, Supreme Court Chief Justice William Rehnquist wrote that "it was the United States Senate—a political body if there ever was one—who stepped in and saved the independence of the judiciary."[82] In Rehnquist's narrative, the legislative branch restored the judiciary's rightful place as a co-equal branch of government.

Viewed another way, however, this historical moment reveals the Supreme Court's inability to respond to executive encroachments without compromise. The Supreme Court assumed a considerably more accommodating posture in the aftermath of FDR's power grab. Though the institutional integrity of the judiciary remained intact, its general propensity to support presidential initiatives persists to this day.

11.5 Judicial Nominations

The president's lawyers have great success, it seems, in legitimizing and defending their boss's actions before the Court. But rather than defend themselves before a hostile bench, presidents would sometimes prefer to reshape the composition of the judiciary itself. The Constitution gives the president the power to appoint federal judges and justices with "the advice and consent" of the Senate. Because federal judges hold office for life, these appointments enable presidents to influence the judicial branch long after they have left office.

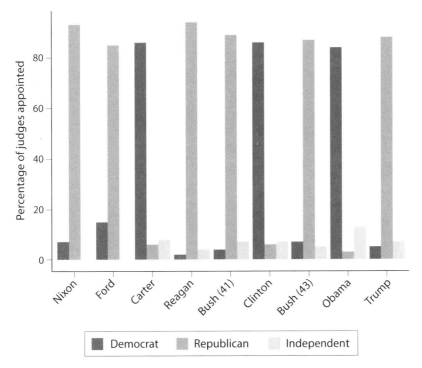

FIGURE 11.5. Appointed judges by partisanship, Nixon to Trump. Though the judiciary is supposed to be apolitical, politics figures prominently in the selection of judges and justices, as the majority of a president's judicial appointments are from the same party of the president. *Sources:* Harold W. Stanley and Richard G. Niemi, *Vital Statistics on American Politics, 2015–2016* (Washington, DC: Congressional Quarterly Press, 2015), 280–82, table 7–5, supplemented with data available at senate.gov.

11.5.1 Appointing Co-Partisans to the Bench

Every full-term president in office since World War II has appointed more than 100 judges and justices to the federal judiciary. Recent presidents have had the opportunity to appoint even more. President Reagan, who served two consecutive terms, set a record by making 402 judicial appointments. Presidents George W. Bush and Barack Obama appointed 340 and 334 judges, respectively. In his four years in office, Donald Trump appointed 245.[83]

Though judges come to the bench with a variety of life experiences, most share some common qualities. All judges, for starters, have been trained in the law. In addition, over the last forty years, nearly 65 percent of appellate court appointees have had some previous judicial experience. And while only 8 to 12 percent of judicial appointees have had a previous career in politics or government,[84] political considerations loom large in judicial appointments. As previously discussed, presidents regularly appoint judges who share their partisan affiliation (figure 11.5). Lower court appointments are fast becoming as politicized as Supreme Court appointments have always been: since Nixon's time in office, upwards of 90 percent of judicial appointments to district and appellate courts have come from the president's own party.[85]

11.5.2 Selecting Judges with Expansive Views of Presidential Power

Presidents clearly evaluate the partisan commitments and ideological outlooks of prospective nominees to the bench. In addition, however, presidents take stock of the nominee's views on presidential power.

During the George W. Bush administration, many appointees to the federal courts were vocal proponents of the Unitary Executive Theory, which holds, as discussed in chapter 1, that the president has nearly absolute control over the executive branch. Supreme Court Justice Samuel Alito provides one high-profile example. Prior to his appointment to the Court in 2005, Alito had spoken publicly for years about his support for the Unitary Executive Theory. Alito had claimed that the theory "best captures the meaning of the Constitution's text and structure."[86] Alito also had a record of pro-executive decisions, such as *Specter v. Garrett*, in which he supported the president's ability to close military bases, and had written and spoken publicly against Supreme Court decisions such as *Morrison v. Olson*, which restricted presidential power.[87]

Of course, appointing judges who support a strong executive branch is not an exclusively Republican habit. In 2010, for instance, Obama nominated Elena Kagan to fill a vacancy in the Supreme Court. Kagan, who at the time was serving as Obama's solicitor general, had in the past published essays supporting expanded power for the executive. In a 2001 *Harvard Law Review* article titled "Presidential Administration," Kagan lauded "the President's ability to trump bureaucracy." In her view, "the President has the ability to effect comprehensive, coherent change in administrative policymaking" when he or she overrules bureaucrats.[88]

Trump's second Supreme Court appointee, Associate Justice Brett Kavanaugh, is perhaps the most explicit proponent of executive privilege on the current Court. Writing in a 2009 *Minnesota Law Review* article, Kavanaugh proposed that Congress "consider a law exempting a President—while in office—from criminal prosecution and investigation, including from questioning by criminal prosecutors or defense counsel," because investigations are "time-consuming and distracting."[89] Opinions like this one do not fit neatly into ideological categories, as presidents of both parties stand to gain from judges who, like Kavanaugh, take a more expansive view of power.

11.5.3 The Politics of District and Appellate Court Nominations

Historically, the Senate has confirmed the vast majority of lower court nominees to the judiciary. In the 1980s and early 1990s, roughly 80 percent of both district and appellate nominees made their way to the bench. Since the Republican takeover of the 104th Congress (1995–96), however, nominees for appellate courts have become significantly less likely to be confirmed than nominees for district courts.

Part of the reason most district nominees are confirmed is that senators play an important role in their selection. When choosing a judicial nominee for a district court, the president will often seek the approval of the senior senator who represents the state in which the court is located. That senator, in turn, will lobby peers in the Senate to ensure that they approve the nominee. This norm, known as **senatorial courtesy**, tends to hasten the process of selecting and confirming district court judges around the nation.

Things get more complicated at the appellate level. Since the stakes are higher, appellate court judges are subject to greater scrutiny by both the president and the Senate. As a consequence, some individuals who are easily confirmed at the district level face objections and delays when they are considered for appellate appointments. Lucy Koh, for instance, was confirmed to the U.S. District Court for the Northern District of California in 2010 by a 90–0 vote in the Senate. When Obama nominated her to the Court of Appeals six years later,[90] her case was reported out of the Senate Judiciary Committee by a vote of 13–7, but the Republican-controlled Senate refused to schedule a floor vote and her nomination expired at the conclusion of the congressional term. Once in office, Trump filled the vacancy on the Ninth Circuit. Koh was eventually renominated to the Ninth Circuit during Biden's first year in office, when she was confirmed by a narrow 50–45 vote.

Koh had to wait five years and a second nomination before securing an appointment on the appellate court. But trouble also can come for presidents who use recess appointments to circumvent the Senate and install their preferred candidate right away. In 1990, when Democrats had control over both chambers of Congress, George H. W. Bush appointed Charles Pickering to a federal district court in southern Mississippi without controversy. Twelve years later, however, George W. Bush nominated Pickering for a position on the Fifth Circuit Court of Appeals. At the time, Democrats still controlled the Senate and refused to confirm Pickering's nomination, levying a variety of charges against him, including racial insensitivity and political views that were "out of step" with mainstream America.[91]

The next year, when the Republicans regained control of the Senate, Bush renominated Pickering. This time Democrats filibustered the nomination, and Republicans lacked the needed votes to cut off debate. Bush waited until the Senate was not in session in early 2004 and granted Pickering a recess appointment that lasted until the end of Congress's next session. When Congress began to formally consider Pickering's case, concerns about his political positions resurfaced. Rather than drag the confirmation out any longer, Pickering withdrew from consideration and retired from the bench.

11.5.4 Increasingly Partisan Supreme Court Nominations

If the politics of appellate court nominations are heated, those of Supreme Court nominations are piping hot. Norms of senatorial courtesy play no role in Supreme Court appointments. Instead, presidents consult directly with their closest advisors and heed the demands of different political constituencies. The goal is to find an individual with just the right mix of judicial experience and policy preferences.

Once the president identifies a potential Supreme Court nominee, the FBI is asked to conduct a full background check on the individual in order to identify any evidence of unlawful behavior. Some recent presidents also have sent the names of prospective nominees to the American Bar Association (ABA), an interest group that represents the legal profession and that provides ratings of the qualifications of candidates. The ABA's

Standing Committee on the Federal Judiciary typically rates nominees as either "well qualified," "qualified," or "not qualified."

A Supreme Court nominee who survives these background checks then must face the public. From the moment the president announces a name, a torrent of media scrutiny follows. Interest groups take out radio and television advertisements to highlight the candidate's strengths or weaknesses. Legal scholars write opinion pieces about the candidate's qualifications, previous decisions, and judicial philosophy. Journalists investigate the candidate's personal and professional histories. Typically, no element of a Supreme Court nominee's past is considered off-limits.

During the 2009 Senate confirmation hearings for Supreme Court Justice Sonia Sotomayor, for instance, the media and politicians focused on comments she had made in a 2001 speech, including, "I would hope that a wise Latina woman with the richness of her experiences would more often than not reach a better conclusion than a white male who hasn't lived that life."[92] The quote was repeated many times by the press, and some Republican members of Congress expressed concern that she believed that race and gender figured prominently in the capacity of justices to perform their duties in office. Like most Supreme Court nominees, however, Sotomayor sidestepped questions about her ideological views. Her record as a district and appellate judge, she claimed, reflected her impartiality.

The official action of the judicial appointment process occurs during the confirmation hearings, which are open to the public and broadcast live on television. At the hearings, members of the Senate Judiciary Committee have the opportunity to interrogate a nominee directly about decisions he or she made as a lawyer or lower court judge. They may ask about his or her views on issues ranging from abortion to campaign finance. Given that the nominee may eventually issue rulings that fundamentally alter public policies, it makes sense that senators would want to question nominees on their views about these issues. Whether the nominees are completely forthcoming in their answers, however, is an altogether different matter. Most are trained to deflect questions with carefully worded responses that reveal as little information as possible.

In general, the Senate is less likely to confirm Supreme Court nominees than appellate or district court nominees. Since the Constitution's ratification in 1789, presidents have formally submitted 165 nominations for Supreme Court justice to the Senate, including those for Chief Justice. Of these, the Senate confirmed 128, and 121 actually took office.* Dissenters can be found in all of the recent Supreme Court confirmation hearings.

In some cases, full-blown controversies erupted. And among these, none compares to the confirmation hearings for Robert Bork, whom Reagan nominated to the Supreme Court in 1987. No fewer than eighty-six different interest groups testified at his confirmation hearings.[93] Critics focused not on Bork's knowledge of the law—the ABA rated him

---

*Seven justices who were confirmed declined to serve, the most recent being Roscoe Conkling in 1882. Data are available online at "Supreme Court Nominations, 1789–Present," United States Senate, http://www .senate.gov/pagelayout/reference/nominations/Nominations.htm.

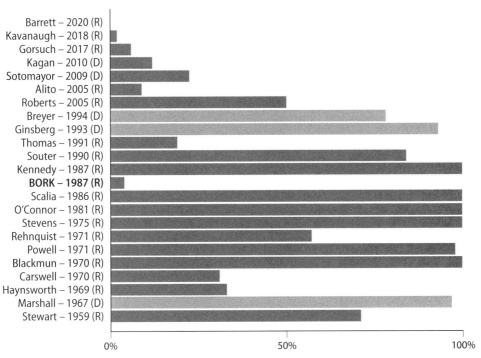

FIGURE 11.6. Party-line support in the Senate for Supreme Court nominees. The names on the left are Supreme Court nominees, which are followed by the year in which they were nominated and the party of the sitting president in parentheses. The bars, colored light gray for Democrat and dark gray for Republican, show the percentage of senators from the opposite party of the president who voted to confirm the nominee. Partisan politics has increasingly become more the rule than the exception, as can be seen by the small percent of opposite party votes that nominees have received since Bork. With the exception of Bork, Carswell, and Haynsworth, all of the listed nominees were appointed to the bench. *Sources:* senate.gov and govtrack.us.

"well qualified"—but on his political views on abortion, civil rights, and civil liberties. Less than an hour after Reagan announced Bork's nomination, Senator Edward Kennedy declared, "Robert Bork's America is a land in which women would be forced into back-alley abortions, blacks would sit in segregated lunch counters, rogue police could break down citizens' doors in midnight raids."[94] For the next three and a half months, an avalanche of criticism descended upon the nominee. On October 23, 1987, the Senate rejected Bork's confirmation by a vote of 58–42. The vacant court seat for which Bork was nominated eventually went to the much more moderate Anthony Kennedy, who was unanimously approved by the Senate, 97–0.

In the aftermath of Bork's failed bid to join the nation's highest court, the two major parties divided in Congress, and the politics of Supreme Court nominations rather suddenly became an extension of partisan politics. Eight nominations garnered the support of less than 50 percent of the opposition party, whereas only two did so before Bork (and neither of them was appointed to the Court). Most recently, the three cases that Trump put forward received, in combination, just four supporting votes from Democratic senators; Biden's first nominee received just three supporting votes from Republican senators.

11.5.5 Eroding Norms of Consideration

Article II, Section 2 of the Constitution states that "[The president] shall nominate, and by and with the Advice and Consent of the Senate, shall appoint . . . Judges of the supreme Court." Note the precise language here: while "shall" is applied to actions the president takes, the Senate does not appear obligated to do anything. Much as Congress is free to table bills the president supports, it need not vote on the president's Supreme Court nominees.

Until quite recently, this distinction did not amount to much in practice. There is a long, unwritten tradition in the Senate of fair dealing with the president's nominees—that even if a nominee is rejected, he or she will at least be *considered*. Thus, what was not compelled by the Constitution was instead encouraged by norms.

In the final year of the Obama presidency, however, this norm was violated by Republican leadership in Congress. When the conservative Justice Antonin Scalia suddenly died in February 2016, Senate majority leader Mitch McConnell announced that he would not even consider a nomination for Scalia's seat on the bench while Obama remained in office. "The American people should have a voice in the selection of their next Supreme Court Justice," said McConnell. "Therefore, this vacancy should not be filled until we have a new president."[95] Undeterred, Obama nonetheless nominated Merrick Garland, an ideologically centrist judge from the DC Court of Appeals.[96] Also undeterred, most Senate Republicans refused to meet with Garland, and Scalia's seat remained open for 293 days—far longer than the average Supreme Court vacancy of 73 days. With Trump's victory in the 2016 election and Republicans still in control of Congress, Garland's chances of ascending to the Court promptly disappeared. Instead, Trump's nominee, Neil Gorsuch, was confirmed on April 7, 2017, by a margin of 54–45.

Examining the history of Supreme Court appointments, it becomes clear just how norm-breaking this series of events really was. Before Garland's nomination, there had been 103 instances in which the Senate considered and voted on a sitting president's Supreme Court nominee—eight of which occurred during election years.[97] By contrast, there were only six instances in which the Senate sought to postpone the appointment process until after an election. These rare cases resulted from questions about the sitting president's legitimacy. Either the president had come to power through the death or removal of a predecessor, or a successor had already been elected. Of course, neither of these conditions applied to the twice–popularly elected Obama. Rather, his defeat reflected a reversal of a clearly established Senate tradition.

But unlike constitutional rules, traditions and norms can change without broad consensus. Democrats were made painfully aware of this fact in 2020, with the death of the liberal Justice Ruth Bader Ginsburg. Former president Obama urged the Senate to delay a nomination and follow the new tradition they had established four years prior—to "apply rules with consistency, and not based on what's convenient or advantageous in the moment."[98] But for the Republicans, who controlled both the Senate and the White House, the opportunity was too enticing to pass up. In one of the quickest confirmation processes in history, the highly conservative Amy Coney Barrett joined the Supreme Court on October 26, 2020—just a week before Election Day and just thirty days after being nominated by President Trump.

What are we to make of these two nominations? It is nearly impossible to discern a cogent principle that justifies the Senate's refusal to consider Garland's nomination in one election year and its rushed approval of Barrett in the very next. To the extent that norms codify public expectations about the roles, practices, and obligations of politicians, and thereby routinize political behavior,[99] a new norm may have emerged: just as political loyalties and partisan affiliations routinely inform the president's choice of nominees, and just as confirmation votes increasingly break along party lines, partisan politics now dictate the Senate's very willingness to even bring a nomination up for consideration.

In both instances, the partisan political incentives for Republicans were reasonably clear. To abide by norms of consideration in 2016 would have established Garland, a left-of-center judge with liberal views on a host of policy issues, as the key median justice whose vote could swing a Court ruling one way or another. Alternatively, to *abandon* these same norms in 2020 would have meant passing up on a solid 6–3 Supreme Court majority, a rare opportunity in the history of the Senate.

The changing rationales for ignoring a president's nominee in one instance and rushing it through in the next ultimately reinforce an understanding of the Supreme Court as a deeply political institution. Though justices frequently claim to stand apart from politics, the hyperpartisan reactions to Garland and Coney Barrett reinforced the opposite view: that the Supreme Court is best understood according to its ideological composition. In this way, the eroding norms of consideration also erode the Court's reputation as an independent constitutional interpreter, its perceived legitimacy, and all that flows from it.

Conclusion

The president holds a number of institutional advantages over the judiciary. Because they have the power to nominate all judges and justices, presidents can populate the judiciary with individuals who share their ideological views and exhibit an expansive understanding of Article II powers. But there is a structural dependence that also defines the relationship between the presidency and judiciary. Judges look to the president, and the executive branch more generally, to enforce their rulings. Lacking the power of the purse or the sword, the judiciary depends on the president, among others, to ensure that their rulings amount to something more than just suggestions.

Judges are usually reluctant to stand in the president's way. When presidential actions and policies are challenged, judges may refuse to take a position one way or another. When they do issue a ruling, more often than not, it comes out in the president's favor.

Still, the judiciary represents an important check on the presidency. In a series of landmark cases, the courts have confronted and constrained the executive branch. In some instances, such as *United States v. Nixon*, the courts forced the president to take actions that proved politically catastrophic for Nixon, and in others, such as *Youngstown v. Sawyer*, the courts undid presidential policies. These cases stand as lasting tribute to the judiciary's continued relevance for executive politics.

Key Terms

legal model	administrative deference
stare decisis	nondelegation doctrine
standing	presidential immunity
ripeness	habeas corpus
case law	Office of Legal Counsel
attitudinal model	solicitor general
cult of the robe	amicus curiae
political question doctrine	senatorial courtesy
judicial review	

Questions for Discussion

1. How might the political question doctrine be used to advance a judge's legal, political, and institutional interests?
2. Under what conditions are presidents most likely to win a court challenge to their policies or actions? When are presidents least likely to do so?
3. Given that presidents have the power to appoint all federal judges, and judges can be impeached by majorities in Congress, does it make sense to think of the judiciary as an independent and co-equal branch of government?
4. If the justices in *Bush v. Gore* ultimately based their opinions on their individual ideologies, does this suggest that personal, as opposed to institutional, considerations proved paramount—or, in this case, do we see the influence of both factors at work?
5. The Supreme Court has the authority to strike down a president's signature legislative package, as almost happened with the Affordable Care Act in *NFIB v. Sebelius*, or a critical executive order, as nearly occurred with President Trump's travel ban in *Trump v. Hawaii*. Do these cases suggest that the Court's inability to enforce its own rulings may be not an especially important impediment to checking presidential power?

Suggested Readings

Bailey, Michael, and Forrest Maltzman. *The Constrained Court: How the Law and Politics Shape the Decisions Justices Make*. Princeton: Princeton University Press, 2011.

Bickel, Alexander. *The Least Dangerous Branch: The Supreme Court at the Bar of Politics*. New Haven: Yale University Press, 1986.

Bonica, Adam, and Maya Sen. *The Judicial Tug of War: How Lawyers, Politicians, and Political Incentives Shape the American Judiciary*. New York: Cambridge University Press, 2020.

Cameron, Charles, and Jonathan Kastellec. 2023. *Making the Supreme Court: The Politics of Appointments, 1930–2020*. New York: Oxford University Press.

Clark, Tom. *The Limits of Judicial Independence*. New York: Cambridge University Press, 2010.

Epstein, Lee, and Jeffrey A. Segal. *Advice and Consent: The Politics of Judicial Appointments*. New York: Oxford University Press, 2005.

Rosenberg, Gerald N. *The Hollow Hope: Can Courts Bring about Social Change?* 2nd ed. Chicago: University of Chicago Press, 2008.

Strum, Philippa. *The Supreme Court and "Political Questions": A Study in Judicial Evasion*. Tuscaloosa: University of Alabama Press, 1974.

Whittington, Keith. *Political Foundations of Judicial Supremacy: The Presidency, the Supreme Court, and Constitutional Leadership in U.S. History*. Princeton: Princeton University Press, 2007.

Yalof, David. *Pursuit of Justices: Presidential Politics and the Selection of Supreme Court Nominees*. Chicago: University of Chicago Press, 1999.

Notes

1. Alexander Hamilton, "Federalist No. 78," in *The Federalist Papers*, ed. Clinton Rossiter (New York: Signet, 2003).

2. This section and the next draw from John J. Coleman, Kenneth M. Goldstein, and William G. Howell, *Understanding American Politics and Government*, 2nd ed. (Upper Saddle River, NJ: Pearson, 2011).

3. Harold W. Stanley and Richard G. Niemi, *Vital Statistics on American Politics, 2015–2016* (Washington, DC: Congressional Quarterly Press, 2015).

4. Rebecca R. Ruiz, Robert Gebeloff, Steve Eder, and Ben Protess, "A Conservative Agenda Released on the Federal Courts," *New York Times*, March 14, 2020, https://www.nytimes.com/2020/03/14/us/trump-appeals-court-judges.html.

5. Lee Epstein and Jeffrey A. Segal, *Advice and Consent: The Politics of Judicial Appointments* (New York: Oxford University Press, 2005), 144.

6. The most comprehensive accounting of this fact can be found in Jeffrey Segal and Harold Spaeth, *The Supreme Court and the Attitudinal Model Revisited* (New York: Cambridge University Press, 2002).

7. Jeffrey Segal et al., "Ideological Values and the Votes of U.S. Supreme Court Justices Revisited," *Journal of Politics* 57, no. 3 (1995): 812–23.

8. Jeffrey Segal, "Separation-of-Powers Games in the Positive Theory of Congress and Courts," *American Political Science Review* 91, no. 1 (1997): 33.

9. "Election 2000 Timeline," *Pittsburgh Post-Gazette*, December 17, 2000, 4.

10. "Contesting the Vote; Excerpts from Gore and Bush Briefs Filed with the U.S. Supreme Court," *New York Times*, December 11, 2000, A.28.

11. *Bush v. Gore*, 531 U.S. 98 (2000) (per curiam).

12. *Bush v. Gore* (per curiam).

13. Evan Thomas, "Reagan's Mr. Right: Rehnquist Is Picked for the Court's Top Job," *Time*, June 30, 1986, 16.

14. *Bush v. Gore* (Ginsburg, J., dissenting).

15. *Bush v. Gore* (Ginsburg, J., dissenting).

16. Akhil Reed Amar, "Supreme Court: Should We Trust Judges?" *Los Angeles Times*, December 17, 2000, M1.

17. Jeffrey Rosen, "Disgrace," *New Republic* 223, no. 26 (2000): 18–21.

18. Hamilton, "Federalist No. 78."

19. Gerald N. Rosenberg, *The Hollow Hope: Can Courts Bring about Social Change?* 2nd ed. (Chicago: University of Chicago Press, 2008), 15.

20. John Brigham, *The Cult of the Court* (Philadelphia: Temple University Press, 1987).

21. Though some believe this quote to be misattributed, it was an alleged response to *Worcester v. Georgia*, 31 U.S. 515 (1832).

22. Rosenberg, *The Hollow Hope*, 21.

23. Matthew Hall, "The Semiconstrained Court: Public Opinion, the Separation of Powers, and the U.S. Supreme Court's Fear of Nonimplementation," *American Journal of Political Science* 58, no. 2 (August 2013): 352–66.

24. *Nat'l Fed'n of Indep. Businesses v. Sebelius*, 567 U.S. 519 (2012).

25. *Hooper v. California*, 155 U.S. 648, 657, 15 S.Ct. 207, 39 L.Ed. 297 (1895).

26. On the "shocked" reaction of Republican legislators themselves to Roberts's decision, see, for example, Manu Raju and Jake Sherman, "Republicans: Et tu, John Roberts?" *POLITICO*, June 28, 2012, https://www.politico.com/story/2012/06/republicans-et-tu-roberts-077962.

27. See Jan Crawford, "Roberts Switched Views to Uphold Health Care Law," CBS News, July 1, 2012, http://www.cbsnews.com/8301-3460_162-57464549/roberts-switched-views-to-uphold-health-care-law/?tag=contentMain;contentBody.

28. *Baker v. Carr*, 369 U.S. 186 (1962).

29. *Marbury v. Madison*, 5 U.S. (1 Cranch) 137 (1803).

30. *Prize Cases*, 67 U.S. (2 Black) 635 (1862).

31. *Oetjen v. Central Leather Co.*, 246 U.S. 297 (1918).

32. *Baker v. Carr*, 369 U.S. 186 (1962).

33. *Goldwater v. Carter*, 444 U.S. 996 (1979).

34. *Youngstown Sheet & Tube Co. v. Sawyer*, 343 U.S. 579 (1952).

35. Gordon Silverstein, *Imbalance of Powers: Constitutional Interpretation and the Making of American Foreign Policy* (New York: Oxford University Press, 1997), 39.

36. *Chevron U.S.A., Inc. v. Natural Resources Defense Council, Inc.*, 467 U.S. 837 (1984).

37. Sapna Kumar, "Expert Court, Expert Agency," *University of California, Davis Law Review* 44 (2011): 1547–1609.

38. Carl Bernstein and Bob Woodward, "FBI Finds Nixon Aides Sabotaged Democrats," *Washington Post*, October 10, 1972, A.1.

39. "Richard Nixon," Spartacus Educational, https://spartacus-educational.com/USAnixon.htm.

40. Eric Weiner, "What Is Executive Privilege Anyway?" National Public Radio, June 28, 2007, http://www.npr.org/templates/story/story.php?storyId=11527747.

41. *United States v. Nixon*, 418 U.S. 683 (1974).

42. *Panama Refining Co. v. Ryan*, 293 U.S. 388 (1935).

43. *A. L. A. Schechter Poultry Corp. v. United States*, 295 U.S. 495 (1935).

44. *Carter v. Carter Coal Co.*, 298 U.S. 238 (1936).

45. Brian Riedl, "The President's Proposed Line-Item Veto Could Help Control Spending," Heritage Foundation, WebMemo #1012, March 30, 2006, https://www.heritage.org/budget-and-spending/report/the-presidents-proposed-line-item-veto-could-help-control-spending; "Save the Line Item Veto," Cato Institute, August 6, 1998, https://www.cato.org/publications/commentary/save-line-item-veto.

46. Helen Dewar and Joan Biskupic, "Court Strikes Down Line-Item Veto," *Washington Post*, June 26, 1998, A1.

47. *Nixon v. Fitzgerald*, 457 U.S. 731 (1982).

48. L. Peter Schultz, "The Constitution, the Court, and Presidential Immunity: A Defense of *Nixon v. Fitzgerald*," *Presidential Studies Quarterly* 16, no. 2 (1986): 247–57.

49. Mary McGrory, "Presidential Immunity Ruling Doubly Ironic," *Toledo Blade*, July 7, 1982.

50. Eric Freedman, "The Law as King and the King as Law: Is a President Immune from Criminal Prosecution before Impeachment?" *Hastings Constitutional Law Quarterly* 20 (1992): 7–68.

51. *Clinton v. Jones*, 520 U.S. 681 (1997).

52. *Trump v. Vance*, 591 U.S. (2020).

53. William K. Rashbaum and Benjamin Weiser, "Trump Taxes: President Ordered to Turn over Returns to Manhattan D.A.," *New York Times*, October 7, 2019, https://www.nytimes.com/2019/10/07/nyregion /trump-taxes-lawsuit-vance.html.

54. *Ex parte Milligan*, 71 U.S. 2 (4 Wall.) (1866).

55. As quoted in Edward Corwin, *Total War and the Constitution* (New York: Knopf, 1947), 78.

56. *Ex parte Milligan*, 71 U.S. 2 (1866).

57. Nelson Lund, "Rational Choice at the Office of Legal Counsel," *Cardozo Law Review* 15, no. 2 (1993): 495. ("Perhaps more than any other agency in the government, and certainly more than any other legal office, the behavior of OLC is determined primarily by its relationship with the White House.")

58. Lund, "Rational Choice at the Office of Legal Counsel," 489.

59. Quoted in Trevor W. Morrison, "Stare Decisis in the Office of Legal Counsel," *Columbia Law Review* 110 (2010): 1454.

60. Quoted in Emily Berman, "Weaponizing the Office of Legal Counsel," *Boston College Law Review* 62, no. 2 (February 24, 2021): 515–69, 536.

61. Jack Goldsmith, *The Terror Presidency: Law and Judgment inside the Bush Administration* (New York: W. W. Norton, 2009), 38.

62. Goldsmith, *The Terror Presidency*, 39.

63. Lund, "Rational Choice at the Office of Legal Counsel," 499.

64. Berman, "Weaponizing the Office of Legal Counsel," 544.

65. Goldsmith, *The Terror Presidency*, 101.

66. "Full Transcript of Mueller's Statement on Russia Investigation," *New York Times*, May 29, 2019, https:// www.nytimes.com/2019/05/29/us/politics/mueller-transcript.html.

67. "A Sitting President's Amenability to Indictment and Criminal Prosecution," U.S. Department of Justice, Office of Legal Counsel, October 16, 2000, https://www.justice.gov/sites/default/files/olc/opinions/2000 /10/31/op-olc-v024-p0222_0.pdf.

68. "The Supreme Court Database," Washington University School of Law, http://supremecourtdatabase .org/data.php. For more on the solicitor general, see chapter 7 of Michael Bailey and Forrest Maltzman, *The Constrained Court: How the Law and Politics Shape the Decisions Justices Make* (Princeton: Princeton University Press, 2011).

69. Michael Bailey, Brian Kamoie, and Forrest Maltzman, "Signals from the Tenth Justice: The Role of the Solicitor General at the Merits Stage," *American Journal of Political Science* 49, no. 1 (2005): 72–85; Michael Bailey and Kelly Chang, "Comparing Presidents, Senators, and Justices: Inter-institutional Preference Estimation," *Journal of Law, Economics and Organization* 17, no. 2 (2001): 477–506.

70. Bailey, Kamoie, and Maltzmann, "Signals from the Tenth Justice."

71. Erwin Griswold, "The Office of the Solicitor General—Representing the Interests of the United States before the Supreme Court," *Missouri Law Review* 34 (1969): 527.

72. Rex E. Lee, "Lawyering for the Government: Politics, Polemics, and Principle," *Ohio State Law Journal* 47 (1986): 599.

73. Kenneth Starr, *First among Equals: The Supreme Court in American Life* (New York: Warner Books, 2008), 144–45.

74. Lincoln Caplan, *The Tenth Justice: The Solicitor General and the Rule of Law* (New York: Knopf, 1987).

75. Kenneth T. Walsh, "The First 100 Days," *U.S. News*, February 12, 2009, http://www.usnews.com/news /history/articles/2009/02/12/the-first-100-days-franklin-roosevelt-pioneered-the-100-day-concept.

76. Walsh, "First 100 Days."

77. Franklin Roosevelt, Press Conference, May 31, 1935.

78. Franklin Roosevelt, "Fireside Chat on Reorganization of the Judiciary," FDR Presidential Library & Museum, March 9, 1937, http://docs.fdrlibrary.marist.edu/030937.html.

79. Roosevelt, "Fireside Chat," March 9, 1937.

80. "Timeline of Polling History: Events That Shaped the United States, and the World," Gallup, http://www.gallup.com/poll/9967/timeline-polling-history-events-shaped-united-states-world.aspx.

81. Daniel E. Ho and Kevin M. Quinn, "Did a Switch in Time Save Nine?" *Journal of Legal Analysis* 2 (2010): 69–113.

82. William H. Rehnquist, "Judicial Independence Dedicated to Chief Justice Harry L Carrico: Symposium Remarks," *University of Richmond Law Review* 38 (2004): 595.

83. Data available at https://www.uscourts.gov/sites/default/files/apptsbypres.pdf.

84. Harold W. Stanley and Richard G. Niemi, eds., *Vital Statistics on American Politics, 2011–2012* (Washington, DC: Congressional Quarterly Press, 2011), 274–76, table 7–5; see also Epstein and Segal, *Advice and Consent*.

85. Epstein and Segal, *Advice and Consent*, 144.

86. Samuel Alito et al., "Administrative Law and Regulation: Presidential Oversight and the Administrative State," *Engage: The Journal of the Federalist Society's Practice Groups* 2 (2001): 12.

87. *Specter v. Garrett*, 971 F.2d 936 (3d Cir. 1992), rev'd, 511 U.S. 462 (1994); *Morrison v. Olson*, 487 U.S. 654 (1988).

88. Elena Kagan, "Presidential Administration," *Harvard Law Review* 114 (2000–2001): 2341.

89. Brett Kavanaugh, "Separation of Powers during the Forty-Fourth Presidency and Beyond," *Minnesota Law Review* 93 (2009): 1461.

90. Howard Mintz, "San Jose Judge Lucy Koh Nominated to Federal Appeals Court," *Mercury News*, February 26, 2016, https://www.mercurynews.com/2016/02/25/san-jose-judge-lucy-koh-nominated-to-federal-appeals-court/.

91. Editorial Board, "The Wrong Judge," *New York Times*, September 4, 2002, A.20.

92. Sonia Sotomayor, "A Latina Judge's Voice," University of California, Berkeley, School of Law, October 26, 2001.

93. Karen O'Connor, Alixandra Yanus, and Linda Mancillas Patterson, "Where Have All the Interest Groups Gone? An Analysis of Interest Group Participation in Presidential Nominations to the Supreme Court of the United States," in *Interest Group Politics*, 7th ed., ed. Allan Cigler and Burdett Loomis (Washington, DC: Congressional Quarterly Press, 2007).

94. Manuel Miranda, "The Original Borking: Lessons from a Supreme Court Nominee's Defeat," *Wall Street Journal*, August 24, 2005, http://www.opinionjournal.com/nextjustice/?id=110007149.

95. Burgess Everett and Glenn Thrush, "McConnell Throws Down the Gauntlet: No Scalia Replacement under Obama," *POLITICO*, February 13, 2016, https://www.politico.com/story/2016/02/mitch-mcconnell-antonin-scalia-supreme-court-nomination-219248.

96. Michael D. Shear, Julie Hirschfeld Davis, and Gardiner Harris, "Obama Chooses Merrick Garland for Supreme Court," *New York Times*, March 17, 2016, A.1.

97. Robin Bradley Kar and Jason Mazzone, "The Garland Affair: What History and the Constitution Really Say about President Obama's Powers to Appoint a Replacement for Justice Scalia," *New York University Law Review* 91 (2016): 53–114.

98. Suzanne Nuyen, "In a Tribute to Justice Ginsburg, Obama Calls on Senate to Delay Naming a Successor," National Public Radio, September 19, 2020, https://www.npr.org/sections/death-of-ruth-bader-ginsburg/2020/09/19/914717463/in-a-tribute-to-justice-ginsburg-obama-calls-on-senate-delay-naming-a-successor.

99. For more on this way of thinking about presidential norms, see Daphna Renan, "Presidential Norms and Article II," *Harvard Law Review* 131 (2017): 2187–2282.

PART IV

Media and Public

12

Relations with the Media

PUBLIC RELATIONS were not built into the job of president. The Constitution says hardly a word about the matter, and eighteenth- and nineteenth-century presidents made little effort to communicate with the American people directly. Even the most democratically minded presidents of this period were reluctant to wade too deeply into the public fray. When running for office, they did not barnstorm the country with public rallies and stirring speeches. Once elected, these presidents did not suddenly command the public's attention with public appeals and directives. Much of their rhetoric, instead, was reserved for written communications addressed to Congress. By modern standards, their public profiles were decidedly reserved.

How things have changed. Modern presidents cannot govern by huddling in sequestered circles with legislators, bureaucrats, advisors, and lobbyists. Rather, presidents must look outward to the broader populace. They routinely engage the American public in conversation about the problems that stand before the country and the policy solutions that now are needed. Presidents do not merely speak *about* the American public; they speak *to* this public. But to reach this public, they must do more than just find the will and the words. Rather, they must navigate an increasingly complex—and increasingly fragmented—media environment that intermittently facilitates and interferes with their efforts to communicate.

12.1 Foundations of the Plebiscitary Presidency

Among the many misgivings the Framers harbored about executive power, they were especially dubious of a **plebiscitary presidency**—that is, a presidency whose orientation and authority derive from its connection and appeal to a broader public. The Framers wanted to be sure that the presidency did not devolve into **demagoguery**, with the executive telling people what they wanted to hear rather than what they needed to hear or, worse still, inflaming popular prejudices in order to advance parochial interests rather than the larger public good. Writing in *Federalist* 49, Madison argued that public appeals would undermine the deliberative work of government, as "The passions not the reason of the public would sit in judgement."[1] For the Republic to survive, the Framers reasoned, presidents and other politicians would have to limit their engagement with those they purported to represent.

Sensitive to such concerns, early presidents communicated only rarely with the general public. When they did, it was usually through proclamations and inaugural addresses, which were intended to instruct rather than appeal. Even Abraham Lincoln, famous for his oratory, used his speeches to convince Americans of the necessity of a policy change only *after* it had been enacted, not to arouse popular support during its consideration on Capitol Hill. In his second inaugural address, one of the most famous speeches ever delivered by a president, Lincoln declared that slavery was the root cause of the Civil War and that the war's ultimate triumph would be slavery's abolition. With the war nearing an end, Lincoln was not rallying the American people to its cause. He was explaining the war's origins and lamenting its great cost. Like presidents before him, in his public speech Lincoln assumed the role of national historian rather than policy advocate, an observer rather than promoter of societal change.

If our early politics discouraged frequent public appeals, modern presidents operate under an entirely different set of rules. Today, public appeals from the White House are not just common; they have become part of the president's informal duties. We expect— no, *demand*—that our presidents actively engage the media, promote a policy agenda, travel the country in support of like-minded candidates, console the nation in times of crisis, and publicly defend their ideas against hostile members of Congress. In *The Rhetorical Presidency*, Jeffrey Tulis characterizes these demands not merely as historical developments but rather as the provisions of a "second constitution" under which the presidency now operates.[2] Under the original Constitution, drafted and signed in 1787, the president would serve as commander in chief and take care that the laws be faithfully executed. Under the second constitution, however, the president would also serve as a popular leader—a rule that was never written down, never ratified by the states, but one that nonetheless binds all presidents who might prefer to carry out their duties in private.

Theodore Roosevelt initiated the turn toward a more engaged public presidency. To be a steward of national interests and ambitions, Roosevelt knew he would have to communicate directly with the people. As such, he legitimized the notion that presidents must make themselves routinely available to a new professional class of reporters and writers. Journalists (at least those who proved their loyalty to Roosevelt) were treated to informal meetings with the president while he received his daily shave, where he was notoriously candid.[3]

At times, Roosevelt also took his message directly to the people, coining the term **bully pulpit** to describe the unique, attention-grabbing power of the president's public appearances. (In those days, "bully" was synonymous with "stupendous" or "magnificent.") The bully pulpit allowed him to circumvent the press—communicating instead with his own words, in a context he could control. Observing these trends, one commentator noted that "Americans felt as if they knew Roosevelt personally."[4]

Roosevelt ushered in the modern plebiscitary presidency, but it was President Wilson who established its conventions.[5] Well before he was elected president, Wilson began

laying out the theoretical justification for increased presidential engagement with the public. Too many crucial national questions were settled behind closed doors, Wilson argued
in his 1885 doctoral dissertation, "Congressional Government." Wilson insisted that public
opinion should be informed by all political leaders, though he ultimately came to the
conclusion that it was the president, not Congress, who was in the best position to educate
the public.[6]

For Wilson, popular leadership relied on a process he called "interpretation"—the ability of the leader to discern the public's desires and convert these desires into policy rhetoric. But interpretation is no easy task; Wilson believed that the public oftentimes was
unsure what it wanted, and it was the president's job to "call it into full consciousness."[7] By
explaining to the public its own desires in a comprehensible way, the president could unite
the nation behind policy initiatives. Not just to educate the public, Wilson drafted his
speeches to gain the public's confidence: to deliver arguments that "find easy entrance into
their minds" and "the palms of their hands . . . in the form of applause."[8]

In line with such thinking, Wilson went out of this way to reach beyond the cloistered
White House, speak directly to elected officials across government, and thereby engage
the broader public. For the first time since Thomas Jefferson, Wilson delivered the annual
State of the Union Address in person—effectively overturning a century of precedent. He
did so, he noted in his first address, in order to "verify for myself the impression that the
President of the United States is a person, not a mere department of the Government
hailing Congress from some isolated island of jealous power, sending messages, not speaking naturally and with his own voice—that he is a human being trying to cooperate with
other human beings in a common service."[9] Wilson sought to break through the separation
and independence that the Constitution took such pains to construct and thereby cultivate
a more open, deliberative, and consensual politics.

Wilson also believed that a "large part of the success of public affairs depends upon the
newspapermen."[10] Thus, he was the first president to hold official **press conferences**. The
structure of this modern ritual came about almost by accident. Shortly after Wilson's inauguration, his press secretary invited Washington reporters to the White House for a
midday chat with the new president. The meeting did not go exactly as planned. Expecting
to hold a series of one-on-one meetings, Wilson discovered the tiny White House press
room packed with over a hundred journalists. He had no choice but to address them all at
once and then take questions.[11]

At the following week's gathering Wilson arrived better prepared, going so far as to offer
reflections on the emerging institution of the presidential press conference. "I want an
opportunity to open part of my mind to you, so that you may know my point of view a
little better than perhaps you have had an opportunity to know it so far," he told reporters.
He stressed that the relationship between the president and the press was a partnership,
one in which the role of the press was not merely to tell the "country what Washington
was thinking" but also to "tell Washington what the country is thinking."[12]

Thus we see the emergence of a new kind of relationship between the president and
public. The elements of this second constitutional presidency, of course, were never

FIGURE 12.1. Woodrow Wilson and the second constitutional presidency. After a century of sending written remarks to Congress, Woodrow Wilson revived the practice of delivering the State of the Union Address in person. *Source:* Library of Congress.

written down. Rather, they became manifest in practices, norms, and expectations that came to define popular notions of leadership. And with the development and growth of new communication technologies, presidents and public would come into ever closer and more frequent proximity.

12.2 New Media Technologies

When Roosevelt and Wilson were rethinking the president's relationship with, and obligations to, the American public, they confronted a media environment that consisted exclusively of print journalists. These journalists, to be sure, represented a rich and diverse assemblage of newspapers, journals, and periodicals. Their only medium, however, consisted of the written word—with all the inevitable delays that accompany its production. Soon enough, though, new technologies emerged that not only expanded the opportunities for presidents to communicate with the public but also, in important respects, reconstituted the plebiscitary presidency itself.

12.2.1 Radio

Radio brought a new intimacy to American politics, as it carried the voices of newscasters, preachers, and politicians directly into people's homes. Starting in the late 1920s and early 1930s, radio sets occupied a prominent place in many American living rooms:

FIGURE 12.2. FDR and radio broadcasts. During his time in office, FDR leveraged the power of radio to speak directly to the American public not only about pressing policy issues but also about their everyday lives. In this photo we see him lauding the Boy Scouts of America for their "physical strength, mental alertness, and moral straightness." *Source:* Library of Congress.

families would gather around the radio to listen to the dramas of the day, both fictional and real.

President Franklin Delano Roosevelt understood the power of this new medium (figure 12.2). Even before he was nominated in 1932 as the Democratic challenger to incumbent Herbert Hoover, FDR had begun using radio as a forum for reaching voters across the country. Seeking to stand out in a crowded field of Democratic candidates, in April 1932, three years into the Great Depression, FDR delivered a speech via radio declaring that the solution to the nation's problems lay in empowering the "forgotten man at the bottom of the economic pyramid" rather than "the big banks, the railroads and the corporations." The nation, he insisted, needed economic plans that "build from the bottom up and not from the top down."[13]

While FDR would focus much of his energy as president on top-down plans that built up banks and corporations, his early identification with these "forgotten" Americans, via a medium that amplified his presence in their everyday lives, cemented his image as a champion of the common worker, and helped clinch his nomination. Almost immediately after taking office, FDR took to the airwaves for the first of what would become known as **Fireside Chats**, informal addresses intended to raise public awareness of key policy issues and, just as importantly, to boost national morale in a time of crisis. The first of FDR's twenty-seven chats was broadcast on March 12, 1933, and it was intended to reassure the public about the nationwide bank closure.[14] Addressing an audience of roughly fifty million Americans, FDR spoke slowly and confidently: "I want to tell you what has been done in the last few days, why it was done, and what the next steps are going to be."[15] And by all accounts, the chat had its desired effect. "Indeed, where, days before, people had rushed to take their money out of the banks, after hearing the first Fireside Chat, they were 'now more eager to deposit cash than to withdraw it.'"[16]

Not all Fireside Chats were successful at moving public opinion. FDR's 1937 Fireside Chat discussing his controversial "court-packing" plan, for instance, did little to bring the nation to his defense. Nonetheless, FDR remained convinced of the value of radio. With print media, the president needed to rely upon sympathetic reporters to convey his message. On the radio, however, there was no middleman. The president could deliver exactly the message he wanted, in exactly the tone he wanted to use, and he could count on significant portions of the American public receiving it.[17] By 1936, when he sought his first reelection, he had a team of radio professionals working full-time on his staff.

Radio occupies a much smaller place in our politics now than it did during FDR's presidency. But it has not altogether disappeared. When President George W. Bush signed a farm bill in 2002, the White House press team worked with the Department of Agriculture to make sure the early morning signing ceremony was covered by farm-only radio stations. Later, Bush's communications director announced that nearly 500,000 farms had tuned in to the special broadcast.[18] More recently, in the 2020 election, Joe Biden spent nearly $24 million on radio ads for his successful presidential campaign.[19] Though radio no longer reaches broad swaths of Americans with a single broadcast, it remains a cost-effective way to target specific audiences.

12.2.2 *Television*

If radio changed the way presidents were listened to, television changed the way they were seen. At the forefront of these developments was John F. Kennedy, who famously used television to his advantage. The veracity of the oft-told tale of Kennedy winning the 1960 presidential debate with television viewers and Richard Nixon winning with radio listeners may be questionable (as discussed in chapter 6), but the story symbolized the growing importance of the president's physical appearance in the age of television. Much of Kennedy's appeal in the early 1960s had to do with the visual aura of his presidency. Kennedy—handsome and youthful when elected at forty-three, with a glamorous wife and two small children—radiated optimism across the airwaves. He was the first president to broadcast press conferences live, and his (tragically brief) tenure in office highlighted the newfound importance of being television-ready—attractive, quick-witted, and charming.

Though Kennedy may have been the nation's first prime-time president, the consummate performer was President Ronald Reagan. A former actor and governor from California, Reagan was known as the "Great Communicator" for his ability to appeal to a wide range of voters. "[His] voice [was] pleasant, [his] confidence, [his] timing sharpened by thousands of speeches and scripts."[20] Seeking to make the most of these assets, his staff

FIGURE 12.3. The Great Communicator. Nearly every day, the president steps before the camera to deliver one message or another. More than most, Ronald Reagan recognized the political value of visual imagery. Copyright 1991 J. David Ake/Getty Images. Reproduced with permission.

meticulously attended to the president's media image and carefully curated the visual backgrounds to his many televised appearances (figure 12.3). Reagan made a point of appearing on television surrounded by American flags and crowds of supporters. "We wanted to control what people saw," said White House staffer David Gergen. "We would go through the president's schedule day by day and hour by hour, and figure out what we wanted the story to be at the end of each day and at the end of each week. And that worked 90 percent of the time."[21]

According to one famous anecdote, a highly critical story on Reagan by *60 Minutes* correspondent Lesley Stahl turned out to be a boon for Reagan's 1984 campaign. Stahl attempted to point out the irony of the president's cutting funding for the disabled and housing for the elderly while showing footage of Reagan at the Special Olympics and at the opening of a nursing home. The imagery, however, proved to be more powerful than the accompanying words. "Nobody heard what you said," Stahl recalled a gloating Reagan aide telling her after the story aired. "They just saw five minutes of beautiful pictures of Ronald Reagan. They saw the balloons, they saw the flags, they saw the red, white, and blue."[22]

Much like FDR's use of radio, television allowed Reagan unprecedented control over how and when he addressed the nation. Reagan's staff oversaw TV press conferences like directors on a film set—with reporters relegated "to the level of actors or even props."[23] When unwanted questions were asked, aides would simply turn the lights off. During televised Oval Office addresses—of which Reagan delivered a record-setting twenty-nine[24]—the press was not allowed, and the president had uninterrupted opportunities to tell tens of millions of Americans what he thought was important.

Unlike the radio, however, television tends to emphasize appearances and impressions over substance—a trait the Reagan White House used to his advantage. Under fire for his administration's cuts to federal student-loan programs, Reagan traveled around the country, holding televised meetings with students and teachers about the need for reform. Though these meetings did not result in concrete changes to education policy, "The polls absolutely flip-flopped," said Reagan's deputy chief of staff. "He went from a negative rating to a positive rating overnight."[25]

Subsequent presidents attempted—with varying degrees of success—to command the television networks as Reagan did. And then, in November 2016, the country elected its second performer-president of the modern era: Donald J. Trump. As a former reality television star, Trump was acutely aware of the power of imagery. Seemingly every executive order he issued during his first year in office was accompanied by a photo-op. In the summer of 2017, the president flirted with the idea of hosting a military parade in the nation's capital. And in 2018, Trump and his team went to considerable lengths to stage his international summits with North Korean leader Kim Jong-un and Russian president Vladimir Putin in ways that highlighted the president's command on the international stage. Having spent years hosting *The Apprentice* on television, Trump entered the presidency with one crucial insight: in today's media environment, viewership may matter almost as much as leadership.

12.2.3 Digital Media

Like radio before it, digital media provides yet another opportunity for the president to sidestep—and in Trump's case, to lambaste—a potentially hostile press.[26] To advance their agenda and shape their image, presidents must work with television, print, and digital media. Concomitantly, presidents forge direct lines of communication with the American public, in whose good graces they wish to stand, and whose support they hope to galvanize.

The advent of the Internet in the late 1980s led to rising online digital media usage among the American public through the 1990s. In turn, the American presidency joined the online sphere. The first president to use email was George Bush in 1992, and the inaugural White House website debuted in 1994 under the Clinton administration.[27] Though rudimentary by today's standards, these platforms signified an age of presidential communications through online spaces—the Internet providing a convenient means for distributing mass press releases and briefings to the public.

Then, in 1997, came social media. During its advent, a mere 5 percent of American adults reported using some online platform. By 2019, that number jumped to 72 percent, with millions of online users. Not only are more people using social media, but the number of social media networks rapidly increased and diversified as well. While only MySpace and YouTube controlled the relatively meager field prior to Facebook's 2008 inception, there are now over 20 sites with more than 100 million active users each.[28]

With the rise of social media, presidents have cultivated an ever-closer relationship with the American public. Twitter users, for example, can send messages straight to the president. They might even receive a response. At the beginning of 2016, Barack Obama had the fourth most popular Twitter feed in the world. Some have attributed his winning the presidency without much political experience or a solid donor base to his campaign's expert use of the Web, which allowed them to create a massive network of small donors and volunteers. Even the nickname of his 2008 website, MyBO, reflected the personalized nature of his campaign.

For Donald Trump, of course, Twitter was not just one among several communication strategies. Rather, it stood at the very center of his presidency. Through tweets—some carefully orchestrated, others impulsively drafted—Trump conducted important governmental business. The world discovered through Trump's Twitter account the planned withdrawal of troops from Syria, and sat uneasy as he publicly mused that the United States should "greatly strengthen and expand its nuclear capability." Because of the official policy nature of Trump's tweets, the Department of Justice revealed that they constituted official presidential statements.[29] Protected by the Presidential Records Act, Trump administration tweets (including deleted posts) are preserved in the National Archives.[30]

In addition to announcing grand foreign policy initiatives, Trump utilized Twitter to manage his administration. On numerous occasions, Trump announced key staffing decisions through Twitter,* hiring and firing cabinet members in sometimes fiery statements that controlled the narrative about goings-on within the White House.[31] Through Twitter, Trump also strengthened his hold on the Republican Party.[32] For example, when Senate majority leader Mitch McConnell considered abandoning Trump, the president showed the entire Senate Republican Conference graphs providing strong evidence that McConnell's approval rating moved directly in response to Trump's tweets, a barely veiled threat that the entire party's electoral fortunes could be decided by 280 of Trump's choice characters.

In addition to controlling his own party, Trump frequently used Twitter to lash out at political opponents, including but not limited to Democrats, athletes protesting for social justice, and the courts.[33] Given its decentralized nature, Twitter and similar social media outlets allowed supporters of Trump to build out large, insular groups and political networks, which helped the president rapidly disperse his message and coordinate supporters.[34] Notably, this also led to echo chambers largely filled with misinformation or misleading claims, many of which came directly from Trump's own tweets.[35]

12.3 The Modern Media Landscape

Let's take a moment to examine the media as it exists today—fragmented, nationalized, and volatile. Perhaps the most striking trend in recent decades is the explosion of consumer choice. Whereas most Americans used to subscribe to a local newspaper, and perhaps tune in to a single national news broadcast, there now exists a cornucopia of

---

* In special cases such as Secretary of State Rex Tillerson, Trump's tweet was the first time even the official heard that they were being fired.

media outlets that cater to increasingly narrow interests. Rather than find all their news in the pages of, say, the *Chicago Tribune*, readers have turned to several online outlets—one for sports, another for politics, a third for global news, and so on—to serve their varied interests.[36] Readers decide not just *where* to consume their information but *how*. In print? On television? As a podcast, email newsletter, or video clip? For some, the answer is "all of the above."

Not all of the options, though, are thriving. In particular, the local news market (be it radio, newspaper, or television) has struggled to keep pace with the countless specialized, easy-to-access outlets found online.[37] By some accounts, circulations and advertising revenues of local newspapers have declined by nearly 40 percent.[38] While consumers have more choices than ever before, the nature of these choices is changing. National behemoths such as the *New York Times*, the *Washington Post*, and the *Wall Street Journal* have seen sharp increases in their monthly subscriptions.[39] More and more, our attention is devoted to national events rather than our local communities.

So, too, has "the golden age of television" come to an end.[40] In 1969, one of President Nixon's press conferences was viewed by 59 percent of households with televisions. Less than thirty years later, a prime-time news conference by Bill Clinton drew only 7 percent of households with televisions.[41] Although some have posited that this decline stems from diminished trust in government,[42] it might be that presidents attract fewer viewers because the public has more choices of what to watch. When presidents hold forth on difficult, challenging, or technical subjects, viewers can simply change the channel.

12.3.1 An Increasingly Polarized Viewing Audience?

Whether this new media landscape exacerbates partisan divisions is a subject of ongoing debate within the discipline. A good deal of evidence points toward the affirmative. Beginning with the rise of cable TV, news sources have become increasingly divided into left- and right-leaning clusters.[43] News channels found that objective reporting was less profitable than catering to the ideologies of their viewers. This catering became central to their appeal, as viewers sought news that reaffirmed their views about politics.[44] Today, consumers continue to report partisan cable TV channels as their primary source of information.[45] Democrats have migrated toward CNN and MSNBC, while Republicans have migrated toward Fox News. Online news media outlets also brandish distinct ideological brands, with sites such as *Breitbart* and the *Daily Caller* anchoring the far right of the ideological spectrum, and sites such as *Buzzfeed* and *Huffington Post* populating the left.

As figure 12.4 shows, the levels of trust in these television and online platforms differ markedly for Democrats and Republicans. If the populations generally agreed about the merits of each media outlet, the news providers would line up on a 45-degree line, with poorly regarded outlets appearing in the lower left of the graph and highly regarded outlets appearing in the upper right. Instead, the location of most political news providers deviates considerably from this line of agreement. A batch of media outlets—Fox News, *Breitbart*, Sean Hannity's and Rush Limbaugh's radio shows—enjoy significantly high levels of trust

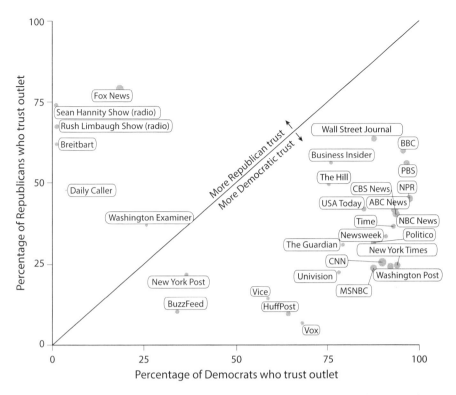

FIGURE 12.4. Partisan trust in different media outlets. The axes depict the trust of popular news outlets by party, while the size of an outlet's point reflects the relative size of its audience—the larger the circle the greater the audience. Notice the lack of outlets trusted on a bipartisan basis. *Source:* Pew Research Center, Journalism and Media, 2020.

among Republicans but extremely low levels of trust among Democrats. Similarly, other media outlets such as the *New York Times*, *Washington Post*, MSNBC, Univision, and *Vox* speak to rapt Democratic audiences while being panned by most Republicans.

In certain respects, the rise of social media has exacerbated these partisan divisions. As of 2019, nearly one in five Americans received most of their news from social networks. Among younger people, 48 percent did so.[46] Social media has made it easier for news organizations to target specific audiences—resulting in outlets that are smaller, less centralized, and often more extreme.[47] Hidden in various corners of the Internet, these outlets face little oversight or accountability for the content they produce. Rife with partisan disinformation, they target readers who are predisposed to believe in the content they produce.[48] It is an unfortunate truth that partisans will often rate sources espousing their views as "more credible"—making them more likely to visit the site, interact with individuals in its comment feeds, and digest its manipulated facts as their new reality.[49]

Other evidence, however, suggests that concerns about the polarizing effects of the modern media landscape are exaggerated. For starters, look at the many media outlets in figure 12.4 that majorities of both Democrats and Republicans profess to trust: PBS, NPR, the *Wall Street Journal*, and the BBC. Democrats, interestingly, endorse many more mainstream media outlets than do Republicans, which could be indicative of either left-leaning bias in the news (as some purport)[50] or a general skepticism toward the media born of Trump's constant haranguing. What is clear, though, is that there remain numerous outlets that are trusted by overwhelming majorities of Democrats and significant portions of Republicans.

Social media, some studies show, exposes its users to a larger variety of news content and disagreement than other communications platforms. Rather than inhabiting "echo chambers" of like-minded co-partisans, most Americans consume a reasonably moderate diet of political news. Up to 30 percent of political news stories that a user sees on social media swing ideologically in the opposite direction of the user.[51] Likewise, other studies show a fair measure of overlap in Democrats' and Republicans' online news consumption habits.[52] On average, the ideological leanings of news sites visited by citizens from opposite parties are not nearly as different as commonly supposed.

12.3.2 Political Disinformation

Another far more insidious risk of media decentralization appears in the spread of disinformation through the Internet and social media. In political media, disinformation refers to deliberately spreading objectively false information, with the end goal of disparaging and disrupting a target's reputation or credibility.

Though concerns about disinformation came into the national spotlight during the 2016 presidential election, their presence in politics is hardly new. In their war for the seat of Roman emperor, Octavian and Mark Antony weaponized disinformation through every medium available, from speeches to poetry, in order to disparage the other's reputation. Octavian even went so far as to mint coins bearing short anti-Antony slogans rather reminiscent of tweets.[53] In the late 1700s, Samuel Adams and his Sons of Liberty ran massive anti-Loyalist disinformation campaigns through the *Boston Gazette*. Thomas Hutchinson, a British Loyalist politician, openly lamented this printing of "every Thing that is Libelous and Slanderous." His house was then burned down for reportedly voting in favor of the Stamp Act, though in reality he had not.[54]

Today, disinformation in the form of false rumors, conspiracy theories, and baseless accusations can be spread rapidly—and often anonymously—through social media. Unlike television ads, almost anyone can purchase ads on social media with little or no disclosure of their identity and with comparatively little content vetting. Facebook, for example, collects data on who created the political ads on its site but, due to its privacy agreements, refuses to disclose this information to viewers.[55]

Though Facebook is not alone among social media platforms in terms of its slack disclosure rules, it does provide the strongest case study of the threat disinformation poses to presidential appeals. In the 2016 election's disinformation campaigns—which extended well into the 2020 race—Russian agencies made massive anti-Democratic ad buys pushing objectively false information across Facebook. The postings then spread rapidly across the platform and onto others, in no small part due to the fake "troll" accounts created to propagate that information under the guise of real users. These disinformation campaigns were also bolstered by their substantial ties to the Russian government.[56] Hillary Clinton, the Democratic nominee, found herself unable to counter the constant drumbeat of disinformation taking place online, and her reputation suffered for it.

The effects of disinformation, of course, are not limited to presidential campaigns. Having already defeated Donald Trump in the 2020 presidential election, Joe Biden found himself tied up in an altogether new web of lies and baseless accusations. Online conspiracy theorists alleged that Biden's inauguration ceremony never happened and that Trump would be sworn in instead on March 4.[57] Another persistent theory held that Biden was a front man and that his vice president, Kamala Harris, was making most decisions inside the White House.[58] These claims are false, but they are not inconsequential. Presidential power rests on the perceived legitimacy of the officeholder. So long as "the darker side of human nature" is bolstered by the anonymity of social platforms and other media developments, this legitimacy may have to absorb increasingly heavy blows.

12.4 Institutionalizing Presidential Relations with the Press

How does the press acquire reliable and relevant information about the president? In the nation's early days, there were no regular press conferences or televised briefings, but reporters were often enmeshed in the daily operations of the presidency to a degree that now seems strange. President Andrew Jackson, for example, counted a coterie of reporters as advisors, comprising an informal "kitchen cabinet" that guided him on the issues of the day. Years later, President Lincoln would readily dole out government jobs to journalists, especially as foreign ministers and consuls.

Though presidents today maintain some informal and congenial relationships with journalists, most White House-press interactions are overseen by a growing administrative apparatus. Teams of media professionals stand between the president and the press, carefully selecting and streamlining the information that reaches both sides. When presidents speak, chances are that their words have already been drafted, revised, and ultimately approved by multiple organizations within the White House.

12.4.1 The President's Press Operation

Since Nixon, the White House communications operation has consisted of two primary units: the Office of Communications and the Press Office. Together, these groups respond to reporters' incessant queries, fend off media attacks, and push the president's agenda forward. The scale of this work, however, has increased over time, such that these offices now lead communications operations across the entire executive branch, not just the White House.

OFFICE OF COMMUNICATIONS

The **Office of Communications** assumes responsibility for longer-term communication planning. As such, its primary tasks involve *message development*, figuring out how to strategically craft a message; *message coordination*, ensuring that everyone involved in conveying messages is on the same page; and *message amplification*, making sure the president's message reaches as many constituents as possible.[59]

The Office of Communications contains a variety of subunits, each of which focuses on a different domain of communication, and all of which are overseen by the director of communication. These subunits include speechwriting, research, media affairs, and, more recently, digital strategy. The institutional flowchart, however, remains an ongoing work in progress. Bill Clinton, for instance, moved the Office of Media Affairs, which specializes in communication with journalists outside of the press corps, from the Office of Communications to the Press Office. George W. Bush then moved it back again. Under Barack Obama's administration, Media Affairs morphed into the Office of Digital Strategy, which focuses on communication through videos, online engagement, digital content, and online platforms.

The **speechwriting department** within the Office of Communications researches, fact-checks, and helps craft the president's major addresses, such as the inaugural, farewell, and annual State of the Union addresses, as well as smaller speeches, such as televised press conferences and radio addresses.[60] Presidents Nixon through Trump each employed between five and ten personnel focused on speech writing and research.[61] Though Trump's speechwriting process was shrouded in mystery for the initial years of his administration, many of his most popular speeches were written by Stephen Miller, his longest-serving senior advisor, who oversaw a team of five writers.[62]

PRESS OFFICE

Whereas the Office of Communications focuses on longer-term strategy aimed at shaping the larger public narrative about politics, the **Press Office** attends to the more immediate concerns of the daily news flow. The **press secretary**, who heads the Press Office, handles the day-to-day media requests, serves as the administration's public face, and delivers near-daily press briefings both on camera and off. Some of these gatherings are formal question-and-answer sessions. Others are casual and unscripted.

The daily press briefing is the most common mode of interacting with the press. During these briefings, which typically run forty-five minutes in length, the press secretary summarizes the president's reactions to recent news, characterizes his positions on key issues, and fields questions from the press.[63] Other gatherings—"gaggles"—are less formal, even impromptu opportunities for dialogue between the Press Office and different media outlets.

Behind what may appear as a journalistic free-for-all there is, in fact, a great deal of stage-craft and strategizing in press conferences. While the White House Correspondents

Association determines the seating chart, and while journalists in the first two rows typically receive the most attention, the press secretary enjoys considerable discretion in fielding questions. And from the morning press gaggle, the press secretary often gleans valuable clues about which issues specific reporters are interested in pursuing. Armed with this information, the press secretary then can choose whom to call upon and in what order.

Though less regular, the president's own press conferences typically garner more media attention. Through these conferences, the president can shepherd news coverage and provide context for his recent policy decisions.[64] Especially important in presidential press conferences is the opening statement, which establishes the president's top priorities and regularly generates headlines in subsequent news coverage. Furthermore, news coverage of presidential press conferences leans heavily on the exact language used by the president, granting him further influence over the media's coverage of his administration.[65]

12.4.2 The White House Press Corps

Not just any journalist with a badge can sit in the White House press briefings. Working with the Senate Press Gallery, the Standing Committee on Correspondents handles the accreditation of daily newspapers, wire services, and electronic news services that cover Congress and the White House. In order to gain accreditation, individuals must be "bona fide correspondents of repute in their profession who are full time, paid correspondents of recognized news organizations."[66] In 2017, 289 news organizations were credentialed, many of which send journalists and photojournalists to the White House, the Senate gallery, and the House gallery. The full list of those individuals with access is published in the *Congressional Directory* and now numbers in the thousands—a far cry from the mere 86 credentialed correspondents first published in 1880.[67]

For much of American history, women and people of color were all but excluded from the White House press corps. It wasn't until 1944 that the first Black White House correspondent, Harry McAlpin from the *Chicago Defender*, joined the press corps. Even then, McAlpin was excluded from the White House Correspondents Association and its now-famous annual dinner.[68] Moreover, McAlpin's access to the White House remained limited, the result of ongoing negotiation to allow minority reporters into the halls of power.

Sixty years later, with the nation's first African American president in office, the White House press corps remained overwhelmingly white. Of the fifty-three regular correspondents during Barack Obama's presidency, only seven were African American or Asian American.[69] Part of the explanation could be attributed to the costs of supporting a Washington correspondent—some African American news organizations like Black Entertainment Television and Jet did not hire permanent White House correspondents. As it always had, though, the press corps' lack of diversity mimicked trends in the field of journalism at large, wherein minority journalists are less likely to be hired, and then less likely to remain on the job, than white journalists.[70]

Though physically located within the White House, members of the press corps are meant to serve their editors and audiences, not presidents or their advisors. Still, the boundaries between the subjects and objects of White House media coverage are regularly breached. Indeed, recent presidents have made a habit of hiring former journalists to fill out their press offices. Tony Snow, previously a television personality, was Bush's press secretary. Jay Carney, formerly a print reporter, became Obama's second press secretary. Kayleigh McEnany, a former producer of the *Mike Huckabee Show* on Fox News, served as Trump's fourth and final press secretary. By making such hires, presidents signal to reporters that journalistic expertise is important and that they, too, may one day be considered for a job in the White House.[71]

Presidents also cultivate relationships with powerful journalists. This practice dates back at least to Andrew Jackson, who relied upon influential newspaper reporters as advisors. In his day, Kennedy was in frequent contact with *New York Times* columnist James Reston, going so far as to share confidential details about one disastrous meeting with Soviet premier Nikita Khrushchev.[72] Sometimes these off-the-record talks are less dramatic, as when Clinton occasionally played cards with select reporters traveling with him on Air Force One, under the stipulation that nothing he said would later be attributed to him.[73] Obama similarly ingratiated himself with high-profile journalists of varying ideological camps through off-the-record talks.[74] Under his administration, Donald Trump frequently spoke with right-wing commentators and shunned journalists who gave him negative coverage. Having granted press credentials to pro-Trump bloggers,[75] the president requested that journalists from unfavorable outlets sit in the back of the White House briefing room.[76] Trump also refused to answer questions from certain journalists, at more than one point saying on live television, "Your organization is terrible" and "you are fake news."[77]

Historical Transformations: Watergate and the Widening Gulf between the Presidency and the Press

Since the beginning of our nation, journalists have criticized and questioned presidents. At the start of his term, the press treated George Washington as if he were all-knowing and infallible, but by its end the press made a habit of calling him a "tyrant" and bemoaned his saint-like status.[78] Thomas Paine, whose pamphleteering had helped spark the Revolution, even confessed to having prayed for the president's imminent death.[79]

Even so, for much of American history certain topics and lines of criticism were broadly recognized by journalists as beyond the pale. The reporters with whom FDR met regularly, for example, overlooked his polio-induced immobility in accordance with the president's wishes.[80] Kennedy's numerous extramarital dalliances, despite being well known in certain social and government circles at the time, never made it to the nightly news.[81] On their own accord, journalists routinely granted presidents a measure of privacy and discretion; and presidents, for their part, could count on a reservoir of deference, if not outright goodwill, from the press.

Those days have clearly passed. With the possible exception of their young children, nearly every aspect of a sitting president's personal life—and the shortcomings of that life—is subject to public scrutiny. From what they eat to where they sleep, the public now demands nearly constant access to their presidents. Journalists, ever hungry for a scoop, work overtime to grant it.

How did this come to be? Lots of factors, of course, contributed to the evolving norms that govern press coverage of the president. The rise of new media technologies, a changing legal landscape that affords journalists and the public greater access to government documents through the **Freedom of Information Act** and the **Presidential Records Act,** and cultural transformations all played a part. But so did the enterprising and dogged journalism of two young reporters who uncovered a scandal that would force a two-term president from office.

The key events began in 1972, when five men were arrested for trying to burglarize the Democratic Party's headquarters in the Watergate office complex.[82] After being tipped off by an informant referred to as "Deep Throat," revealed decades later to be FBI official Mark Felt, *Washington Post* reporters Bob Woodward and Carl Bernstein discovered that one of the burglars was on Nixon's reelection staff, and that Nixon's former secretary of commerce, Maurice Stans, had personally deposited money meant for President Richard Nixon's reelection campaign in the bank account of one of the burglars.[83]

Despite the White House's best efforts to dismiss the scandal as a "third-rate burglary" that its staff had nothing to do with, Watergate turned out to be only the tip of the iceberg. The reporting of Woodward, Bernstein, and other journalists later revealed that the president's reelection team, led in part by his attorney general, had engaged in widespread spying and sabotage of the Democratic opposition. Nixon responded by stonewalling congressional investigators and threatening the *Washington Post* Company's television licenses.[84] By 1974, however, nineteen people had pled guilty to Watergate-related offenses.[85] That summer, after the House Judiciary Committee recommended his impeachment, Nixon resigned.

By demonstrating the professional rewards that journalists could reap from exposing political scandal, and by shaking the confidence of the American public in their elected officials, Watergate helped contribute to important changes in the norms of White House news coverage. No longer would the press defer to the president; no longer would journalists overlook reports of corruption and malfeasance, whether such reports had policy or personal implications.

Presidential scandal was now the name of the game. Among White House reporters after Watergate, a joke circulated: Whenever you aren't sure what to ask, just begin by asking, "But sir, what about the recent charges . . . ?"[86] In this way, a reporter might accidentally stumble across a scandal that had yet to be uncovered.

In the decades after Watergate, multiple administrations battled scandals, many of which were either revealed or amplified by reporters. The Ford administration struggled to assuage the public outcry that followed Ford's pardon of the disgraced Nixon. The Reagan administration labored through Iran-Contra, wherein administration officials used the profits from illegal arms sales to Iran to fund Nicaraguan rebels. Personal

Continued on next page

scandals dogged the Clinton administration, and the president's denial of an extramarital affair with a White House intern led to his impeachment by the House of Representatives. Twice impeached, Trump spent the entirety of his presidency awash in scandals, both large and small. Woodward and Bernstein's stories of that midnight break-in at an otherwise obscure Washington office complex nearly fifty years ago did more than take down Nixon. They permanently altered the relationship between the president and press.

12.5 Navigating the Media Landscape

Media management is not a task that presidents can simply pawn off on a press secretary—or even an entire Press Office. Amid a polarized and fragmented media environment, one in which the administration's critics delight in its public gaffes and stumbles, presidents must be proactive. They must tend to the daily news cycle and deliberately position themselves within it. It is not enough for presidents to speak. They also must manage how they are spoken about. And sometimes, this means ensuring that they are not spoken about at all.

12.5.1 Constraining the Press

The history of president-media relations does not consist purely of accommodation and acceptance. Rather, numerous presidents have sought to punish and control journalists. Long before President Donald Trump berated journalists as "the enemy of the people," presidents wielded the formal powers of the state to suppress the media.

For telling this history, the Alien and Sedition Acts of 1798 are a reasonable starting point. These four laws made it illegal to write, print, or publish "any false, scandalous, and malicious writing with intent to defame the government" or "stir up sedition within the United States."[87] Ostensibly a precautionary measure against the influence of foreign spies, these acts, in practice, served as bludgeons against partisan opponents. Under the acts, the federal government prosecuted fourteen people, most of them journalists who opposed the Federalist Party. Some, like Thomas Cooper and James Callender, were prosecuted for "seditious writings" and political commentary that attacked President John Adams directly. These men were sentenced to six and nine months in prison, respectively, along with $400 fines.[88] Not until Adams left office did the unpopular Sedition Acts finally expire.[89] In his inaugural address, President Thomas Jefferson emphasized the importance of a free and independent press, affirming the right of Americans to "think freely, and to speak and to write what they think."[90]

Over the course of U.S. history, wars have provided the most common pretext for presidents to clamp down on the press. During the Civil War, President Abraham Lincoln not only suspended habeas corpus, he also shuttered more than three hundred newspapers and jailed many of their editors.[91] Unlike Adams, however, Lincoln did all of this without the cover of congressional legislation. Rather, Lincoln simply asserted his independent right to imprison dissenters during this time of national calamity, insisting that he was acting in accordance with the public will and for the ultimate benefit of the country.[92] Ever since, historians and constitutional law scholars have debated the merits of Lincoln's claims, with some offering qualified endorsements[93] and others condemning the president's violation of the First Amendment.[94]

During World War I, President Woodrow Wilson institutionalized the production of media propaganda through the Committee on Public Information. Established in 1917, this committee released pamphlets, articles, posters, and films to foment anti-German sentiment and pro-American patriotism. The committee further encouraged the public to actively support the war effort by purchasing Liberty bonds.[95] Like Adams and Lincoln, though, Wilson also took steps to suppress the press. Under the Espionage Act of 1917 and Sedition Act of 1918, the government censored antiwar rhetoric, banned antiwar publications from the mail, and imprisoned critics of the war.[96] Under these laws, more than two thousand individuals, many of whom were journalists, were prosecuted.[97] Meanwhile, so-called "seditious" newspapers and magazines had their second-class mail privileges revoked and, in some instances, were altogether banned from using the postal service.[98]

Even President Franklin Roosevelt, who maintained a generally healthy relationship with the press, curtailed the media during war. After the 1941 bombing of Pearl Harbor, Congress passed the War Powers Act of 1941, which significantly expanded the president's wartime powers. Under this law, Roosevelt established the Office of Censorship, headed by Byron Price, to monitor media reports about the war.[99] Concerned that the enemy might learn about the U.S. government's intentions and plans from media reports, Price was empowered to take a heavy-handed approach against newspapers and radio stations. In practice, though, he preferred to encourage journalists to exercise independent discretion, and he issued a voluntary Code for Wartime Practices for the American Press that established basic principles for doing so.[100] Meanwhile, Roosevelt himself maintained a rather contentious relationship with the press.[101] Throughout his time in office, he thought that newspapers treated him unfairly, and he tried to work around them through his Fireside Chats and other means.[102] The president "intensely managed his media image" and set rules for what the press could print about his administration, cozying up to favorable reporters and distancing himself from critics.[103]

During the Vietnam War, presidents and journalists once again squared off against one another. In this instance, though, the drama was not precipitated by a congressional statute intended to limit the media or a president asserting his prerogative powers. Rather, it came from the entrepreneurial activities of two newspapers, the *New York Times* and *Washington Post*, which published information that threatened to entirely upend the public's understanding of the war.

The information came in the form of the "Pentagon Papers," a trove of classified FBI reports leaked by Daniel Ellsberg, a military analyst. The papers documented the efforts of successive presidents to mislead the American people about the United States' decisions and involvement in Southeast Asia.[104] Worried about the effect they would have on public opinion, President Richard Nixon sought a court injunction against the papers' publication. The president's lawyers argued the case on the basis of "prior restraint," which, they insisted, justified the papers' suppression before a material harm was done. In *New York Times Co. v. United States*, the Supreme Court did recognize the importance of prior restraint but asserted that the government, in this instance, failed to meet its burden of proof.[105] Following the 6–3 ruling in favor of the plaintiffs, publication of the Pentagon Papers resumed.[106]

The triumph of the *New York Times*, however, did not constitute the denouement of president-media relations. In the aftermath of September 11, 2001, President George W. Bush classified government information at significantly greater rates than previous presidents and systematically denied Freedom of Information Act (FOIA) requests for release of classified documents.*[107] Bush also became especially vigilant about controlling his public image by pre-picking audiences for forums and town hall meetings and dispensing premade videos to news outlets to ensure favorable coverage.[108] In a particularly audacious example, the Department of Health and Human Services produced videos about proposed changes in Medicare legislation that the General Accounting Office concluded were pure propaganda.[109] As a supposed champion of a free and independent press, Barack Obama behaved no better as president. To the contrary, his administration granted substantially fewer FOIA requests than did George W. Bush's.[110] Obama also restricted the press's access to the White House outside of officially sanctioned briefings.[111]

If not in deed, then certainly in rhetoric, Donald Trump took the fight against an independent media to altogether new levels. Even before being elected president, Trump promised to "open up those libel laws, folks," saying, "we're gonna have people sue you like you never got sued before."[112] Via Twitter and public rallies, Trump ranted against the mainstream media, calling it "Fake News," "the opposition party," and "the enemy of the people." And like his predecessors, Trump made a point of excluding from his press briefings those media outlets that offended his political (and sometimes personal) sensibilities.[113]

These tactics paid early dividends: a 2017 Gallup poll found that 62 percent of Americans believed that there was partisan bias in the news media, up from 48 percent in 2003, the last time the question was asked.[114] That Americans distrusted the media, however, is not to say that they endorsed Trump's open disdain for journalists. According to the Pew Research Center, 83 percent of Americans believed that President Trump's relationship with the media was "unhealthy," and 73 percent believed that this relationship compromised voters' access to information.[115]

---

* Signed into law in 1968 by President Johnson, the Freedom of Information Act established procedures by which journalists and citizens could formally request the public release of government information. Subsequent amendments prescribed time frames for government response to FOIA requests and sanctions for improperly withholding information.

12.5.2 *Managing Information Flows*

In trying to control the information that flows from the White House, journalists are not the only ones that presidents must worry about. They also must watch out for their own staffers. But as the prevalence of leaks makes clear, they do not always succeed. Dissatisfied with a proposed course of action or eager to curry favor with a particular reporter, White House staffers and executive bureaucrats occasionally share confidential information with the press.[116] As a result, the president's task of crafting and articulating a single message to the public becomes ever more complicated. "I've had it up to my keister with these leaks!" Reagan was known to lament.[117] And when leaks come in the form of thousands upon thousands of classified documents—as they did with the over 750,000 classified military and diplomatic documents that intelligence analyst Chelsea Manning disclosed to WikiLeaks in 2010 and the troves of National Security Agency data that former employee Edward Snowden hand-delivered to the press in 2013—the policy consequences, from the president's standpoint, can be nothing short of disastrous.[118]

What is a president to do? Whereas the White House press operation typically assumes a posture of support and facilitation, other political actors working on the president's behalf attempt to discipline the press. Under the Obama administration's "zero tolerance policy," the Justice Department prosecuted a record number of journalists and leakers under the Espionage Act.[119] These included Snowden, who was charged but fled the United States and remains on extended asylum in Russia, and Manning, whose thirty-five-year sentence was later commuted. The Trump administration picked up right where Obama left off, focusing not merely on the individuals suspected of leaking classified information but also on the journalists who publish it. Furious over a profusion of leaks that were, by turn, politically embarrassing and damaging to security interests, Trump lashed out on Twitter: "Leakers are traitors and cowards, and we will find out who they are."[120] Jeff Sessions, his attorney general at the time, took notice, initiating upwards of three times as many legal investigations into leaks as had occurred during the Obama administration. And for the first time, during Trump's presidency, these investigations directly implicated journalists themselves when, in late spring 2018, federal law enforcement officials seized a year's worth of emails and phone records of a *New York Times* reporter who, it was thought, had acquired confidential information from the former director of security on the Senate Intelligence Committee.[121]

To be clear, though, presidents are not exclusively in the business of patching leaks. In some instances, they spring leaks themselves—particularly when they would like information to make its way into the public sphere, but neither they nor their immediate subordinates want to speak publicly about it. In 2007, for example, Bush authorized his White House to leak information about a change in Iraq War strategy to *Washington Post* columnist David Ignatius.[122] Bush's popularity, at the time, was at a low point. By surreptitiously enlisting Ignatius to communicate the details of his policy, the president avoided the political liabilities that he himself brought to the table.

Strategic leaks can also abet the president's appointment efforts, giving the White House the chance to see if a possible nominee satisfies or antagonizes key interest groups or congressional blocs. Sometimes called **trial balloons**, these leaks can help a president determine who among the candidates being considered stands the best chance of confirmation. In 2013, for instance, Obama leaked his first choice for chairman of the Federal Reserve, former treasury secretary Lawrence Summers. After encountering stiff resistance from his own party, Obama instead nominated then-Federal Reserve vice chair Janet Yellen, whom Congress subsequently confirmed.[123]

12.5.3 Working around the Press

Sometimes it isn't in the president's best interest to work through the media—better, instead, to work around them. Whether to cultivate their personal image, head off scandals, introduce policy proposals, or shape the contours of public debate, presidents regularly circumvent the media and speak directly to the American people.

When the president's words appear in print or on television, they do not stand alone. Journalists and commentators have tremendous power over the context in which these words appear. This is perhaps especially true on television, where a twenty-four-hour news cycle demands that journalists spend as much time opining about the news as reporting it. To that end, the three major cable television networks—Fox News, CNN, and MSNBC—each hire hundreds of "pundits" (retired politicians, campaign staffers, experts, etc.) to reflect on and debate the news. In the space of a single week, as many as six hundred individual pundits appear on the airwaves of these three networks.[124] When the president speaks, it is their job to interpret and assign meaning to what they hear.

Presidential staffers occasionally lament the shallowness with which White House initiatives are covered. "We have to keep sending out our message if we expect people to understand it," said a deputy press secretary in Jimmy Carter's administration. "The Washington press corps will explain a policy once and then it will feature the politics of the issue."[125] Similarly, presidents and their communications teams have long complained about the media's propensity to distort their messages. President Obama pointed out that when media outlets hire pundits from opposite parties to debate the news, they portray a "false balance" to voters, who are led to mistakenly believe that neither side is right or wrong.[126] And then, of course, there is Trump, who lambasted the press at every turn for delivering fake news—by which he meant news that did not reaffirm the messages he hoped to convey to the American public.

Better, then, for presidents to find opportunities to speak directly to the American people—unmediated and in a context and setting of their own choosing. As discussed, Franklin Delano Roosevelt's Fireside Chats, John F. Kennedy's first live press conference, and Ronald Reagan's reinvention of the televised presidency each opened up new space and opportunities for presidents to communicate directly with the public. The proliferation of social media platforms, too, has given presidents newfound access to their supporters. And as we have seen, Trump, more than any other president, leveraged this access with aplomb and abandon.

In addition to allowing presidents to bypass a media whose interests are not always aligned with their own, these new technologies also afford a second advantage: online platforms such as Twitter and Facebook promote communications in multiple directions. In addition to sending announcements out, presidents can use the Internet to receive feedback in; and through shares, likes, and commentary, these technologies allow people to directly engage and amplify the content sent by the president. So doing, the depth of the exchange between the president and his electorate, and the bonds and commitment that follow, are strengthened.

The George W. Bush administration, for instance, built an interactive "Ask the White House" forum, which included 400 online question-and-answer discussions on everything from Christmas decorations to economic policy.[127] Similarly, during his 2012 reelection campaign, President Obama took questions in a live Twitter Town Hall.[128] In the hour-long session, moderated by Twitter's cofounder, Obama answered questions pulled from 60,000 prior tweets using the #AskObama hashtag. While Obama was criticized for the seemingly cherry-picked questions, the event spurred 161,000 additional tweets reaching over 49 million on Twitter and amassed global media coverage in traditional news outlets.[129]

And of course, President Trump used Twitter to generate a similar (though much less formal) back-and-forth with his base, which is the subject of this chapter's Thinking Institutionally feature. Speaking to a *60 Minutes* host about the platform, Trump said: "It's a modern form of communication. When you give me a bad story or when you give me an inaccurate story . . . I have a method of fighting back."[130] But not only did Trump send more than 25,000 tweets during his presidency; he also frequently *re*-tweeted (nearly 10,000 times) some of his more ardent supporters.[131] A 2019 investigation revealed that Trump retweeted hundreds of small, unverified Twitter accounts, many of which trafficked in conspiracies or extremist content. "I've been retweeted by the President of the United States, President Trump!" tweeted one anonymous account owner, who had promoted lies about Democrats and satanic worship. "Tell me again, how he doesn't care about us."[132]

Of course, Twitter is not a perfect substitute for mainstream media outlets. So long as voters consume traditional forms of televised and print media, presidents will promote good news about their administrations there. And presidents often stand to benefit from these efforts, as the media can amplify the president's voice and communicate messages that his administration would best leave to others. But when trouble comes, as it invariably does, presidents will look for ways to speak directly to the American public. Needing to communicate instantaneously, to avoid misinterpretation, or to open direct lines of communication with a targeted segment of the American public, presidents may opt to work around—rather than alongside—the many journalists, political pundits, and news aggregators that populate the contemporary media landscape.

Thinking Institutionally: The Logic of Trump's Tweets

Donald Trump's relationship with Twitter long preceded his presidency. As shown in figure 12.5, which tracks the daily number of tweets coming from @realDonaldTrump over the duration of his personal account's existence, Trump issued thousands of tweets long before ever announcing his run for the presidency. Indeed, the day on which he issued the most tweets ever came months before he took the political scene by storm, when he sent upwards of 150 tweets in a single day holding forth on his reality television show, *The Apprentice*.

Though Trump, the politician, tempered his Twitter habits, he certainly did not abandon them. During his first year in office, Trump sent 2,606 tweets to his more than 52 million followers. That works out to an average of seven tweets per day. Favorite topics included "fake news," Fox News, global warming, and the many purported errors of Barack Obama. He made a habit of hurling insults like "loser," "weak," and "dummy" at his adversaries, who included the likes of George W. Bush's advisor Karl Rove, Senator Elizabeth Warren, and the entire staff of CNN.

That, though, was just the start of things. Over the course of the next three years, Trump's Twitter feed kicked into higher gear. Trump sent 3,630 tweets in his second year, 7,987 in his third, and 11,998 in his final year—until January 8, 2021, when he was permanently banned from the media platform after repeatedly violating its terms of service.

What are we to make of all this activity? According to many, Trump's brash and impulsive personal character was primarily to blame for his digital outbursts. By this account, Trump's use of Twitter provided "invaluable insight into the workings of the president's mind."[133] His tweeting habits, thus understood, showed Trump to be competitive, unruly, and neurotic.[134] As political scientist P. W. Singer puts it, Trump's use of Twitter revealed his "psychological tics" as well as "what excites him, what angers him, what sets him off."[135] The president's Twitter account also may have revealed something about Trump's news consumption. One analyst followed Trump's Twitter feed closely for months and found that it rather neatly tracked cable news coverage. Tweets that seemed to arrive out of left field, such as his attacks on the National Football League or the Federal Bureau of Investigation, were actually direct responses to Fox News programming.[136]

But might something more be in play? Is it at least possible that Trump's tweeting habits revealed more than just personal impulsivity and a penchant for journaling, 280 characters at a time? Let's consider the possibilities:

1. *Trump used Twitter to rally his political base.* The two most distinctive features of Trump's 2016 campaign were political rallies and tweeting. While some thought that his social media behavior would change as he shifted from primaries to the general election, and then again from the campaign to the White House, Trump maintained the same rhetorical style on Twitter—just as he continued to hold raucous rallies. The

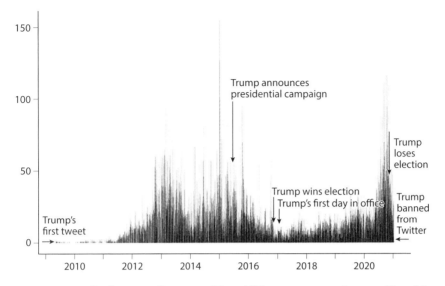

FIGURE 12.5. Daily tweets from @realDonaldTrump, 2009–21. In 2009, Donald Trump launched the account @realDonaldTrump on Twitter. In early 2021, the account was permanently banned. During that twelve-year period, Trump amassed 88 million followers and issued a total of 59,553 tweets, the daily counts of which are presented in this graph.

distinct characteristics of both these activities were popular engagement coupled with populist rhetoric.[137] For his followers, Trump's tweets could be at once affirming and alluring.[138] With insults, bravado, and catchy one-liners, he stirred up the emotions of his followers and then "bind[ed] them in shared righteous anger and victimhood."[139] Unapologetically, he called out the grotesque bias and unfairness of his political opponents and then offered his leadership—sometimes implicitly, other times quite explicitly—as the only available solution. *"That's right, we need a TRAVEL BAN for certain DANGEROUS countries, not some politically correct term that won't help us protect our people!" (June 6, 2017)*

2. *Trump used Twitter to distract attention from other stories in the news cycle.* When the dominant news story was not to the president's liking, Trump dished up plot lines that journalists and their audiences found irresistible. As the president knew too well, "the more outrageous . . . online comments have become, the more coverage they've received."[140] Sometimes the president's tweets were full of personal intrigue and scandal. Other times, they were pure fiction. All, though, had the potential to deflect public attention away from news stories that could have proved damaging to the president. Hence, when domestic political pressure was mounting from the special investigation led by Robert Mueller into Russian interference in the 2016 election, the president announced on Twitter that Trump Tower had been wiretapped by then-president Barack Obama and that an FBI spy was planted in his campaign

Continued on next page

staff.[141] His first tweet on the subject, in March 2017, coincided with the beginning of the Robert Mueller investigation.[142] And as rumors spread a year later that his personal attorney, Michael Cohen, might be cooperating with the Mueller probe, Trump once again complained of "spygate." Through distraction alone, the president seeks to dampen the political fallout of negative news.[143] *"Terrible! Just found out that Obama had my 'wires tapped' in Trump Tower just before the victory. Nothing found. This is McCarthyism!" (March 4, 2017) "SPYGATE could be one of the biggest political scandals in history!" (May 23, 2018)*

3. *Trump used Twitter to discredit the mainstream media.* The president regularly, and quite deliberately, worked to degrade trust in established media outlets, positioning his own Twitter feed as a reliable source of presidential news. Between his inauguration and June 1, 2018, President Trump tweeted about "fake news" 221 times, and he called out major media outlets 140 times.[144] By comparison, during that same time period, he only tweeted 44 times about his signature domestic policy proposal, a wall on the U.S.-Mexico border. Trump's Twitter feed functioned as something of a battering ram against the media establishments that, depending on your political priors, either held him to account or treated him so unfairly. *"The FAKE NEWS media (failing @nytimes, @NBCNews, @ABC, @CBS, @CNN) is not my enemy, it is the enemy of the American People!" (February 17, 2017)*

4. *Trump used Twitter to control messaging.* The president regularly lambasted the "unfair treatment" he was given by the press and media for jumping on slight misphrasings, taking comments out of context, or asking "unfair" questions. As a result, he scheduled fewer and fewer press briefings as his administration wore on, bucking historical trends. Twitter seemed to have largely replaced press briefings as his primary mechanism for communicating information to the public. The distinct advantage of Twitter is control. Reporters have no ability to tailor quotes to their interest or ask potentially damaging questions. Rather, Trump was able to determine precisely what messaging would be released to the public. He successfully wrested control away from the "fake news" and into his own hands. He explained this logic in a tweet: *"As a very active President with lots of things happening, it is not possible for my surrogates to stand at podium with perfect accuracy!"* Trump tweeted in May 2017. *"Maybe the best thing to do would be to cancel all future 'press briefings' and hand out written responses for the sake of accuracy???"*

Which of these logics unlocks the truth about Trump's Twitter habits? It's hard to say. Each has a measure of plausibility, and examples of every one are readily available. These four options, moreover, are neither exhaustive nor mutually exclusive. Depending on the circumstances, the president may have employed any number of political strategies. What is clear, though, is that the president's tweets had as much to do with political calculation and strategy as they did with personality. Even when trying to explain one of the most bizarre behaviors of one of our most unusual presidents, we would do well to resist the temptations of armchair psychoanalysis.

12.6 The Media: Watchdog or Lapdog?

Following the Watergate scandal, the president's *personal* life was no longer regarded as off-limits by the press, but certain *policy* areas—particularly foreign affairs—still received press deference. One large-scale analysis of press conferences dating back fifty years shows that, when it comes to foreign policy, reporters exercise heightened levels of self-restraint and defer to the administration's supposed expertise.[145] Consider, also, the "rally 'round the flag" effect, whereby military conflicts boost public support for the president.[146] Members of the press are not immune to this phenomenon. They rally around the flag, too.

The press's deference to the White House on foreign affairs can have material consequences for the decisions that presidents make. In the run-up to the 2003 Iraq War, for example, the Bush administration chose reporters to selectively leak stories that bolstered the case for the war. The *New York Times* published several front-page articles claiming that Saddam Hussein's regime possessed weapons of mass destruction. After the conflict concluded, and no such weapons could be found, the administration's initial justification for the war—which the press had done so much to promote and publicize—appeared bankrupt. One prominent journalist, former *New York Times* columnist Leslie H. Gelb, chastised the media for failing to offer enough "critical commentary" on the president's claims.[147] By focusing on partisan politics, said Gelb, the media shirked its role as a watchdog of the public interest.

It is not difficult to see why this might happen. In foreign affairs, presidents have a natural advantage over those in the press, stemming from their access to information on the full scope of national security threats. Presidents can always justify a decision or an action on the basis of classified information that neither the press nor public can independently corroborate.

When James Risen, a *New York Times* reporter, presented the Bush White House with a story he had written on their domestic surveillance tactics after 9/11, the White House insisted the paper delay publishing the story. Said the paper's editor, Bill Keller, "The Administration argued strongly that writing about this eavesdropping program would give terrorists clues about the vulnerability of their communications and would deprive the government of an effective tool for the protection of the country's security."[148] The newspaper waited a year before publishing the story. When it comes to foreign affairs, even the most aggressive watchdogs can be held at bay.

None of this is to say, though, that the press has somehow lost its appetite for political scandal or investigative journalism. Indeed, in an age of "alternative facts" and "fake news," the media may now be more consequential than ever for the effective functioning of a democracy. It is the media, after all, that situates the claims of politicians, very much including the president, within a larger narrative. The media assesses the likely consequences of different policy choices, the underlying public support for various courses of action, and, increasingly, the veracity of political claims. This last function, in particular, preoccupied many journalists during the Trump presidency.

Plenty of presidents have been known to lie or mislead the public. Sharing some facts selectively while bending others is, after all, a common artifact of presidential speech and rhetoric. What, though, should the media do with a president who repeatedly espouses verifiable falsehoods?

Right off the bat, Trump and his spokespeople insisted that the news media was deliberately underreporting the turnout for his inauguration, even though all sorts of evidence clearly disproved the president's claims.[149] After four years in office, his relationship with the truth showed little improvement. PolitiFact, a political fact-checking website, ranked 73 percent of its selected statements by Trump as mostly false, false, or "pants on fire." By comparison, only 23 percent of Barack Obama's statements received these ratings.[150]

The challenge is all the more daunting because presidents do not accept such indictments sitting down. As we have seen, presidents take all sorts of actions that are intended to curry favor with some journalists and to discredit others. And, when all else fails, they can try to skate around the Washington press corps altogether. Numerous social media platforms—Twitter, Facebook, Instagram, and the like—enable contemporary presidents to speak to the American people unfiltered. Trump went to great lengths to reap the benefits of every one of these platforms. As he put it, "Much of the news. It's not honest. And when I have close to 100 million people watching me on Twitter, including Facebook, including all of the Instagram, including POTUS, including lots of things—but we have—I guess pretty close to 100 million people. I have my own form of media."[151]

How should the "mainstream" media respond? Beyond keeping pace with presidents' public pronouncements, they must establish objective and fair-minded criteria for reporting on them. Journalists must develop ways of evaluating presidential claims that were never intended to pass through their ranks but, instead, were directed straight to the American people. In a political environment as polarized and distrustful as ours today, the challenge could not be more difficult—or essential—for American democracy.

Conclusion

The president's relationship with the American public, in a very real sense, is mediated. Though the advent of new technologies has allowed presidents, to a limited extent, to target their messaging and speak directly to the American public, it is from the press that most Americans receive their news about the American presidency, and it is through the press that presidents must convey their messages. As a consequence, a growing institutional apparatus within the White House is devoted to managing press relations. End runs and avoidance will not suffice in today's media environment. Rather, presidents and their communications staff must carefully develop strategies for dealing with the press head-on. Through messaging, the selective release of information, careful responses to queries, the managing of leaks, and the shaping of narratives, the institutional presidency confronts the media with all the strategic focus and intentionality as they do Congress, the courts, and the federal bureaucracy.

Success is hardly guaranteed. And given the fragmentation and polarization of the new media landscape, it is no wonder that presidents undertake this work with a profound sense of ambivalence. By turns, journalists are powerful checks on the arbitrary exercise of executive authority and willing abettors of the president's policy agenda; scions of public interest and unwitting propagators of government misinformation; champions of transparency and servile attendants of executive ambitions. Across media outlets and over time, presidents encounter media outlets with very different inclinations. But whether threat or ally, foe or friend, these journalists cannot be altogether ignored. Quite the contrary, presidents must find ways to bend the press to their will—or, more modestly, to mitigate the fallout of their coverage—lest their policy agendas, and with them their presidencies, drift asunder.

Key Terms

plebiscitary presidency   speechwriting department
demagoguery   Press Office
bully pulpit   press secretary
press conferences   Freedom of Information Act
Fireside Chats   Presidential Records Act
Office of Communications   trial balloon

Questions for Discussion

1. In what ways do leaks compromise the president's ability to advance a policy agenda? In what ways do leaks offer assistance?
2. Do structural changes in the contemporary media help or hurt the president's ability to garner support for a preferred policy agenda?
3. Evaluate President Trump's strategy of using Twitter to connect with constituents, sideline the media, and at times distract the public's attention. Was it effective? Did it come with any political liabilities to Trump himself?
4. Which is more important to presidents when they interact with the public: style or substance? What makes the great communicators among presidents (such as Reagan or FDR) stand out?
5. When it comes to public and media relations, is the president in control, or does the communications apparatus predominate?
6. How can a president best advance their own narrative in the modern media landscape?

Suggested Readings

Cohen, Jeffrey. *Going Local: Presidential Leadership in the Post-Broadcast Age*. New York: Cambridge University Press, 2009.

Farnsworth, Stephen, and S. Robert Lichter. *The Mediated Presidency: Television News and Presidential Governance*. New York: Rowman & Littlefield, 2005.

Greenberg, David. *Republic of Spin: An Inside History of the American Presidency*. New York: W. W. Norton, 2016.

Hart, Roderick. *Trump and Us: What He Says and Why People Listen*. New York: Cambridge University Press, 2020.

Kumar, Martha Joynt. *Managing the President's Message*. Baltimore: Johns Hopkins University Press, 2007.

Tulis, Jeffrey. *The Rhetorical Presidency*. Princeton: Princeton University Press, 1987.

Notes

1. James Madison, "Federalist No. 49," in *The Federalist Papers*, ed. Clinton Rossiter (New York: Signet, 2003).

2. Jeffrey Tulis, *The Rhetorical Presidency* (Princeton: Princeton University Press, 1987).

3. George Juergens, "Theodore Roosevelt and the Press," *Daedalus* 111, no. 4 (1982): 114.

4. Joshua David Hawley, *Theodore Roosevelt: Preacher of Righteousness* (New Haven: Yale University Press, 2008), 187.

5. Tulis, *The Rhetorical Presidency*, 118.

6. Tulis, *The Rhetorical Presidency*, 128.

7. Cited in Tulis, *The Rhetorical Presidency*, 129.

8. Tulis, *The Rhetorical Presidency*, 130.

9. Woodrow Wilson, Address to a Joint Session of Congress on Tariff Reform, April 8, 1913.

10. As quoted in Jon Kelly, "The Odd Early White House Press Conferences," *BBC News Magazine*, March 15, 2013, http://www.bbc.co.uk/news/magazine-21761429.

11. John Dickerson, "Meet the Press," *Slate*, March 14, 2013, http://www.slate.com/articles/news_and_politics/politics/2013/03/woodrow_wilson_held_the_first_presidential_pre ss_conference_100_years_ago.html.

12. David Michael Ryfe, "'Betwixt and Between': Woodrow Wilson's Press Conferences and the Transition toward the Modern Rhetorical Presidency," *Political Communication* 16 (1999): 77.

13. Franklin D. Roosevelt, "The 'Forgotten Man' Speech," April 7, 1932, American Presidency Project, https://www.presidency.ucsb.edu/documents/radio-address-from-albany-new-york-the-forgotten-man -speech.

14. Christopher H. Sterling, "'The Fireside Chats'—President Franklin D. Roosevelt (1933–1944)," Library of Congress, 2002, https://www.loc.gov/static/programs/national-recording-preservation-board/documents /FiresideChats.pdf.

15. Franklin D. Roosevelt, "On the Bank Crisis," Franklin D. Roosevelt Presidential Library and Museum, March 12, 1933, http://docs.fdrlibrary.marist.edu/firesi90.html.

16. David Michael Ryfe, "From Media Audience to Media Public: A Study of Letters Written in Reaction to FDR's Fireside Chats," *Media, Culture & Society* 23, no. 6 (2001): 768.

17. Theodore J. Lowi, *The Personal President: Power Invested, Promise Unfulfilled* (Ithaca: Cornell University Press, 1985), 63.

18. Martha Joynt Kumar, *Managing the President's Message: The White House Communications Operation* (Baltimore: Johns Hopkins University Press, 2007).

19. Steve Passwaiter, "Political Ad Spending This Year Reached a Whopping $8.5 Billion," *AdAge*, November 23, 2020, https://adage.com/article/campaign-trail/political-ad-spending-year-reached-whopping-85 -billion/2295646.

20. Michael Deaver and Mickey Herskowitz, *Behind the Scenes: In Which the Author Talks about Ronald and Nancy Reagan . . . and Himself* (Ann Arbor: University of Michigan Press, 1987), 77.

21. As quoted in Richard W. Waterman, Gilbert K. St. Clair, and Robert Wright, *The Image-Is-Everything Presidency* (Boulder, CO: Westview Press, 1999), 119–20.

22. Gil Troy, *Morning in America: How Ronald Reagan Invented the 1980s* (Princeton: Princeton University Press, 2005), 162–63.

23. Steven R. Weisman, "The President and the Press," *New York Times*, October 14, 1984, 6034.

24. Jackie Calmes, "Live from the Oval Office: A Backdrop of History Fades from TV," *New York Times*, July 10, 2013, A.1.

25. Weisman, "The President and the Press."

26. Jesse Helfrich, "Obama Finds Virtual End-Around to Bypass the White House Press," *The Hill*, January 31, 2012, https://thehill.com/homenews/administration/207567-obama-finds-virtual-end-around-to -bypass-the-white-house-press.

27. "The Internet at the White House," White House Historical Association, https://www.whitehousehistory.org/the-internet-at-the-white-house.

28. "Most Used Social Networks Worldwide as of January 2021," Statista, https://www.statista.com/statistics/272014/global-social-networks-ranked-by-number-of-users/.

29. This was decided in the lawsuit *James Madison Project v. Department of Justice*, a 2017 Freedom of Information Act suit.

30. Freedom of Information Act, "Records Released in Response to Presidential Records Act Inquiries, Trump Administration," U.S. National Archives, January 21, 2021.

31. Christina M. Blankenship, "President, Wrestler, Spectacle: An Examination of Donald Trump's Firing Tweets and the Celebrity President as Response to Trump's Media Landscape," *Journal of Communication Inquiry* 44, no. 2 (2020): 117–38.

32. Karin Wahl-Jorgensen, "Media Coverage of Shifting Emotional Regimes: Donald Trump's Angry Populism," *Media, Culture & Society* 40, no. 5 (2018): 766–78.

33. Christopher D. Kromphardt and Michael F. Salamone, "'Unpresidented!' Or, What Happens When the President Attacks the Federal Judiciary on Twitter," *Journal of Information Technology & Politics* 18, no. 1 (2020): 1–17. See also Jemele Hill, "Trump Attacked Black Athletes—And Paid for It in the End," *The Atlantic*, November 10, 2020, https://www.theatlantic.com/ideas/archive/2020/11/black-athletes-should-never-stick-sports-again/617052/.

34. Ángel Panizo-LLedot, Javier Torregrosa, Gema Bello-Orgaz, Joshua Thorburn, and David Camacho, "Describing Alt-Right Communities and Their Discourse on Twitter during the 2018 US Mid-term Elections," in Hocine Cherifi, Sabrina Gaito, José Fernando Mendes, Esteban Moro, Luis Mateus Rocha, eds., *Complex Networks 2019: Complex Networks and Their Applications VIII*, International Conference on Complex Networks and Their Applications (2019): 427–39.

35. Andrew S. Ross and Damian J. Rivers, "Discursive Deflection: Accusation of 'Fake News' and the Spread of Mis- and Disinformation in the Tweets of President Trump," *Social Media + Society* 4, no. 2 (2018): 1–12.

36. Josh Sanburn, "A Brief History of Digital News," *Time*, February 1, 2011, http://content.time.com/time/business/article/0,8599,2045682,00.html.

37. Rasmus Kleis Nielsen, ed., *Local Journalism: The Decline of Newspapers and the Rise of Digital Media* (New York: Bloomsbury Publishing, 2015).

38. "State of the News Media 2016," Pew Research Center, June 15, 2016, http://assets.pewresearch.org/wp-content/uploads/sites/13/2016/06/30143308/state-of-the-news-media-report-2016-final.pdf; "Local TV News Fact Sheet," Pew Research Center, 2017, http://www.journalism.org/fact-sheet/local-tv-news.

39. Michael Barthel, "Despite Subscription Surges for Largest U.S. Newspapers, Circulation and Revenue Fall for Industry Overall," Pew Research Center, June 1, 2020, https://www.pewresearch.org/fact-tank/2017/06/01/circulation-and-revenue-fall-for-newspaper-industry/.

40. Matthew Baum and Samuel Kernell, "Has Cable Ended the Golden Age of Presidential Television?" *American Political Science Review* 93, no. 1 (1999): 99–114.

41. Baum and Kernell, "Has Cable Ended the Golden Age?"

42. "Public Trust in Government: 1958–2014," Pew Research Center, November 13, 2014, http://www.people-press.org/2014/11/13/public-trust-in-government/.

43. Jae Kook Lee, Jihyang Choi, Cheonsoo Kim, and Yonghwan Kim, "Social Media, Network Heterogeneity, and Opinion Polarization," *Journal of Communication* 64, no. 4 (2014): 702–22.

44. Kevin Arceneaux and Martin Johnson, *Changing Minds or Changing Channels?: Partisan News in an Age of Choice* (Chicago: University of Chicago Press, 2013).

45. Mark Jurkowsky and Amy Mitchell, "How Americans Get TV News at Home," Pew Research Center, October 11, 2013, https://www.journalism.org/2013/10/11/how-americans-get-tv-news-at-home/; Tom Rosentiel, "Partisanship and Cable News Audiences," Pew Research Center, October 30, 2009, https://www.pewresearch.org/2009/10/30/partisanship-and-cable-news-audiences/.

46. Amy Mitchell, Mark Jurkowitz, J. Olphant, and Elisa Shearer, "Americans Who Mainly Get Their News on Social Media Are Less Engaged, Less Knowledgeable," Pew Research Center, July 30, 2020, https://www .journalism.org/2020/07/30/americans-who-mainly-get-their-news-on-social-media-are-less-engaged-less -knowledgeable/.

47. Arthur Campbell, C. Matthew Leister, and Yves Zenou, "Social Media and Polarization," CEPR Discussion Papers 13860 (2019), https://papers.ssrn.com/sol3/papers.cfm?abstract_id=3428384.

48. Vidya Narayanan, Vlad Barash, John Kelly, Bence Kollanyi, Lisa-Maria Neudert, and Philip N. Howard, "Polarization, Partisanship and Junk News Consumption over Social Media in the US" (2018), https://arxiv .org/abs/1803.01845.

49. Melissa Tully, Emily K. Vraga, and Anne-Bennett Smithson, "News Media Literacy, Perceptions of Bias, and Interpretation of News," *Journalism* 21, no. 2 (2020): 209–26.

50. See, for example, Tim Groseclose, *Left Turn: How Liberal Media Bias Distorts the American Mind* (New York: St. Martin's Griffin, 2012). But for a very different characterization of political bias in the media, see Yochai Benkler, Robert Faris, and Hal Roberts, *Network Propaganda: Manipulation, Disinformation, and Radicalization in American Politics* (New York: Oxford University Press, 2018).

51. Pablo Barberá, "Social Media, Echo Chambers, and Political Polarization," in *Social Media and Democracy: The State of the Field, Prospects for Reform*, ed. Nathaniel Persily and Joshua A. Tucker (New York: Cambridge University Press, 2020), 34.

52. Andrew Guess, "(Almost) Everything in Moderation: New Evidence on Americans' Online Media Diets," *American Journal of Political Science* 65, no. 1 (2021): 1007–22. See also Matthew Gentzkow and Jesse Shapiro, "Ideological Segregation Online and Offline," *Quarterly Journal of Economics* 126, no. 4 (2011): 1788– 1839; and Seth R. Flaxman, Sharad Goel, and Justin M. Rao, "Filter Bubbles, Echo Chambers, and Online News Consumption," *Public Opinion Quarterly* 80, no. 1 (2016): 298–320.

53. Izabella Kaminska, "A Lesson in Fake News from the Info-Wars of Ancient Rome," *Financial Times*, January 17, 2017, https://www.ft.com/content/aaf2bb08-dca2-11e6-86ac-f253db7791c6.

54. Jackie Mansky, "The Age-Old Problem of 'Fake News,'" *Smithsonian Magazine*, May 7, 2018, https:// www.smithsonianmag.com/history/age-old-problem-fake-news-180968945/.

55. Kevin Roose, "We Asked for Examples of Election Misinformation; You Delivered," *New York Times*, November 5, 2018, A.16.

56. Alexis C. Madrigal, "What Facebook Did to American Democracy," *The Atlantic*, October 12, 2017, https://www.theatlantic.com/technology/archive/2017/10/what-facebook-did/542502/.

57. Devon Link, "Fact Check: No Basis for Claims That President Joe Biden's Inauguration Was Faked," *USA Today*, January 28, 2021, https://www.usatoday.com/story/news/factcheck/2021/01/28/fact-check -president-joe-biden-inauguration-real-well-documented/4268923001/.

58. Amanda Terkel, "GOP Pushes Conspiracy Theory That Kamala Harris, Not Joe Biden, Runs the White House," *Huffington Post*, May 13, 2021, https://www.huffpost.com/entry/gop-kamala-harris-in-charge_n _609a9f6ae4b099ba752f0203.

59. Terry Sullivan and Martha Joynt Kumar, "The Office of Communications," in *The White House World: Transitions, Organization, and Office Operations*, ed. Kumar and Sullivan (College Station: Texas A&M University Press, 2003). See also Martha Joynt Kumar, "The Office of Communications," Report 2017–33, White House Transition Project (2017).

60. "Office of Speechwriting," Clinton Digital Library, https://clinton.presidentiallibraries.us/collections /show/29.

61. "Office Briefs—White House Transition Project," White House Transition Project, https:// whitehousetransitionproject.org/transition-resources-2/office-briefs/.

62. Katie Rogers, "The State of the Union Is Trump's Biggest Speech; Who Writes It?" *New York Times*, February 4, 2020, A.19.

63. For a discussion about the format's persistence—despite occasional dips—see Matthew Eshbaugh-Soha, "Presidential Press Conferences over Time," *American Journal of Political Science* 47, no. 2 (2003): 348–53.

64. Kumar, *Managing the President's Message*.

65. Matthew Eshbaugh-Soha, "Presidential Influence of the News Media: The Case of the Press Conference," *Political Communication* 30, no. 4 (2013): 548–64.

66. "Membership," U.S. Senate Press Gallery, https://www.dailypress.senate.gov/?page_id=8908.

67. Sarah J. Eckman, "Congressional News Media and the House and Senate Press Galleries," CRS Report R44816 (Washington, DC: Congressional Research Service, 2017), https://fas.org/sgp/crs/misc/R44816.pdf.

68. George E. Condon Jr., "The Man Who Integrated the White House Press Corps," *The Atlantic*, May 3, 2014, https://www.theatlantic.com/politics/archive/2014/05/the-man-who-integrated-the-white-house-press-corps/361599/; Earnest Perry, "We Want In: The African American Press's Negotiation for a White House Correspondent," *American Journalism* 20, no. 3 (2003): 31–47.

69. Paul Farhi, "White House Press Corps of Largely White Faces," *Washington Post*, July 25, 2013, https://www.washingtonpost.com/lifestyle/style/white-house-press-corps-of-largely-white-faces/2013/07/25/d8fdacec-f556-11e2-9434-60440856fadf_story.html. See also Stephen Hess, "All the President's Reporters: A New Survey of the White House Press Corps," *Presidential Studies Quarterly* 22, no. 2 (1992): 311–21; and Justin Metz, "The White House Beat, Uncovered," *POLITICO Magazine* (May/June 2014), https://www.politico.com/magazine/story/2014/04/whca-survey-the-white-house-beat-uncovered-106071.

70. "Diversity in the Washington Newspaper Press Corps," UNITY: Journalists of Color, Inc. and the Walter Cronkite School of Journalism and Mass Communication, Arizona State University, July 23, 2008, https://cronkite.asu.edu/news-and-events/news/diversity-072408.

71. Martha Joynt Kumar, "The Contemporary Presidency: Energy or Chaos? Turnover at the Top of President Trump's White House," *Presidential Studies Quarterly* 49, no. 1 (2019): 238.

72. Nathan Thrall and Jesse James Wilkins, "Kennedy Talked, Khrushchev Triumphed," *New York Times*, May 22, 2008, A.31.

73. Richard Benedetto, *Politicians Are People, Too* (Lanham, MD: University Press of America, 2006).

74. Michael Calderone, "Obama Lunches with Journos," *POLITICO*, November 6, 2009, http://www.politico.com/blogs/michaelcalderone/1109/Obama_meets_with_journos_at_the_WH.html.

75. Michael M. Grynbaum, "White House Grants Press Credentials to a Pro-Trump Blog," *New York Times*, February 14, 2017, A.18.

76. Paul Farhi, "The White House Tried to Move a Reporter to the Back of the Press Room," *Washington Post*, April 26, 2020, https://www.washingtonpost.com/lifestyle/media/the-white-house-tried-to-move-a-reporter-to-the-back-of-the-press-room-but-she-refused-then-trump-walked-out/2020/04/25/a5d16cc6-8714-11ea-ae26-989cfce1c7c7_story.html.

77. "Trump Refuses to Answer Reporter's Question on Russia," BBC News, January 11, 2017, https://www.bbc.com/news/av/world-us-canada-38575592.

78. Joseph Ellis, *His Excellency: George Washington* (New York: Vintage Books, 2004), 196.

79. Ellis, *His Excellency*, 245.

80. Hugh Gallagher, *FDR's Splendid Deception* (New York: Vandamere Press, 1985).

81. Seymour Hersh, *The Dark Side of Camelot* (New York: Little, Brown, 1997).

82. Alfred E. Lewis, "5 Held in Plot to Bug Democrats' Office Here," *Washington Post*, June 18, 1972, A.1.

83. See Bob Woodward and Carl Bernstein, "GOP Security Aide among 5 Arrested in Bugging Affair," *Washington Post*, June 19, 1972, A.1; Bob Woodward and Carl Bernstein, "Bug Suspect Got Campaign Funds," *Washington Post*, August 1, 1972, A.1.

84. Mark Feldstein, "Watergate Revisited," *American Journalism Review* (August/September 2004).

85. Feldstein, "Watergate Revisited."

86. "The Watergate Story," *Washington Post*, June 14, 2009, http://www.washingtonpost.com/wp-srv/politics/special/watergate/part1.html.

87. Peter McNamara, "Sedition Act of 1798 (1798)," The First Amendment Encyclopedia, Middle Tennessee State University, http://www.mtsu.edu/first-amendment/article/1238/sedition-act-of-1798.

88. Bruce A. Ragsdale, "The Sedition Act Trials," Federal Judicial Center, 2005, https://www.fjc.gov/sites/default/files/trials/seditionacts.pdf.

89. "The Sedition Act of 1798," History, Art & Archives, U.S. House of Representatives, http://history.house.gov/HistoricalHighlight/Detail/36271.

90. "First Inaugural Address," *The Papers of Thomas Jefferson, Volume 33: 17 February to 30 April 1801* (Princeton: Princeton University Press, 2005), 148–52, https://jeffersonpapers.princeton.edu/selected-documents/first-inaugural-address-0.

91. David W. Bulla, "Abraham Lincoln and Press Suppression Reconsidered," *American Journalism* 26, no. 4 (2009): 11–33; Jeffery Alan Smith, *War and Press Freedom: The Problem of Prerogative Power* (New York: Oxford University Press, 1999).

92. Jeffery A. Smith, "Lincoln's Other War: Public Opinion, Press Issues, and Personal Pleas," *American Journalism* 26, no. 4 (October 1, 2009): 87–117.

93. Geoffrey R. Stone, "Abraham Lincoln's First Amendment," *New York University Law Review* 78, no. 1 (2003): 1.

94. Smith, "Lincoln's Other War."

95. Geoffrey R. Stone, "Freedom of the Press in Time of War," *SMU Law Review* 59 (2006): 1663–70.

96. Eric Arnesen, "Waging War Abroad and at Home," *Cobblestone* 29, no. 9 (2008): 11.

97. Stone, "Freedom of the Press in Time of War."

98. Arthur S. Link, "Letter to President Woodrow Wilson from Postmaster General Albert S. Burleson," in *The Papers of Woodrow Wilson*, vol. 66, ed. Arthur S. Link (Princeton: Princeton University Press, 1992), 92–98.

99. Smith, *War and Press Freedom*.

100. Byron Price, "Governmental Censorship in War-Time," *American Political Science Review* 36, no. 5 (1942): 837–49.

101. David Beito, "Roosevelt's War against the Press," *Reason* 49, no. 1 (2017): 54.

102. Shontavia Jackson Johnson, "Donald Trump, Disruptive Technologies, and Twitter's Role in the 2016 American Presidential Election Symposium: Governing in an Age of Partisanship," *Widener Commonwealth Law Review* 27, no. 1 (2018): 39–82.

103. Lumeng Yu, "The Great Communicator: How FDR's Radio Speeches Shaped American History," *History Teacher* 39, no. 1 (2005): 89–106.

104. Jordan Moran, "Nixon and the Pentagon Papers," Miller Center, University of Virginia, December 27, 2016, https://millercenter.org/the-presidency/educational-resources/first-domino-nixon-and-the-pentagon-papers.

105. David W. Dunlap, "1971 | Supreme Court Allows Publication of Pentagon Papers," *New York Times*, June 30, 2016, https://www.nytimes.com/2016/06/30/insider/1971-supreme-court-allows-publication-of-pentagon-papers.html.

106. Dunlap, "1971 | Supreme Court Allows Publication of Pentagon Papers."

107. Eric Alterman and George Zornick, "The Bush Legacy: War on the Press," Center for American Progress, November 20, 2008, https://www.americanprogress.org/issues/general/news/2008/11/20/5248/think-again-the-bush-legacy-war-on-the-press/.

108. Jacob Weisberg and Isaac Chotiner, "Beyond Spin," *Slate*, December 7, 2005, http://www.slate.com/articles/news_and_politics/the_big_idea/2005/12/beyond_spin.html.

109. Amy Goldstein, "GAO Says HHS Broke Laws with Medicare Videos," *Washington Post*, May 20, 2004, A.1.

110. Julie Moos, "Obama Administration's FOIA Record Worse than Bush's," *Poynter*, September 28, 2012, https://www.poynter.org/news/obama-administrations-foia-record-worse-bushs.

111. Mark Landler, "Photographers Protest White House Restrictions," *New York Times*, November 22, 2013, A.20.

112. Richard Tofel, "Donald Trump and the Return of Seditious Libel," *ProPublica*, November 21, 2016, https://www.propublica.org/article/donald-trump-and-the-return-of-seditious-libel.

113. Ali Vitali, "Multiple Media Outlets Were Excluded from a White House Media Briefing Friday After-noon," NBC News, February 24, 2017, https://www.nbcnews.com/politics/white-house/white-house-excludes-several-outlets-press-gaggle-n725366.

114. Art Swift, "Six in 10 in US See Partisan Bias in News Media," Gallup, April 5, 2017, http://www.gallup.com/poll/207794/six-partisan-bias-news-media.aspx.

115. Callum Borchers, "Analysis: At Least We Agree on Something: Trump and the Media Have an Un-healthy Relationship," *Washington Post*, April 5, 2017, https://www.washingtonpost.com/news/the-fix/wp/2017/04/05/at-least-we-agree-on-something-trump-and-the-media-have-an-unhealthy-relationship/.

116. George Stephanopoulos describes these variations of leaks in *All Too Human* (New York: Little, Brown, 1999).

117. Maureen Dowd, "President of Scandinavia," *New York Times*, May 29, 2013, A.23.

118. Scott Shane and Charlie Savage, "Administration Took Accidental Path to Setting Leak Record," *New York Times*, June 20, 2012, A.14.

119. Peter Sterne, "Obama Used the Espionage Act to Put a Record Number of Reporters' Sources in Jail, and Trump Could Be Even Worse," Freedom of the Press Foundation, June 21, 2017, https://freedom.press/news/obama-used-espionage-act-put-record-number-reporters-sources-jail-and-trump-could-be-even-worse/.

120. Rebecca Morin, "Trump Says Leaks Are Exaggerated but Vows to Track Down 'Traitors,'" *POLITICO*, May 14, 2018, https://www.politico.com/story/2018/05/14/trump-leaks-traitors-white-house-586041.

121. Adam Goldman, Nicholas Fandos, and Katie Benner, "Times Reporter's Records Are Seized in Leak Inquiry," *New York Times*, June 8, 2018, A.18.

122. Steve Myers, "Bush Authorized Leak about Iraq Strategy to *Washington Post*'s David Ignatius in 2007," *Poynter*, August 29, 2011, http://www.poynter.org/latest-news/mediawire/144351/bush-authorized-leak-about-iraq-strategy-to-washington-posts-david-ignatius-in-2007/.

123. Jonathan Bernstein, "Summers and the Proper Use of Trial Balloons," *Washington Post*, September 16, 2013.

124. Paul Farhi, "We Have Reached Peak Punditry," *Washington Post*, June 2, 2016, https://www.washingtonpost.com/sf/style/2016/06/02/pundits/.

125. Sam Donaldson, *Hold On, Mr. President* (New York: Random House, 1987), 26.

126. Amy Chozick, "Obama Is an Avid Reader, and Critic, of the News," *New York Times*, August 8, 2012, A.13.

127. "Ask the White House," George W. Bush White House, https://georgewbush-whitehouse.archives.gov/ask/.

128. Michael Shear, "Obama Campaign Takes Jobs Fight to Twitter," The Caucus (blog), *New York Times*, July 6, 2011, https://thecaucus.blogs.nytimes.com/2011/10/04/obama-campaign-takes-jobs-fight-to-twitter/.

129. Mark Memmott, "Live-Blog: President Obama's Twitter Town Hall @ The White House," The Two-Way (blog), National Public Radio, July 6, 2011; Jenn D, "Ask Obama: The President's First Twitter Townhall," TweetReach, July 6, 2011, https://tweetreach.com/about/2011/07/ask-obama-the-presidents-first-twitter-townhall/.

130. Reena Flores, "In '60 Minutes' Interview, Donald Trump Weighs Twitter Use as President," CBS News, November 12, 2016, https://www.cbsnews.com/news/donald-trump-60-minutes-interview-weighs-twitter-use-as-president/.

131. Brendan Brown, "Trump Twitter Archive," https://www.thetrumparchive.com/.

132. Mike McIntire, Karen Yourish, and Larry Buchanan, "In Trump's Twitter Feed: Conspiracy-Mongers, Racists and Spies," *New York Times*, November 3, 2019, F.6.

133. "Analysis: In Trump's Twitter Feed, A Tale of Sound and Fury," National Public Radio, April 7, 2018, https://www.npr.org/2018/04/07/600138358/analysis-in-trumps-twitter-feed-a-tale-of-sound-and-fury.

134. Martin Obschonka and Christian Fisch, "Entrepreneurial Personalities in Political Leadership," *Small Business Economics* 50, no. 4 (2018): 851–69.

135. As quoted in Nahal Toosi, "Is Trump's Twitter Account a National Security Threat?" *POLITICO*, December 13, 2016, https://www.politico.com/story/2016/12/trump-twitter-national-security-232518.

136. Matthew Gertz, "I've Studied the Trump-Fox Feedback Loop for Months; It's Crazier than You Think," *POLITICO Magazine*, January 5, 2018, https://www.politico.com/magazine/story/2018/01/05/trump-media-feedback-loop-216248.

137. Ramona Kreis, "The 'Tweet Politics' of President Trump," *Journal of Language & Politics* 16, no. 4 (2017): 607–18.

138. Johnson, "Donald Trump, Disruptive Technologies, and Twitter's Role in the 2016 American Presidential Election Symposium."

139. Mark Feinberg, "The Man and the Machine: How Trump Wields Twitter as His Greatest Political Weapon," *The Hill*, March 15, 2017, http://thehill.com/blogs/pundits-blog/the-administration/324001-the-man-and-the-machine-how-twitter-became-trumps.

140. Mathew Ingram and Pete Vernon, "The 140-Character President," *Columbia Journalism Review* 56, no. 2 (2017): 76–81.

141. "Trump's 'Spygate' Is a 'Diversion Tactic': Senator Flake," Reuters, May 27, 2018, https://www.reuters.com/article/us-usa-trump-russia-flake/trumps-spygate-is-a-diversion-tactic-enator-flake-idUSKCN1IS0OQ.

142. Peter Beinart, "Why Trump Is Accusing Obama of Wiretapping," *The Atlantic*, March 7, 2017, https://www.theatlantic.com/politics/archive/2017/03/why-trump-is-accusing-obama-of-wiretapping/518793/; "Timeline of Mueller Probe of Trump Campaign and Russia," Reuters, April 10, 2018, https://www.reuters.com/article/us-usa-trump-russia-timeline/timeline-of-mueller-probe-of-trump-campaign-and-russia-idUSKBN1HH395.

143. Molly Ball and Tessa Berenson, "Donald Trump's Campaign to Discredit the Russia Probe May Be Working; It's Also Damaging American Democracy," *Time*, June 8, 2018, https://time.com/5304206/donald-trump-discredit-mueller-investigation/.

144. ABC, CBS, CNN, NBC, *New York Times*, *Washington Post* (from Trump Twitter Archive).

145. Steven Clayman et al., "When Does the Watchdog Bark?" *American Sociological Review* 72, no. 1 (2007): 23–41.

146. John Mueller, "Presidential Popularity from Truman to Johnson," *American Political Science Review* 64, no. 1 (1970): 18–34.

147. Leslie Gelb and Jeanne-Paloma Zelmati, "Mission Not Accomplished," *Democracy: A Journal of Ideas*, no. 13 (Summer 2009), http://www.democracyjournal.org/13/6686.php?page=all. For a comprehensive analysis of the media coverage and public opinion leading up to the Iraq War, see Stanley Feldman, Leonie Huddy, and George Marcus, *Going to War in Iraq: When Citizens and the Press Matter* (Chicago: University of Chicago Press, 2015).

148. Paul Farhi, "At the Times, a Scoop Deferred," *Washington Post*, December 17, 2005, A.7.

149. Julie Hirschfeld Davis and Matthew Rosenberg, "With False Claims, Trump Attacks Media on Turnout and Intelligence Rift," *New York Times*, January 21, 2017, https://www.nytimes.com/2017/01/21/us/politics/trump-white-house-briefing-inauguration-crowd-size.html, A.1.

150. "Donald Trump's File," PolitiFact, http://www.politifact.com/personalities/donald-trump/; "Barack Obama's File," PolitiFact, http://www.politifact.com/personalities/barack-obama/.

151. As quoted in Adrienne LaFrance, "What Happens When the President Is a Publisher, Too?" *The Atlantic*, March 21, 2017, https://www.theatlantic.com/technology/archive/2017/03/the-pundit-president/520251/.

13

Public Opinion

WHEN PRESIDENTS COMMUNICATE directly with the public, or when they disseminate messages through the media, they inevitably confront public judgment. The unending flow of public opinion polls, some of which are undertaken by the White House, reminds presidents where their power ultimately comes from. Citizens determine who shall occupy the office; and depending upon their assessments of the president's performance, they subsequently determine whether this person shall remain. The public's views also weigh heavily upon the legislators, judges, and bureaucrats who must intermittently decide whether to assist, ignore, or oppose a president—for in various ways, they too are beholden to a public that can either remove them from office or punish them politically for violating their trust.

As in any democracy, state power ultimately flows from the consent of the governed. If we are to understand the powers vested in the institutional presidency, then, we must take stock of the governed—its evaluations of presidents, the forces and considerations that undergird its opinions, and the president's persistent efforts to secure its approval.

13.1 Foundations of Public Opinion

For much of the last seventy years or so, political scientists have devoted a good deal of their energies toward documenting the woeful political ignorance of average Americans. A 1960 study found that Americans were blithely unaware of the contents of their Constitution and had trouble articulating the underlying principles of democracy.[1] Shortly thereafter, in an especially influential article, Philip Converse described Americans as fundamentally confused about the most basic facts of politics: how their government functions, how to decide what issues they support or oppose, and what ideologies like liberalism and conservatism mean.[2] Converse encountered citizens who declared themselves strong proponents of one party while admitting that they didn't know what the party stood for. Emblematic of a broader problem, one man called himself a socialist while simultaneously asserting that private enterprise should solve most problems.

Subsequent studies have corroborated many of Converse's findings. One such study indicated that large numbers of Americans could not name the Chief Justice of the United

States.[3] Still others found that about two-thirds of Americans thought that the basic creed of Marxism—"from each according to his ability, to each according to his need"—appears in the U.S. Constitution.[4] And a 2019 poll found that more than one-fifth of U.S. adults could not name a single one of the three branches of government.[5]

For all the snickering that these survey findings elicit from people who study politics for a living, it would be a mistake to conclude that political ignorance translates to political incoherence. In fact, the U.S. public has definite opinions about what is going on in Washington, and when aggregated, public opinion on all manner of issues reveals remarkable consistencies.[6] Americans do not arrive at their own opinions randomly. Rather, when asked questions about policy or the presidency, they draw on information and experiences that are top of mind, some of which—such as which party they belong to—are relatively constant and others—such as their perceptions about the current economy—are more volatile. By examining these deliberations, we can begin to clarify why some presidents enjoy systematically higher **approval ratings** than others and why, by extension, the political landscape inherited by some presidents is amicable whereas for others it is altogether foreboding.

13.1.1 Party Membership

Perhaps unsurprisingly, voters' support for the president depends upon the party with which they identify. Democrats overwhelmingly approve of Democratic presidents, Republicans overwhelmingly approve of Republican presidents, but across party lines public support for the president rapidly dwindles.

These basic differences define public support for every president in the modern era. As figure 13.1 makes clear, though, the magnitude of these differences appears to be increasing. For every president between Harry Truman and Jimmy Carter, average levels of support among co-partisans and the opposition party differed by no more than 35 percentage points. Under Bill Clinton, however, these differences jumped to 50 percentage points; and they have increased steadily for every president since—topping out at 75 percentage points under Donald Trump.

The differences documented in figure 13.1 are remarkably durable not just across presidents but also within each presidency. Throughout his four years in office, overall approval of Donald Trump fluctuated by just 9 percentage points, from a low of 36 to a high of 45 percent support.[7] (This range is smaller than any president in the history of modern polling, which began in the 1930s.) Moreover, the partisan divide under Trump was unprecedented. Among Republicans, Trump left office with an 82 percent approval. Among Democrats? Just 4 percent. This 78-point partisan gap is the largest recorded in presidential history—and part of a larger trend. Increasingly so over time, the two parties have become entrenched, refusing to change their opinions about the candidates they send to the White House. (This polarization among the public mirrors that of Congress; see chapter 8 for a discussion on party polarization in Congress).

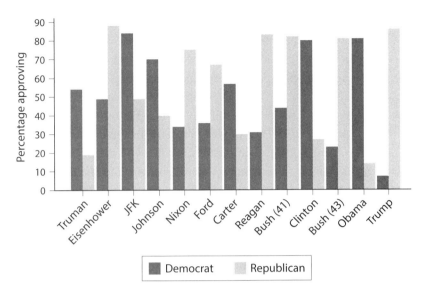

FIGURE 13.1. Partisans' support for the president. Co-partisans routinely register higher approval ratings for the president than do supporters of the opposition party. These differences in average approval ratings, moreover, have only increased, reaching historically high levels under the Trump presidency. *Source:* Presidential Job Approval Center, Gallup, 2021.

13.1.2 *Issue Positions*

For decades, political scientists have investigated the relevance of issue positions for public opinion regarding the president.[8] In a classic public opinion study, Paul Lazarsfeld and his colleagues surveyed a representative sample of American adults about their support for unions before the 1948 presidential election. They then asked these same respondents which presidential candidate they intended to support on Election Day. In doing so, Lazarsfeld found that about 60 percent of Americans who believed unions "are doing a fine job" planned to vote for the Democratic candidate, Harry Truman, as compared to less than 30 percent of those who believed that the country would be "better off without any labor unions at all." On the basis of this and other findings, Lazarsfeld concluded, "An impending defeat for the Democratic Party was staved off by refocusing attention on the socioeconomic concerns which had originally played such a large role in building that party's majority in the 1930s."[9] Issue positions, it would seem, loom large in public evaluations of presidential candidates.

But not so fast. From the simple correlation that Lazarsfeld observed, it is impossible to know whether voters' beliefs about policy issues informed their choice of candidates or if voters merely inferred their issue positions on the basis of signals sent by their preferred candidate. What is unclear here is not whether issues and candidate evaluations are related. They clearly are. Rather, the lingering ambiguity concerns how they are related. And there is reason to believe that the causal arrow points in exactly the opposite direction as Lazarsfeld presumed.

In an important book titled *Follow the Leader*, Gabriel Lenz presents the results of a series of studies that clarify the appropriate causal interpretation about issues and candidate choice.[10] In his surveys of public opinion, Lenz tracked the same people over time and across various upheavals like political campaigns, wars, and natural or man-made disasters. In doing so, Lenz was able to identify whether politicians follow shifts in public opinion or whether, instead, they induce shifts in public opinion.

Lenz's findings do not endorse any single interpretation. On the one hand, he shows that the public does update its evaluations of candidates on the basis of their performance in office. For example, voters became more approving of President George H. W. Bush when they were persuaded that he successfully executed the Persian Gulf War—as opposed to their prior approval of the president determining how they felt about his performance during the war. When it comes to issue positions, however, things look quite different. Lenz finds next to no evidence that individuals shift their votes on the basis of whether politicians' policy stances match their own. To the contrary, Lenz actually finds the reverse pattern. When supporters of a given politician learn that politician's stance on an issue, they come to support that stance, regardless of their prior views on the matter.*

13.1.3 Political Elites

The president is the single most influential political figure in the country. Even so, other elites, such as prominent members of Congress, outspoken governors, and senior party leaders can shape the way the public evaluates the president's job performance. Many political scientists, in fact, argue that presidential evaluations have less to do with specific events and more to do with how elites discuss them publicly.

According to political scientist John Zaller, opinion surveys reflect citizens' recent exposure to elites, which nearly always occur through the media.[11] Like Zaller, political scientist Richard Brody recognizes that public opinion is not a given quantity but instead is constituted and revised by elites.[12] According to Brody, the public defers to "political opinion leaders"—congressional elites, other elected officials, certain members of the press—to guide their assessments of the president at nearly every turn.[13]

If Zaller and Brody are right, public opinions about the president are highly malleable, subject to change over time and contexts. For many issues, it is easy to see why that might be the case. Most members of the public do not directly experience the consequences of

---

*Lenz finds that, rather than adjusting their support for the parties accordingly, those who approved of Bush in 1991 became more conservative by 1992, while those who disapproved became more liberal. Specifically, Lenz finds Bush supporters became about 22 points more conservative (on a hundred-point scale) after learning that Republican politicians were more conservative. For other work with similar findings, see Donald P. Green, Bradley Palmquist, and Eric Schickler, *Partisan Hearts and Minds: Political Parties and the Social Identities of Voters* (New Haven: Yale University Press, 2002).

actions taken by the president. In order for an issue to even be on the public's radar, elites must speak about it, and the media must relay their views to the broader public.[14]

By way of example, consider how reactions by political elites in the aftermath of Hurricane Katrina affected George W. Bush's approval ratings.[15] More than two days before Katrina hit Louisiana on August 29, 2005, the National Weather Service and National Hurricane Center had announced that the city of New Orleans would experience "unprecedented" damage from the storm. As it turned out, Katrina caused nearly 2,000 fatalities and an estimated $81 billion in property damage.[16] It became clear after the storm hit that preparation for the oncoming catastrophe had been woefully inadequate.

The responsibility for responding to this unfolding disaster was split among federal, state, and local agencies, all of which received plenty of criticism in the hurricane's wake. Most elites, though, put the president himself in their crosshairs. When the hurricane struck, Bush was on an extended vacation at his Texas ranch. He was criticized for not returning to DC until more than a day after the hurricane hit. Night after night, political elites, news anchors, and even a few big-name musicians pilloried Bush for nearly every stage of his handling of the storm—from his appointment of a poorly qualified FEMA director beforehand to the inadequate federal response afterward (as discussed in chapter 10).[17] Democrats in particular were quick to blame Bush. Democratic representative and House minority leader Nancy Pelosi called Bush "oblivious, in denial, dangerous."[18]

The scrutiny over Katrina occurred in the midst of a steady decline in Bush's job approval ratings.[19] Many media outlets were quick to report that his approval ratings plunged in the months following the disaster, even though they had been falling pretty consistently since their rally after 9/11 (more on this below). Nonetheless, the president's image as a "strong and decisive leader," typically one of Bush's greatest assets, took a big hit after Katrina.[20] Bush's reputation as an effective manager of the government suffered as well.[21]

The relevance of political elites extends well beyond the public's evaluation of the president during times of crisis. It also helps explain the so-called honeymoon period, when presidents first take office (see chapter 8).[22] During these periods, elite supporters reliably heap all sorts of praise upon the newly elected president, while opponents usually keep their complaints to themselves. Taking its cue from such elites, the public registers high levels of support for the president. As their terms progress, though, elite discourse turns negative, the honeymoon period draws to a close, and presidential approval ratings slip.

When evaluating the relevance of political elites for mass public opinion, it's worth keeping in mind two important caveats. First, political elites both follow and lead public opinion. Knowing that the public stands squarely in the president's corner during the honeymoon period, political elites—particularly those who must worry about their own electoral fortunes—temper their criticisms. We also must remember that presidents can combat the views expressed by political elites. Rather than sit idly by, they can take the offensive, dispute opponents' claims, and steer the national conversation toward issues that better serve their interests.

13.1.4 Economic Evaluations

The public views the president in light of the domestic economy.[23] Whether or not they did anything meaningful to actually cause them, presidents are held accountable for everything from recessions and depressions to booms and busts, the rate of economic growth, the performance of the stock market, unemployment and inflation rates, the government deficit, and the trade deficit.

For all sorts of reasons, the actual performance of the U.S. economy does not depend upon the White House. To begin with, the Constitution grants Congress, not the president, "the power of the purse." Congress has final say over fiscal policy, and the Federal Reserve Board, an independent agency established by law in 1912, sets monetary policy.[24] Factors associated with globalization, meanwhile, further diminish the president's command over the domestic economy.[25]

Still, most empirical studies find that inflation and unemployment drive approval ratings.[26] Some of these effects are larger than others: for instance, one study finds that an increase of 10 percent in the Consumer Price Index (which tracks inflation by measuring the change in price of an array of household goods and services) accounts for a 1.5 percent drop in average approval. The same 10 percent change in unemployment, however, has the effect of depressing approval ratings by 13 percent.[27]

In addition to inflation and unemployment, some scholars have added market volatility to the mix of economic considerations that bear upon a president's job approval rating. According to at least one research team, however, the observed relationship does not correspond with what one might expect based on the larger economic literature.[28] Rather than supporting presidents during times of economic calm and opposing them during times of relative tumult, these scholars argue, the public tends to support a president when markets are in flux. The approval ratings of Clinton and George W. Bush, in particular, closely tracked the Chicago Board Options Exchange's Volatility Index, a standard benchmark of economic uncertainty.

Other scholarship moves past the relatively simple correlations between objective economic indicators and presidential approval ratings to examine how *perceptions* of economic conditions, rather than the conditions themselves, affect public evaluations of the president. Consider, for example, the public's attitudes toward trade relations between the United States and Canada versus its attitude toward trade relations between the United States and other countries. In the 1990s, the U.S. trade deficit with Japan had negative effects on Clinton's approval ratings, whereas a similar imbalance with Canada had no effect. The sheer volume of negative media coverage and harsh elite rhetoric regarding Japan, including comments by Clinton himself, help explain the difference. As one study concludes, "media coverage serves to 'subjectify' the objective economy."[29]

Furthermore, surveys regularly suggest that the public views the economy through distinctly partisan lenses. A week before the 2016 election, for example, three-quarters of Republicans thought the economy was getting worse. Just one week after the election, however, a sudden plurality of Republicans thought it was getting better.[30] During this same period, with political fortunes turned against them, Democrats' perceptions of the economy dropped precipitously. A good portion of these differences may be ascribed to partisan cheerleading, as survey respondents seek to portray their party in the best possible light.[31] Even so, the sheer magnitude of these swings suggests that at least some Americans reason from their partisan affiliations when trying to discern economic realities.

Long-standing debates also persist about the time frames that undergird public evaluation of the president's economic performance. A substantial body of work argues that citizens, both when voting and when evaluating the president, focus on the president's past economic performance. Other research, however, holds that come Election Day, the public evaluates the president according to its expectations about the future performance of the economy.[32] Anticipating economic growth, the public will stand behind an incumbent president, but when an economic downturn is expected, the electorate will look more kindly upon a challenger.

When evaluating the president, different constituents may assign greater importance to different economic indicators. Republicans, for instance, may be generally more inflation-averse, while Democrats may be more unemployment-averse.[33] If trade-offs between these indicators exist, then presidents invariably court the approval of some citizens just as they incur the wrath of others.[34]

13.2 The Shape of Public Opinion

If public opinion really does flow from multiple foundations—rather than the unpredictable whimsies of American voters—we would expect it to follow clear and consistent patterns. And when it comes to the president, this is precisely what we observe. Typically, the public registers the highest approval ratings of presidents early in their terms; and over the course of their time in office, presidents confront an increasingly skeptical—and sometimes downright oppositional—public. Day-to-day changes in approval ratings tend to be modest. If half the public expresses approval of the president on any given Tuesday, half the public is also likely to back the president come Wednesday. Occasionally, however, events intercede that are so threatening to the nation's identity and security that the public's views of the presidents are upended overnight.

13.2.1 General Decline

Since telephone surveys began in the 1930s, public opinion polls have shown that presidents are usually at the peak of their popularity when they first take office. Fresh off of an electoral victory and brimming with promise, presidents enter the White House with great fanfare. As surely as colors fade from sun-washed family photos, however, the perceived vitality of newly elected presidents dissipates over time.

Figure 13.2 tracks approval ratings for every president since Harry Truman. Most—though not all—presidents enjoy their highest approval ratings early in their terms and their lowest approval ratings in the waning months of their administrations. For some

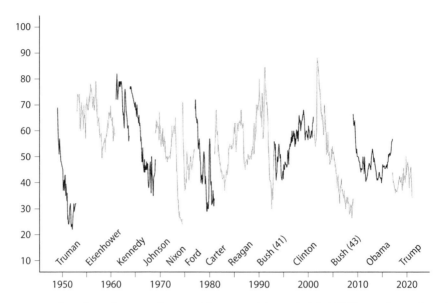

FIGURE 13.2. Presidential approval ratings, Truman to Trump. With Bill Clinton being the sole exception, every president in the modern era left office with a demonstrably lower approval rating than when they started. *Source:* The American Presidency Project, UC Santa Barbara, 2021.

presidents, such as Truman, Ford, Johnson, and Obama, the drop was immediate and precipitous, while for others, such as Nixon and George H. W. Bush, the drop came later in their terms. But with just one or two exceptions—Clinton standing out among them— all of these presidents experienced a steady decline in approval ratings during significant portions of their time in office.

To explain these trends, political scientists offer two explanations, which, interestingly, rest upon almost exactly opposite assumptions. According to one line of thinking, presidential approval ratings decline over time because presidents predictably disappoint their supporters. As Paul Brace and Barbara Hinkley argue, presidents are caught in a "cycle of deflating expectations."[35] Presidential elections invariably create enormous expectations for an incoming new administration, and with them a measure of goodwill. Having spent months on the campaign trail promising a new course and a brighter future for Americans, however, presidents nearly always stumble on the realities of policymaking: members of Congress block their legislative efforts, the bureaucracy proves wayward and recalcitrant, judges deny basic sources of presidential authority, and scandals big and small sap time and energy from governance. Collectively, such forces in our politics make it virtually impossible for any president to fulfill basic campaign promises. Under this first explanation, then, rising disapproval is born of presidential failure and disappointment.

Under the second explanation, however, disapproval arises out of presidential success. The basic storyline of what some scholars call the "coalition of the minorities" runs as follows: at the start of a president's term, Americans tend to rally behind presidents they hardly know, and they read commitments that align with their own preferences into vague presidential pronouncements. When presidents take office and begin making decisions, however, they invariably alienate certain groups of supporters, and with each subsequent action and decision the alienated groups grow in number. Disapproval, then, is born of actions taken and policies successfully enacted.

Both of these explanations have their problems. If the first is right, then those presidents who manage to overcome political obstacles and advance a meaningful policy agenda should maintain their high approval ratings. The data, however, do not appear to bear this out. As discussed in chapter 8, Lyndon Johnson registered the most impressive legislative achievements of any modern president, overseeing such landmark enactments as the 1964 Civil Rights Act, the 1965 Voting Rights Act, Medicare, and Medicaid, the expansion of welfare programs, and much more besides. Yet achievements did not inoculate him from the political fallout of the Vietnam War, which convinced Johnson not to seek reelection in 1968 at a time when his approval ratings were significantly lower than when he began his term. More recently, Barack Obama's first two years in office saw impressive legislative accomplishments including the American Recovery and Reinvestment Act, the Affordable Care Act, the bailout of Chrysler and General Motors, an end to the war in Iraq, and the Dodd-Frank financial reform bill, delivering on much of his campaign agenda. Still, his party was "trounced" in the 2010 midterms, which were broadly interpreted as a renunciation of the first-term president.

The second argument, meanwhile, appears incomplete. That accomplishments breed discontent helps explain why the base of support would shift over the course of a president's time in office. But unless presidential decisions yield more losers than winners—and there is no reason to assume that they do—then it is not at all clear why policy achievements should steadily erode a president's approval ratings.

13.2.2 Rally Effects

Though the general trajectory of a president's approval rating is downward, a curious thing happens in the aftermath of certain crises. Rather than blaming the commander in chief for failing to protect the nation's security, the public rallies in support. The attendant spike in the president's approval ratings may be temporary, and as we shall see, its appearance is not assured. But since the advent of modern polling, a **rally-around-the-flag** phenomenon has constituted an enduring feature of the public-opinion landscape.

John Mueller was first to recognize and then empirically evaluate the short-term boost in popularity a president receives in the immediate aftermath of military interventions and other foreign crises.[36] Since Mueller's groundbreaking work in the 1970s, a number of studies have attempted to document the prevalence of rally effects. Their results vary widely. Canvassing a thirty-year span of American history, one study identified forty-one crises that yielded a mean change in the president's approval rating of just 1.4 percent. But if the sample is limited to crises that received broad media attention, the magnitude of rally effects approached 10 percent.[37] Looking at more than a hundred major uses of force by

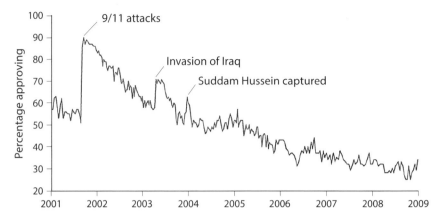

FIGURE 13.3. Anatomy of a rally effect. In the modern era of polling, no event induced a larger or more abrupt change in the president's approval ratings than did the terrorist attacks that occurred on September 11, 2001. Bush's approval rating peaked near the end of September 2001. Other, smaller rally effects occurred after the invasion of Iraq and the capture of Saddam Hussein. *Source:* "Presidential Approval Ratings—George W. Bush," Gallup, www.gallup.com/poll /116500/presidential-approval-ratings-george-bush.aspx.

the United States between 1950 and 1984, the authors of another study found an average change of *zero* percent in presidential approval ratings, leading them to debate not just the significance but the very existence of the rally effect.[38]

Much of the doubt cast on the existence of rally effects, however, was erased following George W. Bush's unprecedented spike in approval ratings following the attacks on September 11, 2001. The post-9/11 rally was the single biggest approval boost in recorded U.S. history. Just days after the attacks, George W. Bush reached not only his personal highest job approval rating as president but also the highest of any president since modern polling began. Figure 13.3 shows Bush's job approval ratings for his two terms in office, including the dramatic rise after 9/11 and the decline that followed.[39]

Overall figures, however, mask interesting partisan differences within rally effects. Take a look at figure 13.4, which tracks Bush's approval ratings among Republicans, Democrats, and Independents.[40] While all three reached similar heights for the initial 9/11 rally, the size of the spike and the rate of decline differ drastically among them. In the three days preceding the attacks, 87 percent of Republicans, 44 percent of Independents, and 27 percent of Democrats approved of the way Bush was handling his job as president. Three days later, 95 percent of Republicans, 84 percent of Independents, and 78 percent of Democrats approved. Democrats and Independents plainly contributed a great deal more to the president's rally: where approval ratings among Republicans jumped just eight points, approval catapulted by forty points among Independents and a remarkable fifty-one points among Democrats.

Democrats and Independents, however, were also the first to abandon the president. Roughly a year and a half after the September 11 attacks, Republican support held strong

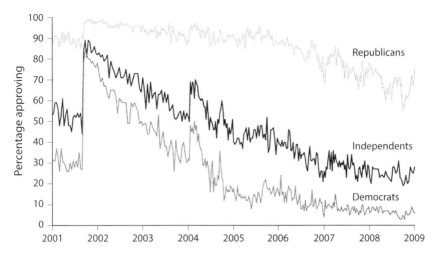

FIGURE 13.4. Rallies by party. The events of September 11, 2001, and after boosted President Bush's approval ratings among all Americans. The fallout, though, created very different trajectories for Democrats, Republicans, and Independents. *Source:* "Presidential Approval Ratings—George W. Bush," Gallup, http://www.gallup.com/poll/116500/presidential -approval-ratings-george-bush.aspx.

in the 90 percent range, while support among Independents dropped to 50 percent and among Democrats returned to pre-attack levels, hovering around 26 percent.

Though more muted, rally effects are also evident during significant foreign crises overseen by other modern presidents. By the end of the Cuban Missile Crisis, John F. Kennedy's approval rating had jumped 13 percentage points. In the aftermath of "Operation Desert Storm," a military coalition of nations to repel Saddam Hussein's Iraq from the recently invaded Kuwait, president George H. W. Bush's approval rating jumped to 89 percent.[41] As routinely happens, though, these gains quickly evaporated and the public approval ratings of both of these presidents rather promptly returned to their pre-crisis levels.

In the face of a crisis or an attack on the nation, why does an otherwise divided public promptly unite behind the president? The answer has little to do with the president's actual performance in office. Bush's approval rating jumped long before he did anything of consequence as a result of the 9/11 attacks. Some political scientists, therefore, attribute rally effects to the activation of otherwise latent patriotic sentiment: crises increase the awareness of national identity and cause citizens to flock to the president, the symbol of the nation as a whole, a kind of "living flag."[42] In this regard, it is noteworthy that rally effects uniquely affect the president. Members of Congress and other elected officials seldom experience comparable boosts in their job approval ratings.

Yet another school of thought draws our attention to opinion leadership. As we discussed earlier in the chapter, when elites rally behind the president, the public can be expected to follow suit.[43] This relationship may be one of either cause or effect—that is, elites may anticipate the public's support or they may actually participate in its creation. The core prediction, though, is much the same: in the aftermath of major crises, the public will unite behind the president as long as political elites do the same.

Thinking Institutionally: Leadership Styles and Public Presentations

The foundations of public opinion point toward the overriding significance of structural factors. As Americans, though, we like to think that we know our presidents—not just for the policies they advance or the messages they craft but for the people they are. This belief is both distinctly odd (since few of us will actually meet or build a relationship with a president) and eminently understandable (since the president's voice and face regularly come into our homes and influence our conversations with colleagues, friends, and family).

How presidents present themselves to the American public—the values they espouse, the personalities they project—amounts to a great deal more than just show. Their behavior determines, at a most basic level, the nature of each president's relationship with the public and media. We do not merely approve or disapprove of presidents; we tend to like or dislike them, and the intensity of our affection or disdain very much depends upon the people we imagine them to be.

A good deal of scholarship attempts to make sense of the various leadership styles and personality traits that individual presidents display before the American public. One of the most famous researchers in this area is James Barber, who in the early 1970s made quite a name for himself by predicting Nixon's downfall on the basis of his personality traits. Barber, though, wanted to do more than just offer idle observations about a president then in office. By developing a typology of presidential personalities, Barber sought to organize our thinking about all presidents.

To this end, Barber emphasized three key components of the image that presidents present to the media and public:

1. *Character*, which is largely synonymous with personality.
2. *Worldview*, by which Barber meant "primary, politically relevant beliefs, particularly . . . conceptions of social causality, human nature, and the central moral conflicts of the time."
3. *Style*, or the president's "habitual way of performing three political roles: rhetoric, personal relations, and homework."

If you can figure out how presidents rate in these three areas, Barber insisted, you will have a strong basis for predicting not only what the public and media will think of them but also their performance in office.[44]

Barber offered distinctly personal explanations for the origins of these traits. The personalities of presidents, argued Barber, took shape long before they assumed office.

Character was forged during childhood, worldview during adolescence, and style during adulthood, particularly at the moment of a future president's first political success. Before an elected president moves into the White House, Barber posited, scholars should have all the materials they need to foretell what kind of leader he or she will be.

Barber's typology may or may not support meaningful predictions about executive politics. To be sure, plenty of scholars harbor doubts about his claims. Leadership styles and modes of public presentation, after all, are not mere matters of psychology or personal biography: rather, they are cultivated and strategically deployed with an eye toward the institutional and historical contexts in which presidents work. For example, whether presidents depict themselves as oppositional or consensual varies according to the partisan composition of Congress and the judiciary, and whether presidents express an intense or relaxed demeanor depends upon the state of domestic and international affairs.

Few scholars have paid more attention to historical forces that shape presidential leadership styles than Stephen Skowronek. According to Skowronek, the posture that a president assumes in office, that is, the "terms of political engagement he projects," derives from the individual's unique place in history.[45] This place in history, in turn, depends upon whether presidents are affiliated with or opposed to a dominant political regime that is either weak or strong.

When affiliated with a regime that is strong, Skowronek argued, presidents have the luxury of appearing open-minded and receptive to competing claims. But when affiliated with a regime that is on the decline, as George W. Bush was throughout his time in office, presidents must work assiduously to stave off opposition and maintain support within the governing coalition. As a result, Bush assumed a posture of what Skowronek called "leadership by definition." At every turn, Bush emphasized that he, and he alone, was the nation's president, and that being president put him in charge. To do otherwise, Bush recognized, would court political disaster, as the remnants of the Reagan Revolution to which Bush was allied continued to wither and fray.

In Skowronek's analysis, it is not altogether clear whether styles and postures are pre-selected or actively formulated—that is, whether history chooses the leader or the leader chooses history. It is possible that the Republican Party first and then the nation as a whole elected Bush precisely because he exhibited the leadership qualities needed for his time in office. Just as plausibly, Bush may have adapted his modes of public presentation in order to meet the particular challenges that he, his party, and his nation faced. In either case, however, the determinants of presidential leadership extend well beyond the individual in office. The person we think we know in the White House, according to Skowronek, and about whom we harbor so many opinions, is very much a product of their historical—not to mention *institutional*—context.

13.3 Taking Stock of Public Opinion

Using the above material as a guide, presidents have a reliable understanding of the forces that shape public opinion and the general trends they face during their time in office. At any given moment, they can assume higher approval among members of their own party, and they may be able to guess which policy stances are broadly popular with the public. But this is not nearly enough to lead a nation. As we will see, past presidents have demanded faster and more reliable means of gathering Americans' opinions, often with an eye toward the next election.

13.3.1 White House Polls

In their public rhetoric, presidents regularly disavow the utility of polling in their daily operations and insist, instead, that their administrations are built on conviction and principle. George W. Bush even campaigned on a promise to disregard public opinion, proclaiming, "I really don't care what polls and focus groups say. What I care about is doing what I think is right."[46] This may have been so, but all modern presidents—Bush included—have sought political guidance throughout their tenures in office, and a good deal of this guidance comes from large-sample, scientific polls.

For much of American history, presidents relied on informal canvasses and newspaper clippings to track public sentiment. Franklin Roosevelt, however, was the first president to use mass survey techniques.[47] Unlike news coverage, which was either devoid of opinion or emblematic of only a fraction of the national population, mass polls provided a snapshot of what all Americans were thinking. Still, it would be several decades before scientific polls became a mainstay of the White House. Though Roosevelt and Eisenhower saw their value, President Truman dismissed them as distracting and unhelpful.

With the election of President John F. Kennedy, the White House's "public opinion apparatus" finally took shape. Having paid for extensive polling during the 1960 campaign, Kennedy entered the presidency with close relationships with national pollsters. Collectively, both he and Lyndon Johnson conducted more than two hundred private polls from 1958 to 1968—often "piggybacking" off surveys that were already being paid for by pollsters' other clients. Johnson was the first to assemble an internal polling team of six members of the Executive Office of the President, overseen by the chief of staff, to administer and advise the president on public opinion.

When President Nixon took office in 1969, he quickly expanded the White House polling capacity, telling his staff to find out "what moves and concerns the average guy."[48] As his chief of staff later expressed in an internal memo, "the President feels very strongly that the most important thing we have to do is find out what people are thinking on the issues."[49] Not only did Nixon increase the number of private polls conducted—to 233 in his first term—he also ended the practice of "piggybacking" off existing surveys. Sponsoring his own polls with money from the Republican National Committee, Nixon's team decided for themselves the wording, timing, and quality of questions submitted to the public.

Roughly half of the White House's polls were conducted via telephone, satisfying Nixon's request that his staff "set up a procedure whereby polls can be taken on immediate issues so that we can get an immediate response."[50] All told, Nixon spent over $1 million on polling in his first term.

With this increased capacity came a shift in subject matter for White House polls. While past presidents had viewed polls as extensions of their campaigns—often asking respondents exclusively about their views of the administration—Johnson and Nixon were far more likely to administer polls during non-election years and to cover subjects that ranged widely. The Nixon White House, for example, used polls to test opinions on Vietnam, taxes, admission of China to the United Nations, busing, and more. These topics were top of mind not just for staffers but for the president himself, who demanded that his polling advisors identify policies "where the president and his team 'aren't getting credit.'"[51]

No longer, then, was White House polling a matter of personal taste for presidents, with some using it and others setting it aside. After Nixon, Presidents Ford through Reagan employed about thirty staff members who "routinely included poll data within their communications."[52] Reagan, for example, spent roughly $1.6 million in his first term on polls, a quarter of which concerned Americans' opinions about policy issues.[53]

And today, presidents and their staff continue to poll the American public. Recent presidents also consult outside pollsters, such as Harris and Gallup organizations, and their administrations work with the national political parties to commission polls, run focus groups, and perform media analyses. During the first two years of George W. Bush's term—despite the president's stated aversion to polls—the Republican National Committee spent $3.1 million gathering the public's opinions.[54] With each additional month Bush spent in office, the RNC's polling budget grew by about four thousand dollars—suggesting not only that Bush took a liking to the White House's polling apparatus but that he saw fit to expand it. Presidents since Bush have acted similarly: in a single month of Obama's 2012 reelection campaign, for example, the Democratic National Committee spent more than a million dollars on polls.[55] There are no signs of any of this changing. Presidents dedicate extensive resources to polls not simply because the capacity exists but because of the many incentives they have to, at the very least, understand what voters are thinking.

13.3.2 *Putting Polls (and the Public) to Use*

Presidents have ample reason to heed the results of White House polls. Should they take positions that upset large segments of the American public, presidents risk a backlash at the next election. If they run for reelection, they can expect a vigorous challenge by an opposition inveighing against an "unaccountable" president who scorns the views of average Americans. If they do not stand for reelection themselves, their party can expect to face an opposition set upon "taking their country back." Public opinion matters because elections matter.

Public opinion also has important implications for the fate of a president's policy agenda. The political debates that precede legislative activity of the sort documented in

FIGURE 13.5. Targeting key legislators. Democratic senator Joe Manchin from West Virginia was the key vote in passing Joe Biden's $1.9 trillion stimulus package in 2021. In the lead-up to the vote, and to Manchin's considerable annoyance, Vice President Kamala Harris appeared on local television stations in his state to sell the recovery plan. *Source:* WSAZ News Channel 3, https://www.wsaz.com/2021 /01/28/exclusive-interview-with-vice-president-kamala-harris/.

chapter 8 serve as a testing ground for each of the sides waging battle. Presidents and their surrogates direct their arguments not just to the members of Congress who will ultimately vote but also to their constituents (figure 13.5). Similarly, members of Congress do everything they can to sway public opinion to their side. Whoever wins this battle for the public's support can tip the balance with a handful of undecided legislators and thus, for particularly close votes, determine whether a bill ultimately becomes law.

Presidents may use polls when deciding which policy issues to tackle. One study, for example, found that the Reagan administration acted in line with public opinion on major domestic issues more than 70 percent of the time.[56] Having set an agenda, polling results further influence how presidents talk about different issues.[57] The Reagan administration (once again) relied upon message testing on foreign policy speeches in the late 1980s: in these sessions, fifty adults recorded their reactions to the delivery, style, and message of several speeches. The analysis of their reactions, done by pollster Richard Wirthlin and his firm, informed future speeches.[58] Similarly, Clinton and his political advisor Dick Morris used polling to test different ways of responding to the Monica Lewinsky scandal.[59]

Public opinion also can affect the contents of the specific policies that presidents ultimately promote. Recognizing widespread opposition to sweeping policy change, presidents may scale back their ambitions. Alternatively, at the sight of an especially restive American public, otherwise cautious presidents may become emboldened to seek major policy reform. For example, polling during the budget debates of the Clinton administration, which are discussed further in chapter 14, consistently demonstrated the public's tendency to blame Republicans in Congress rather than the president for failure to reach an agreement. Such findings encouraged the president to stand firm in his demands of Congress.

Public opinion, therefore, can powerfully shape the bounds of political discourse and the doings of government. Given regular elections and opportunities for citizens to intervene in ongoing policy debates, politicians have ample reason to heed the public's counsel. As British historian and politician James Bryce recognized more than a century ago, "Nowhere is the rule of public opinion so complete as in America."[60] This is every bit as true today. Public support, in one form or another, is a virtual prerequisite for many kinds of policy change.

13.3.3 *The Measured Significance of Public Opinion*

So public opinion clearly matters for presidential governance. The public, however, is hardly a monolithic entity. Citizens are not of a piece. Rather, they distinguish themselves by their partisan commitments, their education levels, their ethnic and racial backgrounds, the attention they give to politics, their involvement in political campaigns, and, perhaps most importantly, their political organization and power. The relevant question, then, is not whether the public shapes the agenda that presidents pursue or the particular positions that presidents assume. Rather, the question is which publics matter most.

In *Who Governs? Presidents, Public Opinion, and Manipulation*, political scientists James Druckman and Lawrence Jacobs investigated the relevance of public opinion for the American presidency. Culling private polling data and official presidential statements from multiple administrations, Druckman and Jacobs were able to evaluate not just whether public opinion corresponded with executive position-taking but whose opinions corresponded most closely. Their conclusions are startling. Presidents, Druckman and Jacobs claim, do not take in the whole of public opinion. They do not seek to represent the views of all citizens equitably and comprehensively. Rather, presidents focus their attention on a relatively small population of politically powerful groups. As the authors put it, "The reality is that on many issues politicians, and presidents in particular, are responsive, but less to general public opinion, and more to party activists, philosophical sympathizers, favored demographic groups, and allied lobbyists and donors."[61] In the pantheon of politically relevant groups, highly organized businesses, trade organizations, and the affluent, as well as active religious and ideological groups, weigh most heavily on presidents.

This isn't to say that the general public fades entirely into the background. Under certain conditions, Druckman and Jacobs recognize, the views of the larger public can weigh on presidents. When the public holds especially strong opinions about an issue, for instance, presidents may have no choice but to abide by its views. Likewise, the appeals of other politicians and the occurrence of real-world events may direct the president's attention to other, more expansive segments of the American polity. During the Vietnam War, for instance, events on the ground and in the jungle prevented presidents from either deflecting the attention of certain publics or changing the opinions of others. Instead, Johnson and Nixon were forced to accept the opinions of much of the American public as given, and adjust accordingly.

Presidential statements, of course, may resemble public opinion either because presidents are informing the public, the public is informing presidents, or both. Much of Druckman and Jacobs's book investigates the first possibility, illuminating the strategies that presidents employ to shape public opinion and deploy its most politically relevant members in the service of some shared cause. In various ways, Druckman and Jacobs show, presidents can raise the salience of certain issues and distract attention away from others. Depending on the circumstances, presidents may choose to inform, activate, manipulate, and even deceive the American public.

As we discuss at further length later in this chapter, presidents are not receptacles of public opinion. Rather, presidents devote considerable resources to shaping it. But public opinion is not merely the product of presidential manipulation. Both the specific views that different sectors hold and the general ideological tenor of public opinion weigh on presidents. And when presidents attempt to remake public opinion, they don't start from scratch. Rather, they devote considerable resources to assessing what the public already thinks about a range of issues—and based on what they learn, they then choose which elements of their policy agenda to act upon and how best to do so. In the case of the Reagan administration, Druckman and Jacobs found, presidential advisors calibrated the "president's public positions to reflect the White House's subgroup polling [that] contributed to the formation of a new and broader conservative coalition."[62] And so do other presidential administrations for their chosen cause. Each takes stock of the views of different segments of the American public, assesses their relevance for policy change, reflects on their capacity for manipulation, and then plots a path forward.

Historical Transformations: From "Institutionalized" to "Individualized" Pluralism

In November 2012—just weeks after Election Day—President Obama was back on the road. Holding a series of rallies in influential swing states, Obama sought to energize his voters in the ongoing tax policy debate. To avoid falling off a "fiscal cliff," the president argued, taxes would have to be raised on the wealthiest 2 percent of earners. Congressional Republicans wanted instead to close various tax loopholes. But in the words of one Democratic representative, "If Republicans refuse to move, if they refuse to cooperate, then you've got to be willing to engage the American public."[63] During visits to small businesses in Pennsylvania, and in meetings with middle-class families in the White House, Obama urged his supporters to share videos on Facebook and Twitter about the necessity of taxing the rich.

Obama, of course, did not invent this strategy of engaging the public. For decades, presidents had enlisted their supporters in policy fights, as Richard Nixon did repeatedly to promote his actions in Vietnam, and as Jimmy Carter did in his four televised addresses on the energy crisis. As discussed in chapter 12, President Reagan also repeatedly used televised national appeals to his advantage.

Though commonplace today, **public appeals** were not always a mainstay of the American presidency. Before the twentieth century, presidential speeches were usually addressed not to the public but to other politicians and government officials. Despite

Theodore Roosevelt's invention of the president's "bully pulpit," policy-based public appeals were rare and usually unsuccessful.[64] But the modern era ushered in an unmistakable upward trend in presidents' public appeals. Whereas in the early 1930s President Hoover averaged only fifteen days of domestic, non-election travel per year, when many of those appeals are delivered, President George H. W. Bush averaged fifty-five.[65]

As with any phenomenon that stretches out over decades, the proliferation of public presidential appeals has multiple origins. It would not have been possible, for instance, without new technologies and changing cultural norms that fed an appetite for a more visible presidency.

Equally important, however, are changes in the institutional environment within which presidents work. In an influential book, *Going Public: New Strategies of Presidential Leadership*, Samuel Kernell offered a cogent institutional explanation of contemporary presidential appeals. Kernell emphasized a transformation in government, beginning in the early 1970s, from a system of *institutionalized* to *individualized* pluralism. Under institutionalized pluralism, Kernell explained, "political elites, and for the most part only elites, matter[ed]."[66] Insulated from public opinion, presidents could afford only to confer with a handful of leaders in Congress. Moreover, presidents were mainly chosen by autonomous delegates to party conventions and relied on party machines for election. This structure of strong institutional actors lent a degree of order to the deliberations that ensued.

In the 1970s, however, parties weakened and interest groups flourished, yielding a system of individualized pluralism—that is, an abundance of political actors with whom presidents would have to negotiate. In addition, Kernell explained, a series of reforms changed the way delegates were selected for national conventions, which opened up the nominating process to a wider electorate and transformed the field of viable candidates. Voters, not the party machines, would be the dominant force in the nomination of presidential candidates. Successful presidential hopefuls, beginning with Jimmy Carter, gained popularity by emphasizing their connection to ordinary voters and promising to prioritize the public over Washington elites.[67]

In an increasingly unstable and diffuse political environment, successive presidents attempted to forge a direct relationship with the public and thereby apply pressure on legislators to cooperate in making public policy. This trend cannot be explained by individual preferences: neither Gerald Ford nor Jimmy Carter took much pleasure in courting the goodwill of either the media or the public. George H. W. Bush famously hated press conferences, and his son, George W. Bush, held much of the media in low regard. Rather, changes in the larger political environment thrust presidents, again and again, before cameras, microphones, and audiences. Forced to adapt, the institutional presidency had less to do with private bargaining and more to do with public relations.

13.4 Influencing Public Opinion

As a result of the larger institutional changes described in this chapter's Historical Transformations feature, presidents directly engage the public with regular frequency. What, though, are they hoping to accomplish? And how successful have they been? Here we consider two possibilities: (1) changing public support for certain policies and (2) brandishing their credentials as president. The evidence on the former, it turns out, is reasonably thin; on the latter, though, public appeals pay dividends.

13.4.1 Evaluations of Presidential Policies

Since Kernell's groundbreaking work, political scientists have attempted to empirically assess the effects of presidential appeals on both public opinion and legislative action. Legislative triumphs by the two Roosevelts and Truman notwithstanding, most research speaks to their limited effects.

According to most systematic studies, public appeals rarely change the content of public opinion.[68] Some of these studies hold that presidential endorsements of specific policies do not resonate broadly because only a narrow portion of the American public actually listens to them; others emphasize that appeals are transmitted by an increasingly critical and politicized media. Under both accounts, presidents do not hold much sway over what most citizens think about health care reform, gun rights, or immigration policy.

Presidency scholar George Edwards, more than most, has cast doubt on the political efficacy of presidential appeals.[69] According to Edwards, presidents who wage extended public campaigns to manufacture public support for a policy objective are on a fool's errand. Rather than trying to change public opinion, strategic presidents leverage preexisting public support for an issue—that is, rather than attempting to transform the polity, these presidents take what already exists and make the most of it.

Edwards's views, however, are not universally held. According to B. Dan Wood, a presidential speech can alter public understandings of certain issues.[70] How presidents talk about the economy can bear on the decisions that citizens make in their everyday lives and produce tangible effects on consumer spending, business investment, and interest rates. Other scholars have offered an even more hopeful assessment of the president's ability to use public appeals to advance policy. By linking presidential appeals to budgetary outlays over the past several decades, Brandice Canes-Wrone shows how such appeals, under well-specified conditions, augment presidential influence. In the aftermath of a direct public appeal, final budgetary allotments across a wide range of policy domains more closely approximate the president's preferences; when presidents remain out of public view, on the other hand, their ability to influence financial appropriations tends to dissipate.[71]

Fueling these scholarly disagreements are formidable challenges to conducting empirical research. Presidents, after all, do not issue appeals at random: rather, strategic deliberations inform a president's decision about whether or not to stand before the American public on behalf of a new policy initiative. It can therefore be extremely difficult to discern causation—are changes in public opinion due to an appeal? Or do expectations about public opinion changes affect the president's decision to issue an appeal in the first place? Nor do presidents make public appeals in a vacuum: presidents join the chorus of voices weighing in on a policy debate, and parsing the separate effects of these voices can be incredibly difficult. For these reasons, many political scientists turn to survey and lab experiments, which allow for the clear manipulation of messages and messengers.[72] Whether these insights illuminate the actual effects of actual presidential appeals, however, is also open to dispute.

13.4.2 Evaluations of Presidents

When presidents issue public appeals, public opinions about specific policies are not all that hang in the balance. The public also updates its views about the individual standing at the center of these public rituals—the president, his character, and his fitness for office. With public appeals, presidents can improve their own approval ratings by projecting strong images of leadership.

The criteria by which Americans evaluate presidents derive, in no small part, from the distinctive role presidents occupy in American political life. Beyond the formal powers they wield and the public attention they attract, presidents also embody all that is distinctly American—the nation's interests, to be sure, but also its values, culture, and heritage. In presidents, many Americans see reflections of their nation's character; they see the vestiges of the Protestant work ethic and Judeo-Christian values; and they see all that they are as a people, and all that they hope to become.* It is no accident that nearly all presidents in American history have been married men. All, too, have been Christian. And with just one exception, all have been Caucasian.†

Though meeting each of these criteria, Trump assumed office with definite liabilities. A political novice and perennial showman, Trump regularly behaved in ways that many viewed as unbecoming of a president. His late-night tweets, personal feuds, crude language,

---

* As the demographics of the U.S. population change, our nation's character also changes. In the years to come, it is possible that the United States may see female presidents, presidents of other religions and cultural backgrounds, Hispanic presidents, etc.

† The one exception, of course, is Barack Obama, whose race and stubborn lies and misperceptions about his religion attracted considerable amounts of scrutiny and criticism. When Obama was first elected in 2008, political scientists began to document the backlash against the nation's first Black president and representations of his "otherness." Quite abruptly, racial considerations infused public understanding of the president and the policies he espoused. Obama's presidency, meanwhile, was dogged by a "birther" movement fueled by a group of Americans who insisted—all evidence to the contrary—that Obama was born in Kenya, making him ineligible to serve in the White House. Very little of this backlash had to do with Obama's performance in office. Rather, it emanated from personal traits of the man himself—the distinctive name he held, his multicultural background, and the color of his skin. For more on this topic, see Michael Tesler and David O. Sears, *Obama's Race: The 2008 Election and the Dream of a Post-Racial America*, Chicago Studies in American Politics (Chicago: University of Chicago Press, 2010).

and propensity not only to criticize but to demean his political opponents made for conduct, many thought, that was unfit for a president. Former secretary of labor and liberal pundit Robert Reich excoriated the president this way: "Let me just say with all due respect, Mr. Trump, you are president-elect of the United States, you are looking and acting as if you are mean and petty, thin-skinned and vindictive. Stop this."[73]

Like all presidents, however, Trump had one thing going for him: the public rituals surrounding the office he occupied. The carefully choreographed addresses that presidents deliver are rather explicitly meant to evoke a sense of veneration. These public displays are not meant merely to attract support for the president and his policies but ultimately to shape the terms by which Americans think about their president—to encourage them, that is, to see him or her as legitimately presidential. The pomp and circumstance that accompany a president's inaugural address, State of the Union speech, and Rose Garden ceremonies leave the distinct impression that the president, as the nation's undisputed leader, deserves the respect, if not the deference, of its citizenry.[74]

To take stock of the effects of such public performances, my colleagues and I administered a set of surveys around the time of Trump's first inaugural address in January 2017. We recruited a large Internet panel of respondents and queried them about whether they thought that Trump would perform the duties of the office of the presidency, govern in the national interest, bring the country together after a divisive election, earn the respect of those who didn't vote for him, and the like. We then told half of them, randomly selected, to watch Trump's speech while the other half of them were told to watch the Food Channel.[75]

After verifying that significant portions of both groups did as they were told, we then resurveyed the same respondents shortly after Trump's speech. The results were striking: members of both groups were more likely to affirm various statements about Trump's presidential qualities in the second survey than they were in the first. The differences for the treatment group, however, were significantly larger than those for the control group. Watching Trump deliver a speech from a platform draped in American flags, with past presidents and dignitaries in the background, with the Chief Justice of the Supreme Court administering the Oath of Office, and with hundreds of thousands of supporters in attendance, did not merely endear Americans to their president—it convinced them that he exhibited the qualities necessary to be president; it made him appear presidential.

Conclusion

The American public does not simply register its opinions about the president—and the presidency—once every four years on Election Day and then blithely return to its everyday activities. Not at all. Throughout their tenures in office, presidents are subject to the public's judgment, which is informed by partisan concerns, issue positions, elite opinions, and economic evaluations. Though their popularity is occasionally buoyed by a foreign crisis or other rallying event, presidents can expect to encounter a growingly skeptical public over time.

Recognizing the importance of public support for winning the next election and for improving the viability of their legislative initiatives, presidents do their best to influence it. On stages small and large, they issue public appeals intended to shape what and how people think about them and their politics. The returns from such efforts, though, are decidedly mixed. While there is some evidence that public appeals can increase the salience of some issue domains, many studies show that presidents have a remarkably difficult time influencing the contents of public opinion about issue positions. Rather than fundamentally altering public opinion about health care or the tax code, these appeals instead may shape how the public understands presidents themselves—the extent to which they are seen as fulfilling their duties in office and upholding national ideals.

Key Terms

approval ratings   **public appeals**
rally-around-the-flag

Questions for Discussion

1. How do citizens formulate judgments about the president's performance in office? What implications do such judgments have for presidential behavior?
2. Figure 13.5 discusses Vice President Kamala Harris's efforts to sway a senator's vote by touting the importance of a key legislative item in an interview in the senator's home state of West Virginia. Was this good strategy? Is it significant that the *vice* president, not the president, participated in the interview?
3. Are presidents' leadership styles determined more by their distinctive worldviews and personalities or by the institutional contexts in which they work and their place in history?
4. In the lead-up to the 2016 presidential primaries, Republican contender Donald Trump made a point of singling out different segments of the American population (e.g., undocumented residents) and his competitors (e.g., Jeb Bush) for special ridicule. What does Trump's behavior say about his personal leadership qualities? What does it say about the structural challenges he had to overcome in pursuit of the party nomination in a crowded field of contestants? And as political observers, how might we go about distinguishing between these two sorts of influences?
5. It's 2031, and climate change is devastating the United States. The American public is skeptical of the president's sweeping $13 trillion infrastructure and climate policy package. Congressional leaders are pursuing a narrow, $4 trillion compromise package, but the Senate minority is threatening to filibuster the deal. Two hurricanes pummel Florida just three weeks apart in the worst natural disaster in recorded American history. The public rallies behind the president, whose approval ratings rocket up to over 70 percent. Should she use her (temporary) popularity in support of an ambitious package that some congressional leaders oppose, or should she attempt to rally public support for the compromise deal?

Suggested Readings

Azari, Julia. *Delivering the People's Message: The Changing Politics of the Presidential Mandate*. Ithaca: Cornell University Press, 2014.

Brody, Richard. *Assessing the President: The Media, Elite Opinion, and Public Support*. Stanford: Stanford University Press, 1991.

Canes-Wrone, Brandice. *Who Leads Whom?: Presidents, Policy, and the Public*. Chicago: University of Chicago Press, 2005.

Druckman, James, and Lawrence Jacobs. *Who Governs?: Presidents, Public Opinion, and Manipulation*. Chicago: University of Chicago Press, 2015.

Edwards, George C. *On Deaf Ears: The Limits of the Bully Pulpit*. New Haven: Yale University Press, 2003.

Kernell, Samuel. *Going Public: New Strategies of Presidential Leadership*. 4th ed. Washington, DC: Congressional Quarterly Press, 2007.

Shogan, Colleen. *The Moral Rhetoric of American Presidents*. College Station: Texas A&M University Press, 2006.

Stuckey, Mary. *Defining Americans: The Presidency and National Identity*. Lawrence: University Press of Kansas, 2004.

Wood, B. Dan. *The Myth of Presidential Representation*. New York: Cambridge University Press, 2009.

Notes

1. James W. Prothro and Charles M. Grigg, "Fundamental Principles of Democracy," *Journal of Politics* 22, no. 2 (1960): 276–94.

2. Philip Converse, "The Nature of Belief Systems in Mass Publics," in *Ideology and Discontent*, ed. David Apter (New York: Free Press, 1964).

3. James L. Gibson and Gregory Caldeira, *Citizens, Courts and Confirmation* (Princeton: Princeton University Press, 2009).

4. "Americans Don't Know Their Constitution," Columbia Law Survey, May 2002, http://www2.law .columbia.edu/news/surveys/survey_constitution/.

5. See "Americans' Civic Knowledge Increases but Still Has a Long Way to Go," Annenberg Public Policy Center, University of Pennsylvania, September 13, 2019, https://www.asc.upenn.edu/news-events/news/appc -civics-survey-2019.

6. Benjamin Page and Robert Shapiro, *The Rational Public: Fifty Years of Trends in Americans' Policy Preferences* (Chicago: University of Chicago Press, 1992).

7. Presidential Job Approval Center, Gallup, https://news.gallup.com/interactives/185273/presidential -job-approval-center.aspx.

8. Bernard Berelson, Paul F. Lazarsfeld, and William N. McPhee, *Voting: A Study of Opinion Formation in a Presidential Campaign* (Chicago: University of Chicago Press, 1954), 270.

9. Berelson, Lazarsfeld, and McPhee, *Voting*, 270.

10. Gabriel Lenz, *Follow the Leader? How Voters Respond to Politicians' Policy and Performance* (Chicago: University of Chicago Press, 2012).

11. John R. Zaller, *The Nature and Origins of Mass Opinion* (New York: Cambridge University Press, 1992).

12. Zaller, *Nature and Origins of Mass Opinion*, 50.

13. Richard A. Brody, *Assessing the President: The Media, Elite Opinion, and Public Support* (Stanford: Stanford University Press, 1991).

14. Brody, *Assessing the President*, 9.

15. Paul Gronke and Brian Newman, "Public Evaluations of Presidents," in *The Oxford Handbook of the American Presidency*, ed. George C. Edwards and William G. Howell (New York: Oxford University Press, 2009), 244.

16. Spencer S. Hsu, "Katrina Report Spreads Blame," *Washington Post*, February 12, 2006, A.1.

17. Sabrina Siddiqui, "A Third of Louisiana Republicans Blame Obama for Hurricane Katrina Response under Bush," *Huffington Post*, August 21, 2013, http://www.huffingtonpost.com/2013/08/21/obama-hurricane -katrina_n_3790612.html.

18. Jeffrey M. Jones, "Bush Gets Negative Views for Handling the Hurricane," Gallup, September 16, 2005, http://www.gallup.com/poll/18550/bush-gets-negative-views-handling-hurricane.aspx.

19. "Democrats Blame 'Oblivious' Bush," *Washington Times*, September 7, 2005, https://www .washingtontimes.com/news/2005/sep/7/20050907-115306-9784r/.

20. Siddiqui, "Louisiana Republicans Blame Obama."

21. Jones, "Bush Gets Negative Views." But see Frank Newport, "Little Impact of Katrina on Bush's Overall Job Ratings," Gallup, August 29, 2006, http://www.gallup.com/poll/24283/little-impact-katrina-bushs-overall -job-ratings.aspx.

22. Brody, *Assessing the President*, 29.

23. Helmut Norpoth, quoted in Michael Berlemann and Soren Enkelmann, "The Economic Determinants of U.S. Presidential Approval: A Survey," *European Journal of Political Economy* 36 (2014): 41–54.

24. Dennis M. Simon, "Public Expectations of the President," in *The Oxford Handbook of the American Presidency*, ed. George C. Edwards and William G. Howell (New York: Oxford University Press, 2009), 146.

25. Gronke and Newman, "Public Evaluations of Presidents," 236.

26. Berlemann and Enkelmann, "Economic Determinants."

27. Paul Gronke and John Brehm, "History, Heterogeneity, and Presidential Approval: A Modified ARCH Approach," *Electoral Studies* 21 (2002): 425–52.

28. Joe Schwartz, Scott Hoover, and Adam Schwartz, "The Political Advantage of a Volatile Market: The Relationship between Presidential Popularity and the 'Investor Fear Gauge,'" *Journal of Public Affairs* 8, no. 3 (2008): 195–207.

29. Barry C. Burden and Anthony Mughan, "The International Economy and Presidential Approval," *Public Opinion Quarterly* 67, no. 4 (2003): 555–78.

30. Philip Bump, "Your View of the Economy Depends on Whether Your Party Controls the White House," *Washington Post*, November 7, 2017, https://www.washingtonpost.com/news/politics/wp/2017/11/07/your -view-of-the-economy-depends-on-whether-your-party-controls-the-white-house/.

31. For more on this point, see John G. Bullock, Alan S. Gerber, Seth J. Hill, and Gregory A. Huber, "Partisan Bias in Factual Beliefs about Politics," *Quarterly Journal of Political Science*, no. 4 (2015): 519–78.

32. Michael B. MacKuen, Robert S. Erikson, and James A. Stimson, "Peasants or Bankers? The American Electorate and the U.S. Economy," *American Political Science Review* 86, no. 3 (1992): 597–611.

33. Douglas A. Hibbs, "The Dynamics of Political Support for American Presidents among Occupational and Partisan Groups," *American Journal of Political Science* 26, no. 2 (1982): 312–32.

34. James N. Druckman and Justin W. Holmes, "Does Presidential Rhetoric Matter? Priming and Presidential Approval," *Presidential Studies Quarterly* 34, no. 4 (2004): 755–78.

35. Paul Brace and Barbara Hinckley, "The Structure of Presidential Approval: Constraints within and across Presidencies," *Journal of Politics* 53, no. 4 (1991): 993–1017.

36. John E. Mueller, "Presidential Popularity from Truman to Johnson," *American Political Science Review* 64, no. 1 (1970): 18–34.

37. John R. Oneal and Anna Lillian Bryan, "The Rally 'Round the Flag Effect in U.S. Foreign Policy Crises, 1950–1985," *Political Behavior* 17, no. 4 (1995): 379–401.

38. Bradley Lian and John R. Oneal, "Presidents, the Use of Military Force, and Public Opinion," *Journal of Conflict Resolution* 37, no. 2 (1993): 277–300.

39. "Presidential Approval Ratings—George W. Bush," Gallup, http://www.gallup.com/poll/116500 /presidential-approval-ratings-george-bush.aspx#1.

40. "Presidential Approval Ratings—George W. Bush," Gallup, http://www.gallup.com/poll/116500 /presidential-approval-ratings-george-bush.aspx#2.

41. The American Presidency Project, UC Santa Barbara, 2021.

42. Bartholomew H. Sparrow, "Who Speaks for the People? The President, the Press, and Public Opinion in the United States," *Presidential Studies Quarterly* 38, no. 4 (2008): 578–92.

43. Richard A. Brody and Catherine R. Shapiro, "The Rally Phenomenon in Public Opinion," in Richard A. Brody, *Assessing the President: The Media, Elite Opinion, and Public Support* (Stanford: Stanford University Press, 1991); Marc J. Hetherington and Michael Nelson, "Anatomy of a Rally Effect," *PS: Political Science and Politics* 36, no. 1 (2003): 37–42.

44. James David Barber, *The Presidential Character: Predicting Performance in the White House*, 4th ed. (New York: Pearson, 2008).

45. Stephen Skowronek, *Presidential Leadership in Political Time: Reprise and Reappraisal* (Lawrence: University Press of Kansas, 2008), 65; Berelson, Lazarsfeld, and McPhee, *Voting*, 270.

46. Kathryn Dunn Tenpas, "Words vs. Deeds: President George W. Bush and Polling," *Brookings Review* 21, no. 3 (2003): 33.

47. Lawrence R. Jacobs and Robert Y. Shapiro, "The Rise of Presidential Polling: The Nixon White House in Historical Perspective," *Public Opinion Quarterly* 59, no. 2 (1995): 163–95.

48. Jacobs and Shapiro, "The Rise of Presidential Polling," 165.

49. Jacobs and Shapiro, "The Rise of Presidential Polling," 174.

50. Jacobs and Shapiro, "The Rise of Presidential Polling," 173.

51. Jacobs and Shapiro, "The Rise of Presidential Polling," 189.

52. Diane J. Heith, "Staffing the White House Public Opinion Apparatus, 1969–1988," *Public Opinion Quarterly* 62, no. 2 (1998): 165–89.

53. Lawrence R. Jacobs and Melanie Burns, "The Second Face of the Public Presidency: Presidential Polling and the Shift from Policy to Personality Polling," *Presidential Studies Quarterly* 34, no. 3 (2004): 536–56.

54. Kathryn Dunn Tenpas, "Words vs. Deeds: President George W. Bush and Polling," Brookings Institution, June 1, 2003, https://www.brookings.edu/articles/words-vs-deeds-president-george-w-bush-and-polling/.

55. Byron Tau, "DNC Drops $1.1 Million on Polling," CNN, March 21, 2012, https://www.politico.com/blogs/politico44/2012/03/dnc-drops-11-million-on-polling-118189.

56. Shoon Kathleen Murray, "Private Polls and Presidential Policymaking: Reagan as a Facilitator of Change," *Public Opinion Quarterly* 70, no. 4 (2006): 477–98.

57. For more on Clinton's "crafted talk" strategy, where public opinion was used to inform approaches to policy issues and their presentation, see Lawrence R. Jacobs and Robert Y. Shapiro, *Politicians Don't Pander: Political Manipulation and the Loss of Democratic Responsiveness* (Chicago: University of Chicago Press, 2000).

58. Robert Y. Shapiro and Lawrence R. Jacobs, "'Source Material': Presidents and Polling: Politicians, Pandering, and the Study of Democratic Responsiveness," *Presidential Studies Quarterly* 31, no. 1 (2001): 162–63.

59. Diane J. Heith, "The Polls: Polling for a Defense: The White House Public Opinion Apparatus and the Clinton Impeachment," *Presidential Studies Quarterly* 30, no. 4 (2000): 783–90.

60. Viscount James Bryce, *The American Commonwealth*, with an introduction by Gary L. McDowell, 2 vols. (Indianapolis: Liberty Fund, 1995), 68.

61. James Druckman and Lawrence Jacobs, *Who Governs? Presidents, Public Opinion, and Manipulation* (Chicago: University of Chicago Press, 2015), 12.

62. Druckman and Jacobs, *Who Governs?* 72.

63. Michael D. Shear, "Trying to Turn Obama Voters into Tax Allies," *New York Times*, November 26, 2012, A.19.

64. James W. Ceaser et al., "The Rise of the Rhetorical Presidency," *Presidential Studies Quarterly* 11, no. 2 (1981): 158–171, 159.

65. Samuel Kernell, *Going Public: New Strategies of Presidential Leadership*, 4th ed. (Washington, DC: Congressional Quarterly Press, 2007), 105.

66. Kernell, *Going Public*, 12.

67. Kernell, *Going Public*, 48–58. For a similar account, see Theodore J. Lowi, *The Personal President: Power Invested, Promise Unfulfilled* (Ithaca: Cornell University Press, 1985), 83.

68. For a review of this literature, see George C. Edwards, "Leading the Public," in *The Oxford Handbook of the American Presidency*, ed. George C. Edwards and William G. Howell (New York: Oxford University Press, 2009).

69. George C. Edwards, *On Deaf Ears: The Limits of the Bully Pulpit* (New Haven: Yale University Press, 2003); George C. Edwards, *The Strategic President: Persuasion and Opportunity in Presidential Leadership* (Princeton: Princeton University Press, 2003).

70. B. Dan Wood, *The Politics of Economic Leadership: The Causes and Consequences of Presidential Rhetoric on the Economy* (Princeton: Princeton University Press, 2007).

71. Brandice Canes-Wrone, *Who Leads Whom? Presidents, Policy, and the Public* (Chicago: University of Chicago Press, 2005).

72. For a general review, see Kim Fridkin and Patrick Kenney, "Laboratory Experiments in American Political Behavior," in *The Oxford Handbook of American Elections and Behavior*, ed. Jan Leighley (New York: Oxford University Press, 2009).

73. Matt Ferner, "Robert Reich Pleads with Trump to Quit It with the 'Petty' and 'Vindictive' Tweets," *Huffington Post*, December 7, 2016, http://www.huffingtonpost.com/entry/robert-reich-trump-twitter-cnn_us_5848bcefe4b064104145b4a2.

74. Bruce Miroff, *Presidents on Political Ground: Leaders in Action and What They Face* (Lawrence: University Press of Kansas, 2016).

75. Additional information about the survey's design and the protocols associated with its implementation can be found in William G. Howell, Ethan Porter, and Thomas Wood, "Rethinking Public Appeals: Performance, Public Opinion, and Donald J. Trump," *Journal of Political Institutions and Political Economy* 1, no. 1 (2020): 137–58.

PART V

Policy

14

Domestic Policy

AS THE SOLE ELECTED representative of the entire country, presidents have a distinctly national outlook on domestic policy. Because of an abiding need for power, presidents take a hard stand on issues involving delegation and executive authority, whereas members of Congress trade away their own authority.* Finally, out of concern for their **presidential legacy**, presidents take a longer view of policy than do most elected officials.

These three qualities of the institutional presidency—national outlook, interest in power, and concern for legacy—are all apparent in presidents' domestic policymaking. These qualities contribute to presidents' policy choices and the strategies they adopt to pursue them. Moreover, they encourage presidents to advance objectives often not shared by Congress or the courts. In these ways, the structural features of the institutional presidency affect the ways in which presidents engage in domestic policy debates—what they choose to emphasize, how they frame policy disputes, and what alternatives they consider.

This chapter is not organized around domestic policy, per se. It is not meant to serve as a primer on the kinds of domestic issues with which presidents must grapple nor a guide through the institutional channels through which domestic policy is crafted. Rather, this chapter uses domestic policy to highlight essential features of the institutional presidency. Each of the three sections, therefore, begins by briefly characterizing one of the distinct perspectives of the institutional presidency. Having done so, it then presents a case study that illuminates the relevance of the institutional perspective for the president's handling of domestic policy.

14.1 A National Outlook

As a nation, we elect hundreds of thousands of people to local and state offices, and hundreds more to Congress, but we have the opportunity to select only one ticket (a president and vice president) that serves a national constituency. It is no accident, then, that the president, more than any other elected official, has a **national outlook** on policy—that is, the president prioritizes the implications of policy change for the country as a whole. When we are

---

* See section 8.5.1 for a discussion on delegations of authority by Congress.

looking for leadership on national problems and for someone to articulate and defend a distinctly national agenda, the president stands apart.

To be sure, presidents do not always see the nation in its entirety. As they govern, presidents may prioritize some interests over others; as we discuss in this chapter's Thinking Institutionally feature, the structure of presidential elections virtually guarantees as much. But to win their party's nomination, presidential candidates must canvass larger portions of the country than any other elected official and, as they do, they work tirelessly to demonstrate their commitment to represent the country as a whole. When discussing the arcane details of ethanol subsidies with Iowa farmers in the lead-up to the first caucus, therefore, candidates do not automatically promise to take the fight to Washington; while acknowledging local concerns, they go out of their way to reaffirm their commitment to represent the interests of all Americans, not just a select few.

Candidates emphasize their commitment to all Americans, in part, because they anticipate facing voters with different concerns in New Hampshire, South Carolina, and all the other states in the primary process. They recognize that the country as a whole is watching them, that national media outlets are judging them, and that voters—all voters—are trying to figure out whether this individual promises to promote distinctly American values and priorities.

Should they secure their party's nomination, presidential candidates then must weather a general election in which national concerns are raised at every turn. In debates, candidates must demonstrate their knowledge about national and world affairs—from the impact on the domestic economy of trade imbalances with China to the security threats posed by extremist groups throughout the world. On the campaign trail, they make their announcements on stages draped in American flags. The media hounds candidates, not over their plans for their hometowns or home states but over their agenda for the country as a whole. In response, presidential candidates roll out policy briefs with titles like "Prosperity for America's Families" (Gore, 2000); "Our Plan for America: Stronger at Home, Respected in the World" (Kerry and Edwards, 2004); "Change We Can Believe In: Barack Obama's Plan to Renew America's Promise" (Obama, 2008); "Believe in America" (Romney, 2012); "Stronger Together" (Clinton and Kaine, 2016); or "Great Again: How to Fix Our Crippled America" (Trump, 2016).

The motivation to represent national interests becomes even more apparent when the president takes office. Electoral pressures certainly do their part to direct the president's attention toward national affairs, but the job description itself demands this care and commitment from the president. As commander in chief, chief administrator, and head of a party, presidents must oversee agencies and personnel who address the needs and interests of the nation as whole. Immediately, presidents find themselves surrounded by White House Office units such as the **Domestic Policy Council** and the **National Economic Council**—both of which serve to advise the president on the crafting and implementation of national policies. The former council is staffed by experts on issues ranging from education and health to immigration and climate change. The latter develops policies related to the national (and even global) economy. In short, the very structure of the White House encourages a concern for the general welfare of all U.S. citizens.

Depending on the issue, of course, the president may pay more attention to some segments of the population than others. Come hurricane season, the lower eastern seaboard receives special consideration. The Department of Education directs a disproportionate share of federal dollars to poorer school districts. The Occupational Safety and Health Administration (OSHA) regulates some industries in some parts of the country a good deal more closely than others. In all these instances, however, the federal government's actions are justified by reference to a basic principle or objective that applies to the entire nation. In theory, the federal government will—and should—intervene when natural disasters strike, when educational inequities grow too large, and when markets fail. In practice, these efforts can be perverted by all sorts of political pressures, leading some groups to get more than their fair share and others to be subject to rampant discrimination. But the underlying principles that guide the executive branch still pertain to the entire nation.

In the president, therefore, we find the most reliable defender of national interests and objectives that our system of government affords. While parties in Congress make special allowances for certain populations and regions of the country, and while individual legislators can be counted on to lobby for their district's or state's interests, the president, as chief executive, must roll out new programs and policies across the entire country. Having attended to certain portions of it, the president cannot ease back into an armchair and declare the work complete. From start to finish, the president must clarify, define, and execute the federal government's policy obligations nationwide.

Constitutionally, it is the president who reports every year to the American people on the state of the union. Having done so, presidents—particularly modern presidents—offer policy proposals aimed at increasing the national welfare. These policies are cast in national terms, meant to solve national problems, and justified by reference to national concerns.

Even the most banal aspects of the job reinforce the president's obligations to the whole nation. It is the president who phones the winning team of the World Series or Super Bowl, whatever their host city or region. It is the president who, when meeting with foreign dignitaries, presents the face of the country. And it is the president who bestows medals of recognition on national heroes and cultural icons.

In the end, though, the president's preoccupation with national concerns does not derive exclusively from a formal job description or daily schedule. Particularly in the modern age, the president embodies all that the nation stands for and aspires to become. When presidents engage in domestic policy debates, therefore, we can expect them to represent these distinctly national sensibilities amid a cacophony of voices lobbying for some preferred industry, population, or region. To see this, we need look no further than the government's efforts in early 2021 to address the health and economic fallout of a yearlong pandemic.

14.1.1 Case Study: Trillions in Pandemic Relief

In January 2021, nearly a year after the country's first documented case of Covid-19, the United States still had a long way to go before defeating the pandemic. At that point, upwards of 350,000 Americans had lost their lives to the virus, and the daily fatalities were rising at a steep incline. Meanwhile, new case numbers had climbed to 300,000 in a single day.[1] Despite what appeared to be a healthy stock market, housing insecurity was rampant, and a record number of Americans relied on unemployment insurance for their survival.[2] For the second time this century, a Democratic president was elected to govern a nation in crisis.

When Joe Biden ran for president in 2020, he did so with an overarching promise to "restore the soul of America." Note that his promise was not to restore the soul of Delaware, or Florida, or North Carolina. To the contrary, his national outlook was central both to his campaign and to the office he would soon inhabit. Standing before a masked, socially distanced crowd at his inauguration, Biden said, "I pledge this to you: I will be a president for all Americans."[3]

In this particular moment, being a president for "all Americans" meant developing a national strategy to combat the pandemic and revive the economy. On January 14, Biden unveiled the American Rescue Plan—a $1.9 trillion stimulus package to support struggling families and local governments. The proposal included $400 billion to accelerate vaccine distribution and testing, $350 billion in emergency funding to states and localities, and $1 trillion in direct aid to families. In what would be among the most expensive bills in U.S. history, Biden's plan also included funding for reopening schools, extensions to unemployment insurance, and—most popularly—payments of $1,400 directly to American taxpayers.[4]

Seeing that a spending bonanza was underway, interest groups quickly got into the game and demanded that more be done on their behalf.[5] The American Hotel & Lodging Association said that additional support was needed for the leisure and hospitality industry. The American Hospital Association requested more resources for the Provider Relief Fund, which goes to hospitals battling the pandemic. The Association of American Medical Colleges called for additional relief to teaching hospitals and research institutions. Of course, these are worthy causes. But unlike presidents, interest groups have no strong incentive to act sparingly. They seek to advance their own specific causes—even if it means that other groups receive less.

The interest groups found a receptive audience in Congress. Legislators, after all, pride themselves on diverting resources back to their constituencies. So, when revising a $1.9 trillion proposal, they laid claim to resources to fund pet projects to placate powerful interests back home. When the American Rescue Plan entered the House of Representatives, seemingly unrelated projects were added by Democrats: $86 billion to bail out failing pension plans, $3.5 billion for Amtrak, and $4 billion for "socially disadvantaged" farmers and ranchers.[6]

Among the most egregious line items were $1.5 million for a bridge between upstate New York and Canada, and a $140 million extension to San Francisco's public transit system. Both projects were later cut from the bill, but not before near-unanimous Republican criticism. "This is the way Nancy Pelosi gets $140 million for her tunnel of love in Silicon Valley," said one Republican senator, pointing out that the transit system was one of the Speaker's pet projects.[7] As for the New York-Canada bridge, Democrats were quick to argue that it was originally part of a funding request from the Trump administration.

Even after these items were eliminated, however, Republicans maintained that the stimulus was a "blue state bailout" that unfairly advantaged Democratic constituents.[8] In late February, despite little evidence that the local emergency funding systematically privileged blue states,[9] every House Republican voted against the stimulus package. In addition to looking out for their own districts, these legislators were also determined to prevent other districts—which they claimed had mismanaged their budgets—from getting too much.

Were these legitimate concerns about responsible budgeting? Or simply a case of the shoe being on the other foot? Just one year earlier, when crafting the first round of pandemic-related stimulus under the Trump administration, both parties sought funding for special projects unrelated to the crisis. For example, the final version of the $2.2 trillion stimulus contained a provision for the FDA to approve "innovative" sunscreens—benefiting a cosmetics company with operations in Kentucky, home of Republican Senate majority leader Mitch McConnell. Other provisions included special deals for casinos and cherry growers, and a "minimum assistance" rule for states that ensured small states like Vermont would receive a disproportionate share of funds.[10]

"Vermont had a front seat in writing and negotiating this bill," said Senator Patrick Leahy, who represents the state. "I am pleased that Vermont will receive this critical assistance, and know more will need to be done."[11] But there is a thin line between critical assistance and parochial interests—a line both parties crossed. In earlier pandemic relief packages, Democrats secured a massive $1 billion for the Smithsonian Institution, $154 million for the National Gallery of Art, and an additional $40 million "for the necessary expenses" of the Kennedy Center of the Performing Arts in New York.[12] Republicans, meanwhile, scored provisions that benefited businesses based in their districts, including handouts to travel agents and the credit reporting industry. One Republican senator, Richard Shelby, won additional funding for the cleaning of harbors in his home state of Alabama. In the words of one Republican aide, it was "an easy give to Shelby, since he's been wanting it for years and now why not give it to him?"[13]

Nonetheless, when the American Rescue Plan reached the Senate, it passed the evenly divided chamber with a total of zero Republican votes. The final version—signed into law on March 11—was not identical to Biden's original proposal (figure 14.1). Certain provisions, including a $15 minimum wage, were cut. Other provisions were merely trimmed, such as the weekly unemployment insurance, which was reduced from $400 to $300 per week. In the main, however, the legislation matched Biden's vision. The stimulus directed

FIGURE 14.1. Biden signs stimulus bill into law. Copyright 2021 Mandel Ngan. Reproduced by permission of Getty Images.

$1,400 checks to more than 85 percent of American households, and according to one analysis, promised to reduce child poverty by more than half.[14]

For legislators, the stimulus was an opportunity to show local constituents the benefits they had brought home. Their press releases shared similar titles: "O'Halleran Secures First District Priorities in American Rescue Plan," read one.[15] "Congressman Gonzalez Secures $920,367,000 for Schools in Rio Grande Valley from American Rescue Plan," read another.[16] Even some Republicans, despite not having voted for the bill, took to Twitter to promote the funding that had been secured for restaurants and other small businesses in their districts.[17]

And somewhere above the fray was Joe Biden. He, too, sought to publicize his accomplishment—but from his own distinctly national perch. "Without the overwhelming bipartisan support of the American people, this would not have happened," Biden said. "By passing this plan we will have delivered real, tangible results for the American people and their families."[18] Remaining mostly in the background of House and Senate negotiations, Biden was never mired down by the fights over local projects. He focused on national planning and obligations—not to please everyone, nor to provide for narrow interests, but to be a president for all Americans.

Thinking Institutionally: The Particularistic President?

Presidents certainly like to present themselves as the only true stewards of the national welfare. At the nation's founding, George Washington professed that his duty as president was to "overlook all personal, local, and partial considerations" and to "consult only the

substantial and permanent interests of our country" when making policy decisions.[19]
Just how far, though, do such declarations take us in understanding actual presidential
behavior? Does a distinctly national outlook on policy matters really distinguish
presidents from other politicians?

The Particularistic President, written by political scientists Doug Kriner and Andrew
Reeves, answers the question firmly in the negative. According to Kriner and Reeves,
presidents exhibit all of the parochial and particularistic tendencies of legislators—at
least when it comes to budgetary matters and emergency declarations. Presidents have
little choice but to do so, as their and their party's electoral fortunes depend upon it.
The very design of the Electoral College keeps presidential candidates focused on a
handful of competitive states, which explains why their vast campaign war chests are
spent almost exclusively in states like Ohio, Florida, and Pennsylvania.

The victors, however, do not promptly abandon these states once they assume office.
To the contrary, Kriner and Reeves argue, presidents make a point of privileging the
policy concerns of competitive states throughout their tenures. By favoring competitive
states during their first terms, presidents improve their own reelection chances. Even
in their second terms, write Kriner and Reeves, presidents continue to pander to swing
states, knowing that the best way to preserve their legacy achievements is to be succeeded
by a member of the same party.

Presidents have additional institutional incentives to shore up the political party
for which they serve as standard-bearer. As we saw in chapter 8, the president's
ability to advance a policy agenda hinges upon having a large number of co-partisans
within Congress. As a result, Kriner and Reeves note, presidents go out of their
way to attend to the material welfare of those constituents who support their
party the most.

To buttress these claims, Kriner and Reeves present a wide array of evidence
revealing that electorally competitive locales that strongly back the president's party
receive a disproportionate share of federal largesse. They show, for instance, that swing
states receive roughly $250 million more in federal grants each year than do electorally
uncompetitive states. During election years, the estimated differences in geographic
spending patterns increase further still. Counties that strongly supported the president
(or the president's party) during previous elections also reap larger shares of federal
outlays, on average. When such counties are located in swing states during election
years, the federal coffers really open up.

If a truly national outlook on domestic policy requires presidents to assign equal
weight to the welfare of every U.S. citizen, then Kriner and Reeves's evidence would
lead us to conclude that presidents certainly do demonstrate particularistic tendencies.
But this takes things too far. That presidents direct disproportionate shares of federal
outlays to select residents does not mean that presidents and legislators share a common
outlook on policy. Rather, their differences in perspectives may be matters of degree
rather than of kind.

Continued on next page

The most obvious point to recognize is that politics of the sort that Kriner and Reeves consider are not representative of all areas in which presidents exert power. Presidents may have strong institutional incentives for favoring some constituents over others when distributing federal grants and disaster aid, but that does not mean that they exhibit the same favoritism in making decisions on entitlement reform, changes to trade legislation, and foreign policy. Indeed, Kriner and Reeves admit as much. As they put it, "plainly, presidents frequently take a more national view than individual legislators tied to more narrow geographic constituencies." It is only when issues involving the distribution of federal dollars are considered, say Kriner and Reeves, that "universalism routinely gives way to particularism."[20]

Two additional points should be mentioned. The first concerns our ability to discern politicians' preferences and perspectives on the basis of their actions. When presidents attempt to pass items through Congress—budgets very much included—they must offer concessions to its members. The **Office of Legislative Affairs** (OLA), in particular, acts as an intermediary between the two branches and seeks to reconcile the president's agenda with the myriad objectives of Congress members. That we observe presidents directing additional federal outlays to districts and counties that strongly support their party may constitute a nod to the core interests and needs of co-partisans in Congress, whose desires presidents must accommodate, at least in part, if they are to make progress on their policy agenda. Rather than indulging their own tastes for particularism, presidents—and more specifically, the OLA—may simply be placating co-partisans whose electoral fortunes, all agree, hinge upon their ability to redirect federal largesse to their home states and districts.

Second, holding a national perspective does not require presidents to attend to the welfare of each citizen in equal measure. Every deviation from universalism need not imply presidential particularism. To the contrary, presidents may believe that the nation's interests, values, and material well-being require that special attention be given to certain citizens.

To understand this, let's revisit Kriner and Reeves's finding that more federal dollars go to counties and districts that strongly support the president's party. It is possible that this finding does not reflect presidential particularism so much as prior policy commitments. Poor and nonwhite citizens, for instance, tend to vote Democratic, and not coincidentally, Democratic legislators and presidents tend to support policies expressly designed to alleviate poverty and reduce the effects of racial discrimination. That Democratic presidents promote policies that disproportionately benefit Democratic citizens, then, may at least partially represent a shared belief that the nation as a whole has a special obligation to its least advantaged members. As such, what looks like particularism may, in fact, represent a deeper and more refined sense of the larger purposes and priorities of national government.

14.2 Power Considerations

If we have learned anything about presidents thus far, it is that they care deeply about power—about protecting the power they have, acquiring new power whenever possible, and expanding their power in new ways and in new domains. In chapter 4, we surveyed the underlying reasons presidents care so much about power, reasons that centered on a basic mismatch between outsized public expectations and the relatively meager endowments of explicit authority awarded to the president in Article II of the Constitution. In subsequent chapters, we then bore witness to some of the many ways in which presidents seek new sources of power, block the efforts of Congress and the courts to encroach on their power, and assert their power at nearly every turn. When assessing domestic policy debates, we must not forget these essential lessons about the institutional presidency.

Some acts of Congress are transparent in their efforts to curtail presidential power. In the spring of 2014, for example, the House passed a measure that would grant lawmakers the ability to sue the president for not faithfully executing the law. Unsurprisingly, the White House quickly issued a statement that the bill would be vetoed should it find its way to Obama's desk.

Other efforts, however, are more veiled. During the same negotiations in which they debate the details of health, welfare, and crime policy, presidents and legislators haggle over the authority they will have to implement the laws; to clarify and amend key provisions; and to fund, oversee, and redirect the final domestic policy agreement. Where they perceive encroachments on their power, presidents erect obstacles to proposed policy change. As a result, when presidents appear inclined (and able) to block a legislative proposal, Congress can occasionally win them over by salvaging the authority that had been subverted.

For example, when Congress came close to passing the National Aeronautics and Space Administration (NASA) Act in 1958, President Dwight Eisenhower—hardly the archetype of a power-obsessed, imperial president—made his objections known. Though the president supported the idea of a civilian group to oversee the U.S. space program, he feared that Congress's proposal left too little room for White House influence. Specifically, he objected to a proposal that would have made the agency's director accountable to a seven-member advisory board rather than Eisenhower himself.[21] Lyndon Johnson, then the Senate majority leader, found a compromise. Wanting to keep the basic structure of the advisory board in place, Johnson simply asked Eisenhower if he would serve as its chair. Eisenhower gladly accepted. Congress passed the final bill on July 16, 1958, and the president signed it into law two weeks later.

This simple insight helps illuminate other dimensions of domestic policymaking. Presidents look kindly upon policy initiatives that confer new powers and leave intact old ones; and presidents occasionally sign power-enhancing domestic policies that, on their separate policy merits, might otherwise attract a veto. Played out over time, these basic dynamics have important implications for the overall balance of power between Congress and the president. Presidents' singular (albeit instrumental) interest in power distinguishes them from legislators, who can be expected to trade away their longer-term power in order to secure short-run policy gains. As a result, power tends to accrue within the executive branch, just as it vacates the legislative.

14.2.1 Case Study: Budgetary Powers

One of the modern president's more important tools in domestic policymaking is the annual proposal of the federal budget. The president has every reason to seek close control over how the budget is conceived and formulated. As the proposer, the president is also the most visible and influential figure in budget negotiations, particularly during periods of unified government. Congress may have the final say over appropriations, but the president sets the terms of debate when it comes to the budget's basic infrastructure, priorities, and policy commitments.

Such was not always the case. Until the early twentieth century, Congress crafted, debated, and passed its own budgetary proposals. This state of affairs perfectly aligned with the Constitution, which grants Congress the power to levy taxes and decide how government revenues are spent. Nineteenth-century congresses might work alongside the secretary of the treasury, who was viewed as an agent of Congress, rather than of the president; and presidents occasionally objected to specific fiscal policies, such as when Jackson started the "Bank War" over Congress's reauthorization of the Second Bank of the United States.* Nearly always, however, Congress maintained the upper hand when it came to raising and allocating government funds.

Through appropriations, Congress worked to constrain and oversee executive spending, usually by giving detailed instructions to executive agencies about how funds should be spent. This practice persisted, in part, because the federal government in the nineteenth century was a lot smaller than it is today—and so was the budget. Federal spending in 1900 was around $520 million, or about $15 billion in today's dollars.[22] Compare that to 2020, when federal expenditures reached approximately $6.5 trillion.[23]

Budgeting decisions also tended to be uncoordinated, even haphazard, with officials in the executive branch submitting funding requests directly to the numerous congressional committees in charge of appropriations. And with America's entry into World War I, legislators were faced with the largest-ever federal government and a deficit that had reached an all-time high. Calls for institutional reform began to gain traction around the nation's capital; and faced with an increasingly large and complex federal bureaucracy that drained more funds than it took in, Congress and successive presidents sought to devise a better system.[24]

---

*Jackson believed government funds should be deposited in state banks—a feat he accomplished after running through a few different treasury secretaries and finally finding one willing to carry out his plan in defiance of Congress. See Louis Fisher, *Presidential Spending Power* (Princeton: Princeton University Press, 1975), 16.

President Taft helped initiate that discussion in 1910 by establishing a presidential Commission on Economy and Efficiency. Through this commission, Taft hoped to expand the president's role in the budgetary drafting process. At least initially, though, the commission's recommendations made little headway in Congress. The powerful Speaker of the House, Joe Cannon, protested that an increase in the president's budgetary powers would violate the Constitution, declaring, "I think we had better stick pretty close to the Constitution with its division of powers well defined and the taxing power close to the people."[25] Uncharacteristically, Taft did not back down. In 1912, Taft announced his intention to submit an executive budget; Congress responded by explicitly prohibiting staff within the executive branch from authoring budget materials unless they were legally required to do so. Taft told his agency heads to go ahead and draft budgetary provisions anyway, which Congress then ignored.[26]

Long after Taft left office, Congress came around to supporting an executive budget. By 1920, many in Congress agreed that putting the president in charge of coordinating the federal budget would help rationalize and limit federal spending. Accordingly, Congress passed a bill that gave the president the power to propose a budget, but with key stipulations ensuring that Congress retained some control over the drafting process. For one, the proposed Bureau of the Budget, while reporting directly to the president, would be located in the Treasury Department rather than in the president's office. The bill also called for a **General Accounting Office (GAO)** to serve as an independent auditing and investigative agency for all government budgetary matters. Overall, the message of the bill "seemed to be that the budget was an instrument for facilitating congressional business, not for the aggrandizement of presidential power."[27]

Though a forceful advocate of an executive budget, President Wilson nonetheless vetoed the bill. The president was suspicious of the plan for the GAO, which he assumed would be beholden to Congress. The bill stipulated that the comptroller general and assistant comptroller general would be appointed by the president, with Senate confirmation, for a period of fifteen years and that they could only be removed through a concurrent resolution of the House and the Senate. From Wilson's perspective, the comptroller ought to serve exclusively at the pleasure of the president.

A year later, President Harding signed into law the **Budget and Accounting Act**, which resolved the impasse by requiring a resolution from the president in addition to agreement from both chambers of Congress in order to fire the comptroller general (thus, in effect, making it difficult for anyone to get rid of the officeholder). More broadly, the Budget and Accounting Act was designed to reduce spending by placing the budget in the hands of a new cadre of government experts.* But over the longer term, the act's most significant accomplishment was to provide the president with a clear entrée into budgetary politics.

---

*For a few years the new budget system did help to contract government debt. The deficit respite, however, proved short-lived. With the onset of the Great Depression in 1929 and the subsequent massive growth of the federal government, spending more than tripled in the 1930s. See Allen Schick, *The Federal Budget: Politics, Policy, Process*, 3rd ed. (Washington, DC: Brookings Institution, 2007), 16.

A recognition of the president's national outlook on policy also informed Congress's willingness to cede budgetary powers to the president.

In 1939 President Franklin Roosevelt had the Bureau of the Budget (later to be renamed the Office of Management and Budget) transferred from Treasury to the EOP, thus augmenting the president's control over the budget process. Subsequent presidents used the budget process to promote sweeping policy change. President Eisenhower, for instance, used the 1955 budget to launch his New Look program for the Department of Defense, which sought to significantly reduce military spending by relying more heavily on nuclear weapons. President Kennedy viewed the budget as a means to stimulate the economy through increased government expenditures, particularly in the area of defense spending.[28]

By the 1970s, Congress became more resistant to the president's attempts to direct policymaking through the budget. The Vietnam War had siphoned off a large chunk of federal revenues, leaving fewer resources for domestic appropriations and engendering a general mood of distrust toward presidential authority. Moreover, the country was entering a long period of stagflation, wherein consumer prices rose amid an economic recession. Blaming the legislative branch, President Nixon claimed in 1972 that the budget crisis was due to the "hoary and traditional procedure of the Congress, which now permits action on various spending programs as if they were unrelated and independent actions."[29] Congress assented, in theory, to a spending ceiling for fiscal year 1973 but could not agree with the president on the details. Nixon responded by unilaterally slashing funding to federal agencies and programs and refused to use billions of dollars Congress had already appropriated.

In 1974 Congress fought back by passing the Congressional Budget and Impoundment Control Act, which sought to wrest back control of the budgetary process. The act not only prevented the president from rejecting, or *impounding*, allocated funds but also established a system for Congress to devise its own budget via the Congressional Budget Office (CBO)—a counterpart and potential rival to the president's Office of Management and Budget. The president is still expected to submit a budget to Congress, but now Congress possesses the authority and institutional support to generate its own.

That Congress reclaimed some authority, however, does not mean that congressional predominance has been restored. In most years, the president's proposal continues to be the centerpiece of budgetary deliberations in Congress. Presidents, moreover, can veto budgets that they do not like, as President Clinton did in January 1995, a move that led to the shutdown of the federal government. Republicans in Congress had proposed massive cuts to social entitlement programs, which went way beyond anything Clinton was willing to support. Republicans in Congress bore the brunt of the political fallout for the shutdown.

When President George W. Bush assumed office, prior budget surpluses promptly disappeared; spending rose on defense, homeland security, and a new entitlement program for drug coverage for seniors, just as revenues dropped due to an economic contraction and the passage of major tax cuts. With Republican majorities in Congress, Bush was able to exert considerable control over the budgetary process, and not just through his proposal powers. The funds for the wars in Iraq and Afghanistan, for example, came largely from emergency **supplemental appropriations**. Sometimes referred to as *blank checks*, these supplementals are routinely vague and offer few details about how money will be spent. The construction of the embassy in Baghdad and an army reorganization plan were each allocated $5 billion from emergency supplemental appropriations, although neither traditionally were part of an emergency scheme.[30] Supplementals expanded so far as to include things like basic military pay, money to develop combat capabilities, and a naval aircraft for future missions. Further, by classifying some items as part of the "black budget," the president managed to undercut Congress's investigatory powers. These items included intelligence and weapons development, which cost between $26 and $47 billion a year between 2005 and 2008.[31]

For the most part, the long history of presidential involvement in budgetary politics is one of expansion. Successive presidents have repeatedly sought to augment their influence over the federal budgetary process by acquiring new proposal powers, by moving the central administrative apparatus for crafting the proposal into the EOP, by using budgetary proposals as vehicles for staging larger domestic policy initiatives, and by exploiting supplemental appropriations to bypass various sources of congressional opposition.

Occasionally Congress does push back, as it did in the early 1970s and again during President Obama's tenure, through repeated threats to shut down the government. Consistently, though, presidents have entered these fights with one eye on policy consequences and the other on power—both the power they claim today and the power they hope to exercise tomorrow.

Historical Transformations: The President's Economy

We have discussed at length the public's extraordinary expectations put before modern presidents. Nowhere are these expectations more apparent (or oppressive) than in the realm of economic policy. The positive relationship between economic conditions and presidential approval is well known, and many voters evaluate the competence of their president according to the domestic economy's performance. Rather than temper these expectations—or remind voters that unemployment and stock prices are largely beyond the chief executive's control—past presidents have actually *reinforced* the perception that the White House pulls the strings of the economy.

The Employment Act of 1946

In 1946, the United States was undergoing a strenuous transition. Hundreds of thousands of unemployed soldiers were returning from the war, and the manufacturing sector struggled to shift its focus away from the large-scale production of wartime goods. With the nation's political leadership anxious to avoid the prolonged unemployment and inequality that had sparked the rise of fascism and communism overseas, President Truman signed into law the Employment Act of 1946.

Continued on next page

Comparatively, past efforts at reform had given presidents little control over the economy. The president's newfound powers over the budgetary process—described at length in the previous section—were critical steps in what would become a gradual accumulation of authority. The 1939 Reorganization Act, for example, brought the Bureau of the Budget into the EOP and streamlined the executive branch's economic decision-making process. Nonetheless, advancements such as these gave the president insufficient authority to affect nationwide economic outcomes.

The Employment Act was different. It legitimized a major role for the federal government—and particularly the president—in improving the nation's economy during times of both crisis and calm. While the act did not specify economic targets, it compelled the executive to forecast the state of the economy in the coming year and set his own objectives for growth. To assist the policymaking process, it authorized the president to establish advisory boards composed of representatives from government, labor, industry, and agriculture.* Most importantly, by placing the president at the center of these policy efforts, the bill reinforced public expectations that the president would exercise control over the economy. This marked the first time the president was formally recognized as the premier steward of domestic policy.

The notion that the president should mitigate (if not solve) the nation's economic woes would shape the future of the presidency. Successive presidents adapted to and welcomed their role as economic stewards. Some boasted from the campaign trail the positive effects their presidency would have on the economy. One such president was Ronald Reagan.

The Tax Reform Act of 1986

President Reagan made tax reform a cornerstone of his 1984 reelection campaign. Heeding recommendations from the **Council of Economic Advisors**—an EOP agency founded in 1946 to provide economic counsel to the president—Reagan believed that tax cuts could increase the country's growth rate by nearly 10 percent over the coming decade.[32] His objectives were hardly new. Many previous presidents had attempted to change the tax code—by altering rates, curtailing abuses, or closing loopholes favored by special interest groups.[33] It was not until Reagan, however, that a president succeeded in making massive revisions to the nation's tax code. In addition to slashing rates, particularly for top earners, the landmark Tax Reform Act of 1986

---

* For example, in 1953 President Eisenhower created an Advisory Board on Economic Growth and Stability, consisting of senior officials of the executive departments and agencies under the leadership of the chairman of the Council of Economic Advisers. This group was directed to "[achieve] a mutual understanding for coordinated action of various departments and agencies to accomplish the objectives of the Employment Act of 1946." See "Report to the President on the Activities of the Council of Economic Advisors during 1953" (Washington, DC: U.S. Government Printing Office, 1954).

took dramatic steps to simplify the tax code. And it would not have passed without the president's involvement.

Reagan aided the passage of the act using the unique powers of the presidency. Speaking to skeptical Republican legislators, he promised to veto any reform bill that did not meet his standards for top tax rates and personal exemptions; and in doing so, he managed to attract an additional 34 votes from the party. Reagan also made prudent use of the resources of the executive office to persuade moderate congressmen. He promised to sign farm legislation for rural districts, grant favorable administrative rulings on tax filing dates, and send popular cabinet members to districts at election time.[34] To assure the bill's passage in the Senate, Reagan promised to support Republican senator Robert Packwood, chairman of the Finance Committee, in his difficult Oregon primary election. Under Packwood's leadership, a coalition of Republicans and Democrats passed tax reform with nearly unanimous support.* On October 22, 1986, Reagan signed the Tax Reform Act into law.†

Thinking only of his interactions with Congress, it may seem that Reagan accomplished tax reform with relative ease. It helped, after all, that Reagan was an immensely popular president. His tax reform efforts took place in the wake of his stunning 49-state electoral victory, when his approval ratings were north of 60 percent.[35]

Putting Congress aside, however, it is worth imagining the political ramifications of Reagan's tax reform promises—or, for that matter, Truman's signing of the Employment Act. When presidents assume greater control over the economy, or promise unprecedented economic expansion as a result of tax reform, voters take note. They form new and more demanding expectations for "the president's economy"—expectations that can go two ways. If the economy is thriving, the president is handsomely rewarded. If not—even if the circumstances of economic decline are well outside the president's control—the president and his party must answer for it. The Employment Act and Reagan's tax reform are transformational moments in a longer trend of presidents inviting responsibility for vast, often unpredictable phenomena. For once responsibility is taken, it cannot be returned.

---

* The final vote was 97–3.

† The *Wall Street Journal* called it "the most sweeping overhaul of the tax code in the nation's history" and said that "the most important player . . . was Ronald Reagan himself." See Jeffrey H. Birnbaum and Alan S. Murray, *Showdown at Gucci Gulch: Lawmakers, Lobbyists, and the Unlikely Triumph of Tax Reform* (New York: Vintage, 1988), 284, 286.

14.3 Legacy

If presidents want power, what do they want power for? To such a question, we might answer simply that presidents want power to accomplish things. But then, you might justifiably ask, why do presidents want to accomplish things? The answers to this question

President	Year	Rank	President	Year	Rank
Ronald Reagan	2022	18	**George H. W. Bush**	2022	20
	2018	13		2018	21
	2010	18		2010	22
	2002	16		2002	22
	1994	20		1994	31
	1990	22		1990	18
	1982	16			
Bill Clinton	2022	14	**George W. Bush**	2022	35
	2018	15		2018	33
	2010	13		2010	39
	2002	18		2002	23
	1994	16			
Barack Obama	2022	11	**Donald Trump**	2022	43
	2018	17		2018	42
	2010	15	**Joseph Biden**	2022	19

FIGURE 14.2. Surveys of presidential greatness. Beginning in 1982, the Siena College Research Institute conducted its survey of U.S. presidents following the first full year of a new president's term. One hundred fifty-seven historians, presidential scholars, and political scientists responded to the latest survey. The figure shows the overall rankings of the most recent modern presidents for each year in which they appear in every survey conducted since 1982. Presidents are rated on twenty categories including integrity, intelligence, relationship with Congress, and handling the economy. *Source:* "US Presidents Study Historical Rankings," Siena College, https://scri.siena.edu/us-presidents-study-historical-rankings/.

are as varied as the presidents who occupy the office. Some presidents may be trying to sate a deep-seated psychological need for achievement. Others want to do things not for their own sake but for the possibility of ushering in a better world. But all presidents want to build a record of accomplishment to secure their places in history—that is, in order to build **presidential legacies**.

Sitting at the apex of the government of the world's most powerful nation, how can presidents not think about how they will be seen by history? Certainly, almost everyone else is doing so. In the media and the discipline of political science, ranking former presidents is something of a parlor game. After nearly every major event that marks a president's tenure in office, the press consults with historians who offer insights into how the current president's speech, policy achievement, or diplomatic initiative stacks up against those of the past (figure 14.2). Presidents, in the regular course of governing, are subject to all sorts of prognostications about how they will compare to their predecessors—whether they will rank among the greats or near-greats, or whether, instead, they will settle among the unremarkable or, worse still, the disreputable.

It is not just what other people say about presidents, however, that matters. At a very deep level, presidents themselves care about how they will be remembered after they leave office. All can find some solace in the fact that by having been elected president, they will not be lost to history. But presidents are expressly concerned with *how* they will be regarded by future generations. On an early Sunday morning in August 1996, for example, while cruising to reelection, President Clinton called Dick Morris, one of his top advisors. As Morris would recall the following year, Clinton talked at length about his place in history. If his second term broke right, the two men agreed, Clinton would be remembered as falling just below the first tier of presidents—men such as Washington, Lincoln, and FDR, who had led the nation during times of peril. In their judgment, Clinton could not join that higher pantheon unless a similarly significant crisis were to occur. The second tier was nothing to sneeze at, however, containing luminaries like Theodore Roosevelt, Truman, and Reagan. For Clinton to join their ranks, the two men agreed, he would have to balance the federal budget, aggressively attack the tobacco industry, and implement the welfare reform bill that he had signed into law during his first term.[36]

Coincidentally or not, Clinton's second-term policy agenda was defined by precisely these items. In 1998, he signed balanced budget legislation.* The same year, thanks in no small part to his prodding, the tobacco industry reached a record-setting $368 billion settlement to help mitigate the hazards and costs of smoking.[37] Over the following decade, the number of people on welfare rolls dropped significantly.[38] A single conversation with Morris about his legacy, of course, did not dictate Clinton's second-term agenda. But the conversation reveals how concerns about legacy intermingle with the tasks of governance.

Clinton recognized the limits of his legacy given the absence of a historic crisis on his watch. The terrorist attacks of September 11, 2001, however, guaranteed that George W. Bush's presidency would be well remembered. Even so, after the president led the nation into the divisive Iraq War, Bush won reelection by the smallest margin of any victorious incumbent in more than a hundred years. During his second term, Bush's average approval rating was 37 percent. When he finally left office, it hovered in the high 20s.[39]

When Bush was weakest, in his second term, the president took solace in the idea that his legacy might be resurrected in the future. In public, Bush repeatedly compared himself to Truman, who was not held in especially high regard while in the White House but was subsequently exalted by historians.[40] In his memoirs, Bush reflected that he was unaffected by the negativity surrounding his tenure in office. For him, thoughts of legacy offered consolation, as when he remembered telling his wife in 2007, "If they're still assessing George Washington's legacy two centuries after he left office, this George W. doesn't have to worry about today's headlines."[41]

---

* Recent historical work shows that Clinton was prepared to go even further in securing America's fiscal future; his impeachment, however, doomed what would have been a far-reaching bipartisan effort. See Steven M. Gillon, *The Pact: Bill Clinton, Newt Gingrich and the Rivalry That Defined a Generation* (New York: Oxford University Press, 2008).

Concerns about legacy have a definite impact on how presidents come to view domestic policy challenges. Worried about their place in history, presidents look beyond the political demands of the moment and focus instead on the more distant horizon. They contemplate the long-term effects of policy initiatives, which will be judged by future historians and future publics. Institutional considerations about legacy, in this way, alter the very terms by which presidents evaluate policy initiatives. More than most, presidents seek policies that will endure, that will benefit citizens not yet born, and that will withstand the scrutiny of observers whose values may differ in important respects from contemporary citizens. For their legacies to prosper, presidents must make history—and in some instances redefine it—through a record of policy accomplishment.

14.3.1 Case Study: Harry Truman and Civil Rights

Today, it is all but cliché: when a president wallows in low approval ratings, he and his aides invoke the story of Truman. During his time in office, Truman's average approval ratings hovered at 45 percent, lower than every other modern president with the exception of Donald Trump.[42] Truman assumed the presidency after Roosevelt's death, just months into the titan's fourth term, and he was scorned from the very start for his perceived lack of experience and naiveté. Nevertheless, subsequent historians have found ample reason to laud Truman, with the 1992 publication of David McCullough's influential biography, in particular, elevating his public stature.[43]

Truman's path to the presidency was circuitous, to say the least. A lifelong member of the Kansas City Democratic Party machine, his political career seemed stalled at the age of fifty, when he had only risen to the level of a county judge.[44] In 1934, he managed to be elected to the U.S. Senate, where his most notable accomplishment was spearheading the Truman Committee, a spending watchdog that successfully saved the U.S. military billions of dollars.* In 1944, FDR enlisted Truman as his third vice president over the course of four terms in office. And just months after entering the White House, Truman was catapulted to the presidency. Famously, when Truman tried to comfort Eleanor Roosevelt on her husband's death by inquiring what he could do to help, the First Spouse replied, "Is there anything we can do for you? For you are the one in trouble now."[45]

The distance between the Capitol Building and the White House is about a mile and a half. The distance between the ambitions of actors housed within them is much wider. As a senator from Missouri, Truman had tended to the specific needs of his state's constituents as well as the political machine that had placed him in office. Now, as president, his constituents were from every state, and *every* issue, especially in the postwar context, had global implications.

As a senator, Truman had charmed visitors by answering his own phone and greeting them personally at the door.[46] Once he became president, such familiarity ground to a

---

* Such an accomplishment was not inconsequential, to be sure, but dwarfed in scale by the extraordinary decisions he would have to make as president.

sudden stop. The attention paid to parochial interests, the patience extended to his local partisan supporters—all the things that had defined him and made him successful—had to be abandoned. First, he had to find a way to prevail in the most catastrophic war the world had ever seen. Within six months of assuming office, he ordered the detonation of atomic bombs over Hiroshima and Nagasaki. (As vice president, he had not even known such weapons existed.) Then, after the surrender of the Axis powers, Truman had to help rebuild Europe and Asia from ashes and simultaneously confront the expansionist impulses of the Soviet Union. If that was not enough, Truman had to help the domestic economy find its peacetime footing and successfully reintegrate millions of returning servicemen and women into American life.

The return of African American soldiers presented particularly acute challenges. During the war, the armed forces had been segregated. Pressed to integrate them, President Roosevelt had demurred, deeming the task impossible, and settled for more modest antidiscrimination policies and oversight measures. Although Truman was known to use racial slurs and tell racist jokes in private, he nonetheless adopted a more progressive stance on this issue than his predecessor. He did so, moreover, at considerable political risk, as the Democratic Party was then divided on civil rights and southern "Dixiecrats" vehemently opposed to any federal attempt to extend new rights and privileges to African Americans. Still, Truman's presidency ended up being a watershed moment for civil rights. More than a decade before Congress enacted the 1957 Civil Rights Act, Truman desegregated the armed forces by executive order.[47]

Truman's commitment to civil rights can be traced to two aspects of the institutional presidency: a concern for the nation as a whole and, relatedly, a commitment to legacy. The southern senators who upheld Jim Crow were not representative of the entire nation. As Truman put it, "for the good of the country," the South had to eradicate its racist practices.[48] He was outraged by reports of returning African American veterans who were physically beaten on account of their race: conversations about "local habits and customs" and the abstract prerogative of states' rights had become, for him, bereft of moral content.[49] And he was certain that history would vindicate him.

Truman insisted that the nation could not tolerate such deplorable treatment of African American veterans, which not only violated basic national principles but also denigrated the nation's standing in the world. In the nascent Cold War, the Soviet Union made much of the ways in which the United States abused its own citizens. In its propaganda, the Soviet Union offered its own alleged practices of ethnic egalitarianism as proof that "the Stalin Way" was the "only correct way" of unifying a heterogeneous population.[50] Truman's secretary of state, George Marshall, informed the president that, given the Soviet propaganda, ongoing racist practices in the nation's South posed a security threat to the United States as a whole.[51]

In 1946, through executive order, Truman commissioned the President's Committee on Civil Rights. In the order, Truman was clear about the committee's charge: "All parts of our population are not equally free from fear. The preservation of civil liberties is a duty of every Government—Federal and local," he wrote.[52] In its 1948 report, the committee

FIGURE 14.3. Remembrance of Truman's desegregation order. At a time when congressional action on the
matter was impossible, Harry Truman unilaterally desegregated the U.S. military. Subsequent generations
would celebrate his actions, which, here, we see honored on a U.S. stamp. Copyright 2005 United States
Postal Services. Reproduced with permission.

recommended the desegregation of the armed forces, which Truman accomplished
through another executive order (figure 14.3). He then championed the report in a dramatic message to Congress and called on representatives to focus "not upon things which
divide us but upon those that bind us together—the enduring principles of our American
system, and our common aspirations for the future welfare and security of the people of
the United States."[53]

Throughout this period, Truman professed not to care about contemporary opinion
polls; and while on the campaign trail in 1948, he actually boasted about it.[54] Later, he put
it colorfully: "I wonder how far Moses would have gotten if he'd taken a poll in Egypt?"[55]
Surely such boasts were good politics, betraying a calculated effort to portray himself as a
public steward rather than a panderer to public opinion. But if there is a hint of truth to
his claims, Truman's presidency was liberated by such disregard. Rather than obsessing
over every moment-to-moment bump and swerve in the public mindset, the president
concentrated on the issues that mattered most to the country at large—a strategy that
would ultimately establish his place in history.

Conclusion

A distinctly national outlook, an abiding interest in power, and a nagging concern for
legacy inform the president's behavior in domestic policymaking.

In domestic policy battles, we witness presidents and members of Congress in conflict
along ideological and partisan lines. But we also see them behaving according to their

institutionally prescribed roles. In his 2021 stimulus bill, Biden focused on the national challenges associated with a global pandemic and a faltering economy, while members of Congress made sure that their constituents back home laid claim to their fair share of the largesse. A preoccupation with power helps explain why, over the course of a half century, successive presidents extended their reach further and further into budgetary matters. Concerns about their places in history convinced a string of mid-twentieth-century presidents—none of whom would be considered liberals on race by today's standards—to take modest steps in support of civil rights.

The institutional presidency, as such, is more than just a set of formal institutions, endowments of authority, and political obligations. The institution of the presidency also shapes how presidents view the world, the ambitions they bring to their work, and the criteria by which they evaluate public policy. In the case studies examined in this chapter, we have an opportunity to learn about more than just the relevance of the institutional presidency for domestic policy. We also can see how presidents distinguish themselves from other political actors working within institutional settings of their own.

Key Terms

national outlook

Domestic Policy Council

National Economic Council

Office of Legislative Affairs

General Accounting Office

Budget and Accounting Act

supplemental appropriations

Council of Economic Advisors

presidential legacy

Questions for Discussion

1. In what ways do presidents, by virtue of where they sit in government, retain a perspective on domestic policy that differs from those of other political actors? Are such differences hard and fast? Are they matters of kind or degree?

2. How is it possible to explain the fact that presidents from across the political spectrum—Carter on the left, Clinton and Obama left of center, George H. W. Bush right of center, and George W. Bush on the right—all supported the North American Free Trade Agreement?

3. Had Truman remained a senator from Missouri for the duration of his political career, would he have advocated for the desegregation of the nation's armed forces? If so, why? If not, why not?

4. How do the outlooks of legislators and presidents differ? Are they both informed primarily by particularistic considerations?

5. Does a focus on public opinion—which Truman eschewed, and many modern presidents embraced—distract a president's attention from the national scope of the executive's duties?

Suggested Readings

Howell, William G., and Terry M. Moe. *Presidents, Populism, and the Crisis of Democracy*. Chicago: University of Chicago Press, 2021.

Kriner, Doug, and Andrew Reeves. *The Particularistic President*. New York: Cambridge University Press, 2014.

Light, Paul C. *The President's Agenda: Domestic Policy Choice from Kennedy to Clinton*. 3rd ed. Baltimore: Johns Hopkins University Press, 1999.

Schick, Allen. *The Federal Budget: Politics, Policy, Process*. 3rd ed. Washington, DC: Brookings Institution Press, 2007.

Warshaw, Shirley Anne. *The Domestic Presidency: Policy Making in the White House*. Boston: Allyn and Bacon, 1997.

Notes

1. "Cumulative Cases," Johns Hopkins Coronavirus Resource Center, 2021, https://coronavirus.jhu.edu/data/cumulative-cases.

2. "News Release: Unemployment Insurance Weekly Claims," U.S. Department of Labor, March 25, 2021, https://www.dol.gov/sites/dolgov/files/OPA/newsreleases/ui-claims/20210574.pdf.

3. "Inaugural Address by President Joseph R. Biden, Jr.," Biden White House, January 21, 2021, https://www.whitehouse.gov/briefing-room/speeches-remarks/2021/01/20/inaugural-address-by-president-joseph-r-biden-jr/.

4. "President Biden Announces American Rescue Plan," Biden White House, March 12, 2021, https://www.whitehouse.gov/briefing-room/legislation/2021/01/20/president-biden-announces-american-rescue-plan/.

5. Alicia Parlapiano, "What 27 Special Interest Groups Said about the Stimulus Bill," *New York Times*, March 6, 2021, https://www.nytimes.com/interactive/2021/03/06/upshot/covid-stimulus-industry-groups.html?searchResultPosition=1.

6. Editorial Board, "Opinion | The Non-Covid Spending Blowout," *Wall Street Journal*, February 22, 2021, A.16.

7. Nicholas Wu, "San Francisco Transit Money, NY Bridge Scrapped from COVID-19 Bill amid GOP Complaints," *USA Today*, March 3, 2021, https://www.usatoday.com/story/news/politics/2021/03/03/san-francisco-transit-money-ny-bridge-pulled-covid-19-stimulus/6900847002/.

8. Sumner Park, "Republicans Slam Biden's $1.9T COVID Stimulus Plan: It's a 'Blue State Bailout Package,'" *Fox Business*, January 22, 2021, https://www.foxbusiness.com/lifestyle/republicans-slam-biden-covid-stimulus-plan-blue-state-bailout-package.

9. Joey Garrison and Javier Zarracina, "How Much Money Will Your State Get If Biden's COVID-19 Relief Bill Passes?" *USA Today*, March 17, 2021, https://www.usatoday.com/in-depth/news/politics/2021/03/04/how-much-money-each-state-would-receive-if-joe-biden-covid-stimulus-bill-passes/6892464002/.

10. Caitlin Emma, Jennifer Scholtes, and Theodoric Meyer, "Who Got Special Deals in the Stimulus and Why They Got Them," *POLITICO*, March 27, 2020, https://www.politico.com/news/2020/03/26/stimulus-coronavirus-special-deals-151108.

11. Megan Henney, "Coronavirus Stimulus Deal Includes Rewards for Special Interests Groups, Lawmakers' Home States," *Fox Business*, March 30, 2020, https://www.foxbusiness.com/money/coronavirus-stimulus-deal-includes-rewards-for-special-interests-groups-lawmakers-home-states.

12. Joe Concha, "Congress's 5,593-Page Porky 'Relief' Bill Is Essence of the Swamp," *The Hill*, December 23, 2020, https://thehill.com/opinion/finance/531294-congresss-pork-filled-covid-relief-bill.

13. Emma, Scholtes, and Meyer, "Who Got Special Deals in the Stimulus and Why They Got Them."

14. Zachary Parolin et al., "The American Rescue Plan Could Cut Child Poverty by More than Half," Center on Poverty and Social Policy, Columbia University, March 11, 2021, https://www.povertycenter.columbia.edu /news-internal/2021/presidential-policy/biden-economic-relief-proposal-poverty-impact.

15. "O'Halleran Secures First District Priorities in American Rescue Plan," Congressman Tom O'Halleran, February 27, 2021, https://ohalleran.house.gov/newsroom/press-releases/o-halleran-secures-first-district -priorities-american-rescue-plan.

16. "Congressman Gonzalez Secures $920,367,000 for Schools in Rio Grande Valley from American Rescue Plan," Congressman Vicente Gonzalez, March 12, 2021, https://gonzalez.house.gov/media/press-releases /congressman-gonzalez-secures-920367000-schools-rio-grande-valley-american.

17. Aaron Rupar, "Republicans Shamelessly Take Credit for Covid Relief They Voted Against," *Vox*, March 15, 2021, https://www.vox.com/2021/3/15/22331722/american-rescue-plan-salazar-wicker.

18. "Remarks by President Biden on the Senate Passage of the American Rescue Plan," Biden White House, March 6, 2021, https://www.whitehouse.gov/briefing-room/speeches-remarks/2021/03/06/remarks-by -president-biden-on-the-senate-passage-of-the-american-rescue-plan/.

19. Jared Sparks, ed., *The Writings of George Washington*, vol. 11 (Boston: Ferdinand Andrews, 1839), 42.

20. Doug Kriner and Andrew Reeves, *The Particularistic President* (New York: Cambridge University Press, 2014), 11.

21. Melanie Whiting, ed., "60 Years Ago, Eisenhower Proposes NASA to Congress," NASA, April 2, 2018, https://www.nasa.gov/feature/60-years-ago-eisenhower-proposes-nasa-to-congress.

22. Allen Schick, *The Federal Budget: Politics, Policy, Process*, 3rd ed. (Washington, DC: Brookings Institution, 2007), 12.

23. "Monthly Budget Review: Summary for Fiscal Year 2020," Congressional Budget Office, November 9, 2020, https://www.cbo.gov/system/files/2020-11/56746-MBR.pdf.

24. Schick, *Federal Budget*, 10, 12–14.

25. As quoted in Louis Fisher, *Presidential Spending Power* (Princeton: Princeton University Press, 1975), 33.

26. William H. Taft, as quoted in Robert Y. Shapiro, Martha Joynt Kumar, and Lawrence R. Jacobs, *Presidential Power: Forging the Presidency for the Twenty-first Century* (New York: Columbia University Press, 2000), 195–96.

27. Stephen Skowronek, *Building a New American State: The Expansion of National Administrative Capacities, 1877–1920*, 7th ed. (New York: Cambridge University Press, 1997), 207.

28. David C. Mowery, Mark S. Kamlet, and John P. Crecine, "Presidential Management of Budgetary and Fiscal Policymaking," *Political Science Quarterly* 95, no. 3 (1980): 395–425.

29. As quoted in Fisher, *Presidential Spending Power*, 175.

30. For more examples of Bush's expansion of presidential budgetary powers, see Irene Rubin, "Budgeting during the Bush Administration," *Public Budgeting & Finance* 29, no. 3 (2009): 1–14.

31. Rubin, "Budgeting during the Bush Administration." For an exposé on the elements of the president's black budget, see Wilson Andrews and Todd Lindeman, "The 'Black Budget,'" *Washington Post*, August 29, 2013, http://www.washingtonpost.com/wp-srv/special/national/black-budget/.

32. Ronald Reagan, "Radio Address to the Nation on Tax Reform," June 7, 1986.

33. John Witte, *The Politics and Development of the Federal Income Tax* (Madison: University of Wisconsin Press, 1985).

34. Jeffrey H. Birnbaum and Alan S. Murray, *Showdown at Gucci Gulch: Lawmakers, Lobbyists, and the Unlikely Triumph of Tax Reform* (New York: Vintage, 1988).

35. George Gallup Jr., ed., *The Gallup Poll, Public Opinion 1985* (Lanham, MD: Rowman & Littlefield, 1986), 233; George Gallup Jr., ed., *The Gallup Poll, Public Opinion 1986* (Lanham, MD: Rowman & Littlefield, 1987), 255.

36. Dick Morris, *Beyond the Oval Office: Winning the Presidency in the Nineties* (New York: Random House, 1997), 305–8.

37. "Clinton Played Pivotal Role in Tobacco Settlement Talks," *Chicago Tribune*, April 21, 1997, SW4.

38. Griff Witte, "Poverty Up as Welfare Enrollment Declines," *Washington Post*, September 26, 2004, A.3.

39. "Presidential Approval Ratings: George W. Bush," Gallup, http://www.gallup.com/poll/116500 /presidential-approval-ratings-george-bush.aspx.

40. Kate Zernike, "Bush's Legacy vs. the 2008 Election," *New York Times*, January 14, 2007, 4.4.

41. George W. Bush, *Decision Points* (New York: Random House, 2010), 122.

42. "Presidential Approval Ratings—Gallup Historical Statistics and Trends," Gallup, http://www.gallup .com/ poll/116677/presidential-approval-ratings-gallup-historical-statistics-trends.aspx.

43. Christopher Shea, "About Truman, the Jury's Out (Again)," *New York Times*, December 21, 2002, B.13.

44. Robert Dallek, *Harry Truman* (New York: Henry Holt and Company, 2008), 8.

45. Dallek, *Harry Truman*, 17.

46. David McCullough, *Truman* (New York: Simon & Schuster, 1992), 282.

47. John D. Skrentny, *The Minority Rights Revolution* (Cambridge, MA: Harvard University Press, 2002), 29.

48. McCullough, *Truman*, 722.

49. McCullough, *Truman*, 719–22.

50. McCullough, *Truman*, 719–22.

51. Skrentny, *Minority Rights Revolution*, 45.

52. "To Secure These Rights: The President's Committee on Civil Rights," Truman Library, http://www .trumanlibrary.org/civilrights/srights1.htm#VII.

53. Harry S. Truman, "Annual Message to Congress," January 7, 1948.

54. Skrentny, *Minority Rights Revolution*, 839.

55. Harry S. Truman, in Robert H. Ferrell, ed., *Off the Record: The Private Papers of Harry Truman* (New York: Harper and Row, 1980), 310.

15

Foreign Policy

ONE PAST PRESIDENTIAL FOREIGN POLICY ADVISOR described the task of the White House as "running the world."[1] It is an apt description of a daunting job. The institutional presidency sits at the very center of U.S. foreign policy. It is the president, after all, who manages the military, directs the diplomatic corps, and negotiates with other heads of state. As the literature on the two-presidencies thesis emphasizes (see chapter 8), presidents enjoy far more discretion in the making and implementation of foreign policy than they do in domestic policy. And when presidents draw upon their unilateral powers, as we discussed in chapter 9, they regularly advance foreign policy initiatives that congressional majorities, left to their own devices, would prefer to leave well alone.

That presidential power increases in foreign policy, however, does not mean that it goes unchallenged. For all their breadth, the president's foreign policy powers are not boundless. In the realm of foreign policy, constraints come in many forms: alliances, international law, congressional hearings and investigations, bureaucratic leaks, military resistance, and more. Though so much in foreign policy is left to executive discretion, a good deal stands between what a president wants and what a president can have.

In this chapter, we investigate how these constraints shape the foreign policy decisions of presidents who seek to project influence abroad while attending to the nation's security at home. And so doing, we revisit a common refrain about the institutional presidency: in our system of government, power is always contested, always provisional, and always partial.

15.1 Presidential Advantages in Foreign Policy

Before we examine the many hurdles presidents must overcome while pursuing a foreign policy agenda, it is worth first acknowledging the significant advantages they have in the process. In chapter 8, we discussed the relative ease with which presidents can sway public opinion on foreign affairs. In chapter 9, we discussed the informational advantages that intelligence communities and national security advisors confer on the president. In this chapter, we recognize two more advantages: America's massive military and advanced economy.

Though it may be easy to see why its military—by far the largest in the world—distinguishes the United States from other countries, the following section illuminates how it positions the president (vis-à-vis Congress) to exert influence around the globe. Likewise, the growth of the American economy has only expanded presidents' power to negotiate favorable agreements with other countries. Together, these two forces depict an executive with near-unlimited authority over foreign affairs—an impression we will reevaluate (and correct) later in this chapter.

15.1.1 Military Capabilities

If presidents cannot find ways to leave a mark on the world, they can at the very least leave a crater. Bombs, missiles, guns, warships, drones, and military planes are the bedrock of American influence abroad. And today's presidents are not afraid to use them. Without Congress's approval—and sometimes despite its opposition—presidents regularly engage in expensive overseas military operations. But it was not always so. Early presidents, believing that the country's best interests were served by keeping to itself, opted to forgo the benefits of an expansive military.

ISOLATIONISM AND EARLY CONSTRAINTS

In his farewell address, President Washington urged Americans to avoid making "political connections" with other countries: "Europe has a set of primary interests which to us have none or a very remote relation."[2] Washington's insistence that U.S. affairs should not be mixed with those of other nations—a doctrine known as **isolationism**—was largely adopted by his successors. President James Monroe, in a speech to Congress in 1823, codified this isolationist tendency with the **Monroe Doctrine**, which held that the United States regarded North and South America as its exclusive purview. Under the doctrine, the United States would keep to its sphere of influence, and Europe would keep to its own. Far from expressing an assertive or expansive foreign policy,[3] the doctrine sought to distance the United States from Europe and thereby maintain a comparatively limited military.

In the decades that followed, on the rare occasions when military mobilization became necessary, it was Congress—not the president—who authorized the effort. To restore the Union during the Civil War, President Lincoln issued a proclamation assembling state militias and blockading southern ports. Fearful that Congress would stand in the way, however, Lincoln convened a special session to request its sanction of the war effort. Only then did Congress boost military spending and pass legislation allowing the drafting of soldiers into the Union Army. And despite the mobilization's success—and the veneration for military superiority it instilled in the minds of a generation[4]—Congress immediately withdrew military appropriations at the end of the Civil War, leaving no significant supply of troops for future presidents to command.

Similar dynamics defined subsequent U.S. military conflagrations. After the Spanish-American War, years of congressional investment in the U.S. Navy left presidents in command of an array of new battalions, battleships, and overseas encampments. Though some

FIGURE 15.1. The Great White Fleet. Eager to flaunt the nation's naval prowess and signal its emergence as a world power, Theodore Roosevelt launched the Great White Fleet, a fourteen-month circumnavigation of the globe conducted by U.S. battleships between 1907 and 1909. *Source:* Library of Congress Prints and Photographs Division [LC-DIG-ppmsca-25942].

presidents sought to use this superior military power to engage the broader world—as Theodore Roosevelt did with his **Great White Fleet** (figure 15.1)—large military operations still required approval from Congress. Thus, in 1916, when President Woodrow Wilson intervened in the Mexican Revolution without congressional authorization, he was forced to withdraw after only one year for lack of federal funds.[5]

After World War I, Congress again demonstrated its reluctance to grant full war-making powers to the president. Having passed the Selective Service Act in 1917, which helped draft more than four million soldiers into the war, Congress quickly reduced military spending to 6 percent of wartime levels when the conflict was over.[6] These cuts served to both promote fiscal responsibility and ensure that presidents would have to win the support of Congress before embarking on costly military ventures.

CHANGING GLOBAL ORDER

All this changed with World War II. The sheer magnitude of the war mobilization effort, which is discussed in this chapter's Historical Transformations feature, along with the altered global order that arose in its wake, permanently altered the federal government's support for its military. Since 1945, the defense budget has never fallen to anywhere near pre–World War II levels.[7] Postwar presidents, as a result, have governed with a fully armed and equipped military at the ready—one that is poised to respond at a moment's notice to orders handed down from the White House.

World War II also set in motion a chain of events that shapes global relations to this day: President Truman's decision in 1945 to detonate newly developed nuclear weapons in Hiroshima and Nagasaki, which resulted in at least two hundred thousand immediate

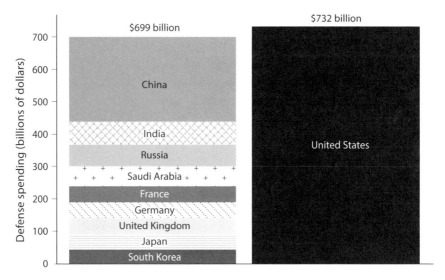

FIGURE 15.2. U.S. military spending in context, 2019. The United States spends more on defense than do the next nine highest-spending countries in the world combined. Breaking it down, the United States spent three times as much on defense as China and more than ten times as much as each of the next eight highest-spending countries. *Source:* www.pgpf.org /chart-archive/0053_defense-comparison, based on data from the Stockholm International Peace Research Institute.

deaths and the surrender of the Japanese, showed the world the capabilities of advanced weaponry. This monumental decision also ushered in the half-century-long **Cold War** between the United States and the Soviet Union. During this period, the two nations built enormous nuclear arsenals that guaranteed their mutual destruction should outright war ever come for them.

The end of the Cold War in 1990 seemed to promise a "peace dividend" that would allow nations to reduce their defense spending. Indeed, in the decade that followed, the American defense budget declined by roughly one-third, and the defense spending of other nations declined as well.[8] Following the terrorist attacks of 9/11, however, the U.S. defense budget returned to Cold War levels—and then some. By 2011, defense spending reached more than $750 billion, its highest level since World War II.[9]

As figure 15.2 shows, U.S. military expenditures in 2019 totaled more than those of the next nine nations combined. That year, the United States spent $732 billion—or 38 percent of the world's total military spending.[10] With these funds, the United States created a permanent supply of arms and personnel that presidents can dispatch at will.

In *The American Warfare State*, Rebecca Thorpe argues that the emergence of this military establishment has fundamentally reshaped the constitutional balance of power in favor of the presidency. According to Thorpe, "Large defense budgets furnish presidents with unprecedented capacity to exercise their military policies independently, and they make it more difficult for Congress to mount effective opposition."[11] Whereas presidents needed Congress to commit the nation to war up until the mid-twentieth century, today's presidents need only employ the vast military resources already at their disposal. With very little outside input, presidents can use these resources to dominate the sea, land, air, and even space—giving them a measure of global influence that would astonish their predecessors.

15.1.2 Economic Considerations

U.S. foreign policy involves a great deal more than just the projection of military strength: economic considerations also loom large. The increasingly interwoven character of the global economy—and the United States' privileged place near the top—has given presidents a large selection of tools with which to promote their national security and political objectives.

TRADE

During the first few decades after World War II, the United States was the world's preeminent exporter, supplying overseas consumers with everything from wheat to washing machines. Starting in the 1970s, Germany, Japan, and, later, China became manufacturing giants themselves. Abetted by deregulation initiatives throughout the world, global financial markets entered a three-decades-long boom that led to—and was finally halted by—the financial crisis of 2008.

The rise of **globalization**, which is the increasingly complex economic and political ties among nations, has been assisted by global economic agreements that increase **economic liberalization**—the reduction of tariffs and other barriers to free trade among nations. Regionally, Bill Clinton fought for and eventually won passage of the North American Free Trade Agreement (NAFTA), a trilateral deal among the United States, Mexico, and Canada that had been initiated by President Reagan. Similarly, the European Union (EU) functions as a single market allowing the free movement of capital, goods, people, and services across its member territories, and the World Trade Organization (WTO) facilitates all manner of interstate agreements that promote the exchange of goods and services among its 164 members.

Globalization has transformed the American economy. Between 1970 and 2006, U.S. international trade more than doubled.[12] Most of that increased trade, however, came in the form of imports to the United States. Whereas in 1970 the United States exported $2.6 billion more than it imported, by 2020 its trade deficit reached an all-time high of more than $915 billion.[13] Meanwhile, of the $26.95 trillion that constituted the national debt at the end of 2020, $7.07 trillion of it, more than one-quarter, was owned by foreigners.[14] All of this led to greater interdependence between the United States and its trading partners.

Make no mistake: despite its apparent dependence on other nations, the United States still dominates the globalized economy. Just as the U.S. military is larger by several orders of magnitude than that of any other country, and just as U.S. political influence verges on the hegemonic, so the U.S. economy stands atop nearly all international rankings. On all sorts of indicators, the U.S. economy is larger and more productive than that of any other nation, with the one (recent) exception of China,[15] which surpassed the U.S. economy in terms of its overall gross domestic product (GDP) in 2014 and has maintained that lead ever since. On a per capita basis, however, the U.S. economy is still vastly more productive than China's. Additionally, the United States boasts the highest income per capita among larger nations, with American wage earners trailing only the peoples of the small nations of Luxembourg, Norway, and Austria.[16]

Presidents can thus draw on the strength of the U.S. economy to champion national interests in an international setting. By threatening to suspend or cut trade relations with another country, presidents find the leverage they need to bolster their military or political interests abroad, and sometimes even fend off political pressure at home. For example, the United States deployed economic sanctions with some measure of success in the early 2000s, when the Libyan government finally caved to American demands that they admit responsibility for the bombing of Pan Am Flight 103 and compensate the families of the 270 victims. Likewise, following a long-standing regime of economic sanctions by the United States and its allies, Iran agreed in 2015 to suspend its nuclear program. In 2018, the United States withdrew from the agreement and reimposed previous sanctions to compel Iran to place even more limitations on its nuclear program.[17] And most recently, the Biden administration coordinated a massive regime of sanctions against Russia in the immediate aftermath of its 2022 invasion of Ukraine.[18] Again and again, the size and strength of the U.S. economy proved instrumental in the undertakings.

FOREIGN AID

Representing the world's most powerful economy, presidents can largely dictate the terms of assistance provided to other nations. Though foreign aid represents only a small fraction of its annual budget—less than 1 percent in 2019[19]—the United States is consistently the largest subsidizer of governments worldwide.[20] Ostensibly, the purpose of foreign aid is to promote peace, stability, and self-reliance in developing nations. And while there is mixed evidence that it achieves these goals,[21] scholars have long noted that the United States administers foreign assistance strategically, serving its *own* needs in addition to the needs of recipient countries.

For example, one study found that countries who hold seats on the United Nations Security Council—a rotating board whose fifteen members vote on matters of international peace and security, including on the authorization of sanctions and military activities—receive substantially more aid from the United States, presumably in return for favorable votes.[22] U.S. aid to these countries increases further as the council approaches especially consequential decisions, such as a 2002 resolution in support of the American invasion of Iraq. When a country loses its seats on the council, aid from the United States promptly drops. Examined this way, foreign assistance is not always akin to charity; in this case, it looks a lot like a reciprocal payment—some might say a bribe—to countries with strategic value to the United States.

As can be expected, presidents have real sway over the tactical decisions that produce foreign aid. Though Congress ultimately sets the foreign aid budget, it has historically let presidents decide how the funds should be disbursed. For example, the 1961 Foreign Assistance Act, which created the current aid system, repeatedly states that the president "is authorized to furnish assistance on such terms and conditions as he may determine."[23] Congress can earmark funds for specific purposes, such as public health, while allowing plenty of room for White House interpretation on how to disburse funds, including transferring funds between programs (see section 8.4.2) or even withholding funds when the president deems it "essential" or "necessary" (impoundment; see section 8.4.3).[24]

The United States represents just 5 percent of the global population but more than 15 percent of global economic activity. Presidents have a great deal of influence over how this economic power is projected abroad. When they use sanctions to deprive countries of American consumers, or redirect the world's largest source of foreign assistance, they advance the nation's strategic interests—economic and otherwise—just as they fortify their own bargaining position with powerbrokers both at home and abroad.

15.2 International Constraints on Foreign Policymaking

Despite its military and economic power, the United States does not confront security challenges alone; and the presidency, for all its considerable advantages in foreign policy, does not navigate a geostrategic landscape entirely of its own making. Rather, presidents must manage a thick network of international alliances and international laws that intermittently facilitate and impede their foreign policymaking objectives. Successive presidents enter and exit alliances and negotiate and renegotiate treaties, all while paying close attention to the ways in which these alliances and agreements affect America's interests abroad.

15.2.1 Alliances

International alliances both establish formal obligations and confer benefits on the states that enter them. As a result, some political scientists argue, nations within an alliance are less likely to either go to war with or impose sanctions on one another.[25] By formalizing the terms of their relationships and establishing well-defined protocols for meeting threats posed by outside aggressors, political alliances rationalize and thereby strengthen diplomacy. Similarly, political allies regularly communicate and exchange information, which mitigates the likelihood that one state will misinterpret another's motives or objectives[26] and forges institutional bonds that reduce the incidence of conflict.[27]

International alliances, however, also come with costs. One school of thought argues that alliances, far from promoting peace, actually fan the flames of conflict. A decades-long project that studied the causes of war found that alliances in the twentieth century were correlated with higher incidences of war.[28] One explanation given for this is that alliances tend to spur counteralliances, thus ratcheting up international tensions. Because many alliances guarantee that signatories will come to each other's aid in the face of a security threat, otherwise localized aggressions can quickly escalate.[29]

Formal treaties and alliances also may limit the choices available to presidents when they formulate U.S. foreign policy. In 2002, for example, when President George W. Bush tried to shore up the domestic steel industry through a nearly 30 percent tariff on imports, the backlash from allies was swift and forceful. After the WTO ruled that the tariffs were illegal, and the European Union threatened retaliation, the Bush administration quickly reversed the policy.

Presidents who refuse to honor the commitments of standing treaties and alliances invite costly sanctions from partner countries and threaten to damage the nation's reputation abroad. In his 2016 campaign for the presidency, Trump championed an "America First" foreign policy, arguing that for too long America's alliances had served other countries at the expense of the United States. He called the European Union a "foe," saying, "in a trade sense, they've really taken advantage of us and many of those countries are in NATO and they weren't paying their bills."[30] Trumped singled out NATO—the **North Atlantic Treaty Organization**—for special reprobation. Founded shortly after World War II to provide collective defense to its thirty signatories, NATO requires that each member nation commit at least 2 percent of its GDP to defense spending—a goal that the United States, nearly alone, routinely meets or exceeds. Bothered that freeloading members weren't "paying their bills," Trump in 2018 questioned whether he would uphold NATO's core mission and come to the defense of a member nation that has been attacked.[31] And in the last year of his presidency, Trump attempted to pull thousands of American troops out of Germany—a NATO member that, in 2020, contributed roughly 1.5 percent of its GDP to defense. "We don't want to be suckers anymore," Trump said of his decision. "We're reducing the force because they're not paying their bills; it's very simple."[32]

But perhaps it isn't so simple. America's military presence in Europe is not a handout to Europeans. This presence serves U.S. objectives in the region and beyond. Pulling troops—and worse, threatening not to defend NATO allies—emboldens America's rivals and puts allies at risk. It is no wonder, then, that these actions degraded America's reputation abroad, particularly in Germany, where a 2020 poll showed respondents evenly divided about who its closest ally was: the United States or China.[33] And when the German chancellor, Angela Merkel, was asked about whether she trusted Trump, she said only: "I work with the world's elected presidents, including, of course, the American one."[34]

In *Shields of the Republic*, Mira Rapp-Hooper argues that American interests suffer when its alliances weaken. To make her case, Rapp-Hooper asks Americans to consider a world in which their alliances never materialized—a world in which allies did not join the United States in every war it fought since the early 1950s; a world with rampant nuclearization, as each nation sought to defend itself by any means necessary. Though Rapp-Hooper believes that alliances should be reimagined and reformed to meet today's challenges, she claims that presidents who eschew international cooperation do so "in no small part because they have been spared the world that necessitated it."[35]

15.2.2 International Law

The terms of international agreements go well beyond formal alliances with individual states. The United States operates within a global system shaped by **international law**. Its rules and conventions cover all matters of foreign policy: trade, immigration, deportation, access to international waters and airspace, and much, much more.

The earliest international law came in the form of trade rules and treaties between states, especially as they pertained to maritime commerce. Since the mid-nineteenth century, however, a growing body of international law has focused on the conduct of war. Most prominent in this area are the **Geneva Conventions**, four international treaties spanning the years from 1864 to 1949 and ratified by nearly every country in the world, which prohibit, among other things, the use of torture against prisoners of war.

International law really took off in the twentieth century, and particularly after World War II. One study finds that of the 779 international legal provisions established since the late nineteenth century, 85 percent have been drafted since the 1940s. These provisions cover issues ranging from children's rights to human trafficking to crimes against humanity.[36]

The most revolutionary change to international law, and the source of much of its recent growth, has to do with the recognition of human rights that transcend state sovereignty. Formerly, political rights had been granted by the nation-state and thus could be revoked without international consequence; today, new international institutions such as the United Nations affirm the "inalienable rights of all members of the human family" regardless of "race, colour, sex, language, religion, political or other opinion, national or social origin, property, birth or other status."[37] In its **Universal Declaration of Human Rights**, the United Nations has laid out the concept of human rights in very broad strokes, offering articles such as, "No one shall be subjected to torture or to cruel, inhuman or degrading treatment or punishment."[38]

Nations have many incentives to adhere to international law. Doing so signals their continued commitment to allied states, as well as their willingness and ability to meet their obligations. This compliance, in turn, can attract increased investment, new alliances, and continued diplomacy.

Despite these incentives, however, holding states and their leaders accountable to international law has proved exceedingly difficult. Nations may choose to break past promises for any number of reasons—sometimes because the domestic costs of international cooperation outweigh the consequences of reneging, and other times because their international reputation is already so damaged that they have nothing to lose. Sanctions for violations of international agreements need not alter the behavior of an aggressor nation.[39] Further, political leaders sometimes face only minimal repercussions in their home countries for disregarding an international agreement. And in others, they may be rewarded for doing so.

The United States has long held mixed opinions about international law. Its legitimacy as a world leader is in many ways based on its historic engagement with international organizations and its respect for international law. Unlike many smaller nations, however, the United States does not need to rely on participation in conventions and multilateral treaties to burnish its global reputation. It can establish guidelines for other nations to follow, and then step back and claim exemption. Thus, over the past few decades, U.S. policymakers have tended to avoid broad international agreements.

The United States' history with the **International Criminal Court (ICC)** offers one such example. After World War II, the United States initially led the effort to prosecute crimes against humanity. Instead of summarily executing the remaining leaders of Nazi Germany, the United States called upon the services of an international court of law at Nuremberg, which became a prototype for the ICC. After years of negotiation over the ICC's establishment, delegations from over 160 nations, the United States included, convened at the Rome Conference in 1998. There, three-quarters of the countries approved the Rome Statute establishing the ICC. President Clinton initially refused to sign the treaty. And when he finally did sign it near the end of his term, he withheld it from consideration for Senate ratification. As the president explained, "In signing, however, we are not abandoning our concerns about significant flaws in the treaty. . . . With signature, however, we will be in a position to influence the evolution of the court. Without signature, we will not."[40] For its detractors, though, the flaws of the ICC were never fixed. Two decades later, when Trump occupied the White House, the United States formally withdrew from the treaty.

In other instances, presidents have rejected long-standing U.S. treaty obligations. Over the course of President George W. Bush's time in office, a series of leaked reports revealed that while interrogating suspected terrorists at Guantánamo Bay and other American facilities located overseas, CIA officers used tactics such as sensory deprivation, waterboarding (simulated drowning), and psychological humiliation. When the Bush administration came under fire for practicing torture, which is prohibited under the Geneva Conventions, it denied that the techniques constituted torture, calling them "enhanced interrogation techniques." Bush's legal experts said torture only referred to "intense pain or suffering of the kind that is equivalent to the pain that would be associated with serious injury so severe that death . . . [or] a loss of significant body functions will likely result."[41] The Bush administration then proposed a bill to Congress that would have revised U.S. obligations under the Geneva Conventions by defining torture as treatment that "shocks the conscience"—a concept arguably much vaguer than what was already outlined in the conventions.

These differences between Clinton, who attempted to strengthen international law, and Trump and Bush, who attempted to limit the restrictions of international law, reflect a larger partisan divide. Democratic presidents broadly support international law and treaties, whereas Republican presidents look more skeptically upon them. Their dispositions, moreover, match those of the larger public. According to one poll conducted at the end of the Trump presidency, 80 percent of Democrats saw as the primary lesson of the coronavirus pandemic that the United States should "coordinate and collaborate with other countries to solve global issues." Meanwhile, 58 percent of Republicans believed the lesson was to "be self-sufficient as a nation so we don't need to depend on others."[42]

Consistent with these trends, President Obama spent the better part of eight years attempting to enhance U.S. involvement in many international organizations. In response to the rising global threat of climate change, his administration played a central role in negotiating the Paris Climate Accords—a set of international agreements meant to limit global warming to under two degrees Celsius above preindustrial levels. Obama also sought to expand U.S. hegemony in the Asian Pacific as he negotiated the Trans-Pacific Partnership (TPP) trade deal.

With the election of President Trump, however, these achievements were summarily overturned. True to his isolationist belief that the United States ought to be sovereign and independent, Trump withdrew from both the Paris Agreement and the TPP during his first year in office, calling the latter "a rape of our country."[43] And the president didn't stop there. Years later, in the middle of the coronavirus pandemic, he withdrew the United States from the World Health Organization (WHO)—a United Nations agency that coordinates global public health efforts.

When President Biden took office, he learned early on that international agreements are much easier to dismantle than restore. Biden carried through on his promises to reenter the Paris Agreement and the WHO, as well as other groups abandoned by Trump, such as the UN Human Rights Council. But in the years since the United States left the TPP, China organized its own Asia-Pacific trade partnership, further expanding that country's influence in the region and limiting the range of possible U.S. countermeasures. And while much of the international community was pleased to see the United States recommit itself to the global fight against climate change, key allies—Germany in particular—were less inclined to defer to American leadership that, in the wake of Trump's presidency, appeared far more precarious than it once had.

15.3 Domestic Constraints on Foreign Policymaking

An adage of American politics holds that "politics stop at the water's edge." The partisanship, ideological disagreement, and infighting that characterize domestic policymaking, we are told, dissipate the moment the president sets foot in the international arena. There certainly is a measure of truth to this received wisdom. Important domains of foreign policy *are* characterized by broad consensus; and Americans *do* occasionally rally behind their commander in chief. But like every other area of policymaking, foreign relations also features consequential political contests both across and within the first two branches of government.

In these political contests, presidents have huge institutional advantages over Congress, particularly in matters involving war. Thanks to the intelligence agencies that report to them, presidents have access to information that Congress simply lacks. Presidents usually are the first to know about developments abroad that warrant a U.S. military response. Just as importantly, presidents set the terms of a possible intervention. Once the president's intention to deploy U.S. troops is announced, members of Congress usually can only react, by lending either support or opposition. If they choose the latter, even with good cause, they risk appearing indifferent to the sacrifices of American troops—an accusation that can weigh heavily on their political fortunes.

That the deck is stacked against Congress, however, does not mean that its members must concede every disagreement when the national conversation turns to foreign affairs. On the contrary, Congress has profoundly altered certain U.S. military entanglements. Through a variety of formal means—spending, appropriations, and legislation—Congress can nudge U.S. foreign policy in directions that the president might otherwise avoid. Members of Congress also can exert political pressure on the president through informal means, as well, by giving speeches and engaging the larger public.

In this section, we survey the various formal and informal ways in which Congress can influence U.S. foreign policy. Having done so, we then shift our attention slightly and take stock of the obstacles presidents face from within the executive branch.

15.3.1 Formal Congressional Checks on Presidential Foreign Policymaking

According to the Constitution, Congress is endowed with a variety of powers that enable its members to shape foreign policy. Occasionally Congress uses them to correct perceived missteps taken by the president. More often, though, the mere threat of congressional action dissuades presidents from pursuing especially controversial foreign policies.

APPROPRIATIONS

The president may be able to *start* a war, but Congress is in charge of *funding* it. As discussed earlier in this chapter, through appropriations legislation, Congress can reduce and sometimes end the deployment of troops overseas. So doing, it can purposefully "clog the road to combat."[44]

Congress used appropriations, for example, to constrain the president's options during the latter half of the Vietnam War. In 1970, six years after a near-unanimous prowar vote on the Gulf of Tonkin Resolution, some members of Congress sought to deescalate a war that had become unacceptably bloody, costly, and unpopular. After officially repealing the Gulf of Tonkin Resolution, the congressional majority sought to make the repeal stick through a series of appropriations bills. In December, for instance, it enacted a supplemental foreign assistance appropriations act that expressly forbade the funding of any American troops in Cambodia.

Over the next several years, Congress continued to press for a permanent end to the war. After the **Paris Peace Accords** in 1973 terminated direct American military incursions into Vietnam and mandated a ceasefire between North and South Vietnamese troops, Congress passed another supplemental appropriations act preventing any funding for possible military actions in Vietnam or in neighboring Laos and Cambodia. By 1975, when North Vietnamese troops were on the verge of defeating South Vietnam, Congress maintained its antiwar posture. Despite the vocal opposition of President Gerald Ford and Secretary of State Henry Kissinger, Congress prohibited the use of American troops to enforce the ceasefire between North and South Vietnam mandated by the accords.

Congress also can use its appropriations power to prevent U.S. military action in the first place. In 1993 and 1994 the United States intervened in Somalia's civil war, but with disastrous consequences, as images of U.S. soldiers being dragged through the streets of Mogadishu by Somali fighters played on American televisions. Thereafter, Congress had no appetite for funding another war—and certainly not another ill-fated humanitarian venture. Soon enough, one would break out in nearby Rwanda, where over 800,000 civilians were slaughtered in a three-month genocidal campaign. When Clinton asked for $270 million in military assistance, Congress slashed appropriations to $170 million, with Senator Robert Byrd, who led the effort to cut funding, remarking, "We had enough of that in Somalia."[45]

TRADITIONAL LEGISLATION

Members of Congress can pass legislation aimed at redirecting American international relations. In 1935 and again in 1937, for instance, Congress passed two **Neutrality Acts** that limited the president's ability to financially support American allies engaged in conflicts brewing in Europe and the Pacific. When Hitler invaded Poland in 1939, FDR beseeched Congress to repeal the legislation, but its members only agreed to rescind the acts' arms embargoes and required that all war materiel be paid for in cash.

Congress also can use legislation to challenge the president's position on trade and diplomatic relations. The Comprehensive Anti-Apartheid Act of 1986, for example, put Congress and President Reagan into a tense standoff. Members of the Congressional Black Caucus had been campaigning for years for the United States to impose economic sanctions on South Africa, an American ally whose white-run government disenfranchised and brutally repressed its Black population. When Congress finally passed a series of punitive measures aimed at crippling the apartheid regime, Reagan vetoed the measure, claiming it would engender Black violence against whites in South Africa. Congress overrode Reagan's veto by a large majority, with one Republican declaring that "the President has become an irrelevancy to the ideals, heartfelt and spoken, of America."[46] It marked the first time since the War Powers Resolution that Congress had overridden a presidential veto on foreign policy legislation.

Through legislation, Congress also can jump-start new programs and initiatives on the global arena. Take, for instance, the legislation enacted just after World War II that was designed to project a positive national image abroad. Immediately following the war, Senator William Fulbright, a staunch internationalist and one of the first supporters of the United Nations, proposed the Fulbright Program, which sponsored international educational exchange with the goal of fostering "mutual understanding" between the United States and the international community. A few years later Congress built on this precedent by passing the Smith-Mundt Act, which shaped up to be one of the earliest efforts in the ideological war with the Soviet Union. Even though the executive branch already had produced wartime propaganda during World War II through the Office of War Information (OWI), many in Congress were uncomfortable with the idea of funding such government-directed propaganda efforts during peacetime. The limited mandates of the Fulbright Program and the Smith-Mundt Act helped allay those fears.

APPOINTMENTS

Another way Congress asserts its authority in matters of foreign policy is through appointments. The president makes many foreign policy appointments that require Senate confirmation, such as the secretary of state, the U.S. ambassador to the United Nations, and the secretary of defense. Most of these appointments are approved. Occasionally, however, the Senate derails a candidacy.

When George W. Bush sought to appoint John Bolton as U.S. ambassador to the United Nations in 2005, key senators from both parties balked at the nomination. Bolton had long been outspoken in his disdain for the United Nations, which he claimed was only useful when it advanced American interests. Bush portrayed Bolton as a reform candidate, but many saw him as a lightning rod who would alienate American allies. Democrats filibustered his nomination, and Republicans lacked the sixty votes needed to break the impasse.

It did not help Bolton that Republican senator George Voinovich urged his fellow party members to join the Democrats, saying that Bolton lacked "the character, leadership, interpersonal skills, self-discipline, common decency and understanding of the chain of command to lead his team to victory."[47] Although Bush would proceed to install Bolton as a recess appointment, Bolton's tenure was short-lived. Unable to secure Senate confirmation the second time around, Bolton stepped down from his post in 2006. Bolton would not serve in public office until 2018, when he was appointed the Trump administration's third national security advisor—a position that does not require Senate approval. Again, his tenure was short-lived, and he resigned in late 2019.

Though congressional revolts against presidential nominees are rare, Congress's right of refusal remains powerful. There are plenty of instances when a president rejects a possible nominee, not because someone else is preferred but because the individual could not survive the Senate's scrutiny. To avoid delay and public embarrassment, a president may choose not to do battle with Congress over controversial appointments.

When Hillary Clinton announced her decision to step down as secretary of state in 2013, many in Washington believed Obama would nominate Susan Rice, then ambassador to the United Nations, to take Clinton's place. Before she could even be officially nominated, however, Republicans condemned Rice for her statements denying that the United States had had knowledge of premeditation in the attacks on the U.S. consulate in Benghazi, Libya. Though Rice was never directly involved in the situation in Libya, her aspirations to the office of secretary of state were ultimately thwarted by charges that she epitomized the Obama administration's laxity on issues of intelligence and security. Fearing

Rice would not receive Senate confirmation, Obama instead nominated John Kerry, a long-time Democratic senator, who, with the support of several powerful Republicans, sailed through his confirmation hearings.

Similarly, in 2019, Trump announced his intention to replace the outgoing director of national intelligence with John Ratcliffe, a Republican congressman from Texas. Ratcliffe's nomination was soon derailed not by Democrats but by Senate Republicans who felt that he was "too political" and inexperienced to be the nation's top intelligence official.[48] Ratcliffe also came under fire for allegedly overstating his qualifications as a prosecutor. Despite his insistence that Ratcliffe was "being treated very unfairly by the LameStream Media,"[49] Trump ultimately decided that he could not win the fight with Congress, and the nomination was soon withdrawn. Trump waited nearly a year before he resubmitted Ratcliffe for the position; and then the Senate relented, confirming Ratcliffe on a party-line vote.

CONGRESSIONAL HEARINGS, INVESTIGATIONS, AND DELEGATIONS

Between 1946 and 2020, Congress held more than twenty thousand hearings on foreign policy matters that ranged from defense budgets to passport regulations. Many of these hearings focused on specific bills, appropriations, or treaties. Others reviewed the operations of various federal agencies and departments.[50] And sometimes Congress used hearings to contest the institutional power of the presidency itself (see section 8.5.2 for further discussion on the topic).

In one of the most sweeping congressional investigations in U.S. history, a Senate committee chaired by Democrat Frank Church in 1975 probed into long-standing practices of U.S. intelligence services. In fourteen reports published between 1975 and 1976, the committee detailed allegations of systematic intelligence abuses going back decades. One of the more notable reports presented evidence of CIA participation in the assassinations and attempted assassinations of a number of world leaders, including the Cuban leader Fidel Castro and Ngo Dinh Diem, the South Vietnamese president killed in a coup in 1963. The committee also exposed the illegal involvement of foreign intelligence agencies in domestic surveillance activities.

In a 1975 appearance on *Meet the Press*, Church warned against the "total tyranny" of the executive branch's intelligence agencies and insisted that congressional oversight was needed to prevent the United States from hurtling into an "abyss from which there is no return."[51] In response to the Church Committee's revelations, President Ford issued Executive Order 11905, which outlawed political assassinations and called for greater congressional supervision of foreign intelligence activities.

Members of Congress occasionally take investigations overseas. Trips abroad by congressional delegations—or *codels*, as lawmakers call them—have a long tradition in Congress. Though critics deride the trips as taxpayer-funded junkets, members of Congress insist that the trips keep them informed about global issues. Codels also provide members of Congress with independent staging grounds for criticizing the president's foreign policy.

In 2013, for instance, a group of lawmakers traveled to Russia to investigate a potential intelligence failure between Russia and the United States prior to the deadly Boston Marathon bombing. Led by Representative Dana Rohrabacher, the mostly Republican delegation claimed that the trip was motivated by reports that Russian officials had attempted to warn the United States that one of the suspected Chechnyan bombers might be a potential terrorist. Rohrabacher called into question the Obama administration's commitment to counterterrorism, a recurrent political attack among Republican lawmakers.[52]

The delegation caused a bit of a stir by speaking to the media and enlisting the help of Hollywood actor Steven Seagal. Although the delegation ultimately failed to find any evidence showing that the bombings might have been prevented, Rohrabacher nonetheless succeeded in shaming the Obama administration before an attentive media. And therein lies the essential power of congressional hearings and investigations: unlike legislation and appropriations, which directly compel the president's foreign policies, investigations can bring public scrutiny to bear on the president. Televised hearings and testimony can train the public's attention on a policy domain that is not typically top of mind for most Americans. And when Congress lacks the necessary votes to overcome a filibuster or veto, investigations (which require only the approval of a committee chairman) may be its only recourse against a wayward president. Thus, even though hearings and investigations do not always result in tangible policy changes, Congress has reasons to investigate when it cannot legislate.

Thinking Institutionally: Congress and the U.S. Withdrawal from Afghanistan

Congress's willingness to brandish its formal oversight powers—much like its willingness to pass certain bills or impeach a sitting president—crucially depends on its partisan composition.[53]

Whereas co-partisans tend to stand by presidents during trying times, the opposition party is relatively quick to highlight their foreign policy failures. When U.S. troops die unnecessarily, when the government fails to achieve its foreign policy objectives, when the president and those who serve him fumble on the international stage, members of the opposition party are reliably among the first to cry foul. And when they control the House and Senate, members of the opposition party can deploy the considerable powers vested in Article I to lambaste and undermine the president.

Recognizing these political dynamics, presidents are more inclined to take risky actions abroad when their party maintains majorities in the House and Senate. On average, they exercise military force with greater frequency, they respond more quickly to foreign crises, and they sustain operations for longer periods of time. This basic relationship undergirds the willingness of presidents, all presidents, to assume the unavoidable costs of war.[54]

This relationship also affects presidents' willingness to *end* certain wars—a decision that comes with costs of its own. When President Biden took office in 2021, he was not the first president to oppose America's military presence in Afghanistan, a country it had invaded shortly after the terrorist attacks in September 2001. Presidents Obama and Trump, too, desired a peaceful conclusion to America's longest war. During Trump's campaign for president, he frequently criticized "endless wars" like the one in Afghanistan: "Are they going to be there for the next 200 years? At some point, what's going on?"[55] Unlike Biden, however, neither of these presidents was willing to initiate a total evacuation of troops. To do so, they recognized, would have required them to concede defeat—admitting that the United States had failed in its objective to build a lasting peace in Afghanistan, and potentially handing control of the country to extremist groups.

Politically, the easy decision for Biden would have been to maintain a modest level of troops and to hand a troubled occupation down to his successor, just as a troubled occupation had been handed down to him. By terminating a decades-old occupation, Biden pursued a path of decisively greater resistance. His willingness to do so, it stands to reason, was buoyed by the knowledge that the Democrats in control of the House and Senate would not deploy Congress's investigatory, oversight, legislative, or budgetary powers to punish the president if the policy's execution deviated from its initial planning.

And deviate from planning it did. Though Biden's team predicted that the Afghan military—after decades of funding and training provided by the United States—could hold their own though the U.S. evacuation, the country quickly fell to the Taliban. The ascendance of the Taliban coincided with the emergence of terrorist groups such as ISIS-K, which carried out a suicide bombing at an Afghan airport that killed 180 people, including 13 American soldiers.

In the immediate aftermath of these failures, however, hardly a word was heard from Congress. Party leaders did not point fingers or dish up recriminations. They did not draft new policies intended to restore order. And they did not call for investigations into Biden's failure to plan for a Taliban insurgency that, within a matter of days, hours even, had toppled a secular government that successive administrations had insisted was up to the task of holding and governing a country. Instead, majority party leaders recast these failures as further justification for Biden's original decision to withdraw. In the words of Senator Chris Murphy, a Democrat, "If 20 years of laborious training and equipping of the Afghan security forces had this little impact on their ability to fight, then another 50 years wouldn't change anything."[56]

Biden's actions in Afghanistan, and the docile response from congressional Democrats, offer two lessons about the institutional presidency. The first points toward the continued relevance of partisanship for whether one branch of government will or will not use its formal powers to curb the actions of another. But the second lesson applies more broadly: the effects of formal oversight powers—indeed, of nearly all powers—are often anticipatory. Congress can guide presidents' actions overseas by passing legislation or, alternatively, convincing presidents that they *would* pass legislation in certain situations. In this way, Biden's willingness to leave Afghanistan was informed not by congressional action but by the anticipation that Congress would not act at all.

15.3.2 Informal Congressional Checks on Presidential Foreign Policymaking

In addition to its formal authority to curb presidential power in foreign affairs, Congress has informal ways of influencing presidential action. Through public appeals, Congress can influence public support for the president's agenda—and the willingness of other nations to accommodate the administration's objectives.

SPEECHES

Public speeches, whether inside or outside the halls of Congress, offer an important platform for members of Congress to challenge the president. Delivered at the right time and by the right legislator, congressional speeches can create all sorts of domestic political trouble for presidents struggling to advance their foreign policy agendas.

For Wisconsin senator Robert La Follette Sr., the Senate floor offered not only a forum for explaining his opposition to America's involvement in World War I but also a chance to defend his personal reputation. La Follette had been an outspoken opponent of the war at a time when few other members of Congress were willing to challenge President Wilson, whose Committee on Public Information and other domestic mobilization efforts had fomented patriotic fervor. Dissent could be dangerous in such an atmosphere, especially in light of the newly enacted Espionage Act of 1917, which gave the federal government broad power to prosecute anyone whose public pronouncements were considered "disloyal" to the war effort.

La Follette's strident antiwar stance and criticism of the Espionage Act made him a target in Congress, where he faced charges of espionage along with formal moves to expel him from the Senate. In October 1917, however, La Follette delivered a rousing three-hour speech defending both his own constitutional rights and those of all "honest and law-abiding citizens of this country" who had been "terrorized and outraged in their rights by those sworn to uphold the laws and protect the rights of the people." In particular, he stressed, citizens had a right "to discuss the war in all its phases" and their representatives in Congress had a duty "to declare the purposes and objects of the war."[57] The charges of espionage against La Follette were eventually dropped, as were some of the more extreme sections of the Espionage Act, when Congress revisited the legislation after the war.

What is not immediately clear from this story, however, is why congressional speeches like La Follette's should hamper a president's wartime powers. When Congress passes laws or refuses to fund certain activities, presidents are understandably constrained. But why should speeches, all by themselves, have any effect on foreign policy?

The answer, it turns out, has less to do with the speaker than the audience. When a member of Congress publicly disavows a war that the president has endorsed, it sends an informative signal to America's foreign enemies and allies who are both trying to gauge the U.S. government's resolve to see a fight through to the end. Enemies, seeing that the president lacks unanimous support for a military venture, may feel emboldened—becoming less likely to surrender to a nation they see as only weakly committed to the fight. Why bother surrendering if the enemy will eventually go home anyway? Allies, meanwhile, may refuse to commit troops to conflicts that they anticipate will be prematurely abandoned—a fact that further increases the costs of military action for the president. Confronting a war against an emboldened enemy without the support of allies, presidents may begrudgingly conclude that military action is no longer worth it. To avoid this fate, presidents must send credible messages to foreign states about the country's wartime resolve—a task that is complicated by the informal statements of lawmakers.[58]

MEDIA APPEARANCES

In an age defined by the twenty-four-hour news cycle, members of Congress do not have to work all that hard to get access to a national audience. Television, in particular, provides an important venue for Congress to communicate with the public. Through appearances on both national and local television shows, members of Congress can indicate to the president and other policymakers how they will likely vote on any relevant legislation, and thus shape presidential policy before it comes up for formal debate.

Members of Congress also serve as important informants for journalists and media outlets. Many aspects of U.S. foreign policy are highly classified, accessible only to a select few in the executive branch and Congress. Foreign correspondents may be able to fill in some of the gaps, but they too must rely on others to clarify the stakes involved in diplomatic talks and foreign policy declarations. (It does not help matters that news outlets are abandoning their foreign desks in an effort to cut costs.) Television news, in particular, leans heavily on congressional sources, as it struggles to churn out large volumes of stories for which there is little opportunity to conduct in-depth research.

So it is Congress that often determines which foreign policy topics get coverage and what information is made available. Media outlets turn to members of Congress to determine which aspects of the issue are discussed, what is considered legitimate criticism, and who constitutes an expert on the subject.[59] In the process, say critics, media reporting becomes a closed system—in the words of political scientist Jonathan Mermin, "a vehicle for government officials to criticize each other, reporting criticism of U.S. policy that has been expressed inside the government, but declining to report critical perspectives expressed outside of Washington."[60]

15.3.3 Intrabranch Checks on Presidential Foreign Policymaking

As we have seen, Congress has both formal and informal ways of checking the president's foreign policy objectives. Sometimes, however, the most frustrating impediments arise from within the president's own branch of government via the actions of bureaucrats, advisors, and military personnel.

LEAKS

The United States has a long history of government leaks, which usually come from a troubled bureaucrat intent upon raising public awareness about a government policy or practice.[61] Such disclosures can shine a bright light on controversial or even illegal actions that might otherwise evade scrutiny.

In modern political history, the most controversial—and possibly consequential—leak came at the height of the Vietnam War.* On June 13, 1971, the *New York Times* began publishing excerpts from a classified Department of Defense study detailing the nature of U.S. military involvement in Southeast Asia. The documents, which became known as the Pentagon Papers, revealed a long history of secret bombings, military invasions, and outright lies about America's involvement in the region since the 1950s. The source of this information was Daniel Ellsberg, a military analyst who had surreptitiously photocopied the reports and then leaked them to the media. Called "the most dangerous man in America" by Secretary of State Henry Kissinger, Ellsberg was charged with theft and conspiracy under the Espionage Act, but the case was dismissed when federal prosecutors were found to have used illegal wiretaps to gather evidence against him.

In terms of sheer volume, though, nothing compares to the deluge of national security leaks surrounding the U.S. government's "War on Terror." Established in 2006 by the controversial and enigmatic Julian Assange, WikiLeaks was an international organization with the expressed mission of publicizing and commenting on government reports and classified information leaked by anonymous sources. In the decade that followed, WikiLeaks released over a million documents from nations around the globe, including a trove of U.S. State Department cables, classified reports on the wars in Iraq and Afghanistan, and internal memos from the National Security Agency (NSA).

WikiLeaks spawned a number of spin-off organizations, such as OpenLeaks and PubLeaks. In some instances, though, rogue employees manage their own release of classified documents. In June 2013, Edward Snowden, a systems administrator at Booz Allen Hamilton, a federal government contractor, shared hundreds of classified NSA documents with journalists Glenn Greenwald and Laura Poitras. Snowden's leaked documents revealed numerous global surveillance programs, many of them run by the NSA with the cooperation of telecommunications companies and European governments.[62] The Pentagon concluded that Snowden's was the largest theft of U.S. secrets in the nation's history.[63] George Brandis, attorney general of Australia, similarly asserted that Snowden's disclosure was the "most serious setback for Western intelligence since the second World War."[64]

Whatever the damage inflicted on national security policy, Snowden's leaks spurred a host of reform efforts both at home and abroad (figure 15.3). In the following years, the

---

*Unlike members of the press, however, government whistleblowers are not afforded any constitutional protections for their actions; as a result, they can face criminal prosecution. See Alexander Kasner, "National Security Leaks and Constitutional Duty," *Stanford Law Review* 67, no. 1 (2015): 241–83.

FIGURE 15.3. Edward Snowden. Stop Watching Us, a coalition of both left- and right-wing groups, rallied in Washington, D.C., in October 2013 to protest NSA surveillance programs disclosed by Edward Snowden. Many demonstrators held signs thanking Snowden for exposing the mass surveillance. *Source:* CQ Roll Call via AP Images.

U.S. House of Representatives passed an NSA reform bill (later defeated in the Senate) meant to curb the bulk collection of phone data.[65] U.S. District Court judge Richard Leon ruled that the NSA's controversial program violated the Constitution's Fourth Amendment, which protects Americans against unreasonable searches and seizures. Large tech firms such as Google and Yahoo finally got serious about privacy, adding encryption technologies to protect customers' information and communications. Great Britain held its first open intelligence hearing. Germany opened an investigation into the tapping of Chancellor Angela Merkel's cell phone. Even President Obama, no fan of Snowden, acknowledged that there would have been no surveillance debate without him.[66]

MILITARY PUSHBACK

Formally, the president commands the military, and the military, for its part, is obligated to obey the president's commands. In practice, though, members of the military need not blindly obey their commander in chief. Military officials may use the media to expound upon the likely costs of a proposed military venture. Sometimes, too, they choose to only partially implement orders from on high. And when media attention spikes, partial implementation may give way to full-blown defiance.

President Truman's experience with General Douglas MacArthur provides a case in point. After North Korea invaded South Korea in June 1950, the United States promptly dispatched air, naval, and (later) ground forces to assist in South Korea's defense. MacArthur, whom Truman had appointed as head of the UN Command in South Korea, achieved some early successes against North Korean troops. MacArthur, however, was not satisfied, and he lobbied the president for an aggressive counterattack into North Korea.[67]

President Truman and his advisors worried that the People's Republic of China might interpret an incursion into North Korea as a threat and respond militarily.[68] Nonetheless, in September 1950, the administration authorized limited operations there.[69] Later that same month, MacArthur advanced into North Korea, testing the limits by some accounts, and, by other accounts, overstepping them.[70]

In November 1950, as Truman had feared, China entered the war. Within weeks, Chinese troops crossed into North Korea and drove the U.S.-led forces south of the nation's border. When MacArthur was asked by a reporter on December 1, 1950, if the president's restrictions on operations against Chinese forces were hampering U.S. efforts, the general replied that they were indeed "an enormous handicap, unprecedented in military history."[71] The not-so-subtle jab caught the attention of his commander in chief. On December 6, Truman issued a directive requiring all military and diplomatic personnel to "refrain from direct communications on military or foreign policy with newspapers, magazines, and other publicity media."[72]

In February and March 1951, MacArthur's forces once again gained the upper hand and recaptured the South Korean capital Seoul, which had fallen on January 4. These developments raised hopes in Washington of brokering a ceasefire. When MacArthur received advance notice of Truman's intention to settle with the North Koreans and Chinese, however, the general issued a communiqué that was sharply critical of the president's plans.[73] Truman later wrote, "This was a challenge to the authority of the President under the Constitution. By this act MacArthur left me no choice—I could no longer tolerate his insubordination."[74]

On April 11, 1951, Truman relieved MacArthur of his command. It wasn't without cost. When the general returned stateside, he received a hero's welcome: ticker-tape parades were held in his honor, and he addressed Congress in person, delivering a speech later known for its memorable reference to the refrain of an old barracks ballad: "old soldiers never die; they just fade away."

Truman had every right to fire the popular general, and by most accounts, he was justified in doing so. The costs of his conflict with MacArthur, however, were unmistakable. Truman's approval ratings at the end of his presidency hovered around the high 20s, and at the end of his term, he would have to vacate his office for another general, Dwight Eisenhower, who won the 1952 election in no small part on a promise to finally end the Korean War.

Historical Transformations: The Emerging "Deep State"

Some readers will look upon leaks and military pushback as evidence of an American "Deep State"—a cabal of unelected bureaucrats who place their own priorities above the president's and nation's. And while this isn't entirely correct—there is no cabal, and supposed Deep State "operatives" are subject to a good deal of oversight and accountability—we should not dismiss these allegations out of hand.

In chapter 2, we surveyed the historical expansion and empowerment of the executive branch, including the foreign policy apparatus. We saw that the most significant increases in federal employment accompanied wartime, when agencies charged with overseeing foreign affairs—the Department of Defense, State Department, and various intelligence agencies—were most active.

But even after World War II, which yielded a vastly more expansive (and expensive) Department of Defense, these agencies continued to proliferate amid an international backdrop in which crises were common and communism threatened to spread westward. In 1940, the Department of State employed 1,128 people. In 1945, that number was 3,700. By 1950, five years after the war's end, the number of State Department employees who were stationed stateside had skyrocketed to 9,000.[75]

Meanwhile, the National Security Act of 1947 established the Central Intelligence Agency (CIA) as an independent, civilian agency within the executive branch, consolidating responsibilities that had previously fallen on the military and other federal bureaus. In the six years after its founding, the CIA would grow to six times its original size and gain the ability to fund operations without disclosing certain details to the public.[76]

In these and similar developments, we see the inception of a modern foreign policy bureaucracy—a Deep State, to some. In important ways, to be clear, this bureaucracy augments presidential power: with a larger State Department, for example, presidents have a greater capacity to negotiate foreign agreements and maintain international ties; with a more expansive CIA, presidents receive more reliable information to guide their decision making.

The growth and maturation of the foreign policy establishment, however, also create challenges for presidents. As we saw in chapter 10, presidents struggle to control an unwieldy bureaucracy not of their making or choosing. And when presidents set their sights on subverting or marginalizing executive branch agencies, those who work within them are more than capable of offering resistance.

When President Trump took office in 2017, he embarked on what seemed like a steadfast campaign to dismantle the country's foreign policy apparatus. His first target was the State Department. He did away with experts and diplomats who had worked there for years, questioning their loyalty and disparaging their contributions. He refused to fill crucial ambassadorships and regional assistant secretaries. And in his first proposed budget to Congress, Trump requested a 31 percent cut to the State Department's funding—a strong message that, wherever Trump's priorities lay, they certainly weren't with the State Department.

To manage and facilitate his attack on the State Department, Trump appointed Rex Tillerson as its secretary. Employees described the former ExxonMobil CEO as uninvolved and dismissive of the department's mission and core functions. At one

Continued on next page

point, Tillerson hired a consulting agency to survey employees about what they felt their work units should "stop doing or providing."[77] And as Tillerson eliminated prestigious State Department fellowship programs designed to recruit talented university students, he grew the size of his personal staff, which he kept in cubicles separate from the rest of the office.

On the rare occasions when Tillerson was responsive to the desires of career State Department officials, Trump himself would stand in the way. In June 2017, with tensions rising between Qatar and other Persian Gulf states, Tillerson traveled overseas to end the standoff peacefully. The president took a different route: he went on Twitter to blame Qatar for the conflict and express his solidarity with Saudi Arabia. Said one department official, "Qatar was seven days of work only to fall apart with a single tweet by the president."[78]

How, then, did the State Department respond to a president who opposed its existence and conducted foreign policy through outside, informal channels? It helped impeach him.

Recall from chapter 8 that Trump was impeached (the first time) after holding up $391 million in Ukrainian military aid in exchange for help with his reelection. Though Democrats in Congress undoubtedly led the impeachment charge, they did so with critical assistance from aggrieved civil servants working within the executive branch.[79] Almost every step of the impeachment process relied on input from government bureaucrats. It began when a member of the CIA alerted Congress of Trump's wrongdoings. After that, a group of sixty executive branch inspectors general signed a letter arguing that Trump could not legally conceal the whistleblower's full report from Congress.

Among these aggrieved parties, bureaucrats from the State Department stood first in line. After years of abuse and neglect from the White House, Trump had yet again undermined their role by conducting a shadow foreign policy in Ukraine. Through his personal lawyer, Rudolph Giuliani, Trump flouted official channels of diplomacy and performed end-around runs against State Department officials stationed in the region. "There appeared to be two channels of U.S. policy-making and implementation, one regular and one highly irregular,"[80] testified William Taylor, the department's interim ambassador to Ukraine. The second channel, Taylor insisted, had "undercut" the nation's foreign policy efforts.

In an impressive and visible reassertion of State Department norms and commitments, the first impeachment trial featured officials like Taylor as well as Deputy Assistant Secretary of State George Kent, who was in charge of the department's policies toward Ukraine, and Marie Yovanovitch, who served as ambassador to Ukraine before Trump removed her. The political value of their appearances as witnesses should not be understated; as distinguished, impartial experts who had served under administrations of both parties, they lent credence to the charge that Trump's actions were not only wrong but that they "undermine[d] the rule of law."[81] Trump himself seemed to understand the damage wrought by their testimonies, at one point tweeting, "What is taking place is not an impeachment, it is a COUP."[82]

For its part, the media ran with the narrative of a Deep State uprising. According to one *New York Times* headline, the "deep state has emerged from the shadows."[83] This storyline reflected talking points from the White House, which alleged that the impeachment was "another example of the 'Deep State,' the media, and the Democrats in Congress damaging our national security."[84] Though Deep State allegations—understood literally—are rarely credible, the moniker seems surprisingly fitting in this context. As Trump tried to exercise unrestricted authority over the nation's foreign dealings, who rose from the depths to stop him? Experienced and aggrieved bureaucrats working deep within the foreign policy establishment.

Conclusion

In foreign policy, the institutional presidency presents a paradox. On the one hand, in this domain presidential power reaches its apex. Through powers Congress has formally delegated and others that presidents have claimed on their own, presidents have situated themselves at the very center of foreign policymaking. It is the president, above all, who decides when and whether we go to war, the president who shapes international trade policy, and the president who represents the nation in all matters of diplomacy.

On the other hand, for all the power they wield in foreign policy, presidents must contend with many constraints. Internationally, they confront foreign states, international alliances and organizations, and a growing corpus of international law, each of which can erect roadblocks to a president's foreign policy agenda. At home, Congress, the foreign policy bureaucracy, and sometimes the military itself can undermine proposed foreign policy initiatives. Against any one political opponent, presidents can expect to triumph. But when fending off so many, presidents often see their foreign policy aspirations wither.

Presidential power, meanwhile, does not necessarily translate into presidential control. In foreign policy, presidents routinely find themselves managing crises not of their making. They struggle at the center of foreign wars launched by their predecessors. They are thrust to the center of foreign disputes they would just as soon avoid. Just when they hope to turn their attention to some cherished domestic policy program, presidents must put out fires, both figurative and literal, erupting around the world.

Key Terms

isolationism	North Atlantic Treaty Organization
Monroe Doctrine	international law
Great White Fleet	Geneva Conventions
Cold War	Universal Declaration of Human Rights
globalization	International Criminal Court
economic liberalization	Paris Peace Accords
international alliances	Neutrality Acts

Questions for Discussion

1. Are there ways in which domestic and international constraints on the president's foreign policy powers reinforce one another? Are there any instances in which they might negate each other?
2. Under what conditions is Congress most likely to take advantage of the foreign policy powers at its disposal?
3. Are there specific features of terrorism that make it an especially difficult foreign policy problem for presidents to solve?
4. In what ways has the democratic peace theory informed the decisions that recent presidents have made about how to respond to emergent foreign crises? In what ways have these presidents justified their decisions by reference to its central empirical claims?
5. In what areas of foreign affairs might an institutional approach to the presidency be most informative? Is an institutional approach more valuable when studying domestic or foreign affairs?
6. Is it fair to say that "presidential power reaches its apex" in the international arena?

Suggested Reading

Baum, Matthew, and Philip Potter. *War and Democratic Constraint: How the Public Influences Foreign Policy*. Princeton: Princeton University Press, 2015.

Bose, Meena. *Shaping and Signaling Presidential Policy: The National Security Decision Making of Eisenhower and Kennedy*. College Station: Texas A&M University Press, 1998.

Fowler, Linda. *Watchdogs on the Hill: The Decline of Congressional Oversight of U.S. Foreign Relations*. Princeton: Princeton University Press, 2015.

Howell, William G., and Jon C. Pevehouse. *While Dangers Gather: Congressional Checks on Presidential War Powers*. Princeton: Princeton University Press, 2007.

Kriner, Douglas. *After the Rubicon: Congress, Presidents, and the Politics of Waging War*. Chicago: University of Chicago Press, 2010.

Kriner, Douglas, and Eric Schickler. *Investigating the President: Congressional Checks on Presidential Power*. Princeton: Princeton University Press, 2016.

Milner, Helen, and Dustin Tingley. *Sailing the Water's Edge: The Domestic Politics of American Foreign Policy*. Princeton: Princeton University Press, 2015.

Rapp-Hooper, Mira. *Shields of the Republic: The Triumph and Peril of America's Alliances*. Cambridge, MA: Harvard University Press, 2020.

Thorpe, Rebecca U. *The American Warfare State: The Domestic Politics of Military Spending*. Chicago: University of Chicago Press, 2014.

Zeisberg, Mariah. *War Powers: The Politics of Constitutional Authority*. Princeton: Princeton University Press, 2013.

Notes

1. David Rothkopf, *Running the World* (New York: Perseus Books, 2005).
2. George Washington, "Washington's Farewell Address—1796," Yale Law Library's The Avalon Project: Documents in Law, History, and Diplomacy, http://avalon.law.yale.edu/18th_century/washing.asp.

3. James Monroe, "Monroe Doctrine—1823," Our Documents, http://www.ourdocuments.gov/doc.php?flash=true&doc=23.

4. Mark Grimsley, "The American Civil War and Civic Virtue," Foreign Policy Research Institute, November 4, 2008, https://www.fpri.org/article/2008/11/the-american-civil-war-and-civic-virtue/.

5. Rebecca U. Thorpe, *The American Warfare State: The Domestic Politics of Military Spending* (Chicago: University of Chicago Press, 2014), 41.

6. Thorpe, *The American Warfare State*, 42.

7. Dylan Matthews, "Defense Spending in the US, in Four Charts," *Washington Post*, August 28, 2012, http://www.washingtonpost.com/blogs/wonkblog/wp/2012/08/28/defense-spending-in-the-u-s-in-four-charts/.

8. Dinah Walker, "Trends in US Military Spending," Council on Foreign Relations, July 15, 2014, https://www.cfr.org/report/trends-us-military-spending.

9. "Military Expenditure (Current USD)," World Bank, World Development Indicators, 2020, Data File, https://datacatalog.worldbank.org/military-expenditure-current-usd.

10. "Military Expenditure (Current USD)"; Nan Tian et al., "Trends in World Military Expenditure, 2019," Stockholm International Peace Research Institute, April 2020, https://www.sipri.org/sites/default/files/2020-04/fs_2020_04_milex_0_0.pdf.

11. Thorpe, *The American Warfare State*, 180.

12. Beverly Crawford and Edward Fogarty, "Globalization's Impact on American Business and Economics: An Overview," in *The Impact of Globalization on the United States*, vol. 3, ed. Beverly Crawford and Edward Fogarty (Westport, CT: Praeger, 2008), xi.

13. "US Trade in Goods and Services—Balance of Payments (BOP) Basis," Foreign Trade Division, U.S. Census Bureau, April 2021, https://www.census.gov/foreign-trade/statistics/historical/goods.pdf.

14. See "Visualizing Federal Government Debt," U.S. Treasury Data Lab, https://datalab.usaspending.gov/americas-finance-guide/debt/, and "Major Foreign Holders of Treasury Securities," U.S. Department of the Treasury, https://ticdata.treasury.gov/Publish/mfh.txt.

15. Dhara Ranasighe, "China to Overtake US Economy; India Trumps Japan," CNBC, April 30, 2014, https://www.cnbc.com/2014/04/29/china-to-overtake-us-economy-india-trumps-japan.html.

16. "Where Are You on the Global Pay Scale?" *BBC News Magazine*, March 29, 2012, https://www.bbc.com/news/magazine-17512040.

17. Many experts, however, debate whether economic sanctions are effective, as in many cases they drive states that flout international norms toward deeper intransigence. See, for example, Daniel Drezner, *The Sanctions Paradox: Economic Statecraft and International Relations* (New York: Cambridge University Press, 1999); David Baldwin, *Economic Statecraft* (Princeton: Princeton University Press, 1985); Dean Lacy and Emerson M. S. Niou, "Theory of Economic Sanctions and Issue Linkage: The Roles of Preferences, Information, and Threats," *Journal of Politics* 66, no. 1 (2004): 25–42; and A. Cooper Drury, "Sanctions as Coercive Diplomacy: The US President's Decision to Initiate Economic Sanctions," *Political Research Quarterly* 54, no. 3 (2001): 485–508.

18. Philip Elliott, "What Russian Sanctions Mean for Joe Biden's Presidency," *Time*, March 1, 2022, https://time.com/6153192/joe-biden-russia-sanctions/.

19. "Fiscal Year (FY) 2019 Development and Humanitarian Assistance Budget: Fact Sheet," U.S. Agency for International Development, March 21, 2018, https://www.usaid.gov/news-information/fact-sheets/fiscal-year-fy-2019-development-and-humanitarian-assistance-budget#:~:text=The%20FY%202019%20President's%20Budget%20for%20the%20State%20Department%20and,Disaster%20Assistance%2C%20and%20USAID%20operational.

20. Nancy Qian, "Making Progress on Foreign Aid," *Annual Review of Economics* 7, no. 1 (2014): 277–308.

21. Craig Burnside and David Dollar, "Aid, Policies, and Growth," *American Economic Review* 90, no. 4 (2000): 847–68, https://doi.org/10.1257/aer.90.4.847.

22. Ilyana Kuziemko and Eric Werker, "How Much Is a Seat on the Security Council Worth? Foreign Aid and Bribery at the United Nations," *Journal of Political Economy* 114, no. 5 (2006): 905–30.

23. Foreign Assistance Act, 22 U.S.C. 2151 (1961).

24. Use of Special Presidential Authorities for Foreign Assistance, GAO/NSIAD-85–79 (Washington, DC: U.S. General Accounting Office, 1985), https://www.gao.gov/products/nsiad-85-79.

25. See, for example, Edward Gulick, *Europe's Classical Balance of Power* (New York: W. W. Norton, 1955); and Bruce Russett and John Oneal, *Triangulating Peace: Democracy, Interdependence, and International Organizations* (New York: W. W. Norton, 2001). For a helpful review of the literature on alliances as instruments of both peace and conflict, see Jack S. Levy, "Alliance Formation and War Behavior: An Analysis of the Great Powers, 1495–1975," *Journal of Conflict Resolution* 25, no. 4 (1981): 581–85.

26. James Morrow, "Modeling Forms of International Cooperation: Distribution versus Information," *International Organization* 4, no. 3 (1994): 387–423; James Fearon, "Rationalist Explanations for War," *International Organization* 49, no. 3 (1995): 379–414.

27. Russett and Oneal, *Triangulating Peace*, 60–61.

28. David Singer and Melvin Small, *The Wages of War, 1816–1965* (New York: John Wiley & Sons, 1972).

29. Levy, "Alliance Formation and War Behavior," 582.

30. Cat Contiguglia, "Trump: EU Is One of United States' Biggest Foes," *POLITICO*, April 18, 2019, https://www.politico.eu/article/donald-trump-putin-russia-europe-one-of-united-states-biggest-foes/.

31. Eileen Sullivan, "Trump Questions the Core of NATO: Mutual Defense, Including Montenegro," *New York Times*, July 19, 2018, A.19.

32. Phil Stewart and Idrees Ali, "U.S. to Withdraw about 12,000 Troops from Germany but Nearly Half to Stay in Europe," Reuters, July 29, 2020, https://www.reuters.com/article/us-usa-trump-germany-military/u-s-to-withdraw-about-12000-troops-from-germany-but-nearly-half-to-stay-in-europe-idUSKCN24U20L.

33. Elliott Davis, "Survey: Germans View China and U.S. as Equally Important Allies," *U.S. News & World Report*, May 18, 2020, https://www.usnews.com/news/best-countries/articles/2020-05-18/survey-germans-view-china-and-us-as-equally-important-allies.

34. Emma Anderson, "Merkel Condemns George Floyd Killing, Dodges on Trump Criticism," *POLITICO*, June 4, 2020, https://www.politico.com/news/2020/06/04/merkel-condemns-george-floyd-killing-dodges-on-trump-criticism-301856.

35. Mira Rapp-Hooper, *Shields of the Republic. The Triumph and Peril of America's Alliances* (Cambridge, MA: Harvard University Press, 2020), 3.

36. Michael Elliott, "The Institutional Expansion of Human Rights, 1863–2003: A Comprehensive Dataset of International Instruments," *Journal of Peace Research* 48, no. 4 (2011): 537–46.

37. From the preamble to the United Nations' Universal Declaration of Human Rights, 1948, https://www.un.org/en/about-us/universal-declaration-of-human-rights.

38. United Nations, "Article 5," Universal Declaration of Human Rights, 1948, https://www.un.org/en/about-us/universal-declaration-of-human-rights.

39. For an analysis of why states comply with international law, see Andrew T. Guzman, "A Compliance-Based Theory of International Law," *California Law Review* 90, no. 6 (2002): 1823–87.

40. "Clinton's Statement on War Crimes Court," BBC News, December 31, 2000, http://news.bbc.co.uk/2/hi/1095580.stm.

41. Mark Mazzetti, "'03 US Memo Approved Harsh Interrogations," *New York Times*, April 2, 2008, A.1.

42. Dina Smeltz et al., "2020 Chicago Council Survey," Chicago Council on Global Affairs, September 17, 2020, https://www.thechicagocouncil.org/research/public-opinion-survey/2020-chicago-council-survey.

43. Andrew Glass, "Trump Scuttles Trans-Pacific Trade Pact, Jan. 23, 2017," *POLITICO*, January 23, 2019, https://www.politico.com/story/2019/01/23/trans-pacific-trade-pact-2017-1116638.

44. John Hart Ely, *War and Responsibility: Constitutional Lessons of Vietnam and Its Aftermath* (Princeton: Princeton University Press, 1993), 4.

45. Terry Atlas, "Clinton Sends US Troops into Rwanda," *Chicago Tribune*, July 30, 1994, 1.

46. Steven V. Roberts, "Senate, 78 to 21, Overrides Reagan's Veto and Imposes Sanctions on South Africa," *New York Times*, October 3, 1986, A.1.

47. Douglas Jehl, "G.O.P. Senator Sends Letter to Colleagues Opposing Bolton," *New York Times*, May 25, 2005, A.10.

48. Maggie Haberman, Julian E. Barnes, and Peter Baker, "Dan Coats to Step Down as Intelligence Chief; Trump Picks Loyalist for Job," *New York Times*, July 29, 2019, A.1.

49. Charlie Savage, Julian E. Barnes, and Annie Karni, "Trump Drops Plans to Nominate John Ratcliffe as Director of National Intelligence," *New York Times*, August 3, 2019, A.1.

50. Data on congressional hearings available online through the Policy Agendas Project (http://www .policyagendas.org).

51. Richard L. Lyons, "Church Warns of US 'Tyranny,'" *Washington Post*, August 18, 1975, A.3.

52. "Congressmen Find Few Clues about Boston Bombings in Russia," CBS News, June 2, 2013, http://www .cbsnews.com/news/congressmen-find-few-clues-about-boston-bombings-in-russia/.

53. This section draws from William Howell, "Presidents, Congress, and the Partisan Politics of War." *Bipartisan Policy Review*, Cornell University, March 2022, 26–28.

54. William G. Howell and Jon C. Pevehouse, *While Dangers Gather: Congressional Checks on Presidential War Powers* (Princeton: Princeton University Press, 2007).

55. Amber Phillips, "Why No American President Followed through on Promises to End the Afghanistan War—Until Now," *Washington Post*, August 19, 2021, https://www.washingtonpost.com/politics/2021/08/18 /why-no-american-president-followed-through-promises-end-afghanistan-war-until-now/.

56. U.S. Senator Chris Murphy, "The Taliban's Latest Gains in Afghanistan Are Not a Reason to Reverse Course on U.S. Troop Withdrawal," Press Release, August 10, 2021, https://www.murphy.senate.gov/newsroom /press-releases/murphy-on-us-senate-floor-the-talibans-latest-gains-in-afghanistan-are-not-a-reason-to -reverse-course-on-us-troop-withdrawal.

57. Robert La Follette, "Free Speech in Wartime, October 6, 1917," in Robert C. Byrd, *The Senate, 1789–1989*, vol. 3, *Classic Speeches, 1830–1993* (Washington, DC: Government Printing Office, 1994), 517–20.

58. Howell and Pevehouse, *While Dangers Gather*.

59. See W. Lance Bennett, "Toward a Theory of Press-State Relations," *Journal of Communication* 40, no. 2 (1990): 103–27.

60. Jonathan Mermin, *Debating War and Peace: Media Coverage of US Intervention in the Post-Vietnam Era* (Princeton: Princeton University Press, 1999), 7.

61. For more on the history and politics of leaks, see Rahul Sagar, *Secrets and Leaks: The Dilemma of State Secrecy* (Princeton: Princeton University Press, 2013).

62. Glenn Greenwald, *No Place to Hide: Edward Snowden, the NSA, and the US Surveillance State* (New York: Metropolitan Books, 2014).

63. Chris Strohm and Del Quentin Wilber, "Pentagon Says Snowden Took Most U.S. Secrets Ever: Rogers," Bloomberg, January 9, 2014, http://www.bloomberg.com/news/articles/2014-01-09/pentagon-finds -snowden-took-1-7-million-files-rogers-says.

64. Cameron Stewart and Paul Maley, "Edward Snowden Stole up to 20,000 Aussie Files," *The Australian*, December 5, 2013, https://www.theaustralian.com.au/nation/foreign-affairs/edward-snowden-stole-up-to -20000-aussie-files/news-story/5c082d0996d2435a412aa603fefa60ae.

65. Julian Hattem and Ramsey Cox, "NSA Reform Bill Dies in Senate," *The Hill*, November 18, 2014, http:// thehill.com/blogs/floor-action/senate/224635-senate-nsa-vote.

66. Matt Sledge, "Edward Snowden Vindicated: Obama Speech Acknowledges Changes Needed to Surveillance," *Huffington Post*, January 17, 2014, http://www.huffingtonpost.com/2014/01/17/obama-edward -snowden_n_4617970.html.

67. James F. Schnabel, *United States Army in the Korean War: Policy and Direction—The First Year* (Washington, DC: Government Printing Office, 1972), 106–7.

68. James I. Matray, "Truman's Plan for Victory: National Self-Determination and the Thirty-Eighth Parallel," *Journal of American History* 66, no. 2 (1979): 314–33.

69. Matray, "Truman's Plan," 326–28.

70. Michael D. Pearlman, *Truman and MacArthur: Policy, Politics, and the Hunger for Honor and Renown* (Bloomington: Indiana University Press, 2008), 119; Schnabel, *United States Army*, 218.

71. Pearlman, *Truman and MacArthur*, 170.

72. Harry S. Truman, "Harry S. Truman to Omar Bradley, December 6, 1950," Harry S. Truman Library and Museum.

73. James D. Clayton, *The Years of MacArthur: Triumph and Disaster, 1945–1964* (Boston: Houghton Mifflin, 1985), 586.

74. Harry S. Truman, *Memoirs by Harry S. Truman: Years of Trial and Hope* (New York: New American Library, 1965), 441–42.

75. "A History of the United States Department of State: 1789–1996," Office of the Historian, Department of State, July 1996, https://1997-2001.state.gov/about_state/history/dephis.html#superpower.

76. "History of the CIA," Central Intelligence Agency, https://www.cia.gov/legacy/cia-history/.

77. Robbie Gramer, Dan De Luce, and Colum Lynch, "How the Trump Administration Broke the State Department," *Foreign Policy*, July 23, 2019, https://foreignpolicy.com/2017/07/31/how-the-trump-administration-broke-the-state-department/.

78. Gramer, De Luce, and Lynch, "How the Trump Administration Broke the State Department."

79. Stephen Skowronek, John A. Dearborn, and Desmond S. King, *Phantoms of a Beleaguered Republic: The Deep State and the Unitary Executive* (New York: Oxford University Press, 2021).

80. Skowronek, Dearborn, and King, *Phantoms of a Beleaguered Republic*, 182.

81. Skowronek, Dearborn, and King, *Phantoms of a Beleaguered Republic*, 180.

82. Skowronek, Dearborn, and King, *Phantoms of a Beleaguered Republic*, 177.

83. Peter Baker et al., "Trump's War on the 'Deep State' Turns against Him," *New York Times*, October 24, 2019, A.1.

84. Skowronek, Dearborn, and King, *Phantoms of a Beleaguered Republic*, 173.

16

Wartime Policymaking at Home

THE PREVIOUS TWO CHAPTERS dealt separately with domestic and foreign policymaking—and with reason. The two domains provide distinct opportunities to clarify the unique perspectives that presidents bring to policy disputes and to appreciate the many impediments that stand in presidents' way, even when their powers seem boundless. Each on their own, domestic and foreign policy provides different lessons into the institutional presidency.

Still, it is important not to read too much into the distinction between "foreign policy" and "domestic policy." There are many policy issues, after all, that operate at the boundaries of these two policy domains. These "intermestic" issues, such as immigration or energy, are not appropriately categorized as either domestic or foreign policy. In truth, they are both.

Meanwhile, other policies that we might be inclined to classify as distinctly foreign have deep domestic roots: protectionist trade policies, for instance, are regularly pursued in order to placate the interests of a domestic industry. And other policies that we might classify as domestic have immediate implications for foreign policy: U.S. agricultural subsidies, for instance, can undermine the capacity of farmers abroad to compete, and thereby reshape trade flows into and out of the country. The globalization of supply chains, the rise of multinational corporations, and rapid development of communication technologies worldwide have further eroded any distinction one might wish to draw between foreign and domestic policymaking.

This chapter investigates still another reason why foreign and domestic policymaking can be evaluated together rather than separately. And this particular reason has preoccupied presidency scholars for decades. It presents itself in the form of a deceivingly simple question: How does war alter the president's ability to remake domestic policy? Or more precisely, can presidents successfully advance domestic policies in wartime that might elude them during times of peace?

16.1 War and Presidential Power: A Brief Intellectual History

In the mid-twentieth century presidency scholars did their most serious and sustained thinking about the relationship between war and presidential power. At that time the topic stood at the very center of studies of the U.S. presidency. And no wonder. The profound

FIGURE 16.1. War and presidential power. Is it possible for presidents to leverage wars to advance controversial domestic policies at home? Or, as this cartoon suggests, are a president's muscles confined to the arm that uses them? Copyright 2007 Mike Keefe. Reproduced by permission of Cagle Cartoons.

political changes wrought by a civil war and two world wars not very long past demanded explanation. So scholars such as Edward Corwin, Clinton Rossiter, and later Arthur Schlesinger set their minds to explaining how wars contributed to the emergence of a distinctly modern presidency. Though their accounts differ in important ways, each of these scholars argued that wars allowed some presidents to exalt their office and to enact federal policy initiatives and change.[1]

EDWARD CORWIN

Edward Corwin devoted an entire chapter of his masterwork, *The President: Office and Powers*, to the issue of presidential power during times of war; he followed it up with a series of lectures at the University of Michigan, later published as *Total War and the Constitution*. Corwin considered the president's constitutional authority to be at its apex during the Civil War, World War I, and World War II. Presidents Lincoln, Wilson, and FDR all flexed their Article II powers during these wars, and Congress and the courts largely let them have their way. In fact, Corwin observed, during these wars Congress actively supplemented the president's constitutional powers, and the courts refused to interfere—at least as long as troops remained in the field. Corwin concluded that **wartime jurisprudence**—relaxed judicial standards for evaluating presidential actions during times of war—takes the place of the principles and standards that typically inform judicial decision making.

Over the course of his career, Corwin appeared to revise his thinking about whether presidential power promptly reverts to its prewar status when fighting ceases. Writing just a few months after the United States' entry into World War I, Corwin suggested that "the powers [war] confers are capable of expanding tremendously, but upon the restoration of normal conditions they shrink with equal rapidity."[2] Later in life, however, Corwin recognized that powers exercised during war may spill over into times of peace, and he suggested that when presidents confront new crises they benefit from the powers claimed during past ones.[3]

The increase in wartime presidential power may be steady, according to Corwin, but the precedent-setting power of some wars is markedly greater than that of others. Largely due to Lincoln's respect for constitutional limits on presidential power, the Civil War, in Corwin's mind, did not fundamentally alter the office of the presidency. Instead, its extensions of presidential power, such as the suspension of habeas corpus, were understood to be exceptional. The two world wars were different. With their development of massive wartime apparatus, sweeping claims of presidential power, and emergency delegations of authority, these wars, according to Corwin, fundamentally changed the presidency.

CLINTON ROSSITER

Clinton Rossiter's views have much in common with Corwin's. "'When the blast of war blows in our ears,'" Rossiter observed, "the President's power to command the forces swells out of all proportion to his other powers."[4] This influence, however, was hardly confined to the conduct of war. By Rossiter's account, it permeated other areas as well: "As proof of this point, we need only think of . . . Franklin Roosevelt as he called upon Congress to extend him 'broad Executive power to wage war' against depression."[5] Rossiter is careful to point out that this expansion is not the result only of the actions of great presidents in great wars:

> Nor should we forget lesser Presidents in lesser crises, for these men, too, left their mark on the office. When Hayes dispatched troops to restore peace in the railroad strike of 1877, when McKinley sent 5,000 soldiers and marines to China during the Boxer uprising, and when Harry Truman acted on a dozen occasions to save entire states from the ravages of storm or fire or flood, the Presidency moved to a higher level of authority and prestige—principally because the people had now been taught to expect more of it.[6]

In *Constitutional Dictatorship: Crisis Government in the Modern Democracies*, Rossiter argued that a state's ability to survive a war depends upon the three criteria of what he called a "constitutional dictator": (1) political power being concentrated in the presidency, (2) government policy reaching beyond its typical bounds, and (3) the executive branch being liberated from constitutional proscriptions. While recognizing that an expansion of presidential power does not, of itself, ensure the nation's survival, Rossiter insisted that "a great emergency in the life of a constitutional democracy will be more easily mastered by the government if dictatorial forms are to some degree substituted for democratic."[7] Should they renounce constitutional dictatorship, in other words, governments conspire in their own—and potentially the nation's—demise.

Still, like Corwin, Rossiter recognized the dangers that accompany an expansive wartime presidency. Constitutional dictatorship puts at risk our form of government and the civil liberties of average citizens, so the people as well as the legislative and judicial branches of government must resist it whenever it takes actions that are not specifically focused on the state's survival.[8]

ARTHUR SCHLESINGER

If the Civil War and the world wars produced a distinctively modern presidency, as many presidential scholars have suggested, later wars, such as those in Korea and Vietnam, yielded additional opportunities for presidents to augment their power.[9] By President Nixon's second term, in the view of some observers, presidents had so distorted the constitutional order that the nation's very system of governance appeared to be in crisis.

In 1973, Arthur Schlesinger expressed the view of many constitutional law scholars and historians when he heralded the emergence of an imperial presidency—that is, a presidency unconstrained by judicial or legislative checks.[10] For Schlesinger, presidential power was "resurgent" in World War II, "ascendant" in the Korean War, and "rampant" in the Vietnam War. In each of these wars, Schlesinger observed, presidents encroached further on Congress's constitutional war powers, until, by the Vietnam War, the practice of war appeared altogether out of sync with the principles laid out in Articles I and II of the Constitution.

This trend, according to Schlesinger, had consequences that went well beyond military matters and into the realm of foreign and domestic policy. After all, Schlesinger asked, "if the President were conceded these life-and-death decisions abroad, how could he be restrained from gathering unto himself the less fateful powers of the national policy?"[11]

In two ways, Schlesinger's argument differs from Corwin's and Rossiter's. First, Schlesinger saw a direct connection between the scale of the war and the amount of power accrued by the president: "The more acute the crisis," he insisted, "the more power flows to the president."[12] Second, whereas Corwin and Rossiter saw successive wars as steadily contributing to presidential power, Schlesinger argued that periods of executive expansion and contraction coincided with periods of war and peace: "While war increased presidential power," Schlesinger noted, "peace brought a reaction against executive excess."[13] For Schlesinger, whether presidents were weak or strong fundamentally depended on whether the nation was at peace or at war.*

Still, Corwin, Rossiter, and Schlesinger essentially agreed on the following premise: wars have catapulted the presidents to the top of the federal government, leaving Congress and the courts to vie for second place in our system of checks and balances.

---

*It was precisely for this reason that Schlesinger, late in life, saw an interminable and pervasive "war against terror" as such a threat to the nation's system of governance. Lacking temporal and physical boundaries, a war against terror might irreparably distort the balance of powers between the executive, legislative, and judicial branches of government.

Thinking Institutionally: Connecting War and Presidential Power
over Domestic Policy

What is it about war that expands presidential influence at home? Why would
members of Congress in wartime support a presidential initiative that, during peace,
they would oppose? Many possible explanations present themselves. Here, however,
we consider two that we've touched upon in earlier chapters: public opinion and the
nationalizing effects of war.

Few forces can shift public opinion about a president more abruptly than war or the
prospect of war.[14] Public support for President Roosevelt in the immediate aftermath
of the Pearl Harbor attacks spiked by roughly eleven points; likewise, just days following
the attacks on September 11, 2001, President Bush's approval ratings jumped by nearly
40 percent, the single greatest increase in a president's approval ratings in the history
of modern polling (see figure 13.2).[15]

It stands to reason that if the public rallies around the commander in chief, it
disadvantages legislators and judges who oppose his policy objectives. Perennially
attuned to their constituents' opinions, this explanation goes, members of Congress
assume a more sympathetic posture to policies originating in the White House.

It is possible, however, that wars expand presidential power through altogether
different mechanisms. One possibility involves the nationalization of public policy
debates. Wars, by this account, increase the relative importance of distinctly *national*
policy outcomes, just as they weaken the kinds of local or regional considerations that,
during peace, are featured so prominently in policy debates. Wars bring the nation's health
and security into stark relief, affirm the American identity of citizens, and underscore
Americans' shared heritage, values, and fates. Wars thereby encourage members of
Congress to prioritize national goals over those that favor their local constituencies. In so
doing, wars align members with the president's policy perspective, which, as discussed in
chapter 14, is distinctly national in orientation. Adopting a national perspective, as
presidents do, members of Congress may look more kindly on the president's policy
agenda, at least until peace is restored and their priorities return to their local constituents.

Both of these explanations allow for the possibility that different wars augment
presidential power to varying degrees. According to the reasoning of the first, a wartime
expansion of executive influence is contingent upon the public rallying behind the
president; according to the second, any expansion depends upon a change in the
terms of the public policy debate. If a war fails to induce significant changes in either,
it would be unlikely to enhance the president's influence at home.

Both explanations also rely on factors that are not confined to war. Though wars
often boost presidential approval ratings, so does a flourishing economy. War is also
not the only event capable of nationalizing domestic policy debates: looming security
threats or belligerent international posturing may have the same effect. Each theory,

Continued on next page

then, emphasizes continuities across peace and war. Rather than reordering and reconstituting our domestic politics, these causal mechanisms imply, wars merely accentuate certain features that play to a president's advantage.

That these explanations have certain commonalities does not mean that they are identical. It is certainly possible for wars to nationalize our politics without increasing the president's approval rating, and vice versa. Such instances present unique opportunities—*critical tests*, in the parlance of social scientists—to evaluate how well each explanation predicts outcomes. As we review the evidence of war's impact on presidential power, we should look for opportunities to discriminate between these two explanations. In so doing we will gain insights not only into whether presidential power expands during times of war but also into *why* it might do so.

16.2 Evidence That Wars Expand Presidential Influence

Are Corwin, Rossiter, and Schlesinger correct when they say that wars tend to augment presidential power? In the main, the answer is yes. But when it comes to the details, as we shall soon see, these three scholars get a number of things wrong.

The following section summarizes the findings of a major research investigation into the systematic effects of war on the president's ability to advance a policy agenda at home.[16] To provide a better sense of the kinds of nettlesome issues that arise when conducting empirical research on the presidency, this section, more than most, also pays a good deal of attention to matters of method. The findings from this study, undertaken by my colleagues and me, show that modern wars did in fact stimulate presidential power but that their effects varied in ways that do not easily comport with the arguments advanced by Corwin, Rossiter, and Schlesinger.

16.2.1 Wartime Appropriations

Appropriations present an especially useful opportunity to assess Congress's willingness to support the president. Presidents, after all, must issue a budget every year, and Congress must subsequently enact a final set of appropriations. Unlike the traditional legislative process, the appropriations process does not permit presidents to remain silent on controversial bills or members of Congress to refuse to cast judgment on presidential proposals.* Examining the difference between proposed and enacted budgets, then, can provide us with a continuous measure of presidential success that can be readily compared across policy domains.

In *The Wartime President*, Saul Jackman, Jon Rogowski, and I set out to examine whether members of Congress were, in fact, more willing to accommodate presidential budgetary

---

* Though Congress can delay formal approval of the budget (and frequently has done so), it ultimately has always passed an annual budget.

proposals during World War II, the Korean War, the Vietnam War, the Gulf War, and the wars in Afghanistan and Iraq than they were during the relatively peaceful interim years. To do so, we tracked budgetary proposals and allotments for seventy-seven agencies over a nearly seventy-year period.* We then compared the president's yearly budget proposal and the actual appropriations allotted to that agency.

Our study found that federal appropriations, perhaps unsurprisingly, increased during times of war. When examining the agencies in our data set, we found that presidential budgetary estimates grew, on average, from $4.1 to $5.1 million (in 1983 dollars) per agency, per year during war; Congress's approved budgets likewise increased from $4.1 to $5.1 million. Note, however, that in times of war, Congress allocated on average slightly *more* money per agency than the president requested (by $19,691), while during peace Congress allocated *less* per agency than the president requested (by $26,629).[†]

Congress's willingness to accommodate the president's requests obviously depended on more than just the presence of peace or war. To tease out estimates of war's independent influence from the data, we had to control for a host of additional economic and political factors that potentially bore on the president's success. In particular, we estimated statistical models that accounted for the size of the president's proposal for each agency in each year, various measures of the partisan composition of Congress, the average unemployment rate during the year when appropriations were proposed and set, the national growth rate since the previous year, and the total budget deficit from the previous year, as well as longer-term characteristics of the agencies themselves.

What did we find? Congress's tendency to approve the president's budgetary requests predictably increased when the nation entered war and declined when peace was restored.[17] During periods of war, the average discrepancy between proposed and final appropriations for our sample of agencies decreased by roughly 26 percent. The effect was negative, substantively large, and statistically significant; and we did not find any evidence that these effects were confined to any particular subset of federal agencies. In short, what Congress gave tended to look a good deal more like what the president wanted during war than it did during peace.

---

*We tracked the same agencies found in D. Roderick Kiewiet and Mathew D. McCubbins, *The Logic of Delegation: Congressional Parties and the Appropriations Process* (New York: Cambridge University Press, 1991) but extended the analysis back to 1933 and up through 2006. In order to extend the data set back to 1933, we also included a handful of the predecessors to agencies in the Kiewiet and McCubbins data set. None of the key findings, however, depend upon their inclusion.

† The same trends hold when these data are grouped into defense agencies and nondefense agencies. During wartime, presidential budgetary estimates increased, on average, from $1.4 to $1.7 million for nondefense agencies, and from $15.4 to $18.3 million for defense agencies. Likewise, congressional appropriations increased from $1.4 to $1.7 million for nondefense agencies, and from $16.1 to $18.2 million for defense agencies. Further grouping the data by agency, we found that 52 of 76 agencies had higher presidential proposals during war, that 53 had higher congressional appropriations, and that the gap between proposals and appropriations diminished during war in 42 of the 76 agencies.

16.2.2 *Congressional Voting in War and Peace*

The fate of presidential initiatives, and with it the potential for presidential influence, does not lie exclusively in budgetary proposals. Presidential power also presents itself in the bills that are enacted into law. As a supplement to the analyses of appropriations, we therefore investigated whether members' voting records during wartime better reflect the president's policy preferences than they do in peacetime. A basic intuition structured this research: if a conservative president takes the nation to war, we ought to observe a shift in members' voting records to the ideological right; and when this war ends, we should then witness a restorative shift back to the ideological left. Correspondingly, when a liberal president is at the helm, members of Congress should shift in exactly the opposite directions.

To assess such possibilities in an ideal research environment, we would have needed identical members of Congress voting on identical bills immediately before and immediately after the outbreak of war, and all potentially confounding factors would be kept constant. Lacking such a natural experiment, we exercised the next best option: we used raw congressional roll-call data and drew upon a variety of technologies designed to summarize each legislator's voting record. These summaries, which are usually referred to as *ideal points*, reflect the general ideological orientation of each member's voting record.[18]

The basic empirical strategy here is straightforward enough.[19] For each of the major wars of the past seventy-five years, we compared individual members' voting records as the nation transitioned either from peace to war or from war to peace and evaluated whether members' votes shifted in a conservative or liberal direction. If Corwin, Rossiter, and Schlesinger were right, we should expect members to shift in the general ideological direction of the president when the nation enters war, and to shift away from the president once peace is restored.

There were lots of reasons, however, to expect that we would not observe any change at all. One reason for this is that, by virtually all accounts, congressional voting behavior has been remarkably stable over time. As political scientist Keith Poole remarked, "based upon the roll call voting record, once elected to Congress, members adopt an ideological position and maintain that position throughout their careers—once a liberal or moderate or conservative, always a liberal or moderate or conservative."[20] Accordingly, the empirical tests that follow constitute a stringent test of the proposition that the voting behavior of members changes during war and during peace.

We had the greatest confidence in estimates associated with the 107th Congress, which ran from 2001 to 2002. The attacks of September 11, 2001, occurred roughly midway through this congressional session, and the transition from peace to war occurred in very short order. Furthermore, the prior legislative agenda had nothing to do with the attacks, a fact that further buttressed the comparison between peacetime and wartime voting behavior.

Figure 16.2 plots the distribution of members' estimated peace and wartime ideal points. The dashed lines indicate the peacetime scores, and the solid lines indicate the wartime

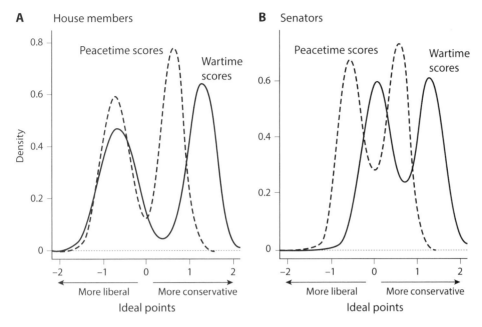

FIGURE 16.2. Aggregate shifts in voting behavior in the 107th Congress. The dashed lines reflect roll-call votes cast before the war in Afghanistan began on October 7, 2001. The solid lines reflect roll-call votes cast after the war began. Positive ideal points indicate more conservative voting behavior, and negative ideal points reflect more liberal voting behavior. *Source:* William G. Howell, Saul P. Jackman, and Jon C. Rogowski, *The Wartime President: Executive Influence and the Nationalizing Politics of Threat* (Chicago: University of Chicago Press, 2013).

scores. Larger values indicate more conservative voting behavior. In both periods in the House (left panel) and Senate (right panel) there are bimodal distributions, with the left hump showing the location of most Democrats and the right hump showing the location of most Republicans. As you can plainly see, the distributions shift markedly to the right. In the House, the movement appears to be concentrated among Republicans, while in the Senate both parties move.

Figure 16.3 again plots the pre- and postwar scores for every member of the 107th House and Senate. This time, however, scores before the outbreak of war are aligned on the x-axis, and wartime scores appear on the y-axis. Members whose voting behavior did not change at all are located right on the 45-degree line. Scores above the 45-degree line indicate movement in the conservative direction, and scores below the 45-degree line reveal movement in the liberal direction.

All members of the Senate and 323 members of the House reveal statistically significant differences in voting behavior, all moving in the conservative direction.* With the outbreak

---

* These estimated differences remained large even after controlling for other possible explanatory variables: party control, the electoral calendar, rising conservatism across all levels of government, and factors that

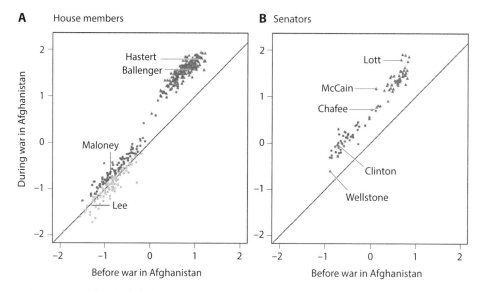

FIGURE 16.3. Individual shifts in voting behavior in the 107th Congress. The x-axes represent member ideal points based on roll-call votes cast prior to the beginning of the war in Afghanistan on October 7, 2001; the y-axes represent ideal points estimated using roll-call votes cast after the beginning of the war. Members whose points fall along the 45-degree line demonstrate consistent ideological voting patterns in the pre- and postwar periods. Republican members are represented by triangles and Democratic members by circles. Members whose pre- and postwar ideal points are statistically different are shown in dark gray. Larger values of members' score signify a more conservative voting record; lower values indicate a more liberal one. *Source:* William G. Howell, Saul P. Jackman, and Jon C. Rogowski, *The Wartime President: Executive Influence and the Nationalizing Politics of Threat* (Chicago: University of Chicago Press, 2013).

of war, the vast preponderance of members of Congress voted more conservatively at a time when a Republican president sat in the White House.

In examining prior wars, we faced a variety of additional empirical challenges. For instance, we could not replicate the exact technique we used for the 107th Congress to compare members' estimated ideal points in World War II and the Korean War. Since the Vietnam and Gulf wars began and ended early in a congressional term, we were forced to examine voting behavior across congresses. Employing a range of techniques to address these and other issues, however, we found that the United States' entry into World War II coincided with a significant shift to the ideological left that was more aligned with the president; the end of the war, meanwhile, brought a significant shift to the ideological right, and therefore away from the president then in office. War, as such, does not automatically induce a conservative response among legislators. Rather, it seems, changes in legislative voting patterns correspond to the partisanship of the president in office.

---

preceded the attacks and precipitated the war. We found similar effects when limiting the sample of votes to purely domestic legislation and to most visible or highly contested bills.

We found limited evidence that the beginning of the Korean War induced Congress to vote in ways that better reflected the ideological leanings of Truman, while the end of the war coincided with a significant shift away from Eisenhower. We found no consistent evidence that the beginnings of the wars in Vietnam and the Persian Gulf induced members to vote in ways that better reflected the preferences of the presidents then in office, while the end of the Vietnam War yielded a Congress less in line with the ideological orientation of the president. Finally, we found no consistent evidence of movement away from George H. W. Bush upon the end of the Persian Gulf War.

It appears, then, that some wars have increased presidential success rates more than others. At the outset of World War II and the Afghanistan War, members of Congress began to vote in ways that more closely reflected the ideological orientation of whichever president was then in office. Evidence regarding the beginnings of the Korean, Vietnam, and Persian Gulf wars is more mixed: members of Congress during these wars did not line up behind the president in consistent ways. With the termination of every war we analyzed, however, members of Congress shifted away from presidents they had rallied behind, suggesting that whatever "honours and emoluments" (to borrow from James Madison) wars had to offer the president were promptly withdrawn when those wars ended.

16.3 Three Cases of Wartime Policymaking at Home

Why is it that some wars make Congress more receptive to the president, while others do not? This section searches for an answer in three prominent case studies: World War II, the Vietnam War, and the post–September 11 military commitments in Afghanistan and Iraq. In these case studies we see how war's effects on the president's domestic agenda depend chiefly on the nationalization of public policy debates. To leverage war to their advantage, presidents must have engaged the entire country in the war effort, as Roosevelt did in the 1940s and Bush did after 2001. If a war does not lead citizens to reevaluate policy in distinctly national terms, we can expect the barrier between foreign and domestic policy to remain firm.

16.3.1 *World War II*

President Franklin D. Roosevelt helped galvanize a once steadfastly isolationist nation to fight—and triumph—in the greatest conflict the world has ever seen. The carnage and destruction that had characterized the world's first modern war were taken to altogether new heights in its second: six times as many Americans fought overseas in World War II as in World War I, and nearly four times as many American soldiers died. It was little surprise, therefore, that citizens were directly engaged in Roosevelt's war effort; many of them had family fighting on its front lines.

The Japanese attack on Pearl Harbor finally upended the isolationist status quo. The most deadly foreign assault on U.S. soil since the War of 1812 convinced Americans and their representatives in Congress to grant unprecedented authority to the executive

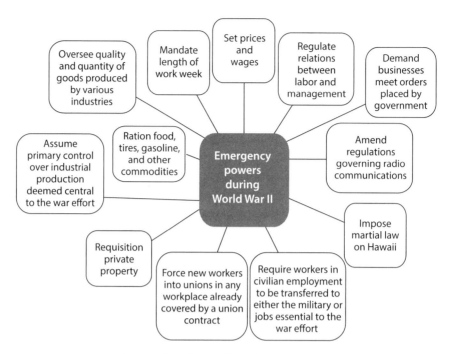

FIGURE 16.4. An abundance of wartime emergency powers.

branch. A few weeks after Pearl Harbor, Congress passed the War Powers Act, followed by a second, expanded version three months later. Together, the acts—"rag-bags into which were tossed all manner of provisions"—gave the president wide-ranging powers to prosecute the war effort.[21]

Not all the powers granted to Roosevelt during this period, however, were directly related to the war. Over the course of World War II, Franklin Delano Roosevelt exerted so much influence over the domestic sphere that critics complained of the emergence of a dictatorship. The charge was not without merit. As Clinton Rossiter wrote in 1948, "Future historians will record that, in the course of World War II, the Presidency of the United States became the most powerful and distinguished constitutional office the world has ever known."[22] Recall from chapter 2 that during the war, with the backing of Congress and the courts,[23] the president independently seized a wide range of emergency powers (figure 16.4). During FDR's wartime presidency, the line between foreign and domestic policy did not merely become blurred: it vanished.[24]

Meanwhile, FDR launched a massive public relations campaign designed to rally support for the war. Citizens were called upon to dedicate themselves to the service of a larger public good and to suppress their individual desires, habits, and routines for the sake of the war effort. One of the most popular series of propaganda posters invoked the president's 1941 State of the Union speech in which he declared that all people should have access to four basic freedoms: freedom from fear, freedom from want, freedom of speech, and freedom of worship. The posters, created by *Saturday Evening Post* illustrator Norman

Rockwell, showed Americans engaging in everyday activities, implying that the war was ultimately about protecting the American way of life. One showed an extended family gathered around a bountiful dinner table, with the caption "Ours . . . to fight for—freedom from want." Another linked religious liberty and military funding, urging Americans to "Save freedom of worship—buy war bonds." Still another wartime propaganda poster beseeched housewives to "buy wisely, cook carefully, store carefully, and use leftovers" because "where our men are fighting, our food is fighting." With a ghoulish image of the Third Reich in the background and a brawny arm wielding a wrench in the foreground, another poster implored, "Stop the monster that stops at nothing. PRODUCE to the limit! This is your war!"

Through such appeals, Roosevelt managed to change the terms under which citizens evaluated the war and, more broadly, the presidency. Rationing coffee and gasoline was not just a patriotic duty that would aid the efforts of American soldiers overseas; it was an investment in a liberal democratic future. These public appeals represented, in the words of historian James Sparrow, a "fusion of liberalism (with its valorization of freedom and equality) and nationalism (with its demand for unity, order, and loyalty)." They helped mobilize the nation for the duration of the war, and they allowed the federal government to "expand its power radically without triggering opposition."[25]

FDR relied upon a battalion of administrative agencies to realize his agenda at home. Some were created to address issues stemming from the Depression, others were expressly modeled after World War I administrative agencies, and still others were created anew (figure 16.5). Most such agencies came into being after Pearl Harbor and were born not from congressional statutes but from executive directives. These included the Office of Price Administration, the National War Labor Board, the National Housing Agency, the Board of Economic Warfare, the War Manpower Commission, the Office of Defense Transportation, the Office of Economic Stabilization (which subsequently became the Office of War Mobilization), the Office of Censorship, and many more. Important elements of the domestic war mobilization effort were run directly through the military. Military purchasing bureaus issued massive contracts for supplies ranging from raw steel and aluminum to aircraft and tanks.

The sheer size of these military orders left a lasting impression on the nation's industries, but it also had an immediate impact on the consumption patterns of average civilians. "By one estimate," notes David Kennedy, "fulfilling all the army and navy orders would cut civilian consumption to 60 percent of its level in 1932, the darkest year of the Depression."[26] Still, overall government war spending had a fantastically positive effect on the standards of living of average citizens. Though citizens had to cut back on staple goods, luxury goods became available to them for the first time. During the war, Kennedy continues,

> most Americans never had it so good. They started half a million new businesses. They went to movies and restaurants with unhabitual frequency. They bought books, recordings, cosmetics, pharmaceuticals, jewelry, and liquor in record volumes. Racing fans wagered two and a half times more on the horses in 1944 than they had in 1940.[27]

FIGURE 16.5. Growth of the administrative state. During the Great Depression and World War II, the president oversaw a massive administrative state filled with administrative agencies, each with an acronym of its own. Copyright Clifford Kennedy Berryman/Corbis-Getty Images. Reproduced with permission.

Government spending during World War II, some economic historians argue,[28] ultimately amounted to a far greater stimulus to the domestic economy than the relatively piecemeal efforts of the New Deal.

As had World War I, World War II unleashed a flurry of presidential orders that curbed First Amendment protections of speech and assembly. Established under an executive order issued less than two weeks after the bombing of Pearl Harbor, the Office of Censorship monitored communications with foreign states and laid out codes of conduct for domestic newspapers and radio outlets. The Office of War Information assumed the responsibilities of World War I's Committee on Public Information to publicize and propagandize the war at home.[29]

Other presidential orders targeted specific ethnic groups. Most famously, in a decision that left the greatest stain on his presidency, FDR ordered Japanese Americans living on the West Coast into internment camps in the months after Pearl Harbor, forcibly detaining and relocating over one hundred thousand people, resident aliens and citizens alike (figure 16.6).[30] The military exclusion order that justified their relocation remained in place for almost the entire duration of the war. When they were finally released, internees were given $25 and a train ticket to their former hometown.

FIGURE 16.6. The Granada relocation center. Located near Granada, Colorado, this World War II relocation center was the smallest of the ten centers constructed for the internment of Japanese Americans and people of Japanese descent. At its peak, more than 7,300 internees resided here; more than two-thirds of them were U.S. citizens. The center is now a National Historic Landmark, open to the public. *Source:* Library of Congress.

Though Japanese Americans absorbed hard blows during World War II, the political status of other racial and ethnic groups, in particular that of African Americans, advanced ever so slightly. Under pressure from the National Association for the Advancement of Colored People (NAACP) and the Urban League, as discussed in chapter 2, FDR issued a series of directives that addressed concerns about racial discrimination in the military. Under Executive Order 8802, enacted in June 1941, a newly established Fair Employment Practices Committee (FEPC) retained modest powers to investigate and, where appropriate, remediate employment discrimination in the defense industries.[31] As originally constituted, the agency had meager resources, operated without clear standards, and lacked direct enforcement powers. Under continued pressure from civil rights groups, however, FDR increased the number of FEPC committee members, required that all government contracts (not just defense contracts) include nondiscrimination clauses, and made the agency directly beholden to the president.

Though limited, FDR's actions here were symbolically important.[32] Most immediately, they demonstrated the gains to be had from organized political action. FDR's executive orders galvanized the civil rights movement and sparked massive growth in the NAACP's membership. Over the longer term, FDR's orders set an important precedent for the federal government's commitment to addressing the plight of African Americans and paved the way for future civil rights legislation.

At every turn, World War II reshaped the terms by which both citizens and politicians evaluated government and its policies. In a very real sense, the war was being waged at home as it was on the battlefields of Europe, Asia, and the Pacific. Virtually every domain of public and private life became tied to the massive war effort. National considerations displaced local ones. And precisely because of the president's distinctly national outlook on policy matters, this shift played to his benefit.

16.3.2 *The Vietnam War and Johnson's Great Society*

Johnson's Great Society programs stand alongside FDR's New Deal initiatives as the most significant twentieth-century domestic policy achievements. Reflecting upon the first session of Johnson's Great Society Congress (the 89th), the *New York Times* concluded, "It is unquestionably one of the most glittering records of legislative accomplishment in history."[33] As David Mayhew observes, the forty-five landmark enactments passed during Johnson's administration exceeded the number passed during any other presidency in the modern era. Of these, twenty-two were passed in 1964 and 1965, the peak years for Johnson's domestic agenda.[34]

Though Johnson enjoyed extraordinary legislative successes during these early years of his presidency, political instability in Vietnam, exacerbated by the demise of French imperialism and rising nationalism, soon commandeered his attention. To show weakness in Southeast Asia, he feared, would imperil the 1964 Civil Rights Act. The president worried that southern Democrats, in particular, would not sit quietly if the Communists triumphed in Vietnam. As Johnson colorfully put it, "If I don't go in now and [the southern Democrats] show later that I should have, then they'll . . . push Vietnam up my ass every time."[35]

After Johnson won reelection in 1964, consensus emerged within his administration for a two-phased bombing campaign against North Vietnam.[36] Johnson authorized an initial round of air strikes in Laos and a second round of bombing operations, which were to be accompanied by the deployment of ground troops. The president refused to make these plans public, however, and took steps to prevent any possible leaks.[37]

As it turned out, a major escalation was just around the corner. On February 7, 1965, Viet Cong—or, more accurately, National Liberation Front—units attacked the U.S. Army barracks at Pleiku and killed eight American soldiers. Within seventy-two hours, Operation Flaming Dart began. The ensuing targeted air strikes shifted into a continuous aerial bombardment program against the North that became known as Operation Rolling Thunder.

The administration continued to justify the air raids as a response to the Pleiku attacks. It also denied any change of policy, although, as George C. Herring put it, "the air war quickly grew from a sporadic, halting effort into a regular, determined program" that included the introduction of 40,000 U.S. troops.[38]

As spring gave way to summer, General William Westmoreland assumed control over American operations in Vietnam. The political situation in South Vietnam worsened as yet another government—the fifth since the death of the Republic's first president, Ngo Dinh Diem—took charge in May. Recognizing the precarious political situation, Westmoreland and the Joint Chiefs called for an increase of 150,000 troops, with General Earle Wheeler, chairman of the Joint Chiefs, arguing that Johnson "must take the fight to the enemy. No one ever won a battle sitting on his ass."[39] At the same time, Johnson's military advisors recognized that the war would be long and costly. According to the Joint Chiefs, winning the war would require 500,000 troops and five years.[40] At the end of July 1965, Johnson approved the deployment of 100,000 soldiers, with an additional 100,000 troops in 1966. The Vietnam War had begun in earnest.

When Johnson convened his military advisors for a summit at the end of July 1965, he was less concerned about what policy should actually be implemented than he was about how it should be presented to Congress and the American public. The reason was simple: Johnson worried that if he rapidly escalated troop levels in Vietnam, "that bitch of a war would destroy the woman I really love—the Great Society."[41] Some components of his Great Society programs had yet to be enacted into law, and others still required funding. Rather than disclose the full extent of the planned military escalation, therefore, Johnson sought to defer financing decisions until the following year, at which point troops would already be in the field and Congress would have little choice but to support them. As National Security Advisor McGeorge Bundy later admitted,

> Johnson knew his Congress, and knew that the practical majority he held in 1965 was a precarious one. Once the Congress got itself involved in direct responsibility for the Vietnam War, conservatives would move from sufferance to opposition and to harsh cutting of domestic funds, and moderates from unstinting support to sympathy for the economy.[42]

The president rebuffed the advice of his defense secretary, which was to declare a national state of emergency and request an increase in taxes to fund the war. Instead, the president ordered his staff to implement his military decisions in a "low-keyed manner" in the hopes of avoiding "undue concern and excitement in the Congress and in domestic public opinion."[43]

Rather than announce the escalation during a prime-time television address, Johnson held a routine noontime press conference on July 28, 1965, in which he said simply that he had increased military forces by 50,000 soldiers. He chose not to acknowledge that 50,000 more troops would be en route to Southeast Asia before the end of the year and that another 100,000 would arrive in 1966. When meeting with congressional leaders the day before the announcement, Johnson insisted that there was no change in policy.

Johnson's understated strategy, as Jeffrey Helsing described it, "was a direct result of his desire to maintain prosperity, contain communism, and create a Great Society. He could not have the latter without ensuring the first two."[44] Vietnam and the Great Society, Johnson believed, were inextricably linked. As he later recalled, "I knew the day it exploded into

FIGURE 16.7. Elusive peace in Vietnam. Here we see a beleaguered Lyndon John-son in late October 1968, after meeting about Vietnam with his military advisors. The war played no small part in Johnson's earlier decision to bow out of the 1968 presidential election. *Source:* National Archives, LBJ Library, Yoichi Okamoto.

a major debate on the war, that day would be the beginning of the end of the Great Society."[45]

Johnson pursued this strategy for as long as he could. But as casualties mounted, it became increasingly difficult for him to deny the true extent of the military operations. After the Tet Offensive in early 1968, Johnson had no choice but to admit that the United States was engaged in a full-blown war. Shortly thereafter, the troubled president an-nounced that he would not seek another term, and the fate of the Great Society would be left to his successors. Johnson spent the remainder of his term working to bring about peace in Vietnam, but despite his efforts, the conflict continued for years after he left the White House (figure 16.7).

16.3.3 September 11, 2001, and Thereafter

The attacks on New York City and Washington, D.C., on September 11, 2001, left the na-tion, public, and government reeling. The stock markets shut down, rumors churned about additional terrorist attacks, and every commercial aircraft stood grounded for the first time since the 1960s. Makeshift memorials popped up on city streets, and flag sales skyrocketed as the country mourned the nearly three thousand casualties from the at-tacks on American soil.

Action clearly was needed, and fast (figure 16.8). Just forty-five days after the terrorist attacks, Congress enacted the **USA PATRIOT Act**, the most wide-reaching antiterrorism

FIGURE 16.8. President George W. Bush at "ground zero." Days after the September 11, 2001, attacks, Bush went to ground zero, where the Twin Towers had collapsed in New York City. A rescue worker at the scene claimed he could not hear the president. Standing atop the rubble, Bush responded, "I can hear you! I can hear you! The rest of the world hears you! And the people, and the people who knocked down these buildings will hear all of us soon." *Source:* AP Photo/Doug Mills.

bill in decades. The act substantially strengthened the federal government's intelligence-gathering activities, surveillance procedures, and controls over money laundering. The act simultaneously centralized power within the executive branch and advanced key components of Bush's domestic policy agenda—border security and immigration—in ways that extended well beyond preventing terrorism.

Long before Bush assumed office in 2001, scholars and politicians had recognized the need for antiterrorism reform. The most recent pre-2001 counterterrorism legislation included the Antiterrorism and Effective Death Penalty Act of 1996 and the Defense Against Weapons of Mass Destruction Act of 1996. These acts increased funding for law enforcement, strengthened penalties for terrorist crimes, streamlined deportation of immigrant criminals, and increased sanctions on weapons used by terrorists.

The rest of America's antiterrorism legislation had been enacted during the Cold War. It included the Foreign Intelligence Surveillance Act of 1978 (FISA), the Electronic Communications Privacy Act of 1986 (ECPA), the Money Laundering Control Act of 1986, and the Immigration and Nationality Act of 1952 (INA), among others. Many observers did not believe that these laws provided an adequate response to evolving terrorist threats. In the late 1990s, multiple blue-ribbon commissions highlighted the federal government's lack of preparedness for a possible terrorist attack. Attempts were made to improve antiterrorism policy, but as Congress scholar David Mayhew notes, "largely due to civil liberties concerns, [Congress] did not pass legislation to correct the problems that would ultimately be addressed in the USA PATRIOT Act.[46]

As a presidential candidate, George W. Bush had not displayed any notable interest in counterterrorism efforts. He had, however, exhibited a long-standing commitment to large-scale immigration reform, largely because of its economic implications. Among many proposed immigration reforms, President Bush emphasized a need for increased border security, the establishment of a temporary worker program, an increase in Immigration and Naturalization Service (INS) funding, and aggressive deterrence programs such as Operation Hold the Line.* Consistent with these objectives, Bush proposed an additional $500 million to fund new personnel in the INS and the splitting of the INS into two agencies, with one focusing exclusively on border enforcement.

Despite his commitment to the issue, Bush made little headway on immigration reform during the early months of his presidency. The high point of his efforts came on September 5, 2001, when he met with President Vicente Fox of Mexico and discussed possible solutions to the problem of illegal border crossings. At the time, though, no substantial reform proposals had made their way onto Congress's legislative agenda.

A week later, the domestic political landscape would shift in the president's favor. Among their many effects in the domestic political arena, the 9/11 attacks "breathed new life" into counterterrorism proposals Congress had previously considered "by turning abstract flaws in terrorism preparedness into stinging indictments of how the system was broken."[47] Concerns about civil liberties, while still present, no longer obstructed new legislation, and members of Congress conceded the need for decisive action. Although the legislative branch had previously stood in the way of antiterrorism policy reform, the events of 9/11 led Congress to act as a "rubber stamp" on Bush's domestic agenda.[48]

The PATRIOT Act moved quickly through Congress. Republican representative James Sensenbrenner introduced the bill on the House floor on October 23, 2001, and the president signed it into law a mere three days later. With the accelerated timetable, the bill bypassed both the committee process and floor debate. The bill received near-unanimous support in both chambers, passing 357–66 in the House and 98–1 in the Senate.[49]

The PATRIOT Act revised and extended existing statutes governing computer fraud, foreign intelligence gathering, wiretapping, and criminal procedure. Many reforms that had previously been derided as civil liberties infringements became prominent features of the act. Title II, for example, drastically expanded the scope and availability of wiretapping and surveillance orders, removed many of the requirements about who could be targeted for surveillance, and diminished the warrant requirements associated with terrorism in-

---

* The goal of Operation Hold the Line was "to prevent illegal immigration through deterrence. This called for more fencing, border patrol agents, technology, lighting, and surveillance equipment to be implemented in four phases." See Andrew Becker, "Mexico: Crimes at the Border. Immigration Timeline," PBS, http://www.pbs.org/frontlineworld/stories/mexico704/history/timeline.html.

vestigations. Title III sought to reduce the flow of laundered money to terrorist organizations by tightening record-keeping requirements for financial institutions and authorizing seizures of terrorist assets.[50] Title VIII increased the criminal penalties for terrorism and redefined terrorism in considerably broader terms. Title IX streamlined communication between the Federal Bureau of Investigation (FBI) and the INS regarding foreign intelligence information and centralized the process through the Director of Central Intelligence (DCI).

The PATRIOT Act also opened the door for significant immigration reform, as one of the troubling revelations of the 9/11 attacks was that hijackers had entered the United States on legal visas.[51] In response, Title IV, Subtitle B, Section 414 imposed a more rigorous screening process for obtaining visas. Additionally, Section 411 retroactively amended the Immigration and Naturalization Act to prevent entry into the United States by aliens who were part of any foreign organization that endorsed terrorist activity.[52]

Consistent with the president's wishes, the act also reformed immigration policy to prevent illegal entry into the United States. The most notable of these reforms appeared in Subtitle A, which increased security along the nation's northern border. Section 401, for example, authorized the attorney general "to waive any cap on personnel assigned to the Immigration and Naturalization Service on the Northern border." Section 402 authorized appropriations for border operations, with special allotments granted to the INS and the U.S. Customs Service. Section 403 amended the INA "to require the Attorney General and the FBI to provide the Department of State and INS with access to specified criminal history extracts."

Each of these provisions sought to protect the country against potential terrorist threats, and by most accounts, they succeeded. The Bush administration had larger goals in mind, however. The PATRIOT Act boosted the number of border troops and funding to border security, but nothing in the act required that these additional resources be tied specifically to antiterrorism efforts. Subsequent reports confirmed that the Justice Department "used many of these antiterrorism powers to pursue defendants for crimes unrelated to terrorism, including drug violations, credit card fraud, and bank theft."[53]

By increasing the number of INS agents and reducing the restrictions on deployment protocols along the northern border with Canada, Sections 401 and 404 provided the raw manpower to install programs very similar to Operation Hold the Line, which Bush had long desired but had not been able to implement. By allocating funding to the INS, the PATRIOT Act and subsequent legislation effectively doubled border security funding from nearly $5 billion in 2001 to over $10 billion in 2007, thereby fulfilling another of the president's campaign pledges.[54]

The PATRIOT Act also allocated additional power to the executive branch. By increasing INS funding and autonomy, the act ensured that future immigration policy would come from this agency rather than from the legislature. Additionally, by giving the attorney general "unfettered discretion to determine who is a terrorist," the act vested in that office extraordinary new powers over the detention of illegal immigrants.[55]

The president's newfound influence over domestic policy, meanwhile, was hardly limited to immigration. As one Democratic aide noted, "The president has so much power as a result of what happened he thinks he can use that to force huge concessions on a range of issues."[56] The president depicted economic growth as "part of the war we fight" and characterized his stimulus proposal, which included a bailout bill for the airline industry, as an "economic security plan."[57] Subsequently positioning tax cuts as a measure of legislators' patriotism, Bush called upon them to "act quickly to make sure that the American people understand that at this part of our homeland defense, our country and the Congress is united."[58] And it seemed to work. Tax cuts ranked among his most significant domestic policy achievements as president. By recasting the terms under which the American public evaluated domestic policy, Bush managed to leverage the war to his distinct advantage.

Historical Transformations: War's Permanence

On April 14, 2021, President Biden gave a major speech on the status of the nation's protracted War on Terror. While promising his audience that "we'll not take our eye off the terrorist threat," the president argued that the nation's primary objective in Afghanistan—to ensure that the country would not become a base for another attack against Americans—had been accomplished long ago. Thus, Biden announced that he would remove all U.S. troops from Afghanistan before the twentieth anniversary of the terrorist attacks on September 11. "I'm now the fourth United States President to preside over American troop presence in Afghanistan," declared Biden. "I will not pass this responsibility on to a fifth."[59]

Given present realities, what exactly would it mean for peace to return? Just months after Biden's announcement, Afghanistan's secular government was overrun by the Taliban—a theocratic organization that had terrorized Afghans for years before being overthrown in 2001. Its resurgence was met with widespread protest and violence: a situation few, if any, would unflinchingly describe as "peacetime."

Distinctions between states of war and peace have always been subject to interpretation, particularly given the steady escalations and de-escalations that characterize modern warfare. In the contemporary world, though, such distinctions have become blurred beyond recognition. War has rooted deeply into the nation's consciousness, becoming, in certain respects, a permanent fixture on the political landscape.

The notion that war somehow stands outside of politics has always been mistaken, but especially so in the post–World War II era. A variety of forces has conspired to make war a mainstay of American politics, three of which stand above all others. The first concerns the web of relationships that typically fall under the rubric of *globalization*. Our interests are too far-reaching, and our dependencies too great, to ignore any region of the world. Civil wars, regional instabilities, humanitarian crises, border disputes, and assassination attempts that once could be written off as someone else's problem have become very much our own. Though politicians disagree vehemently about the proper response to such crises, virtually all concede that lapsing into isolationism would be a terrible mistake.

Perhaps the most important example of this phenomenon is oil. Oil has an outsized impact on the U.S. economy, as small shocks can cause volatility to the stock market. The price of oil, however, very much depends on political circumstances in relatively small, nondemocratic Middle Eastern nations. As such, the United States has become intimately involved with the region. Seeking to promote stability and protect its energy interests, all presidents, regardless of party, have been forced to grapple with Middle Eastern politics and diplomacy.

The second force that has made war a constant in the American political landscape is U.S. hegemony in the international arena. Whether by reference to its economic productivity, military might, cultural dominance, or political influence, the United States continues to wield extraordinary influence abroad. While ongoing debate persists about whether the American "empire" is in ascendance or decline, historians and political analysts broadly agree that, for at least the foreseeable future, the United States will remain, if not the only superpower, then one of a handful. Given its hegemonic status, the United States operates at the very center of international politics. It commands the attention of every foreign state and international organization and often dictates the range of acceptable responses to regional crises.

Finally, there is the nature of contemporary threats to U.S. security. Rarely does the United States square off against a foreign combatant, its soldiers lined up against ours. Rather, battles are episodic and unanticipated, with the enemy striking and then abruptly fading back into civilian populations. Today, the enemy's primary objective is to outlast the United States, not to conquer it or defeat its army.

All of this paves the way for an even more influential presidency in the twenty-first century than the one that came of age in the twentieth. With the possibility of war nearly always present, presidents may loom ever larger over our politics—both for the decisions they make about military deployments and security measures and for the leverage war provides them in domestic policy matters.

Conclusion

As the nation moves into and out of war, the influence of presidents tends to ebb and flow. During war, as we have seen, members of Congress vote in ways that better approximate the president's ideological orientation. They also enact appropriations that better reflect the president's budgetary priorities. Members of Congress fall in line behind the president's domestic policy agenda when the nation goes to war.

Not all wars, however, deliver an equal boost in presidential influence over domestic policy. Some wars, such as the Vietnam War, did not materially improve the president's ability to advance his domestic policy agenda. Smaller conflicts in Panama in the 1980s, Bosnia and Somalia in the 1990s, and Libya and Syria in the 2010s did not endow the presidents then in office with any additional domestic policy influence. Other wars, such as the Iraq War circa 2005, did not augment the president's power nearly enough to overcome the widespread and deeply entrenched opposition to Bush's agenda.

Wars, then, would seem to have the potential—but *only* the potential—to increase presidential power. The realization of power, we have seen, depends upon a host of contextual factors, not least of which is the nationalization of domestic concerns.

These findings imply deeper lessons about the institutional presidency's evolution. In the Historical Transformations features that appear throughout this title, we have considered instances when historical developments altered the institutional presidency. They did so sometimes immediately, other times more slowly, but often irrevocably. The findings in this chapter, however, suggest that the relationship between historical context and the institutional presidency may be a good deal more complicated, and a whole lot more interesting. Wars do not merely alter the presidency. Wars also conjure and shape opportunities for the institutional presidency to assert itself. Wars specifically, and historical contexts more generally, interact with features of the institutional presidency to animate executive politics and intermittently support and hinder the exercise of presidential power. History may directly alter the institutional presidency, but it is through history, and in history, that the possibilities for presidential influence manifest themselves.

As we conclude this final chapter, then, we come to more fully appreciate the principles with which we began this textbook: executive politics are not propelled by the tastes, personalities, or styles of the individuals who occupy the office at any given time; rather, the foundations of the American presidency are institutional in nature; and the ability of any individual president to exercise power depends upon his (and yes, someday her and their) structured interactions with other institutions within the executive branch, across the adjoining branches of government, and in the larger polity. As they advance foreign and domestic policy, as they govern during times of war and peace, presidents must navigate institutional forms; and these forms are continually evolving, the subjects of ongoing political contestation and historical contingency.

To properly understand the presidency, we must take stock of these institutions, which extend all across government, and which do so much to shape a president's political fortunes. A course of the institutional presidency, as such, does more than shine a bright light on the person who occupies this most powerful office. It establishes a station—and with it, a perspective—from which to look out upon the entirety of American politics.

Key Terms

wartime jurisprudence   **USA PATRIOT Act**

Questions for Discussion

1. Why might foreign wars affect and alter relations between the president and Congress at home?
2. In what ways did the experiences of presidents during World War II, during the Vietnam War, and after 9/11 differ from one another? In what ways were they similar?
3. If war has become a more permanent feature of the foreign policy landscape, as some have suggested, what implications does this have for the balance of power across the branches of government?
4. For a variety of reasons, wars may reshape political considerations about domestic policy that have little direct bearing on the nation's security. Will wars necessarily do so, though, in ways that are politically advantageous to the presidency?
5. Many recent presidents defined elements of their domestic agendas in terms of war. For example, Johnson had his War on Poverty, and Ronald Reagan launched a War on Drugs. What do presidents hope to accomplish with this rhetoric?
6. The relationship between Lyndon Johnson's Great Society and the Vietnam War challenges the conventional wisdom surrounding presidential power and wars. Instead of expecting it to improve his position in domestic affairs, Johnson feared escalation overseas would threaten his beloved Great Society. What lessons does this hold for presidents who pursue "never-ending wars"? Does George W. Bush's experience with the War on Terror—augmenting his power in his first term, but crippling his public approval in his second—confirm your intuitions?
7. If presidents are generally preoccupied with power, do they have an incentive to prolong a war instead of ending it? To start a war, even when one may not be absolutely necessary?

Suggested Readings

Corwin, Edward. *The President: Office and Powers*. 5th ed. New York: New York University Press, 1984.

Fisher, Louis. *Presidential War Power*. 3rd ed. Lawrence: University Press of Kansas, 2013.

Howell, William G., Saul P. Jackman, and Jon C. Rogowski. *The Wartime President: Executive Influence and the Nationalizing Politics of Threat*. Chicago: University of Chicago Press, 2013.

MacMillan, Margaret. *War: How Conflict Shaped Us*. New York: Random House, 2020.

Mueller, John E. *War, Presidents and Public Opinion*. New York: John Wiley & Sons, 1973.

Rossiter, Clinton. *Constitutional Dictatorship: Crisis Government in the Modern Democracies*. 1948. New Brunswick: Transaction Publishers, 2002.

Schlesinger, Arthur M., Jr. *The Imperial Presidency*. Boston: Houghton Mifflin, 2004.

Sparrow, James. *Warfare State: World War II and the Age of Big Government*. New York: Oxford University Press, 2011.

Notes

1. This discussion is drawn from research and analysis presented in William G. Howell, "Presidential Power in War," *Annual Review of Political Science* 14 (2011): 89–105.

2. Edward S. Corwin, *The President's Control of Foreign Relations* (Princeton: Princeton University Press, 1917), 153.

3. Edward S. Corwin, *The President: Office and Powers, 1787–1957*, 4th ed. (New York: New York University Press, 1957), 262.

4. Clinton Rossiter, "The Presidency—Focus of Leadership," *New York Times Magazine*, November 11, 1956, 12.

5. Rossiter, "The Presidency," 64–65.

6. Rossiter, "The Presidency," 65.

7. Clinton L. Rossiter, *Constitutional Dictatorship: Crisis Government in the Modern Democracies* (Princeton: Princeton University Press, 1948; New Brunswick, NJ: Rossiter Press, 2007), 288. Citations refer to the Rossiter edition.

8. For eleven criteria by which to identify and then evaluate constitutional dictatorships, see Rossiter, *Constitutional Dictatorship*, 297–306.

9. See, for example, Louis Fisher, *Congressional Abdication on War and Spending* (College Station: Texas A&M University Press, 2000).

10. Arthur M. Schlesinger Jr., *The Imperial Presidency* (Boston: Houghton Mifflin, 2004).

11. Schlesinger, *The Imperial Presidency*, xxvii.

12. Schlesinger, *The Imperial Presidency*, x.

13. Schlesinger, *The Imperial Presidency*, xiv.

14. For a classic study of wartime rally effects, see John E. Mueller, *War, Presidents and Public Opinion* (New York: John Wiley & Sons, 1973).

15. For data on presidential approval ratings, see "Presidential Approval," Roper Center, University of Connecticut, http://www.ropercenter.uconn.edu/CFIDE/roper/presidential/webroot/presidential_rating.cfm.

16. William G. Howell, Saul P. Jackman, and Jon C. Rogowski, *The Wartime President: Executive Influence and the Nationalizing Politics of Threat* (Chicago: University of Chicago Press, 2013).

17. A complete exposition of these findings can be found in Howell, Jackman, and Rogowski, *The Wartime President*, chap. 4.

18. For a useful introduction to these methods, see Keith Poole and Howard Rosenthal, *Congress: A Political-Economic History of Roll Call Voting* (New York: Oxford University Press, 1997).

19. A complete exposition of these findings can be found in Howell, Jackman, and Rogowski, *The Wartime President*, chap. 5.

20. Keith T. Poole, "Changing Minds? Not in Congress!" *Public Choice* 131 (2007): 435.

21. Rossiter, *Constitutional Dictatorship*, 270.

22. Rossiter, *Constitutional Dictatorship*, 266.

23. See, for example, *Yakus v. United States*, 321 U.S. 414 (1944).

24. For detailed treatment of Roosevelt's actions at home during World War II, see Doris Kearns Goodwin, *No Ordinary Time: The Home Front and World War II* (New York: Simon & Schuster, 1995); David Kennedy, *Freedom from Fear: The American People in Depression and War, 1929–1945* (New York: Oxford University Press, 2001); and Harold G. Vatter, *The U.S. Economy in World War II* (New York: Columbia University Press, 1985).

25. James Sparrow, *Warfare State: World War II Americans and the Age of Big Government* (New York: Oxford University Press, 2011), 12.

26. David M. Kennedy, *The American People in World War II: Freedom from Fear*, vol. 2 (New York: Oxford University Press, 2004), 203.

27. Kennedy, *The American People*, 221.

28. See, for example, Michael A. Bernstein, *The Great Depression: Delayed Recovery and Economic Change in America, 1929–1939* (Cambridge: Cambridge University Press, 1987); Herbert Stein, *Presidential Economics: The Making of Economic Policy from Roosevelt to Clinton*, 3rd rev. ed. (Washington, DC: American Enterprise Institute, 1984); Vatter, *The U.S. Economy in World War II*; and J. R. Vernon, "World War II Fiscal Policies and the End of the Great Depression," *Journal of Economic History* 54, no. 4 (1994): 850–68.

29. See Geoffrey Stone, *Perilous Times: Free Speech in Wartime from the Sedition Act of 1798 to the War on Terrorism* (New York: W. W. Norton, 2004), 235–307.

30. For a comprehensive treatment of this subject, see Greg Robinson, *By Order of the President* (Cambridge, MA: Harvard University Press, 2001).

31. For more specifics on Roosevelt's wartime actions on civil rights, see Ruth P. Morgan, *The President and Civil Rights: Policy-Making by Executive Order* (New York: St. Martin's Press, 1970); and Richard P. Nathan, *Jobs & Civil Rights: The Role of the Federal Government in Promoting Equal Opportunity in Employment and Training* (Washington, DC: Brookings Institution, 1969).

32. For a discussion of Roosevelt's efforts to downplay civil rights in order to keep southern segregationists within the New Deal fold, see Ira Katznelson, *Fear Itself: The New Deal and the Origins of Our Time* (New York: Liveright Publishing, 2013).

33. "Editorial," *New York Times*, September 5, 1965.

34. David R. Mayhew, *Divided We Govern: Party Control, Lawmaking, and Investigations* (New Haven: Yale University Press, 1991).

35. Quoted in Brian VanDeMark, *Into the Quagmire: Lyndon Johnson and the Escalation of the Vietnam War* (New York: Oxford University Press, 1995), 60. For more on Johnson's concerns at the time, see David Halberstam, *The Best and the Brightest* (New York: Random House, 1972); and James T. Patterson, *Grand Expectations: The United States, 1945–1974* (New York: Oxford University Press, 1996).

36. David E. Kaiser, *American Tragedy: Kennedy, Johnson, and the Origins of the Vietnam War* (Cambridge, MA: Belknap Press, 2000), 355.

37. H. R. McMaster, *Dereliction of Duty: Johnson, McNamara, the Joint Chiefs of Staff, and the Lies That Led to Vietnam* (New York: HarperCollins, 1997), 195.

38. George Herring, *America's Longest War: The United States and Vietnam, 1950–1975*, 4th ed. (New York: McGraw-Hill, 2001), 155.

39. Quoted in Richard E. Neustadt and Ernest R. May, *Thinking in Time: The Uses of History for Decision-Makers* (New York: Free Press, 1988), 78.

40. Jeffrey W. Helsing, *Johnson's War/Johnson's Great Society: The Guns and Butter Trap* (Westport, CT: Praeger, 2000), 163.

41. Doris Kearns Goodwin, *Lyndon Johnson and the American Dream* (New York: Harper and Row, 1976), 251.

42. Quoted in Helsing, *Johnson's War/Johnson's Great Society*, 171.

43. Herring, *America's Longest War*, 166.

44. Helsing, *Johnson's War/Johnson's Great Society*, 9.

45. Quoted in Goodwin, *Lyndon Johnson and the American Dream*, 283.

46. David R. Mayhew, "Wars and American Politics," *Perspectives on Politics* 3, no. 3 (2005): 437.

47. Michael T. McCarthy, "Recent Developments: USA Patriot Act," *Harvard Journal on Legislation* 39 (2002): 437.

48. McCarthy, "Recent Developments: USA Patriot Act," 439.

49. HR 3162: Uniting and Strengthening America by Providing Appropriate Tools Required to Intercept and Obstruct Terrorism (USA PATRIOT) Act of 2001, 107th Cong. (2001–2), http://www.govtrack.us/congress /bills/107/hr3162.

50. Ted Bridis and David Rogers, "Agency Proposes Much Broader Antiterror Laws," *Wall Street Journal*, September 20, 2001, A.3.

51. McCarthy, "Recent Developments: USA Patriot Act," 438.

52. See HR 3162: USA PATRIOT Act.

53. Nancy Kranich, "The Impact of the USA PATRIOT Act: An Update," Free Expression Policy Project, 2009, https://web.archive.org/web/20091204071302/http://www.fepproject.org/commentaries /patriotactupdate.html.

54. "Immigration Reform," U.S. Immigration Support, https://web.archive.org/web/20111213173126 /http://www.usimmigrationsupport.org/immigration-reform.html.

55. As Stephen Schulhofer notes, "The Patriot Act was enacted in an environment where there was virtually no discussion or careful scrutiny. Maybe there shouldn't have been because we needed to act quickly." See Kranich, "The Impact of the USA PATRIOT Act."

56. Juliet Eilperin, "Bipartisan Approach Faces Tests; As Congress Tackles Tough Issues, Leadership Is Questioned," *Washington Post*, September 27, 2001, A.4.

57. David E. Sanger, "Bush, on Offense, Says He Will Fight to Keep Tax Cuts," *New York Times*, January 6, 2002, 1.

58. Dana Milbank, "Bush Campaigns for More Tax Relief; Some in White House Look to Senate to Cut House-Passed Measure," *Washington Post*, October 25, 2001, A.3.

59. Joseph Biden, "Remarks by President Biden on the Way Forward in Afghanistan," April 14, 2021, https://www.whitehouse.gov/briefing-room/speeches-remarks/2021/04/14/remarks-by-president-biden-on-the-way-forward-in-afghanistan/.

Presidents and Congresses, 1789–2016

Year	President and Vice President	Party of President	Congress	Majority Party	
				House	Senate
1789–1797	**George Washington** John Adams	None	1st 2nd 3rd 4th	Admin. Supporters Federalist Democratic- Republican Federalist	Admin. Supporters Federalist Federalist Federalist
1797–1801	**John Adams** Thomas Jefferson	Federalist	5th 6th	Federalist Federalist	Federalist Federalist
1801–1809	**Thomas Jefferson** Aaron Burr (to 1805) George Clinton (to 1809)		7th 8th 9th 10th	Democratic- Republican Democratic- Republican Democratic- Republican Democratic- Republican	Democratic- Republican Democratic- Republican Democratic- Republican Democratic- Republican
1809–1817	**James Madison** George Clinton (to 1813) Elbridge Gerry (to 1817)	Democratic- Republican	11th 12th 13th 14th	Democratic- Republican Democratic- Republican Democratic- Republican Democratic- Republican	Democratic- Republican Democratic- Republican Democratic- Republican Democratic- Republican
1817–1825	**James Monroe** Daniel D. Tompkins	Democratic- Republican	15th 16th 17th 18th	Democratic- Republican Democratic- Republican Democratic- Republican Democratic- Republican	Democratic- Republican Democratic- Republican Democratic- Republican Democratic- Republican

Continued on next page

Year	President and Vice President	Party of President	Congress	Majority Party	
				House	Senate
1825–1829	**John Quincy Adams** John C. Calhoun	National- Republican	19th 20th	Admin. Supporters Jacksonian Democrats	Admin. Supporters Jacksonian Democrats
1829–1837	**Andrew Jackson** John C. Calhoun (to 1833) Martin Van Buren (to 1837)	Democratic	21st 22nd 23rd 24th	Democratic Democratic Democratic Democratic	Democratic Democratic Democratic Democratic
1837–1841	**Martin Van Buren** Richard M. Johnson	Democratic	25th 26th	Democratic Democratic	Democratic Democratic
1841	**William H. Harrison** (died a month after inauguration) John Tyler	Whig			
1841–1845	**John Tyler** (VP vacant)	Whig	27th 28th	Whig Democratic	Whig Whig
1845–1849	**James K. Polk** George M. Dallas	Democratic	29th 30th	Democratic Whig	Democratic Democratic
1849–1850	**Zachary Taylor** (died in office) Millard Fillmore	Whig	31st	Democratic	Democratic
1850–1853	**Millard Fillmore** (VP vacant)	Whig	32nd	Democratic	Democratic
1853–1857	**Franklin Pierce** William R. King	Democratic	33rd 34th	Democratic Republican	Democratic Democratic
1857–1861	**James Buchanan** John C. Breckinridge	Democratic	35th 36th	Democratic Republican	Democratic Democratic
1861–1865	**Abraham Lincoln** (died in office) Hannibal Hamlin (to 1865) Andrew Johnson (1865)	Republican	37th 38th	Republican Republican	Republican Republican
1865–1869	**Andrew Johnson** (VP vacant)	Republican	39th 40th	Unionist Republican	Unionist Republican
1869–1877	**Ulysses S. Grant** Schuyler Colfax (to 1873) Henry Wilson (to 1877)	Republican	41st 42nd 43rd 44th	Republican Republican Republican Democratic	Republican Republican Republican Republican
1877–1881	**Rutherford B. Hayes** William A. Wheeler	Republican	45th 46th	Democratic Democratic	Republican Democratic
1881	**James A. Garfield** (died in office) Chester A. Arthur	Republican	47th	Republican	Republican
1881–1885	**Chester A. Arthur** (VP vacant)	Republican	48th	Democratic	Republican

Year	President and Vice President	Party of President	Congress	Majority Party	
				House	Senate
1885–1889	**Grover Cleveland** Thomas A. Hendricks	Democratic	49th 50th	Democratic Democratic	Republican Republican
1889–1893	**Benjamin Harrison** Levi P. Morton	Republican	51st 52nd	Republican Democratic	Republican Republican
1893–1897	**Grover Cleveland** Adlai E. Stevenson	Democratic	53rd 54th	Democratic Republican	Democratic Republican
1897–1901	**William McKinley** (died in office) Garret A. Hobart (to 1901) Theodore Roosevelt (1901)	Republican	55th 56th	Republican Republican	Republican Republican
1901–1909	**Theodore Roosevelt** (VP vacant, 1901–1905) Charles W. Fairbanks (1905–1909)	Republican	57th 58th 59th 60th	Republican Republican Republican Republican	Republican Republican Republican Republican
1909–1913	**William Howard Taft** James S. Sherman	Republican	61st 62nd	Republican Democratic	Republican Republican
1913–1921	**Woodrow Wilson** Thomas R. Marshall	Democratic	63rd 64th 65th 66th	Democratic Democratic Democratic Republican	Democratic Democratic Democratic Republican
1921–1923	**Warren G. Harding** (died in office) Calvin Coolidge	Republican	67th	Republican	Republican
1923–1929	**Calvin Coolidge** (VP vacant, 1923–1925) Charles G. Dawes (1925–1929)	Republican	68th 69th 70th	Republican Republican Republican	Republican Republican Republican
1929–1933	**Herbert Hoover** Charles Curtis	Republican	71st 72nd	Republican Democratic	Republican Republican
1933–1945	**Franklin D. Roosevelt** (died in office) John N. Garner (1933–1941) Henry A. Wallace (1941–1945) Harry S Truman (1945) 77th	Democratic Democratic	73rd 74th 75th 76th 77th 78th	Democratic Democratic Democratic Democratic Democratic Democratic	Democratic Democratic Democratic Democratic Democratic Democratic
1945–1953	**Harry S Truman** (VP vacant, 1945–1949) Alben W. Barkley (1949–1953)	Democratic	79th 80th 81st 82nd	Democratic Republican Democratic Democratic	Democratic Republican Democratic Democratic
1953–1961	**Dwight D. Eisenhower** Richard M. Nixon	Republican	83rd 84th 85th 86th	Republican Democratic Democratic Democratic	Republican Democratic Democratic Democratic

Continued on next page

Year	President and Vice President	Party of President	Congress	Majority Party	
				House	Senate
1961–1963	**John F. Kennedy** (died in office) Lyndon B. Johnson	Democratic	87th	Democratic	Democratic
1963–1969	**Lyndon B. Johnson** (VP vacant, 1963–1965) Hubert H. Humphrey (1965–1969)	Democratic	88th 89th 90th	Democratic Democratic Democratic	Democratic Democratic Democratic
1969–1974	**Richard M. Nixon** (resigned office) Spiro T. Agnew (resigned office) Gerald R. Ford (appointed vice president)	Republican	91st 92nd	Democratic Democratic	Democratic Democratic
1974–1977	**Gerald R. Ford** Nelson A. Rockefeller (appointed vice president)	Republican	93rd 94th	Democratic Democratic	Democratic Democratic
1977–1981	**Jimmy Carter** Walter Mondale	Democratic	95th 96th	Democratic Democratic	Democratic Democratic
1981–1989	**Ronald Reagan** George H. W. Bush	Republican	97th 98th 99th 100th	Democratic Democratic Democratic Democratic	Republican Republican Republican Democratic
1989–1993	**George H. W. Bush** J. Danforth Quayle	Republican	101st 102nd	Democratic Democratic	Democratic Democratic
1993–2001	**Bill Clinton** Albert Gore Jr.	Democratic	103rd 104th 105th 106th	Democratic Republican Republican Republican	Democratic Republican Republican Republican
2001–2009	**George W. Bush** Richard Cheney	Republican	107th 108th 109th 110th	Republican Republican Republican Democratic	Democratic Republican Republican Democratic
2009–2017	**Barack Obama** Joseph Biden	Democratic	111th 112th 113th 114th	Democratic Republican Republican Republican	Democratic Democratic Democratic Republican
2017–2021	**Donald Trump** Mike Pence	Republican	115th 116th	Republican Democratic	Republican Republican
2021–	**Joseph Biden** Kamala Harris	Democratic	117th	Democratic	Democratic

Notes: During the entire administration of George Washington and part of the administration of John Quincy Adams, Congress was not organized in terms of parties. This table shows that during these periods the supporters of the respective administrations maintained control of Congress. This table shows only the two dominant parties in Congress. Independents, members of minor parties, and vacancies have been omitted.

Articles I–III of the Constitution

WE THE PEOPLE of the United States, in Order to form a more perfect Union, establish Justice, insure domestic Tranquility, provide for the common defence, promote the general Welfare, and secure the Blessings of Liberty to ourselves and our Posterity, do ordain and establish this constitution for the United States of America.

Article I

Section 1

All legislative Powers herein granted shall be vested in a Congress of the United States, which shall consist of a Senate and House of Representatives.

Section 2

The House of Representatives shall be composed of Members chosen every second Year by the People of the several States, and the Electors in each State shall have the Qualifications requisite for Electors of the most numerous Branch of the State Legislature.

No person shall be a Representative who shall not have attained to the Age of twenty-five Years, and been seven Years a Citizen of the United States, and who shall not, when elected, be an Inhabitant of that State in which he shall be chosen.

Representatives and direct Taxes shall be apportioned among the several States which may be included within this Union, according to their respective Numbers, which shall be determined by adding to the whole Number of free Persons, including those bound to Service for a Term of Years, and excluding Indians not taxed, three fifths of all other Persons. The actual Enumeration shall be made within three Years after the first Meeting of the Congress of the United States, and within every subsequent Term of ten Years, in such Manner as they shall by Law direct. The Number of Representatives shall not exceed one for every thirty Thousand, but each State shall have at Least one Representative; and until such enumeration shall be made, the State of New Hampshire shall be entitled to chuse three, Massachusetts eight, Rhode-Island and Providence Plantations one, Connecticut five, New-York six, New Jersey four, Pennsylvania eight, Delaware one, Maryland six, Virginia ten, North Carolina five, South Carolina five, and Georgia three.

When vacancies happen in the Representation from any State, the Executive Authority thereof shall issue Writs of Election to fill such Vacancies.

The House of Representatives shall chuse their Speaker and other Officers; and shall have the sole Power of Impeachment.

Section 3

The Senate of the United States shall be composed of two Senators from each State, chosen by the Legislature thereof, for six Years; and each Senator shall have one Vote.

Immediately after they shall be assembled in Consequence of the first Election, they shall be divided as equally as may be into three Classes. The Seats of the Senators of the first Class shall be vacated at the Expiration of the second Year, of the second Class at the Expiration of the fourth Year, and of the third Class at the Expiration of the sixth Year, so that one-third may be chosen every second Year; and if Vacancies happen by Resignation, or otherwise, during the Recess of the Legislature of any State, the Executive thereof may make temporary Appointments until the next Meeting of the Legislature, which shall then fill such Vacancies.

No Person shall be a Senator who shall not have attained to the Age of thirty Years, and been nine Years a Citizen of the United States, and who shall not, when elected, be an Inhabitant of that State in which he shall be chosen.

The Vice President of the United States shall be President of the Senate, but shall have no vote, unless they be equally divided.

The Senate shall chuse their other Officers, and also a President pro tempore, in the absence of the Vice President, or when he shall exercise the Office of the President of the United States.

The Senate shall have the sole Power to try all Impeachments. When sitting for that purpose, they shall be on Oath or Affirmation. When the President of the United States is tried, the Chief Justice shall preside: And no person shall be convicted without the Concurrence of two thirds of the Members present.

Judgment in Cases of Impeachment shall not extend further than to removal from Office, and disqualification to hold and enjoy any Office of honor, Trust, or Profit under the United States: but the Party convicted shall nevertheless be liable and subject to Indictment, Trial, Judgment, and Punishment, according to Law.

Section 4

The Times, Places and Manner of holding Elections for Senators and Representatives, shall be prescribed in each state by the Legislature thereof; but the Congress may at any time by Law make or alter such Regulations, except as to the Places of Chusing Senators.

The Congress shall assemble at least once in every Year, and such Meeting shall be on the first Monday in December, unless they shall by Law appoint a different Day.

Section 5

Each House shall be the Judge of the Elections, Returns and Qualifications of its own Members, and a Majority of each shall constitute a Quorum to do Business; but a smaller number may adjourn from day to day, and may be authorized to compel the Attendance of absent Members, in such Manner, and under such Penalties, as each House may provide.

Each House may determine the Rules of its Proceedings, punish its Members for disorderly Behavior, and, with the Concurrence of two thirds, expel a Member.

Each House shall keep a Journal of its Proceedings, and from time to time publish the same, excepting such Parts as may in their Judgment require Secrecy; and the Yeas and Nays of the Members of either House on any question shall, at the Desire of one fifth of those Present, be entered on the Journal.

Neither House, during the Session of Congress, shall, without the Consent of the other, adjourn for more than three days, nor to any other Place than that in which the two Houses shall be sitting.

Section 6

The Senators and Representatives shall receive a Compensation for their Services, to be ascertained by Law, and paid out of the Treasury of the United States. They shall in all Cases, except Treason, Felony, and Breach of the Peace, be privileged from arrest during their Attendance at the Session of their respective Houses, and in going to and returning from the same; and for any Speech or Debate in either House, they shall not be questioned in any other Place.

No Senator or Representative shall, during the Time for which he was elected, be appointed to any civil Office under the Authority of the United States, which shall have been created, or the Emoluments whereof shall have been increased, during such time; and no Person holding any Office under the United States shall be a Member of either House during his continuance in Office.

Section 7

All Bills for raising Revenue shall originate in the House of Representatives; but the Senate may propose or concur with Amendments as on other bills.

Every Bill which shall have passed the House of Representatives and the Senate, shall, before it become a Law, be presented to the President of the United States; If he approve he shall sign it, but if not he shall return it, with his Objections, to that House in which it shall have originated, who shall enter the Objections at large on their Journal, and proceed to reconsider it. If after such Reconsideration two thirds of that House shall agree to pass the bill, it shall be sent, together with the objections, to the other House, by which it shall likewise be reconsidered, and if approved by two thirds of that House, it shall become a Law. But in all such Cases the Votes of both Houses shall be determined by Yeas and Nays, and the Names of the Persons voting for and against the Bill shall be entered on the Journal of each House respectively. If any Bill shall not be returned by the President within ten Days (Sundays excepted) after it shall have been presented to him, the Same shall be a Law, in like Manner as if he had signed it, unless the Congress by their Adjournment prevent its Return, in which Case it shall not be a Law.

Every Order, Resolution, or Vote to which the Concurrence of the Senate and House of Representatives may be necessary (except on a question of Adjournment) shall be presented to the President of the United States; and before the Same shall take Effect, shall be approved by him, or being disapproved by him, shall be repassed by two thirds of the Senate and House of Representatives, according to the Rules and Limitations prescribed in the Case of a Bill.

Section 8

The Congress shall have Power

> To lay and collect Taxes, Duties, Imposts and Excises, to pay the Debts and provide for the common Defence and general Welfare of the United States; but all Duties, Imposts and Excises shall be uniform throughout the United States;
>
> To borrow money on the credit of the United States;
>
> To regulate Commerce with foreign Nations, and among the several States, and with the Indian Tribes;
>
> To establish a uniform Rule of Naturalization, and uniform Laws on the subject of Bankruptcies throughout the United States;
>
> To coin Money, regulate the Value thereof, and of foreign Coin, and fix the Standard of Weights and Measures;
>
> To provide for the Punishment of counterfeiting the Securities and current Coin of the United States;
>
> To establish Post offices and post Roads;
>
> To promote the Progress of Science and useful Arts, by securing for limited Times to Authors and Inventors the exclusive Right to their respective Writings and Discoveries;
>
> To constitute Tribunals inferior to the Supreme Court;
>
> To define and punish Piracies and Felonies committed on the high Seas, and Offences against the Law of Nations;
>
> To declare War, grant Letters of Marque and Reprisal, and make Rules concerning Captures on Land and Water;

To raise and support Armies, but no Appropriation of Money to that Use shall be for a longer Term than two Years;

To provide and maintain a Navy;

To make Rules for the Government and Regulation of the land and naval forces;

To provide for calling forth the Militia to execute the Laws of the Union, suppress Insurrections and repel Invasions;

To provide for organizing, arming, and disciplining the Militia, and for governing such Part of them as may be employed in the Service of the United States, reserving to the States respectively, the Appointment of the Officers, and the Authority of training the Militia according to the discipline prescribed by Congress;

To exercise exclusive Legislation in all Cases whatsoever, over such District (not exceeding ten Miles square) as may, by Cession of particular States, and the acceptance of Congress, become the Seat of Government of the United States, and to exercise like Authority over all Places purchased by the Consent of the Legislature of the State in which the Same shall be, for the Erection of Forts, Magazines, Arsenals, dock-Yards, and other needful Buildings;—And

To make all Laws which shall be necessary and proper for carrying into Execution the foregoing Powers, and all other Powers vested by this Constitution in the government of the United States, or in any Department or Officer thereof.

Section 9

The Migration or Importation of such Persons as any of the States now existing shall think proper to admit, shall not be prohibited by the Congress prior to the Year one thousand eight hundred and eight, but a tax or duty may be imposed on such Importation, not exceeding ten dollars for each Person.

The privilege of the Writ of Habeas Corpus shall not be suspended, unless when in Cases of Rebellion or Invasion the public Safety may require it.

No Bill of Attainder or ex post facto Law shall be passed.

No capitation, or other direct, Tax shall be laid unless in Proportion to the Census or Enumeration herein before directed to be taken.

No Tax or Duty shall be laid on Articles exported from any State.

No Preference shall be given by any Regulation of Revenue to the Ports of one State over those of another: nor shall Vessels bound to, or from, one state, be obliged to enter, clear, or pay Duties in another.

No Money shall be drawn from the Treasury, but in Consequence of Appropriations made by Law; and a regular Statement and Account of the Receipts and Expenditures of all public Money shall be published from time to time.

No Title of Nobility shall be granted by the United States: And no Person holding any Office of Profit or Trust under them, shall, without the Consent of the Congress, accept of any present, Emolument, Office, or Title, of any kind whatever, from any King, Prince, or Foreign State.

Section 10

No state shall enter into any Treaty, Alliance, or Confederation; grant Letters of Marque and Reprisal; coin Money; emit Bills of Credit; make any Thing but gold and silver Coin a Tender in Payment of Debts; pass any Bill of Attainder, ex post facto Law, or Law impairing the Obligation of Contracts, or grant any Title of Nobility.

No State shall, without the Consent of the Congress, lay any Imposts or Duties on Imports or Exports, except what may be absolutely necessary for executing its inspection Laws: and the net Produce of all Duties and Imposts, laid by any State on Imports or Exports, shall be for the Use of the Treasury of the United States; and all such Laws shall be subject to the Revision and Control of the Congress.

No State shall, without the Consent of Congress, lay any duty of Tonnage, keep Troops, or Ships of War in time of Peace, enter into any Agreement or Compact with another State, or with a foreign Power, or engage in War, unless actually invaded, or in such imminent Danger as will not admit of delay.

Article II

Section 1

The executive Power shall be vested in a President of the United States of America. He shall hold his Office during the Term of four years, and, together with the Vice President, chosen for the same Term, be elected, as follows:

Each State shall appoint, in such Manner as the Legislature thereof may direct, a Number of Electors, equal to the whole Number of Senators and Representatives to which the State may be entitled in the Congress; but no Senator or Representative, or Person holding an Office of Trust or Profit under the United States, shall be appointed an Elector.

The Electors shall meet in their respective States, and vote by Ballot for two persons, of whom one at least shall not be an Inhabitant of the same State with themselves. And they shall make a List of all the Persons voted for, and of the Number of Votes for each; which List they shall sign and certify, and transmit sealed to the Seat of the Government of the United States, directed to the President of the Senate. The President of the Senate shall, in the Presence of the Senate and House of Representatives, open all the Certificates, and the Votes shall then be counted. The Person having the greatest Number of Votes shall be the President, if such Number be a Majority of the whole Number of Electors appointed; and if there be more than one who have such Majority, and have an equal Number of Votes, then the House of Representatives shall immediately chuse by Ballot one of them for President; and if no Person have a Majority, then from the five highest on the List the said House shall in like Manner chuse the President. But in chusing the President, the votes shall be taken by States, the Representation from each State having one Vote; a quorum for this Purpose shall consist of a Member or Members from two-thirds of the States, and a Majority of all the States shall be necessary to a Choice. In every Case, after the Choice of the President, the Person having the greatest Number of Votes of the Electors shall be the Vice President. But if there should remain two or more who have equal votes, the Senate shall chuse from them by Ballot the Vice President.

The Congress may determine the time of chusing the Electors, and the Day on which they shall give their Votes; which Day shall be the same throughout the United States.

No person except a natural-born Citizen, or a Citizen of the United States, at the time of the Adoption of this Constitution, shall be eligible to the Office of President; neither shall any Person be eligible to that Office who shall not have attained to the Age of thirty-five years, and been fourteen Years a Resident within the United States.

In Case of the Removal of the President from Office, or of his Death, Resignation, or Inability to discharge the Powers and Duties of the said Office, the same shall devolve on the Vice President, and the Congress may by Law provide for the Case of Removal, Death, Resignation, or Inability, both of the President and Vice President, declaring what Officer shall then act as President, and such Officer shall act accordingly, until the disability be removed, or a President shall be elected.

The President shall, at stated Times, receive for his Services a Compensation, which shall neither be increased nor diminished during the Period for which he shall have been elected, and he shall not receive within that Period any other Emolument from the United States, or any of them.

Before he enter on the execution of his Office, he shall take the following Oath or Affirmation:—"I do solemnly swear (or affirm) that I will faithfully execute the Office of President of the United States, and will, to the best of my Ability, preserve, protect, and defend the Constitution of the United States."

Section 2

The President shall be Commander in Chief of the Army and Navy of the United States, and of the Militia of the several States, when called into the actual Service of the United States; he may require the Opinion, in writing, of the principal Officer in each of the executive Departments, upon any subject relating to the Duties of their respective Offices, and he shall have Power to Grant Reprieves and Pardons for Offences against the United States, except in Cases of Impeachment.

He shall have Power, by and with the Advice and Consent of the Senate, to make Treaties, provided two thirds of the Senators present concur; and he shall nominate, and by and with the Advice and Consent of the Senate, shall appoint Ambassadors, other public Ministers and Consuls, Judges of the supreme Court, and all other Officers of the United States, whose Appointments are not herein otherwise provided for, and which shall be established by Law: but the Congress may by Law vest the Appointment of such inferior Officers, as they think proper, in the President alone, in the Courts of Law, or in the Heads of Departments.

The President shall have Power to fill up all Vacancies that may happen during the Recess of the Senate, by granting Commissions which shall expire at the End of their next Session.

Section 3

He shall from time to time give to the Congress Information of the State of the Union, and recommend to their Consideration such Measures as he shall judge necessary and expedient; he may, on extraordinary occasions, convene both Houses, or either of them, and in Case of Disagreement between them, with respect to the Time of Adjournment, he may adjourn them to such Time as he shall think proper; he shall receive Ambassadors and other public Ministers; he shall take Care that the Laws be faithfully executed, and shall Commission all the Officers of the Unit ed States.

Section 4

The President, Vice President and all civil Officers of the United States, shall be removed from Office on Impeachment for, and Conviction of, Treason, Bribery, or other high Crimes and Misdemeanors.

Article III

Section 1

The judicial Power of the United States, shall be vested in one supreme Court, and in such inferior Courts as the Congress may from time to time ordain and establish. The Judges, both of the supreme and inferior Courts, shall hold their Offices during good Behaviour, and shall, at stated Times, receive for their Services, a Compensation, which shall not be diminished during their Continuance in Office.

Section 2

The judicial Power shall extend to all Cases, in Law and Equity, arising under this Constitution, the Laws of the United States, and treaties made, or which shall be made, under their Authority;—to all Cases affecting ambassadors, other public ministers and consuls;—to all cases of admiralty and maritime Jurisdiction;—to Controversies to which the United States shall be a Party;—to Controversies between two or more States;—between a State and Citizens of another State;—between Citizens of different States,—between Citizens of the same State claiming Lands under Grants of different States, and between a State, or the Citizens thereof, and foreign States, Citizens or Subjects.

In all Cases affecting Ambassadors, other public Ministers and Consuls, and those in which a State shall be Par ty, the supreme Court shall have original Jurisdiction. In all the other Cases before mentioned, the supreme Court shall have appellate Jurisdiction, both as to Law and Fact, with such Exceptions, and under such Regulations as the Congress shall make.

The trial of all Crimes, except in Cases of Impeachment, shall be by Jury; and such Trial shall be held in the State where the said Crimes shall have been committed; but when not committed within any State, the Trial shall be at such Place or Places as the Congress may by Law have directed.

Section 3

Treason against the United States, shall consist only in levying War against them, or in adhering to their Enemies, giving them Aid and Comfort. No Person shall be convicted of Treason unless on the testimony of two Witnesses to the same overt Act, or on Confession in open Court.

The Congress shall have power to declare the Punishment of Treason, but no Attainder of Treason shall work Corruption of Blood, or Forfeiture except during the Life of the Person attained.

Federalist Papers 69–73

FEDERALIST No. 69

The Real Character of the Executive

From the New York Packet. Friday, March 14, 1788. [Alexander Hamilton]

TO THE PEOPLE OF THE STATE OF NEW YORK:

I PROCEED now to trace the real characters of the proposed Executive, as they are marked out in the plan of the convention. This will serve to place in a strong light the unfairness of the representations which have been made in regard to it.

The first thing which strikes our attention is, that the executive authority, with few exceptions, is to be vested in a single magistrate. This will scarcely, however, be considered as a point upon which any comparison can be grounded; for if, in this particular, there be a resemblance to the king of Great Britain, there is not less a resemblance to the Grand Seignior, to the khan of Tartary, to the Man of the Seven Mountains, or to the governor of New York.

That magistrate is to be elected for FOUR years; and is to be re-eligible as often as the people of the United States shall think him worthy of their confidence. In these circumstances there is a total dissimilitude between HIM and a king of Great Britain, who is an HEREDITARY monarch, possessing the crown as a patrimony descendible to his heirs forever; but there is a close analogy between HIM and a governor of New York, who is elected for THREE years, and is re-eligible without limitation or intermission. If we consider how much less time would be requisite for establishing a dangerous influence in a single State, than for establishing a like influence throughout the United States, we must conclude that a duration of FOUR years for the Chief Magistrate of the Union is a degree of permanency far less to be dreaded in that office, than a duration of THREE years for a corresponding office in a single State.

The President of the United States would be liable to be impeached, tried, and, upon conviction of treason, bribery, or other high crimes or misdemeanors, removed from office; and would afterwards be liable to prosecution and punishment in the ordinary course of law. The person of the king of Great Britain is sacred and inviolable; there is no constitutional tribunal to which he is amenable; no punishment to which he can be subjected without involving the crisis of a national revolution. In this delicate and important circumstance of personal responsibility, the President of Confederated America would stand upon no better ground than a governor of New York, and upon worse ground than the governors of Maryland and Delaware.

The President of the United States is to have power to return a bill, which shall have passed the two branches of the legislature, for reconsideration; and the bill so returned is to become a law, if, upon that reconsideration, it be approved by two thirds of both houses. The king of Great Britain, on his part, has an absolute negative upon the acts of the two houses of Parliament. The disuse of that power for a considerable time past does not affect the reality of its existence; and is to be ascribed wholly to the crown's having found the means of substituting influence to authority, or the art of gaining a majority in one or the other of the two houses, to the necessity of exerting a prerogative which could seldom be exerted without hazarding some degree of national agitation. The qualified negative of the President differs widely from this absolute negative of the British sovereign; and tallies exactly with the revisionary authority of the council of revision of this State, of which the governor is a constituent part. In this respect the power of the President would exceed that of the governor of New York, because the former would possess, singly, what the latter shares with the chancellor and judges; but it would be precisely the same with that of the governor of Massachusetts, whose constitution, as to this article, seems to have been the original from which the convention have copied.

The President is to be the "commander-in-chief of the army and navy of the United States, and of the militia of the several States, when called into the actual service of the United States. He is to have power to grant reprieves and pardons for offenses against the United States, EXCEPT IN CASES OF IMPEACHMENT; to recommend to the consideration of Congress such measures as he shall judge necessary and expedient; to convene, on extraordinary occasions, both houses of the legislature, or either of them, and, in case of disagreement between them WITH RESPECT TO THE TIME OF ADJOURNMENT, to adjourn them to such time as he shall think proper; to take care that the laws be faithfully executed; and to commission all officers of the United States." In most of these particulars, the power of the President will resemble equally that of the king of Great Britain and of the governor of New York. The most material points of difference are these: First. The President will have only the occasional command of such part of the militia of the nation as by legislative provision may be called into the actual service of the Union. The king of Great Britain and the governor of New York have at all times the entire command of all the militia with in their several jurisdictions. In this article, therefore, the power of the President would be inferior to that of either the monarch or the governor. Secondly. The President is to be commander-in-chief of the army and navy of the United States. In this respect his authority would be nominally the same with that of the king of Great Britain, but in substance much inferior to it. It would amount to nothing more than the supreme command and direction of the military and naval forces, as first General and admiral of the Confederacy; while that of the British king extends to the DECLARING of war and to the RAISING and REGULATING of fleets and armies, all which, by the Constitution under consideration, would appertain to the legislature.[1] The governor of New York, on the other hand, is by the constitution of the State vested only with the command of its militia and navy. But the constitutions of several of the States expressly declare their governors to be commanders-in-chief, as well of the army as navy; and it may well be a question, whether those of New Hampshire and Massachusetts, in particular, do not, in this instance, confer larger powers upon their respective governors, than could be claimed by a President of the United States. Thirdly. The power of the President, in respect to pardons, would extend to all cases, EXCEPT THOSE OF IMPEACHMENT. The governor of New York may pardon in all cases, even in those of impeachment, except for treason and murder. Is not the power of the governor, in this article, on a calculation of political consequences, greater than that of the President? All conspiracies and plots against the government, which have not been matured into actual treason, may be screened from punishment of every kind, by the interposition of the prerogative of pardoning. If a governor of New York, therefore, should be at the head of any such conspiracy, until the design had been ripened into actual hostility he could insure his accomplices and adherents an entire impunity. A President of the Union, on the other hand, though he may even pardon treason, when prosecuted in the ordinary course of law, could shelter no offender, in any degree, from the effects of impeachment and conviction. Would not the prospect of a total indemnity for all the preliminary steps be a greater temptation to undertake and persevere in an enterprise against the public liberty, than the mere prospect of an exemption from death and confiscation, if the final execution of the design, upon an actual appeal to arms, should miscarry? Would this last expectation have any influence at all, when the probability was computed, that the person who was to afford that exemption might himself be involved in the consequences of the measure, and might be incapacitated by his agency in it from affording the desired impunity? The better to judge of this matter, it will be necessary to recollect, that, by the proposed Constitution, the offense of treason is limited "to levying war upon the United States, and adhering to their enemies, giving them aid and comfort"; and that by the laws of New York it is confined within similar bounds. Fourthly. The President can only adjourn the national legislature in the single case of disagreement about the time of adjournment. The British monarch may prorogue or even dissolve the Parliament. The governor of New York may also prorogue the legislature of this State for a limited time; a power which, in certain situations, may be employed to very important purposes.

The President is to have power, with the advice and consent of the Senate, to make treaties, provided two thirds of the senators present concur. The king of Great Britain is the sole and absolute representative of the nation in all foreign transactions. He can of his own accord make treaties of peace, commerce, alliance, and of every other description. It has been insinuated, that his authority in this respect is not conclusive, and that his conventions with foreign powers are subject to the revision, and stand in need of the ratification, of Parliament. But I believe this doctrine was never heard of, until it was broached upon the present occasion. Every jurist[2] of that kingdom, and every other man acquainted with its Constitution, knows, as an established fact, that the prerogative of making treaties exists in the crown in its utmost plentitude; and that the compacts entered into by the royal authority have the most complete legal validity and perfection, independent of any other sanction. The Parliament, it is true, is sometimes seen employing itself in altering the existing laws to conform them to the stipulations in a new treaty; and this may have possibly given birth to the imagination, that its co-operation was necessary to the obligatory efficacy of the treaty. But this parliamentary interposition proceeds from a different cause: from the necessity of adjusting a most artificial and intricate system of revenue and commercial laws, to the changes made in them by the operation of the treaty; and of adapting new provisions and precautions to the new state of things, to keep the machine from running into disorder. In this respect, therefore, there is no comparison between the intended power of the President and the actual power of the British sovereign. The one can perform alone what the other can do only with the concurrence of a branch of the legislature. It must be admitted, that, in this instance, the power of the federal Executive would exceed that of any State Executive. But this arises naturally from the sovereign power which relates to treaties. If the Confederacy were to be dissolved, it would become a question, whether the Executives of the several States were not solely invested with that delicate and important prerogative.

The President is also to be authorized to receive ambassadors and other public ministers. This, though it has been a rich theme of declamation, is more a matter of dignity than of authority. It is a circumstance which will be without consequence in the administration of the government; and it was far more convenient that it should be arranged in this manner, than that there should be a necessity of convening the legislature, or one of its branches, upon every arrival of a foreign minister, though it were merely to take the place of a departed predecessor.

The President is to nominate, and, WITH THE ADVICE AND CONSENT OF THE SENATE, to appoint ambassadors and other public ministers, judges of the Supreme Court, and in general all officers of the United States established by law, and whose appointments are not otherwise provided for by the Constitution. The king of Great Britain is emphatically and truly styled the fountain of honor. He not only appoints to all offices, but can create offices. He can confer titles of nobility at pleasure; and has the disposal of an immense number of church preferments. There is evidently a great inferiority in the power of the President, in this particular, to that of the British king; nor is it equal to that of the governor of New York, if we are to interpret the meaning of the constitution of the State by the practice which has obtained under it. The power of appointment is with us lodged in a council, composed of the governor and four members of the Senate, chosen by the Assembly. The governor CLAIMS, and has frequently EXERCISED, the right of nomination, and is ENTITLED to a casting vote in the appointment. If he really has the right of nominating, his authority is in this respect equal to that of the President, and exceeds it in the article of the casting vote. In the national government, if the Senate should be divided, no appointment could be made; in the government of New York, if the council should be divided, the governor can turn the scale, and confirm his own nomination.[3] If we compare the publicity which must necessarily attend the mode of appointment by the President and an entire branch of the national legislature, with the privacy in the mode of appointment by the governor of New York, closeted in a secret apartment with at most four, and frequently with only two persons; and if we at the same time consider how much more easy it must be to influence the small number of which a council of appointment consists, than the considerable number of which the national Senate would consist, we cannot hesitate to pronounce that the power of the chief magistrate of this State, in the disposition of offices, must, in practice, be greatly superior to that of the Chief Magistrate of the Union.

Hence it appears that, except as to the concurrent authority of the President in the article of treaties, it would be difficult to determine whether that magistrate would, in the aggregate, possess more or less power than the Governor of New York. And it appears yet more unequivocally, that there is no pretense for the parallel which has been attempted between him and the king of Great Britain. But to render the contrast in this respect still more striking, it may be of use to throw the principal circumstances of dissimilitude into a closer group.

The President of the United States would be an officer elected by the people for FOUR years; the king of Great Britain is a perpetual and HEREDITARY prince. The one would be amenable to personal punishment and disgrace; the person of the other is sacred and inviolable. The one would have a QUALIFIED negative upon the acts of the legislative body; the other has an ABSOLUTE negative. The one would have a right to command the military and naval forces of the nation; the other, in addition to this right, possesses that of DECLARING war, and of RAISING and REGULATING fleets and armies by his own authority. The one would have a concurrent power with a branch of the legislature in the formation of treaties; the other is the SOLE POSSESSOR of the power of making treaties. The one would have a like concurrent authority in appointing to offices; the other is the sole author of all appointments. The one can confer no privileges whatever; the other can make denizens of aliens, noblemen of commoners; can erect corporations with all the rights incident to corporate bodies. The one can prescribe no rules concerning the commerce or currency of the nation; the other is in several respects the arbiter of commerce, and in this capacity can establish markets and fairs, can regulate weights and measures, can lay embargoes for a limited time, can coin money, can authorize or prohibit the circulation of foreign coin. The one has no particle of spiritual jurisdiction; the other is the supreme head and governor of the national church! What answer shall we give to those who would persuade us that things so unlike resemble each other? The same that ought to be given to those who tell us that a government, the whole power of which would be in the hands of the elective and periodical servants of the people, is an aristocracy, a monarchy, and a despotism.

PUBLIUS

1. A writer in a Pennsylvania paper, under the signature of TAMONY, has asserted that the king of Great Britain owes his prerogative as commander-in-chief to an annual mutiny bill. The truth is, on the contrary, that his prerogative, in this respect, is immemorial, and was only disputed, "contrary to all reason and precedent," as Blackstone vol. i., page 262, expresses it, by the Long Parliament of Charles I. but by the statute the 13th of Charles II., chap. 6, it was declared to be in the king alone, for that the sole supreme government and command of the militia within his Majesty's realms and dominions, and of all forces by sea and land, and of all forts and places of strength, EVER WAS AND IS the undoubted right of his Majesty and his royal predecessors, kings and queens of England, and that both or either house of Parliament cannot nor ought to pretend to the same.

2. Vide Blackstone's "Commentaries," vol i., p. 257.

3. Candor, however, demands an acknowledgment that I do not think the claim of the governor to a right of nomination well founded. Yet it is always justifiable to reason from the practice of a government, till its propriety has been constitutionally questioned. And independent of this claim, when we take into view the other considerations, and pursue them through all their consequences, we shall be inclined to draw much the same conclusion.

FEDERALIST No. 70

The Executive Department Further Considered

From the New York Packet. Tuesday, March 18, 1788. [Alexander Hamilton]

TO THE PEOPLE OF THE STATE OF NEW YORK:

THERE is an idea, which is not without its advocates, that a vigorous Executive is inconsistent with the genius of republican government. The enlightened well-wishers to this species of government must at least hope that the supposition is destitute of foundation; since they can never admit its truth, without at the same time admitting the condemnation of their own principles. Energy in the Executive is a leading character in the definition of good government. It is essential to the protection of the community against foreign attacks; it is not less essential to the steady administration of the laws; to the protection of property against those irregular and high-handed combinations which sometimes interrupt the ordinary course of justice; to the security of liberty against the enterprises and assaults of ambition, of faction, and of anarchy. Every man the least conversant in Roman story, knows how often that republic was obliged to take refuge in the absolute power of a single man, under the formidable title of Dictator, as well against the intrigues of ambitious individuals who aspired to the tyranny, and the seditions of whole classes of the community whose conduct threatened the existence of all government, as against the invasions of external enemies who menaced the conquest and destruction of Rome.

There can be no need, however, to multiply arguments or examples on this head. A feeble Executive implies a feeble execution of the government. A feeble execution is but another phrase for a bad execution; and a government ill executed, whatever it may be in theory, must be, in practice, a bad government.

Taking it for granted, therefore, that all men of sense will agree in the necessity of an energetic Executive, it will only remain to inquire, what are the ingredients which constitute this energy? How far can they be combined with those other ingredients which constitute safety in the republican sense? And how far does this combination characterize the plan which has been reported by the convention?

The ingredients which constitute energy in the Executive are, first, unity; secondly, duration; thirdly, an adequate provision for its support; fourthly, competent powers.

The ingredients which constitute safety in the republican sense are, first, a due dependence on the people, secondly, a due responsibility.

Those politicians and statesmen who have been the most celebrated for the soundness of their principles and for the justice of their views, have declared in favor of a single Executive and a numerous legislature. They have with great propriety, considered energy as the most necessary qualification of the former, and have regarded this as most applicable to power in a single hand, while they have, with equal propriety, considered the latter as best adapted to deliberation and wisdom, and best calculated to conciliate the confidence of the people and to secure their privileges and interests.

That unity is conducive to energy will not be disputed. Decision, activity, secrecy, and despatch will generally characterize the proceedings of one man in a much more eminent degree than the proceedings of any greater number; and in proportion as the number is increased, these qualities will be diminished.

This unity may be destroyed in two ways: either by vesting the power in two or more magistrates of equal dignity and authority; or by vesting it ostensibly in one man, subject, in whole or in part, to the control and co-operation of others, in the capacity of counsellors to him. Of the first, the two Consuls of Rome may serve as an example; of the last, we shall find examples in the constitutions of several of the States. New York and New Jersey, if I recollect right, are the only States which have intrusted the executive authority wholly to single men.[1] Both these methods of destroying the unity of the Executive have their partisans; but the votaries of an executive council are the most numerous. They are both liable, if not to equal, to similar objections, and may in most lights be examined in conjunction.

The experience of other nations will afford little instruction on this head. As far, however, as it teaches any thing, it teaches us not to be enamoured of plurality in the Executive. We have seen that the Achaeans, on an experiment of two Praetors, were induced to abolish one. The Roman history records many instances of mischiefs to the republic from the dissensions between the Consuls, and between the military Tribunes, who were at times substituted for the Consuls. But it gives us no specimens of any peculiar advantages derived to the state from the circumstance of the plurality of those magistrates. That the dissensions between them were not more frequent or more fatal, is a matter of astonishment, until we advert to the singular position in which the republic was almost continually placed, and to the prudent policy pointed out by the circumstances of the state, and pursued by the Consuls, of making a division of the government between them. The patricians engaged in a perpetual struggle with the plebeians for the preservation of their ancient authorities and dignities; the Consuls, who were generally chosen out of the former body, were commonly united by the personal interest they had in the defense of the privileges of their order. In addition to this motive of union, after the arms of the republic had considerably expanded the bounds of its empire, it became an established custom with the Consuls to divide the administration between themselves by lot one of them remaining at Rome to govern the city and its environs, the other taking the command in the more distant provinces. This expedient must, no doubt, have had great influence in preventing those collisions and rivalships which might otherwise have embroiled the peace of the republic.

But quitting the dim light of historical research, attaching ourselves purely to the dictates of reason and good sense, we shall discover much greater cause to reject than to approve the idea of plurality in the Executive, under any modification whatever.

Wherever two or more persons are engaged in any common enterprise or pursuit, there is always danger of difference of opinion. If it be a public trust or office, in which they are clothed with equal dignity and authority, there is peculiar danger of personal emulation and even animosity. From either, and especially from all these causes, the most bitter dissensions are apt to spring. Whenever these happen, they lessen the respectability, weaken the authority, and distract the plans and operation of those whom they divide. If they should unfortunately assail the supreme executive magistracy of a country, consisting of a plurality of persons, they might impede or frustrate the most important measures of the government, in the most critical emergencies of the state. And what is still worse, they might split the community into the most violent and irreconcilable factions, adhering differently to the different individuals who composed the magistracy.

Men often oppose a thing, merely because they have had no agency in planning it, or because it may have been planned by those whom they dislike. But if they have been consulted, and have happened to disapprove, opposition then becomes, in their estimation, an indispensable duty of self-love. They seem to think themselves bound in honor, and by all the motives of personal infallibility, to defeat the success of what has been resolved upon contrary to their sentiments. Men of upright, benevolent tempers have too many opportunities of remarking, with horror, to what desperate lengths this disposition is sometimes carried, and how often the great interests of society are sacrificed to the vanity, to the conceit, and to the obstinacy of individuals, who have credit enough to make their passions and their caprices interesting to mankind. Perhaps the question now before the public may, in its consequences, afford melancholy proofs of the effects of this despicable frailty, or rather detestable vice, in the human character.

Upon the principles of a free government, inconveniences from the source just mentioned must necessarily be submitted to in the formation of the legislature; but it is unnecessary, and therefore unwise, to introduce them into the constitution of the Executive. It is here too that they may be most pernicious. In the legislature, promptitude of decision is oftener an evil than a benefit. The differences of opinion, and the jarrings of parties in that department of the government, though they may sometimes obstruct salutary plans, yet often promote deliberation and circumspection, and serve to check excesses in the majority. When a resolution too is once taken, the opposition must be at an end. That resolution is a law, and resistance to it punishable. But no favorable circumstances palliate or atone for the disadvantages of dissension in the executive department. Here, they are pure and unmixed. There is no point at which they cease to operate. They serve to embarrass and weaken the execution of the plan or measure to which they relate, from the first step to the final conclusion of it. They constantly counteract those qualities in the Executive which are the most necessary ingredients in its composition, vigor and expedition, and this without any counterbalancing good. In the conduct of war, in which the energy of the Executive is the bulwark of the national security, every thing would be to be apprehended from its plurality.

It must be confessed that these observations apply with principal weight to the first case supposed that is, to a plurality of magistrates of equal dignity and authority a scheme, the advocates for which are not likely to form a numerous sect; but they apply, though not with equal, yet with considerable weight to the project of a council, whose concurrence is made constitutionally necessary to the operations of the ostensible Executive. An artful cabal in that council would be able to distract and to enervate the whole system of administration. If no such cabal should exist, the mere diversity of views and opinions would alone be sufficient to tincture the exercise of the executive authority with a spirit of habitual feebleness and dilatoriness.

But one of the weightiest objections to a plurality in the Executive, and which lies as much against the last as the first plan, is, that it tends to conceal faults and destroy responsibility.

Responsibility is of two kinds to censure and to punishment. The first is the more important of the two, especially in an elective office. Man, in public trust, will much oftener act in such a manner as to render him unworthy of being any longer trusted, than in such a manner as to make him obnoxious to legal punishment. But the multiplication of the Executive adds to the difficulty of detection in either case. It often becomes impossible, amidst mutual accusations, to determine on whom the blame or the punishment of a pernicious measure, or series of pernicious measures, ought really to fall. It is shifted from one to another with so much dexterity, and under such plausible appearances, that the public opinion is left in suspense about the real author. The circumstances which may have led to any national miscarriage or misfortune are sometimes so complicated that, where there are a number of actors who may have had different degrees and kinds of agency, though we may clearly see upon the whole that there has been mismanagement, yet it may be impracticable to pronounce to whose account the evil which may have been incurred is truly chargeable.

"I was overruled by my council. The council were so divided in their opinions that it was impossible to obtain any better resolution on the point." These and similar pretexts are constantly at hand, whether true or false. And who is there that will either take the trouble or incur the odium, of a strict scrutiny into the secret springs of the transaction? Should there be found a citizen zealous enough to undertake the unpromising task, if there happen to be collusion between the parties concerned, how easy it is to clothe the circumstances with so much ambiguity, as to render it uncertain what was the precise conduct of any of those parties?

In the single instance in which the governor of this State is coupled with a council that is, in the appointment to offices, we have seen the mischiefs of it in the view now under consideration. Scandalous appointments to important offices have been made. Some cases, indeed, have been so flagrant that ALL PARTIES have agreed in the impropriety of the thing. When inquiry has been made, the blame has been laid by the governor on the members of the council, who, on their part, have charged it upon his nomination; while the people remain altogether at a loss to determine, by whose influence their interests have been committed to hands so unqualified and so manifestly improper. In tenderness to individuals, I forbear to descend to particulars.

It is evident from these considerations, that the plurality of the Executive tends to deprive the people of the two greatest securities they can have for the faithful exercise of any delegated power, first, the restraints of public opinion, which lose their efficacy, as well on account of the division of the censure attendant on bad measures among a number, as on account of the uncertainty on whom it ought to fall; and, secondly, the opportunity of discovering with facility and clearness the misconduct of the persons they trust, in order either to their removal from office or to their actual punishment in cases which admit of it.

In England, the king is a perpetual magistrate; and it is a maxim which has obtained for the sake of the public peace, that he is unaccountable for his administration, and his person sacred. Nothing, therefore, can be wiser in that kingdom, than to annex to the king a constitutional council, who may be responsible to the nation for the advice they give. Without this, there would be no responsibility whatever in the executive department an idea inadmissible in a free government. But even there the king is not bound by the resolutions of his council, though they are answerable for the advice they give. He is the absolute master of his own conduct in the exercise of his office, and may observe or disregard the counsel given to him at his sole discretion.

But in a republic, where every magistrate ought to be personally responsible for his behavior in office the reason which in the British Constitution dictates the propriety of a council, not only ceases to apply, but turns against the institution. In the monarchy of Great Britain, it furnishes a substitute for the prohibited responsibility of the chief magistrate, which serves in some degree as a hostage to the national justice for his good behavior. In the American republic, it would serve to destroy, or would greatly diminish, the intended and necessary responsibility of the Chief Magistrate himself.

The idea of a council to the Executive, which has so generally obtained in the State constitutions, has been derived from that maxim of republican jealousy which considers power as safer in the hands of a number of men than of a single man. If the maxim should be admitted to be applicable to the case, I should contend that the advantage on that side would not counterbalance the numerous disadvantages on the opposite side. But I do not think the rule at all applicable to the executive power. I clearly concur in opinion, in this particular, with a writer whom the celebrated Junius pronounces to be "deep, solid, and ingenious," that "the executive power is more easily confined when it is ONE";[2] that it is far more safe there should be a single object for the jealousy and watchfulness of the people; and, in a word, that all multiplication of the Executive is rather dangerous than friendly to liberty.

A little consideration will satisfy us, that the species of security sought for in the multiplication of the Executive, is unattainable. Numbers must be so great as to render combination difficult, or they are rather a source of danger than of security. The united credit and influence of several individuals must be more formidable to liberty, than the credit and influence of either of them separately. When power, therefore, is placed in the hands of so small a number of men, as to admit of their interests and views being easily combined in a common enterprise, by an artful leader, it becomes more liable to abuse, and more dangerous when abused, than if it be lodged in the hands of one man; who, from the very circumstance of his being alone, will be more narrowly watched and more readily suspected, and who cannot unite so great a mass of influence as when he is associated with others. The Decemvirs of Rome, whose name denotes their number,[3] were more to be dreaded in their usurpation than any ONE of them would have been. No person would think of proposing an Executive much more numerous than that body; from six to a dozen have been suggested for the number of the council. The extreme of these numbers, is not too great for an easy combination; and from such a combination America would have more to fear, than from the ambition of any single individual. A council to a magistrate, who is himself responsible for what he does, are generally nothing better than a clog upon his good intentions, are often the instruments and accomplices of his bad and are almost always a cloak to his faults.

I forbear to dwell upon the subject of expense; though it be evident that if the council should be numerous enough to answer the principal end aimed at by the institution, the salaries of the members, who must be drawn from their homes to reside at the seat of government, would form an item in the catalogue of public expenditures too serious to be incurred for an object of equivocal utility. I will only add that, prior to the appearance of the Constitution, I rarely met with an intelligent man from any of the States, who did not admit, as the result of experience, that the UNITY of the executive of this State was one of the best of the distinguishing features of our constitution.

PUBLIUS

1. New York has no council except for the single purpose of appointing to offices; New Jersey has a council whom the governor may consult. But I think, from the terms of the constitution, their resolutions do not bind him.
2. De Lolme.
3. Ten.

FEDERALIST No. 71

The Duration in Office of the Executive

From the New York Packet. Tuesday, March 18, 1788. [Alexander Hamilton]

TO THE PEOPLE OF THE STATE OF NEW YORK:

DURATION in office has been mentioned as the second requisite to the energy of the Executive authority. This has relation to two objects: to the personal firmness of the executive magistrate, in the employment of his constitutional powers; and to the stability of the system of administration which may have been adopted under his auspices. With regard to the first, it must be evident, that the longer the duration in office, the greater will be the probability of obtaining so important an advantage. It is a general principle of human nature, that a man will be interested in whatever he possesses, in proportion to the firmness or precariousness of the tenure by which he holds it; will be less attached to what he holds by a momentary or uncertain title, than to what he enjoys by a durable or certain title; and, of course, will be willing to risk more for the sake of the one, than for the sake of the other. This remark is not less applicable to a political privilege, or honor, or trust, than to any article of ordinary property. The inference from it is, that a man acting in the capacity of chief magistrate, under a consciousness that in a very short time he MUST lay down his office, will be apt to feel himself too little interested in it to hazard any material censure or perplexity, from the independent exertion of his powers, or from encountering the ill-humors, however transient, which may happen to prevail, either in a considerable part of the society itself, or even in a predominant faction in the legislative body. If the case should only be, that he MIGHT lay it down, unless continued by a new choice, and if he should be desirous of being continued, his wishes, conspiring with his fears, would tend still more powerfully to corrupt his integrity, or debase his fortitude. In either case, feebleness and irresolution must be the characteristics of the station.

There are some who would be inclined to regard the servile pliancy of the Executive to a prevailing current, either in the community or in the legislature, as its best recommendation. But such men entertain very crude notions, as well of the purposes for which government was instituted, as of the true means by which the public happiness may be promoted. The republican principle demands that the deliberate sense of the community should govern the conduct of those to whom they intrust the management of their affairs; but it does not require an unqualified complaisance to every sudden breeze of passion, or to every transient impulse which the people may receive from the arts of men, who flatter their prejudices to betray their interests. It is a just observation, that the people commonly INTEND the PUBLIC GOOD. This often applies to their very errors. But their good sense would despise the adulator who should pretend that they always REASON RIGHT about the MEANS of promoting it. They know from experience that they sometimes err;

and the wonder is that they so seldom err as they do, beset, as they continually are, by the wiles of parasites and sycophants, by the snares of the ambitious, the avaricious, the desperate, by the artifices of men who possess their confidence more than they deserve it, and of those who seek to possess rather than to deserve it. When occasions present themselves, in which the interests of the people are at variance with their inclinations, it is the duty of the persons whom they have appointed to be the guardians of those interests, to withstand the temporary delusion, in order to give them time and opportunity for more cool and sedate reflection. Instances might be cited in which a conduct of this kind has saved the people from very fatal consequences of their own mistakes, and has procured lasting monuments of their gratitude to the men who had courage and magnanimity enough to serve them at the peril of their displeasure.

But however inclined we might be to insist upon an unbounded complaisance in the Executive to the inclinations of the people, we can with no propriety contend for a like complaisance to the humors of the legislature. The latter may sometimes stand in opposition to the former, and at other times the people may be entirely neutral. In either supposition, it is certainly desirable that the Executive should be in a situation to dare to act his own opinion with vigor and decision.

The same rule which teaches the propriety of a partition between the various branches of power, teaches us likewise that this partition ought to be so contrived as to render the one independent of the other. To what purpose separate the executive or the judiciary from the legislative, if both the executive and the judiciary are so constituted as to be at the absolute devotion of the legislative? Such a separation must be merely nominal, and incapable of producing the ends for which it was established. It is one thing to be subordinate to the laws, and another to be dependent on the legislative body. The first comports with, the last violates, the fundamental principles of good government; and, whatever may be the forms of the Constitution, unites all power in the same hands. The tendency of the legislative authority to absorb every other, has been fully displayed and illustrated by examples in some preceding numbers. In governments purely republican, this tendency is almost irresistible. The representatives of the people, in a popular assembly, seem sometimes to fancy that they are the people themselves, and betray strong symptoms of impatience and disgust at the least sign of opposition from any other quarter; as if the exercise of its rights, by either the executive or judiciary, were a breach of their privilege and an outrage to their dignity. They often appear disposed to exert an imperious control over the other departments; and as they commonly have the people on their side, they always act with such momentum as to make it very difficult for the other members of the government to maintain the balance of the Constitution.

It may perhaps be asked, how the shortness of the duration in office can affect the independence of the Executive on the legislature, unless the one were possessed of the power of appointing or displacing the other. One answer to this inquiry may be drawn from the principle already remarked that is, from the slender interest a man is apt to take in a short-lived advantage, and the little inducement it affords him to expose himself, on account of it, to any considerable inconvenience or hazard. Another answer, perhaps more obvious, though not more conclusive, will result from the consideration of the influence of the legislative body over the people; which might be employed to prevent the re-election of a man who, by an upright resistance to any sinister project of that body, should have made himself obnoxious to its resentment.

It may be asked also, whether a duration of four years would answer the end proposed; and if it would not, whether a less period, which would at least be recommended by greater security against ambitious designs, would not, for that reason, be preferable to a longer period, which was, at the same time, too short for the purpose of inspiring the desired firmness and independence of the magistrate.

It cannot be affirmed, that a duration of four years, or any other limited duration, would completely answer the end proposed; but it would contribute towards it in a degree which would have a material influence upon the spirit and character of the government. Between the commencement and termination of such a period, there would always be a considerable interval, in which the prospect of annihilation would be sufficiently remote, not to have an improper effect upon the conduct of a man indued with a tolerable portion of fortitude; and in which he might reasonably promise himself, that there would be time enough before it arrived, to make the community sensible of the propriety of the measures he might incline to pursue. Though it be probable that, as he approached the moment when the public were, by a new election, to signify their sense of his conduct, his confidence, and with it his firmness, would decline; yet both the one and the other would derive support from the opportunities which his previous continuance in the station had afforded him, of establishing himself in the esteem and good-will of his constituents. He might, then, hazard with safety, in proportion to the proofs he had given of his wisdom and integrity, and to the title he had acquired to the respect and attachment of his fellow-citizens. As, on the one hand, a duration of four years will contribute to the firmness of the Executive in a sufficient degree to render it a very valuable ingredient in the composition; so, on the other, it is not enough to justify any alarm for the public liberty. If a British House of Commons, from the most feeble beginnings, FROM THE MERE POWER OF ASSENTING OR DISAGREEING TO THE IMPOSITION OF A NEW TAX, have, by rapid strides, reduced the prerogatives of the crown and the privileges of the nobility within the limits they conceived to be compatible with the principles of a free government, while they raised themselves to the rank and consequence of a coequal branch of the legislature; if they have been able, in one instance, to abolish both the royalty and the aristocracy, and to overturn all the ancient establishments, as well in the Church as State; if they have been able, on a recent occasion, to make the monarch tremble at the prospect of an innovation[1] attempted by them, what would be to be feared from an elective magistrate of four years' duration, with the confined authorities of a President of the United States? What, but that he might be unequal to the task which the Constitution assigns him? I shall only add, that if his duration be such as to leave a doubt of his firmness, that doubt is inconsistent with a jealousy of his encroachments.

PUBLIUS

1. This was the case with respect to Mr. Fox's India bill, which was carried in the House of Commons, and reject ed in the House of Lords, to the entire satisfaction, as it is said, of the people.

FEDERALIST No. 72

The Same Subject Continued, and Re-Eligibility of the Executive Considered

From the New York Packet. Friday, March 21, 1788. [Alexander Hamilton]

TO THE PEOPLE OF THE STATE OF NEW YORK:

THE administration of government, in its largest sense, comprehends all the operations of the body politic, whether legislative, executive, or judiciary; but in its most usual, and perhaps its most precise signification. It is limited to executive details, and falls peculiarly within the province of the executive department. The actual conduct of foreign negotiations, the preparatory plans of finance, the application and disbursement of the public moneys in conformity to the general appropriations of the legislature, the arrangement of the army and navy, the directions of the operations of war, these, and other matters of a like nature, constitute what seems to be most properly understood by the administration of government. The persons, therefore, to whose immediate management these different matters are committed, ought to be considered as the assistants or deputies of the chief magistrate, and on this account, they ought to derive their offices from his appointment, at least from his nomination, and ought to be subject to his superintendence. This view of the subject will at once suggest to us the intimate connection between the duration of the executive magistrate in office and the stability of the system of administration. To reverse and undo what has been done by a predecessor, is very often considered by a successor as the best proof he can give of his own capacity and desert; and in addition to this propensity, where the alteration has been the result of public choice, the person substituted is warranted in supposing that the dismission of his predecessor has proceeded from a dislike to his measures; and that the less he resembles him, the more he will recommend himself to the favor of his constituents.

These considerations, and the influence of personal confidences and attachments, would be likely to induce every new President to promote a change of men to fill the subordinate stations; and these causes together could not fail to occasion a disgraceful and ruinous mutability in the administration of the government.

With a positive duration of considerable extent, I connect the circumstance of re-eligibility. The first is necessary to give to the officer himself the inclination and the resolution to act his part well, and to the community time and leisure to observe the tendency of his measures, and thence to form an experimental estimate of their merits. The last is necessary to enable the people, when they see reason to approve of his conduct, to continue him in his station, in order to prolong the utility of his talents and virtues, and to secure to the government the advantage of permanency in a wise system of administration.

Nothing appears more plausible at first sight, nor more ill-founded upon close inspection, than a scheme which in relation to the present point has had some respectable advocates, I mean that of continuing the chief magistrate in office for a certain time, and then excluding him from it, either for a limited period or forever after. This exclusion, whether temporary or perpetual, would have nearly the same effects, and these effects would be for the most part rather pernicious than salutary.

One ill effect of the exclusion would be a diminution of the inducements to good behavior. There are few men who would not feel much less zeal in the discharge of a duty when they were conscious that the advantages of the station with which it was connected must be relinquished at a determinate period, than when they were permitted to entertain a hope of OBTAINING, by MERITING, a continuance of them. This position will not be disputed so long as it is admitted that the desire of reward is one of the strongest incentives of human conduct; or that the best security for the fidelity of mankind is to make their interests coincide with their duty. Even the love of fame, the ruling passion of the noblest minds, which would prompt a man to plan and undertake extensive and arduous enterprises for the public benefit, requiring considerable time to mature and perfect them, if he could flatter himself with the prospect of being allowed to finish what he had begun, would, on the contrary, deter him from the undertaking, when he foresaw that he must quit the scene before he could accomplish the work, and must commit that, together with his own reputation, to hands which might be unequal or unfriendly to the task. The most to be expected from the generality of men, in such a situation, is the negative merit of not doing harm, instead of the positive merit of doing good.

Another ill effect of the exclusion would be the temptation to sordid views, to peculation, and, in some instances, to usurpation. An avaricious man, who might happen to fill the office, looking forward to a time when he must at all events yield up the emoluments he enjoyed, would feel a propensity, not easy to be resisted by such a man, to make the best use of the opportunity he enjoyed while it lasted, and might not scruple to have recourse to the most corrupt expedients to make the harvest as abundant as it was transitory; though the same man, probably, with a different prospect before him, might content himself with the regular perquisites of his situation, and might even be unwilling to risk the consequences of an abuse of his opportunities. His avarice might be a guard upon his avarice. Add to this that the same man might be vain or ambitious, as well as avaricious. And if he could expect to prolong his honors by his good conduct, he might hesitate to sacrifice his appetite for them to his appetite for gain. But with the prospect before him of approaching an inevitable annihilation, his avarice would be likely to get the victory over his caution, his vanity, or his ambition.

An ambitious man, too, when he found himself seated on the summit of his country's honors, when he looked forward to the time at which he must descend from the exalted eminence for ever, and reflected that no exertion of merit on his part could save him from the unwelcome reverse; such a man, in such a situation, would be much more violently tempted to embrace a favorable conjuncture for attempting the prolongation of his power, at every personal hazard, than if he had the probability of answering the same end by doing his duty.

Would it promote the peace of the community, or the stability of the government to have half a dozen men who had had credit enough to be raised to the seat of the supreme magistracy, wandering among the people like discontented ghosts, and sighing for a place which they were destined never more to possess?

A third ill effect of the exclusion would be, the depriving the community of the advantage of the experience gained by the chief magistrate in the exercise of his office. That experience is the parent of wisdom, is an adage the truth of which is recognized by the wisest as well as the simplest of mankind. What more desirable or more essential than this quality in the governors of nations? Where more desirable or more essential than in the first magistrate of a nation? Can it be wise to put this desirable and essential quality under the ban of the Constitution, and to declare that the moment it is acquired, its possessor shall be compelled to abandon the station in which it was acquired, and to which it is adapted? This, nevertheless, is the precise import of all those regulations which exclude men from serving their country, by the choice of their fellowcitizens, after they have by a course of service fitted themselves for doing it with a greater degree of utility.

A fourth ill effect of the exclusion would be the banishing men from stations in which, in certain emergencies of the state, their presence might be of the greatest moment to the public interest or safety. There is no nation which has not, at one period or another, experienced an absolute necessity of the services of particular men in particular situations; perhaps it would not be too strong to say, to the preservation of its political existence. How unwise, therefore, must be every such self-denying ordinance as serves to prohibit a nation from making use of its own citizens in the manner best suited to its exigencies and circumstances! Without supposing the personal essentiality of the man, it is evident that a change of the chief magistrate, at the breaking out of a war, or at any similar crisis, for another, even of equal merit, would at all times be detrimental to the community, inasmuch as it would substitute inexperience to experience, and would tend to unhinge and set afloat the already settled train of the administration.

A fifth ill effect of the exclusion would be, that it would operate as a constitutional interdiction of stability in the administration. By NECESSITATING a change of men, in the first office of the nation, it would necessitate a mutability of measures. It is not generally to be expected, that men will vary and measures remain uniform. The contrary is the usual course of things. And we need not be apprehensive that there will be too much stability, while there is even the option of changing; nor need we desire to prohibit the people from continuing their confidence where they think it may be safely placed, and where, by constancy on their part, they may obviate the fatal inconveniences of fluctuating councils and a variable policy.

These are some of the disadvantages which would flow from the principle of exclusion. They apply most forcibly to the scheme of a perpetual exclusion; but when we consider that even a partial exclusion would always render the readmission of the person a remote and precarious object, the observations which have been made will apply nearly as fully to one case as to the other.

What are the advantages promised to counterbalance these disadvantages? They are represented to be: 1st, greater independence in the magistrate; 2d, greater security to the people. Unless the exclusion be perpetual, there will be no pretense to infer the first advantage. But even in that case, may he have no object beyond his present station, to which he may sacrifice his independence? May he have no connections, no friends, for whom he may sacrifice it? May he not be less willing by a firm conduct, to make personal enemies, when he acts under the impression that a time is fast approaching, on the arrival of which he not only MAY, but MUST, be exposed to their resentments, upon an equal, perhaps upon an inferior, footing? It is not an easy point to determine whether his independence would be most promoted or impaired by such an arrangement.

As to the second supposed advantage, there is still greater reason to entertain doubts concerning it. If the exclusion were to be perpetual, a man of irregular ambition, of whom alone there could be reason in any case to entertain apprehension, would, with infinite reluctance, yield to the necessity of taking his leave forever of a post in which his passion for power and pre-eminence had acquired the force of habit. And if he had been fortunate or adroit enough to conciliate the good-will of the people, he might induce them to consider as a very odious and unjustifiable restraint upon themselves, a provision which was calculated to debar them of the right of giving a fresh proof of their attachment to a favorite. There may be conceived circumstances in which this disgust of the people, seconding the thwarted ambition of such a favorite, might occasion greater danger to liberty, than could ever reasonably be dreaded from the possibility of a perpetuation in office, by the voluntary suffrages of the community, exercising a constitutional privilege.

There is an excess of refinement in the idea of disabling the people to continue in office men who had entitled themselves, in their opinion, to approbation and confidence; the advantages of which are at best speculative and equivocal, and are overbalanced by disadvantages far more certain and decisive.

PUBLIUS

FEDERALIST No. 73

The Provision for the Support of the Executive, and the Veto Power

From the New York Packet. Friday, March 21, 1788. [Alexander Hamilton]

TO THE PEOPLE OF THE STATE OF NEW YORK:

THE third ingredient towards constituting the vigor of the executive authority, is an adequate provision for its support. It is evident that, without proper attention to this article, the separation of the executive from the legislative department would be merely nominal and nugatory. The legislature, with a discretionary power over the salary and emoluments of the Chief Magistrate, could render him as obsequious to their will as they might think proper to make him. They might, in most cases, either reduce him by famine, or tempt him by largesses, to surrender at discretion his judgment to their inclinations. These expressions, taken in all the latitude of the terms, would no doubt convey more than is intended. There are men who could neither be distressed nor won into a sacrifice of their duty; but this stern virtue is the growth of few soils; and in the main it will be found that a power over a man's support is a power over his will. If it were necessary to confirm so plain a truth by facts, examples would not be wanting, even in this country, of the intimidation or seduction of the Executive by the terrors or allurements of the pecuniary arrangements of the legislative body.

It is not easy, therefore, to commend too highly the judicious attention which has been paid to this subject in the proposed Constitution. It is there provided that "The President of the United States shall, at stated times, receive for his services a compensation WHICH SHALL NEITHER BE INCREASED NOR DIMINISHED DURING THE PERIOD FOR WHICH HE SHALL HAVE BEEN ELECTED; and he SHALL NOT RECEIVE WITHIN THAT PERIOD ANY OTHER EMOLUMENT from the United States, or any of them." It is impossible to imagine any provision which would have been more eligible than this. The legislature, on the appointment of a President, is once for all to declare what shall be the compensation for his services during the time for which he shall have been elected. This done, they will have no power to alter it, either by increase or diminution, till a new period of service by a new election commences. They can neither weaken his fortitude by operating on his necessities, nor corrupt his integrity by appealing to his avarice. Neither the Union, nor any of its members, will be at liberty to give, nor will he be at liberty to receive, any other emolument than that which may have been determined by the first act. He can, of course, have no pecuniary inducement to renounce or desert the independence intended for him by the Constitution.

The last of the requisites to energy, which have been enumerated, are competent powers. Let us proceed to consider those which are proposed to be vested in the President of the United States.

The first thing that offers itself to our observation, is the qualified negative of the President upon the acts or resolutions of the two houses of the legislature; or, in other words, his power of returning all bills with objections, to have the effect of preventing their becoming laws, unless they should afterwards be ratified by two thirds of each of the component members of the legislative body.

The propensity of the legislative department to intrude upon the rights, and to absorb the powers, of the other departments, has been already suggested and repeated; the insufficiency of a mere parchment delineation of the boundaries of each, has also been remarked upon; and the necessity of furnishing each with constitutional arms for its own defense, has been inferred and proved. From these clear and indubitable principles results the propriety of a negative, either absolute or qualified, in the Executive, upon the acts of the legislative branches. Without the one or the other, the former would be absolutely unable to defend himself against the depredations of the latter. He might gradually be stripped of his authorities by successive resolutions, or annihilated by a single vote. And in the one mode or the other, the legislative and executive powers might speedily come to be blended in the same hands. If even no propensity had ever discovered itself in the legislative body to invade the rights of the Executive, the rules of just reasoning and theoretic propriety would of themselves teach us, that the one ought not to be left to the mercy of the other, but ought to possess a constitutional and effectual power of self defense.

But the power in question has a further use. It not only serves as a shield to the Executive, but it furnishes an additional security against the enaction of improper laws. It establishes a salutary check upon the legislative body, calculated to guard the community against the effects of faction, precipitancy, or of any impulse unfriendly to the public good, which may happen to influence a majority of that body.

The propriety of a negative has, upon some occasions, been combated by an observation, that it was not to be presumed a single man would possess more virtue and wisdom than a number of men; and that unless this presumption should be entertained, it would be improper to give the executive magistrate any species of control over the legislative body.

But this observation, when examined, will appear rather specious than solid. The propriety of the thing does not turn upon the supposition of superior wisdom or virtue in the Executive, but upon the supposition that the legislature will not be infallible; that the love of power may sometimes betray it into a disposition to encroach upon the rights of other members of the government; that a spirit of faction may sometimes pervert its deliberations; that impressions of the moment may sometimes hurry it into measures which itself, on mature reflexion, would condemn. The primary inducement to conferring the power in question upon the Executive is, to enable him to defend himself; the secondary one is to increase the chances in favor of the community against the passing of bad laws, through haste, inadvertence, or design. The oftener the measure is brought under examination, the greater the diversity in the situations of those who are to examine it, the less must be the danger of those errors which flow from want of due deliberation, or of those missteps which proceed from the contagion of some common passion or interest. It is far less probable, that culpable views of any kind should infect all the parts of the government at the same moment and in relation to the same object, than that they should by turns govern and mislead every one of them.

It may perhaps be said that the power of preventing bad laws includes that of preventing good ones; and may be used to the one purpose as well as to the other. But this objection will have little weight with those who can properly estimate the mischiefs of that inconstancy and mutability in the laws, which form the greatest blemish in the character and genius of our governments. They will consider every institution calculated to restrain the excess of lawmaking, and to keep things in the same state in which they happen to be at any given period, as much more likely to do good than harm; because it is favorable to greater stability in the system of legislation. The injury which may possibly be done by defeating a few good laws, will be amply compensated by the advantage of preventing a number of bad ones.

Nor is this all. The superior weight and influence of the legislative body in a free government, and the hazard to the Executive in a trial of strength with that body, afford a satisfactory security that the negative would generally be employed with great caution; and there would oftener be room for a charge of timidity than of rashness in the exercise of it. A king of Great Britain, with all his train of sovereign attributes, and with all the influence he draws from a thousand sources, would, at this day, hesitate to put a negative upon the joint resolutions of the two houses of Parliament. He would not fail to exert the utmost resources of that influence to strangle a measure disagreeable to him, in its progress to the throne, to avoid being reduced to the dilemma of permitting it to take effect, or of risking the displeasure of the nation by an opposition to the sense of the legislative body. Nor is it probable, that he would ultimately venture to exert his prerogatives, but in a case of manifest propriety, or extreme necessity. All well-informed men in that kingdom will accede to the justness of this remark. A very considerable period has elapsed since the negative of the crown has been exercised.

If a magistrate so powerful and so well fortified as a British monarch, would have scruples about the exercise of the power under consideration, how much greater caution may be reasonably expected in a President of the United States, clothed for the short period of four years with the executive authority of a government wholly and purely republican?

It is evident that there would be greater danger of his not using his power when necessary, than of his using it too often, or too much. An argument, indeed, against its expediency, has been drawn from this very source. It has been represented, on this account, as a power odious in appearance, useless in practice. But it will not follow, that because it might be rarely exercised, it would never be exercised. In the case for which it is chiefly designed, that of an immediate attack upon the constitutional rights of the Executive, or in a case in which the public good was evidently and palpably sacrificed, a man of tolerable firmness would avail himself of his constitutional means of defense, and would listen to the admonitions of duty and responsibility. In the former supposition, his fortitude would be stimulated by his immediate interest in the power of his office; in the latter, by the probability of the sanction of his constituents, who, though they would naturally incline to the legislative body in a doubtful case, would hardly suffer their partiality to delude them in a very plain case. I speak now with an eye to a magistrate possessing only a common share of firmness. There are men who, under any circumstances, will have the courage to do their duty at every hazard.

But the convention have pursued a mean in this business, which will both facilitate the exercise of the power vested in this respect in the executive magistrate, and make its efficacy to depend on the sense of a considerable part of the legislative body. Instead of an absolute negative, it is proposed to give the Executive the qualified negative already described. This is a power which would be much more readily exercised than the other. A man who might be afraid to defeat a law by his single VETO, might not scruple to return it for reconsideration; subject to being finally rejected only in the event of more than one third of each house concurring in the sufficiency of his objections. He would be encouraged by the reflection, that if his opposition should prevail, it would embark in it a very respectable proportion of the legislative body, whose influence would be united with his in supporting the propriety of his conduct in the public opinion. A direct and categorical negative has something in the appearance of it more harsh, and more apt to irritate, than the mere suggestion of argumentative objections to be approved or disapproved by those to whom they are addressed. In proportion as it would be less apt to offend, it would be more apt to be exercised; and for this very reason, it may in practice be found more effectual. It is to be hoped that it will not often happen that improper views will govern so large a proportion as two thirds of both branches of the legislature at the same time; and this, too, in spite of the counterposing weight of the Executive. It is at any rate far less probable that this should be the case, than that such views should taint the resolutions and conduct of a bare majority. A power of this nature in the Executive, will often have a silent and unperceived, though forcible, operation. When men, engaged in unjustifiable pursuits, are aware that obstructions may come from a quarter which they cannot control, they will often be restrained by the bare apprehension of opposition, from doing what they would with eagerness rush into, if no such external impediments were to be feared.

This qualified negative, as has been elsewhere remarked, is in this State vested in a council, consisting of the governor, with the chancellor and judges of the Supreme Court, or any two of them. It has been freely employed upon a variety of occasions, and frequently with success. And its utility has become so apparent, that persons who, in compiling the Constitution, were violent opposers of it, have from experience become its declared admirers.[1]

I have in another place remarked, that the convention, in the formation of this part of their plan, had departed from the model of the constitution of this State, in favor of that of Massachusetts. Two strong reasons may be imagined for this preference. One is that the judges, who are to be the interpreters of the law, might receive an improper bias, from having given a previous opinion in their revisionary capacities; the other is that by being often associated with the Executive, they might be induced to embark too far in the political views of that magistrate, and thus a dangerous combination might by degrees be cemented between the executive and judiciary departments. It is impossible to keep the judges too distinct from every other avocation than that of expounding the laws. It is peculiarly dangerous to place them in a situation to be either corrupted or influenced by the Executive.

PUBLIUS

1. Mr. Abraham Yates, a warm opponent of the plan of the convention is of this number.

GLOSSARY

administrative deference (also known as "Chevron deference") the tendency of the courts to uphold the judgment of the executive branch

ally principle the tendency of politicians to delegate authority to individuals who share their ideological convictions and objectives

amicus curiae legal briefs submitted to the court by interested parties

approval ratings public assessments, as measured in surveys, about whether the president is performing well in office

Articles of Confederation the original agreement among the thirteen colonies to form a national government, which functioned from 1781 to 1789

attitudinal model an understanding of judicial decision making holding that judges base their decisions primarily on ideological considerations

authorization the selection of agencies and programs eligible for federal funding in any given year

Bipartisan Campaign Reform Act a 2002 law designed to limit the flow of funds supporting issue advocacy during elections

blame-game politics attempts by one branch of government (usually Congress) to make another (usually the president) look ideologically extreme

Brownlow Committee commission appointed by FDR in 1936, tasked with offering suggestions for the institutional reorganization and empowerment of the American presidency

Budget and Accounting Act the 1921 law that gave the president the formal responsibility to propose a budget

bully pulpit term coined by Teddy Roosevelt that refers to the president's ability, by virtue of his office, to command public attention

cabinet the most important advisory body to the president on all matters of public policy and government action

career bureaucrats rank-and-file bureaucrats who are not political appointees and are generally valued for their expertise

Case Act (aka the Case Zablocki Act) a 1972 law that established a system for recording executive agreements

case law past courts' interpretations of statutory law

caucuses meetings in which party members openly deliberate about the candidates and then cast votes for them

censure a process by which Congress can formally reprimand the president or any other members of government with a simple majority vote

centralization a presidential strategy of exerting political control over the bureaucracy by transferring key administrative and oversight tasks to the Executive Office of the President

checks and balances a constitutional system of governance in which specific powers are granted to each branch of government in order to guard against the encroachments of others

Citizens United v. Federal Election Commission a 2010 Supreme Court case that eliminated many campaign finance restrictions on corporate donations

closed primary a primary in which only party members can participate in the selection of a party's presidential nominee

cloture a procedure requiring a three-fifths vote of the full Senate that sets a time limit on consideration of a bill, thus overcoming a filibuster

Cold War a decades-long standoff between the Soviet Union and the United States, in which the two waged proxy wars against one another but never launched a direct military attack

Congressional Budget Office the primary agency charged with providing economic and budget information directly to Congress

congressional caucuses formal groups of co-partisans within Congress that make joint decisions about legislative affairs and electioneering

Council of Economic Advisors an agency within the Executive Office of the President that advises the president on economic policy

cult of the robe a view, encouraged by judges, that their judgment on legal matters is inviolable

czars a popular term used to refer to special policy advisors to the president who coordinate and centralize the activities of various executive branch offices

deferrals delays in the spending of monies appropriated by Congress

delegates individuals who cast votes at the party's national nominating committee, usually on the basis of state primary or caucus results

demagoguery the manipulation of public passions for purposes unrelated to—and perhaps even at odds with—the general welfare

departmental order a unilateral order issued by a department secretary or undersecretary acting on the president's behalf

direct primary a system in which voters select a party's nominee through state-administered elections

divided government a period when one political party retains a majority of either the House or Senate and the other party retains the White House

doctrine of acquiescence a judicial principle whereby congressional inaction following an executive assertion of authority is interpreted as tacit consent

Domestic Policy Council WHO group charged with coordinating the president's domestic policy objectives

drift a phenomenon in which bureaucrats work on behalf of interests and objectives that do not align with those of a political principal

economic liberalization the reduction of tariffs and other barriers to free trade among nations

Electoral College a deliberative body constrained by a complex set of constitutionally prescribed rules that stipulate how popular votes translate into the selection of U.S. presidents and vice presidents

electoral mandate authority derived from the outcome of the vote, with the corresponding notion that elected officeholders, particularly those who win by large margins, are entitled to pursue their agendas

enumerated powers powers explicitly granted to the executive in the Constitution

ex ante **influence** an effect on an outcome achieved before the fact

ex post **influence** an effect on an outcome achieved after the fact

excepted service a sector of the civil service that streamlines and bypasses merit-based hiring practices

executive agreements agreements with foreign countries that, unlike treaties, do not require the Senate's formal ratification

Executive Office of the President an umbrella organization that houses the White House Office, the Office of Management and Budget, the Council of Economic Advisors, and other administrative units that report directly to the president

executive orders unilateral directives that enable the president to make policy without securing Congress's formal consent

executive privilege the presidency's claim to immunity from subpoenas and other informational requests made by the legislative and judicial branches

Executive Reorganization Act a 1939 law that enacted many of the formal recommendations made by the Brownlow Committee

Federal Register Act a 1935 law that established a system for recording executive orders, proclamations, rules, regulations, notices, and proposed rules

filibuster any of a variety of stalling tactics designed to block Senate action on a bill

Fireside Chats a staple of FDR's tenure in office, radio broadcasts that brought the president's voice and opinions directly into the homes of Americans

franchise the right to vote

Freedom of Information Act a stand-alone law enacted in 1966 that vastly expanded the public's access to government documents

General Accounting Office an independent administrative agency that investigates how federal money is spent

Geneva Conventions international standards concerning, among other things, the treatment of prisoners of war and the rules of war

globalization a catch-all term used to refer to the increasingly complex economic and political ties among nations

government corporations corporations that are chartered and owned by the federal government but that retain a separate legal status, which affords them a measure of independence from the government

Great White Fleet a fourteen-month circumnavigation of the globe conducted by U.S. battleships between 1907 and 1909

gridlock a condition under which Congress is incapable of changing the status quo

habeas corpus the principle that detained or imprisoned individuals have the right to come before a court to hear the charges brought against them

hearings the primary method by which members of Congress collect information, examine witnesses, and oversee the executive branch

honeymoon period the earliest stages of a president's tenure in office, when politicians, the media, and public are reticent to criticize him or her

Imperial Presidency a presidency that is virtually unchecked by the adjoining branches of government

impoundment a method by which the president could block the spending of particular congressional appropriations

independent agencies administrative agencies within the executive branch that enjoy considerable independence from the political maneuverings of both the president and Congress

inherent powers presidential powers that are neither explicitly delineated within nor implied by the Constitution

institution reasonably stable and binding practices, rules, and relationships that govern the actions and choices of specific individuals

institutionalist someone who takes as a starting point the facts that presidents are embedded within institutions and that presidential power is mediated by those institutions

institutional memory durable knowledge about the protocols and personnel within an administrative unit

institutional presidency an approach to studying executive politics that focuses on the design of the presidency and its attendant powers, resources, and incentives

international alliances formal political and military bonds forged between nations

International Criminal Court an international body responsible for trying state leaders charged with crimes against humanity

international law a set of rules and conventions that govern interstate relations and impose obligations on how states treat populations within their borders

international organizations supranational institutions that consist of member states but that do not report, formally, to a particular country or countries

isolationism a doctrine holding that states should minimize their involvement in foreign affairs and instead focus on domestic matters

judicial review the power to assess the constitutionality of laws enacted by Congress

King Caucus the period roughly between 1796 and 1824 during which party elites within Congress selected the nominees for the two major parties in presidential elections

legal model an understanding of judicial decision making holding that judges base their decisions primarily on legal considerations

legislative oversight the task of monitoring how the executive branch interprets and implements laws enacted by Congress

line-item veto a tool used by the president to excise specific elements of a bill rather than veto the bill in total

literalist theory articulated best by President Taft, the view that presidents may only exercise those powers explicitly granted by the Constitution or congressional delegations of authority

Living Constitution a school of legal thought that views the Constitution as a document whose meaning evolves flexibly over time

McGovern-Fraser Commission a group, formally known as the Commission on Party Structure and Delegate Selection, assembled in the aftermath of the 1968 Democratic Convention to make formal recommendations for democratizing the selection of both parties' nominees in presidential elections

memoranda policy directives that function exactly like executive orders but are not published in the *Federal Register*

modern presidency a contested notion that posits FDR (or possibly Theodore Roosevelt or Woodrow Wilson) as the progenitor of a more powerful and institutionalized American presidency

momentum a feature of presidential primaries that helps the chances of early winners and hurts those of early losers

Monroe Doctrine President James Monroe's declaration that the United States would not tolerate European meddling in North or South America

National Economic Council WHO group charged with monitoring the U.S. economy and making recommendations on how to improve it

nationalization of politics the recent trend whereby local and state politics are increasingly conditioned by voters' attitudes toward issues, politicians, and parties operating at the federal level

national outlook the president's tendency to reflect upon the implications of policy initiatives for the country as a whole

National Security Council a unit of the Executive Office of the President that reports directly to the president on perceived foreign threats and offers policy recommendations on how best to meet them

national security directives classified unilateral orders that relate to the nation's security

negative advertisements advertisements that cast opposing candidates in a critical light by drawing attention to unpopular features of their records, personalities, or histories

Neutrality Acts a series of laws enacted during the 1930s that restricted U.S. involvement in the rapidly escalating crises of Europe

New Deal the collection of domestic policy reforms advanced by FDR that were intended to lift the nation out of an economic depression and that established the template for the modern welfare state

nominating convention the meeting at which a party formally selects its nominee for president

nondelegation doctrine a legal doctrine which dictates that Congress cannot relinquish its core legislative power to executive agencies

norms informal rules that shape how politicians (and others) interact with one another

North Atlantic Treaty Organization a military alliance of twenty-eight North American and European nations, including the United States

October surprise a late-breaking scandal, economic downturn, or other event that can momentarily capture the attention of voters and affect an election outcome

Office of Communications an administrative unit responsible for media strategy that advances the president's policy agenda

Office of Legal Counsel a unit within the Justice Department that provides legal advice to the president and agencies in the executive branch

Office of Legislative Affairs WHO organization charged with overseeing bills making their way through Congress

Office of Management and Budget the largest administrative unit within the Executive Office of the President, charged with producing the president's budget and ensuring that agencies comply with the president's policies

open election an election in which no incumbent politician is running for reelection

open primary a primary in which any registered voters can participate in the selection of a party's presidential nominee

originalism a school of legal thought that views the Constitution as a document whose meaning was fixed once and ever more at the time of the nation's founding

pardon a president's non-reviewable forgiveness of a federal criminal offense

pardon power the president's enumerated power to grant pardons and commutations for federal offenses

Paris Peace Accords the formal terms of agreement that terminated U.S. involvement in the Vietnam War

party bosses elite members of party organizations who, at different stages of American history, wielded substantial influence over the selection of nominees in presidential elections

party polarization the ideological divisions between Democrats and Republicans

personal presidency an approach to studying executive politics that focuses on the distinctive features of the individuals who hold office

plebiscitary presidency a view of the presidency as defined by the speeches, public appearances, press conferences, and the like that presidents perform before the American public

plural executive a panel of elected officials responsible for putting laws into effect

pocket veto a de facto veto deployed through strategic presidential inaction on a bill during the last ten days of a congressional session

pocketbook voting voting based on how an individual's personal economic situation, as distinct from the economy as a whole, has changed during an incumbent's time in office

political action committee (PAC) an organization that pools individual financial contributions and then funnels the funds directly to candidates' campaigns

political appointees members of the federal bureaucracy who were appointed by the president, vice president, or another political appointee

political capital a vague and contested notion that public vestments of trust and approval bestow rights to political accommodation

political patronage rewarding loyalists for party support by appointing them to federal office

political power the capacity to shape government policies through political action, whether threatened or taken

political question doctrine a principle of jurisprudence holding that the judiciary is not meant to settle disputes that are essentially political

politicization a strategy of exerting control over the bureaucracy by appointing loyalists to key positions

Presidential Appointments with Senate confirmation high-level political positions that require the Senate's formal approval

presidential dilemma situation whereby presidents are expected to solve the public's problems despite their limited constitutional powers

presidential immunity the principle that presidents should not be subject to civil prosecution for actions that relate to their official conduct in office

presidential legacy the president's place in history

Presidential Records Act a 1978 law that established the public ownership of all official records of the president and vice president

press conferences structured briefings that allow the professional press corps to direct specific questions to a speaker

Press Office a unit of the Executive Office of the President that attends to the more immediate concerns of the daily news flow and is led by the press secretary

press secretary the primary spokesperson for the president

proclamations unilateral directives that are usually, but not exclusively, ceremonial in nature

professional vetters lawyers, political consultants, researchers, and accountants who research the backgrounds of possible appointees

Progressive Era a period in the late nineteenth and early twentieth centuries marked by an expansion of presidential powers, a growth of civil service protections, and more interventionist government policy

public appeals appeals presidents often make for the public's support of their policy initiatives

quorum the number of members of an assembly needed for a binding vote to occur

rally-around-the-flag the temporary spike in a president's approval ratings following major crises

recess appointment presidential appointment made when Congress is not in session

rescissions the cancellation of budgetary authority before that authority was set to expire

retail politics a style of political campaigning in which candidates interact directly, and usually informally, with voters at public events like fairs and parades

ripeness a principle of jurisprudence holding that the judiciary should only hear cases that constitute actual disputes that are ready for litigation

scientific management a body of knowledge that, during the Progressive Movement, guided reforms meant to improve the efficiency and effectiveness of governing institutions

secretarial order a unilateral order issued by a department secretary or undersecretary acting on the president's behalf

senatorial courtesy a norm that gives considerable weight over a judicial appointment to the views of the senior senator from the state in which the judge is to be appointed

Senior Executive Service (SES) personnel upper-level management positions charged with overseeing agency efforts to implement the president's initiatives

signing statements official commentary on the meaning or significance of legislation that presidents sometimes issue concurrently with the enactment of such legislation

slack the tendency of bureaucrats not to work as hard as elected officials would like

sociotropic voting voting based on how the economy as a whole has changed during an incumbent's time in office

soft money spending and contributions that are not directed to the campaign of a specific candidate

solicitor general a presidential appointee who serves as the federal government's primary advocate before the Supreme Court

speechwriting department communications staff who craft the president's speeches

Stand by Your Ad a provision of the 2002 Bipartisan Campaign Reform Act that requires candidates to declare their approval of ads that are produced by their campaigns

standing a principle of jurisprudence holding that only those parties with a sufficient connection to a harm can bring a suit

stare decisis a principle of jurisprudence binding judges to past precedent

State of the Union Address a constitutionally mandated speech on the condition of national affairs that the president, by tradition, delivers in Congress each year

states' rights authority reserved for state governments rather than the federal government under the U.S. Constitution

stewardship theory a theory of presidential power, pioneered by Theodore Roosevelt, in which constitutional ambiguity surrounding executive powers invites the president to act when the Constitution is silent

structural factors the effects that basic facts about the state of the world, such as the economy and war, have on election outcomes

superdelegates delegates who are not bound to vote in ways that reflect their state's caucus or primary results

super PAC a fundraising operation, formally known as an *independent expenditure-only committee*, that is permitted to raise unlimited sums of money from individuals and from corporations, unions, and associations to support noncandidate-specific political causes

Super Tuesday the Tuesday in February or March of a presidential election year during which the largest number of states hold their primaries and caucuses

supplemental appropriations funds that are provided on an ad hoc basis in order to cover the costs of unforeseen emergencies

swing states states where Republicans and Democrats have similar levels of support, making the outcome of a contest there uncertain

take-care clause the Article II provision that the president shall "take care that the laws be faithfully executed"

Tea Party movement a conservative political movement that advocates a return to what its members see as constitutional principles of government

team of rivals an appointment strategy whereby presidents assemble a diverse team of former political antagonists

three-fifths clause a provision adopted at the Constitutional Convention that counted all enslaved individuals as three-fifths of a person for the purpose of congressional representation

total war massive wars, like World Wars I and II, that require the support and mobilization of an entire citizenry

transition period the period between the election and inauguration of a new president

trial balloon an exploratory measure taken to assess how the public or other political actors will react to a new policy or appointment

two-presidencies thesis a theory that suggests that presidents exert greater influence over foreign policy than they do over domestic policy

unified government a period when one party retains control of both chambers of Congress and the White House

unilateral decisions actions the president carries out on his own, such as issuing pardons or classifying documents

unilateral directives mechanisms by which presidents independently create policies that assume the weight of law

unitary executive a single individual responsible for putting laws into effect

Unitary Executive Theory also called the "unitary theory of the executive," the legal argument that presidents legitimately retain unrivaled control over the federal bureaucracy

Universal Declaration of Human Rights dictates handed down by the United Nations that ban the use of torture and other degradations of humanity

USA PATRIOT Act a law formally known as the Uniting and Strengthening America by Providing Appropriate Tools Required to Intercept and Obstruct Terrorism Act of 2001, which greatly expanded the president's powers to combat terrorism in the aftermath of September 11, 2001

vesting clause the Article II provision that executive power is entrusted exclusively to the presidency

veto a constitutional rule that allows the president to block the passage of a bill, subject to a possible congressional override

veto power the president's power to stop legislation, limited by the ability of both chambers of Congress to override the veto

War Powers Resolution a 1973 law passed by Congress intended to curb the president's ability to wage war abroad

wartime jurisprudence relaxed judicial standards for evaluating presidential actions during times of war

White House Office located in the Executive Office of the Presidency and managed by the White House chief of staff, the administrative unit in which the president and his immediate advisors work

INDEX

Note: Page numbers in *italics* indicate figures or tables.

A NOTE ON THE TYPE

This book has been composed in Arno, an Old-style serif typeface in the classic Venetian tradition, designed by Robert Slimbach at Adobe.